MERCENARY

SOLDIERS OF WAR

Tony Williams
Doug Armstrong
James Halliday

BLITZ EDITIONS

This edition published in 1996

Published by Blitz Editions
an imprint of Bookmart Limited
Registered Number 2372865
Trading at Bookmart Limited
Desford Road, Enderby
Leicester, LE9 5AD

ISBN 1 85605355 5

Typeset by Hewer Text Composition Services, Edinburgh
Printed in Great Britain by Cox and Wyman Limited, Reading

SOLDIER OF FORTUNE 1

VALIN'S RAIDERS

Tony Williams

1

The meeting took place in what once would have been called a bunker. Now it was simply known as basement 101. It was under a small, anonymous building in a small, anonymous town in Virginia. Outside, the streets were sizzling in a heatwave, but in the windowless conference room the temperature was a comfortable seventy degrees.

There were four men present: one FBI, one CIA, one DEA, and one from a government agency in Washington so secret that no one was even sure of its name.

All of the men sitting around the long, glass-topped table wore dark suits, white shirts, dark, striped ties and highly polished shoes. There were no ashtrays because no one smoked. The only refreshment available was bottled water and fruit. It could have been a convention of undertakers. In a way it was.

At precisely four-ten p.m. the man from the no-name government agency called the meeting to order. Not that it had been particularly rowdy before.

'Gentlemen,' he said. 'We all know why we're here today. We may speak freely as the room was swept for bugs less than half an hour ago. No notes will be taken, and as far as I'm concerned none of us are actually here this afternoon. I, for instance, am on the seventeenth green of the golf course at Camp David with our beloved president, as we speak.' He smiled, which was rare for him. 'And I'm sure the rest of you have similarly firm alibis.' The other men smiled too, but with little humour. 'So to the point of this little get-together. As I'm sure we are all aware, we are losing the drugs war. Have been losing it since the mid sixties. Things are going from bad to worse. Some parts of our country are in the grip of pure anarchy.' He paused as the other three men shifted in their seats. 'I know, I know. This is hardly news to any of us. But believe me, gentlemen, our intelligence from the war zones that we like to call the inner cities is that we haven't seen anything yet. New and powerful cocaine derivatives are appearing every day. Derivatives that make crack look as harmless as milk. We are facing a crisis, gentlemen, and I have asked you all to be present today to discuss a solution to at least part of the problem.' Then, turning to the man from the Drug Enforcement Agency, he said: 'Bob, you can take over from here.'

Bob 'Tank' Tankerton rose to his feet and looked at the other men. His nickname may have come from his surname, but it also fitted his build perfectly. He was a little under six feet tall, and in the dim lights that lit the room he appeared to be a little under six feet wide too. At least one of the other men thanked God they were on the same side. 'Gents,' said Tank. 'What our friend here said is perfectly true. We are in deep shit, and believe me, the shit is getting deeper every second. Cocaine is flooding into the country every day from south of the border. It comes in by boat, plane, automobile and truck, on foot, and probably ways we haven't even thought of yet. We manage to halt about ten per cent. We always have, always will. But as our success rate increases, we know that more is being smuggled in. Our only hope is to go to the source. And one of the biggest sources is a factory just outside Bogotá that processes the raw coca leaves into cocaine powder.' Tank saw the FBI man look at the man from the CIA. 'Yes, I'm aware that Bogotá is part of the sovereign state of Colombia. But this factory has been a thorn in my side for years. And that by definition is a thorn in all our sides. Agreed?'

There were nods all round.

'Very well. In that case, I know a man, an old friend of two of us here, and an old enemy of another. His name is Valin. Colonel James Valin. Ex-SAS, and right now a soldier of fortune, first class.'

The man from the CIA sprang to his feet.

'No,' he growled.

'Relax, Jack,' said Tank. 'I know you guys have got a history. But this is no time for old enmities. Valin is the best there is, bar none. We send him in with a squad of his mercs, and he'll blow that coke factory to kingdom come.'

'This is crazy,' said the man from the CIA. 'Do you really expect me to agree to send in a bunch of goddam psychopaths to sort out the business of the United States of America.'

'If we had a flag handy I'd salute it,' said Tank sarcastically. 'Listen, Jack, if you can come up with a better idea, one that doesn't compromise our position on the world stage, then I'll be ready to listen. If not, then with all due respect, shut the fuck up.'

The man from the CIA sat down, then said: 'Why not send in a platoon of Marines?'

'Jesus, Jack,' said Tank. 'We've still got a few ICBMs left under a field in Kansas. Maybe we should just lob a few of those in too.'

'In civilian clothes, I meant,' said the man from the CIA huffily.

'It's a nice idea, Jack,' said Tank. 'Don't think it's not been discussed. But if even one guy got killed or captured, then we'd be in the centre of a political shit-storm that would reach from here right to the UN building.'

The man from the FBI spoke for the first time since the meeting began. 'I agree with Tank,' he said. 'I don't know this character Valin, but I've heard some things about him. He seems like he knows what he's doing. Let's give him a whirl.'

The man from the CIA shook his head.

'At least listen to what he has to say,' said Tank.

'You mean he's here?' said the man from the CIA.

'Right outside,' replied Tank.

'Jesus Christ,' said the man from the CIA. 'You've had this well planned.'

'I had no option,' said Tank. 'A decision had to be made.'

'Shit,' said the man from the CIA.

'So shall I bring him in?' said Tank.

'Do what the hell you like,' said the man from the CIA.

Tank walked to the door of the room, opened it, and beckoned to whoever was waiting outside. The other three in the room looked towards the door as two men appeared, and Tank stepped back to allow them to enter.

The first to enter was a man of about forty-five, tall, with greying hair and a ramrod-straight posture that made him appear even taller than he was. He was casually dressed in civilian clothes, but his military bearing gave the impression that he was dressed in uniform, and probably always would. He shook Tank's hand warmly, then turned to face the room, and the men still sitting at the table saw that the right side of his face was marred with a bright-red scar that ran from his forehead to the lobe of his ear. The man who followed him into the room was younger and taller, but had such a languid air about him that he seemed smaller than his companion. He was blond, with a cowlick of hair that fell down over his forehead almost into one of his pale-blue eyes. He too was casually dressed, in a tartan shirt, jeans and high-heeled brown cowboy boots, and looked as if he would be more at home at a picnic in the park than in a crucial meeting in the war against drugs.

'Gentlemen,' said Tank as he closed the door, 'may I present Colonel James Valin and Lieutenant Mark O'Rourke, both late of the British Special Air Service. Colonel, you have already met Jack Bernard from the Central Intelligence Agency. Sitting next to him is Karl Landers, Federal Bureau of Investigation, and of course you also know General Avery.'

'General,' said Valin to the man from Washington. 'It's been too long, Mr Landers.' He nodded to the man from the FBI. 'Jack,' he said to the man from the CIA, who just shook his head in disgust and said nothing in reply.

'Please be seated, gentlemen,' said Tank to the newcomers. 'Would you care for some water?'

'I'd rather have a Scotch,' said Mark O'Rourke, 'but I suppose that's out of the question.'

'Sorry,' said Tank, 'we don't stock hard liquor here.'

'Never mind,' said O'Rourke. 'I think I can bear to wait until later.'

'Colonel,' said Tank. 'Any refreshment for you?'

'No, thank you,' said Valin. 'I share my young friend's distaste for water.'

'Colonel,' Tank went on. 'You know why I asked you and Lieutenant O'Rourke here this afternoon. I'd like to take this opportunity to show you, in more detail, the target that we wish you to destroy.'

He moved over to a console at the back of the room and pressed a button that hydraulically lowered the wall at the other end, revealing a screen. Another button lowered the dim lights still more, and a third projected a map of Colombia on to the screen, with Bogotá highlighted and a red cross marking a spot some twenty miles outside the city.

'The red cross marks the site of the factory,' explained Tank. 'It is on the outskirts of a small town called Santa Ana. We have informants in the town. Apparently a crack regiment of the Colombian army is based next to the factory to protect it.'

'Crack. Is that a joke?' asked O'Rourke, but no one laughed.

Tank pressed the button again and a picture of an industrial location appeared on the screen. It was surrounded by high fences topped with barbed wire. 'The factory itself,' he said. 'Only one gate in and out, guarded twenty-four hours a day. The fence is heavily electrified, and if you look closely you can clearly see the dead bodies of several small animals that have come too close.' A third click of the button and a larger map of the immediate area filled the screen. 'Should you accept the mission,' Tank said to Valin, 'you will of course be supplied with copies of all our intelligence reports. Now, as I say, we have men on the ground there – locals who know the area well. They tell us that the closest place for you to make landfall is an airstrip about four hours' drive away from Bogotá. Anywhere closer would prejudice the mission itself. Only they and I know exactly where the LZ is. And apart from Colonel Valin here, I think we'll keep it that way for now. Careless talk costs lives, as you all know.'

'How much?' asked Valin.

'Excuse me,' said Tank.

'How much are you prepared to pay for us to complete this exercise?'

'One million.'

'Dollars or sterling?'

'Sterling.'

'Cash?'

'Of course.'

'In what currency?'

'Half and half. Dollars and British pounds.'

Valin looked at O'Rourke. 'What do you think, Mark?'

'A piece of cake, boss.'

'So speaks the voice of the younger generation,' said Valin. 'And I tend to agree.'

'You'll take the job then?' asked Tank.

'I would hardly have bothered to travel to this God-forsaken spot in this unspeakable weather if I didn't intend to,' said Valin.

'How many men will you take with you?' asked Tank.

'We'll be a dozen, all told.'

'Against a regiment?' asked the man from the FBI.

'The odds will be on our side,' replied Valin.

'I really must object,' said the man from the CIA. 'I've never been involved in anything so shambolic in all my life.'

'You must have been,' said Valin. 'Weren't you at the Bay of Pigs?'

'I was *not*,' said the man from the CIA.

'You amaze me. Well, you were certainly in Vietnam. So was I. Briefly during the conflict – or was it a police action? And latterly for a longer time. I saw what you people left behind. If that wasn't shambolic, what was?'

The man from the CIA said nothing.

'Forget it, Jack,' said Tank. 'It's not your decision.'

'Then I'm leaving,' said Jack, who got up from the table and walked towards the door. 'And my report will be on the Secretary of Defence's desk by Monday.'

'So be it, Jack,' said Tank, as the man from the CIA stormed out of the room and slammed the door behind him.

Then they got down to serious business. The deal Tank offered was one-third of the fee down, the other two-thirds on completion.

Valin accepted.

'When will you go in?' asked Landers.

'As soon as we're ready,' replied Valin. 'The exact time and place will be on a need-to-know basis. And frankly only Tank needs to know. No offence.'

'None taken,' said the FBI man.

'So what's your next move?' asked Tank.

'You give us our money, and we go back to England to get the men together.'

'And then?'

'You'll be the first to know, Tank. I promise.'

Later that evening Valin and O'Rourke drove their hire car back to Washington DC and caught the first available flight back to Heathrow, with one-third of a million pounds in mixed currency in their luggage.

2

As dawn broke, four weeks to the day after the meeting in basement 101, an ancient, battered Douglas C47 Dakota, its fuselage patched and frayed, came out of the rising sun, flying under the Colombian radar with its engines throttled back to almost stalling speed, and touched down at the landing zone, four hours' drive outside Bogotá, sending up a puff of dust from the hard-packed earth.

The plane bounced along the makeshift runway and halted with its nose pointing into the dense foliage that surrounded the airfield, before turning to face the way it had come.

When the plane was stationary but with its engines still running, the passenger door in the side opened and a figure appeared. He was dressed in a tiger suit that had been pressed until every crease was like a razor-blade, with sergeant's chevrons on both sleeves, and black combat boots buffed to a mirror shine. He was carrying a Heckler and Koch G3 7.62mm assault rifle. Carefully he checked the terrain that was visible. When he was satisfied that nothing lurked in the undergrowth, he dropped to the ground and turned slowly in the back draught from the propellers, until he was again satisfied that there was no danger. Only then did he relax, and give the pilot the thumbs-up, at which sign he cut the engines. In the silence that followed, and as the dust created by the propellers drifted to the ground, the sergeant hung his rifle over his right shoulder by its sling and stretched. He was massive: fully six foot six, with a physique to match. He reached into one of his pockets and retrieved a purple beret. This he tugged over his blond hair, which was cropped into stubble, and then he banged on the side of the plane, shouting in a heavy German accent: ''*Raus*. Come on, you lazy bastards. Get deplaned, and into some semblance of order.'

One by one, another nine men left the plane and formed a ragged line. They were dressed in a mixture of military uniforms, the colours ranging from sand to deep khaki, to forest green, and civilian clothes, and all were heavily armed. The blond giant walked slowly along the column with a look of deep disdain on his face. 'Homos, all of you,' he said. 'Poofs.'

'You should know, Sarge,' said the man at the far right of the line in an American accent.

The sergeant paused, then walked back until he came to the man who had spoken, and looked him up and down. He was young – maybe twenty-five or six – and wore his dark hair long. He was dressed in a leather bomber jacket over a khaki shirt and mid-green army trousers. On his feet were a pair of dark-brown Doc Marten boots. Over his shoulder was slung an Uzi 9mm machine pistol, and around his waist a belt with a holster containing a Colt 1911 A1 automatic pistol. His GI steel helmet was adorned with a 'ban the bomb' symbol and the word 'PEACE' in black capital letters. He wore two different earrings: in the left ear a plain silver ring, while a red cross made of bone dangled from the other. A Walkman was tucked into a breast pocket of his jacket, and the earphones were around his neck. His eyes were shaded by mirrored aviator sunglasses. He badly needed a shave, and when he smiled his teeth were bright against the stubble that darkened his handsome face.

'What the hell did you say, Angel?' the sergeant demanded.

'Nothing, Sarge,' replied Angel. 'Just remarking what a beautiful morning it is.'

'Don't piss me about, boy,' said the sergeant. 'If you've got something on your mind, get it off now.'

'Not me, Sarge,' said Angel. 'Just waiting to get into some action, get home, and spend some of the dough I'll've earned today.'

'You haven't earned anything yet,' said the sergeant. 'Now straighten up and try and look at least a little like a soldier.'

'No problem, Sergeant Keller,' said Angel and came sloppily to attention. 'No problem at all.'

Keller walked back up the line of men. 'Right,' he said. 'I'm going to talk to the colonel. You men get busy unloading the plane. Angel, keep watch.' He checked his watch. 'Our transport should be here shortly.'

Without another word he turned and returned to the C47, jumped up through the passenger door and vanished. The other men also drifted back in the direction of the aircraft, piled together the weapons they were carrying and opened the door to the hold.

Angel stayed where he was, unslung his Uzi and watched the forest.

Inside the aircraft, Sergeant Keller went up to the flight deck where Valin and O'Rourke had made the latter part of the journey. He found them talking to the pilot. 'Sir,' he roared to Valin. 'All present and correct. The ground seems safe and the men are unloading the ordnance.'

'Well done, Sergeant,' said Valin. 'What time is the transport due?'

Keller looked at his watch again. 'In precisely fifteen minutes, sir,' he replied.

'This *is* South America, Sergeant,' said O'Rourke from his window seat. 'Don't be surprised if they're a trifle late.'

'No, sir,' said Keller. 'I'll be getting back outside to make sure those lumps don't break anything.'

'Carry on, Sergeant,' said Valin, and the German backed out into the main cabin.

'Now, you'll return tomorrow at the same time,' Valin said to the pilot in Spanish.

'*Sí*,' said the pilot, grinning through his moustache. He was himself formerly in the Bolivian air force, and enjoyed earning more in one night ferrying a crazy bunch of ragged soldiers than he did in a week of delivering parcels around the country.

'And if we are not here, you'll come back at the same time the next morning.'

'*Sí*,' said the pilot again. 'But if you are not here then, I am gone for good. To come again would be bad for my health.'

'We'll be here,' said Valin. 'Just make sure that you are. Because if you're not, there are people who know who you are. And for you to abandon us would be bad for *your* health. Do I make myself clear?'

'Perfectly. But believe me, sir, I am an honourable man. An ex-officer myself. I will be here as arranged. Just make sure that you are. It is a dangerous world out there. I would hate for anything to happen to you, so that we do not meet again. You owe me money, remember?'

'How could I forget?' said Valin, and clapped the pilot on the shoulder before leaving the flight deck, followed by O'Rourke, who winked at the Bolivian.

By the time the officers had exited the C47, the soldiers had unloaded the equipment and piled it up beside the runway. Sergeant Keller slammed the loading-bay door, then the passenger door, and whirled his finger to the pilot, who was looking through the window of the aircraft. The pilot replied with a thumbs-up, and taxied slowly away before gathering speed for the take-off. As the plane lifted off then banked away towards the sun, Keller said to Valin: 'I hope he doesn't abandon us. 'Cos if he does I'll have to find him and cut his throat.'

'If he does,' said Valin, 'I hope you're alive to do it.'

Keller grunted and walked over to inspect the boxes and bags that had been unloaded from the plane, while Valin and O'Rourke moved in the direction of the men who were taking a smoke break. Valin looked at them and smiled to himself. These were his troops, and he loved them all, as he had always done the men under his command.

'Everything copacetic?' he asked as he got closer.

'Mellow-D, Colonel,' replied a black man with a London accent, dressed in light-coloured fatigues and with a shoulder holster that held a huge Uzi Desert Eagle pistol under one armpit and spare magazines under the other. His hands clutched a Colt M16 Commando with a collapsed stock.

'Glad to hear it, Stoner,' said Valin. 'Are we treating you better than they did in the Foreign Legion?'

'Couldn't be worse,' replied Stoner, and smiled showing a set of broken front teeth. 'With the cash I'm getting here, I can get my Hampsteads fixed properly.'

'You don't have much luck with them, do you?' said Valin.

'Not a lot,' agreed Stoner, and laughed at the memories.

Johnny Stoner was born in the East End, when he had spent years colliding with the local law for every crime from hot-wiring high-powered cars, to running a string of prostitutes. Finally he skipped the country and after spending some time in jail in Marseilles, he joined the legendary French Foreign Legion, only to learn that the NCOs didn't take kindly to his sense of humour. His cockney wit earned him a severe beating which reduced his face to mush, after which he deserted and stowed away on a ship bound for England. Once back in his home country, he met up with some of his old mates and together they took part in a bank raid in south London where a security guard had been shot and badly wounded. All the members of the gang were caught, and Stoner received a ten-year jail sentence. Once inside, he at last got his teeth fixed by a prison dentist.

He was a model prisoner, but memories were long in the prison service. The security guard who had been shot had once been a screw at Wandsworth, and just before his sentence was complete, Stoner was paid a late-night visit by three warders, who reduced the good work the dentist had done to the rubble that was now visible whenever he opened his mouth.

Once released, and without friends or money, Stoner drifted through the twilight world of criminal London, until one day he found himself in a pub in Fulham where mercenaries were recruited.

As luck would have it, Valin and O'Rourke had been looking for men for the Colombian job, and although Stoner was a complete stranger to them, and even though he had had no experience as a mercenary, they liked the look of him and signed him up on the spot. It had been the same with eight of the twelve men who now waited on the airstrip for their transport to arrive. Even though Valin had been confident of his ability to carry out the mission, times had been hard for the colonel and his lieutenant. A mercenary job in southern Africa had gone disastrously wrong a short time before, so the offer from the Americans had been a godsend.

Valin shivered as he remembered how only he, O'Rourke, Keller and one other member of their squad had got out of Africa alive, and the dead bodies of their comrades that they had left unburied on the cruel veldt.

'Better luck this time,' he said to Stoner.

'I hope we *all* have better luck this time,' said a sardonic voice that Valin knew well.

'Me too, Chris,' Valin replied as a tall, rangy figure

rose from where he had been checking the fastenings of an ammunition box. 'Me too.'

Chris Spenser pushed back the brim of his Boston Bears baseball cap and looked hard at Valin. He was one of the oldest men present – forty-six, though he looked years younger. Born in Los Angeles in the late forties, at the height of the baby boom, as a teenager he had almost made it on the rock and roll scene of the mid sixties. But fate was against him. After seeing his best friend die from a drug overdose, he volunteered for the US army in late 1966, was chosen for the Marines, went through training with flying colours, and was immediately posted to Vietnam. In 1968, at the height of the conflict, he received a battlefield commission in the An Hoa basin, where he was wounded and posted back to Da Nang as a liaison officer. Later, promoted again, he went back into the fray. After his tour of duty was complete, he re-enlisted and stayed in Vietnam until the Americans pulled out in 1975, and it was there that he had first met Colonel Valin. Over countless drinks in the Hanoi Hilton they became firm friends as they bemoaned the state of the war and the calibre of the politicians back in Washington who could not see that it was unwinnable.

Once back in the USA, Spenser resigned his commission and tried to rebuild his life. He was not yet thirty, and again tried to make it in the music business. He grew his hair and joined a band. But bad luck struck once more. When the band broke up, Spenser was left high and dry in New York. One night in a bar on the Lower East Side he heard a young, successful-looking businessman decry all Vietnam veterans as baby-killers. Spenser had been drinking heavily, and an argument broke out that turned into a fist fight. Using the skills he had acquired in South-east Asia, he killed the businessman with a blow of the palm to the nose. Stunned, he sat on the floor by the body until the police arrived, and was arrested. He pleaded guilty to second-degree murder and was sentenced to life imprisonment. During his twelve years in jail he started a correspondence with Valin, and learned of his friend's head injury in a street fight in Belfast, his consequent early demobilization from the SAS on medical grounds and his new career as a mercenary. On his release in 1988, Spenser travelled to Europe, where he hooked up with Valin. Apart from the colonel, he was the only member of the squad to get away from the African débâcle alive, with just a flesh wound to show for it.

'This is the weirdest crew yet,' Spenser remarked. 'You reckon we gonna make it, Colonel?'

'Trust in me and the Lord, Chris,' said Valin.

'Sure will, Colonel,' replied the older man. 'But I tend to rely on my baby more.'

Spenser bent and tapped the gun case that held his 'baby'. A 7.62mm M134 GECAL electrically powered rotary Gatling gun, with six barrels and a cyclical firing rate of up to six thousand rounds per minute, it was powered by a battery pack and had been specially converted to be hand held. Normally a weapon of this kind is mounted on a helicopter gunship or land vehicle, and Spenser loved it all the more for that. Together, Chris and his 'sweet little rock 'n' roller' were like having a platoon of artillery at hand.

'My babies are better,' said a voice with a mid-European accent. It came from one of the men sitting on a nearby pile of boxes. He was smoking a strong-smelling cigar and wearing dark-green fatigues.

'Explosives,' sneered Spenser. 'Where's the subtlety in them?'

Maxim Resnick grinned at the American. 'And where is the subtlety in that oversized popgun you have there? With my equipment and my expertise, I could blow the head off a pimple on your face at a thousand yards and not leave a scar.'

Spenser grinned back. He had met the Russian only a few weeks before, when the group had got together for their first briefing and a short spell of training at the small farm in Norfolk that Valin had bought on his retirement from the SAS as a base for his private army. But already he felt a strong kinship with the leathery veteran of the Afghanistan campaign. Maybe it was the fact that Afghanistan had been as futile an exercise as Vietnam, or perhaps it was simply that he recognized and admired a truly professional warrior.

'We'll see, Max,' he said. 'We'll see.'

Resnick ground out his cigar with the toe of his boot and stood up. He was short. Maybe five foot six, but well built and fit-looking. From his hip hung a Czechoslovakian CZ 75 double-action 9mm handgun, and on his back was strapped a Kalashnikov AK47 with a banana-shaped magazine.

The Russian was a victim of the dramatic political changes in the East since the Wall had come down. When his regiment was disbanded, he drifted west into Germany and then across Europe until he ended up in London. His status as an illegal immigrant had prevented him finding work, but his grasp of English, which he had learned in a crash course as a boy soldier in the bad old days when an invasion of the West was the ultimate aim of his masters in Moscow, soon led him to the pub in Fulham where Valin and O'Rourke had been recruiting.

Resnick was an explosives expert. As he had boasted to Spenser, he could place a charge of Semtex and neatly blow a hole as large or as small as required in any target, or destroy it completely. On this occasion his ordnance was divided up into a dozen or so haversack-sized bags which had been neatly placed in the shade. Even though Semtex was stable, many of the men had seen the effects of heat on high explosive, and were not keen to see it again. They were taking no chances.

'And where the fuck's our transport?' said Spenser testily. 'We're like sitting ducks waiting here.'

'It'll be along,' said Valin, but when he checked his watch he saw that the vehicles were already ten minutes late.

'It's going to be a hell of a walk if they don't arrive,' said Spenser. 'Especially with all the junk we've brought with us.'

'Don't worry about a thing, Chris,' said Valin, and as if to back up his promise, the sound of heavy-duty engines reached them from some way off. The men all scrambled for their weapons and took up defensive positions as the sound of the engines grew louder, and an old British Ford three-tonner with a canvas tonneau over the cargo compartment, closely followed by a World War Two jeep, bounced into view through a gap in the jungle.

The noise of weapons being cocked was the next loudest sound as the two vehicles skidded to a halt about a hundred yards from the squad.

The driver of the jeep dismounted and walked towards the twelve mercenaries, his empty hands held far away from his body. He was wearing the white cotton suit of a peon, and leather sandals, and appeared to be unarmed, but half the squad trained their weapons on him, while the other half kept their guns on the three-tonner.

'Colonel Valin?' said the man as he drew closer, in English with a strong Spanish accent. He was about sixty, wrinkled and grey, but even under the barrels of the weapons that covered him, he had a youthful spring to his step.

'That's me,' said Valin.

A grin appeared on the man's face. 'My name is Jesús,' he said. 'I believe you were expecting me.' He pronounced his name in the Spanish way: '*Hey-zoos*'.

'That is correct,' replied Valin. 'You are very prompt. But as we have not met before, you must excuse me if I am cautious.'

'Of course, señor.'

'There is a question I have been told to ask you.'

'Please, señor.'

'Your army number, date of enlistment, and date of demobilization.'

The Colombian smiled. 'As if I could ever forget,' he said, and reeled off a number and two dates which Valin checked in a notebook that he had already taken from one of the pockets of his jacket.

'Correct,' said Valin. 'Are you armed?'

'No. I felt it safer. Please search me if you wish.'

'Thank you,' said Valin, and expertly frisked the man, until he was satisfied that he was clean.

'Who's in the truck?' asked Valin.

'Only Carlos, my son. He is alone and unarmed also.'

'Tell him to get out,' ordered Valin.

In a burst of rapid Spanish Jesús did as he was told, and a young man in his early twenties, dressed in jeans and a checked shirt, opened the driver's door of the truck and jumped to the ground.

'Angel, Stoner, check out the vehicle,' barked Valin.

The two men walked over to the truck, frisked the driver, searched the cab and opened the canvas cover at the back cautiously. When Stoner shouted: 'All clear, Colonel,' Valin relaxed and said: 'Once again, my apologies, but you realize we must be careful.'

The Colombian nodded. 'Of course, Colonel. I would have been disappointed if you were not.'

'Good. Bob Tankerton said that you knew your stuff.'

'Tank,' said Jesús with a broad smile. 'Have you seen him lately?'

'A few weeks ago.'

'If you see him soon, give him my regards. It must have been my old compadre who came up with the idea of asking me my army number, and those dates.'

Valin nodded.

'It was a good ploy. What other information does a man never forget? Tank, he is as cunning as a fox. But for now, Colonel, instruct your men to load up the truck. There are patrols in the area, and we don't want the army to know that you are here one moment earlier than necessary.'

'Agreed,' said Valin. 'Sergeant Keller, get the men to load the gear pronto.'

'Yes, sir,' replied Keller, then screamed at the men: 'You heard the colonel. Get this stuff loaded at the double.'

Within five minutes the ordnance was in the back of the truck, along with Keller and the rest of the squad, apart from Spenser, who, because he spoke reasonable Spanish, had been ordered to sit next to Carlos. Valin and O'Rourke were in the jeep, with Jesús driving, and as the two vehicles left the airstrip and nosed their way on to the narrow track that ran through the jungle, the jeep led the way.

'It's about four hours to Bogotá, according to Tankerton,' Valin shouted into Jesús's ear above the sound of the engine.

'That is correct, Colonel, but the army presence has become stronger on the roads over the last few weeks. It is almost as if they know that something is going to happen. We should wait until dusk before going the whole way.'

'That was not part of the original plan,' said Valin.

'Plans are made to be changed,' said Jesús. 'We do not want to be stopped for a check by a patrol. I have found a place where we can stay until darkness begins to fall. Believe me, sir, it is for the best.'

'What do you think, Mark?' Valin asked his aide.

'I think we should pay attention to the local intelligence, sir,' the younger man replied. 'We've got until the day after tomorrow to get back to the airstrip. Perhaps it would be better to carry out the operation under the cover of total darkness.'

'OK,' the colonel replied, and then said to the Colombian: 'Very well, Jesús, take us to your secure location. I'll let my top sergeant know what we're doing.'

Valin took a small, low-powered radio from his jacket pocket and spoke into it. 'Valin to Keller, over.'

In the back of the truck, Keller spoke into an identical radio, attached to the lapel of his tiger suit. 'Keller to Valin. Receiving you loud and clear. Over.'

Valin explained the change of plan to the German sergeant, who acknowledged it. 'You heard the boss,' he said to the eight men bouncing up and down on the bench seats along both sides of the truck. 'We go in tonight.'

3

About a quarter of an hour later, Jesús turned off the track and joined a wider road, paved with cracked and buckled concrete and stretching in both directions through the dense jungle. 'We go north here,' he explained to Valin and O'Rourke, 'then to an old ranch I know. We will be safe there until tonight. There is food and drink for you and your men. My wife and daughters are waiting, and they will take care of us.

'Just keep them away from the troops. I don't know everyone I've brought with me on this trip,' said Valin. 'Some of them are a little rough-and-ready, to say the least.'

'I have faith in your ability to keep order, Colonel,' said Jesús. 'Tank assured me of your trustworthiness and honour, in a message he got through to me last week.'

'I admire his faith in me, and yours too, Jesús,' replied the colonel. 'I only hope I can live up to it.'

Christ, I'd better, he thought, as he looked back over the past few hectic weeks. The day after the meeting in Virginia, the pair of them had got back to England, where Keller and Spenser were kicking their heels at the farm, and had started scouring the pubs on the mercenary circuit for fresh recruits. They had money, which was something. But even a third of a million wouldn't last long once they started paying for the men, their keep, arms and ammunition, transport, forged papers for some of them, and somewhere to hole up near their target. It had taken a week to hire eight new men, and Valin had detailed O'Rourke to take them up to Norfolk for basic training under the tender care of Sergeant Keller.

While Keller and O'Rourke were making the new recruits' lives a misery, Valin flew back to the USA to organize transport, weapons, and a hide-out as far south as possible. He found a ranch to rent in New Mexico, close to the Mexican border, where O'Rourke rejoined him. Together they purchased the state-of-the-art ordnance that the troops had recently unloaded from the C47, and made some forays into Mexico, making careful notes as to which roads were heavily guarded by the Border Patrol and which were not. The last thing they needed was to be stopped and searched by the US authorities before they even crossed the border. Valin had no compunction about killing any customs and immigration officers who got nosy, but it was a complication he could do without, and would certainly bring unwanted attention.

Valin and O'Rourke also flew to Mexico City and hired more cars under false papers that they had purchased from a charming gentleman who lived in the *barrio*, before flying on to Panama, where they organized the plane and pilot. When they arrived back at the farm, having been away for a fortnight, they were gratified to find that the men had been forged into some semblance of a fighting unit. Although how good they were going to be when it came to real action, only time would tell.

Under the canvas covering the back of the truck, the temperature was rising as the sun climbed ever higher in the sky. Keller mopped his brow with his sleeve and looked at the men as they lolled on the bench seats. Jesus, he thought, what a bunch. Why can't I find a regular job and not have to get involved with all this crap? Then he smiled to himself. What would I do? Get a milk round in Cologne, marry a fat hausfrau and settle down?

Once again he studied the men under his command, mourning the loss of the old friends that he had been forced to watch die in southern Africa. A pity some of them couldn't be here today, he thought. This is no time to be going into battle with untried troops. He looked up and down the length of the truck, trying to foresee what they would be like in combat.

Angel was OK, he thought. A bit cheeky and rebellious, but he had come through well in the short training period they had spent together. He was a hippie, that was true. But a hippie with a killer instinct if the stories about his basic training at Fort Bragg had been correct. Angel, aka Johnny Angelo, had been another young man who had volunteered for the US army. But in his case it was a peacetime army, and he had been earmarked as a communications operative because he had majored in electronics in college. This was the last thing that Angel wanted. He had craved action, and as if to prove it, he'd fought two military policemen in the last week of his basic. Angel was court-martialled, found guilty of assault and 'conduct unbecoming', slung into the brig and, after he had served his sentence, dishonourably discharged. But soon he went back, found one of the MPs and inflicted even more damage on him, before absconding to Italy, because of his fluency in the language of his father's home country. Hired by a radio station as a technician, he nevertheless soon tired of the job and, like most of the rest of the squad, drifted through Europe until he reached London, where the appeal of the mercenary life led him to the same recruiting pub as the others.

The Russian was OK too. Resnick was a real soldier, professionally trained by other professionals, and although Keller's father had fought on the eastern front during the war, and died soon after his return from the terrible effects of the campaign, the sergeant felt no animosity to the man. In fact he was glad to have him on his side. If Hitler had kept Russia as an ally, he reflected, we would never have lost the fucking war.

And then there was Stoner. Keller was not a great fan of blacks, but as they went he seemed like a reasonable guy. Sitting next to Stoner was the Frenchman. A bit of a mystery, that one. His name was Messelier, or so he said. A good-looking man of about thirty-five, he kept himself to himself, rarely mixing with the other troops. And by the look in his eye, there was something bad, very bad, in his past. But that was his business.

Messelier was wearing blue jeans and a combat jacket. His preferred side-arm was a Sig niner, and cradled across his lap was an Ingram MAC11 machine pistol with two clips welded together end to end, to give it a sixty-round capacity which the little gun could exhaust in about six seconds on full auto.

Messelier noticed the huge sergeant staring at him, and gave him a friendly nod. He could feel Keller's curiosity, but he had no intention of enlightening him. It was nothing personal. Just the way it had to be. Messelier had been a mercenary for some five years, since leaving the French diplomatic corps, where he had received an unusual training. An assassin, he thought. Me. A man with a fine-arts degree from the Sorbonne, and all it got me was a job as a paid killer. For when Messelier finished his studies at the age of twenty-three, not knowing how to use his education, his Uncle Claude suggested a safe, well-paid and permanent job in the civil service, where he himself had spent more than thirty comfortable years growing fat and lazy.

Messelier had applied, and been siphoned off from the other applicants and interviewed by the French secret service. His psychological profile had thrown up some useful insights into his character. He was a born killer, he was told. It came as some surprise, as he had never even been in a fist-fight. The man from the secret service made Messelier an interesting proposition. He would be fully trained in the art of murder, and in exchange for his services in that particular art he would take up the handsomely paid post of a chargé d'affaires in the Foreign Office in Paris.

Messelier jumped at the chance. He knew how popular diplomats were. They drove fast cars, made love to fast women, wore the best clothes and got the best seats at the opera. For a year he trained as a killer, taking to it like a duck to water. Then he took up his government position, and for another year he lived the high life, until one day he was contacted by the secret-service man who had interviewed him earlier. Messelier was given a gun, an address and a name. He was to go there and kill the named person. He did it without compunction. After all, it was what he had been trained for. Over the next five years he did it eight more times. He killed both men and women quite happily. Then one day, after he had knifed the mistress of a minister in the defence department who had been collecting indiscreet pillow talk and selling it to the highest bidder, her eight-year-old daughter had woken up and walked into the room and he had slit her throat too, almost without thinking. It was only afterwards that his conscience began to bother him. He started drinking heavily, and was warned that unless he stopped it would be his turn to be terminated by a fellow graduate of the academy for killers.

Messelier ignored the warning, and when his would-be assassin appeared some weeks later he dispatched him with ease. Then he himself disappeared, just like he had 'disappeared' so many others. He had planned this moment for months. Within the hour he was on a plane to Canada with a false passport. But he could not settle in the suburb of the Francophone city where he had been planning to begin a new life. Within a year he was travelling the world, looking for adventure, and fell in with mercenaries in Africa. He moved about the continent, picking up work where and when he could, under many different names, Messelier being just the latest. If Keller had known some of the other names under which he had operated, he would have realized why Valin jumped at the chance to take on the Frenchman for the current mission. But Messelier had sworn the officer to secrecy when he joined him, and Valin was a man of his word. In fact it was only chance that the Frenchman and the German had not run across each other before, although the likelihood was lessened by the fact that Messelier, knowing that the French government had a very long memory, had schooled himself in the art of keeping a low profile. So low in fact, that in some quarters of the mercenary world his nickname was 'The Invisible Man'.

The Frenchman mentally shrugged at the German sergeant's penetrating look. The German was a professional fighting man, and once hostilities began, all other personal likes and dislikes would be forgotten.

Next to Messelier on the flesh-numbing bench was another new recruit to Valin's private army. Messelier had had little opportunity to speak to him before, and offered him a cigarette, which he accepted. He was very young, nineteen or twenty at the most, and his name was Lenny Packard. He was Australian.

'How the hell did you get involved in all this shit?' Messelier asked him when both their cigarettes were lit.

'My old man,' said Packard. 'He was in Vietnam. He was killed there. I joined up as a boy soldier in the Ozzie infantry. It was boring. I got a three-month psychological discharge and headed for England. I heard there were people who signed up mercs, and I found this bunch in a pub in west London. What about you?'

'A long story,' said Messelier. 'I'll tell you sometime, my young friend. Is this your first time out?'

The Australian nodded.

'I hope you know what you're letting yourself in for.'

'A lot of money and a good time,' said Packard. But he was lying.

'I wish it were as simple as that,' said Messelier.

'Have you been in this game long?' asked Packard.

'Too long. Far too long.'

The Frenchman looked at Packard's fresh, new combat suit, the small holster on his left side holding what looked like a Beretta 1934 model, and the ancient 7.62mm FN FAL assault rifle with telescopic sight that he held between his knees. 'Where did you get your weapons?' he asked.

'They were my old man's. They were shipped back from 'Nam with his body. He was a sergeant. His Top came round and gave them to my mum. I've had them ever since.'

'I hope they bring you luck,' said Messelier.

'Me too,' said Packard.

Suddenly the truck lurched as it turned off the paved road on to what felt like a dirt track again, and Messelier peered through the gap in the canvas back of the truck. 'Looks like we're where we're going to,' he said to no one in particular.

Up front in the jeep, Valin looked ahead at the narrow track that Jesús was negotiating carefully. He picked up and cocked the M16 that was in the well of the vehicle, and O'Rourke took out the Browning 9mm semi-automatic handgun that he carried as a side-arm and worked the slide so that it was ready to fire. 'Just in case,' said Valin casually. 'This looks like a good place for an ambush.'

In the truck behind, Keller was of the same mind, and ordered his men to ready their rifles and machine-guns for action.

The two vehicles bounced along the track until it widened into a clearing that overlooked an abandoned farmhouse. In a dip about half a mile away was a tumbledown ranch house and behind it an equally dilapidated barn. '*Mi casa, su casa,*' said Jesús. 'Welcome to your temporary home.' He put his foot on the accelerator and the jeep, closely followed by the truck with his son at the wheel, headed towards the house. As they got closer, the front door opened and a woman emerged carrying a double-barrelled shotgun. 'My wife,' said Jesús proudly. 'The best cook and shot in Colombia.'

As they drew level with the front of the house, the woman raised her gun in greeting and called to someone inside. 'My daughters are in there, helping prepare your meal,' said Jesús reassuringly. 'We'd better hide these vehicles in the barn. Sometimes helicopter patrols take a look at these broken-down farms,' he said, as he swung the jeep around the house and through the huge double doors of the barn. He pulled up in one corner close to a dark-green VW Microbus, to allow room for the truck. With both vehicles safely inside, Jesús jumped out of the jeep with surprising agility, saying: 'Come along, my friends, let's eat.'

4

The soldiers leapt down from the truck one by one and joined Valin, O'Rourke and Jesús. Everyone then made their way back to the farmhouse. Two of the last three men to exit the truck were the McGuire brothers, Gerry and Daniel, who had come into the mercenary business by way of the IRA, to which they had belonged since their boyhood. The other was Pat Newman, an Englishman who had served in the parachute regiment for ten years before taking voluntary redundancy in the huge shake-up that had occurred in the British armed services in the early nineties. Gerry and Daniel were as alike as twins, even though Gerry was thirty and Daniel twenty-eight. They were large young men, with ruddy faces and bright-red hair that evinced their Irish ancestry.

The McGuires were good-natured and enjoyed a drink and a laugh with their mates, but they were also hardened killers who had demonstrated their loyalty to the Provisional cause with bombs and bullets and had quit their homeland only when they had appeared on the 'most wanted' lists of the British army, the Ulster Defence Force and the Royal Ulster Constabulary. They were dressed alike in British 'greens' and both carried at the waist Colt Combat Commander

.45 automatics, with eight-shot magazines, and, over their shoulders, Czechoslovakian V261 Scorpions in 7.65mm, fitted with suppressors. The weapons had all been supplied by NORAID, which displeased Newman, as he had done several tours of duty in Belfast, and had seen many of his friends brought down by similar weapons. But that, he thought, was then, and this is now. It was in the past and best forgotten, even though he still felt a frisson of anger at the memories. The ex-para favoured straight-legged army trousers, 'monkey boots', an MA1 jacket, a Smith & Wesson Model 59 in 9mm parabellum as a side-arm, and, as a carry weapon, an Ithaca Bear Stopper 12-gauge shotgun with an eighteen-and-a-half-inch barrel, a pistol grip and an eight-shot capacity.

Inside the house, the soldiers found Jesús's wife overseeing the preparation of a huge meal being cooked by her three daughters. 'Colonel,' said Jesús, 'allow me to introduce my wife Maria, and my three daughters, Sofía, Carlotta and Carmen.'

'Delighted,' said Valin, and introduced his men one by one to the four women. Maria was tall, well built and about fifty, her long, dark hair beginning to go grey. She wore a peasant-style black dress and boots, and leant her shotgun against the side of the fireplace as she greeted the men. But their attention was mainly on her daughters. They were beautiful and, as far as Valin and his troops could tell, ranged in age from about seventeen to twenty-two or three. All three were taller than their mother, slim but voluptuous, and had the same long, lustrous black hair. Sofía and Carlotta, who appeared to be the eldest of the trio, favoured simple white blouses with long, dark skirts and sandals, but Carmen wore tight blue jeans, knee boots and a plain, crimson cowboy shirt. The two older girls were unarmed as they went about their chores, although another pair of shotguns stood against the back door. On a cartridge belt around her waist, Carmen wore an open gunfighter's holster which contained an old-fashioned single-action Colt Peacemaker.

All four women spoke English to some extent, and all seemed delighted to greet the arrival of the mercenaries. And so, on a day that was to change the lives of everyone present, the twelve soldiers who made up Valin's Raiders met the six men and women who comprised the Delgado family.

The ground floor of the ranch house was one huge room that combined living, dining and cooking areas. At the back, a wood stove was covered with bubbling pots and pans that exuded a mouth-watering aroma. Next to it was a sink with an old hand-operated water pump. The living area had been swept neatly, and two long trestle tables had been set up, with plain benches as seats. In the opposite corner to the cooking area, a wide staircase led up to the first floor and disappeared into the shadows.

'A drink, gentlemen, to celebrate your safe arrival,' said Jesús, who produced a bottle of tequila, salt, lime, glasses and half-a-dozen six packs of warm Budweiser from under the sink.

'All the comforts of home,' said O'Rourke, who helped himself to a beer, sat at the table, lit a cigarette and watched the daughters as they went about their business.

'There'll be plenty of time for that later, Lieutenant,' said Valin. 'First of all I want guards placed at the perimeters. We'll take it in turns to eat, and replace the guards on a two-hourly basis.'

'Sir,' said O'Rourke, rising smartly to his feet. 'Sergeant,' he said to Keller. 'You heard the colonel.'

'Sir,' echoed Keller, and then turned to the two Irishmen. 'You McGuires take the first duty. We'll get you a snack sent out as soon as we've eaten ourselves. Then you can come back and eat at your leisure in two hours' time.'

'Be sure to save us plenty,' said Daniel. 'We'll have a hell of an appetite by then. Come on, Gerry, we'd better find a comfortable pair of hidey-holes to watch the front and back.'

'Carlos will show you a couple of places we've discovered that give you a good view of the road in and out,' said Jesús. He poured out another torrent of Spanish to his son, who smiled and opened the door to allow the brothers to leave.

'Use your radios if you spot anything suspicious,' ordered Valin as they went through the doorway. 'Otherwise maintain strict radio silence. Understood?'

'Yes, sir,' replied Daniel briskly, as if he had never fought several bitter small-arms battles with Valin's previous regiment, possibly even when Valin was serving with them. 'Leave it to us.'

'And save us a couple of them beers, boys,' was Gerry's parting shot as he left the house.

When the McGuires had gone to take up their guard duty outside, the rest of the men piled their carry weapons against one wall and sat down to eat. The Delgado women had done them proud. On top of the stove were two huge pots of meat stew with chillies that brought tears to the men's eyes, plus a ratatouille of local vegetables and a huge saucepan of rice. In the oven was hot bread, and for dessert a fruit pie. As the men ate, Carlotta boiled up a pot of the strong, bitter local coffee, which Jesús laced with tequila.

Carlos returned, only to be dispatched almost immediately to take the McGuires plates of food, which he did before eating himself, and although the men ate huge portions of everything, there was still plenty for the women, and even some left when the guards came in after their stint.

During the meal, Spenser found it almost impossible to keep his eyes off Carmen, and she could hardly keep her eyes off him. He was amazed. It seemed like years since he had been with a woman. The last one he could remember had been a hard-bitten prostitute in some French port or other before leaving on a mission. He had not enjoyed it much, and had decided there and then that he would not bother again. But the sight of the slim young woman in her tight jeans and shirt, with a handgun slung around her waist, had rekindled something inside him, and it had not gone unnoticed.

'Sweet thang, ain't she?' said Angel as he dug into his stew. 'Trouble is, she could be your daughter, man.'

'I don't have a daughter,' said Spenser, refusing to rise to the bait.

'I'm only kidding, man,' said Angel. 'Hell, I'm jealous. I haven't had a woman look at me like that since I don't know when. Just don't let her momma see, or she might use that shotgun on your ass.'

Spenser smiled. 'I'll take your advice, Angel,' he said. 'I'll be very careful about how I behave.'

'Good idea, man,' said Angel. 'I'd hate to see you get hurt before we even get to the coke factory. Seems like you and me might enjoy sharing a line before we blow the shit out of the place.'

'We just might do that,' agreed Spenser, and went back to trying to look at Carmen without letting the others notice.

When the meal was finished and the plates were stacked in the sink, Valin lit a rare cigarette and said to Jesús: 'Is this your place?'

'No, sir,' came the reply. 'The original owners vanished about a year and a half ago. That often happens in this part of the world. It happened to my own brother too, many years ago. Up until then I was a friend of the regime. But now I would do anything to see them destroyed. Why else would a man who served long and loyally in the army be helping a foreign country to fight a battle on his own soil?'

Valin nodded. 'So you just moved in?'

'That is correct.'

'And do you and your family live far away?'

'No. Eighty kilometres or so, on the road to Bogotá.'

'And what exactly happens tonight as far as you're concerned?'

'Carlos and I will take you in, leave you and the transport, and then vanish.'

'And the women?'

'They will take the VW you saw in the barn,

load it up with all their utensils and leave us before noon.'

'And we just leave the truck and the jeep at the airstrip?'

'Correct, Colonel. Maria, Carlos and I will take a little drive through the jungle in a day or two to see if they have been discovered. If not, we drive them home. If they have . . . well, there are plenty more vehicles around.'

'You have a good attitude, Jesús,' said O'Rourke. 'You should have joined up with our mob. Scrounging is a way of life in the British army.'

Jesús smiled, and was just about to answer when Valin's radio squealed and Gerry McGuire's unmistakable accent came through. 'McGuire to home. There's a vehicle coming down the track. Four bodies on board. They look like army.'

Valin looked hard at Jesús and said: 'This had better not have anything to do with you.'

5

'No, Colonel, I swear,' said Jesús.

'Did you hear me, Colonel? Over,' said Gerry McGuire on the radio.

'I hear you, Gerry,' said Valin. 'What's the story? Over.'

'Definitely army, Colonel. Four in a jeep, all with side-arms, carry weapons and an LMG mounted in the back. An M60. They're coming real slow. I can take them out. What do you say?'

'No. We don't know if they're alone. Just let them come. Give me an ETA.'

'Two or three minutes to you.'

'Stay where you are then. Keep an eye out for reinforcements. We'll take care of them this end. No more radio contact now unless you see any more troops. Over and out.'

Valin put his radio back in his pocket and rapped out a stream of orders. 'Mark. You, Newman and Angel get over to the barn and secure the transport. Keller, take Stoner and Messelier and find cover that gives you a clear view of the front. Now double.' The six men grabbed their carry weapons and ran out of the house. Valin took out his radio again and pressed the send button. 'Daniel, are you listening?'

The younger McGuire came on immediately. 'That's a roger, boss.'

'Where are you?'

'Behind the house.'

'Stay there, and keep down. Over and out.'

'The rest of you come upstairs with me,' Valin said. 'And Jesús, just act as naturally as possible. Tell the army you're squatting here or something. Lose your weapons too.' Then, to the youngest of the four women: 'Carmen, take off that belt.'

'But . . . '

'No arguments, girl.'

Reluctantly the youngest daughter loosened the buckle on her gun belt. Then Valin turned to the remainder of his men. 'Come on, you lot, upstairs,' he barked, and led Spenser, Resnick and Packard up to the top of the house.

The four men ran past three open doors that looked into rooms long neglected and littered with broken furniture, over the bare floorboards to a room overlooking the clearing in front of the house. Valin, Resnick and Packard cocked their carry weapons as they went, and Spenser, who relied on his Gatling, unholstered the Star Model MD.45 ACP selective fire that he had carried since Vietnam and put a round in the chamber. They reached a window covered with torn and dusty brocade curtains just in time to spot a new, long-wheelbase Wrangler jeep painted dull grey and with an open top and a machine-gun mounted on a swivel in the back. Inside were four men in grey army uniforms. 'Militia men,' said Valin. 'Now I wonder what they're looking for.'

'Us?' said Spenser.

'I don't think so,' replied Valin. 'Otherwise there'd be more than just four of them. Unless of course we're losing our fearsome reputation.'

The jeep drove slowly to the front of the house and the four men got out. One, with a captain's chevrons on his shoulders, carried a Walther PPK semi-automatic handgun, while the other three all held Colt AR-15 semi-automatic rifles. They appeared to be ready for combat, though not particularly suspicious of the ranch house.

Then, as Jesús appeared from the veranda and walked towards the soldiers, they cocked their weapons and the officer called out to him in Spanish: 'Who are you?'

'My name is Delgado. Jesús Delgado.'

'What are you doing here?'

'My family and I . . . We have lost everything. We were looking for a place to stay.'

'This house has been put under the control of the Militia. You have no right to be here.'

'My apologies, señor. We will leave immediately.'

'Who else is here?'

'My wife and four children.'

'Let me see them.'

Jesús turned and beckoned, and Maria, Carlos and the three daughters came out on to the veranda and joined him by the jeep, as the soldiers covered them.

The officer stepped forward and said: 'You have very beautiful daughters, señor. Perhaps I can see my way to letting you stay here for a while after all.'

'Thank you,' Jesús replied. 'But we are happy to move on.'

'If I say you stay, you stay,' said the officer, reaching

forward and touching Carmen's hair. Valin heard Spenser catch his breath.

'What is your name, girl?' asked the officer.

'Carmen, señor.'

'Then, with your father's permission, Carmen, you and I will become better acquainted inside.'

'Señor, no,' Jesús protested. 'We will just get our truck and leave.'

'Not at all, Señor Delgado. My sergeant, the corporal and I will go inside, where they will look after you and your family. And Carmen and I will go upstairs for a little while.'

'No, señor, please,' said Maria. 'She is my baby.'

'Be quiet, woman,' snapped the officer. 'Sergeant, Corporal, see these people inside. You,' he said to the private who had been driving the jeep, 'stay here and keep guard.'

'Captain,' said the private, coming to attention, as the sergeant and corporal herded the rest of the family inside, leaving the officer to bring Carmen with him.

'Son of a bitch,' hissed Spenser.

'Cool down, Chris,' Valin whispered. 'Let him bring her upstairs, and you can deal with him.'

The waiting mercenaries heard voices from below, then footsteps on the stairs. They flattened themselves against the wall behind the door of their room, in case he chose it for his tryst, but as they had hoped, he took Carmen into the first room at the top of the stairs. 'Not too many home comforts here,' they heard the officer say. 'But never mind, I'm sure our passion will outweigh the lack of comfort.'

'Please, señor,' said Carmen. 'You are hurting me.'

'Go, Chris,' said Valin. 'But keep it quiet.'

Spenser reholstered his pistol, from under one arm drew the needle-pointed, razor-sharp Marine Ka-Ba knife that he had also owned since his days in the service, and crept out of the room, silent in his rubber-soled combat boots.

He slid down the hall, keeping close to the wall to minimize any creaks from the loose boards, until he reached the room at the top of the stairs, and peered through the open doorway. Carmen was lying on an old, stained mattress, her blouse ripped open to expose bare breasts, with the captain over her, his back to the door, opening his fly.

Carmen saw Spenser in the doorway, knife in hand, but with extreme presence of mind, showed no emotion. The officer started to drop his trousers. Perfect, thought Spenser, as he moved forward, put his left arm around the captain's neck, covered his mouth with his hand, jerked back his head and put the knife into his right kidney, twisting the blade viciously. The officer kicked once and died without a sound. Spenser lowered his body gently to the floor.

'Thank you,' the girl said. 'You saved my life.'

'Thank me later,' said Spenser. 'We're not out of this yet. Now cover yourself up, girl.'

Carmen looked down at her nakedness, blushed, and pulled her shirt across herself. Spenser gave her his hand and pulled her upright, then turned as he heard a sound behind him. Valin was standing in the doorway screwing a silencer on to the barrel of the Smith & Wesson 459 that he carried as a side-arm.

'Good work, Chris,' he said. 'Cover me on the stairs.'

Spenser wiped the blade of his knife on the captain's tunic and returned it to its sheath, then drew his automatic and followed Valin to the head of the stairs, closely followed by Carmen, Resnick and Packard.

The colonel crept down the first couple of treads, keeping in the shadows, and squinted down into the room below. The rest of the Delgado family were sitting on one of the benches under the watchful eye of the corporal, as the sergeant slumped against the door frame smoking a *cigarillo*, his rifle leaning against the wall beside him.

Valin's first shot hit the corporal in the chest, sending up a puff of dust from his jacket, the second punched home an inch or so away from the first, and the man went down like a felled tree. The sergeant barely had time to register what was happening before Valin's third slug ripped through his throat and he died clutching at his neck.

Valin crept down to the ground floor with his finger on his lips, as Jesús, his wife and children rose as one from the bench.

'Quiet,' hissed Valin. 'There's still one outside.'

'Is Carmen all right?' asked Maria, then, seeing her youngest daughter at the top of the stairs next to Spenser, relaxed.

Valin checked the bodies of the two soldiers for signs of life, then pulled the sergeant's body away from the door and looked through the filthy window at the private outside.

The young enlisted man was lounging against the front mudguard of the jeep, his rifle at port arms, unaware of what had just happened inside the house. Valin rapped on the glass to draw his attention, and showing only his hand and the sleeve of his jacket, beckoned imperiously for the private to come to the door. The boy slung his weapon over his shoulder and mounted the steps to the veranda. As he approached the doorway, Valin kicked open the door and shot him straight between the eyes, blowing off the back of his skull and sending a spray of blood, bone and brain across the boardwalk.

Valin stood in the silence that followed the violent death of the young soldier, feeling the heat of the sun as it rose to its zenith and seemed to fill the cloudless sky above the house. The jungle that surrounded the clearing looked dry and dusty in the bright sunlight, and already flies were buzzing around the bodies. He pulled out his radio, pressed the send button to all stations and called in his men. One by one they arrived, and stood in the clearing in front of the house and looked at the body at his feet.

6

'Don't just stand there,' barked Valin. 'There's another three bodies inside. Newman, Stoner. Get them shifted. You McGuires help them. Mesellier, get up to the track and keep an eye out. We still don't know if they were on their own.'

As Messelier doubled away, Angel, who was looking into the Wrangler, said: 'They weren't wearing their body armour or tin hats. And they're still in the vehicle. I reckon they were just looking for a nice, comfortable place to have a drink and while their duty away.' He reached into the back of the jeep and came up with a bottle of tequila. 'See. There's another bottle in here too. I guess our boys were just searching for a place to chill out. They sure found it.' He chuckled. 'Anyway, Colonel, it's a damn nice truck we've inherited. It's even got a si-reen.'

'We might put it to some good use later,' replied Valin. 'You seem pretty keen, Angel. Why don't you try the late private's uniform for size. It looks like it'll fit you nicely, and there's hardly a speck of blood on it. Then you can lead the way into town with the si-reen, as you call it, on, all the way.'

'Jeez, Colonel,' protested the American.

'That's an order, Angel.'

Angel shook his head, put down his carry weapon, climbed up on to the veranda and looked at the body of the private. Meanwhile, Stoner, Newman and the McGuires went inside to remove the other three bodies, and Jesús joined Valin on the corner of the veranda to catch the slight breeze from the north.

'You saved our lives, Colonel,' said the Colombian. 'Not to mention my youngest daughter's virtue.'

Valin smiled at the older man, and his choice of words. 'It was my duty. If we had not been here, you would not have been here. Any of you.'

'That is not the point. We *were* here. And you and your men's actions prevented our women being raped one by one, and all of us killed afterwards. That is the army's way. And for that I thank you.'

'I can only repeat that it was our duty. But it was also a pleasure.'

'If you can call killing four men a pleasure.'

'*Touché*.'

'So what now, Colonel?'

'I think we'd better leave. Sooner or later someone will come looking for these four. I think we'd better make ourselves extremely scarce before they do. We'll hide the bodies behind the barn, then get the transport and leave.'

'Where to?'

'I don't think *we* should go anywhere. You've done enough, Jesús. It'll be safer if we split up. Give us a map and point us in the right direction and we'll find the factory. We've been studying intelligence on it for the past three weeks. If we can't find it by ourselves by now, we deserve to blow the mission.'

'No, señor.'

'What?' Valin growled.

'You have saved our lives. Now we owe them to you. So we will come with you on the mission. There are four hundred men in the barracks next to the factory, and there are just a dozen of you. I think another six soldiers would be most welcome.'

'No, Jesús,' said Valin. 'Four of you are women. And you . . . '

'You think I am an old fool, and my womenfolk are weak?' Jesús interjected.

'I didn't say that.'

'But you thought it.'

Valin made no reply.

'Well, let me tell you, señor. I may be old. But I served my time in the army as you know. When the army was the friend of the people. And when it changed, I took to the jungle and the mountains. And my family came with me. My daughters have been sharpshooters since they were no taller than the rifles they were firing.'

'OK, OK, Jesús,' said Valin, putting up his hands in a gesture of surrender. 'You win. But you and your family will be under my command. And you will take orders from me and my lieutenant, just like the rest of the grunts.'

'Understood,' said Jesús.

'Right. We'd better get back to them then. Tell my men of your new status, and let's work out what we do next.'

Meanwhile Spenser had gone to the other side of the house, away from the stench of death, and lit up a cigarette. He heard footsteps on the veranda and turned as Carmen came round the corner behind him.

'I wanted to thank you, señor,' she said.

Spenser kept his face grim. 'You have already. Anyway, it was nothing.'

'It was.'

He shook his head.

'May I call you Chris?' she said, then paused.

'If you must.'

Spenser could have kicked himself. For the first time in years he was feeling something for a woman. So why was he behaving like this?

He realized he was coming close to blowing it, by the look on Carmen's face. 'Whoa, time out,' he said. 'Listen, I'm sorry. I'm a bit shaky. It's been a while since I've killed a man like that.'

'I understand,' Carmen said quietly. 'I too have killed men.'

'*You* have?'

'Don't be so surprised, Chris. This is a strange country.'

'I'm beginning to see that.'

'So, once again I thank you.'

'I'd do it for you anytime.'

'I know.'

He smiled. 'You're pretty sure of yourself.'

'I am. Do you want to kiss me?'

'How did you know that?'

He realized it was a pretty naïve question, even as he said it. It had been obvious since the moment he first saw her, and he knew it.

She smiled. 'I am a woman, and I saw you look at me when . . . ' She touched her breasts. 'When I was naked.'

'Any man would have.'

'Not the way you did. Not in a dirty way. I could feel you were ashamed for me. That I had been treated that way.'

Spenser nodded, and she came into his arms and they kissed. Then they heard someone running towards them, and before they could part, Angel, dressed in the private's grey uniform, which had hardly been touched by the detritus from his head wound, came round the corner and skidded to a halt. He looked at Spenser and Carmen and grinned broadly. 'Sorry, guys,' he said. 'Didn't mean to break anything up. But the boss wants to talk to all of us.'

7

Valin addressed the troops from the veranda, as they stood in the clearing in front of the house. 'Ladies and gentlemen,' he began. 'It seems that we have acquired reinforcements. Against my better judgement I have agreed that the Delgado family will join us in our mission.'

He heard a rumble of discontent from his men and raised his hands. 'Listen. We can use all the help we can get. Don't knock it. These people are willing to put their lives on the line for us, so I don't want to hear a word against it. They will take orders like the rest of you, and will be treated as such. Understood?'

The men mumbled what could just about be construed as a positive response, and Valin went on. 'Our immediate plan is to move out of here as quickly as possible. Sergeant, contact Messelier and tell him we'll collect him ASAP. The rest of you, saddle up, and let's get gone. From now on we are on full battle alert.'

Valin dismissed them and the troops went to the vehicles. After collecting their weapons from inside the house, Maria and the women took the Microbus. Carlos got into the driving seat of the Ford truck, with Spenser riding shotgun again. Jesús drove the old jeep as before, with Valin and O'Rourke as passengers, and

Angel took the wheel of the Wrangler, with Stoner in the back, looking after the light machine-gun.

As the hands of Valin's old service watch approached eleven hundred hours, the convoy of four vehicles, Angel leading the way, drove along the track through the jungle, picking up Messelier as they went, and headed back to the main road to Bogotá, where they turned north once again.

'There is another jungle track about three kilometres down the road,' Jesús informed Valin. 'We could drive in and bivouac until dusk.'

'Good idea. We don't want to be on the road for a moment longer than necessary. We could meet another patrol at any time, and I don't want to start a fire-fight unless it's absolutely unavoidable.'

Valin called up Angel on the radio and told him to drop back and let Jesús take the lead. Angel complied, and shortly afterwards Jesús aimed the jeep at what looked like a wall of impenetrable jungle. Miraculously, the vegetation opened up to reveal an overgrown track and all four vehicles left the main road.

They drove on for fifteen minutes or so until Jesús brought the jeep to a halt. 'This will do, Colonel,' he said. 'I don't think anyone will follow us in.'

'I'll mount a guard just in case,' replied Valin. 'And this is as good a place as any to check our ordnance.'

Within fifteen minutes, Stoner was on guard duty, the McGuires were tucking into the remains of the meal that the women had brought with them, and the weapons experts were checking their armaments.

Resnick was fiddling with his explosives, well away

from the main party, while Spenser unpacked his Gatling, wiped off the excess oil, and tested the action, before checking the pile of cartridge belts that held his ammunition.

As he was working, Carmen joined him, once again wearing the Colt .45 on her hip. 'That's a hell of a gun,' she said.

Spenser smiled proudly. 'The latest model, and the best. I liberated it from a British depot in Somalia. Don't tell the colonel. But then they shouldn't even have been there. Nor should I.'

'How do you feed the shells?'

'I need a loader. I guess I'll use Packard on this trip.'

'I should be proud to do it for you.'

'You would?'

Carmen nodded. 'Please show me how it's done,' she said.

On the other side of the clearing, Newman sat and covertly looked at the McGuires. They had finished eating and were busy checking their weapons. Bastards, he thought, as he listened to them chatting to each other. Fucking bastards. And in his mind's eye he was no longer sitting in the Colombian jungle smearing insect repellent on every exposed inch of skin to combat the clouds of insects that zeroed in ceaselessly. Instead he was on the streets of Derry on a cold, dark February morning two years before. His squad fanned out behind a heavily armoured Land Rover as it inched its way between the parked cars, and a dismal mixture of rain, sleet and snow drizzled on to the pavement. Next to the paratrooper were his best mates: Corporal Jimmy Reid and Private Lenny Malin. They were on a routine patrol looking for whatever turned up, when Reid took a sniper shot that cut through his body armour as if it were butter and killed him instantly. Newman saw the round hit, and his friend die, and the two steps he took after he was dead, before he tumbled to the hard, wet tarmac, with a rind of ice on the kerbstones, and lay still.

The paras never caught the sniper. They couldn't even locate where the shot had come from, although they suspected it was from the roof of a block of Republican flats that overlooked the street they had been patrolling.

Newman stayed with Reid until the ambulance arrived. The young officer in charge had ordered him to take cover, but for one of the few times in his army career, Newman disobeyed a direct order, and sheltered his dead friend's body with his own. Afterwards he didn't know why. But something told him not to let the cold, hard rain fall on to the corporal's face, and he didn't.

The next day he was up on a charge, and was confined to barracks for a month. He didn't care. He hated going out into town with his mates anyway, especially now there was one less of them. Hated the way that the population treated the British soldiers, spitting on them, deliberately ignoring them in shops and pubs, and shouting obscenities after them in the street.

Lenny Malin did not survive the tour of duty either. He took a shotgun blast in the leg, fired by a fourteen-year-old boy, and was invalided out. In many ways Newman was happy to take voluntary redundancy when it was offered. He had not lost his bottle, but he was close.

And now, thousands of miles away from home, he was being forced to listen to the Ulster brogue again. He touched the Military Medal that he had won in the Falklands, which he kept hidden in the breast pocket of his army blouse, and fingered the trigger of the shotgun he carried, dreaming of using it on the two Irishmen. Trigger, pump, he thought. Trigger, pump. And then maybe some of the pain would go away.

Messelier and Packard were sitting together with their backs to the bole of a huge fern, slapping the bugs that were targeting their hands and necks. 'This is the life, eh?' said the Frenchman sardonically. 'A soldier's life for me.'

'It could be worse,' replied Packard, lighting a cigarette. 'We might both be sitting in an office, earning peanuts and pretending to be scared of the boss.'

'Too true, my young friend. Too true.'

'So what exactly *were* you doing before this?' asked Packard.

'Ah,' said Messelier. 'I told you, it's a long story.'

'I'm sorry,' said the younger man. 'If you don't want to talk about it. I know we're not supposed to ask questions like that. But I thought we could be mates.'

'We will be, I'm sure, if we live that long. And don't apologize. Sometimes a man needs to talk.' Messelier paused and looked up through the thick fronds of the fern. 'I was a killer,' he said. 'A legalized killer for my government. I was like James Bond in those stupid films. Licensed to kill. But I killed once too often. An innocent child. It was not my finest hour.

Afterwards, I went . . . How do you say? Off the rails . . . I was an embarrassment. So my government decided to eliminate me. But I killed the man they sent to kill me, and then I ran away. But I could not stay away from killing. It is like a drug. You may find that too, Packard. But I hope not. So here I am. Back in the killing fields. But at least today, the people we are up against will fight back. No more children, I hope. I couldn't do that again.'

'You may have to.'

'If I do, I do. I just hope it won't come to it.'

'Did you kill many people?'

'Enough. And this is enough talk, my friend. I wonder if there is a drink around.'

'Tequila, I think.'

'Ah, warm tequila. But it will do. Let's go and find Angel. I believe he knows where it is hidden.'

Messelier and Packard found Angel sitting in the driving seat of the Wrangler. 'Angel,' said Messelier. 'What the hell did you do with the booze?'

'A man after my own heart,' said Angel as he produced a bottle from under the seat. 'But don't let the boss see. I don't think he approves.'

'So, how are you doing, Angel?' asked Packard, after all three of them had taken a surreptitious swig.

'Not bad. But I don't think the geek who was wearing this goddam suit before me had taken a bath for a month.'

'You are not exactly the flowers in May,' said Messelier. 'But I thought it would have been impolite to mention it.'

Angel grinned. 'But that's the life in this man's

army,' he said. 'It's a dirty job, but someone's got to do it.'

All three laughed out loud, and the bottle went round one more time.

Valin saw the three of them drinking, but said nothing. Both Packard and Angel had never seen real action before, and he trusted Messelier to take care of them. A drink or two would bond the three together, and in a way Valin envied the two youngsters their innocence. They have a lot to learn, he thought. Please God that they learn it before it's too late.

And so the day went. The sun reached its peak, then started to drop towards the west, and the squad prepared themselves for the night – and the killing to come.

8

As the afternoon lengthened, Colonel Valin called his troops together for a briefing. He spread maps and diagrams over the bonnet of the Wrangler, and the rest of the squad gathered round him. Carlos had replaced Stoner on guard duty, and Jesús would brief his son later in his native language.

'Very well, ladies and gentlemen,' said Valin. 'I believe we are all aware of our objective tonight.' He held up a grainy photograph of the factory complex. 'This is the place. A small factory that quite legally converts raw coca leaves into cocaine, on the outskirts of the town of Santa Ana, about twenty miles from the capital and with a population of some seven thousand. As you can see, the complex is surrounded by an electric fence. There is just one way in and out: a gate guarded by half-a-dozen soldiers from the barracks next door.' He held up another photograph of a grim, block-built structure. 'There are approximately four hundred soldiers billeted here, so our first job is to get as many of them away from the vicinity as possible. That is Resnick's job. Maxim, the floor is yours.'

Resnick rose from the running board of the truck where he was sitting, and walked over to stand next to his commanding officer. 'I have with me, as you are all well aware, a quantity of high explosives,' he began. 'I intend to take some of it and cause a diversion in Santa Ana. I shall be looking for a gas station near the centre, and when I find it, I intend to destroy it in the most spectacular way possible. It that doesn't bring the soldiers out, nothing will. I'll be needing a volunteer to accompany me, and cover my back. Any offers?'

Sofía raised her hand slowly. 'I will come with you, señor.'

'Can you drive?' asked Resnick.

Maria smiled at his question. 'She is the finest driver in Colombia,' she volunteered proudly.

'Can you steal a car?' asked Resnick.

'Any car you can show me,' replied Sofía brazenly. 'I am the queen of the car thieves.'

'We didn't realize that we had such talent available,' said Valin. 'And that's very good. It'll look better if you go into town as a couple. Less suspicious. Can you use a machine-gun, Sofía?'

The young woman nodded.

'Excellent. We have several new Heckler and Koch MP5K personal defence weapons with us. Do you think you could handle one?'

'Show me, and I'll tell you,' said Sofía.

'Lieutenant,' said Valin, and O'Rourke climbed into the back of the three-tonner and came back out holding a stubby, vicious-looking weapon with a folding stock and sound suppressor, complete with a holster and belt. 'Welcome to the future,' he said, as he pulled the MP5K from its holster and punched home a short magazine. 'Thirty rounds,' he explained. 'Nine mill, and it goes some.' He tossed the weapon to

Sofía. 'You'd better get some practice in. Don't worry about anyone hearing. The silencer is very effective.'

'Thank you, señor,' she said, almost curtseying, and O'Rourke winked at her.

'So much for the big diversion,' said Valin. 'At the same time, Stoner and one other will be destroying an electricity substation that feeds the town, plus the telephone exchange that is conveniently located next door. We need to cut communications as much as possible, and keep these bastards in the dark in more ways than one.' He held up another photograph, showing the generator building, with a dark, brick-built edifice next to it. 'They'll take this vehicle.' He slapped the bonnet of the Wrangler. 'And rejoin us as soon as possible back at the factory. Mr Stoner, in a previous life, has had some experience with HE, and Maxim has been giving him a crash course since we got together. Are you happy with that, Max?'

'He is a good student,' said the Russian. 'I'd rather do the job myself, but sadly I can't be in two places at once. Just remember, Johnny,' he said to Stoner, 'to wait for my diversion to stir up the hornet's nest before you blow up anything.'

'You're the boss,' said Stoner.

'I'm going to team you up with Angel,' said Valin. 'Driving an army vehicle, and dressed as he is, you shouldn't have much trouble getting in close. The communications and power complexes are subject to routine patrols according to our intelligence sources.' He nodded at Jesús, who nodded back. 'But I'm going to need you back at the factory pronto. This jeep is the best cover we've got. We're going to have to get through those gates somehow, and we might have to use it as a Trojan horse. So, Angel, try not to lose it.'

'Trust me, boss,' said Angel.

'Meanwhile,' Valin went on, 'Sergeant Keller, with his sniper rifle, will have taken up a position on the hilltop that overlooks both the factory and the barracks.' Keller was lovingly cleaning a .50-calibre Browning Barratt Model 82 A-1 semi-automatic sniper rifle with a ten-round magazine holding shells that could punch their way through the skin of an armoured car, and fitted with a 10x40 Trijicon optical gunsight with tritium-powered red and black dots for night and day shooting. 'The rifle he is caressing is accurate up to two and a half thousand metres, but tonight he'll be less than half that distance away, and he is a good shot, believe me. There are a few of us here who owe our lives to his talent.'

Keller smiled darkly, and carried on cleaning his weapon.

'Gerry,' Valin said to the elder of the McGuire brothers. 'I want you to take a pair of night glasses and act as his spotter. Daniel, you'll be with the rest of us in the main assault team. We'll go in and take the charges with us, which Resnick will set off as soon as he catches up.'

'And if he doesn't?' asked O'Rourke, then looked at the Russian and put his hands up. 'No offence, Maxim,' he said.

'Then I will set the charges,' said Valin sharply. 'Or you, or whoever's around. It's not a difficult job. The preparation's the hard part, isn't it, Max?' Resnick nodded. 'But he *will* return,' said Valin confidently. 'He wouldn't have lasted three years in Afghanistan if he couldn't get across a hick town guarded by an army made up of conscripted old men and boys. And I didn't take on this job to fail, is that understood?'

O'Rourke nodded. 'Just checking, sir,' he said.

'Fair enough, Mark,' said Valin. 'Any other questions so far?' There was silence, so he continued. 'Our main man covering the barracks itself will be Chris Spenser and his Gatling. I believe he has a new ammunition feeder that he's been showing the ropes to this afternoon. Your job, Chris, is to keep the remaining soldiers bottled up in that building. It's not going to be an easy job, so I'm going to put Messelier, Packard, Maria and Carlotta with you. Three of them armed with H and Ks, and the other with the grenade-launcher.' His eyes found the two women. 'It's going to be dangerous – one of the most dangerous jobs of them all. But I need your manpower, or should I say womanpower. I need a lid kept on that place, so if you have a problem with it, speak now.'

The older woman looked at her daughter, and they both smiled. 'Today is as good as any other to die, señor, said Maria. 'We have seen death once already today. Another glimpse will not kill us.' And she giggled like a schoolgirl at her own joke.

'Fine. Good attitude. Newman, Lieutenant O'Rourke and myself, plus Jesús, Carlos and you, Daniel, will go into the complex. We secure it and destroy it. Simple.'

He looked round the clearing at their still faces and paused. 'Afterwards we get out of town fast and get back to the airstrip. We will meet up at this spot here.' Bending over one of the maps on the bonnet of the jeep, he found the location he was seeking. 'There is a crossroads on the south side of the town. That will be our RV. We make our way there as best we can. It's a four-hour drive back to the airstrip. The plane flies in at dawn. That means we need to leave Santa Ana at two hundred hours at the latest. I don't intend to leave anyone behind. The pilot has told me he will make one more trip at the same time next day. But that may be impossible. If the army discovers the location of the airstrip, it *will* be impossible. So I need everyone at that rendezvous on time. I don't care how you get there. Just be there, and we'll all be drinking champagne by noon tomorrow. But we've got to be flexible. The odds are against us, even with the help of Jesús and his family. But we have surprise on our side, and the latest weapons that the American taxpayers' money can buy. We have to get in and out before they even know what's hit them. Just remember that and we'll be OK. There are K-rations in the truck. I suggest we eat now. We don't know when we'll get another chance.' He paused again. 'That's it, ladies and gentlemen. It only leaves me to say good luck, and good hunting.' He began to fold up his maps.

Resnick took Sofía to one side. 'Do you want to try out that gun?' he asked. 'I want to make sure you can cover me properly.'

'I'd love to,' said the girl with a smile. 'Where shall we go?'

'A little way into the jungle,' he said. 'I'll get some spare magazines from the truck. Wait here. Do you want anything to eat?'

'A picnic,' said Sofía. 'How lovely. Yes, please. Whatever you're having.'

Resnick went over to the truck and collected four

spare full clips for the Heckler and Koch, a box of one hundred 9mm bullets, a pocket full of K-ration tins, and a bottle of water. The time for drinking anything stronger was over. He went back and joined Sofía, who by now had strapped the weapon to her hip, and after she had told her mother where she was going and why, they struck off into the jungle.

'This is far enough,' said the Russian after they had gone a few yards. 'Do you want to eat first? Or shoot first?'

'Shoot.'

Resnick took the gun from her and showed her its simple workings. 'Single shot or full auto,' he said. 'Use the auto. If nothing else, you'll scare the shit out of anyone you shoot at . . . Sorry.'

'For what?'

'For my language.'

'I have heard worse.'

'That's no excuse. I apologize.'

'I accept.'

Resnick felt himself redden. 'Right,' he said, to cover his embarrassment. 'Safety off.' He handed her the weapon. 'It's ready to go. Try aiming for that yellow tree over there.' He pointed to a tree some thirty yards away.

Sofía unfolded the stock, wedged it against her hip, flexed her knees, lowered the weapon slightly and pulled the trigger. The 9mm Teflon-coated shells silently stitched a neat line up the bole of the tree, and she moved the gun slightly from left to right and chopped the trunk off neatly about five feet up. By then the gun was empty, and she pulled out the used magazine and stuck it into the waistband of her skirt. 'Next,' she said.

'That's good,' said Resnick. 'You weren't kidding. If you're as good at stealing cars, it's money in the bank.'

'I am,' said Sofía. 'Better. Can we eat now?'

Back in the clearing, the men were talking among themselves. 'What do you reckon?' said Daniel to his brother.

'What the hell do I know?' replied Gerry. 'But I've got to be honest with you, little brother, something in my water tells me we're up shit creek.'

'So what do we do?'

'What the hell *can* we do? We came into this with our eyes open. We've got nowhere else *to* go. We follow Valin or we die where we stand. I reckon there's a couple of guys in the squad would be glad to nail our Republican hides to a tree.'

'Bloody Brits.'

'You never spoke a truer word.'

Messelier and Packard were sharing a can of cold pork and beans, sitting on the tailgate of the truck. 'Glad you came?' asked the Frenchman.

'I wouldn't have missed it for the world.'

'You're a strange guy, Packard. I would like to have met your father.'

'He was a strange sort too, so I'm told.'

'So we're going to be keeping the barracks pinned down. That's good,' said Messelier. 'We can watch each other's backs. I want to come out of this episode alive.'

'Me too,' agreed Packard.

But he was lying again. He didn't want to live. Indeed that was his main reason for signing up with

Valin's Raiders. The same reason he had joined the Australian army, and then worked himself a discharge on psychological grounds when he found out that he would probably never come within a mile of combat. Lenny Packard wanted to die because he was a killer himself, and he hated it.

The first man he ever killed was the driver of an overland truck transporter with three wagons hitched up to its Volvo tractor. The man had been speeding in a cloud of dust along the highway fifty miles from the lonely sheep station that Packard's mother had inherited from his late father. For years, ever since he was a kid, Lenny had practised with his father's rifle, using ammunition illegally bought from a friend of a friend, so that his mother wouldn't find out, and he was a crack shot. He had slaughtered every animal that came into his sights, large or small. But animals were not enough. Now he was hunting for bigger game. And finally, one morning after he had borrowed the family pick-up truck, he had driven alone to the main road, hidden his vehicle behind a clump of scrub, and taken up his position on a ridge overlooking the highway.

Not much traffic used the route, and Lenny had to wait for hours under the burning sun until a target presented itself. But he was patient, and he knew someone would come along eventually.

First of all he saw a dust cloud, far away, which gradually materialized into the mighty roadliner. He smiled and squinted through the telescopic sights at the dirty windscreen through which he could see the head and shoulders of the driver. He exhaled and squeezed the trigger gently. The rifle kicked into his shoulder, and for a second he thought he had missed. Then the big, turbo-driven tractor swerved slightly to the right, then more violently to the left, and the cab and the three containers jackknifed slowly, the front wheels of the Volvo dug into the sand at the side of the road, and the tractor and its trailers began to roll over and break up, until the cab exploded into flames.

Lenny put the FN FAL back into its case and returned to his pick-up. He was not interested in the driver of the juggernaut. He was dead. Strike one.

Messelier had said that he was a strange guy, and Lenny Packard had told him that his father was too. And he'd spoken the truth. But what he didn't know was that his old man often took the rifle out on hunting expeditions, and buried the humans that he had sniped in shallow graves all over the outback. But he wouldn't have been surprised. Not in the least. And the police didn't draw any conclusions from the fact that the mysterious disappearances of tourists and transients in the area ceased when Joe Packard went to Vietnam, only to return in a pine box. They were just grateful. And of course they didn't suspect young Lenny when the disappearances started again some fourteen years later.

But Lenny hated himself for the compulsion that had driven him to kill half-a-dozen people over the next five years. Hated himself, but didn't do much about it. He lacked the nerve to either turn himself in to the authorities or kill himself. But he knew that the only way to stop himself killing more innocent people was for him to die, and as he sat next to Messelier he prayed that it would happen soon.

On the other side of the clearing Spenser and Carmen were going through the procedure to keep the Gatling shooting smoothly once again. 'I've loaded the belts with a mixture of shells,' explained the American. 'High-explosive . . . armour-piercing . . . tracers. You name it. But where we are, it's going to get hot in more ways than one. I hope you can handle it.'

'Trust me,' said Carmen. 'Where are you going after the mission is over?'

'Christ knows. Back to England, I suppose. Until we get another job. What about you?'

She shrugged eloquently. 'Who knows?'

'Have you ever been to England?'

'No, I have never been outside Colombia.'

'Maybe you'd like to.'

'I hear it is very cold and damp there.'

'Only sometimes.'

She nodded. 'Maybe . . . ' she said.

Angel lounged in the front seat of the liberated jeep smoking a joint, while Stoner checked the M60 mounted in the back. 'You reckon we'll have to use that?' asked Angel.

'Chances are,' replied Stoner. 'I was trained on one similar in the Legion.'

'That's good news. I'd hate to go on the mission with someone who didn't know what he was doing.'

'You scared, kid?'

'Shitting my pants. This calm exterior is just a pose.'

'Give us a hit on that joint, then, because I ain't exactly looking forward to tonight myself.'

Newman collared Keller as the sergeant carefully put his Barratt back in its case. 'I need some grenades, Sarge,' he said.

'Help yourself,' said the German.

'I hope that Irish bastard is a good spotter,' Newman muttered.

'He should be. I had a talk with him last night. Seems he spent some time on the south side of the Irish border spotting a Yank who was picking off British troops.' Keller smiled grimly. 'Some of your mates maybe.'

'Don't remind me.'

'Forget it. We're all on the same side now.'

'Sure,' said the ex-para as he went off to fill a sack with grenades and collect another box of cartridges for his shotgun. 'Sure thing.'

Away from the main group, Colonel Valin was giving his lieutenant his final briefing.

'This is it then, Mark,' he said.

'It certainly is, sir.'

'You don't seem too happy.'

'I just don't know if this lot are ready.'

'As ready as they'll ever be.'

'It's not going to be easy.'

'It never was. Just keep them together and we'll be all right.'

'If you say so, sir.'

'I do. I'm going to speak to Jesús. I'm still not crazy about taking the Delgados with us.'

'I think they can take care of themselves, sir.'

'It's not them I'm worried about. It's us.'

Valin left O'Rourke and went over to where the Delgado family, minus Sofía and Carmen, were sitting together, talking in low tones. 'Everything OK?' he asked.

Jesús nodded at him.

'Still determined to come with us?'

'Of course.'

'Then we move out in a couple of hours.'

9

In the jungles of Colombia, the dusk comes early and quickly. By six in the evening, beneath the dense foliage of the tropical forest, it was almost dark, and Valin ordered his men to pack up and move out. There was only one difference in the travel arrangements: Carmen was now in the cab of the Ford truck with her brother and Spenser.

Before they left the clearing, Jesús approached Valin. 'Spenser,' he said. 'What kind of man is he?'

'One of the best,' replied Valin. 'I've known him for years.'

'I think he is interested in Carmen.'

'With all due respect to you, Jesús, who wouldn't be?' said Valin. 'She is a beautiful young woman. And he did kill the man who was going to rape her earlier today. That kind of thing forges bonds.'

'She is beautiful, yes. But crazy in the head, I think. Is he married?'

'No.'

'How old is he?'

'Does it matter?'

'These days, I suppose not. The whole world is going mad.'

'So does it matter if a few more join in?'

'I suppose not,' the old man sighed. 'And what about the Russian?'

'Resnick?'

'Yes.'

'What about him?'

'Sofía is going into town with him to blow up the gas station.'

'Someone had to.'

'I just don't know, Colonel. Here I am with three daughters all of marriageable age, and none of them has shown any interest in men, except now, two of them seem to have fallen for men who may not live through the night.'

'It could be worse.'

'I suppose so. At least neither of them fell for the president,' said Jesús, and he burst out laughing.

Valin laughed too, then said: 'So are you OK about it?'

Jesús shrugged. 'I suppose so,' he said again. 'At least we know they can take care of them.'

'Like I said,' observed Valin, 'it could be worse.'

One by one the vehicles pulled out of the clearing and took the track back to the main road. Only Jesús in the lead jeep showed any lights, and the pace of the convoy was torturously slow. But eventually they made it on to the blistered main road and with a roar of his engine Angel took the lead. While they had been hanging around, Jesús had gone through the maps with the young American and his British passenger. The road to Bogotá was as straight as any in the region, with no turn-offs to negotiate, and the fact that an army vehicle was leading the convoy was bound to ensure a safe passage.

The two jeeps, the Microbus and the old Ford truck, now all with headlights on, clocked up an average speed of just over thirty miles per hour. The surface of the road began to improve as they got closer to Bogotá, and other traffic started to appear, but they saw no sign of any military presence until they had been travelling for just under three hours, when they suddenly came up behind an army convoy.

Angel slowed down to almost a walking pace, and looked over his shoulder at Valin in the jeep behind him, who gave him a hand signal to stop. The young American allowed the jeep to coast to a halt at the side of the road, and his commanding officer exited his vehicle and jogged up to join him.

'What do we do, boss?' asked Angel.

'You overtake that convoy and get into town. Check out the substation and the telephone exchange. Use your siren if you have to. Jesús tells me this is a regular army convoy, not Militia, so they shouldn't be interested in you. Militia and army don't exactly get on in this country. We'll follow behind. You recce the area, and check back with me. Meet us at the crossroads RV just this side of town that we looked at on the map. And another thing . . . '

'Boss?'

'Jesús tells me there's a midnight curfew on the town. It's just come into force. I don't like it a bit. More military activity in the area, and now a curfew. It stinks. I've got a gut feeling we may be expected.'

'Shit, boss,' said Stoner from where he was sitting behind the trigger of the LMG. 'I knew something like this was going to happen. Why didn't the old geezer tell you before? Is he playing both sides against the middle? Because if he is . . . ' He made as if to get out of the jeep.

'He told me this morning,' said Valin. 'I just chose not to share the happy news until now. So relax. Move out, Angel, and take it easy.'

'That's my middle name, Colonel,' said Angel as he jammed the Wrangler into gear, and set off after the convoy, headlights on full beam and the siren already screaming.

I'm too old for all this, thought Valin as he headed back to the other jeep. Far too old.

10

Angel sped past the convoy with the pedal to the metal, and screeched off ahead at about seventy miles per hour.

'Slow down a bit, for Chrissake,' shouted Stoner from the back, above the roar of the slipstream and the scream of the engine. 'Or you'll have us off the fucking road.'

Angel looked over his shoulder with a grin. 'Relax. I used to drive superstocks at the San Marino stadium, back in the good ol' US of A.'

'This ain't the good old US of A,' screamed Stoner. 'And I ain't wearing a seat belt.'

'If you're that worried about your health you shouldn't be here,' Angel yelled back, but slowed down slightly. Even so, they arrived at the outskirts of Santa Ana within half an hour, no longer constrained by the speed of the slower vehicles in the convoy. So the first members of Valin's team made contact with their target at slightly before twenty-two hundred hours on day one of the mission.

As the Wrangler passed the first few scattered dwellings, Angel dropped speed even further, to less than thirty, and kept an eye out for roadblocks.

Stoner moved forward, knelt behind the driver's seat and said: 'Looks pretty quiet.'

'So far,' said Angel. 'Hey, Stoner.'

'What?'

'You speak any Spanish?'

'No. You?'

'No. So what happens if anyone tries to speak to us?'

'We shoot the fucker, that's what happens.'

Both men laughed.

They cruised towards the town centre, and the closer they got, the more military presence they felt. At one point a three-ton personnel carrier, with a full complement of soldiers in combat gear, crossed in front of them, and there were foot patrols every quarter of a mile or so, but non paid them much attention.

'I wonder if this is usual, or for our benefit,' said Angel. 'And where are all the civilians? There's hardly any about, and it's still two hours to curfew time.'

'Christ knows,' replied Stoner. 'Just take it easy, and we'll be cool.'

Angel found the town centre and turned the jeep in the direction of the telephone exchange and electricity substation.

'It should be just down here,' he said to Stoner, as he steered into a side street.

'Keep driving,' hissed Stoner. 'We've got company.'

Parked between the two buildings they were looking for was another personnel carrier, and Stoner had spotted the glow of a cigarette in the back as someone took a drag.

Angel drove by slowly and turned off at the next

corner. 'Shit,' said Stoner. 'It ain't gonna be as easy as we thought to take them out.'

'We'll manage,' said Angel. 'Do you want to take a look at the factory and barracks?'

'Might as well,' replied Stoner, and Angel headed back towards the town centre, then headed west in the direction of the complex. On the way, two jeeps full of soldiers passed them going in the opposite direction, and they spotted three more foot patrols.

The factory was not difficult to find, as it was brightly lit and the glow of the lights could be seen for a mile or so. Angel stopped the jeep at the brow of a hill less than half that distance from the factory, and he and Stoner scoped the view.

The factory and adjoining barracks lay in a depression between two hills. One was the hill where the two mercenaries were parked; the other, behind the complex, had once been cleared of vegetation but now seemed to be partially reclaimed by the jungle.

'Can we get off this road?' said Stoner. 'And up on the other side? Looks like the ideal place for a sniper to cover the whole area.'

Angel nodded, put the jeep into gear and let it drift down towards the factory. About a quarter of a mile before the slip road that led to the complex, he spotted a track off to the right, killed his lights and drove on to it. It was a slow and difficult climb, even with the Wrangler in four-wheel drive, but eventually they found the top of the second hill, and from the cover of the new growth of trees and ferns had an uninterrupted view of both the factory and the barracks beyond it.

Stoner took out his binoculars and swept them across the two brightly lit buildings, which lay close together. The slip road back to the main road sloped gently upwards towards the entrance to the factory, and a side road led off it that, two or three hundred yards down the hill, went up to the barracks. Trucks, jeeps, personnel carriers and a few regular cars painted in army colours were parked on the U-shaped drive in front of the building. There was a fair amount of activity – soldiers moving about on various tasks, vehicles coming and going – but nothing to suggest that they were on any particular state of alert. The factory was busy too, with civilians moving from one building to another, and at the gatehouse that covered the entrance Stoner spotted at least six heavily armed soldiers on guard, and a couple of jeeps parked with their drivers at the wheel.

'This is the ideal place,' he said to Angel. 'Get Keller up here with that rifle of his and he'll have complete control of both the factory and the barracks.'

'Yeah,' agreed the American. 'And once we knock the lights out, it'll be chaos down there.'

'They're bound to have an emergency generator,' said Stoner. 'Now where the hell could that be?'

'Who knows?' said Angel. 'In the basement, probably. Maybe we'll get lucky, and Spenser will knock it out with that Gatling of his.'

'Maybe,' agreed Stoner. 'We'd better get back to the colonel, and tell him what's happening. We've seen all we can here.'

'OK,' said Angel, and he turned the jeep round on the track, drove back down to the road and headed back into town, where he picked up the main road again. He found the rendezvous without difficulty, and swung off the road into the shadows of the jungle, where Messelier appeared out of nowhere like a wraith and led them to where the other three vehicles were waiting, parked out of sight.

'What's the good word?' asked Valin when Angel and Stoner joined him at the command post he had set up in the back of Jesús's jeep.

'Lots of activity,' said Stoner. 'Patrols everywhere. Motorized and on foot. Not much civilian presence, though. I get the distinct feeling that the authorities know something's up, but not exactly when it's going to happen. We found the telephone exchange with no bother. There's a truck full of army watching it and the substation next door. Then we took a shufti at the factory. We found an ace spot for Keller to snipe from. Up on a hill overlooking it. It's ideal.'

'Right,' said Valin. 'Good work.' He called Jesús, Keller and O'Rourke over, who listened as Stoner repeated his story. 'What do you say, Jesús?' asked Valin.

'It's exactly as I thought, Colonel,' replied the Colombian. 'As I told you this morning, I suspected as much.'

'But you don't think we're particularly expected tonight of all nights?' Valin asked Stoner.

'That's not the impression I get. It feels like they're on a yellow alert. Waiting for something or someone, but that's all.'

'It's just as well that only Tank and Jesús knew what day we were due to make our strike, then, isn't it,' said Valin.

'You think someone's tipped them off that you were coming?' asked Jesús.

'That we were coming, yes. But not exactly when,'

replied Valin. 'Otherwise they'd have been waiting at the airstrip this morning to blow the plane out of the sky. But it certainly doesn't make our job any easier.'

'I've got a suggestion, Colonel,' said Stoner.

'Let's hear it then.'

'We're never gonna get four vehicles through the centre of town. It's twenty-three hundred now, and already all the civilians are off the street, and we didn't see one civvy car moving around. I suggest we go in the back way, get Sergeant Keller and his spotter up on the hill overlooking the compound in Jesús's jeep. It's the ideal place. We leave the Microbus here, and put the rest of the Delgados in the truck. That way, at least there'll be one vehicle here to get us back to the airstrip if anything happens to the rest. Not that I think it'll come to that. Then Angel and I take Resnick and Sofía into town in our jeep to set up the diversion. He blows the petrol station, then they steal a motor and get back to you. We wait five minutes or so to give whoever leaves the barracks to see what's occurring time to get away, then we blow the substation and the telephone exchange, and get back over to you. By then you should have the factory and barracks pretty well sewn up, and in we go and blow the place to kingdom come.'

Valin looked at O'Rourke. 'Mark?' he said.

'Sounds good to me, Colonel,' replied the lieutenant. 'Let me check the maps to see what road we need to take to get round to the other side of town.'

O'Rourke picked up a map case, opened it and scanned the contents by the light of his torch. 'Yeah,' he said. 'That works.'

'Good,' said Valin. 'Mark, get everyone together for a final short briefing, and we'll be off.'

A minute or two later the squad gathered together in front of Valin. The Delgado women wore the dead soldier's body armour, which had been in the captured jeep, and had all been issued with Heckler and Koch MP5Ks. Messelier carried a South African-manufactured ARMSCOR 40mm multi-shot grenade-launcher, a semi-automatic six-shot drum revolver – a single-barrelled weapon with a folding stock. It looked like a sub-machine-gun and apart from the cylinder was about the same size. It had a forward and back pistol grip. Its muzzle velocity was 80 metres per second and it had a combat range of 425 metres. It swung open like a revolver for loading and could fire any combination of high-explosive, smoke, gas, illumination and anti-riot rounds. Loaded with a full cylinder, it weighed only 7kg; and the weight was between the hands, where it should be. It was fitted with an occluded sight that was used with both eyes and was self-graduated to 375 metres, where the user picked out a red dot. It was one hell of a weapon and it felt good in Messelier's hands as he slotted in the HE grenades that he would use on the first strike. In his pockets he carried a dozen smoke grenades and more HE for later use. Spenser had his Gatling on his shoulder and Sergeant Keller was nursing his Barratt.

'Revised plan,' said Valin. 'But only slightly. What happens now is that Stoner and Angel lead us in. They've scouted the area, and have an overview. Then they take Resnick and Sofía into town. Sergeant Keller, you take up your position with Gerry on the hill looking down on the factory. Chris, you find a field of fire at the bottom of the hill. We all wait for the diversion explosion, then the electricity to go, and we put a blanket on the barracks, then blow the factory. Rendezvous here, and head back to the airstrip. Any questions?'

There were none.

'OK,' he said. 'Saddle up, people. We're in business.'

11

Everyone piled into their designated vehicle and all three set off, with the captured jeep at the front, leaving the VW safely parked with its keys in the exhaust pipe. They took the road that dissected the highway they had come in on, and headed round the edge of Santa Ana. For this final part of their journey, O'Rourke joined Angel and Stoner in the Wrangler to check the route.

After about twenty minutes the lieutenant tapped Angel on the shoulder and told him to slow down. A quarter of a mile or so further down the road there was a turn-off towards the town, and O'Rourke told him to take it. The two jeeps and the truck turned off into the blackness of the jungle, and with their headlights cutting through the darkness they headed towards the factory.

The road came out the other side of the factory, about two miles from the centre of Santa Ana. Valin got Jesús to flash the lead jeep, and then jumped out and ran forward. 'You go on,' he said to Angel. 'We'll follow in about three minutes, and the truck can come about three minutes after us.'

'The turn-off is about a quarter of a mile past the slip road to the factory,' said Stoner. 'Don't miss it, for fuck's sake.'

'We won't,' said Valin. 'Now go, go, go.'

The lead jeep peeled off down the road, past the factory, and at the last moment Angel killed the lights and spun the wheel so that the vehicle shot off on to the track leading up the hill.

'Perfect,' said Stoner, looking back through the fern fronds. 'No one saw a thing.'

Within six minutes they were joined by the other jeep and the truck, and the squad dismounted. 'Jesús,' said Valin. 'Let Gerry take over and drive your jeep up the hill.'

Jesús tossed the Irishman the keys, and slid in behind the wheel, while Keller, with sniper rifle and twenty spare magazines, climbed into the passenger seat. They took off.

Meanwhile, Resnick had carefully stashed four knapsacks of high explosive into the rear of the Wrangler. Then he turned, and from one of the cavernous pockets of his jacket took three radio transmitters. He handed one to Valin, tossed the second to Stoner, and held up the remaining one in the air. 'Lieutenant,' he said. 'Give me a little light, will you?'

O'Rourke shone his torch on the transmitter in Resnick's hand. 'Stoner, Angel. This is how you blow the packages I will leave with you,' said the Russian. 'Colonel. This is how you blow the rest of the charges in case I do not return. It is simplicity itself.' He paused for effect, then went on. 'In the right-hand corner' – he pointed with his finger – 'is the on/off switch.' He touched the button, and a tiny green light glowed on the face of the remote control. 'It is now armed. Stoner, do not turn yours on until I have blown up the garage, and you have placed your charges where they will do the most damage. Colonel, I hope I will be back here to do the job, but just in case, do not turn *yours* on until you hear the two separate blasts, and you have put the explosives where they will destroy the factory. When they *are* switched on, you simply touch this red button at the bottom and the charges blow.'

Resnick indicated the button in question, but was careful not to touch it. Then he switched off the transmitter and the green light died. 'But be careful,' he warned. 'All three are live, and one could trigger the rest.' He saw the looks on their faces and grinned. 'But don't worry. They won't. They only work up to a distance of a mile or so, and they're all tuned to different frequencies. But just to be on the safe side, keep them turned off until you need to use them. Everyone clear?' Stoner and Valin grunted their assent. 'I want *all* of you to understand,' the Russian said to the rest. 'Who knows what will happen in the next hour or so?'

The others mumbled at his words, and Resnick nodded. 'Now I've also added a hand detonator to each package in case anyone fancies committing suicide in a very spectacular way. Open the knapsacks and you'll see a short length of knotted cord. It works rather like the pin on a hand-grenade. Pull it and the charge blows. But there is no time-delay. When the cord is pulled, the charges blow there and then. So don't pull them. That's my advice. Unless you are in a position where you're going to die anyway.' He looked round at the serious faces, lit by the dim reflection from O'Rourke's torchlight. 'Cheer up,' he said. 'It may never happen. Right. I think we will leave now.'

Then he helped Sofía into the back of the Wrangler, and joined her.

'Just keep the charges out of the line of fire until I get back, Colonel,' the Russian said. 'We don't want any accidents, do we?'

Valin smiled. 'Course we don't,' he said. 'And good luck.'

'Thank you,' replied Resnick. 'See you back here shortly.'

Angel got behind the wheel of the Wrangler and started the engine.

'Drive carefully, Angel,' said O'Rourke, as the American put the vehicle into gear.

'Will do, Ell-Tee,' replied Angel. 'Watch yourselves now.'

He spun the wheel and slowly nosed the jeep through the undergrowth back on to the main road, and was away.

'Right, the rest of you,' said Valin when the sound of the engine had receded into the distance. 'Get yourselves ready.'

12

Angel expertly sent the jeep rocketing towards the town centre. He wanted to get the charges laid and blown as quickly as possible, and make it back to where the real fighting was going to be, as soon as he could.

'You want us to pick you up after?' he shouted to Resnick in the back.

The Russian looked at Sofía. 'What do you say?'

'No,' she replied. 'I'll get us a car. Trust me.'

'Don't bother, Angel,' Resnick shouted back. 'We'll make it on our own.'

Then he pulled Sofía close and said: 'You know of a gas station?'

'Of course. I've been here a thousand times. I know just the place,' she said, grinning. 'It's right opposite the police headquarters. I hate those bastard pigs.'

Resnick grinned back. 'Perfect. We'll give them something to think about too. A little bonus,' he said quietly.

'I hoped you'd say that,' said Sofía, leaning forward and tapping Angel on the shoulder. 'Take the next turn on the left,' she said. 'There's a gas station down on the right.'

The jeep bounced over the cobbles that formed the

side street, and skidded to a halt outside a deserted petrol station. Opposite it was a brick-and-wood building with an illuminated sign that read 'POLICIA'. Resnick and Sofía baled out, taking two of the knapsacks of explosives with them.

'Good luck, guys,' said Angel as he gunned the engine. 'Don't take any wooden nickels.' With a screech of tyres, he was gone.

'Couldn't wait to say goodbye,' said Resnick.

'Who could blame him?' replied Sofía. 'With that lot over the road.'

Resnick cocked his Kalashnikov and smiled at her. 'Don't worry about cops,' he said. 'They're easy meat. Now we need a car.'

'I'll check round the back,' Sofía replied. 'There should be something.' Then she was gone.

Resnick kept a careful eye on the police building as he looked for the cover of the underground petrol tanks. It wasn't hard to find. Between the twin banks of pumps, he found a manhole, sealed with a cast-iron lid. With difficulty he hoisted the cover off, and saw the four line feeds that took the various grades of petrol and diesel into the tanks. He smiled and dropped one of the knapsacks down into the hole, then replaced the lid.

The Russian stood up as he heard the snarl of a powerful engine. An ancient, dusty-pink Chevrolet sedan, with Sofía at the wheel, turned the corner from behind the workshops at the back of the garage and purred to a halt beside him. Sofía wound down the window and leaned out. 'Like it?' she said.

'Very interesting,' Resnick replied. 'But will it get us where we want to go?'

'Count on it,' Sofía replied. 'Are you ready?'

'Won't be long,' Resnick said. 'I just want to give the local police a nice surprise.'

He threw his carry gun into the car and loped off across the road, carrying the second knapsack over his shoulder. The police station was very quiet and he hesitated for a moment before lobbing the sack down into the area in front of it, and then hopped over the metal railing that separated the building from the street. There were no signs of guards. Very lax, he noted. He dropped down about six feet, found the sack and shoved it into a grille that he reckoned was the exhaust for the air-conditioning system. He turned, pulled himself up and over the railings again, and ran back across the street to join Sofía in the Chevrolet, which smelt of damp and cat's piss. 'Drive,' he said. And she took off.

At the end of the street he told her to stop. 'Let me out here,' he said. 'Go at least two streets down before you stop. Then park around a corner, close to a building. Otherwise the concussion will blow out the windows.'

As soon as Resnick was out of the car, Sofía accelerated away again, and the Chevy spun round a corner just as he was taking cover behind the nearest house. There he took out the remote control he carried in his pocket, laid it carefully on the pavement, reached into his pocket again and removed a pair of plugs and carefully inserted them in his ears. He had laid enough charges to know how quickly a demolition expert could go deaf. Then he picked up the remote again, turned on the green light, and touched the red button.

The petrol station and the police headquarters erupted simultaneously. From his position behind the corner of the house, Resnick watched as the package he had placed under the manhole cover in the garage blew it straight up through the roof canopy above, on the crest of a pillar of fire, with an enormous bang. In the same split second, the front of the police station seemed to lift a dozen feet in the air, then blew out, burying the two police cars parked in front in a pile of rubble and broken bodies. There was a frozen silence for an instant, then Resnick heard a deep rumble from the bowels of the earth, and with an explosion that made the previous one sound like a pin dropping, the buried petrol tanks blew out in a sea of boiling fuel, and every window close by imploded as one.

Back at the factory the waiting soldiers heard the explosions echo across the silent town, and watched in awe as the mushroom cloud from the petrol tanks began to rise.

'Shit,' said Packard. 'Was that nuclear?'

'Good job!' said Valin. 'That should stir things up.'

It was not long before he was proved correct. Within half a minute the barracks was like an ant's nest. Troops came out of every exit, hastily buckling on equipment, and dived into the cars, jeeps and trucks that were parked outside, before racing in the direction of the fireball.

'Excellent,' whispered O'Rourke. 'We've just got rid of a hundred and fifty of the opposition.'

'They'll be back,' observed Valin drily. 'Now come on, all of you. Move back to the factory. And keep in the shelter of the trees. We don't want to be spotted yet.'

After Angel had dropped off Resnick and Sofía, he had sped back in the direction of the telephone exchange, and skidded the jeep to a halt on the corner of the main street and the side turning that led to it, just as the Russian slid the manhole cover back into place after laying the first charge.

'You wanna do the thing?' Angel said to Stoner.

'What about the guards?'

'Leave them to me,' Angel growled, and leaving the engine running, he pulled himself out of the driver's seat, hopped into the back and got behind the trigger of the LMG. 'I've used one of these before too. Get up there and lay the charges. If you're spotted I'll give you cover. You can drive when you get back. Quick. I feel a big bang coming on.'

As the words left his lips, the petrol station and police headquarters blew.

Angel and Stoner turned towards the source of the explosions as one, and had an excellent view of the carnage over the tops of the houses in between.

'Jesus Christ,' said Stoner. 'What the fuck's he got in these bags?'

'Plant 'em and let's find out,' urged Angel. 'Look out, here come the sightseers.'

The guards on the telephone exchange and electricity substation had rushed out at the sound of the bombs, and together they ran around the side of the exchange and stood, open-mouthed, in a group gawping at Resnick's handiwork.

Angel squinted through the sights of the light

machine-gun, squeezed the trigger and let go a burst of high-explosive shells that cut the guards down where they stood, hacking lumps of flesh from their bodies as they hammered home. Then he raked the body of the personnel carrier that was still parked where he and Stoner had seen it earlier. One of the bullets hit the petrol tank and the back of the truck bounced up as the fuel exploded and spewed forth a pair of soldiers, their uniforms ablaze. Angel cut them down with another burst.

'Lay the charges,' the American shouted to Stoner, who could hardly hear him for post-explosive concussion, which had set bells ringing in his ears. 'Before any more of the mothers get here! Slash and burn. Slash and burn.'

Stoner didn't have to be told twice. He shot down the street like a greyhound, kicked open the door to the substation and threw a knapsack inside. Then he slammed the door shut, vaulted over the fence that divided the generator from the telephone exchange and did the same there. He turned and sprinted back to where Angel was waiting, leaping over the bodies of the fallen soldiers as he did so. As he ran along the street, Angel was firing at the front of the buildings, where faces had appeared at the windows. He laughed out loud as they vanished, and shouted out to Stoner: 'Come on, you fucker! Get a move on.'

Stoner dived into the driver's seat, crashed into gear and slammed his foot down. As the Wrangler roared off, Angel fired one last, long burst down the street as they went. Stoner almost immediately slammed on the brakes, slewing the jeep to a halt in the middle of the road, and took the radio transmitter from his pocket.

He thumbed the on switch, hit the red button and behind him the street erupted as every electric light in town, and for miles around, went off.

'Fucking A,' yelled Angel. 'Let's get the fuck back to the boss.'

Stoner trod down again as the dust pall settled behind them, and at long last, the citizens of Santa Ana began to show themselves on the streets.

Valin's group heard the second explosion too, a second after the lights went out in the barracks and the factory.

That was Keller's signal to start firing, and his first bullet ripped through the tunic of a young subaltern on his first day of guard duty at the factory gates, which was also to prove to be his last, for he was dead before he hit the ground.

The German's second bullet smashed through the windscreen of one of the jeeps parked by the gatehouse, killing the driver, while the third slammed into the gatehouse itself, sending the inhabitants to the floor in panic.

Good man, thought Valin as he watched the mayhem that Keller's bullets were wreaking on the guards outside the complex. With the rest of his group he was under light cover at the top of the slip road, equidistant between the factory and the barracks next door. Turning to Spenser, he said: 'Chris, let them have it.'

The American smiled, and squeezed the trigger of his Gatling, sending a stream of bullets spewing towards the barracks, where they tore holes in the brickwork and shattered the windows. As he did so, Carmen fed the ammunition belt to the gun as if she had been doing it for years.

Packard, Maria and Carlotta took up their positions, two on either side of Spenser, and added to his barrage of fire a hail of bullets from their Heckler and Kochs. Messelier pulled the trigger of the ARMSCOR grenade-launcher, and the first projectile smashed through a window on the second floor of the barracks, blowing out a chunk of wall as it exploded. The others meanwhile collected the knapsacks of explosive and advanced towards the factory. Resnick knew where they would be when he got back, and if he didn't, well, *c'est la guerre*. Keller kept firing as they went, and when they were close to the gate they dropped to the ground and destroyed the gatehouse with automatic fire and one perfectly placed grenade from Newman.

13

The second, and bigger, explosion at the petrol station knocked Resnick on to his back, and he sprawled into the gutter before he jumped to his feet and ran in the same direction that Sofía had driven the Chevrolet, so that he could escape the intense heat from the blazing motor fuel. He tore round the corner that he had seen her take, and there she was, waiting for him beside the car, the driver's door open and the engine running. He saw a look of relief cross her face in the flickering reflection of the fierce fire that burned behind him, lighting up the street like neon. 'Thank God,' Sofía said. 'I thought you might have been caught in the explosion.'

'An expert like me?' the Russian replied as he dived across the front bench seat on to the passenger side. 'No chance. Now, can you get us back to the factory without getting caught up in all the excitement we've caused?'

'Sure I can.' And she dropped the Chevy into gear and set off. 'You did a good job there. If that doesn't bring out the soldiers, nothing will,' Sofía said as she accelerated.

She took a circuitous route through the narrow streets of Santa Ana, and rejoined the main road to the factory complex. As they were negotiating a particularly narrow street, they saw, heard and felt the explosion that Stoner had detonated, to their left, and the solitary street lamp that illuminated the street winked out. Sofía flicked her lights to full beam and glanced at Resnick. 'You taught them well,' she said.

Resnick grinned back at her. 'Thank you.'

Once on the main road, they passed a stream of army vehicles going in the opposite direction, towards town, and Resnick gave Sofía the thumbs-up. 'Worked like a charm,' he said. 'And our crew seem to be working up ahead,' he added, as he heard the rattle of gunfire from the direction of the barracks and the factory.

Sofía slammed the Chevy through the leaves that hid the side road from the main drag, and skidded to a halt beside the empty Ford three-tonner.

'They've taken the charges and gone to the factory,' said Resnick after taking a quick look inside the truck. 'They didn't have much faith that we'd make it back. Come on, let's find them before someone blows himself up.'

Carry guns at the ready, they set off in the direction of the shooting. As he went, Resnick glanced at his standard-issue Red Army watch. A quarter past midnight.

Stoner and Angel did not have such good luck getting across Santa Ana.

After the explosion had wrecked the utility buildings, Stoner hit the Wrangler's accelerator again and it fishtailed up the street, leaving behind it twin trails of burnt rubber. He sent the vehicle into a four-wheel skid as he joined the main road, almost losing control, but he straightened up and roared off towards Valin and the rest of the squad.

'Whoa,' yelled Angel. 'Easy, man. Hang loose a little.'

'I thought you liked hot-rodding,' Stoner said. 'What's the problem? Scared?'

'Bastard,' shouted Angel, grinning manically.

Stoner glanced behind him and the pair exchanged looks of exultation. 'Did you see them go?' he shouted. 'Amazing.'

'Awesome,' agreed Angel. 'She-it. One to the visiting team.'

Then, as they reached another crossroads, from the right a jeep appeared containing four soldiers of the regular army. The one sitting in the passenger seat hit the siren and motioned for Stoner to stop. Instead Angel opened fire with the LMG, exhausting one belted magazine of ammunition, and rapidly reloading a second. Two members of the patrol were hit, but a third loosed off a burst from the M16 he was carrying. Half-a-dozen bullets rattled off the Wrangler, and two caught Stoner. One hit his left shoulder, just above the edge of his flak jacket, sending a spurt of blood across the dashboard; the other penetrated his left side. Three more of the heavy lead slugs punched through the windscreen.

At the moment he was hit, Stoner lost control of the jeep, which hit the low kerb, careered across the pavement, slammed into a house front, bounced back across the street again, and scraped along the body of a parked Nissan saloon in a shower of sparks. All the while, Angel poured bullets into the grille of the army jeep, which suddenly lost its radiator in a cloud of steam and pulled over, disgorging the two uninjured soldiers, who stood and poured a hail of lead at the back of the retreating Wrangler.

'You OK, man?' asked Angel after they had taken the next corner on two wheels, sped down the road and into the shadows behind a small block of flats, where Stoner halted the jeep and slumped forward over the steering wheel.

'I'm hit, man. I need a medic,' he said through gritted teeth.

'Is it bad?'

'Bad enough. Is there a medical kit on board?'

'Sure,' said Angel. There was a padlocked box with the Red Cross symbol on it, attached to the inside of the vehicle. He broke off the padlock with the butt of his Colt .45 and looked rapidly at the contents, then lifted out several items to examine them more closely by the flame from his Zippo lighter. 'Good,' he said. 'This stuff is written in American, at least. Now let's see.' He picked up a handful of disposable hypodermics, full of liquid. 'She-it,' he said in amazement. 'Morphine. Want some?'

'No. Any bandages?' asked Stoner.

'Some.'

'Then take a look at my fucking shoulder and side, I'm losing blood here.'

Angel did as he was asked, ripping open the material of Stoner's jacket and shirt to inspect the wound. The first bullet had passed straight through Stoner's shoulder. The entry wound was blue and puckered in the light of the Zippo, but the exit was the size of his fist and weeping blood. And he could see the white of bone splinters inside the wound.

'I'll do what I can,' said Angel, 'but you need a doctor.'

'And there's never one about when you need one. I've been hit in the side too.'

Angel investigated the second wound. The bullet was still inside Stoner's body. There was not much blood visible, and Angel feared serious internal injury and bleeding.

'Man, I'm not up to this,' he said.

'Do what you can, man, and let's get the fuck out of here before another patrol shows up.'

'You in pain?' said Angel.

'Not yet. Just numb. Like when I got hit with a baseball bat a couple of times.'

'You will be.'

'Thanks.'

Angel helped Stoner across to the passenger seat, then collected what he needed from the medical kit and got to work. Speedily he treated both wounds in Stoner's shoulder with antiseptic powder, then put a dressing in the front and back and hastily wrapped a bandage round his upper arm and under his armpit. As for the wound in his side, he simply attached a dressing with tape. 'That'll have to do for now, bro,' he said. 'We'll get someone to look at you later. How you feeling?'

'Like shit.'

'That's the shock. Here, swallow a painkiller.'

'Morphine? I don't want to be knocked out.'

'No. I'm saving that for me. This is just regular drugstore stuff. Come on, quick, man. We need to get out of here.'

'I told you, I'm not in pain.'

'And I told you, you will be. Just take these and shut up.'

Stoner swallowed the pills, washing them down with a mouthful of water from the canteen slung around his waist, and Angel got behind the wheel. The Wrangler was running smoothly enough, but as soon as he moved off he knew something was wrong. He got out and walked to the back of the jeep. 'Shit,' he said. 'We got us a flat.'

'What do we do?' asked Stoner weakly. The pain was beginning.

'Well, I ain't no grease monkey. I ain't about to change the fucker. And I don't think we belong to the local branch of the Automobile Club, so I reckon we just drive it as it is. It'll be bumpy, and mess you up, but it can't be helped. Sorry, man.'

'Just drive, Angel. Don't worry about me,' said Stoner. 'I'll survive.'

'You got it, Stoner.'

Angel put his foot down and the jeep bumped across the pavement, slowly gathering speed, but he felt the drag of the flat tyre and knew that pretty soon he would be driving on bare metal.

He managed to get up to about twenty miles per hour before the bumping got too bad, and he kept at that speed to save Stoner from too much pain.

Shit, he thought to himself as the jeep limped along in the direction of the fire-fight at the factory, this could take for ever. He glanced up at the face of a church clock lit by the moon. A quarter past twelve.

By midnight the soldiers left in the barracks had got themselves organized and were returning fire. They were sending up flares which bathed the area in a dull red glow, and tinged the smoke from Messelier's grenades pink, as it drifted down the hill towards them. Spenser and his team had dropped back slightly to gain cover from the trees at the edge of the jungle. 'Keep firing,' he yelled. 'Keep them interested in us and let the boss get inside the complex.'

The Gatling ate up another belt of ammunition, and in the comparative silence as Spenser threaded in a new one, the three mercenaries and the three women with them heard a clanking sound from the road beside the barracks. Spenser, Messelier and the women had heard the sound before and knew what it was. Packard just looked at them in the darkness. 'What the hell . . . ?' he said.

The noise got louder, and gun barrel first, a late-model American M1A1 tank rumbled round the corner. It was armed with a 120mm main gun, the M256 smooth-bore cannon using either kinetic-energy, armour-piercing, fin-stabilized tracer, or high-explosive anti-tank multipurpose chemical. It was perfect for the climate, as it was fitted with a cooling system that allowed the crew to wear normal combat suits rather than chemical suits, for it was fully equipped for chemical and/or nuclear warfare. The tank was painted in camouflage green, and as its treads clattered across the tarmac, the gun turret swung in the direction of Spenser and the rest. The American recognized it for what it was: a sixty-seven-ton monster with a 1500hp motor, driven through a four-speed automatic transmission. Known as 'Whispering Death', the tank could reach a top speed of forty miles per hour on tarmac. It had a thermal sight, laser rangefinder, and also carried a coaxial 7.62mm machine-gun. It was not to be messed with, as Saddam Hussein and his cronies had discovered to their cost in the Gulf War.

'Fall back,' Spenser screamed. 'Fall back and take cover.'

The group split and dived back into the jungle as the tank fired its big gun, and earth, trees, and bushes were thrown twenty feet in the air.

The squad fell back even further as the tank fired again, and Packard grabbed a grenade from the half a dozen hanging on the front of his body armour and raced towards the tank and the barracks. This was the moment he had been waiting for, and he felt a crazy elation as he ran.

'Packard,' yelled Messelier. 'Don't.' But it was too late: he was gone.

The Australian ran out from the shelter of the trees, across the cleared area in front, across the slip road, over the low wall that separated it from the front of the barracks, across the parking area towards the tank, whose machine-gun chattered and ripped up earth and tarmac all around his feet. He pulled the pin from the grenade, kept running, jumped up on to the side of the vehicle above the tracks, and popped it deftly into the machine-gun slot. When the grenade exploded, and the tank lifted an inch off the ground, smoke and flame roaring out of every orifice in its armour plating, he was already running back towards his mates.

He never made it. A sharpshooter inside the barracks, using the lull in the shooting coming from the foliage, took careful aim and fired. The bullet hit Packard square in the back, and went through his flak jacket like a knife through butter. He leapt into the air, fell, rolled and was still.

Spenser stepped out from the edge of the jungle and poured half the contents of an ammunition belt into the window from which the sniper had fired.

'Bastard,' he screamed as he sprayed the window. 'Fucking bastard.'

At the factory gates, Valin and his squad had been pinned down by fire from the complex itself. Either there was a squad of Colombian army inside, or the management and workers had been issued with weapons, and knew how to use them. Valin broke radio silence and called up Keller as the tank opened fire on Spenser's group, and Packard made his suicidal run.

'Keller. Come in. Over,' he said.

'Colonel, Keller. They've got a fucking tank over there. Over.'

'Forget that. Spenser will sort it. Who the hell's inside the factory? Can't you see? Over.'

'I'll try, Colonel. Over and out,' said Keller, then, to Gerry McGuire: 'You heard the colonel, McGuire. What can you see?'

'A whole lot of nothing, Sarge . . . Wait. Third window along, second floor. Gun flash.'

Keller let the red dot of the sight creep along the wall of the factory until it found the window. He saw a shadow move in the light from the flares and the burning tank, and fired.

'Hit,' hissed McGuire. 'I saw him go down.'

14

As Resnick and Sofía were racing towards the rest of their party, they heard the reports from the tank's big gun as it fired on Spenser and his crew, and the deeper thud as Packard dropped the grenade through the machine-gun port and killed it.

'What's that?' said Sofía, sliding to a halt.

'Artillery of some kind,' replied the Russian. 'Christ knows what kind of ordnance they've got up there. Keep going, but be careful.'

They snaked through the jungle, until Sofía almost ran over her mother, who was standing by the bole of a tree, gun at the ready.

'Mama, what's happening?' she demanded.

'My darling, you're back. Thank God. Get down, there's a tank firing on us.'

Resnick peered through the foliage and saw the M1A1 burning, and Packard's body lying where he had fallen. 'Relax,' he said. 'One of ours dealt with it.'

'Is he all right?' asked Maria.

'No. It looks like he paid the ultimate price.'

'The poor young man. He had no life.'

'But he gave it to save the rest of us,' said Resnick, not for a moment suspecting Packard's deeper motive. 'For that we must be grateful. Where are the others?'

'Hiding from the tank's guns. Has it really been destroyed?'

'Yes. Have no fear, Señora Delgado. Now come on, let's find Spenser, and hope there are not other casualties.'

Angel was worried about Stoner. The Brit seemed to have gone into deep shock, and the way the jeep was handling was not helping.

'Hey, Stoner, you all right, man?' he asked.

Stoner didn't respond, so Angel pulled to the side of the road. Up ahead, he could see the light from the flares and hear the popping of rifles and light machine-guns, plus the heavier booming from the tank. It wasn't sounding good. And from behind he heard more explosions, as the havoc that Stoner and Resnick had wreaked spread. But one thing was sure. Before long, the soldiers who had left the barracks to check out the diversion in town would be alerted to what was going on back at the factory and barracks, and come looking for them.

'Stoner,' said Angel again, more alarmed than he pretended. 'Come on, man. Talk to me.'

Stoner opened his eyes and groaned. 'Jesus,' he said. 'I feel terrible.'

'Listen, man,' said Angel. 'We're caught between a rock and a hard fucking place. Sounds like our buddies have got troubles of their own up ahead. There's bigger guns than ours being used. And those fucking army guys are going to be hot on our tails, PDQ. And this fucking jalopy is going nowhere fast.'

'How far's the factory?' asked Stoner.

'Ten klicks, maybe less.'

'How much ammo is left for the LMG?'

'Coupla belts. A few thousand rounds.'

'Then get me into the back and I can hold the army off for a while. You go ahead on foot. I'll be useless in a fire-fight. I can do more good here as a diversion.'

'Are you sure, man?'

'Sure I'm sure. Just give me some more of those pills, and I'll hold off the bad guys until hell freezes over. You go on ahead. They need more troops up there by the sound of it.'

'OK, man, if you're really sure.'

'Got any cigarettes?'

'Cigarettes, joints. You name it.'

'Leave me what you've got.'

'I'll just keep a coupla Js for myself. I might need them later, the way things are going. I can scrounge some smokes when I get up ahead.'

'Whatever. Just give me what you can spare and go.'

Angel took a pack of Marlboro from his pocket and gave it to Stoner, plus half-a-dozen ready-rolled joints that he had in his shirt pocket.

'Jesus, man, that uniform you're wearing stinks,' said Stoner.

'I know. But orders is orders. I hope someone's takin' care of my leather jacket. It cost me five hundred bucks.'

Angel steered the Wrangler towards the ditch at the side of the road, slewed it round side-on, so that it half-blocked the road, and helped Stoner out of the front passenger seat and behind the machine-gun. He checked that there was a fresh belt of ammo ready to fire, that Stoner's M16 was loaded and cocked, and finally he took the Desert Eagle from its holster under the Londoner's arm without disturbing the bandage, worked a cartridge into the breech and put it into his lap. Then he hopped out of the vehicle and stood beside it. 'You gonna be cool, babe?' he asked.

'Cool as ice. Thanks for the medical treatment, Angel. You did fine.'

'Any time, man. Any time at all.'

'I hope it's a long time before I need it.'

'Me too.'

'Gotta light?'

Angel hesitated. 'Only my Zippo. My old man gave it to me . . . Oh, what the fuck. Here.' He thrust the lighter into Stoner's hand, then helped himself to a cigarette from one of the packs, and Stoner lit it for him.

'Thanks, pal,' said Angel. 'See you later.'

'Hope so,' said Stoner.

'I'd better,' retorted Angel. 'I want my fucking lighter back.'

Then, with his Uzi slung over his shoulder, he set off at a trot towards the factory.

Spenser's squad had regrouped at the edge of the jungle, joined by Resnick and Sofía. They were all safe, apart from the unfortunate Packard.

'And I promised to watch his back,' said Messelier. 'Damn good job I did of it.'

'It wasn't your fault,' said Spenser, with one eye on the barracks, which had fallen silent since he had shot the sniper.

'What do you think is happening?' asked Resnick.

'I reckon they're deciding whether to come out and try and overrun us,' replied the American.

'You'd better give Sofía and me some covering fire, and we'll join the boss. Sounds like he's having trouble over there,' said the Russian.

'No problem,' said Spenser. 'Come on, guys. You heard what the man said. Let's shape up here.' As he moved towards the open space, his Gatling at the ready, he shouted: 'Carmen, come and feed me.'

The girl showed a mouthful of white teeth as she did what he said. 'Come on, mama,' she chided. 'We're needed.'

Valin and his squad were indeed in trouble. It was proving more difficult than he had thought to get inside. Cutting the electrical power to the complex had not killed the current to the perimeter fence. There had to be an auxiliary generator inside the factory, but he had no idea where, and being pinned down outside by withering fire from the factory buildings, despite Keller's sharpshooting from up on the hill, was not going to help him find it. He had suffered no casualties so far, but it was just a matter of time.

It had been quiet at the barracks for a few minutes, but suddenly Spenser and his troops opened fire again, and within a minute Resnick and Sofía came zigzagging across the open space behind them as bullets tore up the tarmac about their feet.

'What's the hold-up, Colonel?' said Resnick as he dropped down next to Valin.

'The sodding fence is still live, and we're pinned down here.'

'Give me one of my charges,' said the Russian. 'I'll soon sort this out.'

He grabbed a knapsack, took out the remote control

he still had in his pocket, made some deft changes, jumped up and ran towards the perimeter of the factory, where he slid the bag next to one of the fence supports, wormed his way back, and switched on the control. 'Heads down,' he said, and pressed the red button.

The support was torn from the ground by the explosion and the fence itself split open in a shower of sparks.

'Come on,' said Resnick. Let's get inside and find some cover.'

Valin, O'Rourke, Daniel McGuire, Newman and Sofía didn't need to be told twice. They sprang to their feet and hared through the gap in the fence, firing their carry weapons as they went, with Resnick in the lead.

From their position up on the brow of the hill, Keller and Gerry McGuire had a good view of what was happening down below, and so far no one on the other side seemed very interested in returning their fire.

'They're in,' said McGuire. 'Resnick must've got back and planted a charge.'

'Thank Christ for that,' said the German. 'I thought we were going to be here all night. If we're going to catch that plane, we'll have to get out of here before long. He looked at the luminous dial on his watch. A quarter to one. Time was passing quickly, and he too was aware that soon the troops who had gone into town would be back to reinforce the men in the barracks. 'Come on, Colonel,' he said almost to himself. 'Get a move on.'

He was not wrong. At the same time as Keller was

whispering to himself, Stoner saw the lights of the first troop carrier as it made its way back to the barracks.

He flicked away his fifth cigarette on the trot and checked the action of the LMG as the truck turned the corner, a quarter of a mile or so away, and started to lumber towards him.

By luck or by judgement, Angel had picked the perfect place to leave the disabled jeep. The road narrowed as it reached the top of an incline, and both sides were flanked by dense vegetation and strung with barbed wire. Unless troops were prepared to make a full-frontal assault up the metalled road, take to the jungle or try to use the ditch on the right-hand side as cover, they would just have to shoot it out.

Stoner pulled back the bolt and fired the LMG. Bullets ripped into the front of the big truck, killing the driver and passenger instantly, and the vehicle slid to the side of the road and nosed into the barbed wire. Stoner kept on firing, strafing the canvas-covered cargo area where the soldiers were sitting, and sending those he didn't hit looking for safer cover.

'Number two for the visiting team,' he said to himself as he lit another of Angel's cigarettes with the Zippo.

Angel heard the bark of the LMG as he arrived back at the track leading off the main road and found the three-tonner, parked and empty, next to the ancient pink Chevrolet. His leather jacket was in the cab of the Ford where he had left it. He looked back and wished Stoner good luck as he ripped off the stinking army tunic he was wearing and slid the jacket on, checking the pockets to see if the Walkman was still there.

He stopped for a moment to admire the lines of the Chevy, and check out the paint job. Pure rock and roll, he thought, as he picked up his Uzi and headed off towards the fire-fight.

He found Spenser, Messelier and the three women where they were still pinning the barracks down. 'Yo, man,' he said to the other American as he joined them. 'Nice work.'

'Where's Stoner?' asked Spenser, giving the red-hot Gatling time to cool down.

'He's been hit. He's keeping an eye on the road between here and the town.'

'Hit bad?'

'Twice. One bullet broke his shoulder up, and he took another round in his left side. It isn't looking good. He's in a lot of pain.'

'And you just left him?'

'Had to make a judgement call, Chris. You know how it is. He told me to leave him. He's a brave guy. So how's it going here?'

'Fine. You going to join the boss?'

'Seems like that's where I'm needed. You guys seem to be managing here all right.'

'Well, get going then.'

Taking advantage of the fresh hail of bullets that Spenser pumped at the barracks, Angel tore across the slip road in the direction of the factory. He saw the hole in the electrified fence and charged through, his machine pistol ready to cut down anyone who got in his way. He slid to a halt at the corner of one of the buildings and peered round just in time to see Valin's distinctive form entering a door into the next.

15

Stoner lit another Marlboro, and looked down the hill. There was a lot of activity going on there, as the army vehicles piled up behind the wreck of the first personnel carrier, which was blocking the road.

He grinned to himself. His shoulder and side hurt like hell and he swallowed more painkillers, then listened to the sound of the battle for control of the factory that was going on behind him.

Shit, he thought, I wonder if I'll get out of this one alive, as his fevered brain replayed events from his life over and over again.

He remembered his first brushes with the law when he was just a teenager, stealing from Woolworth's, then his move into more serious crimes as he climbed the underworld ladder. He recalled his time as a runner for a drug-dealing syndicate – ironic, considering the mission he found himself on now. Cocaine had been the drug of the early eighties, and Stoner had dealt his fair share round the West End and City, and sampled enough of his own product too, with the yuppies who made up his clientele at the time.

Then he had graduated to running a string of high-class whores to service the very same wheeler-dealers with too much money to spend, whom he had met when he had sold them drugs. It had been an easy life. Money, sex, fast cars, and as much dope as he could use. But he'd been too flashy, made a lot of enemies, and eventually one had grassed him up to the police.

While on the run, he'd made his aborted attempt to join the French Foreign Legion. What a dummy! A black cockney who didn't speak a word of the language, and who'd been used to getting up at noon, spending all day and night in relentless hedonism, trying to join the toughest army in the world. But at least they'd taught him how to use a variety of weapons, and some basic martial arts. If only he'd been able to keep his mouth shut, he might still have all his own teeth.

You've got to laugh, thought Stoner, as he lit the first of the joints that Angel had left, made himself more comfortable on the metal seat behind the LMG, and wished that the troops down the hill would do something before he died of boredom. Or my wounds, he said to himself. I wonder just how bad they are.

Not that learning to shoot and stab, garrotte and gouge in the Legion had done him much good. If he hadn't been willing and able to use a gun, perhaps he wouldn't have taken up armed robbery when he came back to England, which culminated in the shooting of the security guard, and his spell in prison.

Stoner's gloomy thoughts were rudely interrupted when the troops below opened fire, sending bullets ricocheting off the jeep. At last, he thought, a bit of action, and he pulled two grenades off the clips that secured them to the front of his flak jacket, released the pins and lobbed them down the hill. One exploded between the front wheels of the abandoned personnel carrier, which began to burn as the fuel caught, and the second bounced into the ditch where three soldiers were taking cover and burst in a shower of shrapnel that tore their bodies apart.

Slash and burn, he thought, as the grenades went off. Slash and burn.

Back at the barracks, what Spenser thought was going to happen, happened. The soldiers inside had got over their surprise at the attack and the efficiency with which the lights had been cut off. Someone had managed to get an emergency generator working, and now that they had light to see by once more, they regrouped at the back of the building. By sheer force of will the commanding officer, a major, calmed the conscripts who had seen their friends cut down before their eyes, and their armour destroyed, and split them into two groups, which advanced up the roads on either side of the building.

Spenser and his group slaughtered them as they came. It was almost too easy to cut them down in droves as they tried to get across the open area between the barracks and the edge of the jungle.

The women retched at the sight of the blood and guts that their bullets were producing, and almost stopped firing.

'Keep going,' screamed Spenser. 'Keep firing. Don't let them get close.'

Reluctantly they opened fire again and the sound of their weapons joined with the hammering of the Gatling and the explosions from the grenades that Messelier kept lobbing from the ARMSCOR in their direction, while the slugs and shrapnel tore through the advancing men again until they fell back. 'Well done,' said Spenser as he ordered his troops to cease fire. 'That's evened the odds a bit.'

Angel raced after Valin, through the open door that the boss had used, and into the factory proper. It was illuminated with dim emergency lights from the same source that had kept the outside fence live. He could hear the sporadic rattle of gunfire as the defenders put up a last bid to fight off the invaders. As Angel looked round the room, he saw one civilian and a couple of soldiers sprawled across the floor where they had fallen, their clothes bloodstained and their weapons still clasped in their hands. He ignored them, well aware that Valin and his men would not have passed without checking that they were dead. He was more interested in the equipment that filled the room. It was packed with all sorts of vats and tubes that he didn't have a clue about. But one thing he knew he would recognize: pure cocaine. And if he had anything to do with it, before the factory was destroyed he would make sure that he took some with him.

Suddenly he heard a sound from behind a bench that had been dragged to one side of the room. He walked towards it, finger on the trigger of the Uzi, and kicked the bench aside. Cowering on the floor was a man; he was small and dark, and wore a lab coat.

What have we here? thought Angel. Someone the others missed; that was rather careless. With the toe of one combat boot, he pushed the man, who looked up fearfully. 'Don't worry,' said the American. 'I won't shoot you unless you try and shoot me first. Are you armed?'

The man let go with a stream of breathless Spanish.

'English? *Inglés*?'

The man shook his head, and rattled on again in Spanish.

Shit, thought Angel. Sure wish I'd paid more attention to my Spanish lessons in high school. He held up his hand to silence the man. 'Come on,' he said, pulling him up by the arm. He marched the trembling man ahead of him with the tip of the barrel of his machine pistol close to his back. Up ahead he caught sight of Newman covering the backs of his comrades. The former para spun round when he heard the footsteps of the American and his prisoner, and brought up his shotgun ready to fire. 'Steady, man,' said Angel. 'Friend.'

'Angel!' said Newman, and gave one of his rare smiles. What little he had seen of the American hippie, he'd liked, even if they were as different in outlook as was humanly possible. 'You made it. You and Stoner did a good one on the electrics. Where is he?'

Angel frowned. 'I don't know, man,' he said. 'He took a couple of hits, and the jeep's U/S, and I left him up on the road taking care of business. I sure wish I could get back with some transport. Listen, check this guy, will you? See if he's carrying.'

Newman did as Angel asked, and frisked the man in the lab coat expertly. 'Clean as a whistle,' he said. 'Not even a nail file.'

'Good. Let's find the boss. He might be able to get something out of him.'

They moved forward past smashed equipment and more bodies, until they caught up with the main party.

'Hey, Angel,' said O'Rourke. 'Good to see you.'

'Likewise, Ell-Tee.'

'Who's this?' asked the lieutenant, nodding at Angel's prisoner.

'Fuck knows, he doesn't speak English. Or won't.'

'Colonel, Jesús,' O'Rourke called. 'Over here. We need a translator.'

Valin and the Colombian joined them.

'Angel. Good job,' said Valin. 'Where's Stoner?'

Angel explained about the jeep and Stoner's wounds, and Valin said: 'We're nearly finished here. As soon as we are, you and Newman get the transport and go and pull him out. Meanwhile, let's have a word with our friend here. Jesús, will you do the honours?'

Jesús questioned the prisoner in Spanish, and listened intently to his answers. After a minute or two he held up his hands and the prisoner fell silent.

'He is a scientist, Colonel,' said Jesús. 'A chemist, and he is here under duress. Also, he is a pacifist. That is why he did not join in the fighting. He hates the government. They have murdered his family. You were correct: the authorities knew that someone was coming to try and destroy the factory.'

'Yes, I got most of that,' said Valin. 'How did they know?'

'A moment,' said Jesús, and started talking in Spanish again.

The chemist spat out an answer.

'An American came here.'

Valin smiled grimly. 'I thought as much,' he said. 'Ask him if he knows who.'

Once more there was a stream of Spanish from both men.

'He saw him. You heard the description. Does it ring a bell?' said Jesús.

'Yes,' said Valin. 'It does.'

He then spoke to the chemist in his native tongue, and everyone understood his affirmative reply.

'He's coming with us when we leave,' said Valin. 'Back to the States. Lieutenant, I'm putting you in charge of his safety for now. We need him to positively identify the man who informed on us. Take good care of him. Right, let's finish up here. We'll clean up the last of the resistance. Resnick, start placing the charges. And all of you, be careful.'

16

O'Rourke stayed with the chemist, who said his name was Ramón García, while the rest of the group moved through the factory, Resnick laying charges as they went. They met more sporadic resistance, but soon dealt with it. Angel and Newman worked together, the American keeping a sharp eye out not only for armed men, but also for the drugs he was seeking. He finally found what he was looking for in a small store-room. It was a junkie's dream. Plastic bags of cocaine were piled floor to ceiling, and even the air seemed imbued with the drug.

'Shit,' said Angel. 'Christmas Day, and the snow is on the ground.'

He picked up a bag and weighed it in his hand – a kilo, he guessed – and put it inside his leather jacket, which he zipped up tightly.

Newman gave him a questioning look. 'Purely for personal consumption,' said Angel as he ran his finger along a shelf, picked up the residue of coke on his finger and rubbed it on his gums. 'She-it. Ninety-eight per cent pure, or I'm a monkey's uncle.'

'You will be if you take too much of that stuff.'

'Want some?' asked Angel.

'Not for me, thanks.'

'Suit yourself . . . Hey, and don't tell the boss. I don't think he's into dope.'

'I'm sure he's not,' said the Englishman. 'How much is that little lot worth?'

'On the streets back home? Cut? Shit. A quarter of a million bucks maybe. Maybe more.'

'Is that what you came here for?'

'No. I came for the foreign travel, adventure and to make new friends. What about you? This is just a bonus. Take one for yourself.'

'No thanks, Angel.'

'Your loss. Come on, let's go. I want to finish up here, and pick up my man Stoner.'

By the time they had found the rest of the team, the battle for the factory was almost over. The last few defenders had surrendered to Valin's men and stood sheepishly under the guard of Carlos and Daniel McGuire, and Resnick was busily setting the charges where they could do the most damage.

Angel looked at his watch as he joined them. Twenty past one. Time was running out fast.

'Angel, Newman,' barked Valin. 'Get a vehicle from somewhere and go and fetch Stoner.'

'Right away, Colonel,' said Angel.

'And be quick,' underlined Valin. 'We've got to get out of here fast.'

Stoner had exhausted the ammunition in the LMG, and used up the half-a-dozen grenades he had with him. The soldiers below had fanned out into the jungle by the light of the burning vehicles on the road, and were advancing up the hill.

His wounds were giving him a lot of pain, and he took his M16 and the Uzi automatic and left the jeep. Although he didn't know it, single-handedly he had managed to kill or wound thirty men, and destroy or disable six vehicles.

He scrambled into the ditch that ran parallel to the road and took stock. His movement had drawn fire from even closer, confirming that the opposition was moving up on him. Behind him he could still hear the battle of the barracks and factory, and wondered if any help would be forthcoming from the team. He guessed that it would, but had no way of telling how soon.

Better move my black arse, he thought to himself. Keeping himself low, he started wriggling back towards the crest of the hill, which was a few hundred yards behind him, in order to put it between himself and the Colombians below.

Even more bullets thudded into the ground around him as the enemy realized that they were no longer threatened by the LMG, and Stoner fired a warning blast from his M16, using the lull it caused to scuttle back further.

Come on, Angel, he thought, as he checked his watch. Let's see some action.

Angel and Newman ran back through the factory and across the slip road to where Spenser and his group were still keeping the lid on the barracks.

'How's it going over there?' said the Vietnam veteran.

'Pretty good,' replied Newman. 'No casualties, and the place is ours. What about here?'

'We've been lucky. We only lost Packard when he took out the tank.'

'Any sign of anything from the direction of the town?' asked Angel.

'Nothing,' replied Spenser. 'Stoner must be still blocking the road. But it can't last.'

'We're off to get him,' said Newman. 'We need transport.'

'The truck's still where we left it, and there's an old jalopy like something out of *American Graffiti* there, too,' said Angel. 'Resnick and his partner must've requisitioned it. We'll use that.'

'Come on then, Angel,' said Newman. 'We're wasting time. If we don't get out of here quick, we'll miss our airlift out of this God-forsaken dump.'

'Keep up the good work,' Angel said to Spenser, and the two men vanished into the darkness, equipment jangling as they went.

They ploughed through the undergrowth towards where the vehicles were parked until suddenly they came under automatic fire from their left.

'Shit,' they groaned in unison as they hit the ground, and brought their carry weapons up into firing position.

'Who the fuck is it?' hissed Angel.

'Christ knows,' whispered Newman, as he tried to get a fix on whoever was shooting at them. 'Either Stoner's copped it, or it's a pincer movement from the barracks.'

'I hope it's the barracks,' said Angel. 'Otherwise there'll be soldiers all over us like a rash. Come on, let's move.'

As they did so, the firing started up again. Newman

spotted a muzzle flash and returned fire, then heard a hoarse scream as his shotgun load hit home.

'Gotcha,' he said triumphantly.

There was more firing immediately, bullets whistling through the leaves around them, thudding into the trunks of trees and kicking up dirt. Both men returned fire as they tried to outflank the ambush in order to reach the vehicles. They might never have made it, except that from behind they were joined by Messelier and Maria Delgado, who gave them the advantage of the extra firepower of his Ingram and her Heckler and Koch. A brief but heavy gun battle followed before the ambushers finally dropped back.

'Thanks,' said Newman when the four made contact. 'Who the hell was that?'

'God alone knows,' said Messelier, as he heard gunfire from further down the road in the direction of the centre of Santa Ana. 'But it sounds like Stoner's still keeping someone pinned down. Go and help him. We'll cover you.'

Newman and Angel didn't waste another moment. They pushed through the undergrowth, keeping their ears and eyes open for any further opposition, but none was forthcoming, and within a few minutes they found the two vehicles parked where they had been left, seemingly undisturbed.

Angel made straight for the Chevrolet. The wires under the dash, which Sofía had stripped and used to start the engine, were still hanging free. He touched one to the other and the motor turned over, missed, caught, and then, as he jammed his foot on the accelerator, roared into life.

'GM,' said Angel proudly. 'Made with union labour

on American soil, and still starts first time, old as she is.'

'Can we discuss the pros and cons of car manufacturing at another time?' suggested Newman as he got into the passenger seat. 'We've got work to do. Drive the fucker, will you?'

Without another word, Angel shoved the Chevy into gear, put his foot down, wrestled the wheel round, and joined the main road, heading towards where he had left Stoner. The wounded man was by then putting up a desperate rearguard defence against the soldiers who were swarming up the road to where he had left the jeep. They looked as if they were in danger of overrunning him where he lay in the ditch at the brow of the hill, using his remaining ammunition in a frantic attempt to stay alive.

Suddenly he heard the sound of the motor from behind him, turned and saw the Chevrolet, lights blazing, heading his way at top speed. He didn't recognize the car, but considered any alternative to where he was an improvement.

As he got closer to where he had left Stoner, Angel banged his fist on the horn. The Londoner emptied the last of the M16 magazines down the hill at the advancing troops, then dropped the rifle, dragged himself to his feet, ignoring the pain from his wounds. Desert Eagle in hand, and blasting a few shots downhill, he turned and staggered in the direction of the speeding Chevrolet.

Angel recognized him as he stood upright. 'He's there,' he screamed at Newman. 'My buddy made it.' He put his foot down harder, and the old car almost seemed to leap up the incline in Stoner's direction.

As Angel and Newman looked through the windscreen at Stoner's halting advance, troops appeared at the top of the hill and started firing down at them. Angel slammed on the brakes, spun the wheel, jerked on the handbrake and felt the back wheels break away as he slammed the heavy car into a perfect one-hundred-and-eighty-degree turn almost in its own length.

'Open the back door,' the American shouted to Newman as he held the car still on the foot brake, waiting for Stoner to get to it.

The wounded Englishman was hobbling down the road as fast as he could, firing his Uzi automatic over his shoulder as he came, and Newman added shotgun fire from his Ithaca.

'Come on, Stoner,' Angel screamed out of the open window on his side. 'Come on, man. You can make it.'

Bullets were tearing at the ground near Stoner's feet as he made for the Chevy, and others were slamming into the back of the car, until Angel feared that the petrol tank would be hit.

'Come on, man,' he screamed once more, and saw Stoner make the final effort to reach the open rear door, when a slug hit him in the thigh and he stumbled.

Angel feathered the accelerator as, almost in slow motion, Stoner put out his hand to pull himself into the car. Just then, a burst of bullets stitched up his back, neck and head, and finally blew his face away as he dropped to the ground, slid along on his front and lay perfectly still, the Zippo lighter he held in one hand slipping from between his lifeless fingers and bouncing in front of him.

'Beat it, Angel,' said Newman between shotgun blasts. 'He's copped it.'

'No, man, he'll be OK. Just let me get him inside.'

'No, you bloody fool. His head's gone. He's dead.'

'I want to see.'

Newman turned the shotgun round and stuck it into Angel's face.

'It was your fault we were too late,' he growled. 'If you hadn't stopped to pick up those drugs, we could've got him out. Now drive, before we get killed as well.'

Angel stared at him for a few seconds in the light from the dashboard, a terrible look of guilt on his face, then stamped on the accelerator again. The bonnet of the big old Chevrolet lifted and the car took off back in the direction of the factory with a scream of protest from its rear tyres.

17

Inside the factory everything was set. The prisoners that Valin's men had taken had been disarmed and sent off into the night. The last thing he wanted was any more spare baggage. He realized that he could not leave any of the Delgados behind. With a traitor operating back in the States, the family's cover could be blown at any moment, so they had to be taken out if at all possible. And then there was Ramón García. He alone could positively identify the turncoat, even though Valin had a fair idea of who it was from his description. The only witness. As such the chemist was indispensable.

'Right, Colonel,' said Resnick as he checked the last of the charges. 'Time to go.'

'Everyone,' roared Valin. 'Get back across the road. But be careful. There'll still be some resistance. And I haven't lost any of you . . . Yet.'

The troops bailed out, taking García with them under the watchful eye of O'Rourke. They sped across the road, bent double and zigzagging as they went, attracting only sporadic fire from the barracks – where for the present at least, the defenders seemed to have lost interest in the battle – until they were all back in the safety of the jungle, where they met up with Spenser's crew.

'OK, Resnick,' said Valin when they were all accounted for. 'Let her go.'

'A pleasure, Colonel,' said the Russian. He switched on his transmitter for the third time that night and calmly touched the red button.

The entire factory complex shuddered, as the charges that Resnick had so carefully placed exploded simultaneously. A brilliant flash, almost bright enough to blind them after the dim light that was all the attack force had seen for hours, burst through the windows as a thunderclap rang around the valley where they stood. Slates, bricks, wood and glass shot upwards, as the full force of the blasts was felt by the building, then rained down in a cacophony, as if a giant orchestra of tone-deaf musicians was tuning up.

Everyone ducked at the explosion, except Resnick, who watched proudly as the roof of the factory dropped between the walls as they were blown apart.

Excellent, he thought.

Up on the hillside, Keller and Gerry McGuire watched the explosion too, and felt the blast of hot air pull at their clothes.

'Time to go,' said the German, starting to pack away his sniper rifle. 'Money for old rope, wasn't it?'

'We're not home yet,' replied the Irishman.

'Too true. But at least we've done what we came for.'

Angel and Newman were about halfway between where they had left the dead Stoner and where the truck was parked, when the explosion occurred. They watched the pillar of fire, smoke and debris rise up in front of them, and Newman, in triumph, simply said: 'Yes.'

For once Angel had nothing to say. He knew he was at least partly to blame for Stoner's death, and the knowledge filled him with anger. Anger at himself, anger at the Colombians, and anger at the people who had sent both of them to risk their lives for money. He put his foot down violently, and the Chevy rocketed back towards the others.

'Let's go,' said Valin as the factory crumpled. 'Everyone back to the truck, and watch out for soldiers in the jungle.'

The thirteen of them, Valin, O'Rourke, Spenser, Daniel McGuire, Messelier, Resnick, Jesús Delgado, his wife, son, and three daughters, and Ramón García, who had thrown away his lab coat and was now less conspicuous in blue jeans and a dark-green shirt, set off back through the jungle in the direction of the track that led off the main road.

But their troubles were just about to start. They were met by a murderous hail of bullets, and Carlotta Delgado's white blouse blossomed red as a round hit her above her left breast and knocked her to the ground. The brief lull in resistance was over, as soldiers from the barracks joined the men who had ambushed Newman and Angel earlier, and who had been scattered when Maria and Messelier came to their comrades' assistance.

'My daughter,' screamed Maria, dropping her Heckler and Koch and rushing to Carlotta's aid.

'Daniel,' shouted Valin. 'First aid.'

Valin had always prided himself in having a medic

with the squad when they went into a fight. But the last soldier with real battlefield first-aid experience who had been part of the group still lay somewhere in southern Africa, felled by a bullet from a tribesman's muzzle-loading rifle at the end of their last, ill-fated excursion into enemy territory. And for this mission, there had just not been time enough to recruit another, so Daniel McGuire, who had picked up his knowledge by patching up the wounds of his IRA brethren on the streets of Belfast, had been appointed official medic.

The Irishman dodged bullets to get to Carlotta, flinging off his backpack and digging out the medical kit that he had been given. Valin, Maria and Daniel dragged Carlotta behind the shelter of a tree, trying hard to ignore the gasps of pain she made as they did so. Only there, out of the direct line of fire from whoever was preventing them reaching their transport, did Daniel dare to show a glimmer of light from the torch that he carried.

What he saw filled him with trepidation. He knew that it was beyond his meagre skills. A bullet had ripped through the young woman's body armour and torn open an artery in her chest, from where rich, red blood pumped in sync with the beating of her heart. And with every second that passed, the rhythm was becoming weaker.

He pulled her flak jacket open, and tore the flimsy material of the blouse below, to expose bare breasts streaked with gore, and examined the wound. But he knew, even as he looked at it, that there was nothing he could do. She was too far gone. What she needed was a hospital, blood transfusions, treatment for shock, and an expert surgeon to patch her up. Out here in the field, in half darkness, with his mud-caked hands, no proper equipment, and under fire, he knew that she had only minutes to live.

'Colonel,' Daniel said. 'I can't . . . '

Maria Delgado looked at him. 'Save her,' she cried, as the bullets from the ambushers drove them to take further cover. 'Please, señor. In the name of God.'

'I can't,' Daniel repeated, holding a pad of gauze over the wound in an attempt to staunch the flow of blood. 'She's too badly hurt. It's impossible.'

And as if to underline his words, the young girl stiffened, rattled deep in her throat, and was still.

'Christ Jesus,' screamed Maria, made the sign of the cross, and threw herself across her daughter's body.

'I'm sorry, Colonel,' said the Irishman. 'It was no good.'

'I understand,' said Valin. 'There was nothing you could do. Now come on, both of you. We've got to get out of here.'

As he spoke, Jesús scrambled to join them, and when he saw his wife covering his daughter's lifeless body with her own, tears sprang to his eyes.

'Jesús,' said Valin, touching the man's shoulder. 'I'm so sorry.'

'Lord,' said Jesús. 'Have mercy on her eternal soul.'

'Amen to that,' said Valin. And ours too, he thought. The situation seemed desperate. His men, and the civilians he had promised to care for, were pinned down by the ambushers, who had had time to dig themselves in. Valin looked at his watch. It was almost two o'clock, their deadline to get away, and they were in big trouble.

* * *

Angel and Newman and Keller and Gerry McGuire arrived back at the truck at almost exactly the same time. They got out, stood beside their three vehicles and listened to the sound of gunfire coming from the jungle.

'Goddam,' said Keller, 'that's not from the barracks. It's too close. They must've met some resistance on the way back here.'

'Angel and I were ambushed in the jungle before,' said Newman. 'We chased them off, but they must have regrouped. And it sounds like there's more of them now. We'd better go and give the rest a hand.' He took a hand-grenade from one of his pockets. 'A little reinforcement from the rear. That'll shake the bastards up.'

Keller nodded his agreement, and the four men readied their carry weapons, the German once again trusting to his Heckler and Koch G3, and in single file they snaked into the thick foliage to seek out the enemy.

Although the ambushers had made themselves as secure as possible, they were not seasoned campaigners, and were not expecting to be attacked from behind. So when the four mercenaries came up from the rear, guns blazing, and Newman dropped his grenade into their midst, panic swept through them. The soldiers were caught in the crossfire from in front and behind, and within a matter of seconds their line broke and they retreated towards the barracks, inflicting no more losses on Valin's people.

The soldiers, the Delgados and García stood together looking down at Carlotta's corpse, and O'Rourke switched on his torch. The light was very faint in the enormity of the jungle, and she looked very small. Maria bent and pulled the torn edges of her blouse over her naked breasts and the dreadful wound that had killed her. Jesús, Carlos, Carmen and Sofía had tears running down their cheeks, but Maria remained dry-eyed.

'We should bury her here,' said Valin.

'No,' said Maria firmly.

'No,' agreed her husband. 'We shall take her with us, and bury her somewhere better.'

'None of us may get out of here alive,' said Valin. 'You may not be able to bury her at all.'

'Then at least we'll all be together in death,' said the dead girl's mother.

'Carlos will carry her,' said Jesús, and spoke in Spanish to his son, who nodded back. 'And if he falls, I will carry her. If I fall, Maria, and so on. This place is bad. We will find a good place for her to lie.'

'Very well,' said Valin, knowing it was useless to argue. 'But let's go . . . Now.'

Maria and Jesús helped Carlos hoist Carlotta's body on to his back, where her blood stained his shirt. Valin found Maria's Heckler and Koch and handed it back to her, while Daniel replaced the useless first-aid kit in his backpack. Once ready, the sixteen survivors of the battle for the factory, plus one of the three casualties, made their way back to their transport.

18

The Delgados walked together, Carlos leading, carrying Carlotta's lifeless form, followed by Carmen and Sofía, supporting their mother, with Jesús bringing up the rear, head bowed.

'What happened?' Gerry McGuire said to his brother, who looked shaken and ill.

'What do you think happened? She copped one, and I couldn't do a thing for her.'

'Poor wee bitch.'

'She bled like a stuck pig, Gerry. I tried to help, but she died on me. Just like our sainted sister all those years ago on the Falls Road.'

'No, Dan, don't.'

'We were there, Gerry. Both of us. You tried to help, but could do nothing. You know what it's like to lose someone. To feel their life trickle through your fingers.'

Gerry McGuire did. Very well indeed. He hardly needed reminding, and he knew that his little brother had to be feeling deep pain to bring up the subject at all. When the elder of the McGuire brothers had been a lad of thirteen at the height of the Troubles, he had been sent on an errand by his mother to fetch some bacon for his father's tea.

'Take your wee sister with you for a walk, Gerry,' his mother said.

'Oh, Mam, she's a baby. I don't want the boys to see me with her.'

'The devil take the boys of yours, and you take your sister. You've got to look after her. You're getting to be a man now, Gerry, and you should take on some responsibility for others. And I've put twenty pence in the envelope with the list for you. On the way back buy some sweeties. And share them. But don't give Bridie enough to make her sick.'

Gerry McGuire had very little intention of giving his sister any sweeties at all. If he was going to be forced to run the gauntlet of his mates' jeers as he went down the street hand in hand with someone who was little more than a toddler, and a girl to boot, sister or no sister, then at least he'd get his just reward.

'OK, Mam,' he said. 'I'll take her,' he said, picking up the envelope into which, for safety, his mother insisted on putting the shopping list and the money for his father's supper.

Bridie was playing in the tiny front garden of their council house. When Gerry took her hand, she came willingly. She worshipped both her older brothers, even though they teased her mercilessly and always hid their sweets from her prying eyes. So when Gerry wanted to take her for a walk, she was as pleased as Punch. *He* wasn't, however, and hardly made any reply to her constant prattle as they headed towards the grocer's. Then he saw them. Half-a-dozen poorly dressed boys astride bicycles that for the most part had been cobbled together from stolen parts. And all waiting at the corner as if they just knew that he was on his way, ripe to be teased.

Oh no, he thought, as he saw them. Not now. As he drew level with them, the gang started to whistle, shout and laugh at their unfortunate friend's predicament.

'Got your wee girlfriend with ya, eh, Gerry?' said one.

'He loves his little sister, right enough,' said another. 'Look, he can't bear to be parted from her for a minute.'

'Stop it, will ya?' said Gerry. 'I'm doing an errand for me mam. Now what's wrong with that?'

'So you are, Gerry,' said yet another of his pals. 'But who's taking who for a walk?'

And the boys dissolved into laughter.

'Jeez, but you're impossible,' said Gerry, and hurried his sister past the gang, his ears burning and continuing to do so all the way to the shops, where, kicking his heels outside a newsagent's on the other side of the street, was his eleven-year-old brother.

'Hey, Dan,' Gerry shouted. 'Get yourself over here and look to Bridie. Our mam's made me bring her, and I've got to go for our dadda's tea.'

'Look to her yourself,' replied Daniel, not looking up.

'Dan, I'm warning you.'

'Don't make me laugh.'

Gerry let go of Bridie's hand and left her standing on the pavement as he made to get hold of his brother. But she didn't realize what was happening. She thought that it was a trick to lose her, and she ran after her brother as fast as her little legs would carry her. Across the pavement, down the kerb and into the road, where a motorcyclist, doing a very legal twenty-eight miles an hour, tried to swerve to avoid her, but skidded on the slick surface, wet from recent rain, lost control, his back wheel swinging round to scoop up Bridie and fling her against a lamppost, head first. Her skull split open with a sound like a paper bag full of water being dropped on to a hard surface, and Gerry, hearing the screams of the women in the street, looked round to see his sister lying in the gutter, blood and brains sliding out of the hole in her head. He couldn't believe what he was seeing, and ran back to her, his little brother just a few steps behind. Gerry threw himself down next to Bridie, and tried to scoop the warm mess back inside her skull, spitting and kicking at the passers-by who tried to stop him, as Daniel looked on in horror.

There were a dozen witnesses who said that he'd abandoned the little girl on the pavement, and she in her innocence had chased him into the street, and a dozen more to say that the motorcyclist had been obeying the speed limit. So, hard as he had tried in the years since, he could never forgive himself for what he had done to the child that he had been charged to take care of. The little sister that deep down inside he'd loved, and would never watch grow up.

No, he didn't need reminding what it was like to lose someone. And though he'd seen sudden death dozens of times since, nothing could ever blot out the horror of that day. And he knew that it was the same for his brother.

'It wasn't your fault, Dan,' he said, touching him on the shoulder. 'You did what you could, didn't you?'

'Course I did. But it was precious little.'

* * *

The soldiers got back to the transport and climbed in. Carlos put his sister's body into the back of the truck, before going back to the driving seat, and the rest of the family climbed into the back too, with García, Keller, Resnick and Spenser joining them. The McGuires got into the Chevy with Angel driving again, and Valin climbed in beside Carlos. Messelier and Newman got into Jesus's old jeep with O'Rourke at the wheel, leading the convoy, and they set off.

As the three vehicles reached the main road, O'Rourke, up at the front, saw the glare of headlights from the direction of the town. The vehicles that Stoner had wrecked had finally been cleared off the highway, and the cars, jeeps and personnel carriers that had been bottled up there started the remainder of their journey back to the burning factory, their occupants bent on destroying the perpetrators of the outrage against the Colombian economy.

'Jesus, they're after us,' O'Rourke said to his passengers, 'and we've still got to get past the bloody barracks.'

The three vehicles sped back towards the track that led to the ring road round Santa Ana, and comparative freedom.

But as O'Rourke had so truthfully pointed out, the barracks was between them and it.

A roadblock had been set up across the main road, manned by the last of the troops Valin's men had left alive, and they were more than ready to avenge their fallen comrades and their lost honour.

O'Rourke spotted the roadblock at about the same time as the troops guarding it saw the convoy and opened fire. He slewed the open-topped jeep to the side of the road before it was properly in range, and the truck and the Chevy pulled in sharply beside him.

'Looks like we've got a little problem,' said Valin laconically from his perch on the passenger side of the three-tonner.

'Don't worry, boss, I'll get through,' said Angel through the open window of the Chevrolet. 'You guys,' he said, turning to Gerry and Daniel, 'you wanna get out? I'm going straight through, and it'll be a bumpy ride.'

The two brothers looked at each other, and each for his different reasons, some recent, and some long in the past, grinned strained grins, and said: 'Let's do it,' in chorus.

'We probably won't make it,' said Angel, picking up his steel helmet from the seat next to him and putting it on.

'What the hell?' said Gerry. 'No one's going to live for ever.'

19

The Chevrolet leapt forward, and the McGuires poked their silenced Scorpions out of the rear windows into the slipstream, as the defenders of the roadblock raked the highway with fire.

Back at the truck, Valin buttonholed Resnick, saying, 'Haven't you got anything to slow down that lot?' as he pointed at the headlights of the vehicles coming up behind them and getting dangerously close.

'Just the thing, Colonel,' said the Russian. 'I brought along a few land-mines, just in case. I was going to leave them as a goodbye present when we turned off the main road.'

'I think you'd better leave them as a goodbye present now, don't you?'

'Anything you say,' said Resnick, who grabbed a knapsack out of the truck and ran to the jeep, dived into the back and shouted to O'Rourke: 'Get me back a bit.'

The lieutenant hauled on the wheel of the jeep and headed back the way they had come, his passengers hanging on to the sides for balance.

Bullets were tearing at the Chevy as it got closer to the roadblock, which consisted of a five-ton truck and a Ford staff car. Angel ducked down over the steering wheel, and the McGuires let go twin volleys of bullets from their silenced machine-guns.

Half a mile or so back down the road, Resnick shouted for O'Rourke to stop the jeep, and he leapt out carrying the knapsack, pulling out its contents – three flat, disc-shaped, NATO-standard M-19 anti-tank mines – as he went. These he placed on the road in a Z-shaped pattern. Then, as O'Rourke turned the jeep round again, he threw the knapsack to the side of the road and ran back to the jeep, leapt in, and yelled: 'Go, go, go!'

Meanwhile the Chevy was just a couple of hundred yards from the roadblock, and a hail of bullets was ripping through its bodywork. The windscreen imploded in a shower of glass, the radiator blew up in a cloud of steam, the bonnet flew upwards and both front tyres exploded, but still it kept going. By a miracle, no one in the car had been hit, but it couldn't last. A 9mm bullet slammed into Gerry McGuire's left elbow, but he kept firing his Scorpion, changing magazines every few seconds. Then his brother felt a terrible blow to his chest. He looked down and saw blood, but assumed that his body armour had prevented serious injury, and laughed out loud as he carried on pumping bullets out of the window.

A second bullet hit Daniel in the groin, but his adrenalin was flowing, and he felt nothing. When a third ripped into his neck he fell back against the seat behind him.

Another bullet hit Angel's tin helmet and his head rang, but the thick bulkhead of the Chevy was protecting him from fire as he aimed the dying vehicle at the side of the staff car. The heavy old saloon slammed into it, knocking it off the road, and then itself spun in a full circle, sending soldiers flying, hit the edge of a ditch, bounced back on to the road, and then rolled over half-a-dozen times in a shower of sparks, before coming to rest back on its wheels.

Angel sat at the wheel, almost mesmerized, before he made a move. The driver's door was jammed, but the passenger door sagged open, and, grabbing his Uzi from the floor where it had finished up, he kicked it open. 'You guys in the back OK?' he shouted to Gerry and Daniel.

'I've been hit in the arm,' said Gerry in a dazed voice.

'What about your brother?'

'He's been hit too.'

'Bad?'

Before Gerry had time to answer, the first vehicle in the convoy of Colombian soldiers coming from the town, an armoured personnel carrier, hit one of the land-mines that Resnick had laid, and was tossed up into the air before landing broadside and bursting into flames. Behind it was a jeep. The driver of the jeep swerved as the first land-mine exploded, and hit another. The vehicle was flipped right over, spilling men and guns, and landed on its top next to the personnel carrier, and the two of them completely blocked the road.

'What the fuck was that?' said Angel.

'Christ knows,' said Gerry.

'We'd better get out of here, Irish. Come on, and bring your brother,' Angel said urgently.

'The door's stuck.'

'Use the window.'

Gerry leant over and touched Daniel on the shoulder, but his head slumped down, and when the elder of the two brothers felt for a pulse on the younger's neck, there was nothing.

'Daniel,' he shouted. 'Daniel, are you all right?' But there was no answer.

'He's dead,' Gerry moaned. 'Oh Christ, my poor little brother's dead.'

The troops back at the jeep and truck saw and heard the first vehicle in the pursuing convoy hit the landmine too. 'Nice work, Resnick,' said Valin, as he watched the truck burning.

'Your confidence in me is most gratifying, Colonel,' replied the Russian. 'But shouldn't we press on and see what has happened to Angel and his comrades?'

Valin looked towards the roadblock. 'Of course. Mount up, people,' he said. 'We have more work to do.'

At first Gerry refused to leave his brother, and Angel had to lean into the car and almost drag him away from the body. 'It's no good, man,' the American insisted, after he too had felt for a pulse. 'He's gone.'

'I can't leave him here.'

'We can't take him with us.'

Christ, thought Angel. At this rate we'll have more dead bodies with us than live ones. 'Come on, Gerry, let's find some cover and wait for the rest,' he said firmly.

As more bullets thudded into the body of the Chevrolet, at last Gerry forced his way through the window and joined Angel on the road.

'This way,' said the American, and dragged Gerry across to a slight knoll, where they threw themselves down and started to return fire at the remnants of the defenders of the roadblock, as the Ford three-tonner and the jeep headed in their direction.

'I'm going back for him,' declared Gerry, when the firing died down as some of the enemy guns were turned on the approaching vehicles. He stood up, only to be cut down by a bullet in the leg.

'You fucking crazy bastard,' screamed Angel as he loosed the remains of a magazine on to the road. 'Why couldn't you wait a minute until they got here?'

That was all it would have taken, as the truck and the jeep screeched to a halt at the other side of the roadblock, and Valin's troops threw themselves into battle, Maria's Heckler and Koch automatic spitting lead up at the front, for she was determined to avenge the death of her eldest daughter.

The last of the defenders who stayed to fight were cut down within seconds, while the rest fled. For a moment silence reigned.

'I'll be back,' said Angel to Gerry. 'Hold on.' He quit the knoll and ran towards his comrades.

'Angel, you made it,' said O'Rourke. 'Where are the McGuires?'

'Daniel's still in the car. He's dead. Gerry's up there,' Angel said, gesturing back the way he had come. 'He's been hit. Don't know how bad.'

'Are you OK?'

'Can't seem to be anything else.'

'You're lucky,' said Newman, who had been standing next to the lieutenant. 'I'll go and see how he is.' He melted away towards the knoll that Angel had indicated.

So one of them's dead, the ex-para thought as he went. Good job. I wish it had been me who'd done it. Let's see if the other survived. From his pocket he drew a knife, a Randall No. 1, as sharp as a razor from constant honing. He found Gerry McGuire lying where he had fallen, his Scorpion still clasped in one hand. Gently he knelt beside the Irishman, took his gun from him, and said: 'Are you all right?'

McGuire looked up at Newman through eyes glazed with pain. 'Thank God you're here,' he said. 'Help me. I've got to get back to my brother.'

'Too late for him, old son,' said Newman. 'He's dead.' He lifted the knife and kissed the blade. 'And so are you.' The last words he whispered almost lovingly as he slit McGuire's throat. 'That's for my mates,' he cooed as he cleaned the knife on the dead man's tunic. 'The ones you and your like murdered for that shithouse called Northern Ireland, you Republican scum.'

He looked down at the dim form of McGuire's body, put his knife away, then removed several playing cards from another of his many pockets. There were a dozen or more of them, all from different decks. But they all had the same motif: the Ace of Spades. He removed one, tucked it into the collar of the Irishman's jacket and stood up. Then he walked down to the Chevrolet, wrested open the back door and checked Daniel's body to make sure he was dead. He was. Newman took another of the cards, slid it into the pocket of the dead man's blouse and slammed the door shut on him.

20

Newman returned slowly to the others, a feeling of well-being suffusing his whole body after what he had just seen and done. Even if he didn't make it back himself, he thought, at least he'd done something to avenge all those friends who'd been brought home from Ulster in wooden boxes, or invalided out to spend the rest of their lives becoming increasingly bitter, and trying to live on army pensions.

'How is he?' asked Angel.

'Dead.'

'He can't be.'

'He is. How many more bodies do you want to see tonight? He was hit at least three times. There's nothing you can do – any of us can do.'

'I want to see him.'

'I told you, there's nothing you can do. He's dead, Angel. Get it through your head.'

'What's going on here?' It was Valin.

'The McGuires. Newman says they're both dead,' said Angel. 'But Gerry was alive when I left him.'

'Why would he lie?' said Valin harshly, sensing the panic in Angel's manner. 'Now mount up, soldier. We're late.'

It was almost two-thirty and they still hadn't left

Santa Ana for the long drive back to the airstrip. They were late, and Valin knew the pilot would not hang around.

'But, Colonel,' protested Angel, 'Gerry might still be alive.'

'They're *both* dead,' said Newman. 'Take my word – I've seen enough dead bodies in my time.'

'I just want to be certain,' said Angel.

'OK,' said Valin, beginning to lose his patience. 'Check.'

Newman said nothing as Angel went up to the ridge, where he found McGuire's body and the card. He knew what it meant, and that it was too late to do anything about it. He went back to where Newman and Valin were waiting. 'So?' said Valin.

'Dead,' said Angel. 'Just like he said.' He looked at Newman, who looked straight back.

'Satisfied?' asked Valin.

'Sure.'

Newman's eyes narrowed, but he said not a word, and all three got back into their vehicles, and the convoy, now reduced to just the truck and the jeep, moved off.

They sped down the road nose to tail, O'Rourke in the lead again, until they came to the jungle track that led to the ring road. For the next few miles it was slow going, and Valin, sitting next to Carlos in the truck, could hardly contain his impatience. They would need to be very lucky to reach the airstrip on time. It meant a straight run with no more delays, and the way their luck was running, that seemed more and more unlikely.

They returned to the rendezvous point they had

chosen, but which they had not had to use, and picked up the Microbus.

Jesús carried his dead daughter to it, and the rest of the family, apart from Carlos, joined him inside.

Valin went over for a word, and the Colombian joined him outside the bus.

'What are you going to do with Carlotta's body?' Valin asked.

'We have decided to take her home.'

'But I thought you were coming out with us and García.'

'It is impossible, Colonel. We have to bury our daughter.'

'But you may all be in danger. You know there is an informer back in the States.'

'So be it.'

'Jesús, I beg you to reconsider. Bury your daughter by all means. But do it out by the airstrip, then come on the plane with us.'

'Without the benefit of a priest?'

'If necessary. She's dead now, and words mean nothing to her.'

'They mean much to Maria and me.'

Valin realized once again that it was pointless to argue with the Colombian, and changed the subject. 'We're going to need petrol and diesel soon,' he said.

'We have laid stashes all along the highway,' said Jesús. 'The first is about forty kilometres away. We can be there in a little while and fill up the tanks.'

'Bless you.'

'It is nothing.'

Valin looked through the window of the bus and saw the body of the Delgados' daughter laid out on the back seat, and knew what a gigantic lie her being there made of the old man's words.

'Your other children maybe. Let them come then. They could make a fresh start in America,' he said.

'Carlos? He speaks no English.' Jesús then saw Valin's face, and said: 'All right, I will ask them. But for now, we had better leave. Time is passing, and there are many soldiers between us and our destination. And all of them will be looking for us.'

Don't remind me, thought Valin tiredly. 'Of course,' he said, and returned to the truck.

The convoy reached the fuel dump without any problems. Once there, Jesús and Carlos busied themselves with refuelling the three vehicles, helped by Newman, Messelier and Angel. Maria, Carmen and Sofía sat together in the Microbus, and Spenser, after a brief word with Valin, went over and tapped on the glass next to where Maria was sitting. The three women inside all looked at him, and Maria wound down the window.

'I'd like to speak to Carmen, please,' said the American.

Maria turned to her daughter and said: 'Do you want to?'

'Yes,' the girl replied.

'Then do so.'

'I'm sorry for your loss,' Spenser said to Maria.

She nodded. 'Thank you,' she said.

'I'll say a prayer for her.'

'Say a prayer for yourself. You will need it before you leave here. If you are not killed first – you and all your friends.'

'Mother,' said Carmen. 'It was not his fault. We knew what we were getting into.'

The older woman nodded again. 'I'm sorry,' she said to Spenser. 'That was ungracious of me. One life among so many that have been lost is worth little. But she was my eldest daughter. I had such high hopes for her. And look what has happened.'

'I understand,' said Spenser. 'I have lost people too. Friends, family, comrades. Too many. I know what it's like to mourn. I don't blame you for being angry.'

Maria touched Spenser's hand through the open window of the bus, as Carmen climbed out, and she and Spenser went to the edge of the clearing where they were parked.

'The colonel tells me that your family are staying here. Not coming out with us as planned,' he said.

Carmen looked up at him and nodded.

'I want you to come with me to America,' Spenser said. 'On your own if necessary.'

'Why?'

'You know why. You've known since the moment I first laid eyes on you.'

'Yes, I've known. But my parents . . . '

'They would want what is best for you.'

'And you know what that is?'

Spenser smiled. 'No, I can't say that I do. But there is a chance that you might find it with me.'

'*You*. A soldier of fortune. A paid mercenary, who fights for whoever has the biggest purse.'

'Yes, me. I've been alone a long time, Carmen. Years. *Too* long. I don't make a habit of this, believe me. But as soon as I saw you, I wanted you to be with me. That's why I kissed you before. I thought you enjoyed it. I hoped you did.'

'You are an attractive man, Spenser. I can't believe there has been no one for as long as that.'

'Take my word for it. And take my word that I only want the best for you.'

'I do.'

'Then will you come with me?'

'Let me think about it. I will speak with my mother. Perhaps she does not want to lose two daughters in one day.'

'Of course.'

Carmen went up on tiptoe and kissed Spenser briefly on the mouth again. 'Of course I enjoyed it,' she said. 'More than you know.'

'I'm glad.'

'You could always stay here with us,' said Carmen.

'And be on the "most wanted" list of every law-enforcement agency in Colombia? Not to mention the army.'

'There are places we could go where no one would ever find us.'

'You make it sound very tempting.'

'So you'll think about it?'

'I will.'

'I must go back to my mother.'

'Of course.' And he watched as she walked back to the Microbus, looking wistfully over her shoulder once as she went.

Spenser stood alone and considered what Carmen had said. What the hell did he have to go back to in the States? Money. Sure. There was money waiting. Plenty. If they ever made it out, that was. Maybe life wouldn't be too bad in Colombia. Not with a woman like Carmen. But did he want them both to live in fear of a knock on the door at midnight for the rest of their lives? He shook his head wearily. Jesus Christ, what a decision.

Over at the truck that Jesús and Carlos were topping up with diesel from a huge can, Resnick was smoking a cigarette and watched Spenser and Carmen as they talked. He saw their brief kiss and envied their obvious attraction to each other, and looked through the side window of the Microbus at Sofía's lustrous hair.

Jesús saw him looking. 'She is beautiful, is she not?' he said.

'Sofía?'

Jesús nodded.

'She is,' said Resnick.

'If only you could have met under different circumstances . . . ' said the old man.

'I was thinking the very same thing.'

'Your friend: the American with the sad eyes. He also has those thoughts – about Carmen.'

'I think he does.'

Just then, Valin came and joined them. 'About finished, Jesús,' he said.

Jesús and Carlos put the heavy can on the ground, and Carlos screwed on the cap, before returning it to its hiding place under camouflage netting at the side of the clearing, with the rest of the stash of fuel.

'All done, Colonel,' said Jesús, rubbing his hands down the sides of his trousers. 'All the vehicles have full tanks. Certainly enough to get us where we're going.'

'Will you reconsider?' asked Valin. 'About staying, I mean.'

'I think not.'

'OK, I won't argue. But remember what I said about your son and daughters.'

'I will,' promised Jesús. 'We'd better go.'

Everyone climbed back into their vehicles once again, to begin the long haul through the night to the airstrip. By then it was almost four o'clock, and they had only two hours left to make a journey that needed more than three. Valin looked at his watch again as Carlos bumped the truck on to the road, bringing up the rear of the convoy, and in the pit of his stomach he knew they were not going to make it.

21

The miles rolled under the wheels of the three vehicles as they headed towards the airfield, and in the back of the truck Keller broke out rations for himself and Spenser, Angel, Resnick and García.

As Spenser thoughtfully munched on tinned sausage and vegetables, and drank from a canteen of water, he said: 'Sergeant, I may not be coming out.'

'What?' said the German, almost dropping his own can of K-rations.

'I may not be coming out with you,' Spenser repeated. 'I'm thinking about staying.'

'Christ, man. In this God-forsaken hole? After what we've done? Are you mad? Why would you want to stay here?'

'*Cherchez la femme*,' said Resnick.

'What?' said the sergeant again.

'I think our man has lost his heart,' explained the Russian.

Realization dawned on the German's face. 'One of Delgado's girls?' he said.

'That's right. Where have you been, Sarge, that you haven't noticed?' asked Resnick.

'Mostly sitting on top of a hill watching your arses,' said the sergeant. 'But Chris. What are you thinking about? Love 'em, by all means. Fuck 'em if you can. But stay with 'em? Where the hell would the world be if every man did that?'

Spenser and Resnick laughed at Keller's indignation, and even Angel, still deep in gloom from what had happened to Stoner and the McGuire brothers, managed a faint smile.

'I'll have to speak to the boss,' said Spenser.

'I should think you would. What are you doing with your life?' said Keller.

Christ knows, thought Spenser. Christ alone knows.

His mind rewound back to Vietnam. Dust-off at dawn for a strike at a village deep in lush jungle that was so similar to the scenery that was flying past outside. The chopper dropped the patrol close to a village called . . . What the hell did it matter what it was called? It was just another gook village: a dozen hovels, chickens digging in the dirt, and a headman who claimed to love the Yanks. Sure he loved them. Just like all the rest. 'GI, number one,' they called out to soldiers as they went past, then shot them in the back. But hell, who could blame them? It was their country, after all.

They approached the village as a cock crowed, and found cover, then called in for the mortar attack to begin. There were guerrillas in the village, or so intelligence told them. But intelligence had been wrong before, and probably would be again.

Lieutenant Christopher Spenser, aged twenty-one, was in command of a six-man patrol out on a search-and-destroy mission. His radio-man had his headset stuck in his helmet. There was a muffled squawk and he reached for it. 'Go, ten,' he said, then listened. 'Roger that.'

'Guns up on the TOT, Lieutenant,' he said.

'Tell 'em to go for it.'

'Ten, five. Let her eat.'

Then the mortars started to fall on the villages. Huts burst into flames and the occupants, both male and female, ran out screaming. The women carried babies, the children carried cooking pots and bedding and the men carried nothing.

When the last mortar had hit its target, the patrol rose to their feet as one and headed into the village.

Spenser led the way, with to his right a veteran sergeant called Hope. To his left was PFC Beaumont. Behind him, the radio operator, Hopkins, and three more privates, Bennett, Kawolski and Simpson. Beaumont and Simpson were black and Kawolski was a second-generation Pole. Not that it mattered. It just was. It didn't matter either that Beaumont and Simpson were just eighteen.

As they came up to the settlement, something moved in the undergrowth and Kawolski fired off a short burst from his M16 without looking. It was a dog, and died like one: noisily.

As they came to the main street of the village – if you could call a flattened mud path a main street – a black-clad figure appeared from behind a burning hut. Spenser fired on full auto, and the figure vanished into the smoke. 'Check it out, Bennett, Simpson,' he ordered.

'You got it, Ell-Tee,' they chorused, and stealthily went to the corner of the hut and squinted round it.

'It's a woman, Ell-Tee,' said Simpson. 'And she's pregnant. Or at least she was.'

Spenser went to see for himself. The black-clad

figure was indeed a woman, and was indeed pregnant – or had been. His bullets had hit her in the stomach, and she was busy miscarrying and dying at the same time.

'Shit,' said Spenser. 'Medic. Medic.'

Beaumont was the medic, but there was nothing he could do. As the sun rose higher, and the smoke drifted across the paddy-fields, all he did was shoot the woman full of morphine and cradle her head as she and the baby died in the dirt.

The patrol stood around in the morning heat haze and looked at her as she breathed her last. 'Shit, man,' said Simpson. 'What are we doing in this fucking hole? A coupla months ago I was in Philly, and the only thing on my mind was what record to buy on Sat'day. Or what chick to ask to dance. Now look what they done to me. They dumped me out here in a place where we kill pregnant women in the name of the USA.'

'*You* didn't kill her,' said Spenser. '*I* did.'

'Shit, Ell-Tee,' said the young black again. 'We all in this shit together.' He lit a Lucky Strike, and offered Spenser one. The lieutenant accepted and as Simpson gave him a light, he could see that the boy was crying.

Boy, he thought as the truck bounced along the bumpy highway in Colombia. I was nothing but a boy myself. A boy with the blood of a pregnant woman and her unborn baby on my hands. Among others.

There had been no Vietcong in the village. It had been friendly, and the intelligence had been wrong. The patrol dusted off again at nine hundred hours, leaving the destroyed community to fend for itself. The last thing Spenser saw as he looked out of the open door of the Huey was a smudge of smoke against the blue sky, and they were all back at base camp in time for a late breakfast.

The base camp was a little slice of the US transported to South-east Asia. A place where the troops could buy Budweiser and Coca-Cola, Hostess Twinkies and *Playboy* magazine. And listen to Tamla Motown records on the radio: Smokey, Marvin, The Supremes, The Isleys. Tamla Motown: 'The sound of young America.' That was a joke. To Spenser and Simpson, Beaumont, and all the rest, the sound of young America was the rattle of an M16 on full auto.

Spenser's daydream was so real that he imagined he could hear the sound of the Huey as it prepared to land, and he jumped when Keller kicked his foot and screamed, 'Wake up, man. There's a chopper upstairs. Get your fucking gun, for Chrissake.'

Even as Spenser scrambled for the Gatling, the first bullets from the machine-guns mounted in the helicopter began to hit the convoy.

22

The chopper was a Sikorsky HH-S 3C gunship, better known as 'The Jolly Green Giant', because of its size, and had been used to great effect by the American army, notably in Libya in 1986. It had a crew of five, and three 7.62mm mini-guns, similar to the one used by Spenser, poked obscenely from its body, which in this case bore Colombian air force markings.

The first vehicle to bear the brunt of the machine-gun fire from the powerful weapons mounted inside its open doors, and in a gun port underneath its huge belly, was the Microbus in the middle of the convoy. Bullets slammed into it, and Jesús, who was driving, swerved across the road as they punched through the windscreen, killing Maria instantly, stitching a line along the empty seats behind her, next to where Sofía and Carmen were sitting, and pounding into the already dead body of their sister.

Jesús saw the bullets tear through his wife's body, and he let out a roar of pain as the Microbus veered off the road and ploughed into the jungle.

The chopper swept around and came back to strafe the jeep and the truck as Keller and Resnick ripped the canvas cover above them from its metal supports, and Spenser aimed his Gatling at it and began firing. The pilot sheered away as the shells punched through the air, tracers helping Spenser's aim.

O'Rourke, at the wheel of the jeep, skidded to the side of the road, and in the cab of the three-tonner Valin yelled at Carlos in Spanish to stop too, which he did, as Spenser and his companions in the well of the truck kept firing.

The helicopter swept back towards them, its thirty-million-candlepower Night Sun searchlight illuminating the road as if it was day. O'Rourke, Newman and Messelier had left the jeep and taken cover among the trees, and O'Rourke and Newman were firing up at the helicopter with their carry weapons, while the Frenchman reloaded the ARMSCOR with fresh grenades.

Spenser's next burst slammed into the fuselage of the aircraft and one gunner stopped firing as a slug ripped into his leg, which spouted blood.

Messelier fired the grenade-launcher upwards, and by sheer luck, the first projectile went straight through one of the Sikorsky's open doors, hit the roof and bounced back inside the cabin, where it exploded with maximum force. Trailing smoke, the stricken helicopter veered away over the jungle, where it suddenly dropped like a stone and exploded a few hundred yards away.

'Yes,' yelled Messelier, punching the air. 'We killed the fucker.' He did a dance of triumph.

Carlos drove the truck to where the jeep had stopped. 'Status report,' yelled Valin, as he jumped out of the cab. 'O'Rourke, Keller. Any casualties?'

'We've lost the bus,' shouted O'Rourke. 'Angel, Newman, get back and find it.'

The American jumped out of the back of the truck, and he and the ex-para ran back down the road to where the Microbus had pushed into the undergrowth.

There they found Jesús cradling his dead wife, and Sofía and Carmen, white and shaken, holding on to each other for comfort.

'Oh no,' said Angel as he tugged open the door. 'Is she . . . ?'

'Dead,' said Jesús. 'My family is being ripped apart.'

The two mercenaries stood beside the bus in silence. There was nothing they could say, and they knew it.

'I can't go on,' sobbed Jesús. 'This is too much.'

'I'm real sorry, Mr Delgado,' said Angel, and he reached inside the bus to touch the Colombian, who shook off his hand angrily.

'Leave me,' he said. 'Leave us all.'

'We can't do that, sir,' said Newman. 'They know where we are. If there are any jets close by, they'll be looking for us at first light, and we'll really be in trouble. And even if there aren't, the chopper pilot will have radioed through, and some of his buddies might come looking, or send ground troops. We have to move off, and soon.'

'Just leave us. Haven't you done enough? First my daughter, now my wife. I should have listened to your colonel and taken them home this morning when I had a chance.'

'But you didn't, sir,' said Newman. 'And I'm afraid it's too late for you to change your mind. Is the vehicle driveable?'

'I don't know,' said Jesús.

'Here, let me,' said Angel and he slid into the driver's

seat, which Jesús had vacated, and tried the stalled engine. It started first time.

'Do you want me to drive, sir,' asked Angel.

The Colombian nodded, but said nothing.

Angel reversed the Microbus out of the thick vegetation where it had stopped, back on to the road, selected first gear, and with Newman clinging to the outside, drove back to join the others.

When they got back, Newman jumped off the bus and went to report to Valin.

'Oh hell,' said the colonel. 'I told him not to come.'

'He wishes he hadn't, believe me.'

'It's a bit bloody late for that.'

Newman said nothing in reply.

Valin trotted over to the Microbus with Carlos and Spenser close behind, and when the young Colombian saw his mother's body, he wailed and fell to his knees.

Christ, thought Valin. This is all we need. Hysterics from the bloody driver. What next?

Spenser leaned through the window and looked at Carmen. She looked back at him with empty eyes, and said nothing. He didn't speak either, but just walked on to the road and bummed a cigarette off Resnick.

'Tough,' said the Russian.

'And getting tougher,' replied Spenser.

Back at the bus, Valin told Carlos in his native tongue to get in with his family, and said to Angel: 'You drive.'

'Sir,' replied Angel.

Valin then turned to the rest of his men. 'Newman, can you handle the truck?'

'No problem, sir. I've got my HGV.'

'Good, though I don't think anyone will ask to see your licence,' and he looked at his watch as the first faint hint of dawn appeared in the sky towards the east. It was five a.m. – only an hour until take-off.

'Mount up, men,' he said. 'But I think we're right royally screwed.'

23

Angel couldn't believe what was happening to him as he slotted the Microbus with bullet holes in the windscreen into the middle of the convoy. Blood and dead bodies everywhere. And some of them innocent. This was not the way he'd expected it to be when he'd joined Valin's team. Christ, he thought wearily as the Microbus picked up speed. Christ help me.

What he'd wanted to be was a soldier. A regular soldier in the US army. Just like his father had been, and his father before him. Sonny Angelo had fought at Guadalcanal, and Angel's old man, Bobby, had done his time in Vietnam. But by the time Angel had enlisted there were no more wars to fight. Grenada and the Gulf were finished, the Iron Curtain was down, and all there was for him overseas was a short haul in Germany with the drug addicts, unless Clinton got the country involved in some UN shit in Bosnia or Somalia. To be transferred to communications was the last straw. Angel wanted to be out where the fighting was, gun in hand, gum in mouth, wearing shades, just like the photos of his dad in Saigon, *circa* 1970.

So he'd looked for a way to be discharged, and the fight with the MP had been the answer, although he could have done without the time served in the military prison. The fight really wasn't all his fault. He'd fallen in with a bunch of recruits who drank too much, smoked dope, and ingested as many other drugs as they could get their hands on. He had got into a lot of debt, which he could only pay off by acting as chauffeur to one of the dealers who'd heard about his prowess at the wheel.

On Friday and Saturday nights Angel had to drive the guy around a succession of army and civilian bars close to Fort Bragg. The dealer was the proud owner of a restored cherry-red 1959 Plymouth Fury with white leather upholstery, which was not the most discreet vehicle for delivering drugs, but both of them were so zonked it made little difference.

That particular Friday night, Angel had just come off guard duty and was still in uniform. At about ten o'clock he was sitting outside the quaintly-named Stand and Deliver bar, sinking a Bud Lite and smoking a joint, when a jeep with two MPs inside pulled up in front of the Plymouth.

Shit, Angel thought as they got out, settled their equipment belts more comfortably on their hips and walked towards the car.

'Hey, soldier,' said the first MP. 'What's up?'

Angel looked around. 'The sky,' he replied.

'Very funny, man,' said the other MP, a black dude who seemed to be about five feet wide.

'Yeah, man,' said Angel, taking another sip of his beer and a toke on his joint, 'I'm a funny guy.'

'Who says so, your mother?'

'Among others.'

'Gimme your army number and regiment, boy,' said the first MP.

Angel reeled off the information.

'This your car?' asked the black cop.

'No, man,' said Angel. 'Just driving it for a friend, is all.'

'What kinda friend has wheels like this.'

'A rich friend.'

'How did he make his money?'

'Running slaves,' said Angel, looking the black MP straight in the eye.

'Get out the car, motherfucker.'

'You want to make me?'

'Angelo, you're under arrest.'

'In a horse's ass.'

When the big black MP dragged Angel out of the Plymouth, the young recruit lost his temper. He caught hold of the baseball bat he kept under the driver's seat in case of trouble and landed a huge whack just under the rim of the cop's steel helmet, where his neck met his shoulders. The cop went down and Angel began to kick him, as the other MP unholstered his side-arm and dived into the fight.

Angel lashed out at him too, but the MP struck Angel a massive blow on the side of his head with the barrel of his Colt .45, laying him out cold.

Angel got six months in the brig for the escapade, plus a dishonourable discharge. But he got his revenge when he went back to Fort Bragg on his release, and lay in wait for the MPs. He still had a few friends in the town, including the dope dealer, and one night they staged an ambush outside the very same bar. The dealer made a call to the MPs, telling them that a fight was about to break out between the military and a bunch of redneck civilians. Angel had made some enquiries and knew that the white cop, by the name of Jones, was on duty that night. When his jeep turned up, siren wailing, Angel was there waiting. He was dressed in civilian clothes, and the MP hardly gave him a second glance, until Angel walked up to him and smacked him in the face with the brass knucks he was wearing on his right hand, breaking the cop's nose and cheekbone with one blow.

Jones's partner, not the black guy who had been with him on the first occasion, tried to retaliate, but Angel's friends moved in and started to mix it, while Angel made his escape and took the first plane to New York. The episode went down in the legend of the camp.

Soon after, Angel heard about the mercenary scene across the pond, and took a trip to Europe, where he met Valin and O'Rourke and signed up for the mission to Colombia. Now he wasn't so sure it had been the right thing to do, and as the sun peeped over the mountain top, he pulled his sunglasses from his top pocket and put them on, and wondered if any of the mercs would ever get out of the country alive.

24

Valin called O'Rourke on the radio at five forty-five. 'We're never going to make it,' he said tersely. 'Pull over. Out.' O'Rourke did as he was ordered, and Angel in the Microbus, which stank of blood and human tissue brutally exposed to the humid air, did the same, as Newman brought the truck to a halt behind them.

Valin hopped out and ran to the Microbus. 'How much further, Jesús?' he asked.

The Colombian looked at him through eyes still curtained with grief. 'Too far,' he said. 'Another hour at least.'

'Damn it,' said Valin. 'We're never going to catch that plane.'

'He will be back tomorrow.'

'I hope so. Is there anywhere you can think of that we can hole up for the rest of the day?'

'My land is about forty-five minutes away. We can go there, and I will bury my wife and child.'

'Will you come out with us then?'

'Maybe.'

'Your place it is, then. Are there other people about?'

'No, it is quiet and secluded.'

'Angel, you take the lead,' said Valin. 'Will someone show him the route?'

'I will,' said Carmen.

Valin ran to tell O'Rourke what was happening, then headed back to the truck. He was surprised that the party had met no more resistance on the road, and to tell the truth, a little worried. But he mentally shrugged as he took his seat next to Newman and the small convoy set off again.

At six o'clock precisely, as the three vehicles carrying Valin's Raiders were still an hour or so away, the ancient C47 made a pass over the airstrip where it had dropped off Valin's Raiders twenty-four hours earlier, lowered its undercarriage and came in to land. The pilot taxied up to the end of the makeshift runway, feathered his engines and turned the plane round for take-off again. He sat in his patched leather seat and surveyed the clearing. There was nothing to see but the edge of the jungle that surrounded him, and no one emerged to board the Douglas.

The pilot wiped a thin sheen of sweat from his brow, took off his headset and walked back into the body of the plane, where ten men in green fatigues were sitting. They wore no insignia of any kind, and each held an Israeli Galil assault rifle, snouted with a suppressor, as a carry gun, and wore Sig Sauer P228s in holsters on their hips. One of them had been monitoring a powerful radio since the plane had crossed the Colombian border.

The one who had done all the talking so far, and who, the pilot assumed, was their leader, turned from the window that he had been peering through, and said: 'Any sign?' He, like the rest of the men, had an American accent.

'Not a thing,' replied the pilot. He had not been a happy man since the unmarked military transporter had landed at his base and disgorged fourteen anonymous soldiers the previous evening. They had taken command of the C47 and insisted, with the aid of the heavy ordnance they carried, that he take the ten soldiers now sitting in the cabin to meet Colonel Valin and his men, leaving the other four behind to make sure of two things. First, that the pilot returned the next day if by any chance he had to leave them in Colombia; and second, if the worst happened and Valin's men defeated the soldiers, there would be a welcoming party when they got off the plane in Panama.

The leader had paid the pilot handsomely, but even the sight of so many US dollars had not calmed the flier's fears that Valin might object. Physically.

'Well,' said the leader. 'They did the job and got out. At least some of them did. Plus some civilians. A stupid bastard in a chopper dive-bombed them a while back, and copped it. But since then they've been allowed free passage. I've made sure of that.' He gestured towards the radio. 'These dumb Colombians don't know who they've been taking on.'

'The colonel said that they might be delayed,' said the pilot.

The leader smiled. 'That's a nice choice of words,' he said.

'And if they weren't here today, I was to come back tomorrow at the same time.'

'You've told me that already,' the leader said impatiently. 'I wanted this all over and done with by then. Can't you raise them on *your* radio?'

'I don't know what frequencies they're using.'

'You should have asked.'

'*Sí, señor.*'

'We'll wait fifteen minutes, then if they're not here, you get going back across the border and try again tomorrow. We'll stay. Of course, they may have run into something we don't know about yet. A patrol maybe. This is a mess. Why the hell Washington agreed to send them . . . ' He stopped speaking, as if he realized he might be saying too much. 'OK, compadre. Back to your seat and keep a weather eye out. If you see anything – I repeat, anything – sing out.'

'*Sí, señor*,' said the pilot.

When he was safely back on the flight deck with the door closed, the leader, who was referred to by his men only as 'Number One', stood up and addressed them.

'Right,' he said. 'You know why we've been sent down to this hell-hole, and what we have to do now we're here. It's not the most pleasant of jobs, but it has to be done. There are a bunch of half-assed mercenaries running around this apology for a country, creating mayhem in the name of the USA. It was a bad decision made by those fools in the civilian agencies, and we've been sent to clean up their mess the same as we've been doing for the last fifty years. When in doubt, call up the army. You also know that we have no official jurisdiction down here, and if we're caught, no one will admit that we exist. I've been able to use some juice on the military as you heard when I was talking on the radio. But how far it goes, Christ alone knows. These bastards could turn at any moment. And I can tell you they're not crazy about being ordered around by me. The only reason I've got away with it so far is that our orders came down from someone very powerful. Powerful enough to put the fear of God into these Hispanics. What he's got on them I don't know, and I don't think I want to. So I warn you now, as I've warned you before: if this all goes wrong, and any of us – I repeat, any of us – fall into the hands of the Colombians, we'll just disappear. And these guys are expert at the art. So stay close, watch your backs, keep your weapons close, and trust no one except us ten. Understood?'

The nine soldiers all replied in the affirmative.

'Good,' said Number One. 'And God be with you.'

25

Carmen showed Angel the turn-off to her father's land at almost exactly the same time that the C47 was flying back across the border into Panama. The Microbus bumped down a muddy trail that seemed to be leading nowhere, until suddenly it opened out on to flatlands that dipped until they met a small range of foothills, beyond which reared up an imposing cluster of mountains. The jungle had been cleared to provide arable land, and beside a small stream stood a low farmhouse with a large barn behind it. It was an idyllic scene, and for the first time in hours Angel felt himself relax. He drove towards the building and parked in the barn on Carmen's instructions.

The jeep and truck followed the Microbus inside, and everyone disembarked. Immediately Valin sent Messelier to stand guard on the track that they had taken to enter Jesús's land. The Frenchman was under strict orders to maintain radio silence. The rest of the men stood silently as Carlos and Jesús took the bodies of Maria and Carlotta from the VW. Valin offered to help, but he was rebuffed. The two women were carried gently into the farmhouse and Carmen spoke to the colonel. 'We will prepare some food, when we have made my mother and sister comfortable. But until then, please stay out of the house. You are free to go anywhere else on the land but this is a private moment. I'm sure you understand.'

Valin nodded. 'Of course,' he said. 'You know you have all our sympathies. We won't stray far. In case another chopper comes looking for us.'

'There will not be room for you all to sleep inside the house, but you are welcome to bed down in the barn.'

'We're very grateful to you,' said Valin.

After the Delgados had gone, the men began cleaning their weapons, eating and smoking. Angel found a quiet spot and took the bag of cocaine out from his jacket. It was amazing to him that it had survived all he had been through, but it was undamaged. He poked the point of his knife through the plastic wrapper and took a hit. It was good stuff. The best he'd ever tried, and he got an immediate rush which made him feel better.

That was when Newman found him. 'The spoils of war?' he asked.

'Give it a rest, bud,' said Angel.

'I don't give a fuck,' said Newman. 'Every man is free to be the architect of his own downfall. Just as long as you can do your job when we get out of here.'

'I'll do it,' said Angel. 'Don't worry about that.'

'Good.'

'And what about your job?'

'What do you mean?'

'I saw what you did to Gerry McGuire.'

'Me?'

'Who else?'

'One of the Colombian soldiers.'

'Give me a break, man.'

'You didn't say anything to Valin?'

'What would've been the point?'

'He would probably have shot me, there and then,' said Newman.

'But we need you and that Ithaca you're toting.'

'Self-preservation first, huh, Angel?'

'The McGuires were dead. You're alive. I just wanted you to know that I know, and I'm wondering whether I should watch my back when you're around.'

'You're Italian, aren't you?' asked Newman.

'Fourth generation.'

'Then you've got nothing to worry about, son.' And Newman smiled an evil smile. 'They're better off dead, those two. It's their sort that killed mates of mine,' he went on. 'They should never have been allowed to mix with real soldiers. Irish fucking Republican Army. I shit on them.' He smiled again. 'I'm only sorry that the other one was dead before I got to him.'

'Cool,' said Angel. 'You keep quiet about this' – he tapped the bag of cocaine – 'and I'll keep quiet about McGuire.'

'Deal,' said Newman. 'I'm off for a kip. I imagine you won't want one.'

'I'm fine,' said Angel. 'Just fine.'

At the airstrip, the leader had gathered the men round him in the jungle. It was getting hotter, moisture dripped from the trees, and the bugs were using the men in the green fatigues for target practice.

'You know the deal,' said the leader, wiping the perspiration from his brow with a green rag that he then tied around his head as a sweat band. 'We wait here until dawn tomorrow. The pilot's going to make one more trip. That was the arrangement with Valin. If this little band is not here by then, the pilot has no obligation to return. End of story. And as far as anyone will know, they *didn't* make it. These men are the scum of the earth. They will not be missed. But we have to make sure that there are no loose ends. We have to see to it that not one of them, or anyone they've teamed up with, is still alive to talk about what happened last night in Santa Ana.'

'Why didn't someone do something about it before they even got here?' asked one of his men.

'Valin has friends in high places. If they'd never got here, questions *would* have been asked. But they completed their mission more by luck than by judgement, I imagine. So it's just a tough break that they never made it back to be picked up.'

The man who had asked the question nodded.

Back at Jesús's farmhouse, Carmen was staring out of an upstairs window at the barn where Spenser was standing in the shadows smoking a cigarette and looking at the house. I wonder if he will come for me, she thought. I hope he does. Oh please, Chris, just walk up here and take me away. I don't care what happens. Even if we don't live to see another day, it would have been worth it to spend my last few hours with you.

But he didn't. He dropped the cigarette butt and ground it into the earth with the toe of his combat boot, then turned and went back into the barn.

Inside, Valin was talking to O'Rourke and Keller.

Spenser walked over and joined them. 'What's up, Colonel?' he asked.

'To use a phrase from some of those old films, I don't like it; it's too quiet.'

'Can't be quiet enough for me,' said the American.

'Listen, Chris,' said Valin. 'We were spotted on the main road out of Bogotá by that chopper we shot down. Don't tell me he didn't get a message through about our position before he crashed. Since then, nothing. We could have been bottled up half-a-dozen times. Why weren't we? I think something's going on that we don't know about. So we keep a permanent guard on that road coming in here.'

'You can't suspect Jesús. Not after all he's been through.'

'No, of course not. Jesús could've had us all on slabs any time since we arrived. He's one of the few that I don't suspect.'

'Present company excepted, of course,' said O'Rourke.

'This particular part of the company, yes,' said Valin. 'You three I'd trust until hell freezes over. But who knows about the others. They've only been with us for a few weeks, and we didn't exactly seek references.'

Too true, thought Spenser. Maybe now was not the best time to tell him he was thinking about staying.

'Then why put the Frenchman on guard,' said Keller, 'if he's one that you don't trust?'

'But I do,' replied Valin, remembering Messelier's *nom de guerre*, 'The Invisible Man'. 'He's been around the block. Anyway, someone had to be first on. You can have the next turn if you want.'

'I don't mind,' said the German. 'I've always been

happy to take my share of the shit jobs, as you well know, Colonel.'

'I know, Franz,' said Valin. 'Nobody's casting aspersions on you, of all people. Now go and get some sleep, and I'll wake you if you're needed.'

'OK, Colonel,' said Keller. 'That's not a bad idea.'

'So who's screwing us?' said Spenser.

'We'll find out when we get back to the States,' said Valin.

'*If* we do,' Spenser corrected him.

'Pessimism, Chris,' said Valin. 'Isn't that always the way with you?'

'At least I'm never disappointed,' said Spenser.

'I don't know about that,' said O'Rourke. 'Seems like you and a certain lady are both very disappointed right now.'

'Meaning?'

'From the way you've been gazing up at that house, and the way Carmen's been gazing down here, I'd say that if you two don't get together pretty soon there'll be tears before bedtime.'

'Very funny.'

'Not funny from where I'm standing. More like tragic.'

'Mark. Leave it,' said Valin.

'OK, Colonel,' replied the young lieutenant. 'I just figured that life was too short, that's all.'

And with a wink at Spenser he wandered off.

'But he's not wrong, is he?' said Valin, when the lieutenant had gone.

'Colonel, this is hardly the time and place,' protested Spenser.

'You never said that in Saigon.'

'That was a lifetime ago.'

'And how long's a life?'

Spenser looked at his old friend for a long while, then said: 'You don't think we're going to make it out of here, do you?'

'Anything's possible.'

Spenser nodded. 'I get the picture, Colonel. See you later.' And with that he turned on his heel and walked out of the barn, up the track, on to the farmhouse veranda, and knocked on the door firmly.

Carmen opened it. 'I saw you coming,' she said.

'I don't mean to disturb your family,' said Spenser. 'But I wonder if you'd like to take a walk.'

Carmen smiled. 'In the park?' she said.

'I know it sounds stupid, but we don't know who's going to be coming down that road after us today. I'd just like to talk to you for a few minutes. Just in case.'

'In case?'

'In case I don't make it.'

'And if *you* don't, do you think I will?'

'You must. You must take care of yourself.'

'My place is here with my family – what's left of it.'

Spenser nodded. 'Whatever you say. But will you come?'

'A moment,' she said, and went back inside, closing the door gently behind her.

Spenser turned and looked across the clearing to the entrance to the track. 'Come out, come out, wherever you are,' he said quietly to himself.

The door opened again and Carmen emerged. 'Let's go,' she said. 'This way.' She took him around the side of the house and down another set of steps.

They made their way towards a huge old tree that stood alone. 'This was my playhouse when I was a child,' said Carmen, looking up. Pieces of wood had been nailed to the trunk to make a crude ladder. 'Up you go,' she said.

'Will it support me?'

'Baby,' she said with a smile.

Spenser shrugged, and climbed up into the leafy haven, to find a platform of wooden planks jammed into a support made by four thick branches.

'See,' said Carmen as she joined him. 'That wasn't too bad, was it?'

'You speak very good English.'

'I studied hard. Some of us in the family speak it better than others.' She hesitated. 'Or some of them used to.' She began to cry.

Spenser sighed, and awkwardly took Carmen in his arms. She sobbed gently on his shoulder as he stroked her ebony hair.

Eventually she pulled back and looked at him. 'I'm sorry,' she said.

'Sorry? What's there to be sorry about?'

'You were looking for some happiness. I only gave you grief.'

'Grief with you is like happiness with anyone else,' Spenser said.

'Oh, Chris,' she replied. 'No one has ever said anything like that to me before – in Spanish or English.'

He reddened under her gaze. 'I'm glad,' he said. 'I meant it.'

Carmen leant forward and kissed Spenser, and he clasped her to him again.

26

Fifty yards inside the jungle, beside the track that ran down to the Delgados' land, Messelier leant against a tree and considered the situation. It wasn't looking too good, he thought, as he lit a cigarette, and wondered, like some of the others back at the farm, whether or not any of the group would get out of the country alive.

Of course it wasn't the first time the Frenchman had looked death in the face. Not by a long shot. He thought about all the people he had killed while working for his government as an assassin, and latterly as a mercenary, in the pay of anyone who could afford his services.

Death was familiar to Messelier, as familiar as the feel of wood to a carpenter, or the smell of the sea to a fisherman. But one particular death always remained with him. The one that had made him relinquish his comfortable life in France and ultimately brought him to this humid, stinking jungle: the murder of the child, the daughter of a small-time spy and whore. And although he knew that as a merc he'd killed children since – or at least been involved in the deaths of children – he had felt so close to death on that particular day.

It had been a beautiful spring afternoon in Paris,

and the trees along the Seine were in blossom as he parked his Citroën at a meter and set off to kill the woman who had been selling the confessions of her lover to whoever would pay the most. Messelier strolled along the boulevard where she had her apartment and stopped often to gaze into the windows of the high-priced boutiques where he loved to buy his designer clothes. He was in no hurry. It was a lovely day for a stroll, and his information was that she rarely rose before noon, then spent the afternoon pampering herself before meeting her *amour* for supper.

He picked up a bunch of flowers at the florist's on the corner of the avenue. A spring mixture: carnations, daffodils, roses, lilies. An expensive bunch, as befitted a woman of her reputation, and he carried it to her block, with the flowers covering his face in case the concierge was peering out from behind the shutters. The street door was wide open and Messelier took the lift to the fourth floor, then walked along the wide, carpeted hallway to the woman's door and knocked.

'Who is it?' said a female voice after a minute.

'The florist, mademoiselle,' he replied. 'A delivery.'

'One moment.'

He heard the chain go on, then the door opened a fraction. In the gap between it and the jamb he saw a pretty face topped with blonde hair, and he showed her the flowers.

'*Très jolies*,' she said, pushed the door to, unfastened the chain and opened the door all the way. 'Come in, monsieur.'

Messelier did as he was asked and went into the hall of the apartment. The woman was about thirty, very beautiful, wearing a long, black negligée.

'Take them through to the kitchen,' she said. 'My maid will arrange them when she returns.'

She's alone, thought Messelier. Excellent. He went in the direction she indicated, into a large, light, airy kitchen with a view of the Eiffel Tower.

He laid the flowers beside the sink and turned to look at the woman. She *was* beautiful, and it seemed a shame to mar such beauty with death. But he had a job to do.

He smiled at her and said: 'It's a beautiful day, isn't it?'

She agreed, and went to look for a card attached to the bouquet.

Messelier, who was armed with a silenced .38 automatic pistol and a switchblade, looked around the kitchen. On the wall hung a set of carving knives, and it seemed to him appropriate that he should use one of them to dispatch her. He was wearing thin, black-leather gloves and he reached for the longest, most wicked-looking of the utensils as she searched among the foliage of the flowers for the message she expected.

'Your lover?' he asked.

She spun round on one heel. 'What?' she demanded, then saw the knife he was holding, and suddenly looked ten years older.

'They're not from the minister,' he said, 'but perhaps from some of his colleagues. The ones that do not appreciate you selling their most precious secrets.'

'I don't . . . ' she said, and put her hands up to her mouth.

'I am sorry,' said Messelier, and sunk the blade of the knife into her abdomen and twisted it viciously.

The woman let out a stifled scream like a pig being slaughtered, and stepped back, pulling herself off the blade of the knife, which dripped blood on to the immaculate black-and-white tiled floor. She grabbed at her wound, but blood welled between her fingers and she looked down at it and fainted.

Messelier finished the job by lifting up her head and slashing the tempered steel of the blade across her throat. He dropped her body and stepped back to avoid his clothes being stained by her vital fluids.

He washed the knife under the tap and was just about to return it to its place when he heard footsteps in the hall. The maid, he thought. But I didn't hear the front door . . . A little flaxen-haired girl came into the kitchen.

'*Maman* . . . ' she said, then saw the body, stiffened and screamed. Messelier grabbed her and covered her mouth with his gloved hand. There was only one thing for it. She had to be killed too, for he knew, by looking into her wide, terror-filled eyes, that she would remember the man who had been in the room with her dead mother. Messelier lifted her cleanly with one arm and sliced through her windpipe with a single blow of the knife with the other. Then he dropped her next to her mother, where she twitched twice before her heart stopped beating and the blood stopped flowing from the cut.

This time he didn't bother to wash the weapon, but just dropped it next to the two bodies and walked unhurriedly out of the flat.

Once in the fresh air again, he breathed deeply and walked down the avenue to the first café he came to, where he ordered a large brandy.

The assassin was still there an hour later, three empty glasses in front of him, when he heard the scream of ambulance and police sirens, and knew that the maid must have returned to make her grisly find. He watched the public utility vehicles as they skidded to a halt in front of the apartment building where he had done his evil work.

Messelier was so deeply engrossed in his thoughts, and neglectful of his guard duty, that he heard nothing of the faint footsteps on the soft ground, and when the hand on the end of a bare, brown arm grabbed him by the hair from behind, and the other came round his neck and slit his throat from ear to ear with a long-bladed knife that closely resembled the one he had used on the two females so long ago, he almost welcomed it.

When two hours to the minute had passed since they got to the farm, Valin called Newman out from the barn and sent him to relieve Messelier.

The former para jogged off and vanished into the undergrowth. Five minutes later he came through on the radio to Valin. 'Colonel, Newman,' he said. 'Receiving? Over.'

'Newman, Valin. I thought I ordered radio silence. Over.'

'You'd better get up here, Colonel, right now. Over and out.'

'Shit,' said Valin. 'What now?' He picked up his carry weapon and went to find O'Rourke.

Together they headed towards the spot where Newman had vanished, and pushed into the bushes. They heard Newman's whistle as they pushed further into the jungle, then came out to where he was waiting. From a branch of the tree immediately in front of him, Messelier's body dangled on a length of thick wire. The slash in his throat resembled a red-lipped grin, and his uniform had been split open at the crutch and his genitalia cut off and stuffed into his mouth.

27

They left the Frenchman where he was hanging and faded back into the jungle. 'Who the hell got him?' said O'Rourke. 'I thought he was an expert.'

'The only experts in these jungles are the natives,' said Valin. 'I don't think this was soldiers' work.'

'Who then?'

'Bandits,' said Valin. 'Let's get back quick.'

From the direction of the farmhouse they heard the first crackle of gunfire.

'Shit,' said Valin. 'Go, go, go. At the double.'

It was not clear how long the bandits had been watching the farmhouse, or if they had been sent on their mission by some outside agency. Or whether, simply, they were in the wrong place at the wrong time. But what was clear was that there were more than half a dozen of them: small, brown men dressed in rags, all carrying various derivatives of the Kalashnikov AK47, side-arms, swords, knives, bows and arrows, and crossbows, and all determined to kill everyone in their path.

The first volley of bullets slammed into the barn and house, and Keller, who was asleep on two bales of hay, woke with a start, grabbed his G3 and dived towards the door, yelling orders as he went. He didn't know what the hell was going on, but whatever it was, it was trouble.

Spenser, who was still in the tree house with Carmen, came bolt upright as the firing started. They were both naked and he cursed as he struggled into his clothes in the confined and uncomfortable space. 'Christ,' he said. 'What's happening?'

'I don't know,' said Carmen, also pulling on her clothes.

'You stay here,' Spenser ordered, slipping his Star .45 from its holster. 'I'm going to see what's happening.'

'I'll come with you.'

'*No.* You stay right where you are.'

The American dived down the ladder and peered round the side of the tree. What he saw was Keller appearing at the door of the barn, spraying the bandits with shells from his automatic rifle, and the farmhouse door opening, and Carlos appearing in the threshold holding a pistol, only to be cut down by a hail of bullets from among the trees.

For a confused moment the bandits looked like Vietcong to Spenser, and once again he was back in 'Nam, until he pulled himself together, steadied his handgun, and popped off half a magazine in their direction.

One of the bandits threw up his arms and fell face forwards on to the ground, and two more immediately turned their guns in Spenser's direction and bullets ripped up the earth around him and slammed into the tree trunk where he was sheltering.

Shit, he thought. I wish I'd got the Gatling.

Jesús appeared at the doorway of the farmhouse and dragged Carlos back inside, then knelt and fired one of the Heckler and Kochs that Valin had given to the women, and another of the bandits hit the dirt, just as Valin, O'Rourke and Newman came out of the jungle a hundred yards or so to their right and added their fire to that coming from the farm.

The bandits turned their fire on the newcomers, who dived to the ground and rolled behind what cover they could find, still shooting. Another of the bandits was hit and he lay where he had fallen, and Spenser could hear his screams from where he was taking cover.

He hated that. It was always one of the worst memories he had of the war: lying in cover, listening to a fallen comrade or enemy screaming for help. Sometimes the sound went on for hours, or what seemed like hours, until the wounded man lost consciousness or died.

Spenser tried to reckon the distance from where he was to the barn. He reckoned about five hundred yards. He wanted to get hold of his sweet little rock 'n' roller, and as the bandits were occupied with Valin's trio, he kicked away from where he was kneeling and zigzagged towards the barn and his gun. One of the bandits spotted his run and turned his gun in Spenser's direction. The American saw the bullets stitching a line across the ground towards him and threw himself down and felt earth patter across his back. Just as quickly he was up and running again, as the bandit ran out of ammunition and had to change the magazine in his Kalashnikov. Spenser put on a spurt, and saw Keller, Resnick and Angel pumping out covering fire. Then suddenly he was between the corner of the barn and the enemy, and threw himself inside and fell against the wall, panting hard.

'Enjoy the exercise?' said Angel conversationally.

'Fuck you.'

'Nice to see you too, Chris. Where's the little woman?'

'Halfway up a tree if she knows what's good for her,' said Spenser, as, still breathless, he hurried to the back of the three-tonner and retrieved his Gatling.

'This'll do for those fuckers,' he said grimly. 'Who the fuck are they anyhow?'

'Fuck knows,' said Angel. 'They look like a bunch of Crips looking to do some gangbanging, from the state of the threads they're wearing.'

'You wanna feed me?' said Spenser.

'Always a pleasure,' said Angel, and he connected the ammunition belt to the feed of the Gatling.

'Run with me, Angel,' shouted Spenser, and the two of them dashed through the open door and Spenser started to fire towards the bandits' cover. His shells smashed into the trees and undergrowth, cutting a huge swath of destruction through the lush greenery. Branches flew from trees, and others were chopped to the ground completely, as his bullets ripped into the jungle.

Two more of the bandits went down in the onslaught, and Angel screamed above the hammering of the weapon: 'Way to go.'

Keller, Resnick, Jesús, Valin, Newman and O'Rourke added their fire-power to the onslaught and the remaining handful of bandits were mowed down. All except one, who, when his AK47 jammed, threw it to the ground, drew a curved machete from his belt and made a kamikaze charge towards Valin's group. They poured fire at his diminutive form, and saw the shots chopping lumps out of his body. But still he came. The hail of fire they were pumping at him was relentless, but still he wouldn't fall, until finally, with the last of his strength, from ten or fifteen yards in front of their position, he hurled the evil-looking blade he was holding. Its surface caught the sun as it flew through the air, and as it left his hand the bandit himself pitched forward and skidded along the ground face down. The machete struck the side of Newman's neck, and he toppled backwards, dropping his Ithaca and clutching at the obscenity sticking out of him.

28

In the silence that followed the fire-fight, the birds that had risen from the jungle at the sound of gunfire began to settle back into the trees.

Valin dropped his M16, and went to Newman, but it was too late. The ex-para had torn the blade from his neck, but he was drowning in his own blood as the terrible sucking wound took its toll.

Valin clamped his hand over Newman's windpipe, but he knew he was wasting his time, and the man died as he knelt over him.

'Shit,' he said, and wiped his bloody hand on Newman's tunic.

O'Rourke picked up the dead man's shotgun and went over to the fallen body of the bandit who had thrown the machete and fired a round into his head.

'He's dead too. Must be,' said Valin.

'Not dead enough,' said O'Rourke, and fired again and watched the bandit's lifeless body kick as the shot smashed into him.

'Come on, Mark,' said Valin. 'Let's go and see what's happened down there.'

Together they walked back towards the farmhouse.

Carlos was dead from a bullet to the heart. There seemed to be no end to the tragedy that was striking the Delgado family that day. Valin told the rest what had happened to the Frenchman. 'We'd better bury our people,' he said.

'I need a priest,' said Jesús.

'No priest, Jesús. Sorry,' said Valin. 'We bury our dead, leave those bastards out there to the carrion, and get out of here.'

'No,' said Jesús firmly.

'I'm sorry,' said O'Rourke. 'But what Colonel Valin says, goes.'

'Spenser, Resnick, burial detail. Angel, Keller, O'Rourke, let's go and collect Messelier and Newman,' said Valin.

'I will dig my family's graves myself,' said the Colombian.

'As you wish,' said Valin. And with that, they set about their grisly tasks.

It was almost noon before the work was done. Everyone lent a hand with the work, even García. Carmen and Sofía prepared food for the men, as Valin watched the road and the skies for the enemy that he knew could come from anywhere, any time.

The day was hot, and as he watched the men under his command sweating as they toiled, it reminded him of other times when he had seen graves being dug. The graves of Argentinians in the Falklands, where the earth was cold, and the merciless wind blew from Antarctica; graves in the Gulf for the civilian victims of that insane regime; and graves in Britain to bury the soldiers killed in Northern Ireland. He touched the scar on his face. It was a constant reminder of his days in the service of his country before he had been cast aside like an old shoe when the powers that be considered him of no further use.

It was almost as if it were yesterday. Belfast. Christmas, three years earlier. A convoy was heading towards the barracks where Valin's regiment was billeted. In the lead was an armoured Land Rover with bulletproof glass and skirts to prevent hand-grenades being tossed underneath. Then came a dark-blue Rover containing men from the RUC, followed by a ministerial Jaguar carrying Valin and the politician who was bringing seasonal greetings from the people comfortably ensconced on the mainland. Bringing up the rear was another Land Rover, bristling with guns.

As they passed a Republican estate, Valin remembered, the politician turned to him and said: 'It's not as bad as the people back home think it is over here. These houses are really quite respectable.' Just then the first Land Rover hit a land-mine against which even its skirts couldn't protect it, and the vehicle was heaved over on to its side, as the blue Rover swerved to avoid it.

'Get down, sir,' roared Valin, pushing the politician to the floor and drawing his Browning 9mm pistol, as the driver braked hard, and the firing from the ambush began.

The Jaguar was also fitted with bulletproof glass, but nothing could prevent the heavy-calibre bullets that were splintering the car. Valin fired at the muzzle flashes until his face took the force of a ricocheting slug that tore a long groove in his flesh and knocked him unconscious. One man in the lead Land Rover was killed and another two seriously wounded. The RUC officers were unhurt, as were the passengers in the second Land Rover. The minister sustained only minor cuts, as did the chauffeur of the Jaguar. Valin's were the most serious injuries and he was flown back to England. He missed his Christmas dinner, but O'Rourke, who had been on leave, managed to smuggle a bottle of brandy into his hospital room on New Year's Eve. Valin had never been back to Ireland since, and he wasn't sorry.

When the work was complete, Jesús brought a bible from the house and read the burial service in Spanish as the bodies of Maria, Carlotta, Carlos, Messelier and Newman were lowered into the ground.

The mercenaries stood bare-headed in the humid breeze that blew across from the jungle to the mountains, and Valin recited the Lord's Prayer before they began to fill in the graves.

When they were complete, and the rough crosses that Carmen and Sofía had fashioned from odd pieces of wood that they had found in the barn had been set up over the scars in the earth formed by the graves, Valin said: 'I think it's time we moved out.'

'To go where?' said Jesús.

'Anywhere that we can lie low until tonight. It's not far to the landing strip, is it?'

'An hour or so.'

'I don't want to draw attention to it until we have to,' said Valin. 'Any ideas?'

'There is a mountain road,' said Jesús. 'There are caves up there that no one knows about.'

'And you'll come with us?'

'What is there here for me now?' said the Colombian.

'To America?'

'The land of golden opportunity?'

'That's right.'

'And revenge on the man or men who double-crossed us.'

Valin smiled, and the scar on his face stood out. 'But of course.'

'If we make it.'

'We've made it so far.'

'But at what cost?'

'To you more than the rest of us.'

'So the revenge will be all the sweeter.'

Valin touched Jesús on the shoulder. 'Yes, my friend,' he said. 'All the sweeter.'

29

The phone lines in Washington were red-hot.

Bob 'Tank' Tankerton called General Avery in his office near the White House. 'They did it, General,' he said. 'Mission accomplished. I've heard that they razed the factory and most of Santa Ana to the ground.'

'Is this a secure line, Tank?'

'Certainly.'

'Good. Are they out?'

'That's all I know, General,' replied Tank. 'Nothing further. And I've heard nothing from Valin or any of his troops.'

'Any casualties?'

'I heard that the locals dragged some bodies through the town and hanged them from lampposts.'

'How many exactly? Alive or dead?'

'The reports are sketchy on that. But I should imagine they're dead by now.'

'Jesus.'

'Valin always knew that could happen. It goes with the territory.'

'Keep me informed of any further developments.'

'Of course, sir. You'll be the first to know.'

Next, Tankerton spoke to Karl Landers from the FBI, and told the same story.

'That's good news,' said Landers.

'Sure,' replied Tank.

'Worth the money.'

'Yeah.'

'*If* we don't have to pay the balance.'

'Meaning?'

'Meaning that if they don't come out, we're free and clear, and two-thirds of a million pounds better off.'

'Not a nice thought, Karl.'

'But a practical one.'

'I suppose. But then you don't know James Valin like I do. I'd stake my pension on him surviving.'

'I hope you never have to.'

'Nor you.'

'Keep in touch, Tank.'

'Count on it.'

Tankerton's final call was to CIA headquarters at Langley, Virginia, where he was put through to Jack Bernard.

'So they did it,' said Bernard, after listening to Tank. 'Frankly, I'm amazed.'

'I'm not.'

'You always were a fan, Tank.'

'And you never were.'

'Cor-rect.'

'Maybe you'll change your mind now.'

'Maybe. But it goes deeper than that. I always thought that goddam Limey went round with a broom handle stuck up his ass.'

'That's the way they do it in the British army.'

'Sure is.'

'Listen, Jack, I'll keep you up to speed on developments.'

'You do that little thing.'

Tank smiled as he put down the phone, sat back in his seat and remembered how he, Jack Bernard and Valin had met.

It had been in Saigon, in May 1970. Tank had been a captain in the Marines, Jack Bernard had been part of the CIA task force involved in the Air America scheme, flying into Cambodia. And First Lieutenant James Valin, as he was then, was one of the many British SAS personnel who were wearing American uniforms and fighting illegally in South-east Asia.

It wasn't only the British either. German and French soldiers fought side by side with the US troops, mainly on covert missions, while their countrymen sat at home, comforted by the knowledge that their governments were not involved in the costly action in Vietnam.

Like hell. They had all been young men then, pumped up at the promise of action. Who cared that the war was going to hell in a handcart? Who cared that, without the proper back-up of men and equipment, and Nixon doing his usual prevaricating in Congress, and the general public at home becoming even more anti-war with every day, there was no way they could win?

It was a paradise for a professional soldier. Guns to play with. And a bunch of gooks to use as target practice. A free-fire zone for every gung-ho maniac in the land.

It wasn't so much fun for the conscripts, but that was the way the ball bounced. Tough.

The three of them met for the first time at a morning briefing, then went to an off-limits bar that stank of cooked fish and stale sweat, and was packed with girls hawking their wares, drug dealers, currency speculators, souvenir salesmen, and every other kind of low life imaginable. The Rolling Stones were on the jukebox and the beer was cheap. Paradise.

'You're never going to win this war without the full backing of all sections of your government,' said Valin. 'And the opposition is growing. Your president has to put the full weight of his authority behind it, or you'll be sent home with your tail between your legs. The chances are you will anyway. You're fighting a fanatical opposition on their own territory. A territory alien to ninety-nine per cent of your personnel. The North Vietnamese regard it as a privilege to die for one inch of soil. Do your men feel the same?' The question went unanswered. 'Of course they don't,' the Englishman said. 'The same thing is going to happen to the British government in Northern Ireland if the past three years are anything to go by. Look at military history if you don't believe me. The only way to conquer anyone in their own country is complete destruction, or the fear of it, swiftly followed by economic integration. Look at Germany and Japan after the Second World War. The way you're going, you can't win. And it won't be long before you find that out. A matter of a year or two at most.'

'Then we will lose,' said Tank, 'if we're relying on Nixon. The guy's an asshole.'

'Don't talk about the president like that,' said Bernard pompously. Even at twenty-two he'd been a bumptious conservative. 'Especially not in uniform. And you know we shouldn't be in this place. It's dangerous. The VC infiltrate.'

'Just like the base,' said Tank.

Valin grinned, and ordered more beers.

'That's the kind of talk that *will* lose us the war,' Bernard admonished his fellow countryman.

'No. What you're doing in Cambodia will lose the war,' said Valin decisively.

'Not so loud,' said Bernard looking round. 'That's classified.'

'Then how come every hustler in town knows about it?' asked Tank.

'People like you blabbing their mouths off in bars,' said Bernard. 'That's how.'

Tank and Valin looked at each other and pulled faces.

It was one o'clock, and stiflingly hot. Both Tank's and Valin's tropical uniforms were sodden rags, as was Bernard's summer-weight suit, and the fan that turned lazily above their heads did little but move the humid air around the place.

Sgt. Pepper was now on the hi-fi, and Tank hummed along, and ordered more iced beer.

The afternoon wore on, and they continued arguing about the rights and wrongs of the US involvement in the war. Tank knew that Bernard was mentally noting everything that he and Valin said, for future reference, but the more beer he drank, the less he cared. Around two-thirty everyone in the bar heard the buzz of a small motorcycle, and the screech of tyres as it pulled up outside. Suddenly, a fragmentation grenade was lobbed through the hole that acted as a window, hit the back wall, and dropped, to bounce along the stained surface of the bar and come to rest in front of the three of them.

The place began to empty in a second, women screaming and everyone scrambling to get out.

Jack Bernard dived under a table, and Tank and Valin just looked at each other, before Valin calmly picked up the grenade. 'It's amazing how often amateurs forget to take out the pin,' he said in a conversational tone, as he reached over the bar and appropriated a bottle of rice wine. 'I think we deserve this for being so brave,' he said, and removed the cork with his teeth and took a slug, before passing it to Tank, who did the same.

Valin looked around the room for their CIA comrade. 'Hey, Jack,' he called. 'Fancy a snort?'

Bernard had never forgiven Valin for that. Or for being right about the outcome of the war. Or Tank, for that matter.

But the Americans had been forced to work together occasionally since they returned to the USA and Tank had joined the DEA, and they maintained an uneasy truce.

It still made Tank laugh to think of the look on Bernard's face as he crawled out from under the table, and how, when Valin had tossed him the grenade, Bernard had flinched, even though it was safe.

As soon as Tank put down the phone after one of his calls, the person at the other end dialled a number in Leavenworth, Kansas, and was put through to someone who owed him more than one favour.

'Everything copacetic?' he asked.

'As far as we know.'

'Let me know if it isn't.'

'Sure will.'

30

The troops abandoned the bullet-scarred VW Microbus, and took only the ancient jeep and the Ford three-tonner. O'Rourke drove the former, with Keller and Jesús as passengers. The two Delgado daughters, García and the rest of the troops travelled in the truck, Angel driving, Valin riding shotgun, and the rest in the back. All weapons had been checked and Resnick carried his last knapsack full of explosives.

The two vehicles drove up the narrow track through the dense jungle with all personnel ready for trouble, but none was in evidence. They turned in a westerly direction and soon the road started to rise. The jungle receded as the foothills became mountains, and the road narrowed and began to corkscrew. The air thinned, the temperature dropped and the views over the countryside became ever more spectacular the higher they climbed.

They saw little traffic for the first hour, apart from the occasional donkey cart, farm vehicle or pedestrian, until, as they crossed another mountain pass, two black Buick sedans with silver insignia on the doors, blue-and-red panniers mounted on the roofs, and long whip aerials at the back, sped past them in the opposite direction, headlights blazing in the afternoon sunlight.

'Shit,' said Angel as the cars sped past. 'Cops.'

In the jeep in front O'Rourke looked over his shoulder at Jesús.

'State Police,' said the Colombian. 'Bastards.'

The two police cars took the next bend and screeched to a halt with a stink of rubber. There was a brief radio conversation between the cars and then they both made hasty three-point turns on the narrow road before setting off in pursuit of the small convoy of mercenaries.

Angel, in the cab of the truck, and Spenser, who was watching from the back, were the first to see the lead police car coming up behind them. Angel glanced in his mirror and said: 'Trouble, Colonel. The fuzz are behind us.' Spenser shouted at Resnick to tell Valin through the window that divided front and rear of the Ford that trouble was looming.

'Affirmative,' said Valin, who had seen them already.

Angel blasted the horn and flashed his headlights at the jeep in front, and accelerated the cumbersome three-tonner as much as he could on the steep and twisting climb, and O'Rourke responded by putting his foot down in the jeep, to get as much power to the four drive wheels as he could.

But both the jeep and the truck were old, and their engines, although well maintained and tuned, were tired. By contrast, the police Buicks were almost new, both with turbo-charged, five-litre V8 lumps, and were coming up fast.

Spenser and Carmen loaded the Gatling and steadied it on the tailgate of the truck.

'Blow them away,' growled Resnick, and Spenser opened fire. The heavy slugs tore lumps out of the road, stitched a line up to the oncoming bumper of the first

Buick, ripped through the radiator, destroyed the block, imploded the windscreen, and killed both driver and passenger. The heavy sedan swerved, hit the low retaining wall at the side of the road, somersaulted, and flew into space, to tumble down the mountainside and explode in flames. 'Easy,' said Spenser, and winked at Carmen.

The second Buick dropped right back. Valin, squinting in his wing mirror, was in no doubt that frantic radio messages were flying across the airwaves to police headquarters.

'We're in trouble,' he said to Angel. 'We've got to disable that other car. They can follow us for ever, out of range of our guns, and let their pals know exactly where we are.'

'We'll just have to fuck 'em, then,' replied his companion.

'Very succinctly put.'

'Count on me, boss.'

'So how do we do it?'

'Radio through to the jeep. Get them to pull ahead fast. I'll slow down. That guy behind us isn't going to get too close, in case the same thing happens to him as to his buddies. When the jeep comes to a turn-off, it pulls off the highway. Then, when the cops have gone past, it pulls out behind them, and we've got the sons of bitches bottled up. I slow down, the jeep speeds up, I block the way forward, O'Rourke blocks the way back, and we catch them in the crossfire.'

'Good idea, Angel,' said Valin. 'As long as the police don't pick up our call. Or if they do, they don't speak English.'

'Nothing's infallible, Colonel.'

Valin smiled grimly, reached for his radio and called

Keller in the jeep. He explained the plan and the German raised his right arm and leant forward and shouted in O'Rourke's ear. The lieutenant lifted his hand off the wheel and when he did, Angel allowed the three-tonner to slow slightly, and the jeep pulled away.

Angel saw the Buick drop back as the truck's speed decreased, and he made a circle with his thumb and forefinger to Valin. 'Got the suckers, Colonel,' he said. 'The guy who's driving that cop car would last no time in East LA. It's the oldest trick in the book. Bookend the cops and shoot shit out of 'em.'

'Nice friends you've got, Angel.'

'I get around. East Coast, West Coast. You know how it goes.'

'One step in front of the law.'

'That's what shoes are for, boss.' And Angel laughed, keeping one eye on the mirror.

Up at the front, O'Rourke kept the pedal to the metal until Jesús, whom Keller had filled in on the plan, leant forward and shouted: 'Two hundred metres ahead on your right. Mining road.'

O'Rourke put the jeep into a four-wheel skid that sent dust and pebbles flying as he expertly steered the jeep into a narrow lane that was hardly more than a ditch leading to an abandoned mineshaft.

O'Rourke drove the jeep round a slight bend and slammed on the brakes. 'Sergeant, check the progress of the police,' he shouted, and Keller hopped out of the jeep and ran back down the track, taking advantage of all possible cover until he could get a clear sight of the road without being seen himself.

First the three-tonner went past, and then a minute or so later, the Buick with four officers aboard.

Keller sprinted back to the others, gave a thumbs-up and O'Rourke turned the jeep round, and after the German had got into the back, they returned to the main road in pursuit of the police car.

'What a surprise they're going to get,' Keller shouted to O'Rourke.

'Not as big a surprise as we'll get if another carload come up behind us,' O'Rourke shouted into the slip-stream. 'You look out the back.'

And as Keller complied, the lieutenant radioed ahead to inform Valin that the police car was boxed in.

Valin and Angel heard the message and looked at each other in triumph, then the colonel relayed the news through to the well of the lorry, and Spenser prepared to fire again.

'Slow right down, Angel,' said the colonel. 'Let O'Rourke and the rest catch up.'

Angel did as his commander ordered, and gave the labouring engine a respite.

Behind them the Buick slowed too, until O'Rourke saw its red tail lights ahead of him.

'Got 'em, boss,' he said into his radio.

'Stop,' yelled Valin, and Angel slewed the big truck across the road. Spenser, Carmen, Resnick and Sofía dropped down from the tailgate and fanned out, as Valin and Angel joined them, guns at the ready, and García threw himself down behind the first cover he could find.

The police driver saw what was happening, slammed on his brakes and threw the Buick into reverse, just as O'Rourke turned the bend behind him and pulled the jeep into the side of the road and his two passengers tumbled out.

Spenser was crouched behind the retaining wall and opened fire as the Buick's four doors flew open, and the officers inside scrambled for cover. Spenser's burst hit the car broadside and both tyres went down and flames licked from the engine compartment. Then he turned the Gatling on the four policemen, backed up by fire from the rest of his party, and crossfire from the three guns in the jeep. The first of the policemen threw up his arms and fell heavily as the heavy-calibre bullets cut him off at the knees. The second walked into a volley from Keller, O'Rourke and Jesús that left him bleeding his last on to the cracked tarmac. The third and fourth were more fortunate, and reached cover on the hillside, from where they returned fire.

Valin was just about to radio O'Rourke to bring up the jeep, when the Buick exploded, bouncing sideways and sending out a sheet of flame that sealed off the highway.

'I hope to Christ they can get the jeep past,' Valin said to Angel, who was crouching next to him, as bullets zipped past their ears. 'The road's very narrow there. I don't want to stick around here for a moment longer than necessary.'

'They'll have to come in the truck if they can't,' replied Angel. 'Are you going to call them up? We can keep those two pinned down with covering fire while they make it.'

'Yes,' said Valin. 'But thanks, Angel. I might never have come up with that on my own.'

'Sorry, boss,' said Angel. 'It was just a thought.'

'Don't apologize. It was a good one. If we get out of this alive I'm going to make you up to sergeant, if you're interested,' said Valin, keying the radio to reach O'Rourke.

It was decided that the lieutenant would attempt to drive the jeep up to the truck under the cover of fire from Valin's group. And if he couldn't get it past the burning Buick, to abandon it, and leg it up to the truck. Valin was worried about having to rely on only one vehicle. He was well aware that if they came under attack from another helicopter, having just one target made it easier for the opposition to kill and injure the maximum amount of troops in one go. And as for mechanical failure, he dared not think about the consequences. The truck had as many holes in it as a tea-strainer, from their previous engagements, and it was a miracle that nothing vital had been hit so far.

'Right, people,' said Valin. 'Now!' He took aim and fired a short burst at the rocks where he had seen one of the policemen take cover. The rock exploded into chips, and the other members of the squad with weapons opened fire too. García, who refused to fight, hid behind the low wall with his arms over his head, and wished, not for the first time, that the young British lieutenant was still acting as his personal bodyguard.

At the first crackle of gunfire, O'Rourke, who had already fallen back to the jeep, started the engine, slammed it into gear and took off up the hill. He skidded to a halt, to allow Keller and Jesús to dive on board, before he accelerated away with a screech of tyres and made for the Buick, which by then was burning less fiercely. At that point, the level area on the side of the mountain was so narrow that the road on the right-hand side was only separated from thin air and a thousand-foot drop by the retaining wall. Further on, where the truck had stopped, there was a slope behind the wall before the cliff ended, where Valin's people had taken cover.

The jeep's nearside wing rammed into the Buick's back bumper and pushed it slightly out of the way, but the police car was too heavy and the jeep bounced back, its offside front wheel demolishing the crumbling wall, and lifted off the ground as O'Rourke frantically spun the wheel anti-clockwise. The vehicle lurched, and Valin and the rest of the squad held their collective breath as the jeep teetered towards disaster.

Flames licked at one side of it, as the other began to tilt away, until suddenly the front wheel hit rock again and the tyre found purchase. The engine screamed as O'Rourke upped the revs and the jeep leapt forward, only to be caught by a burst from an automatic weapon held by one of the policemen.

Keller took bullets in both legs and his groin, and Valin's soldiers poured fire on to the mountain again, forcing the policeman to duck back into his hidey-hole. O'Rourke pulled up in front of the truck, stopped and helped Jesús attend to the German.

Valin, his men, and the Delgado girls, with Sofía dragging García, made a run back to the truck, Spenser halting in the middle of the road to empty his cartridge belt at the mountainside to give his friends covering fire.

Angel and Valin dived for the cab, and the rest leapt into the back. Angel fired up the engine, and gesticulated to Spenser to get on board, which he did. The young American gave a blast on his horn, and O'Rourke left Keller to the ministrations of Jesús, jammed the jeep into gear and sped off, closely followed by the truck and twin bursts of fire from the two policemen on the mountain.

31

A quarter of a mile down the road, round another bend and well out of range, O'Rourke stopped the jeep for another look at Keller's wounds. He was a mess. It looked like some of the bullets had ricocheted off the metal of the jeep, judging from the jagged holes they had ripped in the flesh on entry, and others at the exit points. All were leaking blood, and the sergeant's face was white with shock and pain.

'This is not good,' Jesús told the lieutenant as he finished tying tourniquets, which he had made from the sleeves of his jacket, around Keller's upper thighs to try to slow the loss of blood. 'I can't do a thing for those,' he said, pointing at the wounds to Keller's groin. 'He needs a doctor.'

Valin jumped down from the truck and ran to the jeep. 'How is he?' he demanded.

'I'm OK,' the German said through clenched teeth.

'No, he's not,' said O'Rourke. 'He needs urgent medical attention.'

'What, here?' said Valin, looking round. 'In the back of beyond? Not to mention that he's one of the most wanted men in the country right now. What do you suggest? That we drop him off at casualty, and leave him to the gentle care of the nearest hospital? This is not the Edgware Road on a Saturday night.'

'No, sir,' said O'Rourke stiffly. 'I suggest that we try and save his life.'

'Sorry, Mark,' said Valin. 'Point taken. You're right, of course. Where *is* the nearest hospital, Jesús?'

'Bogotá. We'd never get within a hundred kilometres of it.'

'A doctor?'

'There is a village about thirty kilometres away. There is a doctor there. But there is a military post too.'

'So we take out the military post, then get the medic to look at Keller.'

'But . . . '

'No buts, Jesús. This is one of my men. I won't have him bleed to death on the side of a mountain in Colombia. We go to the village and get him looked at. Now mount up. Jesús, you show Mark the way. And be careful. We don't know who those police alerted that we were in the area.'

Valin ran back to the truck and O'Rourke, with Jesús directing him, led the way to the village.

About a mile before they reached the outskirts, at an empty crossroads, Jesús asked O'Rourke to stop the jeep. Keller was lying in the back, his face contorted with pain, and blood was dripping from his trouser legs and forming a puddle on the floor. The Colombian got out of the leading vehicle and went back to the truck.

'The military post is on this side of the village,' he explained to Valin and the rest. 'It is nothing much. Just a blockhouse and a small barracks for maybe four or five men.'

'Right,' said Valin. 'Jesús, get back to the jeep and get Mark to pull into the side road and out of sight. We'll follow.'

Jesús went back to the jeep and O'Rourke steered it off the main road and behind a ruined cottage that was the first sign of civilization they had seen for miles. Angel drove the truck after him, and everyone gathered together for a final briefing.

'The jeep and Keller stay here,' said Valin. 'Sofía, if you will, I want you to stay with him. And you, García.'

Jesús explained to the chemist what the colonel had said, and the prisoner nodded.

'The rest of us go into the village and disable the guard post,' Valin continued. 'Then we get the doctor and come back.' He addressed Sofía again: 'If anything goes wrong and we don't return, do what you can for Keller, García and yourself. I know it will be difficult, but whatever you do, don't follow us. Take the jeep as far away as possible and try and help the sergeant. We should be OK, but if it goes all wrong at least there's a chance that the three of you çan get away.'

Sofía nodded. 'I understand,' she said. 'I wish you the best of luck.' She kissed her father and sister and embraced them fiercely.

García raised his hand and saluted Carmen and the men. '*Hasta la vista*,' he said. '*Vayan con Dios, compadres*.' Then he and Sofía went to the jeep, where the girl sat in the back next to Keller and held his hand, and García sat behind the steering wheel.

The rest went back to the truck, but before they got on board, Valin asked: 'What's the ammunition situation?'

'Not too good,' said Spenser, and the others grunted in agreement. 'We didn't expect this kind of opposition, did we?'

Valin shook his head. 'So be sparing, people,' he urged them.

'Yeah,' agreed Angel. 'We don't want to come up against any of these guys with just our dicks in our hands.' He nodded at Carmen. 'Begging your pardon, ma'am. Not that you'd have that kind of a problem.'

Carmen smiled back at him. 'I think I get the picture,' she said.

'Saddle up, then,' said Valin. 'Back into the breach. Jesús, you come up front with us, and show us the lie of the land.'

Once in the truck, the Colombian explained that the military post straddled the main road into the village. It was a deterrent to the kind of bandits that they had met at his farm earlier, and who roamed the bleak mountainside, looking for prey.

The truck nosed along the road until the post came into sight. As Jesús had said, it controlled the main thoroughfare of the hamlet, which drowsed lazily in the afternoon sun. Angel pulled up to the barrier that blocked the road and a National Guardsman, uniform jacket mis-buttoned, came out of the hut yawning, and carrying a Thompson sub-machine-gun.

Angel unholstered his side-arm as the guard approached the driver's side and spoke to him in Spanish.

'*No comprendo*,' answered Angel, then poked the pistol over the edge of the window and shot the man in the face, as Valin slipped out of the passenger door, closely followed by Jesús, and the rest of the squad dived out from under the canvas at the back of the truck.

At the sound of the shot, another soldier poked his head out of the hut, only to collect a burst of bullets from Valin's M16. The troops rushed the guardhouse and the barracks beyond, meeting little resistance. Two of the soldiers were enjoying a siesta, and the third raised his hands in surrender as they burst into the guardhouse.

'Ask him if there's any more around,' Valin said to Jesús.

The Colombian did, and the soldier shook his head.

'OK,' said Valin. 'Tie them up, and let's go and find this medic. And listen, see if there's an ammunition store with anything useful.'

32

After the task of securing the soldiers had been completed, and the ammunition store had been plundered for as much ordnance as Valin's team could use, they went in search of the doctor.

His house was behind the main street of the village, if indeed such a title could be bestowed on the tiny, dry and dusty thoroughfare that they found when they pushed on. The shooting from the guard post seemed to have caused little excitement in the small collection of dwellings, and Angel followed Jesús's directions without seeing another human being.

'Some burg,' he said. 'The Las Vegas of Colombia. A one-horse town, and the horse died.'

'Shut up, Angel,' said Valin. 'Just drive.'

''K, Colonel,' said the American. 'Just making a comment.'

'The people will have been frightened by the gunfire,' said Jesús. 'It is not advisable to be too inquisitive in these circumstances. They are probably hiding beneath their beds with their hands over their ears.'

'Let's hope they stay that way,' said Valin.

On Jesús's instructions, Angel stopped the truck outside a tiny brick-built house with a tarnished brass nameplate screwed to the wall, and Jesús and Valin jumped down.

They stepped on to the porch and Valin hammered on the door. After a moment he hammered again, until it was opened by a wizened old woman in a long, black dress and a white apron.

'*Médico*,' he demanded. '*Llame al médico*.'

The frightened woman ran back into the house and within thirty seconds a distinguished-looking elderly man in a black suit, white shirt and black tie came to the door.

Jesús told him in Spanish that a man with bullet wounds in his legs was needing assistance on the edge of town.

The doctor looked at him and shrugged, and then they rattled away at each other in their native tongue.

'He does not want to come, Colonel,' said Jesús.

'You amaze me. Tell him he has no choice.'

'He says that he has retired from medical practice.'

'Tell him he just got back into it.'

Jesús rattled another half-a-dozen sentences.

'He says no, Colonel.'

Valin took the Smith & Wesson auto from its holster on his lap and stuck it into the doctor's midriff. 'Tell him we'll go with him to get the necessary bandages and medication,' he said. 'Or he'll be treating himself.'

When Jesús had spoken again, the doctor shrugged once more, and the three men went into the house, to reappear a few minutes later, the doctor now wearing a dark overcoat and carrying an ancient medical bag.

All three squeezed into the cab, and Angel drove to the next corner, then back to the main street and headed out of town past the disabled military post. Within a few minutes they got back to the jeep.

Keller was delirious, and Sofía was supporting his head on her lap, while García stood by helplessly. 'Thank goodness you've come,' the young woman said to the doctor in Spanish. 'He's getting worse.'

The doctor looked at the state of Keller's wounds, shook his head and opened his bag, but Valin stopped him. 'We're not staying here,' he said. 'It's too risky. You were saying something about some caves, Jesús.'

'Yes. There are a number about fifteen minutes' drive from here in that direction.' He pointed down the road that cut across the highway they had travelled in on.

'Let's go then,' said Valin. 'The doctor can look at him there. Another few minutes won't make much difference.'

Jesús told the doctor what Valin had said, as O'Rourke got back behind the wheel of the jeep and started the engine, and then climbed into the front passenger seat. The doctor got in the back with Keller and Sofía, and gave the German a painkilling injection as they drove.

The mountain reared up again in front of them, and Jesús pointed to a track that led off the road they were following. 'Down there,' he said to O'Rourke. 'Just a few more minutes.'

Before long they came to a towering cliff punctuated at ground level and above by a number of large holes. 'In there,' said Jesús, pointing to one of the openings. 'The cave runs under the mountain like a natural tunnel. We can pass right through, and the airstrip is only a short drive from the other side.

'Sounds good to me,' said O'Rourke, and, flicking on his lights, steered the jeep into the darkness. Angel followed slowly in the three-tonner. The jeep's yellow beams showed a large, domed cave, and O'Rourke stopped the vehicle on the smooth rock floor.

The doctor rattled off something in Spanish to Jesús, who shouted for Angel to bring the truck round so that his headlights would give the doctor some illumination to work in. As soon as he was satisfied, the doctor ripped the unconscious Keller's trousers off and examined the wounds more closely, all the time talking to Jesús.

'He's very bad,' Jesús relayed to the group, while the doctor began to dress the wound. 'Bones have been shattered, and he's lost a lot of blood.'

'Resnick,' said Valin, 'go and keep an eye on the entrance. I want to know if anything's going on out there.'

'Colonel,' said the Russian, and jogged towards the light-filled entrance to the cave.

The doctor finished bandaging Keller's legs and groin and stood back to survey his handiwork.

'That is all I can do,' he said in Spanish. 'Maybe he will live. Maybe not. He is in God's hands. Now may I go home?'

Valin understood what he was saying and shook his head. 'I'm sorry,' he said in the same language. 'But you will stay here until we leave. My man needs care, and you will give it to him.'

The doctor let forth a torrent of words that was too fast for Valin's limited understanding of Spanish, but he got the drift and grinned. 'Tell him to shut up, Jesús, or we'll have to gag him.'

As Jesús gently explained what Valin had said, and the doctor scowled angrily, Valin had a word with

O'Rourke, then went to join the rest of his troops. 'We stay here until tomorrow morning, then set off for the airstrip,' he said. 'Apparently we go straight through this mountain, then head downwards.'

'Sounds OK to me, Colonel,' said Angel. 'I can't wait to get back home.'

'Me neither,' said Spenser.

'Soon,' said Valin. 'Very soon, I promise. And then we can have a gentle word with the person who spoiled what could have been a very clean exercise.'

'And collect our cash,' said Angel.

'That too,' agreed Valin. 'That too.'

Back in the USA, the man who had betrayed Valin's men was making another call to Leavenworth. 'Any news yet?' he asked.

'The plane has returned to Panama, empty. My men have stayed down in Colombia. The pilot will return tomorrow under escort.'

'What *is* happening down there?'

'The remains of the strike force escaped from Santa Ana, then shot down a Colombian air force chopper. A Jolly Green Giant.'

'They have the luck of the devil.'

'Their luck will run out tomorrow, if not before.'

'I hope so.'

'Count on it.'

'No, you. I will be very angry if you fail.'

Then the line went dead.

33

The afternoon dragged into evening, and the party ate a desultory meal of the remains of their rations, leaving only enough for a snack before their departure.

Spenser, sitting next to Carmen in the chilled air of the cave, gave her his jacket to wear. She looked hard and long at him before she spoke. 'Did you mean what you said before?' she asked.

'Of course.'

'Then it seems we have very little choice. I have to come out with you.'

'Collectively? Or me personally?'

'I don't understand.'

'Come out as part of the team, or as a couple.'

'You know very well.'

'Good.'

He leaned over and kissed her, and for the first time in years offered up a prayer. A prayer that it would happen, and nothing else would go wrong.

Sofía continued nursing Keller, who was drenched in sweat and moaning softly. In his delirium he was back in post-war East Berlin, a child of the Nazis and forced to scavenge for food for his mother on the bomb-sites that covered the city like the empty sockets in a toothless mouth.

Franz Keller's father had come back from Russia, a shadow of the proud SS officer who had gone off to destroy Stalin's armies. He sired his only son before dying of tuberculosis in the unheated flat that the small family occupied. Franz Keller had grown up fast. Before he was five he was scrounging supplies from the American servicemen who guarded the Brandenburg gate. He exchanged chewing gum, cigarettes and nylon stockings for black-market food and fuel for the paraffin heater that kept Frau Keller and her son alive during the bitter winters of his childhood.

His mother passed away when he was eleven and he was alone. It was the mid fifties, and while the free world held its collective breath for the economic boom that was to come, young Franz slept in deserted bunkers, discovered the remains that the rats had left of the bodies of his countrymen, fought with other children for the rotting remains of other people's refuse, and learnt to defend himself against the ghouls and monsters who roamed the city in search of human prey.

By the time the wall went up, he was in his teens, and just before the authorities clamped down on travel between the east and west he moved to free Berlin, where he joined a gang of black-marketeers as a runner. He was unusually strong, even after years of poor nutrition, and that, combined with his natural cunning and the ruthlessness he had learnt after years of fending for himself, soon brought him to the attention of his bosses and he moved fast up the ladder. He went all over the country, helping oversee the import of contraband. Especially at the seaports, where one evening in the Star Club in Hamburg, he befriended a young man from Liverpool who was a guitarist in one of the beat groups who played there. They ended up drunk and stoned, swapping a couple of prostitutes all night long, until eventually, hung over and suffering from their debauchery, they breakfasted together in a café down by the docks. Swearing eternal friendship, they parted, never to meet again. The musician was John Lennon, and Keller had never forgotten that night.

By the time he was twenty, Keller was a gun-toting bodyguard to one of the most powerful hoodlums in the gang. He had a flat in one of the smartest parts of the city, a Mercedes, women, clothes and, most important of all to the orphan from the east, more than enough to eat and drink.

As the sixties wound down, and the black market dwindled, a large-scale gang war broke out in West Berlin, as control of the city's burgeoning drug trade came up for grabs.

One night, Keller entered a smart restaurant with his boss, and one of the dozen working girls that the boss squired round the town and then took back to his flat and used for sexual gratification. The kind of sexual gratification that involved abuse and sodomy, where the woman was tied up with leather straps and beaten with a horse whip. Meanwhile Keller would sit in the next room, reading a magazine or watching TV, ignoring the screams from the bedroom.

To Keller it was routine. A night like a hundred others. He would sit at the next table to his boss and his whore, and listen to his boss boast of the week's achievements, and how much money he had made. He would watch him stuff his mouth with goose and potatoes, and run his greasy hands up the whore's legs until he reached her underwear, with no concern about who might be watching. Keller's boss was a pig. But a pig with a big trough. Big enough for Keller to get more than his fair share of the swill.

But that night was different. As they waited in the foyer to be shown to the best table in the place, three gunmen appeared in the doorway behind him. All three carried powerful automatic handguns, and opened fire. The woman took three shots to the abdomen and one to the neck. Keller's boss took eight bullets in all: two to the head, five to the body, and one in his right arm. Miraculously, Keller was left untouched, and he hardly had time to reach under his jacket and unholster the Colt Lightweight Commander .45 auto that he had liberated from an American serviceman late one night, before the gunmen were gone.

Pandemonium broke out in the restaurant. Twenty-one shots had been fired in all. One waiter had been killed by a bullet to the heart. Another had collected a spare slug in his buttock. A female diner was bleeding her last on to the deep-red carpet, which soaked up her blood and hardly showed a stain. One man, who was dining with a woman who wasn't his wife, choked to death on a piece of steak. And at a nearby table, the host at a dinner party for six was killed by a bullet that hit him in the liver before he had settled the bill, much to the disgust of his guests.

Keller's boss was dead before he hit the floor, and the woman died a few minutes later. Keller left before the police arrived. He had checked on the man in his charge, and he knew a dead body when he saw one.

Keller was in big trouble. His other bosses would want to know why he didn't return fire at the gunmen, and would brook no excuses. A couple of bullets in his own body might have mitigated his laxity. But probably not completely. Only his own death while saving his boss's life would have truly exonerated him. But he was unhurt, and he knew that people would soon be asking questions. Embarrassing questions like how much money had he taken to allow his charge to be gunned down. He probably wouldn't be allowed to live long enough to offer an explanation. It would be shoot first and ask questions later, when the news of the assassination got around.

There was only one answer. To get out – fast.

The limousine in which the three of them had arrived at the restaurant had vanished by the time he got outside, but anyway he would have ignored it. He took a taxi to his flat and was packed and gone within twenty minutes. He went straight to the airport, carrying the little money that he had stashed away there, and a passport in a fake name that he had bought months before in case of just such an eventuality as this. Life was cheap in West Berlin in the sixties, and Keller's motto had always been: 'Be Prepared'. He booked a one-way ticket on the first flight to Madrid, ditched his gun just as his flight was called, and no one had come looking for him. He didn't need the hassle of being caught trying to carry a weapon through the departure lounge or through customs at the other end, and he knew he could pick up a new weapon in Spain within a few days. The only problem was cash. He dared not touch his bank account. The gang had key bank employees in their pocket, and Keller knew it would only be a matter of days before his bosses would be after him if he made a withdrawal.

So he arrived in the Spanish capital with just the minimum of luggage and a few thousand marks in his pocket. He stole a car and drove to the coast, where he mingled with the few holiday-makers who were just discovering the Costa del Sol, and he robbed and burgled his way along the strip, until once again he could afford the best hotels and a hired Mercedes.

But luck was not with him. The Germans were also taking their holidays in Spain, and one evening when Keller was enjoying a quiet drink after dinner, he was recognized by one of his old gang. Keller recognized the man too, and left town without even checking out of his hotel. He drove along the coast, dumped his car, bought a one-way passage on a fast PT boat that was smuggling cigarettes, gold, medical supplies and guns both ways between Spain and Africa, and the next day found himself once again penniless, this time in Morocco. He headed south, picking up a car and money on the way, by the same means he had used in Spain, leaving a trail of dead and dying people behind him.

Eventually, when he got to newly independent Burundi, part of the Belgian Congo until 1962, he was captured by a marauding band of tribesmen, and only released when they fought and lost a pitched battle with a group of mercenaries who had been brought in by the president.

Keller was given the option of joining the group or

being summarily shot. Naturally he joined, and fought behind their leader, a former Scots Guards major, for the next five years. The major granted Keller the honorary title of sergeant, and taught him to handle weapons from all over the world.

The major was killed by a stray shot on the South African border in 1974 and Keller caught a boat to the USA, once again using forged papers. His visa stood up to scrutiny in New Orleans and he started a one-man crime wave that took him right across the country to California, where he worked in Hollywood as an armourer and stunt man.

But the German found life on the West Coast boring, and after a few years he drifted across the Midwest, picking up jobs where he could. Finally, he pushed on further, until he got to New York, where, on a whim, he took a boat to Europe, where he ended up one cold winter's night in London. That was how he met Colonel Valin and Mark O'Rourke, and the three had been together ever since.

As Keller lay in the back of the jeep in the dark and frigid air of a cave somewhere in Colombia, it was as if it were only yesterday, not years ago, that he had met the pair of them.

'Another brandy, Colonel?' he shouted, startling Sofía out of her half doze. 'And a pint for you, Lieutenant,' he called, as if across a busy bar.

'Shh,' she said, and stroked his forehead, which was pouring with sweat. 'Shh. Everything's going to be all right.'

Resnick, who had been relieved by Angel at the cave entrance, watched Sofía as she ministered to the sick man. And he watched Spenser and Carmen too.

Resnick was another loner who had not had a steady woman in his life for years. If we both get out of here alive, he thought as he gazed at the young woman, perhaps we could make it a double wedding.

Night fell fast again, and soon after it got dark, Angel found and spoke to Valin.

'There's a lot of noise and light back where we came from,' he said. 'I think there's choppers up with searchlights.'

'They could hardly ignore us killing those police and destroying their cars,' said Valin. 'And then taking out a guard post. If they get close, come and let me know.'

Angel touched the rim of his tin hat, and went back to his post. The sound of helicopter engines rose and fell, but he knew that they were safe unless the spotlights got closer.

Jesús and Valin sat together on a rock shelf, and the Colombian said that the next morning's drive should take no longer than an hour or so, and that they should leave about four-thirty.

'How are we off for fuel?' asked Valin.

'There's enough,' said Jesús. 'Both the truck and the jeep have extra fuel tanks.'

'And if we don't meet anyone on the ride home, we should be back in the USA in three or four days,' said Valin. 'There are three cars waiting in Panama, and three more in Mexico City, complete with our papers.'

'What about us?' asked Jesús. 'My girls, García and me? How are we going to get into the States?'

'I think you'll have to go in illegally. But don't

worry. We know some back roads. Some of the stuff we brought out wouldn't pass muster with the Border Patrol, so we had to cross by covert means.'

'So be it,' said Jesús philosophically.

'And then we get down to business. There's money to be collected, and I know that the rest of the men would agree that you deserve your fair share. You *and* your daughters.'

'Do you think money could replace what we've lost?'

'Of course not. But it will help you all to build a new life. And at least one of them seems ready to do it with one of my men.'

Jesús looked over at Carmen and Spenser, and shook his head. 'It's crazy,' he said. 'Women. What can you make of them?'

34

To the eleven people waiting in the cave, the night seemed to go on for ever. The moon hung in the corner of the sky, hardly moving as the temperature dropped like a stone.

Spenser and Carmen were together under his thin cotton jacket. He had fallen asleep; she could not. Her sense of loss was too great. Angel had been relieved and was snorting coke behind a rock at the back of the cave, while Valin took his turn on watch. Resnick was working on a timing device by the light of a pencil torch close to the jeep where Sofía was still sitting next to Keller, who had dropped off into a fitful sleep. O'Rourke was dozing in the back of the truck on the opposite bench to García, who was asleep. The doctor sat alone, still wearing his coat, and with his battered bag between his legs, while Jesús kept an eye on all of them, a cigarette cupped in one hand and a cocked Heckler and Koch in the other.

Carmen looked at her father's face by the glow of the cigarette each time he took a drag. His features could have been carved out of dark ivory. Poor man, she thought. What he's gone through today. What all of us have gone through. Silent tears began to run down her face as she thought of her mother, sister and brother, laid to rest in cold graves that she would probably never see again. She thought too of the two mercenaries, Newman and Messelier, who lay next to them, and the other four men they had left behind in Santa Ana.

She remembered her mother's work-roughened hands, with which she had gently cared for her as a child, and her brother's strong back as he'd helped with the meagre harvest that was their livelihood, and the way that Carlotta had been a friend as well as a sister, all her life, and her tears flowed harder. She moved closer to Spenser for comfort and warmth in what was turning out to be a cold, hard world.

Outside the cave, Valin looked back across towards the hamlet where they had kidnapped the doctor, and up towards the mountains where they had fought the pitched battle with the police. There was still light and noise from the choppers, but he was convinced they had no idea where his small band was hiding.

A bit of luck at last, he thought. If only it can hold.

As all nights must, eventually this one passed, and at a few minutes to four Jesús and Valin roused the rest of the group.

'Tell the doctor he can go now,' said Valin to Jesús. 'Tell him he'll have to walk. Give him my apologies, but I have no choice in the matter. I don't want him telling the authorities where we spent the night until we are long gone.'

Jesús did as he was told. Naturally, the doctor objected vehemently. But eventually he realized he had no choice, and he picked up his bag and left the cave. Before he went, O'Rourke gave him his torch.

'Don't want the old boy falling down and breaking his neck,' he said.

As he left, the doctor checked Keller, who was awake and in dreadful pain, for the last time, and his prognosis was not good. 'He will never walk again,' he told Valin. 'And there is a chance of gangrene. More than a chance.' He gave the German a final shot, and left pills for him, should the pain get any worse.

As soon as the doctor had walked out of the cave, Valin gave the order for the rest to mount up. Jesús, Sofía and Keller were in the jeep, with O'Rourke driving, and the rest got into the truck, with Valin and Angel in the cab as before. At four-twenty the drivers started their engines and set off through the tunnel. The journey was as easy as Jesús had predicted, and they came out on a mountain road just as their synchronized watches showed four forty-five.

35

The two vehicles began the hairpin descent towards the carpet of jungle below, which was black in the pre-dawn light, their beams cutting a yellow path in front of them.

'Won't be long now,' Valin said to Angel. 'Let's just hope those choppers have gone back to their base, or that they don't get inquisitive if they haven't.'

'Can't be soon enough for me,' said the American. 'Clean sheets and ice in the drinks.'

'Your idea of civilization?'

'Fucking A, Colonel.'

'So what are you doing here?'

'Civilization pales next to this kind of experience.'

'It's like a drug,' said Valin candidly. 'And you know all about that, don't you?'

Angel looked over at the colonel in the dim light from the dashboard. 'What do you mean?'

'You know very well. The little package you've been carrying around in your jacket since we blew up the factory.'

'Well, I'll be damned. You're smarter than I gave you credit for.'

'I just keep my eyes open. Do you intend to sell it when you get back to the States?'

'I know some people who might be interested.'

'I thought you might.'

'There's nothing wrong with making a profit. That's what we're all risking our lives to do here.'

'I could make you dump it,' said Valin.

'And I'd do it, sir. If you ordered me to.'

'What the hell?' said Valin. 'What difference will it make? It's a bad world.'

'Glad that you see it that way, Colonel,' said Angel, and put a cigarette in his mouth.

'But I might need you to do something special for me one day,' Valin went on. 'Are you ready for that?'

'Depends on what it is.'

Valin shook his head. 'No,' he said. 'Whatever it is. You do it without question. That's the only way it can be.'

The cab of the truck was silent except for the roar from the tired old engine.

'I dig, Colonel,' said Angel. 'Just say the word.'

'I will. Count on it,' replied Valin.

Angel slammed down a gear as the incline got steeper, and said nothing more.

The sky began to lighten in the east and with it the spirits of the party. Surely nothing much more can happen, they thought. If, the harder hearts added, the fucking plane turns up.

Meanwhile, back in the jungle beside the airstrip, the soldiers who were waiting had been awake for more than an hour, keeping watch for any sign of movement on the track leading to it.

'What do you say, sir?' one of them said to Number One.

'Who knows?' he replied. 'Maybe something *has* happened on the way here. Maybe they won't turn up at all. There's been a lot of traffic on the police and military radio channels. Our boys seem to be causing mayhem wherever they go. But we've not heard that they've been stopped. Not so far at least.'

'Or maybe they've called in at McDonald's for an Egg McMuffin,' said the soldier.

'Jesus,' said another 'I hope they get a take-out.'

'Me too,' said a third. 'What the hell do they put in these combat rations?'

'Nutrition for our nation's youth,' said Number One. Then he stopped, one hand raised. 'Can you hear anything?' he said.

They could. From across the jungle came the faint sound of heavy-duty vehicles, and from the fading darkness, heading east to where the sun was just about to rise, came the deep roar of twin-prop aero engines.

Then the soldier the leader had posted along the track as a look-out raced from the trees and towards them. He gave a swift salute and said: 'Someone's coming, sir.'

'Time to go time,' said Number One. 'Let's kick butt.'

The journey down the mountain had been uneventful, and as it got lighter, first Angel, then O'Rourke, killed the lights on their vehicles.

They found the entrance to the track with no difficulty, and O'Rourke, closely followed by Angel, turned into it, just as the soldiers at the airstrip heard, first their engines, then those of the Douglas C47 Dakota.

The soldiers spread out to wait for the new arrivals, who happened to turn up more or less simultaneously, the nose of the jeep poking through the jungle, followed by the truck, as the rising sun's rays caught the dull surface of the plane and muddily reflected it across the look-out's eyes.

The soldiers were under strict orders to hold their fire until their leader's signal, and they all sat tight as the plane made its final run and came in to land.

When the truck and jeep came to a halt, everyone disembarked. O'Rourke and Jesús lifted Keller, who was now awake and seemingly slightly better, from the jeep, and laid him gently on the ground. The rest, carrying weapons and equipment, watched as the C47 lost height, and there were relieved smiles all round as their fatigue disappeared at the thought of their imminent departure.

Then one of the soldiers lying in ambush, nervous after his long wait, hot, tired and covered in insect bites, touched the trigger of his machine-gun and loosed a single burst. His bullets tore into the side of the three-tonner, and Valin's team split apart, and dived for cover.

'What now?' said O'Rourke as he found himself next to Valin, behind one of the double rear wheels of the truck. 'What the hell's going on?'

'Don't know,' said Valin calmly, as he let off a burst of shells himself at a green-clad figure he had seen move his position, and fired the last grenade from the ARMSCOR that he had taken from Resnick when the truck was unloaded. It exploded just within the trees, sending the soldiers there diving for cover.

The pilot of the C47, meanwhile, who had not been

too pleased to be forced to return to the airstrip under threat not only from Valin, but also from the leader of the soldiers, was becoming less pleased with every passing moment. If it had not been for the four soldiers Number One had left at the pilot's home base to convince him that an early-morning flight was good for his health, he would have taken a chance and not come back at all. One of them was now sitting in the co-pilot's seat with a Sig Sauer 228 pointed at the pilot's belly, another was peering through one of the windows of the main cabin, and the other two were waiting back there, just in case the unthinkable happened, something went wrong, and Valin's people managed to get out somehow.

'Just for insurance, you understand,' the soldier sitting next to him had explained during the flight, holding up his pistol. 'But I do have a pilot's licence, so don't think I won't use this.'

At the moment of touchdown, the pilot saw the muzzle flashes from the jungle as the soldier opened fire prematurely, watched Valin's group throw themselves into cover, and then jammed on the brakes and slewed the C47 to one side of the runway. Then he turned it as tightly as he could in a full circle, and prayed that he had enough runway to take off again, which he would have been sorely tempted to do if it wasn't for the damned gun that covered him steadily.

Resnick, unaware that the pilot was not alone, and assuming that the fire from the jungle was coming from Colombian soldiers, National Guardsmen or police, saw the plane turn and heard its engines revving, and assumed again that it was about to take off and leave him and his comrades stranded. He was determined to stop it. Grabbing his last pack of HE, he stood up and ran to the jeep, flung himself into the driver's seat, started the engine, jammed it into gear and sent it in the direction of the C47. He skidded to a halt close to the side of the plane, jumped out of the jeep without switching off the engine, grabbed the pack, slung it over his shoulder, and carrying his CZ 75 semi-automatic pistol in his left hand, yanked open the door in the side of the fuselage, and leapt inside as bullets thumped into the skin of the plane beside him.

'Don't shoot at the plane,' yelled Number One to his troops. 'We need the fucker to get out of here.'

The soldier in the cabin of the plane had watched Resnick's dash, and smiled. He stood up as Resnick hauled himself and his knapsack inside. The Russian sensed a presence and looked up into the soldier's eyes and they both pulled the triggers of their guns simultaneously. A burst of 7.62mm bullets from the soldier's Galil hit Resnick in the chest, knocking him down in the aisle, where he lay still, and the soldier took a single shell in his neck and died instantly.

The other soldier kicked open the connecting door between the flight deck and the cabin, and poked the snout of his Sig through the doorway. Through the smoke from both guns he saw his comrade lying dead, and Resnick sprawled on his back, with blood bubbling out from the multiple wounds in his chest. The soldier cursed the mercenary, walked down the aisle, kicked his pistol out of his hand, and was just about to finish the Russian off, when the radio in the cockpit burst into life and he heard Number One's unmistakable voice cut through the static: 'Number One to C47. Come in.'

The soldier left Resnick where he lay and ran back to the flight deck, tore the mike off its hook and said. 'C47 to Number One. Receiving.'

'What's going on in there? Over.'

Outside, Valin's people were by now a little more organized and were returning fire steadily as Spenser readied the Gatling. The only problem was that he was very low on bullets, as the cartridge belts for the weapon were heavy, and only so many could be taken on a mission. And for days he'd been using ammunition like it was going out of fashion.

Carmen was at his side again and they smiled at each other like veterans, which in a way they were.

They had taken refuge in a shallow, dry ditch at one side of the runway, and when the gun was ready they stood up together and swept the soldiers' position with a hail of fire, then dropped down again as their fire was returned.

The soldiers had not fared well in the exchange. Of the ten of them on the ground, three were hit: one dead, one seriously wounded and one with just a flesh wound.

Their leader was furious as he talked on the radio with the soldier on board the plane, the radio man kneeling beside him. Everything would have been fine if some damn fool hadn't fired too soon, he thought to himself as Spenser opened up with the Gatling.

The bullets cut through the thick jungle cover and he heard a man cry out, and for the first time considered the possibility that his mission to exterminate Valin's team might not succeed.

Back on the plane, Resnick opened his eyes to find himself lying on the floor with his chest on fire with pain, and the soldier he had shot lying next to him, his eyes staring sightlessly up at the roof of the cabin. Resnick's blouse was soaked with blood, but his body armour had deflected most of the force of the shells, so that the wounds looked a lot worse than they really were. The other soldier was standing in the doorway to the cockpit with his gun on the pilot, his back to the cabin, talking on the radio handset to whoever was on the ground.

Resnick's side-arm was lying a yard or so from his right hand and he picked it up, pulled himself into a sitting position and then on to his feet, trying not to make any noise, as pain lanced through his chest. Maybe the wounds *were* as bad as they looked, he thought. He was afraid to shoot inside the plane for fear of hitting something vital, so he held his gun by the barrel like a hammer and pulled himself towards the soldier, using the backs of the seats as supports.

He was within a yard of the door when the soldier sensed that all was not right behind him, and began to turn. Using all his strength, Resnick lunged forward and brought the butt of the pistol down on the soldier's neck just below the rim of his steel helmet, and he slumped to the floor.

Resnick holstered his own weapon, picked up the soldier's Sig, steadied himself against the wall of the plane and looked in at the pilot. He was fine. Obviously a pragmatist, he showed little emotion at the way the tables kept being turned.

Using the soldier's belt, Resnick trussed his hands behind his back and went to see the state of play, dragging the pilot with him. The firing was spasmodic by then, and no one was shooting at the C47, much to Resnick's relief.

'We've got to make that plane,' said Valin, firing single rounds into the jungle. 'I'm almost out of ammo.'

'Me too,' said O'Rourke. 'If the bastard thing waits for us.'

Not knowing what had happened inside the cabin of the C47, Valin said confidently: 'Resnick's on board. He'll make sure it does. Come on, let's get Keller and make a run for it.'

They snaked along the ground underneath the body of the truck to where Keller was lying beside the front wheel. He was awake and held his Heckler and Koch across his body.

'We're off,' said Valin. 'Come on, we'll give you a hand.'

Keller shook his head. 'You go, I'll give you cover,' he said.

'Don't be stupid,' said O'Rourke. 'One goes, we all go.'

'I can't walk.'

'We'll carry you.'

'We'll be dead before we get ten yards. Leave me. Give me the ARMSCOR. I've got ammunition and grenades, and I'll give you covering fire. Get the civilians to the plane.'

'I'm not leaving you,' said Valin.

'You've got no choice. I'm not coming. I'm dying. And even if I'm not, my legs are never going to be any use again. I heard what the doctor said. There's no future for me. I'd rather die like I lived, with a gun in my hand. I've got some rounds left. Now go.'

'Keller . . . ' Valin implored.

'Go, Colonel. And thank you for all the good times. We'll never see the likes of them again.' And he pulled himself up on to one elbow and poked his gun around the side of the tyre.

Valin looked at the German and made his decision. In similar circumstances he would do exactly what Keller was doing, and they both knew it. He tossed the ARMSCOR down beside the sergeant and said: 'Goodbye, Keller. It's been a pleasure, my old friend. You're a brave man. Come on, Mark, let's get out of here.' He touched Keller on the shoulder before heading towards the ditch where the rest of the group were sheltering.

O'Rourke tried one more time. 'Keller,' he said, 'that doctor doesn't know what he's talking about.'

'I think he does,' said the sergeant. 'I can feel it. Now go, Mark, and have a drink for me when you get back to London. In that pub in Paddington where we met.'

'I will,' said O'Rourke, and he squeezed Keller's arm and followed Valin.

36

Valin dived for cover as bullets from the soldiers in the jungle whined around him, and he added his fire to that of the rest as O'Rourke left Keller and zigzagged across the open ground towards them. Valin bluntly explained what was happening, and looking at his expression, no one argued. It was that kind of war. Personal. Where friends died, and mourning came later.

Valin saw Keller raise his hand and make a 'Go' gesture, and he shouted: 'Come on. Get to the plane.' On Valin's order, Angel, O'Rourke, Spenser, Carmen, Sofía, Jesús and García scrambled to their feet and, closely followed by Valin himself, made their final run.

Keller opened fire with his Heckler and Koch as they went, and all of them blasted off their remaining ammunition in the direction of the jungle. Keller had loaded the ARMSCOR, and started lobbing fragmentation and smoke grenades. Anything to give his friends the few seconds they needed to get to safety.

Number One, from his position behind the bole of a thick vine close to the edge of the jungle, saw the plan and screamed for his remaining five men to make for the plane. They broke cover and Keller smiled through the pall of smoke that was drifting towards him. 'Come on, you suckers,' he shouted, as he smacked home a fresh magazine, aimed and opened fire, forgetting the pain from his injuries in the excitement of action.

Three of the soldiers went down with the first burst, and the rest dropped into cover and fired back at Keller. Then Resnick got into the act. Using both his pistol and the Sig he had captured, he fired two-handed from the door of the plane while the pilot cowered next to him.

Valin, his men and the civilians sprinted towards the plane, and Keller kept up the hail of covering fire. Luckily for the mercenaries and their companions, the soldiers were trying to avoid hitting the plane in case a stray bullet ignited one of the fuel tanks and they were all stranded in South America. As the group got closer to the C47, Keller hauled himself to his feet, despite his appalling wounds, and pumped round after round at the enemy. He hardly felt the first bullet hit him in the shoulder, his adrenalin was pumping so fast. But a second smashed into his arm; the gun was knocked out of his grasp, and the bullet that ended his life tore through his skull as he scrabbled to retrieve it.

The leader saw him go down and lie still, and he screamed: 'Get after them.' The remaining soldiers scrambled to their feet and set off after Valin's group.

Resnick jumped down from the doorway of the plane. He knew that the bullets from the Galil had done more damage than he had at first thought, and he was beginning to hallucinate. He saw the figures running towards him as the friends he had lost in Afghanistan, and urged them to go faster. They dived through into the cabin one by one, and, seeing the soldiers advancing towards the plane, he knew that he must destroy them.

The pilot ran back to his seat and revved up the engines, keeping one careful eye on the gauges in front of him in case some vital part of the plane had been hit and he might not be able to take off. But everything seemed fine. The oil pressures were up, and the fuel tanks were three-quarters full.

'Go,' shouted Valin, as he dived through the door behind the others. 'Resnick,' he yelled at the Russian. 'Get back in.'

But Resnick was in a world of his own. Deep down he knew that if they tried to take off, the soldiers would destroy the plane out of sheer spite, and as he walked towards them he dropped the guns he was carrying, and put his hands into the knapsack slung around his back and pulled the knotted cord inside that set the detonator to blow.

The three soldiers casually shot him down as they went, but as they passed him by the charge blew, killing Resnick and two of them, and mortally wounding their leader.

As Resnick died, the last impression in his mind was of a night in Afghanistan at another airfield, where he and his comrades had just finished loading the hold of the huge cargo plane known as the 'Black Tulip' because of its paint job. Every evening as dusk descended, it was loaded with the plywood coffins of dead soldiers and flew back to the homeland with it grisly cargo. It was not a job to relish as some of the bodies were days old and decomposition had set in. The smell was horrendous and attracted swarms of black flies that bit at the exposed skin of the men loading the plane. They were issued with masks, but as the heat of the day had hardly diminished, they were more of a hindrance than a help, and most of the loaders dispensed with them. On that particular night, as Resnick was holding one end of a coffin, the soldier at the other end, a corporal of infantry, slipped and fell, the box they were carrying burst open, and the horribly disfigured corpse of a young conscript fell into the dirt. As Resnick and the corporal gingerly loaded the body back into the coffin, one of his arms broke off to expose a heaving mass of maggots that had claimed the body for their own. Resnick had never forgotten the stomach-clenching feeling as they threw the bits of the soldier into the box. As the explosive charge blasted Resnick to eternity, he once again stared death in the face – but this time it was his own.

Valin saw what the Russian had done, and realized that they would never have got away without the sacrifice of him and Keller. He slammed the door and shouted: 'Take it away.' The pilot opened the throttles and started the C47's final take-off from Colombia.

37

Valin watched as the smoke from Resnick's suicide drifted across the airstrip, and the pilot, under the watchful eye of O'Rourke, who had taken the co-pilot's seat, banked the C47 away, and headed for Panama.

The inside of the fuselage shook from the vibrations from the twin engines and boomed from their noise and the slipstream outside, so that talking in normal tones was impossible. 'What about this one, Colonel?' shouted Angel, poking the nameless soldier in the ribs with the barrel of his Uzi.

'I think we'll have a little chat.'

The soldier looked at Valin scornfully. 'You'll be wasting your breath,' he yelled.

Valin shook his head. 'I don't think so.'

'Try then.'

'I assume you were with that lot,' Valin said, gesturing behind him to indicate the dead and wounded soldiers back at the LZ. 'Who sent you?'

'Give me a break.'

'All right. Let's start with a simple question. Name, rank and serial number.'

'Fuck you.'

Valin's hand lashed out and caught him around the

side of his face, and the soldier's head snapped back. 'No profanity, please. There are ladies present.'

'Call them ladies. Fucking spic whores.'

Spenser made as if to get up, but Carmen restrained him. 'Ignore him, Chris,' she said.

'Don't stop him,' said the soldier. 'The odds are just about right. Him armed and me tied up. Spenser, isn't it? Renegade officer. Murderer.'

'And that little welcome back there was a fair fight, was it? A nice little ambush,' hissed Valin.

'Fuck you.'

'And you know who at least one of us is,' said Valin. 'How interesting.'

The soldier shook his head in disgust, then looked away. Valin grabbed him by the chin and turned his head so that their eyes met. 'I'm not playing,' he shouted. 'I want to know who sent you.'

'You never will.'

'Then you'll never live to see your home and family again. You do have a family?'

The soldier was silent. Valin looked at the dead body of the soldier's comrade. Still lying on his back, blank eyes staring upwards, and blood crusted around the wound in his neck. 'Throw that body out,' Valin said to Angel. 'It's making the place look untidy.'

'Sir,' said Angel in reply.

'And him too,' said Valin. 'The live one.'

The young American's eyes widened. '*What?*'

'You heard. Open the door of the plane and throw them both out.'

'We don't have any parachutes,' said Angel.

Valin pulled a 'couldn't care less' face. 'Throw him out anyway, Angel. He's excess baggage.'

'I'll do it if you won't,' said Spenser. 'I was getting kind of fond of Resnick, and Keller's been a friend for a long time. And this dude called Carmen and her sister rude names. I hate that kind of disrespect. Specially from an American. Throw the shit out and let's be done with it.'

'Angel will do it, won't you, Angel. After all, you have to earn your bonus,' said Valin.

Spenser, Jesús, Sofía and Carmen looked puzzled. García was looking around the faces in the cabin trying to figure out what was going on.

Angel shrugged, remembering the bargain he had struck with his commanding officer back in the cab of the truck. 'OK, Colonel,' he said. He poked the soldier again. 'On your feet, pal.'

'You can't do this,' shouted the soldier, for the first time looking worried.

'It's done, babe. You heard the man,' said Angel with a cheery grin.

'Look, I don't know anything. I'm just a grunt.'

'You knew all about Spenser,' said Valin. 'And I'm willing to bet you know exactly who else came into Colombia two days ago with me.'

'Gossip. Scuttlebutt,' stammered the soldier. 'You know the kind of thing. We just got talking.'

'We?'

'Special Services. Out of Leavenworth.'

'You're a long way from home, soldier.'

'Listen, Colonel Valin . . . '

'You know me too?'

'Course I know you. All of you. They gave us a full briefing before we left the base.'

'And they issued you with uniforms without insignia,

and even took your dog tags off you.'

The soldier's hand went instinctively to his neck.

'Nothing there,' said Valin. 'Or did you just lose them?'

The soldier didn't answer.

'Covert activities,' Valin said, and shook his head. 'Naughty, naughty. Now who sent you?'

'Christ, I don't know. We just followed orders.'

'From?'

'Captain Skelton. You left him back there.'

'Shame,' interjected Spenser. 'What exactly was the mission?'

'Terminate with extreme prejudice.'

'All of us?' Valin again.

'Everyone in your party.'

'Civilians too?'

The soldier nodded.

'You came out of Panama with the plane yesterday?'

'I didn't. The ten did. I was left behind with him.' He gestured at the body. 'And two others to make sure the pilot came back. I can fly a plane.'

'So there's a little reception party waiting.'

The soldier didn't reply. He didn't have to.

'Damn it,' said Valin. 'We'll have to land somewhere else.'

'Shit,' said Spenser. 'Is this operation ever going to go right?'

'It will,' said Valin. 'We haven't started yet.'

He looked long and hard at the soldier. 'Sorry,' he said. 'Angel. Do it.'

'Up, motherfucker,' said Angel. 'Spenser, open the door.'

'No,' said the soldier. 'Please. My family.'

'I gotta family too,' said Angel. 'Think how my mom would've missed me if you'd managed to kill all of us. At least *your* mom'll get a letter from your commanding officer telling her that you died in an unavoidable accident. So move your ass, son.'

'My wife. My kids.'

'I'm inconsolable,' said Angel. 'Chris. Door.'

'I'll just warn the pilot,' said Valin, and went to the door to the cockpit and told him that he'd have to trim his craft, as Spenser rose to his feet and pulled the door inwards and the slipstream whipped through the inside of the plane.

'Move it,' said Angel, pushing the soldier with his gun. 'Say a prayer.'

'You bastard,' said the soldier as Angel hustled him towards the open doorway. 'Please. No.'

'Have a nice trip,' said Angel, and shoved the soldier through the opening. The man grabbed the edge, his fingers white with strain, and Angel reversed his gun and slammed the butt down on to his knuckles, making him cry out as the mercenary shoved him through the doorway.

His scream was lost in the roar from outside, and Angel looked down as his figure diminished until he was no longer visible, then he and Spenser picked up the dead soldier's body off the floor and tossed it out too. Angel slammed the door shut and turned toward the colonel and said: 'Done, sir.'

'Good man, Angel. I'm going forward to have a word with our pilot about a change of flight plan.'

He moved to the cockpit door, opened it and went inside, slamming the door behind him.

'Welcome to the real world, Angel,' said Spenser.

'It's been real enough for me these last few days,' he replied.

'How do you feel?'

Angel shrugged and pulled a face. 'Shit happens,' he said, and slumped down into his uncomfortable seat, his Uzi cradled on his lap.

Valin stood between the pilot's and the co-pilot's seat.

'Change of plan,' he said to the pilot in English.

The man looked up at him and said: 'How?'

'We figure we might be met if we go back to your home base. Of course, you know nothing about that, do you?'

The pilot's eyes widened. 'Me, señor?'

'You, señor. Before he took a little walk in the fresh air, our friend told us that there was a little welcoming committee back at your airfield.'

'I know nothing . . . '

'Except how to play both ends against the middle and take a little baksheesh from both sides.'

'It is a hard world.'

'And getting harder all the time. You know what happened to him. How would you like to make the same last journey?'

'Then who would land the aeroplane?'

'We may have lost a lot of men. But there are still some talented people aboard. Talented enough to land this bucket anyway.'

The pilot paled beneath his tan.

'I see you get my drift,' said Valin. 'Now I want you to fly us to Mexico.'

'Mexico. Impossible.'

'Nothing's impossible.'

'Air traffic control.'

Valin laughed mirthlessly. 'You mean you've never done any smuggling in this wreck. Fly under the radar like you did coming in and out of Colombia.'

'Fuel. I'll need more fuel to get us there.'

'What's your range?'

The pilot shrugged. 'Fifteen hundred miles,' he said. 'But I only have enough fuel for a thousand.'

'And how far is Mexico City?'

'Maybe sixteen hundred.'

'One stop then.'

'But we'll need money.'

'I've got American Express,' said Valin.

O'Rourke looked up to the roof. Christ, he thought. Only Valin could hijack a plane and pay for the gas with plastic.

38

'I'll send someone to relieve you soon,' said Valin to O'Rourke. 'But in the meantime keep an eye on our treacherous friend here. I don't trust him any further than I can throw him.'

'You threw the other ones quite a way,' said O'Rourke with a grin. 'About twelve thousand feet if the altimeter in this crate is accurate.'

The pilot paled even more and Valin went back into the passenger section. 'You'll be glad to hear we won't be driving from Panama to Mexico City,' he announced.

'Shame,' said Spenser. 'I was really looking forward to it.'

'I'm sure you were, Chris. No. We've extended our charter, and the brave captain of this low-rent airline is going to fly us all the way there.'

'And we leave the welcoming party twiddling their thumbs in Panama.'

'Exactly. While we fly on over, give them a cheery wave and head towards Mexico.'

'We've got to cross a lot of countries.'

'We'll take the scenic route over the water for some of the way.'

'I hope no one thinks we're muling drugs,' said Angel.

Valin gave the young American an old-fashioned look. 'It's a risk we're going to have to take.'

'If we get spotted by some Latin American air force we could be shot down and all end up being deep-sixed,' said Spenser gloomily.

'Pessimism, Chris. I've told you about that before,' said Valin.

The plane droned on and O'Rourke waited to be relieved so that he could get some rest. He was dog-tired and the noise from the engines was sending him to sleep. It had been fifty-six hours since he had slept properly and he slowly dozed off.

He was in a car being driven down a street in Dublin. In his pocket was a tiny Russian-made .20-calibre PSM. It was very small and slim, with a bullet that could penetrate all known practical body armour. It had been developed for the KGB special ops personnel, especially for 'wet' operations.

And that was precisely what the young lieutenant was embarking on. He and his female driver had crossed the border the previous evening posing as tourists. Now they were looking for the address of a notorious IRA assassin who had fled to the safety of the south, and the hit-and-miss extradition orders that were passed there. He knew that even if he was arrested there, the chances of his being sent north again were slim.

'So be it,' O'Rourke's commander had said. 'You are going down there to fix the bastard. He's been thumbing his nose at us for too long. He's back and forth across that border like a dog at a fair. We're fed up with him. Go and deal with the bugger.'

'That's it,' the driver said, and nodded at a

terraced house with a stone-clad front. She braked the Montego to a halt just around the next corner.

O'Rourke got out of the car, walked back round the corner and up the front path of the house where his target lived, and pressed the doorbell.

A light came on behind the glass quarter-light above the door, and a man's voice said: 'Who's there?'

'Garda,' answered O'Rourke.

There was a rattle of chains and the door opened on a chain. 'Let me see.'

O'Rourke had a forged Garda ID in the name of Hardman. He thought that was amusing. And he held it up to the gap between the door and jamb. The door was pushed to, the chain was removed and the door opened all the way. 'Whaddya want?' said the man who appeared.

O'Rourke identified him from the photos he had seen. 'Pat Davies?' he asked, just to be sure.

'That's me,' said the man. 'What do you want?'

'This,' said O'Rourke, and produced the gun from under his coat and shot Davies three times. At that range he couldn't miss, and the Irishman fell backwards. The reports of the shots had been no louder than hand claps, and O'Rourke pulled the door to before walking to the car without a backward glance.

'Done,' he said when he got into the passenger seat and the driver pulled smoothly away.

On the way back north, she asked: 'How does it feel?'

She was a sergeant. 'Like shit,' said O'Rourke, and lit a cigarette. 'I didn't join up to become an assassin.'

'It had to be done.'

'Oh yeah? In whose name? The great British public. If this ever came out I'd be in jail faster than you can sneeze. And our lords and masters in Whitehall would deny having even heard my name.'

'It's better than patrolling the streets, dodging snipers.'

'Is it? I don't know so much. At least I could get to sleep without feeling like a murderer when I was doing that.'

'Don't worry about it, Mark.'

'I worry that they'll order me to do it again.'

'That's the risk we take doing this sort of duty.'

He shook his head sadly at the truth of her remark. 'I need a drink. Find somewhere decent-looking,' he said.

She did, at an anonymous motel that was part of a large chain. The drink became a late dinner, and O'Rourke suggested that they stay out another night, and when the sergeant agreed, he booked a pair of adjoining single rooms.

O'Rourke woke up at three o'clock with a scream dying in his throat. He had been dreaming about the bloody body of Davies pursuing him through some nightmare landscape.

He lay back down again and wiped the sweat off his body with the sheet.

A minute later there was a tap at the door. He switched on the bedside lamp, got out of bed, pulled on the robe he had packed, then opened the door.

The sergeant was standing outside, her blonde hair down and wearing a robe of her own. 'I thought I heard you cry out,' she explained.

'Bad dream,' he said. 'Come in.'

'Tea?' he said, as she sat down.

'Please.'

He filled the kettle that had been on the sideboard, from the tap in the tiny bathroom, plugged it in, and threw two tea bags into the cups provided.

When the kettle boiled he made the tea and he took her cup to where she was sitting on the only chair, an uncomfortable-looking thing with a straight wooden back. Mark took his own cup and sat on the bed.

'Davies?' she asked when they had both lit cigarettes.

He nodded.

'Bad?'

'Enough.'

'I'm sorry.'

'Me too.'

She put down her cup, stood up, unfastened her robe, pulled if off her shoulders and let it fall to the floor. She was naked underneath. Her body was firm and for the first time he could be sure that she was a natural blonde. 'I'll make you feel better,' she said and walked across the bedroom towards him.

O'Rourke's dream was broken when the Bolivian pilot, who had seen his eyes close, made a grab for the Browning automatic that had almost slipped from his fingers.

The young lieutenant woke with a start and lashed out at the pilot, whose other hand slipped off the joy-stick. The plane nose-dived. They fought for control of the gun as the plane dipped even more steeply.

Behind, all was chaos as all seven passengers were flung out of their seats.

'Christ,' shouted Angel, 'what the hell's happening?'

Back in the cockpit, the pilot gave up the fight and dived for the controls and managed to pull the C47 out of its dive, just a few hundred feet above the tops of the trees that formed the jungle below.

'You stupid bastard,' said O'Rourke as he regained his seat and Valin came to the cockpit on the run, his Smith & Wesson in his hand, ready to fire.

'What happened?' he demanded.

'Our friend here decided to play the hero,' said O'Rourke.

'The bloody plane nearly crashed,' growled Valin.

'Tell me about it.'

Valin leant over the pilot. 'Are you mad?' he asked.

The pilot shrugged, but his hands were trembling on the controls.

'Go on back, Mark,' said Valin. 'I'll take a turn here.'

39

The unscheduled stop for fuel was in Panama, but at an airfield about two hundred miles from the pilot's home base. He was apparently well known there, and called in on the radio with Valin, gun cocked and pointing at him, and Jesús standing between the seats listening for any hint of treachery in the message. But the pilot seemed to have learnt his lesson, and merely asked for permission to land to refuel. The air traffic controller in the tower casually gave him the OK, and the C47 touched down just after eight o'clock and taxied to where a bowser, manned by two yawning men, was waiting.

They were happy to accept Valin's American Express card in exchange for the fuel, and within thirty minutes the plane was airborne again. Jesús had stayed with the pilot throughout, and nothing more than some macho remarks seemed to have passed between them.

The pilot followed the coastline of Honduras, up towards Mexico, flying low, and the radio was silent.

They landed for the last time at an airstrip just outside Mexico City. The pilot reported to the ATC that he was doing a short-hop charter, and that his compass had broken, and requested an emergency landing.

The request was granted, and everyone offloaded, their weapons broken down and stashed away neatly, and resembling nothing as much as a party of hunters who had been on an excursion and lost their way home.

Valin hired three taxis at the airport, and they drove to where their cars were garaged, taking the pilot with them. No one at the airfield, which drowsed in the afternoon sunshine, seemed too worried at their arrival, and that suited everyone fine. As Angel commented: 'They're too busy having a siesta to worry about little old us.'

At the garage, Valin paid the pilot the remainder of his fee, plus a sizeable bonus, changed cars and headed north towards the USA. They drove through Durango and Chihuahua on main roads, but before they reached the border, they struck off into the desert, the way they had entered the country, and by nightfall of their second day on the road, they had crossed the border on an unpatrolled secondary road.

40

When they got back to the temporary base that Valin had set up in the rented ranch in New Mexico they felt that they could relax for a while. They were all exhausted and went off for some much-needed sleep. But sleep didn't come easy for any of them, and within a couple of hours they were all gathered together in the huge kitchen at the back of the ranch house, where O'Rourke made pot after pot of strong coffee.

'What now, Colonel?' said Angel, lighting a cigarette. 'Where do we go from here?'

'We go to Virginia to collect the money that's owed us for completing our mission. And we find the man who tried to sell us out, and sent those troops to kill us.'

'And?' Angel again.

'And we kill him.'

'More killing?' said Jesús. 'Hasn't there been enough?'

'Yes,' said Valin. 'More than enough. But we left a lot of good people down in Colombia. I can't rest until they have been avenged. I'll understand if any of you don't want to come with me. If necessary, I will go alone. You will still be paid. This was not part of the deal. Everyone here fulfilled their obligations tenfold down there.'

'I'm with you, sir,' said O'Rourke.

'Me too,' said Angel. 'I nearly had my butt shot off half-a-dozen times. Anyway, what else is there to do?'

'Count me in,' said Spenser.

'Where he goes, I go,' said Carmen, putting her arm around Spenser's shoulder.

'And where she goes . . . ' Jesús didn't finish the sentence. 'Besides, I have a little unfinished business of my own.'

'And me,' said Sofía going to her father and embracing him.

'And you, García,' said Valin in Spanish, and explained the situation to the Colombian, who rattled off an answer.

Valin smiled. 'Ramón is up for it. So that means we all are. I'm proud of you. Now what I suggest we do is split up for the journey back north. I won't be happy about our security until we've finished this business once and for all. I'll go with O'Rourke and Ramón. Spenser, will you take Jesús, Carmen and Sofía with you?'

The American nodded.

'And Angel, I imagine you'll want to be off on your own.'

'Yessir,' said Angel.

'Then we'll meet again at a designated time and place and bring this thing to its logical conclusion.'

'I'll go and check the cars,' said Angel.

'Good man,' said Valin, and Angel left through the back door and headed to the barn where they'd left their cars on arrival.

At the start of the mission, Angel had flown into Phoenix, Arizona, and hired a Lexus for the drive to New Mexico. Valin, O'Rourke, Keller and Spenser had come into Albuquerque together and picked up a Chevrolet Caprice station wagon at Hertz, which they had used to ferry the rest of the mercenaries, who had come in on domestic flights, to and from the airport.

Angel checked on the fuel, oil and water on both vehicles, and everything was OK. But they would need another. The three other station wagons that had been rented legitimately for the drive to and from Mexico City were parked under the shade of some stunted trees outside the ranch house, and he figured one of them would do. He went back into the kitchen and said as much.

Valin agreed.

'I'm going to drive to Miami,' Angel said. 'I got me a little business there.'

'How long will that take?' asked O'Rourke.

'Coupla days. Three at the most. Then I'll drop the car off and catch a plane, and meet you in Virginia.'

'Good enough,' said Valin. 'What about you, Spenser?'

'We'll go back to Albuquerque. We'll get a plane to New York, check into a hotel. Maybe do a little sightseeing. Then we'll fly to Virginia too, and catch up with you there.'

'Good. I think we should meet each other there a week today in the bar of the Hilton in Richmond. But don't check in. Just get some transport, and find a motel locally. We'll only be there twenty-four hours.'

Or maybe for ever, thought Spenser, but didn't say so.

41

Once they were all safely away, from the anonymity of a gas station pay phone Valin called Tank Tankerton in Washington.

'Christ, James,' said the American. 'We thought you were all dead.'

'No such luck, Tank.'

'I don't get you.'

'We were stitched up.'

'What do you mean?'

'Sold a pup. Betrayed.'

'By whom?'

'Such perfect grammar. Not by you.'

'Well thanks, James.'

'Don't mention it.'

'Who then?'

'You'll find out.'

'But only you, your men, Jesús Delgado and his family, and the four of us who hired you had any idea . . . '

'Exactly,' interrupted Valin. 'So work it out for yourself. It wasn't my men, or any of the Delgados.'

'What happened to them?'

'The survivors are back here.'

'With you.'

'Not right now.'

'Shit. How do you mean, survivors?'

'Jesús's wife, one of his daughters and his son are buried down in Colombia. And some of my men. Too many. Some of them didn't even get a decent burial.'

'My God. So you're saying . . . '

'I'm saying nothing right now. Got the rest of our money?'

'Sure.'

'The mission was a success, by the way.'

'I know that.'

'No "Congratulations on a job well done"?'

'Sorry, James. I'm just a bit surprised to hear from you like this.'

'I'll take it as read, then. Are you ready to deliver?'

'Of course. When?'

'Soon. I'll be in touch. And make sure everyone's there. We don't want any truants. Same place as last time. Just let them know we'll be in town. I think they'll all want to come to the party.' And with that Valin hung up.

Tank rang Landers, Bernard and General Avery straight away, and told them the news. Within fifteen minutes a telephone rang in Leavenworth.

'What's happening?' asked a voice.

'They're still in Colombia.'

'Like hell. Valin's somewhere in the United States. He's on his way to Virginia.'

'But the plane never came out. A couple of my guys are still waiting in Panama.'

'Bring them home. I think you can draw a line under

the rest. The whole deal's gone to shit. You'd better find out what went wrong.'

'I will.'

The phone went dead.

42

On the day of the rendezvous the cocktail bar of the Hilton in Richmond, Virginia, was dark and air-conditioned cool in comparison with the streets outside, where the heatwave had not abated, and the state capital shimmered in the heat haze.

Valin, O'Rourke and García were the first to arrive at the rendezvous. After leaving the ranch in New Mexico they had driven across country to Los Angeles, where they had booked into the Château Marmont, and spent a week living in room-service luxury, and catching up on their sleep, before flying to Washington DC, then driving down to Richmond overnight, where they were booked into a Howard Johnson. Spenser and the Delgados came into the bar about half an hour later. They had gone to New York as planned, and rented a service apartment in a block overlooking Central Park. Spenser and Carmen had decided to get married in the city when the mission was finally finished. Angel rolled in about twenty minutes after them.

The eight of them looked very different from the last time they had been together. Colonel James Valin was wearing a three-piece suit in cream linen that he had picked up from his tailor in Savile Row the last time he had been in England. O'Rourke was wearing faded blue jeans, cowboy boots, a white shirt and a brown suede waistcoat. Perched on his nose were a pair of sunglasses with purple lenses. García was pure Ivy League in a blue Brooks Brothers suit, pale-blue Oxford button-down shirt and a plain, navy-blue knitted tie. On his feet he wore shiny black loafers. Spenser still wore his baseball cap, and with it, a leather jacket and chinos. Carmen and Sofía were out-and-out *haute couture*, Carmen wearing a pink Versace suit, black nylons and matching pink, low-heeled pumps. Her hair had been put into one thick, dark pigtail and she wore huge sunglasses. Sofía was a vision in yellow: dress by Albertini, accessories by Chanel. Spenser had obviously not stinted with his money. Jesús was wearing a black suit, white shirt and thin black tie in memory of those he had lost. His white hair was cut short and he looked like a Mafia Godfather on his way to church.

Both Carmen and Sofía had wanted to wear mourning too, for their mother, brother and sister, but Spenser didn't want to draw attention as they arrived in town, where they'd made reservations at the local Holiday Inn, and had argued that it was better for the two women to look as though they were simply on holiday. Jesús had reluctantly accepted Spenser's logic, but insisted that he would wear black, and Spenser had concurred.

Angel was wearing a pale-blue Hawaiian shirt, a pink *Miami Vice* suit, white deck shoes with no socks, and his usual reflector shades. He sported a two-day growth of stubble, and his hair was long and unkempt. He had found a Sheraton hotel on the edge of town, and had booked in.

'Watch out,' said O'Rourke as he entered the bar. 'It's Don Johnson.'

Angel sashayed over and joined them, ordered a Bourbon with ice and water for himself from the waitress, took off his shades and winked at her.

He was rich now that he had sold the Colombian coke to a contact in Miami. And he'd be even richer when he collected the remains of his fee for the mission. But not rich enough to forget the friends he had made under fire.

'You're looking well,' said Valin drily.

'Never better, sir,' said Angel. 'But I can't get used to the quiet life.'

'It should get more interesting now,' replied Valin.

'Any chance of another mission?' asked Angel.

'You're a glutton for punishment, aren't you,' said O'Rourke.

'Your next mission is now,' said Valin. 'Maybe later we'll talk about the future.'

'Good enough, Colonel,' said Angel.

'Is the meeting set?' asked Spenser.

'Yes,' replied Valin. 'I had confirmation over the phone this morning.'

'When?'

'Tomorrow afternoon at two.'

'Were they surprised to hear from you?' asked Angel.

'A little.'

'Who did you speak to?' Spenser said.

'Tank Tankerton. Three times. Once on the road soon after we left the ranch. Yesterday afternoon. Then again this morning.'

'My old friend,' Jesús said.

Valin nodded. 'I didn't tell them about García.'

The Colombian perked up at the sound of his name, and Jesús quickly translated.

'No one knows that he came out with us. Or indeed that he even exists,' said Valin.

Jesús carried on whispering quietly to the Colombian as Valin spoke.

'And they'll all be there?' said O'Rourke.

'The same four as last time,' confirmed Valin.

'And they'll have our money?' asked Angel.

'That was the arrangement,' replied Valin. 'One-third up front, the rest on completion.'

'Did he say anything about the welcoming committee that was sent to meet us?' asked Spenser.

'Not a word. But I doubt that Tank even knew about it.'

'One of those bastards is gonna pay,' said Angel.

'Are you armed?' asked Valin.

Angel touched under the arm of his pink jacket. 'I always am these days, Colonel. It's a dangerous world out there.'

'Bring it tomorrow,' said Valin. 'I want everyone but García armed. They searched us thoroughly last time and we went through a metal detector. We're going to have to take that place.'

'Sounds good to me,' said Spenser. 'Pay-back time. I can hardly wait.'

They met for the last time the next afternoon in a diner on a corner close to the building that housed basement 101. They were all casually dressed except for Jesús and García, who wore suits. Sofía and Carmen wore jeans and leather jackets. Everyone but García carried concealed handguns. Between them they had enough fire-power to wage a war, which was exactly what they intended to do if necessary.

They sat together in the diner under the draught of a huge ceiling fan until they were all present, then paid for the Cokes they had drunk and walked together to the building.

The reception area was large, and scrutinized by twin video cameras: one covered the entrance, the other the doors to the lift that connected it with the floors above and below. In front of the lift doors was a walk-through metal detector, similar to those used at airports. There were two men at the desk – both big, in tight, black suits with bulges under the right armpits – and they stood when they buzzed Valin and his companions through the front door.

'Colonel James Valin and party,' said Valin in his most British accent.

'You're expected, sir,' said one of the security men. 'But first we have to search you.'

'Of course. I think this is what you're looking for.' And the colonel took a Glock niner from the shoulder holster he wore under his casual jacket and covered both men. 'Mark,' he said, and O'Rourke took a can of black spray paint from one of his pockets, grabbed a chair from behind the desk and, climbing on it, blanked out the lenses of the cameras. As he was doing so, Angel and Spenser relieved the guards of their weapons, and Carmen summoned the lift.

'We'll all go down together,' said Valin calmly when the lift appeared. When the doors whispered open, six guns were trained on it, but it was empty. They all managed to squeeze in, and Valin touched the button marked 'B101' and they descended to the basement. When the doors opened, the corridor was empty, and the party walked along it, guns at the ready, their footsteps silent on the carpet, with the only noise the hum of the air-conditioning system.

The door to the room that Valin and O'Rourke had visited before was unguarded and Valin gestured for one of the men in dark suits to open it.

The same four representatives of the US government were sitting at the same table as before, fruit and bottled water in front of them, and they all looked up when it opened without a pre-emptive knock. Valin stepped into the room, gun in hand, closely followed by his seven companions and their two prisoners.

'For God's sake, James,' said Tankerton, half rising to his feet. 'What's going on?'

'We've come to settle our accounts,' said Valin quietly.

'But why with guns? What the hell's wrong with you?'

'There's nothing wrong with us. Not that I can say the same for our companions who we left to rot on Colombian soil. But we're fine. A little older, a little wiser, perhaps, that's all. But I'm forgetting my manners. Allow me to introduce you all. You'll forgive me if I'm telling you something you already know. The gentleman who's done all the talking so far is Bob 'Tank' Tankerton, who represents the Drug Enforcement Agency. Next to him is Jack Bernard from the Central Intelligence Agency, based at Langley. Next to him is Karl Landers, Federal Bureau of Investigation, and finally, all the way from the White House itself, is General Ethan Avery.' Then in turn he introduced the survivors of Valin's Raiders and the Delgados, but not Ramón García.

Tankerton looked over at Jesús Delgado. 'Jesús, my old friend,' he said. 'It's been too long. I heard what happened to your family. I'm so sorry.'

'I too am sorry,' said Jesús.

'And your daughters,' Tankerton went on, looking at the young women. 'The last time I saw them they were only babies.'

'I remember, Mr Tankerton,' said Sofía.

'Tank, please. All my friends call me Tank.'

'Tank,' she repeated.

'We didn't know which of you, if any, had made it out until you called,' said Tankerton. 'There were such confusing reports coming out of Colombia.'

'We almost didn't make it,' said Valin. 'Any of us.'

'And who is this?' asked Tankerton, referring to García.

'Someone we linked up with down there. His name is Ramón García. He was a chemist at the factory complex. The Colombian government coerced him into working for them. We brought him out.'

'You did a wonderful job, James,' said Tank. 'Our spies tell us the factory was completely destroyed.'

'They'll rebuild it,' said O'Rourke. 'With help.'

'What kind of help?' For the first time, the man from the CIA spoke.

'The help of this government,' said O'Rourke. 'The kind of help that almost killed us all.'

'I don't know what you're talking about,' Tankerton said.

'*You* probably don't, Tank,' said Valin. 'But at least one of the rest of you does.'

The DEA man looked genuinely puzzled. 'What are you talking about?'

'A traitor. Someone who flew down to Bogotá from the USA, visited the factory and told the authorities down there what was happening. That we were coming, though not the exact place, date and time. Thank Christ only a few people knew that, including you, Tank, which puts you in the clear. Otherwise the plane that took us in would have been shot out of the air, and none of us would be here today. But once in, *everyone* knew where we were, and certain contingency plans were made to stop us coming out again.'

'I still don't understand,' said Tank, looking at the other three men who sat at the table.

'Tank,' said Valin. 'Are you losing your touch? Getting old? When the plane came back to pick us up, along with it came a force of US personnel. No uniform insignia. No dog tags. But US all the same. Special Services out of Leavenworth.'

The man from the FBI interrupted: 'If what you say is true, wouldn't it have been easier just not to pick you up altogether, or to let the Colombian authorities know where you were being collected from, and let them mop you up.'

'No,' said Valin firmly. 'If that had happened it's possible one or more of us might have escaped, to eventually get back here and tell you exactly what I'm telling you now. Unfortunately, the men sent down weren't as good as us. But it was very close.'

His words hung in the air like smoke.

'So who *is* the traitor?' asked Tankerton.

'Like I told you on the phone, Tank, it's one of the three here with you. It has to be.'

'I don't like this,' said the man from the FBI. 'Not one bit. I didn't come here today to listen to this sort of thing.' And he made as if to rise from his seat.

'Stay where you are,' ordered Valin, moving his gun round to cover him.

'Have you got any proof?' asked Tankerton.

'Yes. Do you speak Spanish?'

'A little.'

'Gentlemen?' said Valin to the others. The man from the FBI shook his head. The other two nodded.

'When the traitor went to Santa Ana he was seen by García here,' said Valin. 'And what he told the authorities down there was passed on to the factory personnel. Of course no one down there, or our traitor, ever thought that we'd complete the job, or in doing so bring out the one man who could and would identify him.' He paused for effect, then said: 'Jesús, you know what to do.'

Jesús turned to García, and in Spanish asked: 'Is the man who came down to Santa Ana in this room?'

'*Sí*,' said García.

'What exactly did he do when he came down?'

'He talked to the factory boss, and the military leader from the town.'

'What did he say?'

'He told them that a force of unofficial soldiers was coming to destroy the factory.'

'Did he say when?'

'No. That he did not know. Not exactly. Only that it would be soon.'

'And what happened?'

'We were put on orange alert at the factory, and the military commander drafted in extra troops.'

'And he is definitely here?'

'*Sí.*'

'Would you point him out?'

All the time, between question and answer, Jesús translated for the non-Spanish speakers, and at the last question García dramatically raised his finger and pointed it at General Avery.

'This is nonsense,' Avery spluttered. 'Are you going to believe some Colombian whom no one has ever seen before, over me? A man who has fought for his country in three wars. Who has been decorated for bravery a dozen times.'

'Shit, General,' said Spenser. 'I believe him. I remember you from 'Nam. Always in the DMZ with a freshly pressed uniform and a couple of young WAACs in tow. Hey, man, you enjoyed your wars, as long as there was someone else to fight them for you.'

'Things never change, do they?' said Valin.

'Tank,' Avery pleaded. 'You don't believe this nonsense, do you?'

'Check with Leavenworth, Tank,' said Valin. 'Even our gallant general here couldn't send those men down to Colombia without leaving some record of it. There must be an order in triplicate somewhere. And at least some of them were stranded at an LZ in Panama, waiting in case we did manage to get the plane out. They might be still down there, waiting for further orders.'

Without warning, one of the guards grabbed at Valin's gun and tried to wrestle it from his grasp. Spenser chopped at his neck with his own gun barrel, and the man slumped to the floor with a groan, but before order could be established, Avery stood up from his seat, an automatic pistol in his hand that seemed to have appeared from nowhere, and grabbed Carmen, twisted her gun out of her hand and held her in front of himself as a shield, his arm around the throat, and his gun at her head. 'Put down your weapons,' he ordered. Everyone did as Avery said, weapons thumping to the carpet, and as the general looked at Valin, his mouth curled in contempt. 'You think you're very clever, don't you?' he spat.

'Not at all, General,' replied Valin. 'Anything but. But we did what we were sent to do, despite your efforts to the contrary.'

'Damn you,' said Avery, and tightened his grip on Carmen's throat. 'I should shoot you where you stand, like a dog.' He shook his head. 'Another time, Colonel. I'm sure we'll meet again.'

'It will be my pleasure,' said Valin.

'I'll be leaving now,' said Avery. 'If anyone follows, she's dead.'

'You'll never get out of here alive,' said Tankerton.

'I think I will,' replied Avery. 'But if I don't, nor will this bitch.'

'You bastard,' said Spenser, and made a lunge for Avery, who shot him in the shoulder. As the shot rang out, and while Avery's attention was elsewhere, Jesús bent down and picked up the gun he had dropped earlier and fired once without seeming to aim. The bullet hit Avery in the head, blowing out the back of his skull, and splashing bone splinters, brain and blood across the wall behind him in a red crescent. He fell to the floor, blood gushing from the gaping wound, letting go of Carmen. The girl ran to Spenser, who was leaning against the wall, his hand staunching the blood from his wounded arm.

'That was for my family,' said Jesús.

'Good shot,' said Valin coolly. 'Do you believe me now, Tank?'

Tankerton looked down at the general's body and shook his head. 'Christ, James,' he said. 'I would never have believed it if I hadn't heard it from his own lips.'

'I'm glad you did,' said Valin. 'Are you going to be all right, Chris?'

'Thanks for the thought, Colonel,' said Spenser wryly, as Carmen tore the tail off her shirt to make a rough bandage. 'It's not the first time I've been shot, but I think a doctor might be in order.'

'I'm sure we can get you one, just as soon as Tank completes his side of our bargain.'

'What?' said Tankerton, furrowing his brow.

'Our fee,' said Valin. 'Not only did we destroy the cocaine factory, as per instructions, but we've just saved your government the cost of twenty years for General Avery in a safe little prison somewhere with cable TV piped in and *nouvelle cuisine* three times a day. Not to mention the scandal of a trial. So come on, Tank, cough up. There's a good chap.'

Tankerton took a suitcase from under the chair he had been sitting in, and slid it across the table.'

'There you are, James,' he said. 'Spend it in good health.'

SOLDIER OF FORTUNE 2

THE KOREAN CONTRACT

Doug Armstrong

1

It was ironic, he thought, that he was about to die so near the graves of his ancestors. Of course he had been promised all sorts of things if he talked, but he knew, in his heart of hearts, that the only real fate awaiting him was death.

He wasn't afraid of it, but he hoped it would come quickly. He had already suffered enough at the hands of his captors. He had hoped that vengeance would be his, but it was not to be. As he hung on the damp wall, he remembered that one of his uncles had once called vengeance the highest of all honours, but it was an honour that would now fall to someone else. He had come to accept it.

There had been plenty of time for such thoughts during the night. It was strange how the most forgotten of things surfaced from the memory when you were about to die. Nothing profound, but little pictures from his boyhood visits to Sokch'o and the family tombs where he had been taken on festival days to make the offerings and say the prayers that he had long since scorned as so much wasted energy. Why did he have to remember them now? Was it his conscience, or was there really some unseen spirit, finally making a half-hearted attempt to console this lost and broken piece of humanity that was about to be crushed?

A smile creased his cracked and swollen lips and he shifted awkwardly in the shackles that chained him to the cellar wall. He raised his head and flinched at the bolts of sudden pain that shot through his body with the effort. He could tell that outside it was daybreak, for the slenderest crack of light penetrated under the heavy wooden door, despite the filthy blanket that had been nailed across it on the inside to deprive his senses and destabilize his mental equilibrium. Again he smiled.

Over the last three days, that crack of light had become almost a friend. None of the guards had noticed it because whenever they came into the cellar they first turned on the light from outside. Every time, he would first hear their footsteps approaching from across a gravel-covered yard, then the bolts of the outer door. Then there were some steps descending to a narrow corridor and lastly some more bolts and the heavy, ill-fitting key grinding in a lock. There must be a skylight of some sort in the outer chamber which had not been properly covered, and through this came his secret friend and ally, to comfort him and help him remind himself that whatever horrors were going on in the cellar, outside the day was coming and going as it always had.

Whenever he was being interrogated, he tried to distance his mind from his body and to focus on the world outside that was going about its business oblivious to the sufferings of this one tormented soul. Again, the teachings of his boyhood had come to his rescue. Separate the mind from the body. Look upon the broken flesh if you must, but view it as someone else's. Take your inner self elsewhere.

It had been impossible at the start and although he

had steeled every nerve and sinew, he had screamed despite his efforts at control. That had given them satisfaction, he had seen. It seemed to be an essential part of the process for the tall one: to inflict pain for its own sake and not merely to extract the information that they repeatedly said he must give them.

Then he had finally managed it. He had taken his mind away and floated across the surrounding hills, seeing the colours of the rich woodland and the hot springs, entered the houses of the hill farmers, walked invisible through the busy streets of Sokch'o and Yangyang, looking into the shops where people lived and breathed, talked and bartered, all oblivious to his presence in spirit and to the empty body being torn apart in the squalid secrecy of the nearby hills.

His captors hadn't noticed at first and had continued with the interrogation assuming that he was simply being stubborn. Of course it had been the tall one, the boss, who had first noticed the change in his prisoner's mind-set. The other two guards were as tough as oxen, but also as stupid. The tall one had then tried new techniques and each time, for a while, they worked. But once the separation of mind and body had been mastered, it became ever easier to effect.

Finally, giving up in exasperation, the tall one had subjected him to a merciless and uncontrolled beating that had left him in his present state, hanging in his chains, convinced that the end would not be long in coming. Unable to get the information they had wanted, they would now dispose of him quickly.

In a sudden realization that shocked him to his core, the prisoner understood that, mixed with the riot of terror and other emotions flooding through his brain, was a slender thread of gratitude. For somehow, over the period of his imprisonment, he had been put in touch with things that he had thought lost for all time. It was as if, in the extreme suffering inflicted by his tormentors, he had managed to link hands across the years with the family he had betrayed so long ago. But, more importantly, he had linked hands with the person he had once been and had thought dead. That person was not dead – simply waiting in some hidden place deep within himself to be contacted and given new life. Again the irony struck him that such new life should only come now, moments before his bodily death.

But at least the contact had been made. In his agony he had reached out and found them all there, waiting for him. His ancestors. Perhaps this was the only way to find them. Or rather, it was only at such moments of death that they drew near in readiness to gather another family spirit into their arms. The prayers and mantras he had mumbled through as a boy, usually bored and waiting for the ritual to end so he could go racing through the trees to play hide-and-seek with his brothers, gathered about him now and made a strange kind of sense.

Once more he raised his head to look across the darkness at the crack of light. He could hear footsteps coming across the yard, crunching on the gravel, and then the outer door being opened. There were several of them, the tall one in the lead as usual. They came down the steps, muttering to each other, and then the bolts were being pulled back and the key was turning in the lock. Suddenly the prisoner was blinded as the light was switched on and the guards burst into his room. He knew it was useless to pretend to be asleep – he had tried it before. So he simply looked from one to the other. And he knew that this was it. The two stupid ones refused to meet his eyes. Only the tall one stared back. There was no hatred on his face, just complete indifference as if the whole terrible episode had, for him, been an exercise or a game. Unfortunately it was a game that he had lost and he didn't like losing. He wasn't used to it and the prisoner was about to pay dearly for his victory.

Francis Kwang didn't like to think of himself as an impatient man but as he stared out of the broad french windows that led from the modern but tastefully furnished open-plan ground floor of his country villa on to a large, sweeping, wooden balcony, he clenched and unclenched his fists, clasped behind his back. It was a sign that anyone who knew him would instantly recognize as a warning signal. From the bedroom at the top of a wrought-iron spiral staircase he could hear Lulu humming to herself; she had put on a Frank Sinatra record that she had obviously found while going through his cupboards, so, while old blue eyes was busy doing it *My Way*, Kwang was being kept from doing things to Lulu his way by that idiot 'Babs' Butler. What kind of name was that for a soldier? He snorted in derision at the thought of the white fleshy major attempting to do anything even remotely military.

From upstairs the humming stopped as Lulu changed the record, managing to bounce the needle across at least three other tracks in the process. In the delectable moments of peace before Tom Jones ground into another number, a woman's voice called down from the top of the banisters.

'Francis, aren't you coming upstairs?'

Kwang turned round and the forced smile was

startled into a genuine glow of pleasure when he saw that Lulu had already undressed and was wearing the nightgown he had bought her on his last trip into Seoul. Standing at the top of the stairs, she posed for him, twirling this way and that, pulling open the hem to reveal a tantalizing glimpse of her long, olive-coloured thigh.

'Do you like it, darling? It suits me, doesn't it?'

Kwang nodded. 'Yes, my dear. I'll be with you in a minute. Go and warm the bed for me. That's my kitten.'

With a pout of disappointment Lulu flounced out of sight but a moment later was humming her inane tune again. She was like a rabbit, Kwang thought. One minute her entire attention was focused on something as if her life depended on it, and the next she had completely forgotten what it was and was pursuing some altogether different and vapid thought. Still, that had its advantages. Conversation, such as it was, was effortless. But then he hadn't acquired her for her conversation.

Looking once more out of the expanse of window, he cast his eyes over the stunning vista before him. At this time of year the tree-covered hills were a beautiful patchwork of greens and golds. Rising into jagged peaks, they were clad to the summits with pines, spruce and birch, and all manner of bushes and shrubs. From down in the deep valleys wisps of smoke rose from the few farmsteads and monasteries that lay between his villa and the coast many miles to the east. Looking to the north, he noted how they rose ever higher until they seemed to melt into the sky. But in that direction lay the border and the ridiculously termed demilitarized zone, the DMZ, or 'D M Zee' as the Americans called it. It was one of the most militarized areas on the planet but with a double-speak worthy of Orwell, it was referred to with clinical detachment as the DMZ.

Kwang sighed. Ever since the Korean peninsula had been partitioned along the 38th Parallel at the end of the war in 1953, the heavily armed truce had frozen the two states in unrelenting but impotent hostility. Backed by their foreign allies throughout the decades of the Cold War, neither side was strong enough to overcome the other, nor indeed would they have been allowed by those same allies to try.

But with the collapse of the old Soviet Union and with China embroiled in the uncertainties of reform, all of that was changing. The old pieces of the political jigsaw were inexorably shifting and soon the greatest of prizes would once again be up for grabs.

Glancing for the hundredth time at his Cartier watch, Kwang was about to give way to a combination of impatience and mounting lust when the phone rang. In two strides he was bending over the glass-topped coffee-table.

'Yes?'

'Mr Kwang?' The voice on the other end of the line was instantly recognizable. Coiled like a snake about to strike, Kwang forced himself to relax, sinking on to the white sofa and crossing his legs with effeminate grace.

'You've kept me waiting again. I hope it isn't always going to be like this, Major Butler.'

'Babs. Everyone calls me Babs,' said the voice a little uncertainly, and then, remembering the threatening tone of the renowned Francis Kwang: 'No, of course not. It's taken me quite a while to get what you wanted, that's all.'

Kwang revelled in the hint of submission, feeling sufficiently appeased to allow himself to relent.

'So tell me, Babs, have you got what I want?'

'Yes. The team's almost complete.'

'Almost? I don't think you realize the urgency of what we're attempting here.'

There was a flutter at the other end of the line before the voice replied: 'I do, believe me. But these aren't the easiest men to get hold of. You don't find them in the Yellow Pages, you know.' And then, regretting the stab at humour, it went on: 'I mean, they . . . Look, Mr Kwang, the team's virtually together. There's just one other guy I can't get hold of.'

'What do you mean?'

'I mean, I'm waiting for his reply.'

'Then get someone else instead.'

For the first time in the conversation the voice of Babs Butler took on the ring of authority, at home on his own ground at last.

'There is no one else. At least not of the same quality as this guy. You said you wanted the best in the business, and that's what I'm getting you. But it takes time, a bit of negotiating here, some encouragement there . . .'

'Spare me the advertisement, Major Butler, if you please.'

With the nub of their conversation complete, Kwang felt his concentration wandering. He had waited all morning for his chauffeur to return from the airport with Lulu and now she was here again he was being prevented from getting his money's worth by this mumbling idiot of a Westerner. The man was being paid an obscene amount of money simply to hire a bunch of marginally capable thugs. But oh no, he had to inflate himself to the status of professional. A connoisseur. It was really quite pathetic.

Lulu, on the other hand, was a real professional. Ever since Kwang had met her in the cocktail lounge of the Hyatt Regency in Seoul, he had been besotted by her. Her look of sweet innocence had captivated him instantly but he had quickly been enlightened as to the standard of her hidden talents. Since then he had flown her across to his villa in the Sorak-san National Park numerous times, and on each occasion she had never failed to surprise him with her variety and guile.

The voice on the phone droned on and on and was in the middle of something about someone flying in from Australia or South Africa when Kwang's patience snapped.

'Just tell me one thing. Will they be at the camp and ready in time? Yes or no?'

'Erm . . .'

'Yes or no?'

'Ye . . . es.'

'Right then. I'll see you there as planned.'

Kwang was about to hang up when the voice hurriedly stammered something down the line.

'What was that?' Kwang snapped.

'My money, Mr Kwang.'

Kwang sighed in exasperation. This current project had occupied him for several months already and his concerns about it centred on matters of far greater import than mere finance. The stakes were possibly the highest he had ever gambled for and to lose would mean . . .

But his mind automatically veered on to a safer track. Failure was out of the question. He wasn't altogether an unreasonable man and he appreciated that not everyone was fortunate enough to be called upon to shape history and the fate of nations. In a voice that could be mistaken for kind, he replied: 'I suggest you check your account again, Major Butler. You might have a very pleasant surprise.'

When he had replaced the receiver, Kwang felt the need to wash his hands. This part of the business was so sordid and vulgar. He crossed the fur rug to the bar and ran the tap until the water lost its mountain-spring iciness and steamed pleasantly. Then, cracking several cubes of ice from their tray in the freezer, he poured himself a generous Scotch and watched it swirl around the smooth blocks in pale-golden luxury. He gently shook the tumbler from side to side, listening to the chink of the ice and, holding it up to the light, watched the patterns shimmering through the perfectly cut glass.

This was the way to begin, he thought. A slow alerting of the senses to the pleasures to come. The music from upstairs had stopped and he knew that Lulu would have heard his conversation end and would be preparing herself to receive him. He wondered how she would surprise him this time.

Sipping the whisky, he was about to make his way to the bedroom when he remembered something. He pushed a small button and spoke into the intercom.

'Yi, could you come up to the house for a moment.'

He had almost forgotten. That wouldn't do at all. The operation was now far too advanced to allow anything to go wrong, not even if Lulu was waiting for her lover. It was already beyond the point of no return. The countdown had started and over the coming days he would have to keep his wits about him. Even while making love.

There was a knock at the door and when Kwang pressed the security button it opened to reveal a fit, lean man in his early thirties. Comfortably over six foot tall, Yi Soong walked like a cat, perfectly balanced, the natural spring of each step disguised in part by military bearing ingrained during his years as an officer in the Republic of Korea special forces. His trim waist and broad shoulders spoke of strength and agility, but it was somehow from his gait and very core that the sense of immense physical power emanated.

'Still no luck?'

Yi Soong's shake of the head was barely perceptible.

'Hm.' Kwang hadn't really believed that they would get anything out of the infiltrator. They were always the toughest individuals to crack, selected, as much as anything, for their ability specifically to resist interrogation.

'It's not good for the men to see, sir. They might start to fear the mettle of the enemy.'

There was a surprising quality about Yi's voice, a sophistication that was masked by his imposing appearance. Kwang had always known that Yi had a first-class brain beneath his close-cropped, jet-black hair. In fact he was an awesome character altogether and Kwang was grateful, not for the first time, that Yi was in his employment. He thought a moment longer.

'Finish him.'

Yi nodded again.

'Rid us of every trace that he ever existed. We can't afford the slightest risk of compromise.'

He gazed out of the window and took another sip of his drink. When he looked back at the door it was closed. Yi had gone without a sound.

Kwang shuddered. Tipping back the glass, he drained it in one gulp, closing his eyes and holding his head back, luxuriating in the twin sensations of the liquid, at once ice-cold and pure fire. Mounting the steps to his bedroom, he pushed open the door and gazed at Lulu. She had removed her nightgown and fallen asleep on the bed. He went and sat down beside her, gently stroking her smooth, unblemished skin, soft and warm. She moaned in her light sleep and, half-waking, rolled on to her back with eyes still closed.

As his hand moved over her stomach and up on to her breasts, Kwang felt them harden beneath his palm. Circling the nipples with his fingers, he felt Lulu wriggle with delight. With eyes still closed she reached up to his neck and pulled his mouth down to hers, opening her lips as they met.

When Babs Butler put down the phone from his conversation with Francis Kwang, he too poured himself a stiff whisky, but for very different reasons.

'The bastard,' he said to himself, his palms moist with nervous perspiration. 'That slant-eyed, gook-fucking bastard.'

He could tell from the Korean's evident impatience that his whore was probably loafing in the background. Babs had seen her when he had been graced with an audience with the great Kwang the other week. He was reluctant to admit that there was a high degree of envy rolled up in his resentment. She was a stunner, one of those gorgeous little Asian tarts that Babs had come to love seeking out on his visits to the brothels in the It'aewan district where the American GIs hung out.

She was called Lulu or something, but who cared about her name? The price-tag was the problem. Kwang had doubtless found her in some high-class joint and for now she was his and his alone. But sooner or later she would end up where girls like her all ended up in Seoul, flogging her raddled wares to some spotty teenaged Yank doing his stint in the army to pay his way through college. By then Kwang would be deep in the knickers of his next young thing, and probably even richer and more powerful than he was now. It made you want to spit.

Babs took a gulp of whisky, refilled his grimy beaker and sank down into a frayed armchair, the centrepiece and only significant furnishing of his sitting-room. He allowed himself the luxury of wallowing for a further five minutes in colourful daydreams of lurid and impossible sexual exploits with Lulu, sinking ever deeper into the shapeless armchair and staring into the middle distance through dull, half-closed eyes.

Starting into full consciousness, he blinked, wiped his mouth with the back of one hand and reached across to a bulging file on the side table. Leafing through the pages, he made a mental tally of the team so far. For once in his life he was proud of himself. Kwang had asked him to recruit the best and he really believed that he had. As he skipped from page to page Babs counted them off, grinning with self-satisfaction.

'Jee-zus,' he said. 'He's going to get the Magnificent fucking Seven and the Dirty Dozen rolled into one!'

He leaned back in his chair and stretched towards the ceiling feeling his joints crack in surprise at the effort.

'The Ghostbusting sodding A-Team!'

Chuckling at his own wit, he pulled himself out of the chair and waddled over to the whisky bottle. He had done it. He had really and truly, bloody done it! When the first discreet enquiries had been made some weeks ago by Kwang's henchman, Babs had marvelled that a guy like that should need a guy like him. Sure, Babs had been good in his day. He had been in the Congo with Mike Hoare, hadn't he? In fact, there was hardly a colonial war or brush-fire campaign that he hadn't seen in one capacity or another. But it had been a while since he had last bloodied his hands. Babs Butler had been an agent for some time, a middleman and go-between, setting up deals and putting together teams for various hirers.

Surveying the miserable suite of rooms that he called home, he found himself wondering where all his earnings had gone. None of it ever seemed to stick. Only shit did that.

Then, one evening when he had been half-cut in a bar near the Wonhyo Bridge, this evil sodding monster with a smile to chill a vindaloo had approached him with a proposal that had set his head spinning. There had followed the meeting with Kwang and . . . Babs your uncle!'

Of course he hadn't a clue what Francis bloody Kwang was up to or what he wanted with the biggest band of cutthroats since Henry Morgan sailed the seven seas. But why should he bother? Kwang had promised him good money and Babs knew he could deliver. The team was due to assemble next Monday. Babs had laid on a little surprise reception for them before they all moved up to a secret training camp near the border where they would be equipped and briefed on the mission. Kwang had said that his own aide would then take charge; Yi the monster was apparently going to lead the expedition himself.

'So, he's not just a pretty face,' Babs had been rash enough to say. By that time his meeting with Kwang had been nearly at an end and Babs had enjoyed several large tumblers of remarkably fine Scotch. Even so, through the haze of his blurring vision he had seen a sweet smile spread across Kwang's face as he repeated Babs's comment to the monster who had been hovering in the background like the earth-bound spirit of some dead relative.

The monster had glided forward without seeming to use his legs and, placing a hand on either arm of Babs's chair, had bent over him, grinning broadly, revealing a perfect set of glistening white teeth that reminded Babs of a Dracula movie he had seen, although this titbit of information he thought it best to keep to himself.

'My name is Yi Soong,' the monster had said with surprising friendliness.

'And what do your friends call you?' Babs had replied, offering him a pudgy hand and hoping that he'd get it back intact. The monster was obviously puzzled by the question, answering it obliquely.

'You can call me Mr Yi,' he had said after a moment's pause, his grin freezing into something much less pleasant.

Babs's hand had hung limply unacknowledged in the air for a second or two before he had replaced it on the reassuring familiarity of his glass. He had smiled meekly at the time, thinking to himself, Well, fuck you, Mr Yi. I'll call you Odd Job if I want.

Remembering the meeting, he chuckled to himself. Almost everything was ready. Looking at his watch he decided to lash out on a decent meal in It'aewan, so pulling on a shapeless jacket and thumbing through his wallet to check his resources, he bounced out of the apartment, locking the door as an afterthought. He didn't have anything worth stealing, but it would be best to keep the file secure.

Once out in the street he took a deep breath of the fumes. The traffic was particularly heavy at that time of day and, having decided to take the subway, Babs pushed through the crowds to the nearest station, bought a ticket and fought his way on to an escalator. Once a month the government held civil-defence drills and for anything up to half an hour the entire city would grind to a halt. Cars were abandoned where they stood and people would pack into the basement shopping arcades and subways, anywhere under cover and out of sight of the notional threat of North Korean aircraft. As they were only a few minutes' flying time from the border, it was essential that the drills were efficient and disciplined. Disciplined? Standing on the escalator and looking around him Babs thought that the people of Seoul made the Germans look like a bunch of pissed Millwall supporters. It never ceased to amaze him how, within seconds of the first siren, the streets would be utterly deserted. But then they would have to be if ever the North really did decide to attack. In that event, the good Lord himself would be hard pushed to deliver the city. The last time it happened, in 1950, Seoul had been fought over at least twice and been flattened in the process. Hardly two bricks had been left standing on top of each other; the next time, who could tell? The North might even play the final card and use nuclear weapons. If they had them, that is.

* * *

Yi had enjoyed his morning workout. It was always so much more enjoyable having a real person to practise on. But then in some respects the prisoner was a disappointment. He had barely uttered a sound and Yi was ashamed to find himself even respecting the man. He seemed to have deep inner reserves that Yi hoped he also possessed.

After leaving Francis Kwang, Yi had decided it was such a beautiful day that he would go for a run before carrying out the directive. He was no simple henchman and enjoyed considerable leeway in the execution of his orders. So, after changing into a trim-fitting tracksuit and trainers, he had strapped on ankle and wrist weights and jogged out of the compound towards the unmade path that led across an area cleared of undergrowth, through a tall barbed-wire fence topped with razor wire, and off down the wooded hillside.

The air was wonderfully fresh and crisp. He fully appreciated his boss's preference for the countryside over the city. Seoul was full of American servicemen and Western or Japanese tourists. The heart of the city had been prostituted to the foreigners, but it wouldn't be for ever.

Having reached the foot of the hill, Yi pushed on up the far side of the valley, selecting a narrow trail that wound through the trees and crossed a stream of crystal-clear water. At the top of the far crest he stopped and looked back over the two miles he had come. The villa was well concealed and could hardly be seen until you were almost upon it. Only the pointed wooden roof could be detected protruding from the green and golden treetops. Yi sought out a branch at exactly the right height, jumped up to grab it and did fifty rapid pull-ups, changing his grip from under to over, halfway through.

Then, down on the forest floor coated with pine needles, he burned through a hundred press-ups and two hundred sit-ups before jumping to his feet and setting off on the return jog back to the villa. It would soon be time for the next international Taekwondo championship and Yi very much hoped that he would be able to compete as usual. But the mission obviously took top priority and if that meant that his competing days were over, then so be it. The need for absolute secrecy might well prevent him taking such a prominent role in the games again, but he had had his day: six times national champion, and world champion twice. His skills these days had a more practical bent. There was a huge difference between facing an opponent across the bare wooden boards of the arena and tackling a sworn enemy, possibly armed, in some backstreet at night.

But he had taken to it like a natural. His time in the ROK special forces had been the first step; there it was not unusual for men to be killed in training. But after that he had met Francis Kwang and nothing had been the same again. It was as if his whole life had been a preparation for this: from his long hours as a serious-minded youth in the training gyms, to his military service, officer selection and special forces work, then his triumph in numerous tournaments and at last the approach by Kwang, one of the top figures in the South Korean intelligence service.

Yi entered the compound and loosened up with some stretching exercises, before steadying his breathing as he had been taught to do long ago by his instructors. Then, with joints and muscles loose and supple, and feeling powerful enough to uproot a tree and snap it in two, he adopted a low fighting stance and went through a few basic punches and kicks.

A door opened on the other side of the yard and one of the guards coughed politely. Yi ignored him for a full two minutes before bringing his exercises to a close.

'What is it?'

The guard bowed from the waist and with a jerk of the head towards the open door behind him, asked: 'What are we to do with him?'

'You are to do absolutely nothing with him. Not yet.' But as an afterthought he asked: 'Have the pigs been fed yet?'

'No.'

'Good. They'll be getting a little extra protein in their diet today.'

The guard looked puzzled for a moment until the light dawned and a thin smile spread across his pock-marked cheeks.

'OK,' Yi said. 'Let's do it.'

Unbuckling his weights, Yi grinned with pleasure at the wonderful sudden lightness of his limbs. He looked full into the sun as if daring it to take him on, and with a final glance around the compound, he followed the guard down into the cellar.

After days of interrogation he was suddenly bored with the prisoner and the whole business of the infiltration into the network. Who cared what he had discovered? In all likelihood he had been found out before he had time to do any real damage. The mercenaries were arriving in a few days, the camp was prepared, and he, Yi Soong, was at the height of his powers.

Placing himself in front of the pathetic creature chained to the wall, he beckoned the two guards aside. Then, after sinking once again into the fighting stance, he waited until, with a great effort, the prisoner raised his head, before speaking softly to him.

In the house overhead, Kwang supported his upper body on clenched fists, his neck muscles hard and glistening, gasping as his pelvis drove forward in urgent spasms. Lulu twisted beneath him on the bed, her tanned legs locked at the ankles in the small of his back, forcing him down and in. She bucked, ever faster, ever softer, then froze, a shriek escaping from her gritted teeth as her nails dug into the taut shoulders of Kwang, who was transfixed on his own summit, suddenly motionless save for the subsiding pulse of his hips, ebbing like a quiet sea.

The motion, when it came, was swift and beautiful in its fluidity and power but terrible in its effect. Yi Soong seemed to draw on some invisible reserve of untold strength, spinning into a reverse back-kick of lightning speed and ferocity.

As his heel made perfect contact with the centre of the prisoner's chest, the dark cellar resounded with the sickening crack, and before the guards had realized what had happened, gaping in mesmerized fascination as if watching a cobra with its prey, the sternum had shattered, puncturing the exploding heart with jagged ribs.

2

Without appearing to, Terry Williams was carefully gauging his opponent. Some new kid who had been watching too many Chuck Norris videos, no doubt replaying particular fight sequences again and again, freeze-framing them to practise later in front of his bedroom mirror when his mum had given him his tea and buggered off to watch *Eastenders*.

The image was so depressing he felt like laughing out loud. Yes, here it came, a bloody great clumsy step forward in preparation for an attack, so obvious to even an untrained eye, he wondered if he had time to slip out for a cup of tea before the kick was landed. What made it worse was the expression on the youth's face, a sort of grimace that might suit Steven Seagal in *Marked for Death*, but smeared across the gob of this pimply git, it made Terry want to throw up.

In it came, the kid's rear leg rising with painful slowness off the floor and coming round at waist height with a final effort to crank it up at the last moment and hit Terry in the face. He was even having a stab at a *kiai*, the shout that was supposed to come from the gut, but in the kid's case was uttered feebly from his throat, sounding more like a newt being stepped on.

Trying hard to disguise his impatience, Terry

brushed away the approaching limb, grabbing the trouser leg as he did so. A look of alarm appeared on the kid's face, replaced a second later by shock as Terry executed an *ashi-barai* footsweep, knocking his opponent's supporting leg from under him and taking him down to the floor. Being a decent bloke at heart, Terry let him down lightly, keeping a firm grip on his clothing. The finishing move would have been a drop-punch to the face, shattering the bone and, if done with full force, fatal. But instead, with one effortless heave, Terry yanked the kid to his feet again and slapped him on the shoulder.

'That *mawashi-geri* is coming along nicely, Matthew. Keep at it.'

With his self-esteem salvaged in front of his mates, the kid blushed and swaggered back to his place on the dojo floor among the other kneeling students. Tossing back greasy locks, he rolled his shoulders as he walked. Get a shift on, Popeye, Terry thought. Run home to mummy for your spinach.

'Right. Let's have you, Barry.'

The training sessions always finished like this. At the end of formal practice, the *kata* and some free-fighting, Terry would take on a few selected students to give them a chance of going all out. In answer to Terry's command, a youth in his late teens sprang to his feet and leapt into the arena. Taking up his position opposite Terry, he bowed from the waist, but kept his eyes alert and fixed on his instructor. Good, Terry thought. Stay alert, stay alive.

'*Hajime*!' With the command to begin, the youth danced backwards to the edge of the arena and moved round to the left, circling, looking for an opening in Terry's guard. Good! Terry was pleased to see the youth's style, his awareness of his opponent, his measurement of the distance between them and his use of the different hand positions.

Terry tried a couple of exploratory moves forward and on each occasion the youth responded as Terry would have hoped, always moving, always changing his position and stance. To remain static was to offer yourself up as a target. What was more, whenever he moved he shifted his weight carefully, maintaining his balance at all times, ready for any attack that Terry might try to throw at him.

OK, Terry thought, come to daddy. After circling a few more times and trying several unoriginal attacking moves, he purposely froze on the spot, breathing heavily as if winded. He allowed his eyes to wander to the clock on the wall behind his opponent. The youth, who also knew it was there, fell for the ploy, hook, line and sinker. In a flash he had closed the gap and was lunging at Terry's face, dropping his centre of balance at the last moment, turning his attack into a feint and using his other fist for the real attack to the solar plexus.

Terry saw it coming but even so the kid was fast and he only just managed to step back in time, dropping his right hand and deflecting the blow with the heel of his right palm in a downwards block. Then, with the youth's momentum still carrying him forward into the space where his target should have been, Terry sidestepped and executed a left punch to the temples. He felt the youth was good enough to take a little pain, so he delivered the blow, albeit at greatly reduced power.

'Good!' he said as the youth sprawled on the floorboards. 'You'll get me yet.'

When the class had been dismissed and the last of them had changed and gone home, Terry turned off the overhead lights and went to his office by the gym's entrance and the notice-boards. It was dark outside and rain swept across the car park. Coming off the Bristol Channel, it drenched the bleak Swansea streets and petered out somewhere over the Black Mountains. He had pulled a tracksuit over his karate *gi* and stepped into a pair of flip-flops. He kept a kettle in the large bottom drawer of his desk, and after making himself a cup of black instant coffee, he sat back and blew on the steam before sipping the strong, dark liquid.

A light flickered in the night outside and he made a mental note to fix the sign over the doorway.

'Karate Dojo – Terry Williams, Fourth Dan. Children's classes every Saturday,' it read.

Yes, there was many a toddler in Swansea simply dying for someone to kick sand in their eyes. Go on punk, make my day.

Terry smiled. He'd be lucky if he could afford this month's rent, let alone buy a new strip light for the sign. The trouble was that kids just didn't have the self-discipline nowadays. He knew he sounded like a dull old fart, but he didn't care; just let anyone say it to his face. Oddly enough, he enjoyed taking the children's class the most. At least they never pretended it was anything but a game. The older kids were the worst. All they wanted to learn were the fancy moves, the stylish spinning and jumping kicks and all that shit. No one ever used that crap in competition, or if you did, you only did it once.

He leafed through some papers in the plastic 'Pending' tray. Most were bills. Since he'd lost his job and had been obliged to rely on the earnings of his karate dojo, things had gone from bad to pig-awful.

Then, out of the blue, he had received the letter from Babs Butler. Terry cursed him for getting in touch again. It wasn't so much that he had specifically told Babs after the last time that he was retiring from that line of business; more that the devious fat bastard should catch him at such a low point when he was vulnerable to a good offer. And the offer was certainly good, suspiciously so.

Terry had never been to Korea and the idea of seeing the Far East again was a big attraction. He had been based in Hong Kong some years back when in the British Army, and had got as far as Okinawa, where he had spent several months training under Master Nishime Higashi, one of the greatest karate masters in the world.

The rest of his army career had been spent among the featureless towns and training areas of the north German plain, preparing for a war that no one ever really believed would come. Disillusioned to the point of despair, he had chucked in his hand and after a period of trying to hold down a job in Civvy Street, had answered an advert in a flashy magazine. Before he knew what was happening, he found himself bouncing along a dust track in central Africa in the back of a Nissan pick-up truck, being fired at by guerrillas with an RPG 7 rocket-launcher.

But all that was several years ago now, and like the world itself, he had changed or, more to the point, grown up. When he was younger he was able to excuse his participation in other people's wars by saying that they would be fighting each other whether he was there or not. Later, however, he grew tired of the sight, sound and smell of death and went home to Wales wanting no more part of it.

He had even married and now had two kids of his own, but it hadn't lasted and his wife had taken the kids with her. He knew that he wasn't the easiest bloke in the world to live with but he bitterly regretted the separation. He kept telling himself that he would patch it up somehow, make it up to his wife and kids, but in his present state, when he couldn't even afford a new strip light for the dojo sign, he was hardly much of a prospect.

Balancing back in his chair sipping his coffee, he jumped when the phone rang. He knew before he picked up the receiver who it would be and, sure enough, a moment later he was listening to the familiar voice again, the sentences punctuated with the unnerving gaps of a long-distance call from the other side of the planet.

'Terry? Is that Terry Williams?'

He didn't answer. Let the bugger guess.

'Have you considered my offer?'

'Yes.'

'I don't like to press you, but I need an answer.'

Terry remembered hearing that everything before the word 'but' is a lie.

'Yes.'

'You'll come, then?'

'Who's putting up the money?'

There was a chuckle at the other end of the line and Terry could imagine the loose, thin lips slobbering into the mouthpiece.

'An old hand like you knows better than to ask questions like that.'

'I just want to be sure that the money's up front, not like that Peruvian fiasco.'

'It's there, trust me.'

'I really would be fucked if I did that.'

The same chuckle repeated itself. 'Look, come over and see for yourself. I'll send you a return ticket and if you don't like the set-up when you get out here, you're free to leave at any time. Can't say fairer than that.'

Terry let Butler stew for a while. What the hell? The rain was lashing against the window, the flickering light had gone out altogether, and he felt suddenly very alone.

'OK, Babs. You've got me.'

'Terrific. I've put together a great team, you'll see. How's Liz?'

'We've split up.'

'Oh, I'm sorry. But at least you're a free man again.'

Before Babs condemned himself with any more 'buts', Terry brought the conversation to a close. Afterwards he sat in the dark for a long time and then did something he hadn't done in a while. He stopped at The Bull on the way back to his bedsit and got horribly drunk.

Pushing himself up the hill into the teeth of the blizzard, Andy Buchan cursed himself to keep going. The pack on his back was almost as big as he was but it was mainly his exhaustion and the biting wind that doubled him over as he laboured up the slope, each step draining his dwindling reserves of energy.

The moment he had heard the weather forecast announce that heavy snow and high winds were expected in the Grampians over the next three days, he had packed his bergen and taken the bus north out of Glasgow. All the way along the banks of Loch Lomond and right on until it finally laboured into the Cairngorms, he stared morosely out of the misting window. The bus was nearly full of tourists and some stupid English bastards had tried to start a sing-song with a selection that even Kenneth McKellar would have spurned. Well, maybe not. But it put Andy in a vile mood anyway.

Not that that was difficult. His temper had been his downfall on many occasions and he had never really bothered to try to master it. For a while the Paras had provided a fitting home for his anger. Selection had been a piece of piss, especially the 'milling', when you had to go all out for the other bugger and do as much damage as you could before the whistle. He'd loved that. The best thing was to get put against an officer. In P Company there was no rank among the candidates and the officers always thought that when it came to milling they were supposed to box. They could handle the assault courses and the tabs but milling was something else. Getting the shit punched out of them by a squaddie was not what they had gone through Sandhurst for.

Sure enough, Andy had been paired with a six-foot artillery captain. He could see the bloke smiling as he sized up the grubby little Glaswegian the PTIs were about to feed to him. Dashed fine of you, he'd probably thought; I promise I'll go easy on the fellow. The silly bugger even had a toothbrush moustache and some of the lads had christened him Aldershot Adolf.

Andy had come out spitting like a scalded cat stroked the wrong way, arms and feet flailing. His opponent had blinked in consternation and attempted a combined jab and hook, by which time Andy was in under his guard and kneeing him in the balls like there was no tomorrow. For the captain there wasn't. He was casualty-evacuated off the course the same afternoon and Andy was threatened with being RTU'd if he tried that again. But he was buggered if he'd return to his unit. The chief PTI gave him a sly wink when he came out of the OC's office.

'Don't worry, lad,' he said. 'It's stuff like that took Goose Green.'

That was just about the only compliment anyone had ever paid Andy and he didn't know how to react. He remembered feeling appallingly shy and embarrassed, and felt like laying one on the PTI himself for being nice to him.

After that he had enjoyed the only stable period in his life and over the next five years had done as many courses as he could, compensating in some way for the truancy that had wrecked his education. Most of them were physical: combat survival, mountaineering, Arctic warfare. He had tried an unarmed-combat course but came away with the conviction that it was purely for wankers. If you had to drop a bloke, simply nut him. Why ponce about with fancy footwork and hand techniques? The instructors had probably never been in a real fight. When it came to a rumble the outcome would depend on guts – that and nothing else.

Eventually he had been recommended for SAS selection and had pushed himself to the limit of his physical ability. He had sailed through all the 'tabs' and endurance tests and everything had been going fine until, yes, his temper got in the way. One of the instructors had cracked a joke at his expense and Andy had seen red. It had taken four of them to get him off the tosser. But that had been that. After returning to his regiment he had gone rapidly downhill. Everyone seemed to pick on him after that and it wasn't long before he decked a subaltern. Then it had been a spell in Colchester and out of the forces.

He didn't even try getting an ordinary job but went straight out and bought a paper to find out where there was a war on, then dropped into his local branch of Thomas Cook, bought a ticket and was off. If Thomas Cook do it, do it. His latest escapade had been in Bosnia with a Muslim militia, but when a bunch of mujahidin had turned up from Afghanistan, they had taken exception to being called rag-heads, even though Andy had meant it as a joke. They had ended up threatening to kill him, whereupon his Bosnian commander had politely notified him that his services were no longer required.

Coming over the crest of the hill, he was almost knocked off his feet by the force of the wind. He sank to his knees and clawed his way forward, the hurtling snow stinging his cheeks and eyes. Pulling on a pair of goggles, he begun to surge ahead, rising once more to his feet as soon as he was over the top and heading down towards the next valley, invisible behind an impenetrable white mask.

His heart thrilled at the challenge. He was out on the edge, the only place where he could feel alive. He felt it every time he approached the brink of death in combat, but here at home this was the closest he could get. Denied an enemy, he pitted himself against the elements; he became his own enemy. And Andy Buchan needed an enemy. It was what kept him going, what convinced him he was alive. He despised a lot of things but most of all he despised anyone who only wanted a cushy life, a soft option. They were the pits and he would die before he became like them. That was why he had leapt at the chance of going East. Major Butler had spelled out the terms as if Andy was some kind of moron. Well, screw him. He would play Babs's little game if it got him what he wanted. And right now he wanted the Korean contract more than anything else.

Reaching the foot of the hill, Andy pushed back his goggles and looked across the valley floor. For a few brief moments the wind dropped and the snow cleared, revealing the lie of the land ahead. The hills had disappeared and instead he found himself facing a snowscape of farmland and distant cottages. A mile away a snowplough was clearing a road down which people would soon be gingerly driving, complaining about the weather and the local council's lack of preparation. Andy Buchan had made it through. He had broken the back of the mountains.

Clearing his throat, he spat savagely in the snow and pulled his goggles down again. He tightened the straps of his bergen, turned and looked at his footsteps in the snow, already disappearing under a renewed fall, and as the wind lashed at him with raging force, he started up the mountainside the way he had come.

Danny Grey Wolf knew there was going to be trouble the moment he saw the row of bikes outside Dog's Diner on the edge of town. For a moment he thought about going elsewhere, but only for a moment. After cutting the engine of his pick-up, he stepped out into the night, the deep treads of his Chippewa boots crunching on the wet gravel of the car park. Driving north from Tacoma to Seattle, he had pulled in off the highway for a drink and some food and there wasn't another place as good as Dog's until you got into town. A Montana man, Danny looked upon cities as places for passing through. Do what you've got to do and get out. If you stayed, you were lost, especially if you were an Indian.

He had seen the Indian drunks down near the waterfront of Puget Sound: sad old men, mostly Nisquali, Yakima and Chinook, with long, black, matted hair, beer guts hanging over shapeless jeans and eyes dulled by the white man's liquor. Danny had last been there to trade in his hunting rifle for a new Winchester. The shelves had been full of automatics, pistols, assault rifles of every kind: M16s, Colt Commandos, Ingrams. How could anyone be surprised that the country was in the state it was? Sure, the right to keep and bear arms was enshrined in the Constitution, but didn't anyone realize that the frontier days had been over since before the turn of the century? What the hell.

He walked along the row of bikes, taking in the *Easy Rider* handlebars, the tassels, the chrome. Eat your heart out, Dennis Hopper. He could almost smell the unwashed hair and picture the overweight, bearded, out-of-condition slobs that would own these surrogate penises. Shaking his head, Danny Grey Wolf sunk his hands in his pockets and slunk into the diner. Right every time, he thought a moment later.

To an observer, the tall, powerful, square-jawed man who entered the diner simply minded his own business, went to the bar and relaxed on a stool. But anyone who had worked with Danny Grey Wolf before would know that within two seconds of opening the door he had evaluated the whole situation, noted every individual present, and correctly divined from which quarter the first trouble was likely to come and in what form.

The man behind the bar looked up. 'Oh shit.'

Knowing Danny as well as he did, Dog cursed his luck that he should come in just now. The bikers would have been going in a few minutes, but with Danny's arrival the writing was on the wall. He had often dropped in when he had been based at Fort Lewis with the Rangers. There were only two Ranger battalions in the whole US Army, one in Georgia and the other here in Washington State, Dog's backyard. The competition was fierce to get into such a small élite and Danny had been one of the top instructors, at least until four years ago. Dog had only heard that Danny had been obliged to leave in a hurry, but he could guess why. His furniture had been reduced to matchwood on more than one occasion.

'Hi there, Dog. Been a long time.'

Dog slid along the bar. 'Shame it wasn't longer.'

'Hey, what kind of a welcome's that? What's the special?'

'Same as ever.'

'Better give me one of those then, fries on the side and a coffee.'

'Coming up,' Dog said, and trying to disguise his one concern as if it was an afterthought, added: 'Be good tonight, Danny. Please, for my sake.'

Danny smiled warmly. He liked old Dog and besides, he was in a good mood. He had received his air ticket that morning and tomorrow would be flying back to his old stamping grounds in It'aewan. God, it was so long since he had been based up on the border alongside the ROKs. There were a few old friends he would have to look up. A few old mamasans too.

He reached up and swept off his baseball cap. There was a hoot from the far corner.

'Well, if it ain't the last of the fucking Mohicans!'

Danny ran his fingers across his scalp. His head was shaved clean except for a two-inch-high ridge of jet-black hair running down the centre from front to back. In the middle of pouring the coffee Dog glanced round, screwing up his face as he saw the approach of the inevitable, swearing as he spilt the scalding coffee on his fingers.

Danny ignored the bikers and thanked Dog when he had the mug between his large hands. It was warm and he relished every sip. He had driven a long way and still had quite a few miles to go before he reached the motel. Farther along the bar another Indian had already drunk himself into a stupor. His eyes were glazed, and tears ran down the deep wrinkles of his face, dropping in pools that mixed with the stale beer.

There was muttering and giggles from the corner and two of the bikers got up from their table and rolled across past the pool table and up to the bar. Flanking the old man, they looked in disgust at his dishevelled hair and grimy coat. He was wearing a battered old hat with an eagle feather stuck in the band.

'You're one sorry son of a bitch. D'you hear me, Hawkeye?'

The old man's head wobbled as he tried to focus on the nearest of the bikers, then snapped back as the other one kicked his stool from under him, sending him to the floor with a crash.

Dog came hurrying over. 'Easy, boys, I don't want any trouble.'

But their real target all along had been the new

arrival, who carried on sipping his coffee. The nearest biker planted his hands on his hips.

'Ain't you goin' to help the old fucker? He's one of yours, ain't he?'

Danny looked down at the old man, now being helped to his feet by Dog.

'Why should I? He's a Nisquali. You've done me a favour. Dog, give these men a beer on me.'

The biker's face reddened. 'Hear that, boys? This Injun's going to share a drink with us.'

From their corner table the other bikers sauntered over to the bar. Danny looked across at Dog and shrugged apologetically.

'Listen, boys,' he tried once more, 'let's all cool down. You go back to your table and I'll move on.'

Shock and surprise registered on Dog's face. He had never seen Danny smile as sweetly before. Nor, for that matter, had he ever seen Danny walk away from a fight. There must be something big on. But by now the bikers could smell blood; and the four of them were spread in a semicircle around Danny.

Danny slowly swivelled round on his stool to face them, his elbows leaning back on the bar, relaxed and casual.

'Do I take it we've got a problem here?' he asked.

'No, Redskin. You've got the fucking problem.'

With that, Danny's stool was kicked out from under him. Landing face down on the floor, he used the spring in his upper arm muscles to absorb the shock of the fall, grunting loudly as if winded. I can do without this, he kept thinking. I can really do without this. Not tonight, not on my last night in the country. Perhaps they've made their point. If I let them have just a little bit more . . .

Encouraged by the ease with which he had put the big Indian down, the biker moved in close to kick Danny in the ribs. Seeing it coming, Danny tilted on to his side and allowed the kick to land in the heavy folds of his woollen jacket. But he was starting to get angry. The bikers had so far been enjoying their stop-over at the diner. They had each had several beers, the best hamburger and fries in Washington State – according to Dog's sign outside – and they had beaten the shit out of two Indians. But when Danny rolled on to his side to take the kick, their luck ran out.

Some years ago Dog had hung a big mirror on the ceiling over the bar, angled down so that whenever a drunk slipped off his stool, Dog could check he was all right without having to come out from behind the counter. But now the man on the floor was Danny Grey Wolf. Still groaning, Danny inadvertently caught sight of himself in Dog's mirror.

'Fuck it,' he muttered. He didn't mind his jacket and trousers being dirtied but what really pissed him off was the spectacle of four white men standing over a Blackfoot Sioux whose forefathers had fought under Crazy Horse at Little Big Horn.

Seeing there was no need for caution, the other bikers had closed in.

'Give it to him, Frank,' one of them goaded.

'Yeah, take his fucking scalp off.'

Rolling on to his back, Danny glared up at the nearest biker, who was about to kick him again. Releasing the full power of one heavily muscled leg, Danny propelled the sole of his boot into the biker's testicles, lifting the man clean off the ground as the underside of the boot made contact. As his attacker toppled forward with a squeal like a stuck pig, Danny caught him by the shoulders and adding the man's forward momentum to the power of his own substantial neck muscles, shattered the biker's nose with his forehead.

Before the others realized that the odds had drastically changed, Danny shoved the semi-conscious biker to one side and drawing up both knees to his chest, sprang to his feet in a single movement. Going straight into a forward roll, he dived through the gap he had created and spun to face the three remaining bikers, whose surprise was already turning to red-hot anger.

The next to come at him was the biggest of the gang, but his size in no way compensated for his lack of speed. Swinging wildly, his fist sailed through the empty space where, a second earlier, Danny's calm, expressionless face had been. Ducking below the punch, Danny brought his balled fist up hard into the man's gut, driving behind it with the full weight of his body and kicking the biker's legs out from under him at the same time. As the man went down like a giant redwood, Danny pushed him from behind so that his chin met the bar on the way, smashing his lower teeth and snapping his neck back with a sickening crack.

Seeing the turn of events, the other two had made a snatch for weapons. One had grabbed a cue from the pool table, the other had taken a lock-knife from his pocket and flicked open the seven-inch blade. Facing them across the writhing bodies of their companions, Danny judged it was time to even the odds. Without taking his eyes off the two bikers, he reached behind him, lifted the tail of his jacket and pulled out a tomahawk.

'Holy shit!' one of the bikers muttered, lunging at Danny's throat with the sharp end of the pool cue. But Danny was already sidestepping and with a single swing of his tomahawk severed the cue and then, changing his grip on the handle with a spin of the wrist, whiplashed the flat of the blade first into the biker's nose and mouth, then into his windpipe.

By now the man with the knife should have been scared, but he wasn't, and Danny instantly changed his tactics to match. Let him come to you, Danny-boy, he thought. See what he's got to offer first. Don't spoil it now. He might look like a fat asshole, but a knife's a knife, whoever's on the other side of it.

The two men circled each other and Danny noted that the biker was surprisingly agile. Twice he feinted with the knife but Danny kept moving back, judging his opponent's proficiency before committing himself to a counter-attack. Then, as the biker lunged again, Danny knocked the blade aside with his tomahawk and lashed viciously at the man's forearm, slicing through the black leather and denim, severing flesh and the tendons underneath. The man winced and leapt backwards. In a wild effort to save himself, he heaved a kick at Danny's groin, but the Indian swung his tomahawk again, this time directing the razor-sharp blade downwards on to the biker's shin. There was a dull thud as it found its mark and for a second it lodged in the bone, then sprang loose as Danny yanked it out and the man went down into a foetal position, hugging his wounded arm and leg.

With the last of the bikers out of commission, Danny walked over to the bar, paused and drained his coffee mug. Dog stared at the bodies.

'I suppose you're going to fuck off now and leave me to make the peace with these assholes?'

Danny grinned at him. 'I've got a plane to catch. You know how it is.'

'Sure I do. Has anyone ever told you you're one mean son of a bitch?'

'Only my friends.'

Danny grabbed his cap off the bar and stuffed it in his pocket.

'Be seeing you, Dog. Take it easy.'

He wiped the blade of his tomahawk on the sleeve of his jacket and was sauntering towards the door when a shout split the air.

'Danny! Look out!'

The deafening roar of a gunshot filled the diner and a bullet cracked past Danny's head, splintering the edge of the door frame. The biker who had pulled the knife was still lying on the far side of the room where Danny had left him, blood pouring from his arm and leg. But with his good hand he was levelling a snub-nosed Magnum at Danny and already steadying his aim for the second shot.

In one fluid movement, Danny spun and dropped, his right arm reaching back over his head, pausing for one frozen moment as he locked eyes with his attacker. Then, with the power of a steel spring, he unleashed his terrible weapon, the blade and handle tumbling end over end towards the biker. It struck with deadly accuracy, finding its target and splitting the man's forehead clean open. With a single grunt, he sank back against the wall, eyes fixed on the ceiling, dead.

Danny slowly got to his feet and walked across to the biker. Dog stared at the figure sprawled on the floor of his diner with a tomahawk sticking out of his head.

'If you're thinking of checking for a pulse, I wouldn't bother.'

Danny sighed. 'I could have done without this.'

'I reckon he could, and all,' Dog added wryly.

Retrieving his weapon, Danny wiped the blade again and made to leave.

'Can you give me a couple of hours before you call the cops?'

'You know I can't do that, Danny,' Dog replied. 'You'd best get going.'

Danny nodded. Why did it always seem to end like this? He eased himself into his pick-up, gunned the motor and pulled out on to the highway. Looking at his watch, he made some quick calculations. He had hoped to relax at the motel in front of the TV, but he could forget that now. Best move on. That seemed to be the story of his life. Always moving on.

3

The rush-hour traffic in Washington DC clogged the air with a thick pall of smoke that made Alex Leitner wish he was back at his desk, but ever since Bill Clinton had taken office it had become the norm for senior executives in both government and business to skip lunch, zip themselves into outrageously expensive designer track suits and be seen jogging in the park instead. Being seen was the crucial part. No one did it to get fit. Who the hell needed to be fit in this day and age? What was the point of screwing the ozone layer with carbon monoxide if you then went and used your legs?

'Hi there, Jack!' he panted as he passed a fellow fifty-five-year-old jogger. 'When the going gets tough, the tough get going.'

'Fuck . . . off,' the senior foreign affairs adviser wheezed.

Another one bites the dust, Alex thought. If this goes on I'll get that promotion after all. Every other sucker will have dropped dead. But in his saner moments he knew that promotion was no longer on the cards for him. His boss had seen to that. Before the arrival of Eliot Masterson, the CIA's Washington office had been staffed with OK guys, but Masterson had changed that seconds after walking through the door. He was one of those characters who was going to rule the world, or so he thought. If ex-CIA boss George Bush could make President, why couldn't Eliot Masterson? Alex hated his kind and all he stood for.

Coming to the end of the park, he slowed to a walk, even though a casual observer would have been hard pushed to see the difference. It was the arms that gave it away: when he was jogging they bounced up and down, his clenched fists level with his hollow chest, but when he walked they just hung down uselessly.

He had managed to park his car near the main gate, and he collapsed into the driving seat, his sodden pants squelching on the blue imitation leather. He had taken longer than expected today and would have to hurry if he was going to be back at his desk by two. Still, he had been seen by a couple of big shots, the first of whom had even told him to screw himself – a sure sign that Alex was liked. It was all good networking.

A short while later, when he was towelling himself after a shower, he found himself thinking about the satellite photographs that had arrived on his desk the week before. It had only taken him a few seconds to realize the significance of what he was looking at. As an intelligence photographic interpreter, he had been working closely with the Korean desk for some months and felt he knew every square yard of the Communist North as if it was his home town.

The first cursory glance had been enough to set the alarm bells ringing in his head as he saw the evidence on the small squares of paper laid out in front of him. It was considerably less sophisticated than a Soviet rocket site, yet the ramps and rails were plain to see and could mean only one thing, that the North Korean nuclear programme was nearing completion.

The bomb might not yet exist, but they were making damn sure that as soon as it did, they would have the facilities in place to launch it.

Naturally Alex had filed an immediate report to Eliot Masterson, the head of department, for onward passage up the line, but it was strange that he hadn't yet been summoned to the full briefing that usually followed any such new discovery. He had sounded out Masterson's secretary, but she had given him the brush-off.

'Ours not to reason how,' she had told him.

'Ours not to reason why.'

'What?'

'I said, it's "Ours not to reason why",' he had repeated as if talking to an idiot, which he felt was probably the case. She had giggled and left it at that. Well, now that a week had gone by he was damn well going to ask the reason why. He had made an appointment and intended to get an answer.

Straightening his tie, Alex was shown into Eliot Masterson's office and left standing in the middle of the carpet while his boss finished reading a letter. OK, you bastard, Alex thought, I've got the message. I'm dirt under your feet. Now get on with it.

Eventually Masterson raised his head and feigned surprise to find one of his subordinates standing there.

'Why, Alex, forgive me. I was engrossed.'

Like a glutton with his lunch, Alex thought.

'What's the problem?'

'No problem,' Alex replied, remembering the golden rule: never admit there's a problem, even if King Kong is on the loose and a rocket full of Martians has just landed on the White House lawn. 'I was just wondering whether you had had time to look over the report I sent in last week about the North Korean nuclear programme. It seems they've been busy.'

'Haven't we all, Alex. Yes, I read it thoroughly and found it deeply interesting. A fine piece of analysis. Well done.'

'And?'

'And what?'

'When are you going to need me to brief the chiefs?'

'I think you can leave that to me. As a matter of fact I don't think it'll be necessary.'

Alex was thunderstruck. The North Koreans were possibly within weeks of acquiring a nuclear weapon and this asshole didn't seem in the slightest concerned.

'If you'll excuse me, sir, if the government in Pyongyang gets its hands on . . .'

Masterson leaned across his desk, the colour draining from his cheeks, and interrupted him brusquely.

'Alex, you've made your point. I think the matter's quite safe in my hands, don't you?'

Alex looked back into the chilling, pale-grey eyes that bored into him. Whatever this bastard was, he wasn't incompetent. Everyone knew that Eliot Masterson was a fast-stream high-flier who was going places. It was just a pity he had stopped off here on the way. But if he said he had things in hand, then who was Alex Leitner, a passed-over loser, to contradict him?

Without another word Alex left the office. It would be Friday soon and then he would be free for two whole days to do what he wanted. He had promised to take his son fishing. They would probably drive down to the Potomac at Chesapeake Bay, or maybe go up to Annapolis. Stephen loved it there and desperately wanted to pass the entrance exams for the Naval Academy next autumn. They would watch the cadets go by in their crisp new uniforms and joke about Alex coming to pick him up at the end of term in his derelict Chevy. Those were the real things, the things that mattered.

But then, with a son in the Navy, the last thing Alex wanted was another war. His own father had fought in Korea the last time round and although Alex had only been a scrawny twelve-year-old, he remembered as if it was yesterday the arrival of the telegram from the Marine Corps and his mother's scream, which had echoed through the house moments later. The last thing he wanted was another Korean war.

As soon as Alex had left his office, Masterson swivelled round in his chair, put his feet up on the window-sill and stared out bitterly at the city skyline. Why should he bother about Leitner? The guy was a burnt-out shell whereas he was the man of tomorrow and it wouldn't be long before tomorrow dawned and he found himself one of the most powerful men in Washington, and therefore in the world.

The sound of the traffic was muffled by the thick reinforced glass of the windows. It was a murky day, partly because of the smog but partly because the grim wastes of the Atlantic were so near. He would far rather have been in California, sunbathing by a pool with the red-roofed villas of Santa Barbara spreading out below instead of this dismal mediocrity. Still, this was the seat of power and to Eliot Masterson power was as essential as oxygen. Later perhaps, he would land some prize political fish like the California governorship as another step on his path to glory, but for now he would have to endure the grey smog of Washington and the pedantic narrow-mindedness of clerks such as Alex Leitner.

He reminded Masterson of the idiots in the UN inspection teams who had been trying for months to gain access to North Korea in order to inspect its nuclear facilities. Did they really expect the world's last hard-line Communist regime to give them a conducted tour of its most highly guarded secrets? Couldn't they see that so long as the government of President Kim Il Sung thought it had one card left to play it would sit it out, happy in its dangerous isolation?

Masterson got up from his desk and walked across to a sideboard where a pot of coffee steamed below a large oil painting of General Cornwallis surrendering to George Washington at Yorktown. He poured himself a cup and stood contemplating the picture for a moment, stirring the coffee with a solid-silver spoon. He had come to this new post as a result of rapid promotion and was set on proving himself one way or another. Let the UN fool themselves if they wished; let them believe that fanatics are open to persuasion and reasonable argument from reasonable men. He knew otherwise. There was only one way to deal with a bunch of maniacs like the North Koreans, even if it involved gambling with the highest of stakes. Unless you were prepared to accept a high risk, you couldn't expect to receive the high gains that came with it.

Back at his desk he pressed the intercom button.

'Julie, I'm not to be disturbed until further notice.'

'OK, Mr Masterson.'

Picking up a handset from the bank of phones, he flicked back a small panel and stabbed at the buttons underneath, before settling back in his chair to await the arrival of his radio signal on the other side of the world. He toyed with the spoon, fascinated by the whirlpool he was able to create and control with a turn of his wrist.

'Hi there, it's me. We'd better turn turkey.'

He reached back to the panel, punched in a code and waited for a small green light to appear, along with the gobbling sound of a scrambled voice at the other end.

'Are you hearing me OK? Terrific.'

It's not so much like a turkey, Masterson thought; more like the guy's got his head underwater. Even so, the words were clear enough and the speaker was easily recognizable as Francis Kwang.

Diving through the thick undergrowth, the two Korean boys flung themselves down the embankment, sending a cascade of loose stones tumbling down the slope faster even than their own bruised and aching bodies. Behind them, shouts and screams echoed angrily through the forest and the harsh white beams of torches criss-crossed in the overhead branches as the guards drew closer.

Little Chiao sobbed as he ran, fighting with all his pathetic might to suppress the terror that had seized him the moment they had vaulted from the trucks as they slowed to take yet another hairpin bend on the painfully slow climb away from the labour camp. Glancing sideways at him, Liang wondered if it had been a mistake to bring the younger boy. By himself he might even have got away unnoticed and then, by the time the idiot guards had done a head count, he would have covered a reasonable distance and would be well on his way to the border and to the freedom that he had heard his father speak of so often.

But since Little Chiao's own brother had been murdered he had attached himself to Liang for the protection that was vital to survival in the brutal environment of the camp. Against his better judgement, Liang had brought him. Then, just as they were easing towards the tail of the truck, Little Chiao had slipped on the wet boards and gone down on his face. Liang should have covered it up by pretending that he was simply helping his friend back to his seat, but journeys outside the compound were rare and he was desperate to try his luck. It hadn't lasted very long. The guard had been sitting up behind the cab and by hammering on the roof had managed to bring the whole convoy to a halt in the space of a hundred yards. Why was Liang cursed with such bad luck?

Suddenly one of the torches locked on to them. The screams rose to a frenzy and a second later the guards opened up with their Kalashnikovs, sending a wild hail of bullets crackling through the forest. All around them branches splintered and whistled. Little Chiao cried out and for a moment Liang thought he had been hit, but catching sight of his friend's terrified face in the torchlight, he realized the shout had been a warning. Liang turned back a moment too late, missed his footing and pitched head first over the drop and into the darkness.

He must have passed out for a few seconds because the next thing he knew was the feeling of an arm around his neck, holding him above the freezing water of the river. He tried to speak but a small hand was clamped over his mouth and he twisted round to see Little Chiao grimacing and pointing upwards. Torch beams still swept the undergrowth but seemed farther away now. There were bursts of gunfire as the guards fired into the dense bushes and anywhere that might conceal the two runaways.

It was a cloudless night and the moon cast a silvery glow on the water's surface. In the ghostly light Little Chiao's wide eyes were as huge as saucers and Liang felt a sudden flood of gratitude for his friend, who had probably saved his life. He was just about to risk a hushed thank you, when he heard a new sound, still far off but, unlike the bursts of gunfire, getting closer. Dogs.

A sob burst from Little Chiao before he could help himself. Then he put his mouth close to Liang's ear and said: 'What are we going to do now? The dogs will find us and you know what they'll do.'

Liang knew only too well. Barely a month had passed since the whole camp had been paraded to witness the punishment of a youth who had been recaptured only hours after escaping from a work detail. They were made to form up in a hollow square and then, as they watched in horror, the fugitive's hands were tied behind his back, he was led into the middle and the dogs were set on him. Liang thought the youth was still alive when the dogs were pulled off some minutes later and the body was dragged away, but it would have made no difference. The medical facilities at the camp were reserved for the guards; prisoners were forced to make use of whatever herbs they could smuggle in from outside, and for the sort of wounds that the youth had sustained there wasn't a medicine in the whole of North Korea that would have helped.

'We must stay in the water,' he hissed. 'Follow me.'

And then, without believing it himself, he added: 'We'll be all right, I promise you.'

Pushing away from the bank, Liang allowed the current to take him. With his left hand he gently swam with the river while his right fist kept a firm hold on Little Chiao. In the centre of the river the current was powerful and it took all of Liang's strength to keep his head above the surface. Trailing behind him, the younger boy paddled furiously, spluttering and gulping for air.

As the current took them faster and faster, it was strangely comforting, as if an invisible force was whisking them to safety. Liang even found himself wondering at the events of the whole extraordinary day. The trucks had arrived without warning soon after their breakfast of rice and watery tea. There had been twelve of the big Chinese vehicles and he had quickly seen that all but four of them were already full. In one of the trucks a man had peeled back the canvas side and was peering out. He was an old man with white hair and Liang had also been able to see that the other people in the truck were a mixture of men and women, old and young; there was even a baby which a woman was holding to her breast. But then the man had been spotted and the guards had screamed at him to sit down as they rushed to refasten the flap.

About forty of the boys from Liang's youth labour camp had been selected and told to board the trucks. Liang had overheard two of the guards talking. One of them had asked if he should order the boys to pack their few personal items, but the other had just laughed in response. Liang had thought about this as he had climbed aboard but his mind had soon been sent spinning in a new direction as he peered occasionally through a rip in the canvas and contemplated his escape. It had been rumoured that some of them were soon to be moved to a new camp and the bundles of new clothing that they found in the truck convinced them that this was now happening. Liang knew that any new camp would be just as heavily guarded as the last one, maybe even more so, and that as the son of a well-known political prisoner he could never expect to be released. Escape was his only chance of freedom.

Floating downstream, Liang was suddenly jolted by the realization that the current was taking them towards the sound of the barking dogs. In a panic he swung himself around and tried to kick against the river, but it was useless. He and Little Chiao were now firmly in its grasp. The next moment they heard voices from the bank behind a screen of trees.

'I don't care. The trucks have got to be at Wonsan by dawn.'

'But we were specifically told to deliver a set number, divided up by age and sex.'

'I don't give a stuff. If the Commandant doesn't take delivery by midday at the latest you'll be floating face down in the river yourself.'

Liang couldn't see the speakers but as he tried to ease his way towards some drifting branches for better concealment, a shout from behind pierced the night.

'There they are, the little fuckers! Get the dogs over here!'

A burst of fire from a sub-machine-gun rattled across the water, the bullets stinging into the river in tiny trails of spray.

Yanking Little Chiao by the hand, Liang dragged him back towards the middle of the river, where the current was strongest, and kicked with all his might, shouting: 'Swim! Swim for all you're worth!'

Twenty yards away, on the nearer bank, a handler thrust through the bushes, a brace of huge black dogs tugging at their leash, berserk and almost roaring with the excitement of the hunt. Then another guard appeared, aimed his Kalashnikov and emptied a full thirty-round magazine into the water at Liang and Little Chiao.

Liang's ears were ringing with the noise of the bullets, the water and the terrified screams of Little Chiao.

'It's no use, Lan-Lan! It's no use! They've got us!' And as if to confirm it, another spray of bullets whined all around them.

Exhausted by the river and half-deafened, Liang felt the last of his strength draining from him. He turned to look at his young friend one last time, smiled weakly, tightly clasped his hand, and dived.

Thirty thousand feet over the Bay of Bengal, Terry Williams was trying to decide whether to have the lamb dish or the chicken chasseur. He couldn't remember if the chasseur was the one in the red wine sauce. He had had it once at a restaurant in Cardiff and liked it, but looking across the aisle at the passengers who had already been served, he settled for the lamb and sat back ready to order.

His seat was right at the front of economy class, and peering through the dark-blue curtain he could see that the business-class passengers were well into their meal and being served with champagne in real glasses. That was just typical of Babs bloody Butler. A man could risk his life for truth and justice and a better world, but Babs would still send him a sodding economy ticket. Terry had never travelled business class in his life and every time he flew he made a promise that one day he would treat himself to it. First class was another world altogether and he scarcely bothered to contemplate it.

Once in his army days, he had been flying back from Germany with a captain from his own regiment. There had been some mix-up over the allocation of seat numbers and Terry's had been double-booked. The officer had sat there grinning, saying that Terry would have to fly in the baggage compartment, when the steward had come along to sort it out. There had been some spare seats in business class, but instead of upgrading Terry's ticket, they moved the captain forward and gave Terry his economy seat. The bastard had gloated about it for weeks. Still, Terry had got his own back at the next Christmas party when the officers came to the sergeants' mess for drinks. He had roped several of his mates in on the plan. They had laced the captain's drinks, got him pissed as a rat, stripped him stark bollock naked in the toilets and sent him wandering off through the barracks. The officer's wife had not been amused, particularly by the photos in the next edition of the regimental magazine.

With his meal finally in front of him, Terry set to work, fighting to hold his elbows down in the confined space. He would have a word or two to say to Babs when he arrived.

Just before the meal had arrived, Terry had made a trip to the toilets at the back of the jumbo. Scanning the sea of faces on the way, he had recognized the vicious little Scot. Andy something, he thought. They had worked for the same side in Angola. What a bloody mess that had been! Training the UNITA guerrillas of Jonas Savimbi had not only paid badly, but the end result had not been up to much. Even when most of the Cubans had left, Terry's team had still been unable to better the opposition. He had seen the writing on the wall and got out soon afterwards when the war deteriorated into just another intertribal feud, with the innocents caught up in the middle as usual.

The Scot, on the other hand, had had a terrific war. Terry remembered some of the stories circulating about him, most of them no doubt originating from the twisted little bugger's own relentless gob. How he had foiled an enemy ambush, how he had captured a position single-handed, how he had cleared a path through a minefield with his commando knife while the engineers looked on from the sidelines. But not all of it was bullshit. Terry had seen him in action in the bush near Mussende. A bunch of South Africans had got themselves pinned down and the Scot had led his team on a wide flanking move that caught the enemy by complete surprise. Terry's platoon had been held in reserve on a hillock on the Umpolo road and had enjoyed the grandstand view as the Scot went screaming in from the side, rolling up the enemy position and winning the day.

The South Africans had given the Scot first pick of the captured weapons, which Terry thought was jolly decent of them, seeing as they would all have been butchered if he and Andy hadn't shown up. There had been a real mixture of stuff, piles and piles of it. Russian AK74s, the brand spanking new 5.45mm assault rifle, RPK light machine-guns, some Chinese Type 56s – their own version of the older Russian AK47 – and the thing that had been doing most of the damage: an AGS 17 grenade-launcher that had a very nasty habit of accurately lobbing 30mm grenades over half a kilometre.

But what had appalled Terry was the Scot's treatment of the enemy wounded. He had mumbled something about not having the rations to feed extra mouths and had gone through the scrub finishing them off with a captured Chinese Type 59 9mm pistol. Terry had not arrived on the scene until the killing was over and had been incensed, but the South Africans had sided with the Scot and the UNITA guerrillas didn't seem to know what the fuss was about, so there hadn't been anything Terry could do.

Except leave, which he did soon afterwards. Since then he had only taken part in specific missions. Brush-fire tribal wars were too open-ended and brutal for his liking. Some mates had tried to persuade him to go with them to Bosnia, but things had been going fairly well with the dojo at the time and he and Liz had been trying hard to make a go of their marriage once again. So, while some of the lads had packed up and gone off to what was now cryptically called 'the former Yugoslavia', he and Liz had left the kids with her mum and gone for a weekend in Snowdonia. It had hardly been a great success; Terry wanted to shin up the mountains while Liz insisted on spending hours in the bloody visitor centres. They had made love twice, but the first time the walls of their room in the bed and breakfast had been paper-thin and they could hear the couple on the other side attempting to do the same, and the second time Liz kept talking about the cost of a cream tea they had eaten that afternoon. It had all ended up in a huge row and another split.

When Terry had finished his meal and searched

every little envelope and plastic container to make sure he had eaten everything, the air hostess collected his tray and pulled back the blue curtain leading into business class to give Terry a clear view of the overhead screen.

'Your seat's too far forward to see the screen in the economy section, sir, but it's exactly the same movie in business class,' the hostess said.

'Are you sure I won't contaminate them, love?'

The hostess laughed and walked away, smiling stiffly as if she had just trodden in corgi shit at a Buckingham Palace garden party.

After plugging his headphones into the armrest, Terry turned the dial to the correct channel and settled back to enjoy the film, which he had been dying to see. After the preliminary advertisements reassuring everyone that they had made the best possible selection in their choice of airline, the titles rolled, the action began, and Terry discovered that the soundtrack being broadcast to his economy seat was out of sync with the pictures on the business-class screen. As the heroine opened her mouth to speak, a deep male voice boomed in a Germanic accent: 'Screw you, asshole.'

Fighting to control his temper, Terry took a couple of deep breaths and took off his headphones, dreaming blissful images of Babs Butler tortured by the Spanish Inquisition.

As the plane droned high over central China, Terry tipped his head back, closed his eyes, steadied his breath, and went through the basic hand techniques. Resting lightly on his knees, his hands became a series of deadly weapons, one after the other, each pair of weapons perfectly suited to a particular lethal task. The basic fist *seiken*, the knife hand *shuto*, the palm heel *shotei*, *haito* the ridge hand, *boshiken* the thumb fist, *yubi hasami* the finger pinch, *washi de* the eagle hand, *kuma de* the bear's paw, *keiko ken* the phoenix-eye fist, on and on. And then the whole list was repeated. The techniques had been ingrained through years of training and relentless self-discipline until they were part of his very being.

Startled by a hand pulling gently at his sleeve, Terry opened his eyes to see a little girl leaning across from her seat on the other side of the aisle, grinning at him.

'I can do that too,' she said, interweaving her fingers. 'Look. Here's the church and here's the steeple. Open the door and here's all the people!'

Terry smiled at her waggling fingers.

'Come on, you try it,' the girl persisted, and a moment later Terry's favourite *nukite* finger-thrust, capable of crushing a man's windpipe, had dissolved into a chapel full of pious Welshmen.

Kneeling astride Babs Butler's naked thighs, the woman moved rhythmically, driving forward in sharp lunges, grinding her buttocks downwards, forcing him deeper into her. Grasping her by the hips, Babs rocked back and forth, reaching up to caress her breasts, the wine-dark nipples taut and quivering. He circled one with his thumb until she threw back her head and moaned, her long, black hair cascading down her arched back, thrusting her breasts sharply forward into his coaxing palms.

Nearing the end, the woman doubled forward, dropping her head and bucking furiously, racing, flattening her stomach against his. Their bodies glistened with sweat and as Babs thrust savagely into her, he clasped at her buttocks, thighs, shoulders, frantic in the final moments as lights exploded behind his eyes and he shot into her moments before she cried out, shuddered and collapsed across his chest, panting hard.

Opening his eyes, Babs looked up at the fan circling lazily on the ceiling, then lifting the woman's head, stroked back her hair, kissed her and held her face between his hands.

'Michelle, you're getting bags under your eyes. Too much shagging's not good for you.'

The woman bared a broad set of white teeth, her almond eyes narrowing at him like a cat's.

'Babs will be good to me. You take care of me, no?'

'Sure I will. When Babs got plenty money, he give you very special present.'

Michelle's face lit up. Babs nodded.

'Just you wait and see.'

She reached down between his legs and took him lightly in her hand.

'This present?'

'No. Other special present.'

A look of puzzlement crossed Michelle's face. 'I no understand. We go holiday?'

'How would you like long, long holiday?' Babs asked, watching her changing expression with delight.

'You mean we go away? Leavey Seoul?'

'Yes,' he nodded. 'We leavey Seoul. For good. You, me. Like real couple.'

Unable to contain her joy, Michelle threw herself on Babs and hugged him tightly until he could hardly breathe. Easing out of her arms, Babs slid out from underneath, swung his legs off the bed and reached for a cigarette. He stared down at his soft, flabby stomach, where no sign remained of the muscles that had once coated it. His legs were still strong but he winded quickly. There was no denying it: he was way out of condition. What was more, he knew that he would never again be properly fit. His life from now on would be a steady decline through a series of illnesses to eventual and inevitable dissolution. What a bitch, he thought.

Michelle had sprung off the bed and was sitting naked in front of a mirror combing her hair. Babs looked at her back and long, brown legs. She too had seen better days, but he still felt a thrill whenever he saw the genuine delight in her eyes when she opened the door and saw him standing there. He knew that she really liked him. 'Loved' would be too strong a word perhaps, but then again, why not? Stranger things had happened. Watching her brisk movements and listening to her shrill humming, he resolved to stick to his word this time. He really would come for her. They would be a couple and make something of themselves with whatever time they had left.

She caught sight of him in the mirror and smiled warmly.

'Babs, you good man. You know that?'

He smirked. 'Don't you believe it.'

Wrapping himself in a sarong, Babs walked over to the window and peered through the slats. It was raining outside and the coloured neon lights blurred in the puddles as people splashed through them. The thought of stepping out into the bustling crowds depressed him. He went over to the stool and sat beside Michelle, taking one breast in his hand and kissing the nipple.

She closed her eyes with pleasure but gently pushed him away.

'No time now, Babsy. No time.'

There never was, he thought, getting to his feet with a heavy sigh and shuffling to where his dishevelled clothes littered a corner of the spartan room. He would rather go now while there was still the illusion of love, before the tentative knock at the door, reminding them both that they lived in a harsh world and that her next client would soon be stumbling up the poorly lit stairs, drunk on his own brand of dreams.

4

Looking around the large private dining-room of the Golden Carp restaurant, Babs Butler smiled at the sixteen mercenaries assembled before him.

'Welcome to Seoul, gentlemen. I think I'm right in saying that you all know me, or at least know of me, so I won't bother with a lengthy introduction.'

Sprawled in a chair at the back, a large Australian shouted: 'Thank buggeroo for that.' A couple of men laughed, but most sat stony-faced. Babs nodded good-naturedly.

'Thank you, Ken. Remind me to fuck up your account number when I sort out the bank drafts.'

'There'll be a draught between your eyes if you do, mate.'

'Be that as it may,' Babs continued, 'I welcome you all to Seoul and to what I'm sure will be a profitable and successful enterprise. Now, for obvious reasons I am going to keep this short. You're all here to do a job and you'll be fully briefed on the task in a few days. But for now there are just a couple of points I want you to take in. Firstly, security. It won't come as any surprise to you that you're being sent somewhere where you really oughtn't to be.'

A ripple of cynical laughter spread around the tables.

'That being so, there are going to be a lot of people trying to make sure firstly that you don't get there, and secondly that you don't make it back. I hardly need emphasize that you'll stand a better chance of fucking up their plans if you all keep your traps shut. So tonight, when you're pie-eyed and in the voluptuous arms of your latest conquest, don't start mouthing off about what a big-shot mercenary you are and how you're going to do this and that to so and so. Get the message?'

'Yes, Mr Butler, sir,' came the chorus from the floor.

'Good. My next point is an admin one. I've put you in different hotels around the city, all part of my fiendishly clever plan to avoid drawing attention to ourselves. Don't whinge that Fred's in a better hotel than you are, because if you were all at the Hyatt or the bloody Savoy, it'd be rubble by the time we moved on.'

'That's all very well,' piped a South African, 'but why the hell do I get the bloody YMCA?'

'Hey, mun. Got the bleddy YMCA, hev you?' the Australian hooted in imitation.

The South African turned round, glowering darkly, and said: 'That's ripe coming from a bloody sheep-shagger like you, man.'

'. . . a bleddy ship-shegger like you, mun,' echoed the Australian.

'I'm glad to see you all getting on so well,' Babs continued quickly. 'Now, before this ends in tears, to conclude my admin points, you've been split up for a reason and I would be grateful if you would keep it that way. So, even if you recognize a mate that you haven't seen since butchering babies ten years ago, say hello now, but when you leave this room, go your separate ways.'

He paused to take a sip of whisky. 'Lastly, you are all to rendezvous at the address on the card I will shortly give to each of you, at the day and time stated. Transport will pick you up at the spot and take you to our next meeting place. Anyone who's late or decides to sleep in and misses the RV is on his own and his contract's terminated. Is that clear?'

Heads nodded.

'Sorry, gentlemen, I can't tell if that's an affirmative or if you're falling asleep.'

'Yes, Mr Butler, sir!' came the unanimous answer.

'Lovely. What happy campers we all are! By way of an appetite-whetter, I will simply say that after being picked up you will be transported to a training camp where you will be equipped and do some warm-up and familiarization training.'

'Bloody 'ell,' a cockney voice called out. 'They came in search of paradise and found . . . Babsy.'

'Not quite,' Babs continued once the laughter had died down. 'I'll be at the camp but sadly I won't be accompanying you on the mission.'

'Who's in charge, then?' someone shouted.

'A gentleman you've yet to have the pleasure of meeting,' Babs answered with some satisfaction. Yi Soong will shut the buggers up, he thought. We'll see how verbose that Aussie git is by the time Yi's finished with him.

'Are there any questions?'

One or two of the men asked about the method of payment and someone else started probing for details of the mission. When he had answered the pay queries and deflected the operational question,

Babs stood up and clapped his hands theatrically.

'Right then, you've been a wonderful audience and I love you all! Tonight is for merriment, so I've arranged a little treat for you. Maestro, play!'

With that, the double doors behind him swung open and a line of girls in Korean national dress danced into the room, followed by drummers and a line of waiters balancing trays of food.

As the girls twirled and spun in time to the music, the Australian groaned loudly. 'Christ, I didn't come all the way from Oz for a fucking cultural show.'

But before anyone else could agree with him, the girls loosened the ribbons that fastened their flowing pink dresses, which gently slid from their shoulders until they were dancing naked. An enormous cheer went up, and as beers and dishes heaped with food were distributed to all the tables, Babs sat slumped in a chair, mopping his brow with an unusually clean handkerchief and watching with pride the team he had assembled, a selection of some of the most dangerous men in the world.

When Terry Williams saw the dancers slip out of their dresses he knew it was time to go. At first he had thought he was in for an entertaining evening and had been on the verge of congratulating Babs on his planning. But as he looked at the expression on Andy the Scot's face, leering at the closest of the girls, he realized that Butler was still the same old Babs. Why can't he realize that we're not all a bunch of animals, he thought. Some of us have got principles even if they are a bit flexible at times.

Declining an offer from one of the girls to dance, and

negotiating his way around the tables from which his fellow mercenaries were being pulled on to the floor in what seemed to be turning into an orgy, Terry weaved across to Babs.

'Why, Dojo!' Babs shrieked, opening his arms wide as if welcoming the prodigal son. 'Long time no see.'

Terry winced at his old nickname. Hearing it on Babs's lips conjured up images from the past, not all of which were pleasant to remember. They had seen a few wars together and been in a number of tight corners. The nickname had been coined by a Londoner, himself a karate instructor. He had once overheard Terry saying how much he would like to open his own karate dojo, and for no particular reason the name had stuck, long after the Londoner had died in an African ditch from a stomach wound and Babs and Terry had moved on to other countries and other wars.

As Babs was obviously not about to be parted from his chair, Terry crouched beside him.

'Listen, Babs, this isn't really my scene,' he said, indicating the girls and the mercenaries, most of whom were already well on their way to being horribly drunk. 'I think I'll slope off and take in some of the sights.'

'Same old Dojo, I'm glad to see. As you please. You'll miss a great show. I've got a few other surprises in store for the lads.'

Terry had a fair idea what they might be. He also noted with distaste the way Babs said 'the lads'. It reminded him of the sort of officer in his old regiment who employed the term in the belief that it would somehow make him one of the lads. It never had and it never would. Looking at Babs's floor show, Terry couldn't help feeling like a citizen of ancient Rome, fêted with games and vulgar morsels by an emperor trying hard to conceal an underlying contempt for his populace.

He forced a smile that Babs, his senses blunted by two double whiskies, took to be genuine warmth. Making his way to the door, Terry went out into the corridor, down a flight of steps and out into the street. He had picked up a street map from the dressing-table in his hotel room, so once he had got his bearings and pinpointed the restaurant in the Seoulin-dong nightclub district, he decided to walk a few blocks north and have a look at the Kyongbok Palace.

Strolling through the crowded streets, he soaked up the battery of sights, sounds and smells. He always relished the first impressions of a country, and did his best to open his senses wide and take it all in without prejudice or expectations. In many ways Seoul reminded him of Hong Kong. On the surface, it was one of those modern prosperous Asian cities that were springing up all around the Pacific rim and which were tipped to be the dominant trading centres in the next century. Terry could well believe it. There was a vibrancy and sense of urgency and direction that had long vanished from the streets of London, Paris and Berlin; everywhere he saw people getting on with life. They didn't have time to moan about what was owed to them or about how terrible it was that the government wasn't doing more to help them solve their own personal problems. Perhaps it was because over the centuries they had grown accustomed to survival under a series of tyrants. To them, democratic government was an unknown concept, and by the time it arrived their tradition of survival and of driving ahead using their own wits and determination was ingrained.

As he scanned the high-rise buildings, the packed

markets and shops, and the streets clogged with the latest Japanese cars, Terry found it hard to believe that forty years ago the city had been rubble. After crossing Samchong-no Street, he entered the park surrounding the Kyongbok Palace and gardens. There appeared to be no one in the gardens at this late hour, which made it all the more enjoyable as far as Terry was concerned. As he strolled along the tree-lined pathways he could make out the rise and roll of the surrounding hilltops. His route wound through old-style pavilions, statues of Buddhist deities, and ornamental ponds, and eventually led him to the foot of steps that climbed through a series of levels up to the imposing five-tiered roof of the National Museum. He stared up at it and whistled. Nothing like this in Swansea, he thought. Brushing past some rhododendron bushes, he moved towards the steps.

The speed with which his reflexes operated never ceased to amaze Terry. After years of training they had acquired a life of their own; it was rather like having an ever-watchful bodyguard on hand at all times, almost a separate person who was ready to spring to his defence when required. So it was now.

Although he was hardly conscious of the knife and the dark shape of a man looming behind it, even as it was being thrust towards his side Terry's body was moving to face the attack, his right arm scything down, his hand open in a *shotei otoshi uke* palm-heel block. His head whipped round, eyes seeking out his opponent and locking on to him with the speed and precision of a missile. In a fraction of a second, Terry Williams had switched from being an inquisitive Western tourist, easy prey for a mugger, to the lethal fighting machine that had earned him the nickname of 'Dojo'.

Driving into the attacker's wrist, Terry's block pushed the knife harmlessly aside as if it was a toy. Calculations spun through his brain as he did so, evaluating the enemy and the situation, deciding on his own response. There was no question of pulling his counter-punch; the attacker's intention was as clear as if it had been written on the blade itself. As Terry's reflex defensive block flowed into an automatic counter-attack, his thigh and leg muscles locked in place, fixing him to the ground as solid as a launching platform, and his left fist powered away at lightning speed, the twin knuckles of the index and middle finger clenching into the *daikento*, the concentrated area of bone into which Terry focused his entire strength and life-force. As it met the space immediately below the attacker's nose, Terry's *kiai* shattered the night and the mugger was flung backwards like an unwanted doll.

Before the body had hit the ground, Terry was turning, executing a *mawashi-uke* double block as he did so. The standard precautionary measure paid off as he found himself facing two more men, both short and powerful, the nearest of whom was already delivering a ferocious front kick that might have caught Terry in the small of the back, shattering his spine. Instead, the Welshman's right forearm swept it up and with a forward drive from the hips, he tipped the man off balance, dropping him to the ground.

Terry had no time for a drop-punch to finish off the third mugger. However, having seen how he dealt with the two previous attacks, the man faltered and held back, preferring to size up this unusual tourist before trying for an opening. That was his big mistake. Switching from defence to attack, Terry went into action. His blood was up and he was out to fix the bastards who had spoiled what might otherwise have been a pleasant stroll.

Gliding forward with swift, measured steps, Terry feinted at the retreating mugger with a blinding series of punches and kicks, dazzling him with the display until it was impossible to guess from which quarter the real attack would come. When it did it was a roundhouse kick from an unexpected direction, and as the ball of Terry's foot slammed into the man's jaw he crumpled in the dirt, his eyes rolling in his head and shutting out the image of the Welsh tornado.

Fully aware that the second man would by now be on his feet again, Terry went into a forward roll, turned and lunged forward at the point where he judged the man would now be. Instead he was barely able to avoid launching himself at a tall, thickset man with a Mohican haircut.

'What the . . .?' Terry shouted as he pulled his punch an inch short of the man's face. The man grinned and Terry noticed that he was holding a tomahawk. The second mugger was lying silent and unmoving on the floor at his feet.

'Oh shit,' Terry groaned.

'It's OK,' the Indian quickly reassured him, 'he's just getting some shut-eye.' And by way of explanation he smacked the flat of his tomahawk blade on his other palm.

'That's a relief,' Terry said, smiling. 'I thought you'd bloody scalped him.'

The Indian kicked at the man's jacket with the toe of his boot and a pistol slid out on to the pathway.

'This one had a sting in his tail, I heard the noise and saw him pulling the pistol from his pocket while you were busy rearranging his buddy's face.' He gestured to the nearby body. 'Nice footwork.'

Terry shrugged, then remembering the first attacker, went to look among the rhododendrons.

'I'm afraid that one got away,' the Indian called over, checking the other muggers for signs of life. Terry scratched his head.

'Oh dear. Must be losing my touch.'

'I don't think he'd agree. I caught a glimpse of him and his nose seemed turned inside out.'

Wondering what to do with the two unconscious men, they decided to heed Babs's warning about drawing attention to themselves. Instead of calling the police, they dragged the muggers back to the main road, stripped them naked and used their clothing to tie them securely to a lamppost.

'Let them talk their way out of that when the next patrol car passes by,' said Terry with a wicked grin.

Checking that they hadn't been seen, they jogged across the road and headed off down Taepyong-no Street, back towards the hotel district, several blocks away. As they parted, Terry held out his hand. 'Terry Williams. Thank you for what you did back there.'

The Indian grinned. 'I'm glad you're on my side. The name's Danny. Danny Grey Wolf.'

Terry whistled. 'Not many folks in Swansea with a name like that. Well, Danny, this could be the start of a beautiful friendship.'

The camp consisted of a cluster of wooden huts in the bottom of a steep, forested valley. An assault course had been built along one side of the camp, and along the other white-painted stones marked out a rifle range some six hundred yards long. A firing point was similarly marked every hundred yards to enable firers to practise with different weapons from a variety of known ranges.

Andy Buchan felt immediately at home the moment he set eyes on the huts as his truck rumbled over the crest and began its descent to the training camp.

'Now that's what I call a hotel,' he bragged. Ken, the Australian, spat over the side.

'Listen to him. Fucking beam me up, Scotty. I don't know what planet you're from, mate, but down here we call that a shit-hole.' He leaned across and thrust his face towards Andy's.

'Repeat after me: shit-hole.'

Andy reddened and the men on either side of him had to hold him in his seat as Ken laughed and said: 'Only kidding, mate. Nothing personal.'

To Andy Buchan any slight was deeply personal. He would remember the Australian and sort him out. He always did, sooner or later. Consoled by the thought of future revenge, he slumped back on the bench and grinned.

'Sure, mate. Nothing personal.'

With the mercenaries concentrated at the training camp, Babs put them through a couple of days of simple warm-up exercises before Yi Soong arrived to take over the real training. A daily routine was quickly established whereby the men were woken early and pushed over the assault course three or four times before a light breakfast. During the rest of the morning they practised on the firing range.

The basic personal weapons issued to the men were the American M16 and the Colt Commando, both using interchangeable 5.56mm ammunition. In addition there were four of the tried-and-tested British general-purpose machine-guns, a seemingly endless supply of M72 single-shot disposable rocket-launchers, boxes of grenades, M79 and M203 grenade-launchers, an M202 Fireflash, and two American 60mm light mortars complete with a range of ammunition, high-explosive, white-phosphorus smoke bombs, and para-illuminating shells.

Andy Buchan was in his element, pitting himself against the assault course and then, after breakfast, being handed an array of the best weaponry in the world and ammunition to match, and told to blaze away on the range. He passed each day like a schoolboy on the loose in a toy shop; until the third day and the arrival of the new commander, Yi Soong.

The moment he set eyes on the tall, broad-shouldered Korean ex-special forces officer, Andy Buchan felt an intense dislike that was, in a matter of hours, to distil into hatred. For his part, Yi Soong was scrupulously polite, tactful and almost too solicitous of the welfare of his men. He seemed displeased that Babs had them running over the assault course, and immediately ensured that they finish each day's training two hours earlier. He arranged for a truckload of beer from Seoul and set up a canteen where everyone was entitled to four free cans of San Miguel before they had to start paying.

'This is more like it,' Ken said one evening. Andy was silent, staring into his mug. Ken prodded him lightly, having learnt that it was best to tackle the little Scot with caution.

'What's the matter, Scotty? Don't you like his face?'

'No. He's a smooth bastard and I'd like to stick one on him.'

Ken chuckled, popping open another can. 'I wouldn't try it if I was you, mate. You might not like his face, but there's one big fucker underneath it. Inscrutable fucking Orientals, that's what I say.' He belched. 'Don't trust 'em if you like, but there's nothing wrong with their money.'

The next day Terry Williams and Danny Grey Wolf were cleaning their rifles after a session on the range. Since their encounter in the park they had become friends and whenever a team effort was required for any of the tasks they naturally drifted together. Andy Buchan had tried to join in but neither of the other two men seemed particularly keen to encourage him.

They had stripped down the rifles and were scraping the carbon off the breech-blocks before oiling them, when Yi Soong came up and started to chat. He asked where they came from and about their military qualifications and battle experience.

'I can expect you boys to keep me on my toes then,' he quipped. 'It sounds as if you should be in charge.'

Terry smiled. 'Double my money and I'll consider it.'

Yi Soong wagged a finger at him. 'You'd put me out of a job. By the way, I hear you're pretty good with your hands?'

'You'd better believe it,' Danny grunted, snapping the butt of his rifle back in place and ramming home the locking pin. 'Damn near killed three guys who jumped him in Seoul. Luckily I came along and saved them.'

'Is that so?' Yi Soong said, smiling easily. 'You and I should do some sparring some time.'

Terry shook his head. 'Not me. I've seen you Taekwondo boys in action before. We've only got stumpy little legs in Wales, you see. Haven't got the reach.'

'That's too bad. Maybe one day.'

'Maybe,' Terry agreed doubtfully.

Yi Soong laughed and slapped him on the back a little harder than necessary. As he strolled away with a cheery wave Danny eyed his friend.

'I'd watch him, if I were you. I think Mr Yi likes to be the biggest fish in the pond.'

'Yeah,' Terry said thoughtfully. 'I was thinking more of the biggest turd in the bowl.'

The next evening the whole camp gathered for a briefing. As they trooped into the main dining-room the men found that the chairs had been rearranged in rows and a large bed sheet had been hung on the wall at the front. Babs was fussing about getting everyone seated and when this was done, Yi Soong appeared, strode straight to the front and pulled down the sheet to reveal a large map of Korea with the border indicated by a thick red line and the main towns on both sides marked by coloured pins. Yi stood aside and watched his audience for a while before speaking.

'Gentlemen, the time has come to explain to you the reason why we are all here. As some of you will know, the North has been attempting to build a nuclear weapon for quite some time. This is no big secret. The UN has been trying to persuade them to open their facilities for inspection.'

A ripple of laughter ran through the room. Yi smiled.

'Exactly. I am glad that you all seem to agree with me. It is a futile approach. Worse than that, it strengthens the North because they see the West as both weak and gullible, and by the West I include my own South Korea. They will never allow the UN access, and if they do they will show them factories making baby food or condoms. Which brings me to one Professor Lim Choy.'

He pressed a button on the remote control of a slide projector and the face of a stern, bespectacled, middle-aged man grimaced down at them from a screen.

'Professor Lim is, quite simply, the most brilliant man in North Korea.'

'Is that like the wisest man in Ireland?' someone called out, following it with a convincing impression of a mental defective. Yi smiled politely.

'Not exactly. He is the head of the North Korean nuclear weapons programme. Without him, even at this stage in the development process, the whole edifice tumbles. The wheels stop turning and, with luck, the North suffers a delay from which they will not recover.'

'By now the room was completely silent. Terry raised his hand.

'Excuse me, I might be being thick, but surely any delay will be just that, only a delay.'

Yi nodded and said: 'That is correct, but it is all that we will need.'

'For what?'

Yi shrugged as if the answer was obvious. 'For our own bomb to be ready, of course.'

There was a subdued muttering until Yi waved his hands for silence.

'Let me reassure you, South Korea is not going to start any nuclear war. We are going to prevent one. It's simply what you in Europe have been doing for the last forty years. A balance of terror, if you like.

Don't hit me or I'll hit you back, you say to your enemy.'

He waited until his words had sunk in before continuing.

'You and I, gentlemen, are going to rescue Professor Lim. Or to put it another way, we are going to enable him to defect. So you see, for those of you with scruples, it is a rescue mission. For the others' – he shrugged – 'the money is even now being transferred to your accounts.'

During the ensuing outbreak of chatter Yi unrolled another map and a large diagram, and pinned them both to the wall. When the room was again silent he picked up a long pointer and indicated the diagram, which showed a compound.

'This is where we will find Professor Lim. It is a government holiday resort for the use of the top members of the politburo only. President Kim Il Sung himself uses it.' He grinned. 'Maybe we'll even find him in residence when we drop in for tea.'

There was a nervous laughter from the men, all of whom now leaned forward to absorb every detail of the forthcoming operation. As the significance and the risks involved burned into the minds of the mercenaries, each in his own way focused his full attention on the task ahead.

'The resort is south of Wonsan, here,' Yi said, pointing to the map. 'The insertion phase will be by sea and under cover of darkness. Once ashore we will march inland, lie up throughout the hours of daylight, carry out a covert close recce, finalize plans and assault the following night as soon as it is dark. If our secrecy is compromised we can expect some stiff resistance from the guards but I hope to accomplish entry to the compound undetected. Professor Lim will be ready and waiting; the RV and time have been arranged by one of our agents. We will then exfiltrate, get back to the coast and be away long before first light.'

Proud with himself, Yi Soong stood back with folded arms. He ran his eyes over the assembled mercenaries, anticipating the volley of questions that was sure to come.

'And before you all start shouting, I will now explain the details of the plan.'

In response to another press of the buttons the slide projector covered the screen with a mass of timings and grid references.

Two hours later Yi Soong knocked on the door of the office and waited for permission to enter. Seated in the red plastic chair behind the desk, Francis Kwang was talking with Babs Butler. Ignoring Babs, Yi reported that the briefing was complete and that rehearsals for the infiltration of the compound would begin the following morning.

'We'll use this camp as a model to practise on. It's far from perfect but it'll do. I want to run them through some set procedures that we'll use at the objective.'

'Of course,' Kwang agreed, full of admiration for his subordinate and right-hand man. 'A dry run will be invaluable.'

'Oh, not just one. I intend to get them working together as if they were one of my old special forces groups.'

Kwang nodded, then turning to Babs, suggested politely that the men might have some final queries about administration that he may be able to answer. Taking the hint, Babs left the office. Once he had heard the outside door close, Kwang turned back to Yi.

'And will they all do?'

'Major Butler has produced exactly the team we knew he would.'

Kwang tipped back his head and laughed. 'You mean, the toughest bunch of killers ever to walk the earth.'

Yi joined in, mimicking Babs's voice: 'Of course. The top men in their field, every one.'

Suddenly serious, Kwang examined his fingernails. 'Good. Well then, there's nothing more to be said.' He picked up the slide of Professor Lim and held it up to the light.

'Good night, Professor Lim Choy. This time next week you'll be enjoying the freedom of Seoul.'

In the back of his limousine, Kwang helped himself to a drink from the cabinet. Yi had done a good job, but then he always did. Kwang had slipped in and out of the camp unnoticed, but while he had been waiting in the back office, he had studied the assembled mercenaries through one of the security cameras that had been installed for the purpose. He had seen pretty much what he had expected: a sad collection of losers. Still, he thought as he stirred the ice in his gin, they were good enough for the task in hand. He had read through a selection of their dossiers and had found several who sounded very interesting. In other circumstances he might even have been willing to offer some of them more permanent work with his organization. It was something to bear in mind.

His car sped through the night along the east–west Yongdong Expressway, whisking him back to Seoul, where he had some last-minute business to attend to. Ideally he would have liked to return straight to his villa, where Lulu was waiting for him, but she would just have to wait. If he found himself at a loose end in Seoul he could easily look up someone else. There was never any shortage of women ready to do anything for a man like Francis Kwang. It was true what they say: power is the best aphrodisiac.

Watching the cars and trucks speed by, Kwang marvelled at the life of the ordinary man. What on earth motivated such people? He found it impossible to imagine a life without intrigue. He had acquired most of the things that he had ever desired. He had power, wealth, a beautiful mistress; he was in good health, and he was feared. Fame was less important. Indeed, in his line of work it was highly undesirable. He took a far greater satisfaction in being anonymous, walking through the busy streets of Seoul, driving like this along the expressways, as if he was just another good and law-abiding citizen. The delight came in the secret knowledge that he, Francis Kwang, was far from average and ordinary. He could look through anyone with the sweetest smile masking his contempt, knowing in his heart that he could topple governments. Let the politicians strut like peacocks, mouth their bold words like fish behind thick glass. He was the real kingmaker. He was the mover of mountains.

As he passed a sign indicating that Seoul was fifty kilometres away, Kwang eased back in the leather seat. Yes, he would give Linda a call when he got in.

5

In the final days at the training camp, the sixteen mercenaries were divided up into four teams of four. Yi Soong did the selection, basing his decisions on observations made throughout the training period. He had noted which groups of men gravitated together and by the time of his final preparations, the teams had virtually formed themselves. Everyone was happy with the choice, recognizing that it would be the most efficient way of operating.

As always, there were one or two loners. Rather than stick them together in a group of their own, Yi divided them between the teams who would be best able to absorb them. Since the fight in the Seoul park, Terry and Danny had stuck together throughout the warm-up course. As Ken had antagonized everyone except Terry, who seemed extremely slow to anger, and Danny, who didn't care, Yi grouped the three of them together and completed the team with Andy Buchan.

'Fuck a stoat,' Ken said loudly when he heard the news. 'Why do we have to get lumbered with Bonnie Prince Charlie?'

'Well, why not?' Terry said good-naturedly, noticing Andy's warning scowl and anxious to avoid a dangerous rift before the operation had even begun. 'We've already got Robert the Bruce.'

'Ha!' Andy bellowed. 'You tell him, Dojo.'

Although he kept himself to himself, Andy liked the look of Terry's team. The Welshman was a smooth operator, as Andy had seen before in Africa. OK, so what if he was a soft touch when it came to sorting out the prisoners: he remembered the run-in they had had, with Dojo screaming and him standing over the bodies, pistol in hand.

'It's a dirty job, but someone's got to do it,' Andy had said. Dojo hadn't liked that. For a moment Andy had thought he would have to shoot him too, but then the South Africans had turned up and cooled him down. Nevertheless, the Scot had felt a grudging respect for the Welshman. He recognized that it had taken guts to put a stop to the killing, even if Dojo was wrong to try.

He had also been impressed by the big Indian. Danny Grey Wolf was obviously a natural – anyone could see that. Andy hadn't liked to admit it to himself, but he had longed to join their team. It was a shame about the loud-mouthed Aussie but nothing was perfect.

Yi had announced that he would make up a fifth team with three fellow Koreans. They had arrived at the camp only the day before departure and a couple of the men voiced concerns that the newcomers had missed out on all the preliminary training.

'Let me worry about that,' Yi had answered. 'They're in my team and if I'm happy to trust them with my life I don't think it should bother you.'

'More to the point,' Terry had said quietly to Danny afterwards, 'why isn't Yi prepared to commit himself to a team made up of our boys?'

But he never got his answer because the next

morning four large trucks pulled into the camp and the operation began. After loading all the weapons, stores and ammunition, the convoy set off for the coast, arriving in darkness at a small fishing village north of Konsang. As the trucks drew up beside the walls of what appeared to be a schoolhouse, they were met by a man who waved them to a halt with a torch and then led them down to the waterfront. At the end of a long, narrow pier a large fishing boat lay at anchor. The captain leaned from a window on the bridge, looking at the trucks with only mild interest, while below him the crew scuttled about their tasks, making space for the mercenaries.

'Why did I ever break my golden rule: never travel by sea?'

Hanging his head over the side of the fishing boat, Jules Merkoen, the South African, was in a bad way, his voice muffled by the waves breaking over the prow and slicing along the rusty, green-painted sides in foaming crests. With a violent convulsion he retched and vomited again, his knuckles white from grasping the railings.

'Here you are, mate,' Ken said, handing him a packet. 'I saved you an egg-and-cress sandwich.'

'Oh shit . . .' Jules heaved again, ending with a fit of coughing as his empty stomach rebelled.

Elsewhere in the boat every member of the little force was busy. Weapons were being stripped, cleaned and checked for the hundredth time; ammunition was being packed and repacked in pouches and bergens in the search for the most efficient method of distributing the weight; and webbing was being adjusted to sit securely but comfortably on the wearer, allowing him freedom of movement, but not fitting so loosely as to rattle and give him away.

Danny was sitting on the deck, leaning against one of the five inflatable dinghies, one for each of the teams. He had spread a cloth over his lap and was oiling the pieces of his M16.

'You'll wear them out,' Terry said, dropping down beside him. 'Here, have some coffee.'

He gripped the plastic mug between his knees, unscrewed the cap of the vacuum flask and poured as carefully as he could against the pitching of the boat.

'Bit rough, isn't it?' he said passing the mug to Danny.

'Thanks.'

Danny took a swig of coffee, paused to let it cool in his mouth before swallowing, took a second swig and handed the mug back.

'Did you make that yourself?'

'Do you like it?' Terry asked eagerly.

'Tastes like shit.'

'Now there's gratitude for you. I slave all day over a hot stove and that's all the thanks I get.'

From the other side of the inflatable Ken called over: 'Shut the fuck up. I'm trying to get some kip. You sound like an old married couple.'

Since leaving the jetty, Yi and the captain had insisted on a complete black-out. Not a single light showed from anywhere in the boat; only the stars shone on the water, glinting on the tossed waves and dimly lighting the distant horizon. At one point another vessel was sighted far away to the north-east and the skipper swung his fishing boat towards the shore in case it was a North Korean gunboat on patrol and he needed to seek the shelter of the inlets and coves.

Ken swore under his breath. 'Just our luck to get caught in the middle of this bloody lot. We're sitting ducks out here in a tub like this.'

Danny Grey Wolf peered long and hard through his binoculars and when he eventually lowered them, he looked puzzled.

'What's up, Danny?'

Without looking at Terry he examined the horizon again, scanning from side to side.

'Nothing, I hope. It's gone now anyway.'

'What was it?'

'An Osa missile-attack boat.'

Ken whistled. 'Thank God it missed us.'

Danny nodded slowly. 'Yeah. Stroke of luck, wasn't it.'

In the early hours the fishing boat turned towards the shore again, only this time going to within half a mile of the beach. The captain hissed from the bridge.

'What's that fat bugger on about?' Andy said, scowling.

Danny listened carefully, then translated. 'He says he can't go in any closer. It looks like this is our stop.'

'Your Korean might come in useful,' Terry said.

Danny shook his head. He had picked up a rough understanding of the language when he had been based just south of the border.

'If it does it probably means something's gone wrong.'

At Yi's command, the inflatables were dropped over the side and two men from each team climbed down into them. While one handled the dinghy, keeping it close alongside the boat, the other stowed the kit that the remaining members of each team handed down to him. Throughout the operation Yi stood calmly on the other side of the boat, occasionally checking his watch, then looking up at the horizon for any sign of the returning gunboat.

'Cool customer, isn't he?' Jules said, heaving a box of bombs overboard for the 60mm mortars.

Terry looked across at Yi. He had to admit that whatever they thought of their commander as a human being, it was rapidly becoming clear that he was a highly professional soldier. His training at the camp and the detailed rehearsals had demonstrated a thorough grasp of low-level tactics, while his superb physical fitness was beyond question. During a break in one of the range practices Yi had laid on a little Taekwondo demonstration, executing various fancy spinning and jumping kicks. As usual he had tried to coax Terry into a sparring match, but Terry had joked his way out of it. He had a gut feeling that he and Mr Yi might one day do more than simply spar together, so while he took careful note of the Korean's style and favourite techniques, he took care to give away nothing of his own considerable ability.

When the dinghies were loaded and the last of the men had clambered over the side, Yi signalled to the skipper and swung himself down into his own dinghy with his three fellow-countrymen. As the five inflatables bobbed in the water the fishing boat turned away ponderously and headed out to sea, leaning into the waves towards the south and home.

Each inflatable was fitted with a small outboard motor, easing the short trip to the shore and giving each of the teams greater control over their tiny craft in the heavy sea. When they were about two hundred yards from the shoreline, Yi held up his arm as the signal for the dinghies to swing out into an extended line, so that when they hit the beach a minute or two later they did so in line abreast, disgorging their teams of heavily armed mercenaries simultaneously.

Leaping over the sides, two men from each team raced ashore, sprinted across the bare stretch of sand and dived into the sparse tufts of grass at the foot of a wall of dunes. Scanning the beach and searching inland with the aid of night-vision goggles, they prepared to give covering fire to their mates if necessary. Meanwhile the other half of each team manhandled the dinghies across the sand and pulled them in among the dunes, where a thick tangle of mangrove provided sufficient cover to hide the boats from any patrolling aircraft that might fly over the beach in daylight.

While some of the men hacked at the mangrove and camouflaged the dinghies, others went back over the beach, sweeping away their tracks until all sign of their arrival had been eradicated.

Finally, when he was satisfied that everything had been done according to the plan, Yi called together the other four team leaders.

'All OK?' he asked.

They nodded.

'Let's go, then. Same order of march as in rehearsal. I'll take the lead, then you Dave, followed by Dominic's team, Jules, and you Terry to bring up the rear. Any questions? Then move.'

As he doubled back to where Danny, Ken and Andy waited by the mangrove, Terry felt a thrill of excitement course through his veins. It happened every time he approached combat. Later on would come the ruthless self-control and cool nerve that had made him one of the best in the business, but for now he allowed himself the adrenalin. It was what kept him coming back.

Waiting until the other teams had headed out through the dunes, Terry hand-signalled his men into position, himself leading, followed by Ken, then Andy, with Danny bringing up the rear. If anyone was able to detect a tail it was the big Indian. Terry had witnessed Danny Grey Wolf's tracking skills on the warm-up course and he seemed to have a sixth sense when it came to bush work.

The track leading inland from the beach soon started to climb and it wasn't long before the men were sweating under the weight of their heavy bergens and webbing.

'Jesus,' Ken muttered, 'we must have brought enough kit to start a fucking war.'

'If we fuck this up that's exactly what we could end up with,' Terry answered, plodding resolutely forward, head down, his breathing steady and deep.

Having crested the first ridge, they went down into a valley, leaving the track and striking out across rough, scrub-covered country. By now the moon had risen and Yi was careful to keep the line of march below the skyline lest they be silhouetted against the velvet-black sky for any chance security patrols to see.

Clumps of pine trees dotted the hillside and as the column began to climb again, Terry knew from his previous study of the maps that they were scaling the last of the ridges before the final descent towards the resort, the objective that had brought them together from the four corners of the earth.

With the first hint of a glow beneath the eastern horizon, they rounded a summit and dropped sharply across two hundred yards of open gorse before Yi signalled a halt, put out sentries and summoned the team leaders.

'OK, this will be the lying-up position. We'll be staying here throughout today. Adopt the triangular harbour formation as we rehearsed. Dave, you take twelve o'clock. No lights, no fires, no cigarettes, not even after first light. Nothing. Is that understood?'

This is just like a bloody exercise, Terry thought. If it goes on like this it'll be money for old rope.

'Terry, you'll come with me on the close recce later this morning,' said Yi. 'Cam up and get Danny to come too. I want to select our exact route in for the infiltration.'

'Right you are,' Terry answered, regretting his complacency.

'Jules, work out sentry stags and anyone not on duty is to sleep. Tomorrow's a busy day,' Yi continued, looking at the blackened faces of the men crouching around him. 'So far so good, gentlemen. Let's hope we've caught the Commies napping.'

He smiled broadly and sent his team leaders away to organize their rotas. Watching from the shadows, only Andy, the cynical loner, noticed how the smile disappeared a little too quickly from Yi's face the moment the last back was turned. But then Andy had never liked the bastard anyway.

Slumped in a deck chair, Alex Leitner gazed across the choppy waters of Chesapeake Bay. There must be some kind of race on, he thought, judging by the number of brightly coloured sails that bobbed and whizzed back and forth in front of where he and his son sat fishing. Windsurfers darted across the water like skimming pebbles, hands holding fast to the boom, backsides sticking dangerously over the edge.

He nudged his son. 'Can you imagine your old man doing that?'

Stephen laughed. 'Nope,' he said, and a moment later he shouted and grabbed the rod as the line was tugged sharply downwards.

'You've got something, Pop! Here, you play him. Careful now.'

Struggling out of his chair, Alex was almost sorry. Now he'd have to get his hands all wet and slimy on some poor creature that was swimming along minding its own business, thinking it had just found a nice little snack to take home for the kids.

It was only a short mental step from a slimy fish to Eliot Masterson. After the unsatisfactory interview with his boss, Alex had tried to put the photographs and the report from his mind, but it wasn't easy. The habits of a lifetime in intelligence work were not easily bypassed and ever since Masterson's cursory dismissal of the affair Alex had been deeply troubled. Against his better judgement he had been making a few discreet enquiries but so far had found nothing unusual in his boss's past.

Masterson had graduated from Harvard with just about the finest degree known to man, had been recruited by the CIA while doing a doctorate in Far Eastern Affairs, and since joining the organization he had sky-rocketed, keeping his nose so clean it almost squeaked. Still, Alex wasn't done with him yet.

He laid the cod on the bank and worked the hook from its lip. Stephen had run over to the car and was rummaging in the boot for a basket to put it in. They had taken the old route past Annapolis and cracked the usual jokes. Alex had enjoyed the day.

Holding the fish in his hand, he turned round to check that Stephen wasn't looking then tossed it back into the water. In a flash of silver it was gone. Alex's hands hung limply between his knees. What kind of an agent was he? He didn't even have the heart to kill a goddam fish.

When Stephen came back he looked at the empty space on the grass where the fish had been, then at his father.

'Shit, Dad. You didn't throw it back again?'

'The one that got away?' Alex shrugged.

'But they all do!'

Alex peered out across the windswept waves. The leading windsurfer had just overbalanced and toppled head first off his board, the sail crashing down on top of him.

'Not all of them,' he said.

Hugging the ground, Terry nudged his way through the undergrowth. In his day he had been one of the best stalkers in the British Army, passing his sniper course with flying colours. He had had to carry out a one-mile stalk across a bare-arsed stretch of Salisbury Plain, with the Directing Staff watching for him with binoculars. He had not only completed it successfully, but had then put a single shot through the centre of the target's chest at eight hundred yards and withdrawn, still undetected.

He regretted not having brought his custom-made

gillie's suit with him, but had improvised just after first light by shredding a spare combat jacket and then rapidly stitching strips of camouflaged cloth, branches and undergrowth into the fabric. He had been particularly careful to crawl a little way forward with his binos and study the ground that he would have to cross, selecting his route and gauging the right combination of colours he would need if he was to stand a good chance of remaining undetected.

Yi, Danny and another of the Koreans had done likewise, and the four of them had set out at mid-morning, moving as quickly as possible over the first leg of the journey, crawling only to cover gaps in the undergrowth. But as they neared the resort itself, they found themselves having to crawl more and more often until by the time they were within six hundred yards of the outer fences, they were wriggling on their stomachs at a painfully slow pace.

'This is as close as I dare go for now,' Yi whispered in Terry's ear. 'We'll have a good look from here and then circle around to see if there are any better approaches. I also want to select an emergency exit point in case we have to get out in a hurry.'

Terry hand-signalled Danny to crawl forward beside them, and while the Korean guard stood watch the three of them studied the compound buildings, fences and guard posts.

Having made a sketch map for use in the planning meeting that would be held in the afternoon, Terry was surprised to find the layout was just like that of any large Mediterranean hotel, only with a few security fences and watch-towers. He could see a pool with a couple of people floating lazily in the clear water; others were sunbathing while the guards kept a discreet distance from the holidaymakers. So the Communists, for all their talk about equality, are just like the rest, Terry thought as he sketched in a guard position that he had just spotted. It's one rule for the rich and one for the poor. Those fat cats round the pool are full of bullshit about the proletariat, but when they're on holiday, God help any worker who strays too close. Still, that would work to the mercenaries' advantage. If the guards were ordered to keep away from the VIPs, then they wouldn't be around when Terry and the other teams infiltrated after dark.

He looked across at Danny, who was obviously thinking the same, and they exchanged grins.

'Candy from a baby,' said Terry.

When they had gained all the information they could from their present position, they crawled around to the west with slow, agonizing precision, Yi leading, the other Korean following behind, guarding the rear. Once established in another observation post, they refined the sketch, adding in details that had not been visible from the other part of the hill, gradually building up a detailed plan of the resort.

There were five main buildings in the complex, all substantial accommodation blocks, with balconies and terraces where the recce party could see powerful North Koreans dozing in the sun or reading the newspapers that only they would have access to. There were three swimming pools in all, and an open-air restaurant that reminded Terry that he was starving.

'Have you seen enough?' he asked Yi, who was scribbling in a notebook. He looked up and smiled.

'More than enough. Let's get back.'

If anything, the return journey took longer than the

outward stalk, as every member of the recce party fought against the desire to switch off and rush. They were all experienced enough to know that many a close recce had been compromised at the withdrawal stage, when team members' guard went down because they thought it was as good as in the bag.

It was only when they were back within the relative safety of the lying-up position that Yi spoke again and they relaxed, slipping out of their sweat-soaked jackets and shirts. Ken thrust his water bottle into Terry's hand.

'Nice going, mate. Give some to Tonto as well,' he said, pointing at Danny. The Indian looked up slowly and for a moment Terry felt his stomach muscles tighten. The last thing they needed before an action was a bloody split in the team. It was bad enough already coping with Andy's moods.

Danny got to his feet and stood over Ken. Slowly he took the bottle and took a swig.

'Thank you, Kimosabe,' he said quietly.

Terry felt the tension drain from him in a flood of relief. Ken laughed and clapped Danny on the back. They were happy. It had been a good recce, the operation was going according to plan and with luck they would all soon be back in Seoul and considerably richer.

Francis Kwang really didn't see why he had to explain his behaviour to anyone, least of all to a call-girl. But he had and it disconcerted him. It had started when Lulu discovered a piece of paper with Linda's name and telephone number on it, and it had finished with several of his Chinese vases shattered on the sitting-room floor of his villa. Having spent her wrath in the only way she knew how, Lulu had padded upstairs and collapsed on the bed in a flood of tears, leaving Kwang wrestling with a range of emotions that he was uncomfortable to discover in himself.

He had considered the reflex action that he had used before with other women, of having her put in a cab by one of the guards, roughed up a bit, driven back to Seoul and dumped in It'aewan. But halfway to the phone he had stopped. The thought of not seeing her again suddenly struck him as unpleasant, inconceivable even. With a chill feeling that was partly dread and partly excitement, he realized that he had allowed Lulu to become special to him. So, taking a bottle of Veuve Clicquot from the icebox, he had gone quietly upstairs and attempted to appear contrite.

Since that unforgettable night, the balance of power in their relationship had undergone a radical shift and Kwang knew that Lulu knew it. It was intolerable. She was as happy as a child and moved about the villa with a new ease as if she was truly the mistress of the place. But she was also wise enough not to push her luck. She had discovered an Achilles heel in her lover, but unlike the Greek hero, Lulu could not be sure that Kwang's weak point would remain vulnerable for ever. The result was a deepening of their relationship as both partners felt their way forward as if in a pitch-black room, hands outstretched, but moving inexorably closer together from their opposing sides.

Tonight of all nights, Kwang wanted to keep a clear head, but he had returned to the villa to find that Lulu herself had prepared dinner, having dismissed the cook and dimmed the lights.

Instead of the Sinatra record that she loved, she had put on one of Kwang's favourite Pavarotti CDs. The food by candlelight had been surprisingly good and although he had tried to stick to just one glass of red wine, Lulu had refilled it without him noticing, so that by the time she produced a dessert made with fresh lychees, cream and an unidentifiable liqueur, he could feel himself expanding from his customary reserve into an extremely pleasant torpor.

Lulu slipped round the side of the table and stood behind Kwang's chair, draping herself over his shoulders like a fur stole, warm and soft. Kissing him at first on the cheeks, she ran her fingers through his hair, pulling his head gently back and pressing her lips to his. As he opened his mouth Kwang felt her silky-smooth tongue flick the tip of his, and her hands caress his chest, seeking the buttons of his shirt.

'Lulu,' he whispered, pulling away from her and looking in her eyes. 'Can we do this later? There are things I have to do.'

But she smiled as if she hadn't heard and pulling open his shirt, slid around him and straddled his lap.

'Lulu, please,' Kwang moaned, feeling the heat rising through him. Against his will he found his hands sliding down her legs, stroking the little hollows behind her knees, then rising again, pushing her dress up over her thighs. Lulu was kissing his ears, her hands unfastening the front of her dress and a moment later he caught the sweet scent of her breasts and tipped his face forward into them.

Somewhere in the villa a clock chimed. Now would be the time, he told himself, fighting to order his brain before Lulu's irresistible onslaught. But her weapons were such as had no counter, and as she felt the palms of his hands slide under her buttocks, and as she wriggled and brought him into her, she heard him gasp and knew that she had mastered the most powerful man in South Korea.

After crawling up the last slope below the compound fence, Terry elbowed slowly through the undergrowth and peered over the top. The base of the fence was a mere ten yards in front of him, across an open strip of close-cropped grass. Christ, he thought, this is a piece of piss. A bloody holiday home for important invalids. Not a guard in sight and, as far as he could tell, no dogs either.

He signalled to the other members of his team, who were waiting below, and crawled across the narrow lawn until he reached the bottom strand of barbed wire. According to Yi, their intelligence had reported that the fence was not electrified but as Terry was the one who had to cut it, he tested it first. The report was correct. Unable to suppress a feeling of disgust at the appalling security of the camp, he spat in the dirt and prepared to cut the wire as Danny wrapped pieces of sacking around the point of the cut to muffle the noise.

When Terry had cut a hole big enough for a man to crawl through, he rolled aside and Ken and Andy slithered through and doubled across to the outside wall of the nearest accommodation block. Then Danny and Terry themselves crawled through and signalled for the other teams to close up. Jogging out of the darkness, the remaining twelve mercenaries and the four Koreans came up the slope and through the wire while Terry's team provided close protection on the inside.

Kneeling beside Terry, Yi glanced up at the lights,

shaking his head in disgust when Terry scoffed at the lack of video cameras or trip-wires. They had entered at a point that Terry had found, a complete blind spot, out of direct line of sight of any of the watch-towers.

'Fuck 'em,' Yi hissed. 'Whoever designed this show will be facing a firing squad tomorrow.'

Under the plan that Yi had drawn up after the recce, he and his team would enter the accommodation block that was known to house Professor Lim Choy. The Professor had arranged an RV, Yi said, and they would wait there for only two minutes. If the Professor didn't show, they were to withdraw immediately. While they were gone, the other four teams were to move to a garden and pool area that would be deserted at that time of night, and await Yi's return. In the event that his team was compromised, the mercenaries were to withdraw to an emergency RV halfway back to the lying-up position and wait there for five minutes in case Yi and his Koreans were able to escape. If not, they were free to return to the dinghies and the pick-up point.

When Yi and his team had gone, Terry led the others round the edge of the building, steeled and ready to silence any guard they encountered. Danny had slung his M16 and carried his tomahawk in the throwing position. Terry preferred to use his hands, and grinned back at Ken, who had picked up a feather and stuck it behind his ear.

'Christ alive, it's like Dances with bloody Wolves,' he whispered as he came alongside Terry, waiting for Danny to clear the next corner. There was a dull thud and they raced forward to see Danny lowering the body of a guard to the floor, a savage gash at the base of his skull where the tomahawk had severed the spinal column.

'Nice work,' Terry whispered. But Danny was frowning.

'What's up?'

Danny turned the guard's face to the light and studied it.

'He's only a fucking kid, Terry.'

Ken patted him on the shoulder. 'He can still pull a trigger, mate.'

'That's not what I meant. It doesn't add up, raw kids guarding a resort used by the President himself.' He stooped and picked up the Kalashnikov.

'No security cameras, no noise of partying. Fuck it, Terry, this is supposed to be a holiday camp where these bastards let their hair down. Why wasn't there anyone in the restaurant when we saw it on the recce? It was midday; it should have been packed. And that patrol boat veering off like that. It just doesn't add up.'

He sprung open the cocking handle of the assault rifle and tilted the chamber towards the light. The magazine was empty.

'Shit,' Ken murmured, as one of Jules's team jogged up to them out of breath and said: 'Dojo, Jules said you'd better come and have a look.'

'What is it?' Terry said, feeling the hair rise on the back of his neck.

'Just come and have a look.'

Leaving Andy and Ken to cover their backs, Terry and Danny followed the mercenary to one of the pool areas. Jules had also come across one of the guards and silenced him. But like the one Danny had killed, he was no more than a teenager and his magazine was empty.

'What's going on?' Terry asked.

'That's not all. Look at this,' said Jules.

The South African and Terry came out on to a lawn where deckchairs were laid out ready for sunbathers. Although it was late at night, several of the chairs were occupied, men and women in brightly coloured trunks and swimsuits lazing in the darkness, some with papers over their faces as if fast asleep, others tilted on their sides, eyes closed.

Despite his training and despite his years of combat, Terry felt a wave of sickness sweep through him, followed by a chill iciness that gripped his chest. As he took in the distended bellies, swollen and bloated with the build-up of gases, and the limbs mottled and stiff in death, his body reacted first, as it always did in extreme danger. He spun on his heel, raising his voice from the whisper of the past hours to the full pitch of a battle cry.

'Ambush!'

6

'Headlights coming up the main road, Dojo. Looks like a convoy of troop carriers.'

'Strength?'

'At least two companies. About a mile away.'

Terry cursed. Why the hell hadn't he smelt it? It had all been far too easy. The coastal insertion, the approach march and recce, no perimeter patrols, cameras, trip-wires or dogs. They had walked straight into a trap.

Even under his cam cream, Terry could see that Jules had gone pale. 'What the hell's going on, Dojo?'

'No time for that now. Let's get the fuck out of here.'

A couple of the men called out for Yi.

'That bastard'll be miles away by now,' Andy said bitterly.

'What do you mean?' Ken growled.

'Who do you think set us up?'

Terry felt the pieces slowly starting to fit. 'Let's see if he's still around. Danny, Ken and Andy, come with me. Jules and Dominic, you and your men cover the main entrance. Force the gooks to debus from the trucks and slow them down. Dave, give them your mortar and ammo and get your team back to cover the entry point.'

Dave Bedford looked doubtful. 'You're not going out that way, are you?' he asked.

'No fucking way; they'll have ambushed our route by now, hoping to catch us making a run for it. But make sure they don't come in the same way we did. I'll check for Yi, then recce a new exit point on the opposite side.'

'Right.'

Terry spoke quickly, trying to sound calm and in control, masking the thoughts and fears tumbling through his brain. He realized they were probably in the tightest corner any of them had ever been in and that they were going to need all their skills and co-operation to escape. Deep inside a hostile country, their mission had been compromised and if they weren't already surrounded, then they soon would be, just as soon as the troop carriers arrived.

'Listen in, lads,' Terry shouted as the teams sorted themselves out, swapped kit and mortars, and filled their pockets with spare magazines and grenades. 'From now on, any Koreans you see, blast them,' he ordered. 'And that goes for Yi too. If they think we're going to be a pushover they've picked a fight with the wrong bunch. OK, move!'

The teams jogged away from the pool area and disappeared to their various tasks. With a final check on the grenades attached to his webbing, Terry led the way towards the accommodation block that Yi had indicated. A central staircase climbed up through the four levels, with a balcony on each floor dividing to both left and right. Rows of doors led from the carpeted corridor into the plush holiday suites.

Moving in pairs, the team leapfrogged forwards in a series of short tactical bounds, Terry and Danny going first and then covering Ken and Andy when they moved. Dropping into a kneeling position and aiming his Colt Commando, Terry shouted for Andy to move.

'Go!'

Opposite him Danny was pressed into an alcove, his M16 covering the other direction, tensed and ready to fire at the slightest sign of movement. Darting between them, Ken and Andy burst up the last flight of stairs, dived for cover and a moment later Ken's voice echoed down the stairwell.

'All clear!'

Bounding up three steps at a time, Terry and Danny split left and right at the top, dropping again into an aiming position, their eyes sweeping the corridor on either side, taking in every detail and evaluating possible targets.

Locating the nearest door, Terry hand-signalled Danny to cover him, and cradling his assault rifle for a forward roll, shouldered his way straight through it, dived across the carpet and came up ready to fire. The room was empty, but Terry's nostrils were filled with a stench that made him retch. On the hotel lawn he hadn't noticed the smell of the bodies, but here in the confined space of a bedroom it was overpowering.

'Jesus Christ,' Danny muttered, coming in after him. 'Where the hell's that coming from?'

Terry went carefully over to the bed and flicked back the sheet with the tip of his rifle. Staring up at the ceiling with glazed lifeless eyes, a man and a woman lay in each other's arms. Between them a baby clung to its mother's breast, from which it would never again draw life. Even through the mass of blood that soaked the mattress, Terry could see that it had been shot, like its parents.

A shout came from the adjoining room and they ran in to find Ken and Andy staring at a similar spectacle, only this time the man was fully dressed and propped in an armchair while the woman lay in a half-filled bath, the water pink and stagnant.

Ken held his hand over his nose. 'I wonder if they'll get a refund?'

'Shut it, Ken,' Andy snapped.

'Do you think there's a mini-bar?'

'I said shut it!'

Terry laid a hand on Andy's shoulder. 'Easy. Come on, lads. Let's get out of here.'

Having made their way to the end of the corridor, they found more corpses in the other rooms but no sign of Yi or his team.

'He'll be under the wire by now,' Danny said. 'Waiting to guide in his friends.'

Terry nodded. 'We'd better find an exit quick or we'll end up like these poor buggers, whoever they were.'

'One thing's for certain,' Danny said, 'They're no government honchos. Look at their hands.'

He bent down beside the body of a white-haired old man and pointed to the calluses covering his palms.

'And there's no luggage. They've all been dressed in bright holiday clothes but where are the cases?'

'Yeah, and no toothbrushes or razors in the bathrooms,' Ken said. 'Nothing. What the fuck happened to them?'

Terry led the way back down the corridor. 'I don't know and right now I don't care,' he muttered.

Halfway to the perimeter fence, the noise of a mortar

firing shook the ground, followed a few seconds later by the crump of the distant explosion as Jules and his men opened fire on the North Korean troop carriers.

Jules had waited until the leading truck had slowed to negotiate a hairpin bend on its descent to the resort before signalling the mortar team to open fire. Judging the range as best they could, they had set the elevation and then sited for direction along the barrel towards the target, waiting for a signal from Jules for exactly the right moment to slide a dark-green HE bomb down the short black tube.

As the cartridge in the base of the tail fin hit the firing pin and detonated, launching the bomb on its arcing flight towards the unwary troops, the team were already preparing to adjust the elevation and bearing.

Scanning the road through his binos, Jules waited for the fall of shot. A moment later there was a bright flash followed by the thump of the exploding shell.

'Nice shooting, lads,' he called across to the others. But the round had landed a hundred yards from the intended target, spraying its fragments of splintered metal harmlessly into the darkness as the truck lumbered on. Stretching his arm towards the target, Jules squinted along it, using the knuckles of his clenched fist to measure the distance from the round's point of impact to the place where the truck would next be forced to slow for another bend. In this way he estimated the degree of adjustment necessary.

'Go right two clicks, up one click,' he shouted. 'Repeat.'

As the two men adjusted the mortar, Dominic allocated arcs of fire to the rest of the men, concentrating on the machine-guns, which would do most of the long-range killing. The M16s would come into their own when the battle got to closer quarters.

'Hold your fire until they debus. Get the fuckers when they're milling around in the headlights. Once they're into cover we've lost them.'

Planting the bipods of their GPMGs firmly in the grass, the gunners tucked the butts into shoulder and cheek, aligned the sights and shuffled into comfortable positions to steady their aim. Meanwhile each gun's number two laid a belt of ammunition across the breech, slammed shut the top cover and clipped fresh belts on to the end ready for a prolonged fire-fight. With a series of metallic rasps, the gunners cranked back the cocking handles, slid the first rounds into place, and huddled down to wait.

Again the mortar fired, its 60mm HE bomb climbing almost vertically into the night sky, high above the valley, turning lazily at the summit of its trajectory, then accelerating down towards the convoy of trucks. The driver of the lead vehicle had stepped heavily on the brake and was fighting with the gear stick when the bomb drove into the gravel beside his cab, exploding in a blinding flash of light, showering the truck with white-hot splinters of shell case that pierced the fuel tanks, igniting them in sky-rocketing clouds of flame.

A cheer went up from the two teams of mercenaries at the main entrance and with the range determined, the mortar went fully into action, bracketing the convoy with a shower of HE bombs. As the first truck exploded, those following behind screeched to a halt in the dancing light of the flaming wreckage, helplessly nose to tail as the officers screamed to regain control of the panicking drivers, leaping from their cabs for the cover of the roadside. Ordered to debus, the soldiers tumbled from the back of the trucks on to the tarmac, but in doing so entered the killing ground of the GPMGs.

'Fire!'

Dominic's voice carried above the noise of the pounding mortar and each of the gunners squeezed his trigger, tightening the metal butt-plate into his shoulder as the guns juddered into life. A stream of empty brass cases spilled on to the ground as lines of tracer snaked gracefully away from the compound, their arcs shallower than the mortar's but even more lethal. Sweeping back and forth, the streams of copper-coated 7.62mm machine-gun bullets chewed through the canvas, wood and metal of the stationary trucks, tearing flesh and splintering bone.

When the soldiers dived for cover in the grass verges, the continuing rain of mortar bombs sought them out. To add to the confusion, Jules ordered the mortar team to intersperse the HE rounds with white-phosphorus smoke bombs. Detonating in livid balls of orange flame, the smoke added to the chaos while the phosphorus particles stuck to flesh and material, burning with merciless efficiency.

With the column successfully halted some eight hundred yards from the main entrance, Jules and Dominic brought the fire of their teams under tight control to conserve their limited stocks of ammunition.

'Steady, lads. Keep it topped up but don't let them recover. Rifle group, hold your fire. Wait for them to close to three hundred yards and then fire on my command.'

The tiniest movement in the bushes brought Dave

Bedford to full alert. He and his three men had been listening enviously to the ferocious fire-fight at the main gate, their trigger fingers itching, anxious to get stuck in and release the tension that had built up over the last hours.

Taking cover to the flank of their original entry point, Dave had selected a pool of darkness for his team's position, in welcome contrast to the flood of spotlight beams illuminating the breach in the wire on which their weapons were trained.

The first man to emerge from the undergrowth moved cautiously with the wide-awake tenseness of an animal, sniffing the air for danger.

'Not good enough,' Dave muttered to himself, bringing his M16 into his shoulder and silently thumb-flicking the safety-catch on the pistol grip to automatic.

'So the road was a diversion, was it? Draw our fire, reveal our strength, then hit us in the rear with the big boys. Well, it didn't fucking work, mate. We're too bloody good for the likes of you.'

Behind the first man, a second and then a third and a fourth emerged into the full glare of the light and approached the foot of the slope below the wire fence. Dave hand-signalled his man with the M203 grenade-launcher to prepare to fire into the cover from which the enemy had come. He guessed that this new threat would be of at least platoon strength. Good old Dojo. Trust him to know what to do, even in a monumental fuck-up like this. Lots of other blokes would have bolted for the boats, straight back the way they had come. Not Dojo. He had been around too long for such basic mistakes. One route in, a different route out. Never follow a track, always blaze a new trail; that way you were harder to ambush.

When an eight-man section were out in the open and the lead scout was nosing up to the wire, Dave squeezed off the first round, the signal for his whole team to open fire in controlled four to five-round bursts. But while two of his men took on the enemy point section, he and the M203 fired in depth, directing their 5.56mm M16 rounds and the deadly 40mm grenades from the M203 into the cover where Dave knew the platoon commander would be watching and waiting, tensed and ready for the all-clear signal from his point-section commander.

Not this time, mate, Dave thought. This time you play it our way.

Scythed down where they stood, the point section crumpled, the ground at their feet dancing with impacting bullets while the undergrowth behind them jumped and crackled, shredded by the jets of high-velocity bullets and the grenades' jagged fragments.

As Dave had anticipated, the Korean officer staggered out of the bush and tumbled into the dust, his face a pulp of ripped flesh and bone. But these were not the simple regular troops that had been used as a decoy on the road; they were a special forces detachment from an élite North Korean parachute division, every bit the equal of the mercenaries behind the wire. Unlike the chaotic leadership on the main road, the platoon sergeant instantly took command and rallied his men for a frontal assault.

But fanatical courage was no match for the ice-cold steadiness of Dave's fire control. Unmoved by the sight and screaming ferocity of the attacking paratroopers, the four men of Dave's team swivelled on their bellies to face the new threat, each man picking his target with cool deliberation, aiming and firing, working inwards from the outer ends of the charging line. Soon only a handful of North Koreans were left, stumbling up the slope, where they were met at point-blank range by the two Browning pump shotguns that Dave's team carried for close-quarters jungle work.

As the bodies rolled back down the slope, Dave's team took advantage of the lull to tear off half-expended magazines and clip on fresh ones.

'Change your fire positions!' Dave called, rolling to his left and seeking a new angle from which to cover the clearing. Already he had spotted a dark line of figures winding down the hillside, and estimated their strength to be at least another two companies of paratroopers. They would take a bit more stopping. They would have seen the reception their scout platoon had been given, and forewarned was forearmed.

Turning to one of his riflemen, Dave whispered: 'Reckon you've got enough time to set out some Claymores?'

Even in the darkness he could see the answering grin.

Out on the main road, the officers had managed to regain some semblance of control and were now pushing towards the resort compound. Although they were attempting to move using the tactic of fire and manoeuvre by platoons, the troops had been unsettled by the ferocity of the mercenaries' resistance and by the deadly accuracy of the mortar and machine-gun fire. With one company strung out in an extended assault line on either side of the road, their own return fire was desultory by comparison. Striding at the back, the officers brandished their 9mm Type 59 Chinese pistols more at the soldiers themselves than at the enemy mercenaries.

As soon as he had heard the noise of battle from Dave's team, Jules had ordered the mortar out of action in case their scarce ammunition would be needed on another flank. But the GPMGs continued their steady chatter, hosing the oncoming ranks that were nearing the three-hundred-yard line, coming nicely into the battle range of the M16s.

'Come on, Jules,' Dominic shouted. 'We're going to sleep over here.'

Muffling his South African drawl with the best English accent he could manage, Jules called across: 'OK, old boy. Rifle group, carry on.'

'Fire!' Dominic yelled, and the concentrated bursts from four M16s skimmed over the scrub, seeking out the infantry, who were just enjoying the first sense of relief that the mortar had fallen silent.

After leaving the accommodation block, Terry and his team went quickly back through the pool and restaurant area towards the far side of the compound. Moving in pairs, they still used short tactical bounds to cover the ground, ever aware that Yi and his three Koreans might be somewhere in the vicinity and convinced by now that it was Yi who had double-crossed them.

Terry's main concern now was to locate a new exit point from the compound. He had expected the noise of firing from the main gate and had only detached Dave's team to the breach in the wire as a standard precaution. However, it was obvious from the weight of fire that Dave was now engaging a considerable force there and Terry's worst fears were proving correct. The North Koreans already had their two main exit routes covered and were moving quickly to encircle them completely. He knew that he could trust Dave, Jules, Dominic and their men to impose a good delay on the enemy and to make them pay dearly for every yard of ground, but there was a limit to what a small force could do against overwhelming odds with far greater supplies of ammunition, even if that small force was made up of the best mercenaries in the world.

Beyond the restaurant, the ground fell away through an area of gardens, the bushes becoming increasingly dense until at the foot of the slope, where they met the wire outer fence, the undergrowth was almost impenetrable. Using their machetes, Terry's team hacked a way through to the wire. Then, cutting the strands one by one, they peeled back the loose ends to make a hole big enough for a man in battle gear to get through.

'Andy and Ken, stay here,' Terry said. 'Danny and I will get the others to break clean and move back. One of you keep an eye on the garden in case our old friend Yi turns up; the other one watch the outside. The Koreans may try another angle of attack if Dave's giving them too much trouble at the breach.'

But the situation at the breach had deteriorated rapidly. The depth companies of Korean paratroopers had learned from their comrades' mistakes and were not going to take the mercenaries so lightly. Instead of putting in another direct assault across open ground, they had detached two platoons as a diversion while the main force worked its way around the side in an effort to outflank Dave's team. Approaching stealthily through the forest, the two platoons came to the edge of Dave's killing ground but refused to enter it. Instead they put down a withering fire, drawing the four mercenaries into a battle of attrition that the latter couldn't hope to win. If they tried to withdraw, the Koreans edged forward, threatening to come through the breach, but so long as they remained locked in the ferocious fire-fight Dave was painfully aware of the threat developing to his flank. He could see figures moving far off to the left but the moment he tried to detach half his team to deal with it, the Korean platoons to his front pushed forward again. He was locked fast in a pincer and knew that the Koreans would squeeze it ever tighter until the two points met and destroyed him and his men.

Racking his brain for a solution, Dave knew that he couldn't break clean and withdraw until the two teams at the main gate had pulled back. If he bugged out now the Koreans would flood in and Jules and Dominic would be cut off. Somehow he had to hold his line.

'Are the Claymores set?' he shouted back over his shoulder.

'Yes, boss.'

'Fix a grenade necklace fifty yards behind them and set it to a trip-wire.'

'Wilco.'

If anything, the main-gate position was under even heavier pressure. The assaulting infantry companies had faltered the moment the M16s had opened up and one or two of the younger soldiers had even turned to run. But the officers had reacted with clinical efficiency, shooting them down in full view of the rest of the troops and threatening to do the same to anyone else who thought they could sit out the attack hiding in a ditch.

Trapped between the mercenaries and their own officers, the infantry had pressed on, realizing that their only hope of salvation was to eliminate the intruders in the resort compound as quickly as possible. With a renewed determination born of desperation, the Korean soldiers surged forward into the hail of fire, learning their manoeuvre skills the hard way, living or dying according to their use of the sparse cover available.

'These bastards don't give up, do they?' Jules yelled.

'You're not kidding. We'll have to withdraw in contact by teams,' Dominic shouted in reply, slamming a new thirty-round magazine on to his M16. 'I'll set up an intermediate fire position by the first accommodation block. You move back through me on my command and when they reach the gate I'll hit them with the Fireflash. That should give us enough breathing space to break clean and fuck off out of here.'

Dominic had just fired a couple of rounds from his new magazine when his team took its first casualty. Vince Paulis was wriggling across an open patch of ground to a new fire position when a burst from a Kalashnikov caught him full in the face and chest. His body jerked with the impacting rounds and lay still.

'Vince is down!' cried his mate Jimmy Hughes, who had been paired with Vince in the warm-up training in the south. He edged across and checked the carotid artery for a pulse. Finding nothing, he rolled the body over and stripped the pouches of ammunition and grenades, stuffing them into his own.

At that moment Terry and Danny rounded the corner. Seeing the foremost Koreans rush forward in the lull Vince's death had created, they brought their own assault weapons into the aim and blazed off a full magazine each. Terry pulled the hard-plastic butt of his Colt Commando into his shoulder and felt the recoil judder through his entire body like an electric shock. Beside him Danny's M16 poured out a stream of empty cases, the red-hot brass tinkling on the paving stones.

'Pull back!' Terry shouted across to Jules.

'About bloody time, man.'

'Danny'll lead the way. I'll blister on to Dominic's team. Move!'

By now Dominic had got the surviving members of his team into their intermediate position fifty yards back and had set up two Claymore mines to cover the main gate. In preparation for the first stage of their withdrawal, every man in Jules's team emptied a full magazine into the enemy, spraying every piece of bush and scrub where the assaulting Korean infantry might be taking cover. Then, throwing a grenade each, they waited for the detonating blasts and the screams of the wounded, before turning and bolting for the cover of the first accommodation block, reloading as they ran back through Dominic's team.

'We'll go firm between blocks two and three,' Jules shouted as he jogged past, following Danny and disappearing round the corner.

'OK, Dojo,' Dominic said, 'let's show them what this little beastie can do.'

Opening his pack, he took out a two-foot-high rectangular green box resembling a huge biscuit tin, unclipped and folded open the front flap and with a stiff tug telescoped out the back end to double the overall length.

'Give us a hand, Dojo.'

Terry hoisted the huge box on to Dominic's shoulder.

'What setting?'

'Let's give the fuckers the full house,' Dominic replied, flicking out the sight.

'Right you are. Don't expect to use your ears again.'

Unable to hold his position any longer, Dave had just started to pull back when he took two casualties in quick succession. First to go down was Mike Timmis, shot in the throat by a single round from a Kalashnikov. But the 7.62mm bullet not only tore through the cartilage but shattered his neck, killing him stone dead. Then, when the survivors were almost at the cover of their first fall-back position, Kevin Hughes screamed and clutched his leg where a grenade fragment had ripped into the flesh and lodged itself, still white-hot from the explosion.

'Help him back!' Dave shouted. Grabbing the wounded man's shoulder straps in one powerful hand and dragging him backwards, Alan Steers clasped his M16 in the other and blazed away at the Koreans at the edge of the trees.

Pulling the pin on two grenades, Dave lobbed them over the wire and into the nearest trees, waited for the explosions and then bolted for cover. The paratroopers who had attempted to outflank him had disappeared and Dave was worried that they were about to give him a nasty surprise. But for now he was powerless to do anything about it: his hands were full with the platoons to his front. They were already inching up the slope, pressing him hard and would soon be through the wire and on to him. He had to get back to the Claymores.

Diving over a low wall, he almost landed on Alan, who was frantically knotting a field dressing on Kevin's leg.

'Where're the fucking clappers?' Dave shouted, scrabbling around for the Claymore firing triggers.

'On the wall.'

Peering round the wall, Dave waited until at least a full eight-man section had come through the wire. He would have loved to have caught more of them, but the first men would soon be pushing out from the breach and leaving his Claymore killing ground. Grasping a clapper in either hand, he squeezed them shut, shooting the electrical pulse on its split-second journey down the hair-thin wires towards the detonators plugged into the top of the mines. With an ear-splitting roar, the 680gm of plastic explosive in each mine exploded, rocketing a jet of ball bearings towards the Korean section. The directional mines had been sited by an expert and as the seven hundred steel balls from each Claymore tore into the flesh and bone of the Korean point section, not a single man escaped alive.

But the ambush had created little more than a breathing space. The depth sections were already closing up, knowing that the Claymore was a one-shot weapon and prepared to gamble that the mercenary commander had expended his limited supply.

'Look!' Alan shouted, pointing to the far side of the compound a couple of hundred yards away. 'Jules is pulling back. Let's get the fuck out of here.'

Dave was getting to his feet when a series of explosions rocked the compound and from the direction of the main gate a mushroom cloud of flame and smoke erupted into the night sky.

'Jesus Christ,' Kevin gasped. 'They've gone nuclear!'

'No, mate. The Koreans have just had a taste of the Fireflash.'

The 60mm anti-armour rocket of the M72 was a lethal enough weapon, adaptable for use against bunkers and dug-in machine-gun emplacements. The big biscuit tin of the M202 contained four of them in a block, capable at the flick of a switch of being fired singly or in a ripple of all four, one after the other, the firing option that Terry had selected. However, unlike the HE of the M72, the four rockets of the M202 Fireflash were each packed with napalm.

When the Korean officers had seen the men of Jules's team pulling back they realized that the time had come to urge their troops forward into the final stages of the attack. With threats and screams, they pistol-whipped their men out of cover and drove them towards the gates of the compound.

Leaving Dominic free to handle the Fireflash, Terry had taken command of his team, ordering them to hold their fire and lure the enemy into the trap. Watching the first of the Korean soldiers reach the gate, they ducked out of sight as he sprayed the courtyard with bullets, smashed the locks and burst the gates open.

'Hold your fire,' Terry hissed at his men as their fingers tightened the triggers of their automatics to second pressure.

'Steady . . . steady . . . Fire!'

A shock wave rocked Dominic on his feet as the first

of the Fireflash rockets exploded from his shoulder, spouting a jet of flame into the massed ranks of the terrified infantry. As the second and then the third rockets shot away from the launcher, Terry and the rifle group fired from the hip, raking the gateway with a hail of high-velocity bullets. Slamming into the killing ground, the last of the rockets sent a spiralling torrent of flame skywards and the gateway vanished in a seething orange ball.

Tossing aside the empty M202 case, Dominic took up the two Claymore clappers and detonated the mines, pumping the open gateway with a searing mass of steel ball-bearings that cut short the screams of the human torches and tore into their fleeing comrades who had broken and run. Shooting the fugitives at random, the Korean officers were themselves overwhelmed, cut down by their own men, who were desperate to escape from the tornado of the gateway where the mercenaries stood firm, awaiting the next onslaught, the barrels of their weapons smoking like sated dragons.

'Move now!' Terry shouted, pitching his voice to carry above the noise of battle.

Leapfrogging back in pairs, the team jogged through the resort complex until they reached Jules's men, who were lying in wait, weapons in the aim, ready to give covering fire and take over the battle at a moment's notice.

'No probs,' Dominic called jauntily as he hopped over a low hedge, following Terry back to the exit point where Andy and Ken were waiting. 'We've broken clean. They've had enough.'

But as he landed on the grass Dominic was flung forwards as if hit by a sledgehammer between the shoulder blades. A voice seemed to be screaming in his ear, but it was coming from very far away. He wondered why everything had suddenly gone so quiet and peaceful. They had given the North Koreans a licking at the gate, but he was baffled by this complete silence. Then he was being rolled on to his back and looking up at the stars. Terry was staring at him, stern and serious, both hands pumping at his chest. But now Terry was fading too, and as Dominic's lifeblood seeped from the gaping wound in his back he was left to spend the last seconds of his short life alone, while Terry and Jules and every member of the team desperately scanned the surrounding buildings for the sniper.

7

An eerie screech rebounded off the compound walls and was followed a moment later by the rasping voice of a PA system.

'Well done, gentlemen, well done. But I'm afraid your little game's over.'

'Yi,' said Danny, catching the same recognition and cold hatred in Terry's eyes.

'Lay down your weapons and surrender. You've had a good run for your money. You will be treated as prisoners of war with more honour than you deserve. You have my word on it.'

'Fuck you!' Jules shouted, firing a burst at a speaker attached to one of the accommodation blocks. But the voice went on relentlessly, echoing throughout the resort and into the surrounding countryside.

'Even now you are being cut off. Surrender and you will live. Fight on, and you will die.'

'Not before a lot more of you bastards!'

The speakers chuckled, there was the crack of another single shot and the mercenary cried out, toppling on to his side, clutching his arm. In response the mercenaries fired at random, blazing at windows, shadows, into doorways and across rooftops.

Terry glanced from Dominic to the wounded mercenary. 'There's more than one sniper.'

Danny checked the angles of fire. 'I'd guess there'll be at least one more. Yi on the mike and those three fuckers from his team – all trained snipers. We really fell for that one.'

'We're smack in the middle of their killing ground. If they've got night-sights they can pick us off one by one.'

'Then why don't they?' Danny asked.

'I don't know. They haven't used mortars or artillery either. For some reason they want at least some of us alive, but I'm not about to stick around to find out why.'

Hand-signalling to Jules and the remainder of Dominic's team to get ready to move, Terry shouted out to Yi.

'What are your terms?'

'None. Surrender unconditionally or die. I would have thought even a dull-brained *karateka* like you could understand that.'

Holding his temper in check, Terry checked his assault rifle, slipped two white-phosphorus smoke grenades from his webbing, then signalled to Danny and Jules to do the same.

'OK. Give us a moment to think it over.'

Grasping both grenades in one hand, he gripped the two pins in his teeth and yanked them out. Next to him, Danny did the same and across the pathway Jules nodded that he was ready.

'You're not playing for time, I hope,' Yi's disembodied voice echoed. 'It would be very silly of you to think that I'm bluffing.'

'Throw!' Terry screamed. In one convulsive motion he lobbed his grenades over the wall, Danny throwing his to the left and Jules his to the right. Exploding in a cascade of brilliant flashes, the six grenades created an instant semicircular screen of dense white smoke.

'Move!' The breath was hardly out of his lungs before the mercenaries sprang into action, following Danny who zigzagged back through the pool area towards the restaurant.

'Go! Go! Go!' Terry screamed, emptying a full magazine from his Colt Commando into the smoke to deter any follow-up. He was about to turn and follow when across to the left he caught sight of Dave and Alan helping a wounded man between them.

'Shit,' he muttered. The smoke was already thinning and he had used his last WP grenade.

'Run!' he screamed, and slamming another magazine on to his assault rifle, fired single aimed shots into selected windows and doorways that might be sniper firing positions. But there were too many even for a whole platoon to cover and as the smoke began to clear, first one shot and then another rang out. There was a scream and Kevin toppled forward into a swimming pool. He floated to the surface a moment later, to turn in slow circles, as a film of blood spread across the water, further rounds pocking the rippled surface, nosing towards the dead body like piranhas.

Terry provided wild covering fire as Dave sprinted towards him, weaving and ducking, a rain of sniper bullets kicking up showers of fragmented plaster and concrete around him.

'Jee-zus!' he screamed as he streaked past and on towards the restaurant.

With him in the clear, the snipers turned their attention to Terry. However, with Jules and the rest of the men now safely through the wire, Danny had returned with Ken and Andy and together they put down a withering fire into the compound. Tearing straight through the middle, Terry moved faster than he had ever moved in his life. On reaching the outer ring of scrub at the top of the slope above the new exit point, bullets thudding into the soft grass and cracking in the air, he dived over the edge and plummeted down into the thick bushes. A moment later, Danny, Ken and Andy followed in a hail of arms and legs.

Picking themselves up, they pushed through the gap in the undergrowth they had cut earlier and wriggled under the wire to be met by Dave, Jules and the others, hastily organized for all-round defence.

Terry checked his assault rifle and did a head count. Four dead, and almost everyone else had at least one light injury, ranging from multiple cuts and scratches to puncture wounds from grenade fragments. Dave was the first to speak.

'There's a company of paratroopers unaccounted for, maybe two. They sent a couple of platoons to probe at the old entry point but the rest cut round us. They could be between us and the beach.'

'You can bet on it,' Terry said, his mind racing. Well, if they expected him to walk into an ambush, they would be sadly disappointed. But as he was about to speak, Jules cut in.

'If we do a wide hook we can outflank them and still reach the boats by daybreak.'

Terry stared at him dumbfounded. 'What boats? You don't think they'd allow us to waltz along the beach, jump in the dinghies and sail away, do you? They'll have destroyed or booby-trapped them by now.'

'How do you know? And anyway, who said you're in charge?'

Terry felt himself go taut inside but fought to keep control. 'Listen, Jules, we're all in this together. We've been double-crossed and must count the beach hiding-place as compromised as well.'

'Well, what do you suggest?'

Terry was aware that every pair of eyes was on him. He hadn't been prepared to take the lead – it had just happened, and in the heat of battle the men had listened and followed. But now would come the real test. If they followed Jules, he felt certain they had a good chance of walking straight into an ambush.

'We should go north,' Terry said as calmly as he could. Jules was incredulous.

'North? Deeper into Korea? You're fucking barking, man.'

Danny chipped in on Terry's side. 'I reckon Terry's right. It's exactly what they'd least expect. We could hook south later.' He looked around at the others. 'I'm with Terry.'

Ken stepped forward. 'I'm sorry, Terry. Jules gets my vote. I think it's worth trying for the dinghies. Even if that fishing boat doesn't turn up, they'll get us further down the coast and closer to home.'

One by one, the other mercenaries declared for Jules and the boats until Terry shook his head in desperation. 'You're mad, all of you. Raving fucking mad.'

But there was no more time. As Jules gathered the men together and prepared to set out for the boats, the sound of renewed firing came from the main gate where the surviving officers had finally regained control of their men and had restarted the assault. Finding the mercenaries gone, they were moving rapidly through the compound.

'Move out,' Jules ordered. Turning to Terry, he asked: 'Are you coming with us?'

Danny looked at Terry. 'I'd rather strike out on my own than go with this asshole. Will you come too?'

Jules's men were already snaking down into the forest away from the compound. Maybe Jules was right, Terry thought. Maybe they could give the paratroopers a wide berth and arrive at the beach to find the boats intact. Then, as Ken had said, they could be well down the coast by daybreak, even with those little motors.

'Well, are you coming?' Jules prompted.

'Come on, Dojo,' Ken called over, setting off down the hill. 'Leave Tonto to dance with his shagging wolves on his own.'

Terry looked at Danny. 'Maybe they're right,' he said, glancing away to avoid the look in Danny's eyes, which was too painful to take. It was a mixture of contempt for a professional who has taken a wrong decision, but tempered with pity for a middle-aged man trapped in a younger man's profession.

'OK, Terry. Good luck. I'll see you in Seoul, Danny said, and without a backwards glance he cradled his M16 in the crook of his arm and set off for the north, his long, steady stride taking him away from the boats and into the teeth of the enemy.

Throughout the journey to the beach, Terry was tormented by doubts. What the hell was he doing tagging meekly along at the back of the column like some Tail-end Charlie raw recruit, mind in neutral, a lamb to the slaughter? His every instinct told him that he had made the wrong choice, but now it was too late. Perhaps it was time to admit that he was simply too old for this game. When the crunch had come, the lure of a nice easy boat trip down the coast had been too great a temptation to resist. He had weighed it in the balance of his judgement against the prospect of a hard slog through mountains and forests with Danny and the soft option had won. What was the old saying about the road to hell being the easy downhill one?

However, about half an hour out from the compound, they heard the sound of an almighty fire-fight in the north, a deafening and continuous roar from a hundred Kalashnikovs and the thin, pathetic reply of a single M16. There were a couple of muffled thuds from detonating grenades and then silence. So that was the end of Danny Grey Wolf. Terry didn't doubt he had gone down fighting.

Jules fell back alongside him. 'No hard feelings, Dojo. We all make mistakes.'

'Fuck off and leave me alone.'

'Have it your way, man,' he said with a shrug, returning to the head of the column.

The wide hook added at least two hours to their journey but shortly before first light they came over the crest of a hill and saw the shimmer of the Sea of Japan below them.

'We've done it.'

Terry turned to see Andy beside him. His face was the usual impenetrable mask, but in his own feelings of isolation Terry sensed a new kinship with the tough little Scot.

'You're thinking about Danny, aren't you?' Andy asked.

'I'm wondering why I didn't go with him,' Terry replied. 'It was my idea.'

Andy chortled. 'Fucking stupid one too. No offence, mate.'

'Well,' Terry said thoughtfully, his eyes scanning the peaceful beach laid out below them. 'We'll see, won't we.'

Winding down the steep hillside, the exhausted mercenaries made quickly for the beach. There was no sign of the fishing boat which should have been there to pick them up, but that came as no surprise. But even without it they estimated that the outboard motors of the dinghies would be sufficient to get them out of the immediate danger area before running out of fuel. If their luck was in they might even make it past the 38th Parallel and then they could land safely on South Korean territory. If not, they would have to attempt a crossing of the land border. Either way they would be beyond the reach of the Communist paratroopers.

Terry didn't like it one bit. They were moving much too fast, lowering their guard, convincing themselves that the dinghies were clear and the enemy far behind. He dropped back from the main body, Andy staying with him, and carefully surveyed the beach as the lead man stepped out of the cover of the trees and on to the bare sand.

'Come on, lads,' the man called back, 'it's as clean as a whistle.'

He broke into a jog with the others following him, heading for the hiding-place where the dinghies had been concealed in the mangrove. Reaching it, he tore at the branches.

'They're fine!'

A couple of the men cheered.

'Let's get cracking.'

'Seoul here we come!'

Andy moved out on to the beach. 'Come on, Dojo. Better get a shift on.'

Terry was still uneasy, but why should he be? The Koreans had fully expected to catch them in the compound. The wide hook of their escape march had probably worked, taking them round the edge of the paratroopers' ambush. For all Terry knew the Koreans were still sitting back there waiting for them and in a few minutes they would be out on the water and hurtling down the coast towards home. Sure, it was wise to take precautions but it wasn't always necessary. Not every enemy soldier was as cunning as that.

With a sickening roar, the detonating booby-trap sent the mercenary's body cartwheeling into the air with the force of the explosion, ripping him apart and shredding the inflatable rubber dinghies. The fuel tanks ignited and burst in a series of lesser explosions, but by the time the lifeless body slumped back on to the sand everyone's attention was on the line of scrub-covered sand dunes from where a fusillade of gunfire was pouring.

The sand at Jules's feet danced with impacting bullets and as the mercenaries returned fire, they were forced back towards the waterline, bunching together involuntarily, defenceless in the open and at the mercy of the ambushers.

Concealed at the edge of the trees, Terry looked on in horror. But as he watched he noticed that apart from the single man killed by the booby-trap, none of the others was hit. The hail of bullets had driven them into a tight bunch like sheep herded by a dog, until they stood helpless in the water, the sea foaming with bullets around them.

As suddenly as it had started, the firing stopped, and a loud-hailer barked at them from the cover of the mangrove.

'Lay down your weapons.'

No one moved. Terry shrank back out of sight. The voice was not Yi Soong's. Presumably he was still back at the compound and the paratrooper commander was in charge of the ambush.

A second hail of bullets struck the ground at the mercenaries' feet and Andy doubled over, hit in the leg.

Again the firing ceased and again the loud-hailer blared out.

'Lay down your arms. This is your last chance.'

One by one the mercenaries dropped their weapons and raised their hands in surrender. From the cover of the dunes a line of North Korean paratroopers emerged, their Kalashnikovs at the ready, levelled at the mercenaries in case of any tricks.

Cursing himself, Terry ducked back deeper into the trees. He would now have to make it on his own, without even the help of Danny Grey Wolf, whom he had deserted and left to die on the hills behind the compound.

'And where do you think you're going?'

Terry spun at the sound of the familiar voice. With his full attention concentrated on the plight of his comrades on the beach, he had missed the approach of someone behind him. As he spun he tried to execute a precautionary block as he had done in the park in Seoul, but the strap of his Colt Commando was looped on his wrist for a safer grip, and his feet were shifting on the loose sand. The vicious roundhouse kick caught him full on the jaw and he went down, his last sight being the focused concentration on the face of Yi Soong.

The first thing Terry saw when he regained consciousness was the naked light-bulb in the middle of a bare ceiling. His head was pounding and his eyes felt as if someone was inside his skull trying to push them clean out of his head.

'Ah, Sleeping Beauty awakes.'

Recognizing the voice of Yi Soong, Terry tried to get to his feet but discovered that he had been securely tied to a wooden chair, his arms straight down by his sides, wrists and ankles tightly bound with cord.

Lifting his head, the first person he saw was Jules, similarly tied, his face swollen and bleeding, his head hanging limply down. On either side of him, two other prisoners stared back at Terry: Andy and Ken. Terry noticed that no attempt had been made to dress Andy's wound and although the blood had crusted and dried, fresh blood seeped from the gash, running down his ankle and on to the floor, where it was forming a dark pool.

From somewhere else in the building a piercing scream was cut suddenly short, followed by raised voices shouting some unintelligible command.

'What the hell's going on?' Terry asked.

From behind him, Yi's voice answered calmly. 'You're being tortured, what do you think? You're safely back at the resort.'

Ken raised his head. 'They want us to admit we're an American special forces unit on an authorized mission. They're trying to pin the murder of all those people in the resort on us.'

Terry tried to turn his head to look at Yi, but the Korean remained out of sight.

'But you know that's not true. You were in on the recruiting as well as Babs Butler.'

'Why, so I was. Perhaps it's all been a mistake and you can go home. Do forgive me.'

A fist slammed Terry's head forward, then grabbed him by the hair and yanked him back. Yi stared contemptuously down at him.

'What do you take me for? I don't give a damn who you really are, or what particular kind of scum. You'll say what I tell you to say.'

Terry sucked his lip and tasted blood. 'OK. What's so difficult about that?'

Yi chuckled. 'Let me clarify that. Your confession will be televised and broadcast to the world.'

'I see.'

'I doubt it, Mr Williams. Or can I call you Dojo?'

Again Yi's fist crashed into Terry's head.

'I've been looking forward to this little chat.'

'I bet you have,' Terry said, spitting blood on the floor. 'This is the only way you'd dare hit me.'

'You're not trying to goad me into untying you, are you? I can beat you any time I choose. I don't give a damn for your insults.'

'Good, 'cos that's all you're going to get out of me.'

'Wonderful! I was afraid you were going to do what we wanted and that would have spoiled my fun.'

Yi shouted for the guards and two men burst through the door and moved to the side of Terry's chair, tipping it back until he was lying on the floor staring up at the ceiling.

'You'd better agree to say what they want, Terry,'

Ken shouted. 'We all have. They've killed Dave Bedford.'

Terry felt himself go hot with anger. He struggled against the ropes, but the guard stepped on the chair back, fixing him in place.

'You bastards!'

'Really, Dojo. I didn't realize you were as stupid as David. I finished with him just before you came round. Let's see if you're prepared to go the distance.'

As Terry struggled on the floor, Yi took a sodden towel from a bucket of water and wrung it out. After shaking it loose, he draped it over Terry's face, straightening the ends so that his eyes, nose and mouth were all covered.

'You've heard of the Chinese water torture, I suppose? Well, we like to flatter ourselves that they got it from us.'

As Terry tried to inhale, the damp towel tightened on his face, suffocating him. The only way he could loosen it was by blowing out, but as he did so he emptied his lungs, which were already gasping for air. As he gulped in again, the towel once more tightened, choking him slowly.

'Fun, isn't it?' said Yi as he took a metal cup from the bucket and poured a trickle of water on to the towel. Soaking through the saturated material, droplets of water ran into Terry's nose and throat. He coughed and choked as it penetrated his windpipe, but whenever his aching lungs contracted, struggling for air, the towel was sucked closer to his face in a merciless grip.

When Terry's body started to convulse, Yi plucked the towel away and Terry gasped and choked. But before he had properly regained his breath, Yi flopped the towel back again, having poured a fresh cup of water over it.

'You see, we can go on like this all day if you wish. As they say in the old movies, we have ways of making you talk.' He laughed, enjoying the sport immensely.

Steady, Terry thought, fighting to control his mounting panic. He had steeled himself to face the physical pain of a beating, but this was beyond his wildest nightmares. While his lungs screamed for air his mind battled for control. Drawing on his inner reserves of will-power, he forced his muscles to relax, countering every desperate survival instinct and reflex. Focus on the mind, he thought. The mind is apart, separate. It doesn't need to breathe. He had almost managed it and felt himself slipping into the blissful release of unconsciousness when the towel was removed and, against his will, his body gulped in the air, undoing all the efforts of his concentration.

Eventually he lost track of how many times the towel had been placed over him until, finally, his body showed him the mercy that his captors would not and he passed out.

He was woken by Ken, who was kneeling beside him and holding a cup to his lips.

'Here you are, mate. Have a drink of this.'

Terry choked as the water slipped down his throat. 'A drink's the last bloody thing I need, you daft Aussie bugger.'

'Well, it didn't take you long to get back to your old self, did it?'

Leaning against the far wall of the cell, Andy

chuckled. Slumped against him, Jules was in a bad way.

'What did they do to him?' Terry asked as he crawled across the floor.

'Old Julesey wouldn't say what they wanted him to,' replied the Scot. 'I guess he felt responsible for going against you and leading us into this shit.'

Terry examined the South African. 'There don't seem to be any bones broken.'

'No, but he's been unconscious for too long. He should have come round by now. I reckon his brain's fucked.'

Andy gently turned Jules's head and showed Terry the bruising on the back and side of the scalp.

'That bastard'll pay for this. Somehow,' Terry said.

Ken laughed. 'We've got to get out of here first.'

His mind racing, Terry just nodded.

Right now, Yi Soong and his goons held all the cards, he reasoned. They had said what they wanted: a confession. So what if it was all a load of crap? Unless the mercenaries did what they were told they were going to die. Dave had already been killed, Jules was badly hurt, and Terry himself wasn't sure how much longer he could hold out. Just before he had passed out he had felt himself cracking. Next time perhaps he would break and then where would all his stubborn resistance be?

OK, give them what they want. But then what's to stop them simply killing the prisoners when they have made their confession? Perhaps they couldn't just finish them off that easily, though. Yi had said that the confession would be televised to the world. If the mercenaries were then murdered, the North Koreans would lose their propaganda victory. They wouldn't be able to set them free because they would tell the truth as soon as they reached the South, so the mercenaries would probably be imprisoned in a labour camp in the hope that the outside world would eventually forget about them. But at least if they were prisoners they would be alive. And if they were alive, they could find a way to escape.

'Right,' he said. 'Let's give them their confession.'

When Yi next visited the cell he found Terry in a more co-operative frame of mind.

'OK, you win. Just keep that towel away from me, that's all,' Terry said as he huddled in the corner, staring at the floor.

'Well, this is a surprise,' Yi replied. 'You disappoint me. I'd thought you were tougher than this. I was looking forward to our next session. In fact I'm almost tempted to continue with it regardless.'

Terry looked up, tears welling in his eyes. 'Please, no! I'll say whatever you want, just leave me alone.'

Yi stared at him with contempt. 'And you were so full of bullshit. The big *karateka*, grovelling in the corner like a whipped dog.'

He lashed out at Terry with his foot, hitting him in the ribs. Terry cried out with the pain and rolled away from the towering Korean.

'Be ready in an hour. Here's what you've got to say.' Yi threw a sheet of paper into the middle of the room. 'Learn it by heart or you'll be having another little drink with me.'

'Tell me one thing,' Terry asked. 'Why did you go to all this trouble?'

Yi stopped in the doorway. 'Why? I would have thought even you could work that out. When the world witnesses the blatant aggression of the United States on a tiny Asian country, the UN will forget its demands to inspect our nuclear facilities.'

'Only for a while, surely?'

Yi grinned. 'That's as long as we'll need.'

'And us. What'll happen to us?'

'You'll be released, of course. After a brief time as our guests.'

Terry thought for a moment. 'Who were the people outside in the compound? The bodies?'

'Trash, like you. Political prisoners. You might even find yourselves occupying the labour camp they've vacated.'

Laughing, Yi left the room, then shouted an order to the guards to take the prisoners for a shower and to bring fresh clothes for them to change into.

Thirty minutes later the mercenaries were handcuffed and lined up in a corridor. Chains bound their ankles, linking them together like convicts, but they had all had a hot shower and been dressed in brand-new prison clothes. When all was ready Yi and a paratroop officer marched slowly along the line to inspect their charges, stopping here and there to comb someone's hair or straighten a shirt collar.

'We want you looking smart for the world's press.'

Jules, still unconscious, was propped between Andy and Ken. When Yi came to the South African he rounded on the paratroop officer.

'What do you mean treating a prisoner of war in this way?'

The officer blinked in confusion as Yi's hand lashed across his face.

'Take him to the medical centre immediately.'

As two of the guards dragged Jules away, Yi smiled

sweetly and said: 'You see, we are men of principle too.'

He strode to the end of the corridor and with a final glance at the line of mercenaries, opened the door and led the way into the glare of lights. Emerging into the room, Terry was dazzled by the storm of flash bulbs and spotlights. The prisoners were led on to a stage and ushered into seats at a long table covered with a white cloth on which stood jugs of water and glasses.

A North Korean officer stepped up to a microphone and began his address, detailing with the aid of maps, diagrams and slides the American plan to assassinate the country's élite nuclear scientists. Projected on the screen, Terry saw the bodies, photographed where he had seen them in the bedrooms and on the lawn outside, but photographed at an earlier time when freshly killed, before they had become swollen and discoloured.

Minute by minute the evidence of the massacre was spelt out to the assembled press, all of whom had been carefully selected from countries or organizations sympathetic to the North Korean regime, or at least antagonistic to the United States.

Finally, a microphone was passed along the row of mercenaries, who one by one admitted that they were members of an American special forces unit, infiltrated in from the South with the full connivance of the South Korean puppet regime.

When it was over they were hustled away before the journalists were able to ask further questions. But instead of returning to the cells, they were led out into the compound, where a large crowd of civilians had been assembled. Still in the glare of the television cameras, they were made to walk through the crowd as women and children jeered and spat at them. An American flag was ceremoniously burned, but as an old woman leapt forward to attack Terry with feeble kicks and punches, a Korean guard restrained her, assisting for all the world to see, the inhuman butcher who had slaughtered the innocents in the resort.

When Andy stumbled, another guard leapt to his aid, supporting him under one arm and evoking a storm of protest from the civilians, who were now hysterical and screaming for vengeance. But the paratroopers moved in to bar the way, shepherding the criminals of the US special forces team to the safety of a waiting bus. There, as they were ushered to comfortable seats, the briefing officer explained that the criminals would now be taken for a fair trial by a panel of independent judges, after which they would be sent back to South Korea or sentenced to a term in prison to atone for their murderous crimes.

The United Nations should desist from its absurd claims that the peace-loving people of North Korea were constructing a weapon of mass destruction. It was absolute nonsense. Instead it should focus its attention on the clandestine activities of the so-called free world and on the United States of America in particular. They were the real enemies of world peace. He made a special appeal to the non-aligned nations of the Third World, urging them to free themselves from the capitalist yoke that had kept them economically enslaved since the end of the colonial era. They were being dominated even more than before, he proclaimed, his voice rising to fever pitch and breaking with emotion.

Under careful supervision the cameras were allowed forward to film the captured special forces unit through the bus windows. Ken shoved two fingers up at them and a guard went to restrain him, but Yi Soong, mingling inconspicuously with the crowd, gestured to him to leave the prisoner alone. Having butchered innocent children in the resort, it was fitting that the unrepentant American soldier should demonstrate his contempt for world opinion so graphically. It had all turned out better than Yi could have wished, and as the bus drove off he allowed himself a moment of self-congratulation.

The only thing that puzzled Yi Soong was the sudden breakdown of Terry Williams. The Korean was seldom wrong in his judgement of character and it had truly surprised him when the Welshman had caved in. Still, Terry Williams wasn't motivated by political conviction like Yi himself. In fact, Yi couldn't imagine what did motivate him. But then, Dojo was only a mercenary after all. Worthless trash.

8

In his Washington office, Alex Leitner had never known it so busy. Since the news had broken of the armed incursion into North Korea by an alleged American special forces team, the phones had never stopped ringing. He had heard it rumoured that the President himself had been grilling the high-ups. Probably even missed his lunchtime jog, Alex chortled.

One thing was for sure, Eliot Masterson was looking a worried man. Alex didn't have a clue what the son of a bitch had been up to but because he had been dismissed from the great Masterson's office the other day, he didn't give a damn about his fate.

Leaning back in his chair, feet on the desk, he tried to pitch another ball of screwed-up paper into the waste-bin, missed and idly rolled up another. Yes, nothing would please him more than to see Eliot in the shit, the deeper the better.

He knew that the idea of the CIA being behind the whole caper was absurd. Why the hell would they want to insert a band of cutthroats to massacre nuclear scientists and their families while they were skinny-dipping in the Sea of Japan. Hell, the UN had almost gained admittance to the goddam country by the front door. The whole thing just didn't make any sense.

He looked at his watch and tossed another ball of paper at the bin.

'Ah, Alex, I'm glad you're here.'

Alex leaned round to see who it was and sprang to his feet as Masterson walked into his office and shut the door behind him.

'I've got some bad news and I see it as my duty to give it to you personally.'

Looking into his boss's cool blue eyes, Alex felt as if a hand had reached inside his chest and grabbed hold of his heart. The concerned expression that had masked Masterson's face since the news first broke had vanished and in its place had returned his customary icy arrogance.

'I'll come straight to the point. When I was appointed to this job I was given a free hand to improve efficiency and get results. I know you've been with the organization for most of your career, but I've come to the conclusion that you're in need of a rest.'

Alex stared at him dumbfounded, the hand tightening its grip on his heart.

'This is as hard for me as it is for you, believe me, but I'm sure it's for the best. This is a job for younger men and I'm sure you'll agree it's time you moved over and gave someone else a chance.'

Masterson paused a moment, somewhat perturbed by the sudden paleness of Alex's complexion.

'It's got nothing to do with this Korean business. In fact I'm leaving for Seoul in a couple of hours' time to find out what the devil's going on. I expect they've got a mole in their organization. You know what the gooks are like. Anyway, I'd like you to clear your desk and be out of the office by . . .' – he looked at his watch – 'let's say three o'clock. I hate doing things in such a rush but it's standard procedure, as you know. Security. We can't afford a leak like the Koreans. There's a guard outside who'll help you tidy up. Alex?'

But Alex could no longer hear what he said. He was fishing in Chesapeake Bay with his son, joking about the time when Stephen would be an officer cadet at Annapolis. Nor did he hear the hurried steps of the security guard as Masterson flung open the door and screamed down the corridor that Leitner was having a heart attack.

After leaving the compound, the bus carrying the mercenaries wound its way painfully out of the valley, escorted by two truckloads of paratroopers. But when it came to a fork in the road just out of sight of the resort, instead of taking the main highway north to the city, it turned down a narrow lane that led through ever-thickening forest.

Staring blankly out of the windows, the prisoners were still in a daze, bewildered by the events of the last hours, most of them in deep shock. Only Andy and Terry took careful note of the route, wondering why the column was heading into the heart of a forest on a track that both of them knew from their map briefings led down to a steep-sided river and a dead end.

Without alerting the guards Terry glanced across the aisle and caught Andy's eye. The Scot frowned and raising his chained hands, drew a finger across his throat. Terry nodded solemnly. So this was how it was to end. He had miscalculated again. Yi Soong had got his confessions and no longer gave a damn what happened to the mercenaries. By the time the world woke up to the fact that they had been massacred, if it even cared, the North Korean nuclear-weapons programme would be complete and, thanks to them, the UN would have been outmanoeuvred and the South would be wide open for ransom. Accept Communist rule or face destruction.

Terry desperately tried to think of a way out but it seemed hopeless. Each truck would be holding about fifteen paratroopers, each armed with a Kalashnikov and a plentiful supply of ammunition and grenades. One truck was leading the way, the other following the bus, escorting it to a new and terrible killing ground. Perhaps there would even be others already waiting to receive them on the river bank.

Although in the bus itself there were only the driver and four guards, they were fully alert, their weapons levelled at their prisoners, safety-catches off and fingers on the trigger. The slightest pressure would let loose a torrent of fire. Furthermore, the mercenaries were chained together and without so much as a toothpick between them. They were exhausted and Terry wondered if any of them had any fight left. He would have to find out.

On the seat in front, Ken was starting to doze. Slowly Terry edged forward.

'Here, Ken. Wake up, you dozy bugger.'

'Fuck off.'

'Listen, mate, if we don't do something we'll soon be having the big sleep.'

Ken shifted and without turning round, leaned closer.

'What do you mean?'

Terry explained about the track and the dead end. 'Pass it on.'

Ken yawned loudly and leaned forward as if going

back to sleep, muttering instead under his breath to the man in front. God, don't go on the stage, Terry smiled to himself. You'd never win an Oscar like that.

While the message was being passed round the bus, Terry tried to figure out a way to distract the guards. The sun was pouring in through the windows and inside it was warm and comfortable. Although the mercenaries had been chained together, the chains were long enough to allow each of them to sit in a row on his own, the loose chains trailing down the central aisle. There were two guards at the front of the bus beside the driver, and two at the back. OK, Terry thought, here goes.

'Come on, lads, what about a little sing-song,' he said heartily, and before the guards could react, he began.

Row, row, row your boat, gently down the
  stream,
Merrily, merrily, merrily, merrily, life is but a
  dream . . .

Ken turned round and winced with horror. 'Is that the best you can do?'

'Sing, you bugger!' Terry hissed at him, and burst into the next repetition.

Row, row, row your boat, gently down the
  stream,
Merrily, merrily, merrily, merrily, life is but a
  dream . . .

One by one the others joined in. The guards were on

their feet immediately, shouting at them to stop and lashing out with their feet and rifle butts.

The bus had reached the steepest part of the descent and was winding laboriously down the hairpin bends through the forest. The turns were now coming every sixty or seventy yards and were so sharp that the bus was almost doubling back on itself. But more importantly, Terry had noticed that for long stretches at a time they were out of sight of the escorting trucks.

By now every prisoner was singing and, despite the beatings of the guards, they persevered, endlessly repeating the simple tune. Then, as the bus rounded another bend and lurched forward down the next stretch of track, Terry realized that both escorting trucks were out of view, the one in front having rounded the next bend and the one in the rear not yet having appeared from behind. He estimated that he had only a few seconds in which to act.

'Sing up, lads,' he shouted and shrugged at the guard who rushed to silence him. Terry smiled sweetly up at him as he raised the butt of his Kalashnikov.

'Now or never,' he said. The guard paused, a puzzled frown creasing his brow, and Terry's foot shot up between his legs, driving the guard's testicles deep into his body. His eyes bulged and he doubled forward, collapsing across Terry, who looped his handcuffed wrists over the man's neck, gripped his temple with one hand and his shoulder with the other and twisted viciously, breaking the neck with a loud crack.

'Rumble!' Ken shouted. 'Now that's what I call a sing-song.'

Before the other guards could react, the mercenaries struck. In their attempts to silence the prisoners the guards had carelessly spaced themselves along the bus, leaving their positions of relative safety at the front and back. Swamped by the mercenaries, they were dragged to the floor and killed before they had a chance to fire a single shot.

At the front of the bus the driver tried to bring the bus to a halt, but Andy's fist swung out of nowhere and spread him across the steering wheel.

'No you don't, mate. This isn't my stop.'

Lifting the stunned driver out of the seat, Andy flung him aside for another mercenary to finish off. But, as he clambered into the driving seat himself, he found that with the chains on his ankles he was unable to reach the brake and stop the bus from careering out of control down the hill.

'Dojo, get these fucking chains off!'

Ken rummaged desperately through the guards' pockets.

'Forget it,' Terry shouted. 'They won't have a key. Where we were going they wouldn't have needed to take them off – just dump us in the river.'

'Then shoot the bastards off!'

Ken grabbed at the dead guard's Kalashnikov but Terry snatched it from him.

'No. The escorts'll hear the shot.'

'Do something!' Andy screamed. The bus was now hurtling towards the next hairpin bend and at its present speed would go straight over the edge and down the precipice into the trees below.

Tugging against his own chains, Terry shuffled forward to Andy and raising the butt of the Kalashnikov over his head, brought it down with all his might on a single link of the chain an inch short of Andy's ankle. The chain sprung apart and Andy jerked his foot free and hit the brake, spinning the wheel to regain control of the bus and bring it into the turn. A cheer went up from the rest of the mercenaries as it lumbered round the corner and entered on the next stretch of road.

'Here, put this on and keep your face down,' Terry said, stuffing the driver's cap on Andy's head. 'Don't get too close to the truck in front. If they see your ugly mug behind the wheel it'll all be over.'

Back in their seats the mercenaries were smashing their chains. One of them had found a way of using the bayonet clasp to break open the handcuffs and went from man to man springing them free.

'Right, back in your seats everyone, quick. Everything's nice and normal,' said Terry.

Donning one of the guards' hats, he sat at the front of the bus beside Andy, cradling a Kalashnikov. Ken went to the back with another and sat in the guard's seat, checking that no one in the rear truck had noticed anything. When it rounded the bend a moment later sixty yards behind, it was motoring easily as if nothing had happened. The driver in the cab gave Ken a cheery wave.

'Up yours too, mate,' Ken murmured as he waved back.

Two of the other mercenaries also now had weapons but with half their number still unarmed, Terry didn't like the idea of getting embroiled in a fire-fight. The bus guards had only been carrying four spare magazines apiece and two grenades, and the driver had been unarmed, so it was hardly an arsenal with which to take on the escorting platoon of paratroopers.

'Think, man, think,' Terry murmured to himself. You've taken over the bus but it won't be long before you reach the clearing at the bottom of the hill and then it'll be too late. Sure, you would have the element of surprise and in the first few seconds you might be able to account for half a dozen of the paratroopers, but even with surprise your fire-power's no match for their greater numbers. The odds are they would eventually win.

OK then, what if we stop the bus? If we time it right the truck in front won't notice and will carry on and the four of us with weapons can ambush the one behind. With only fifteen of the buggers to deal with the odds are better. But the front truck would hear the firing and be on us before we could get away into the forest. It would only take a couple of survivors from the rear truck to keep us pinned down until their mates arrived.

He was just wrestling with a third option when Andy shouted down the bus.

'Hang on!'

A second later they were shooting down a footpath, Andy's foot hard on the accelerator, branches whipping and cracking against the windscreen.

'What the fuck are you up to?' Ken screamed from the back.

Andy stamped on the brake and the bus skidded and slewed to a juddering halt, flinging everyone to the floor. He sprang to the door and flung it open, shouting: 'Shut up! Listen.'

As the dust settled and the peace of the surrounding forest reimposed itself, they could all plainly hear the sound of the truck engines receding, the front one continuing steadily down the zigzag road, the other bringing up the rear. Suddenly Ken burst out laughing.

'You canny Scottish git.'

Andy shrugged modestly. Noticing a path leading

off the main track, he had reacted on impulse. Seeing that the lead truck had already rounded the next bend and glancing in the mirror to check that the other one hadn't yet appeared, he had swung the bus on to the footpath and ploughed deep into the thick forest.

Picking himself off the floor, Terry grinned and clapped Andy on the shoulder. 'Nice work. Of course I was just about to suggest something like that myself.'

Ken's hat spun the length of the bus, hitting Terry on the back of the head, and everyone cheered. But Terry realized there wasn't a moment to lose. As they negotiated the bends, the truck drivers would only have to miss a few more glimpses of the bus to become suspicious, and when the rear truck caught up with its partner at the bottom of the hill the game would be up. Shouting for everyone to debus, he and the other seven mercenaries tumbled out into the heart of the forest, and as the sound of the trucks grew fainter the river's distant roar rose up from far below.

'What's the betting we'd have ended up floating in it?' Ken said as Andy limped up beside him, the wound in his leg smarting from the sudden exertion.

'Aye, pumped full of holes and strung together like a fucking daisy-chain.'

Back at the resort, the press had been taken to see the unconscious Jules in the medical centre before being given coffee and driven back to Pyongyang. Standing by the bed, the briefing officer looked at the wounded man with tenderness.

'We don't blame the men themselves,' he said. 'They have been brainwashed by their corrupt political system. It is their government that must answer for their crimes. This poor individual was wounded in the battle with our victorious forces, but he will have the best medical care that North Korea can provide.'

A correspondent from an African state asked what would become of him when he regained consciousness.

'He will receive a fair trial, like his comrades, but in the meantime our prime concern is to ensure his full and speedy recovery.'

The journalist nodded approvingly and one or two members of the gathering applauded.

'Now come this way, please. I'm afraid that I must now show you the bodies of the innocents they murdered, helpless men, women and children enjoying a holiday here at the resort.'

Leading the crowd of reporters and cameramen out of the ward, the officer took them to see the bodies of the dead, unrecognizable in their garish holiday clothes as the inmates of labour camps from which they had been plucked several days ago and taken to their deaths.

When the ward was quiet again a door at the far end opened and Yi Soong came in. Dismissing the nurse, he went to Jules's bed and sat down on the edge.

'Can you hear me, Mr Merkoen?' he said.

Then, with his thumb, he pulled open one eyelid, looked into the unfocused pupil and let it drop shut.

'Pity. I was hoping this would be more fun,' he said aloud.

With his fingers under Jules's chin, Yi gently tipped his head back until the windpipe stood out bare and exposed.

Now, Yi pondered, how best to do this?

He searched around the bedside table as if looking for some implement to help him.

'Oh, never mind,' he said, finding nothing suitable.

Turning to face the unconscious body, Yi braced his knee on the mattress and drew back his clenched fist, couching it level with his breast. With the speed and force of a whiplash, he snapped the fist down, pulverizing the cartilage of the windpipe, and as Jules Merkoen choked to death in his sleep, his murderer stepped back like an artist surveying his latest creation.

As he walked out into the bright sunlight, Yi looked around at the compound and cursed the wretched mercenaries who had made such a mess of the place. It would be some time before it was fit once again for the use of the President and members of the ruling élite. The walls were pock-marked with bullet holes and grenade splinters, there were phosphorus scorch marks on the flagstones, and the main gate had been completely destroyed by the Fireflash.

Nevertheless, the operation had been a brilliant success. The press were eating out of his hand and would soon be filing their reports to every corner of the globe. The nuclear-weapons programme would be completed in a matter of weeks and to add to it all, he had advanced his own career in the North Korean intelligence service immeasurably. He smiled. What would Kwang and his whore have to say about that?

He gazed at the surrounding hills. The forest and mountains were certainly beautiful at this time of year. By now the remainder of the mercenaries would also be dead, their blood-soaked bodies tumbled into the river to feed the fish. What a pathetic bunch they were. But something still niggled at the back of his mind and he couldn't pin it down, something about Dojo Williams.

'Comrade Yi, Comrade Yi!'

He turned to see an officer, red in the face, hurrying towards him across the compound, nervously waving a scrap of paper in his hand. The spectacle struck Yi as extremely vulgar and as he accepted the message he wondered why the officer was standing as far away as he decently could.

Terry first realized that the North Korean paratroopers were on to them when he heard the distant crack of two pistol shots down in the valley, where the trucks would by now have stopped.

'Some poor bastard getting the blame,' he said to Ken, panting as they pushed up the hillside.

'My heart bleeds for him.'

He could imagine the shock and panic when the rear truck finally closed up with the leader and they looked stupidly at each other, gaping at the empty space in between, terrified to admit the worst. Couldn't happen to a nicer bunch of blokes, he smirked.

After leaving the bus, he had sent two of the lads back to the end of the footpath where it left the track, to camouflage the tyre marks as best they could. It might just buy them an extra half hour if they could force the paratroopers to search the whole length of the winding road for the bus's exit point. They would find it eventually, but all the while they were searching they would be unable to start tracking the escaped prisoners themselves.

Andy was having a hard time of it, the gunshot wound from the beach ambush was bleeding again and although he had bandaged it as best he could with a strip of shirt from the dead driver, he was limping badly and had fallen back from his usual place at the front of any difficult tab.

Terry had taken the lead, with Ken close behind him; both were armed with Kalashnikovs. He had given the remaining Kalashnikovs to the two men at the rear, the three unarmed mercenaries and Andy walking in the middle in single file, feeling naked without so much as a knife. Whoever was at the front of the column had the unenviable role of pathfinder, forcing a way through the thick undergrowth and overhanging branches, and when they reached a part of the forest that was particularly dense and tangled, Terry decided to swap over the lead scouts every few hundred yards.

They had decided to march due west, heading deeper into Korea in accordance with Terry's earlier plan before the disaster at the beach. Eventually they would swing south and attempt a crossing of the land border, but to do so now would be to walk right into the blocking position that the paratroopers would be bound to place in their way as soon as a reaction force could be gathered together.

With neither compass nor watch, it had only been possible to estimate the direction roughly, but it would have to do for now. Terry regretted not having the time to get a more accurate fix by setting up a shadow stick. He could even have improvised a compass with a piece of wire and something magnetic from the bus, but the paramount need had been to get moving and put as much distance as possible between themselves and the hunter force. For now, a quick glance at the sun would have to do. When darkness came he would find a clearing and check the stars. Then, locating his direction of travel, he would seek out a prominent feature or landmark on the skyline and use it as a reference point by which to navigate.

'This is almost as bad as secondary jungle,' Ken

said, tripping over a hidden root and going down on his knees.

'Were you ever in 'Nam?' the man behind him asked.

Ken winked at Terry.

'Sure, mate. Birming'nam.' He spat in the dirt. 'Stupid pom. How old do you think I am?'

Terry chuckled. 'When were you really last in the jungle?'

'Philippines. Helping the government winkle the Commies out of the bush. You?'

'West Africa. Some stinking bloody bush that was, I tell you.'

Terry looked at the pines and silver birches, smelt the fresh air. 'This is luxury compared to that. We lost most of the team from malaria and some eventually went down with Aids after some R & R on the coast. Jesus, what a God-forsaken hole.'

'Lucky you kept your flies done up. Kept that Welsh willie of yours nice and clean. What do you feed it on?'

'Laver bread, what do you think?'

'Might have guessed. The original Welsh rarebit.'

'Don't you ever shut up?' Andy snapped, panting heavily.

'Not so long as there's someone I can piss off by talking,' Ken said, grinning at him broadly.

At the crest of the hill they stopped for a break, the four without weapons sitting miserably in a huddle while the others with Kalashnikovs kept their backs to the group, facing outwards and each covering a quarter of the arc.

'Don't just sit around, lads,' Terry said when they had rested. 'We can get some cam on at least.'

The clothes they had been given were brown prison fatigues, loose and shapeless but the right colour for a walk in the forest. Normally prisoners would have been issued with light canvas shoes, rope-soled and quick to wear out, but unable to find sizes big enough for the Westerners and wanting to create a good impression for the press, the Koreans had allowed them to keep their boots.

By smearing their fatigues with mud and streaking the material with crushed leaves and grass stains, they gradually converted their prison outfits into a passable set of combats. This done, Terry crawled forward and checked the terrain they were about to enter.

'Looks like the same mix of pine and birch. There's a fair bit of bracken too. Much like the stuff we've come through.'

Cutting branches and uprooting clumps of bracken, they worked in pairs to cam themselves up further, breaking the sharp outlines that could easily be identified at a distance, until at last they resembled a gang of runaway pantomime trees.

Finally Terry redistributed their small stock of weapons so that those without Kalashnikovs at least carried a bayonet and a grenade each.

'And if it comes to a fight make every one count,' he told them.

With this done, rested and feeling more like soldiers, they set off in a well-spaced single file, two Kalashnikovs front and rear as before.

As they marched, Terry put his mind to the question of food. Water was no problem: they had already forded several streams and it tasted beautifully fresh and cold. Looking around at the woodland, he reckoned that a man with the right training could live on the run for weeks or even months. They wouldn't be able to risk the noise of shooting game, at least not until they were deeper in the *ulu*, but they may be able to get some fish and there was an abundance of plants. They had found mess tins in the webbing they had taken from the guards, and if they could build a fire and boil the young bracken shoots and nettles, they could make an edible stew. Add in some berries and fungi and they could march all day. It might not give them enough protein to go the distance with Frank Bruno, but it would keep them alive.

It was towards evening that Terry began to feel uneasy. It started as a slight wariness. First he slowed the pace and increased the spacing between the men. Next he pushed two lead scouts fifty yards ahead. Then, as the sun got lower in the sky, he executed a standard ambush procedure, breaking track and doubling back to ambush their own trail; if they were being followed, the pursuer would walk right along the muzzles of their waiting guns. Nothing.

Andy edged closer. There weren't many men in the world he respected, but Dojo was one of them.

'What's up?'

Terry shook his head, puzzled. 'I'm not sure. Something.'

Ken shifted on the bed of brown leaves. 'Got the spooks, have you?'

Andy shut him up with a glare.

'OK, from now on we move for ten minutes, listen for five. I'll increase it if I have to.'

By now Terry was accepted by everyone as the natural leader. They had learnt the hard way that the shortest route is rarely the safest, and from now on, if Dojo said wait, they would wait. Half their number had already perished since landing in North Korea, and they knew that if Yi Soong had his way, the rest would soon follow.

'Get these miserable shits out of my sight.'

Yi Soong stood at the roadside in full combat gear, a new AK74 slung across his chest. The latest Russian 5.45mm assault rifle, it was the weapon borne by every man of the North Korean special forces company that had just deplaned from the Hip helicopters in the field behind him.

At Yi's feet, the two paratroop officers from the prisoners' escort lay in the dust, their faces bleeding from his interrogation.

'What do you want done with them?' the special forces officer asked with contempt.

Yi didn't even bother to answer, but shook his head in disgust as he walked away. Drawing his pistol, the officer stepped up to each man in turn and fired one round into the base of his skull.

Calling the platoon commanders together, Yi briefed them on the pursuit operation that was now in full swing.

'The paratroopers who allowed the mercenaries to escape have been sent on their trail. Having managed to lose the bus, they have now found it and are following up. If they fail to recapture the enemy, they have been told that they will be shot – a good enough incentive, I think.'

He spread his map on the ground. 'We are now here, some kilometres to the west of the escape point, and before any idiot asks me why we are not cutting off the direct route due south, let me say that I know now who's leading the mercenaries. I underestimated him once before and I don't intend to do it again. He'll be heading into the heart of Korea, probably intending to cross the rail line at Singosan and then cut towards the border opposite Kumhwa.'

Yi stared at the faces around him. 'Believe me, I know this man. Our border forces have all been alerted but apart from the miserable paratroopers, I have ordered everyone out of the area. I don't want us tripping over our useless infantry. They made a big enough mess of the attack in the first place. No. We, gentlemen, will track these fuckers ourselves.'

When he had dismissed the commanders and they had dispersed to brief their platoons, Yi folded his map and slid it into the pocket of his combat jacket. Checking his watch, he estimated that there was an hour at the most to darkness. Good. A hard night march into the hills would be an excellent warm-up for the company. Not that they needed one. These were the best troops in the country, better even than their opposite numbers in the American puppet state of South Korea. He should know. He had served in both, rising to the rank of officer in the ROK special forces, laughing secretly at their lax training under American instructors.

Their Achilles heel was their reliance on a sophisticated back-up. Without massive air support, packs full of the latest high-energy rations, satellite communications, instant casevac – without the trappings of civilization – they were like lost sheep.

But Yi Soong had always been the wolf. He realized that civilization itself was the enemy of the man of war. It softened him and if he relied on it for support it would betray him. Let the Americans keep their helicopter gunships and rations and casevac, their waterproof clothing and rucksacks crammed with candy bars and clean underwear. He had always trained his men to live with nothing but their wits. They could kill with their hands and feet, live off the land, navigate by the stars, sun and moon, and disappear like the wind itself.

Most of all he had trained their will, and when the final war came between the North and the South, it would be strength of will that would decide the outcome. His government would call the bluff of the southern regime, which, with its allies, would collapse. In their souls, Yi Soong knew, they were weak.

'And what of you, Dojo?' he said aloud to himself as he studied the moon rising in a dark, icy-blue sky. 'How strong are you in your soul?'

9

Half an hour before dawn Terry woke the others. They had stopped for the night on the side of a heavily wooded, steep-sided hill. Thrashing through the bushes, with branches whipping in their faces, some of the men had complained that they should find somewhere on flatter ground with easier access. But Terry was not to be moved; this was exactly the sort of place he had been looking for to harbour for the night. It was the type of country that no one would attempt to move through in darkness, and if they did the mercenaries would hear them coming from a mile away. Furthermore, it would be necessary for only one man to remain awake on stag. With eight in the party, the sentry would have to do no more than an hour on watch and everyone could therefore expect to get plenty of rest.

Terry had always loved the hour before dawn, a time of complete peace and stillness, so, reserving the last stag for himself, he enjoyed a good night's sleep before he was shaken awake at the start of his duty. Having risen and moved silently to one side of the others, he went through a simple warm-up routine to loosen his muscles, aching and stiff from the day before. He slipped into the *sanchin* hourglass stance, his arms coming up in the position of a double block, his breathing deep and powerful. Normally he would have used the thunderous *ibuki* breathing technique, but in the circumstances he executed each move in total silence.

Step by step he worked through the whole *sanchin kata*, feeling his mind come fully awake and the power flood back into his limbs. Each punch was executed in slow motion in perfect synchronization with the movement of the legs, hips and the breathing, Terry's concentration being on the complete focus of energy into the striking point of the two knuckles. At full speed it would smash bricks or shatter wood, but in the dark silence of the forest, Terry's fist moved with the controlled strength and precision of a stalking tiger, the energy locked deep within ready to be unleashed in a split second.

When he had finished *sanchin*, he worked through the fluid movements of the *tensho kata*. Here, instead of confrontation of power against power, the aim was avoidance, the deflection of the opponent's own strength and aggression back against himself. In place of the solid arm blocks, the defences were executed with rolling wrist movements, and gentle hooks that would gather in the enemy like corn to be cut down with open hand blows, each one capable of scything through bone.

Completing the routine, Terry shook himself loose and sat cross-legged to focus his mind, now fully awake. This day would be crucial. He hoped that a good march would take them out of the immediate danger area, but they could not afford to relax their guard for a moment. It was probable that Yi Soong himself would take charge of the hunt, for that was what it was. This was no exercise on the Brecon

Beacons or Dartmoor. This would be a savage, ruthless pursuit, with death the price of failure.

Terry knew that Yi would have limitless resources at his disposal, but would he use them? He thought not. Yi had tried that at the resort and the soldiers had made a complete mess of it. This time, Terry guessed, he would use the stealth of specialists. He might well use the army and border guards to throw some kind of cordon around his quarry, but cordons were easy to slip through if you knew how. The border would be another matter; Terry had heard that it was one of the most heavily guarded in the world, but that would be the problem for another day. For the moment they would have to concentrate on avoiding Yi's specialists.

When everyone was ready to move, they filed out of the harbour position and contoured round the hill. Then, breaking track, they climbed fifty yards and silently doubled back until they were above and parallel to their exit route. When they reached a position that offered good visibility down the hillside, they crept into cover to lie motionless and alert for fifteen minutes, observing their own tracks from this new ambush position in case they had picked up a tail.

Terry still didn't know why he was uneasy. Being on the run behind enemy lines was enough to unsettle anyone, but he had never been the jumpy type. Whenever he had felt like this in the past it had always been for a reason. This time as well, he was sure that his sixth sense was firing on all cylinders; he just hoped that he would discover the cause before it discovered him.

The fifteen minutes were almost up and the men were starting to shuffle restlessly, anxious to be on the move, when something caught Terry's eye, springing his senses to full alert. His hand signal for enemy contact instantly brought everyone back to the present and eight pairs of eyes strained through the undergrowth, seeking out the hostile tracker. The safety-catches of the four Kalashnikovs were silently eased down into the automatic firing position, and the remainder of the party clutched their grenades in preparation for the coming fire-fight.

On the track that they had created when leaving their night harbour, a single bush moved. Terry was right: there had been someone tracking them. But whoever he was, he had just made his last mistake. There was another rustle, and the sound of muffled voices, but just as Terry squinted through the aperture of his weapon sight, closing his left eye and tightening his trigger to second pressure, two thin boys stepped into the open.

Barefoot and filthy, they were dressed in rags and moving with the stealth and terror of cornered animals. The smaller of the two was stuffing into his mouth something that the elder boy had just handed to him. It was hard to be sure from fifty yards away but Terry thought it was a shoot of bracken that Andy had spat out as inedible the previous night.

Ken reached across and tapped Terry on the shoulder.

'What the fuck do we do?'

Terry looked back at the boys, but catching the movement of Ken aiming his Kalashnikov, quickly pushed the barrel aside. There had been enough killing of children at the resort. He was damned if he was going to kill any himself; leave that to Yi and his cronies.

Thinking through his options, Terry reckoned that

they could simply lie still and let the boys move on, but he was sure that they had been tracking him for at least a day now, and if they felt the mercenaries were going to leave them a trail of food, they would continue to follow them. Then, if they ran into Korean troops, the boys might give them away.

But the matter was decided for him by Ken, who angrily flicked his selector switch back to safe, disgusted that Terry had weakened and stopped him from firing. In the silence of the forest the metallic click resounded as a clear warning of another human presence, and before the mercenaries could react, the boys had whipped around and shot away into the trees.

'Get them!'

Bounding out of cover, Terry shouted and threw himself down the hill. Although the boys had had a fifty-yard start, the smaller of the two had caught his jacket sleeve on a thorn bush. Wriggling free, he darted underneath a bush but not before Terry was able to grab one of his ankles and drag him out kicking and screaming. Getting to his feet, Terry lifted the boy upside down by the ankles and held him at arm's length, as he struggled like a demon. But a second later something slammed him in the back and he staggered forward as the older of the boys leapt at him, flailing with his puny fists and bare feet.

'Help me, someone. Get these little buggers off me!'

The rest of the men gathered in an amused circle to enjoy the spectacle of Dojo Williams being beaten up by a couple of ragged kids.

'Now there's a sight,' Ken mused happily. 'Dojo and the Karate Kid.'

One of the men stepped forward and with a swipe of the hand sent the older boy sprawling.

'He's got some guts, that one. Coming back to save his little brother.'

The others nodded approvingly and as Terry dropped the smaller boy to the ground, the men crowded round to inspect their captives, who clung together with eyes as big as saucers, the older one gabbling something in Korean.

'What's he saying?' asked Ken.

'How the hell should I know?' replied Terry.

'Maybe it's Korean for "Take me to your leader."'

'Or "Who's that fat, ugly bastard with the big mouth?"'

Terry crouched in front of the boys and looked closely at their clothes, trying to examine the material underneath the layers of dirt.

'Prisoners? Are you prisoners too?' He fingered the hem of his own fatigue jacket and held it beside their own. The boys looked at Terry's clothes, then at the others standing around them and nodded suspiciously.

'Well what the hell do we do with them now, Dr bloody Barnardo?'

'I say finish them. The first sign of the gooks and they'll give us away.'

Terry looked round at the speaker, a big Geordie. 'Don't act as dumb as you look. They wouldn't be wandering around in the bush if they weren't on the run as well. I bet they're more scared of the paratroopers than you are.'

'And that's saying something,' Andy piped up.

'We'll have to take them with us,' Terry said after a moment's thought, raising his hand to cut the storm of protest.

'Listen, if we leave them behind they'll simply trail after us and then they're far more likely to give us away. At least this way we'll know where they are.'

Ignoring the grumbles from the men, Terry placed the two boys in the middle of the little column, allocating one mercenary to keep an eye on each of them. When they were ready to set off, he checked everyone's camouflage, detailed the order of march, nominated two lead scouts, and passed the word to move. For the next few hours he couldn't help turning round every hundred yards to check that the boys were still there and that the men hadn't quietly disposed of them along the way, but whenever he looked the boys appeared to be quite content. They moved completely without sound, in sharp contrast to the tall Westerners flanking them. Previously Terry had thought that his men's fieldcraft was second to none, but in comparison with the two Korean boys they sounded like a herd of elephants. Even the men themselves noticed it and began to view their captives with a new and grudging respect.

It was also the boys who, towards the middle of the afternoon, gave the first warning of the paratroopers. Handing over their positions as lead scouts, Terry and Ken were taking their turn at the rear of the column, enjoying a break from the constant tension of pathfinding, where every sense was on full alert for the slightest hint of ambush or contact. But they had barely settled into the new movement procedure, each one turning alternately to check their tracks for an enemy follow-up, when there was a scuffling further up the column and the mercenary guarding the elder of the two Korean boys let out a curse as he wrestled with the boy, who was kicking him vigourously in the shins and chattering away unintelligibly.

Leaving Ken to watch the rear, Terry hurried forward to put a stop to the row. In the silent forest the smallest noise was amplified out of all proportion and travelled far. Furthermore, the column had just left the thicker cover of the trees and emerged into a clearing of stumps where the felled timber lay stacked in neat piles. The mercenaries could ill afford to be heard or spotted by woodsmen who could then alert the local police as to the whereabouts of the escaped prisoners.

'What the hell's going on?' Terry asked.

'God knows. The little bugger went all quiet and then ran amok. Needs a good hiding,' the man said.

But Terry could tell fear when he saw it and the boy had clearly been terrified by something. Passing the word quickly up the line, he ordered the column to stop, but being intent on their own task, the lead scouts had missed the commotion behind them and were already well across the clearing, becoming ever more isolated from the others. Suddenly there was a shout, followed a second later by a burst of Kalashnikov fire.

'Contact!'

Terry cursed his luck as the cry echoed back from the lead scout. He had thought that they were travelling too fast for their own good but had let it go, happy with the good progress they had all made since the escape. He had even allowed himself to dream of reaching and crossing the border unhindered. Some hope.

What was more, he now had his fire-power split in two at the exact moment when he could least afford it: a frontal contact with an enemy force of unknown size. In the normal contact drill, he and Ken would have moved forward through the relative security of the bush to add the weight of their own fire to the two Kalashnikovs of the lead scouts. Lobbing a grenade, they would have been able to break contact and bug out; they weren't in any position to get embroiled in a fire-fight. But now it would be suicide to cross the clearing, leaving behind the rest of the party with only bayonets and a couple of hand-grenades to defend themselves. The thick tree stumps made it impossible for Terry or Ken to even see the lead scouts, let alone expend their valuable ammunition in a useless blanket of covering fire. The only way would be by standing up and firing short, accurate bursts over the stumps, but already the air around them was crackling with the enemy's return fire, indicating a force of at least section strength. Whichever way he looked at it, Terry kept returning to the same terrible conclusion: his scouts were on their own.

'Pull back.'

'What do you mean?' Andy shouted above the noise.

'Do as I say!' Terry barked. 'Back to the cover of the trees. Move!'

At the first sound of shots the two Korean boys had hit the ground and huddled together behind a thick silver-birch stump. Grabbing them both by the collar, Andy shoved them along the ground in front of him towards the edge of the trees. With his Kalashnikov slung across his shoulders, Ken crawled forward on hands and knees, dropping into position beside Terry.

'Bit of a bummer, eh?'

'You're not kidding. Those two have had it.'

'I was thinking more about their guns and ammo. The other lads could have used them.'

'Has anyone ever told you you're all heart?'

'Never.'

There was a scream from the far side of the clearing, where the two lead scouts had gone to ground, and a moment later the dull thuds of exploding HE sent showers of wood fragments into the sky as grenades bracketed the remaining scout.

'Get the lads back to the last rally point,' Terry snapped. 'I'll hold them up for as long as I can.'

For once in his life Ken didn't argue. Every few hundred yards Terry had nominated a prominent feature, rocky outcrop or distinctive tree as a rally point for use in just such an emergency as this. In the event of ambush and the party getting split up, everyone was to return to the last rally point and wait for the others. After ten minutes they were to assume that no one else had made it and they were to proceed on their own. Ken knew that without the delay that Terry would impose on the pursuing paratroopers, the fleeing mercenaries would be lucky to get more than a hundred yards before the enemy rushed forward and got in among them. They would be cut to pieces.

'Right, mate. Don't keep us waiting,' Ken said, then turned and was gone.

Searching anxiously around, Terry located a good firing position about thirty yards to his left. At present he was dangerously close to the place where the two lead scouts had been killed. It would only take the paratroopers a couple of minutes to regroup and continue the pursuit and unless he moved, he would find himself directly in their path. Somehow he had to slow them down and he reckoned that he could best achieve this and conserve his precious supply of ammunition by sniping at them from a flank.

'What I'd give to be another six hundred yards away with an L96 rifle and a gillie's suit,' he muttered under his breath as he leopard-crawled through the wood chippings that littered the soft earth. But there would be no time for that, and besides, the ground didn't allow for it. If he was any further than fifty yards the trees would prevent him from identifying his targets. Instead of the sniper's stealth and unwavering patience, he would have to rely on speedy footwork and snap shooting.

Having reached his selected firing position, he had barely checked his magazine when the first paratrooper stepped into the clearing and moved clumsily into Terry's new line of fire.

'Dumb bastard.'

Terry tightened the butt into his shoulder and aligned his Kalashnikov sights on the unwary soldier. Flicking his selector switch to single shot, he waited until the figure had paused as if wondering which way to go, and squeezed the trigger. The round caught the paratrooper squarely in the chest knocking him backwards.

'Wales, one: North Korea, nil.'

Rolling to his right, Terry changed his position, the clusters of tree stumps obscuring him from the enemy's view. There was a shout from the far side of the clearing, where he estimated the rest of the paratroopers were gathering, and a fusillade of random shots ripped through the overhead branches.

You'll have to do better than that, Terry said to himself as he prepared to take on the next Korean.

But with Yi Soong's threats fresh in their minds,

the paratroopers were desperate to prove themselves to their absent commander. In a wild rush they burst from cover and surged forward, firing from the waist as they ran. One of them stumbled over a root and went down, accidentally firing his Kalashnikov as he did so. Thinking they were being engaged from a new angle, the paratroopers froze and bunched, blazing wildly around them. Steadying his aim, Terry levelled his sights at the only figure wearing the rank insignia of an NCO and fired. The sound of his single shot was lost in the torrent of noise from the paratroopers' weapons and the NCO crumpled and dropped to the floor.

'Just a couple more ought to do it.'

Estimating that there were at most half a dozen men left from the paratrooper section, Terry flicked his selector switch to automatic. In their panic and without the guidance of an NCO, they had allowed themselves to become bunched in the open, presenting a tempting target for the opportunist. An accurate burst would have a good chance of taking out several of them. Drawing up his right knee, Terry shifted on to his side and primed himself for action.

Using the pistol grip of the Kalashnikov to screw the weapon securely back into his shoulder for a rock-solid aim, he jack-knifed into a kneeling position and squirted two five-round bursts into the packed soldiers. Three of them went down, at least two of them dead, but the remainder, in the flood of relief at seeing their assailant for the first time, screamed with a mixture of hatred and fear, and charged at the kneeling mercenary behind the tree stump.

Bounding over the roots and fallen trunks, they rapidly closed the gap, but keeping his breath measured and even, Terry aimed at the nearest man and fired again. Both shots of the two-round burst caught him in the chest, although his momentum carried him forward until he hit a stump and collapsed dead on the ground.

Switching his aim calmly to the next soldier in line, Terry again squeezed the trigger. Nothing happened. Flicking the weapon on to its side, he stared in horror at the empty brass cartridge case jamming the mechanism. The front end projected out of the ejector slot, but the base was held fast by the breech-block. Snatching at the cocking handle, Terry tipped the weapon over and shook it violently to dislodge the empty case, but even as he let the spring slam shut, carrying the next round into the breech for firing, he knew that it was too late. The paratroopers were upon him.

Ducking under the slashing bayonet of the leading man, Terry cursed himself for having given his own bayonet to one of the lads who had been unarmed. Swinging his Kalashnikov, he caught the paratrooper behind the knees and brought him down, then, reversing his grip on the wooden stock, he crashed the metal butt plate into the bridge of the man's nose. Glimpsing a blur of steel to his left, he flung himself aside just in time to avoid a vicious lunge from the second paratrooper. In a fit of rage, the Korean raised his rifle above his head and hacked at Terry, who edged away on his back, wriggling to right and left to dodge the rain of blows. Then, allowing the man to close within range of a hand grip, Terry brought his foot up into the man's stomach, gripped the lapels of his combat jacket, and using his foot as a lever, hoisted the surprised paratrooper over his head in a perfect *tomoenage* somersault throw.

Even as the man was landing with a grunt in the dirt behind him, Terry was on his feet, darting to the side of his fallen opponent. As the man tried to get up, Terry slashed downwards with a *shuto* open-hand blow to the jugular, instantly following it with three devastating drop-punches, one to the bridge of the nose, the next to the upper lip, and the last to the point of the chin.

The immediate threats neutralized, Terry dropped to his knees, gasping for breath.

'Jesus, man, you're getting too old for this lark,' he muttered as he mopped the sweat from his forehead and slung the extra two Kalashnikovs over his shoulder. He then rummaged through the webbing of the two paratroopers for the spare magazines and grenades, which he stuffed into his own pouches.

'These'll do nicely, thank you.'

He was just standing up to go forward and check that the lead scouts were dead and to retrieve more equipment, when a bullet snapped past his ear. Dropping into cover, he looked across the clearing to see an extended line of paratroopers advancing steadily towards him.

'Bloody hell, where did you lot come from?' he said as he snapped a fresh magazine on to his Kalashnikov. 'I reckon this could be it, Terry my lad. One fire-fight too far.'

By now he estimated he had bought enough time for the other mercenaries to make good their escape to the rally point. They would only wait a few more minutes before setting off without him, presuming him dead. But glancing round, he saw that he was a good fifty yards from the relative safety of the trees and his position had been clearly identified by this new force of paratroopers. He gritted his teeth, promising himself that the Koreans would pay dearly for his death.

Suddenly, there was a burst of fire to his right and he ducked by reflex.

This is it, mate, he thought. They've got you cut off now as well.

But as he searched for this new enemy, Terry noticed that far from pressing home their attack, the paratroopers had gone to ground and were returning fire, not at him but at the new fire position. Adding his own fire to the bursts from his unknown helper, he created an overlapping arc with the Korean paratroopers caught in the middle. But something else was bothering him: the sound of the rifle fire was different; it was not a Kalashnikov but an M16.

With the paratroopers hugging the ground and unable to hit him because of the stumps, Terry made his way slowly back to the edge of the trees. As soon as he reached the welcome shade of the towering pines and birches, he fired a last burst at the paratroopers and then turned to sprint away into the depths of the forest. But what was more, as if at a signal the M16 of the other firer fell silent, and Terry knew that he too, whoever he was, would similarly be running for his life. Since he had been in Korea it was a drill that Terry had only practised with one man: Danny Grey Wolf.

Even from a distance of several miles the sound of the battle was music to the ears of Yi Soong. In the forest shadows around him every member of the special forces team instantly froze, melting into the shapes and colours of the woodland, tensed and ready for anything.

Yi listened carefully, counting the guns, accurately

picturing the engagement in every grenade burst and return of fire as if reading a sheet of music, building his mental image into a precise symphony of battle. With closed eyes he saw the initial contact, the panic of the answering fusillade and the pinning down of the lead scouts with a series of short, sharp bursts. In the silence that followed he imagined the confusion among the escaped mercenaries as they matched their inadequate weapons to the task, and then, yes, just as Yi had known he would, Dojo Williams offered himself up as a sacrifice and Yi could imagine the deliberate sniper fire from the Welshman's rifle taking a terrible toll of the miserable paratroopers.

Nor could he help smiling when he heard the Kalashnikov fire from the second section of paratroopers, imagining Dojo's surprise in the face of this new and unexpected threat. But the smile froze on his lips when he heard the unmistakable crack of an M16, knowing that it could stem from only one man. When the paratroopers had contacted Danny Grey Wolf north of the resort, they had assured Yi that he had been killed; he had fallen into the river and been carried away. No, they hadn't found his body, but there had been bloodstains on the rocks at the top of the cliff on to which they had driven him, and in the water below they had seen his body, turning face down in the swell, pulled under by the current and swept out of sight. With a painful effort, Yi forced the episode from his mind. He would deal later with the officer responsible.

Jogging across to a bare knoll, Yi walked out on to the rock, unzipped a small pouch on his web belt, and pulled out a compass. Taking a fix on the direction of the firing, he noted the bearing, plotting it on the transparent cover of his mapcase, and matching it to the ground below him. Across the valley the roof of the forest was a brilliant sea of greens and golds, but today there was no pleasure in it for Yi. Today it was an obstacle to be crossed and the site of a possible future cut-off position to ambush the mercenaries when they neared the border.

He outlined his plan to the special forces officer.

'We won't catch them today. Maybe not even tomorrow. But we will catch them. Right here.'

His finger stabbed at the map on his knee, and the officer looked with some surprise at the point indicated, in the desolate wilderness of minefields and razor wire of the border DMZ.

After Terry and Danny met up, they made their way back to the rally point to find that the rest of the party had already given Terry up for dead and left. But with Danny's tracking skills they soon located the trail and by nightfall everyone was celebrating the return of not one, but two spirits from the dead.

'What about the blood on the rock?' Andy asked as Danny recounted his escape to the crowd of eager listeners.

'I killed a rabbit, slit its throat and daubed the blood on the ground beside my empty cartridge cases. Once I was in the water I reckoned if I could convince them I was dead they wouldn't bother coming all the way down to check me out. The current was pretty fast and by the time I had to stick my face up for air, I was in the clear.'

Ken whistled in admiration. 'I take back everything I said about you, mate.'

Danny smiled and reached into his bergen.

'You guys look like a bunch of skeletons. Don't they teach you anything in the army these days?' He pulled out a bundle and unwrapped the grubby cloth. 'I don't have any wampum, but how about some nice rabbit jerky?'

As he handed round the strips of dried meat, he grinned, for one by one the faces all about him glowed with the pleasure of the taste of meat. He waited until they had finished and then pulled out another bundle, this time of dried fish.

'I'm afraid I don't have any ketchup.'

There was a cough from the back of the group and Danny saw two huge pairs of eyes boring into the bundle of fish. He selected two of the largest strips and passed them to the boys, who stuffed them in their mouths and chewed ravenously. When they had finished, Danny fired a couple of questions at them in Korean.

After questioning the boys further, interspersing their answers with further bribes of dried fish, Danny repeated their story to the others, telling them of their time in the labour camp and escape from the trucks, their flight to a forest hide-out and eventual contact with the mercenaries.

'They thought you were ghost spirits,' Danny said, laughing. 'They had never seen Westerners before, and when you came clumping through the forest covered in twigs and camouflage, they reckoned their time had come and they were supposed to follow you into the next world.'

'It might still come to that,' Terry added morosely. 'Have you any ideas about how to cross the border?'

Danny thought for a while. 'Some. I did a number of tours of duty in different sectors, and the Rangers ran an escape and evasion exercise that might come in handy. We all learnt quite a few lessons.'

There was a buzz of excitement around the encampment.

'Thank fuck someone knows what to do,' Ken said, sighing with relief.

'What's that supposed to mean?' Terry asked.

'No, I didn't mean it to sound like that, mate. We wouldn't have made it this far without you,' Ken replied hastily to background murmurs of assent from the others.

'What about the boys?' someone asked. 'It'll be difficult enough for us to make it by ourselves, let alone bogged down with a couple of brats.'

'We can't just leave them here. The poor little buggers'll starve to death, or get shot by those Korean bastards.'

'Yeah, you heard what they told Danny about having the dogs set on them.'

Terry looked across at Danny. 'You know the border. What do you think?'

Oblivious to the turn of the conversation, the two boys were picking the last shreds of dried fish from their teeth, happy for the first time since being picked up by the mercenaries. Danny called across to the eldest of the two and asked him some questions.

'What did he say?' Terry asked when they had finished.

'Well, he doesn't seem to know the immediate border area, but they sure as hell want to come with us. They might even be useful. It's fine up here in the forest, but once we're out in the open we'll stick out like sore thumbs. If we have to go near any villages we could use them to scout out the land for us.'

'Can they be trusted?'

Danny shrugged. 'Why not? We were dumb enough to trust that asshole Yi and look where it got us. These kids have got a vested interest in escaping to the South, just like us.'

Terry looked around the gathering: everyone was nodding in agreement.

'OK, then. The boys come too.'

Danny called to the boys, translating the news. Liang sat up, wiping his mouth and beaming, and whispered hurriedly to Little Chiao.

'What's he saying?' asked Terry.

Danny smiled. 'He says they were right about you being ghost spirits. He says you are going to lead them into another world.'

10

When they came to the edge of the forest Terry ordered a change of cam. They had been marching due south for some time and when the trees at last began to thin out they knew that they would soon be forced to leave the relative security of the wooded hills. Putting the men in a temporary defensive harbour, Terry and Danny stalked forward to the brilliant sunlight that dazzled their eyes after days in the shadows and gloom. Danny had taken Liang and as they dropped into the grass to crawl the final yards, the boy surged eagerly ahead as if expecting to see the free world laid out before him.

Instead, he only just managed to duck back into cover as a truck thundered past, spraying clouds of dust into the air from the surface of the unmade road that skirted the forest. Grabbing him by the ankle, Danny yanked him back into the shadows.

'Someone's coming,' Terry whispered, and crouched as low as he could, hugging the ground. But a moment later, an old man sauntered past, leaning heavily on a walking stick, oblivious to the three people watching him intently.

'There must be a village near by,' Danny said. 'Let's see if we can get a better look.'

Using their sniper training, he and Terry leopard-crawled out of the trees, the boy following, imitating their movements. Peering across the dusty track, they saw a cluster of houses some two hundred yards away. Beyond them, the ground stretched into the distance, where a low line of hills rippled the horizon.

'According to my estimates, the border's just the other side of those hills,' Terry said, thinking back to the maps that he had studied and memorized back in the training camp. 'If we're going to cross tonight, we'll have to get over this farmland this afternoon.'

'In broad daylight?'

Terry shrugged. He didn't like it any more than Danny did, but he knew that Yi was likely to have located their approximate position from the noise of the contact battle with the paratroopers. Ideally he would have liked to lie up for a few days, march by night and attempt a border crossing in a totally different sector, but without proper food the men were getting weaker by the hour and their ability to cover long distances was now seriously curtailed.

'I think it's time for a little deception plan.'

Back at the harbour, the men were restless, anxious to get moving with the border and the freedom of the South so close. When Terry, Danny and the boy entered the clearing, they were met with a barrage of questions. How far was it? Would they get over tonight? Had Dojo spotted any more paratroopers?

'Hang on a minute, lads,' Terry said, waving for silence. 'First things first. Strip off your cam and wipe off as much of the shit as you can. We've got a couple of miles of fairly open farmland to cross and folks'll get suspicious if they see a shagging forest strolling along. When you've done that, use the bayonets to cut two or three stacks of saplings, the longer the better. Nice leafy ones.'

'I knew it,' Ken smirked, 'we're going to pole-vault over the fucking border. The Welshman's finally flipped his lid. Couldn't hack the pressures of command.'

'Shut it. There're some farm buildings and a small village off to the left and anyone in it will have a clear view out across the fields. We'll keep as far away as we can but there's no way we can stalk it. The only way is to brazen it out.'

Having gathered the men around him, Terry explained his plan, and half an hour later a tired but successful group of woodcutters emerged from the forest and walked happily back to their homes on the other side of the valley. Each pair of men carried a stack of saplings between them, balanced on their shoulders, their heads and faces hidden behind the bright-green leaves.

One farmer, pausing by his herd of cows on the outskirts of the village, thought it was strange how the shadows at this time of day made a person seem taller than he actually was, but then it was hard to tell when, like the group of peasants, they were bowed under the weight of such loads. Two of them had brought their sons, who played and sang in front of the work party. The farmer smiled to himself. It was always the same with the young these days. They had no sense of responsibility; not like in his day.

'I blame the parents,' he said to his friend, who had come out of his cottage to watch. 'If I was their father I'd whip them if they didn't help.'

His friend nodded. 'A spell in the army would sort them out.' And the two of them shook their heads in disgust and went inside to moan to their wives about the lax villagers of Hamdok on the opposite side of the valley, who had been cutting fence posts and beanpoles.

Sweating under his burden of saplings, Terry shifted the weight, careful not to dislodge the Kalashnikov, which he had secured by the shoulder strap in the middle of the bundle. He had thrown away his webbing, keeping only the belt, slinging the pouch with his spare magazines over his shoulder like a satchel. Reluctantly, Danny had also thrown away his bergen, and stuffed his pockets with the most essential items of survival kit.

'Just keep that haircut out of sight,' Ken called over. 'One look at you and they'll think it's the brush salesman.'

They were almost across the belt of open farmland when directly in front of them an old farmer appeared out of nowhere, ambling towards them along the same narrow footpath. At the front of the column Terry swore under his breath, turning round to see Danny slip his tomahawk from his belt. Why did the old fool have to appear just now? The last thing Terry wanted was to take an innocent life. Also, if there was a scuffle it might be seen from the village. And how long would it be before the old fellow was missed? In addition to Yi Soong and his men, they would have the whole district out hunting for them.

The old man had been dozing behind a low earth bund and had been invisible until getting to his feet. He looked up and squinted at the approaching woodcutters, narrowing his eyes to focus on their bowed heads, hidden beneath their loads. He wondered why they were hesitating. Still, maybe they could let him have some water, for he was thirsty after being out in the fields all day. He was just about to start towards them, when a small boy ran past and snatched his hat.

'Here, grandfather. See what I've got,' Little Chiao called out as he tossed the black stovepipe hat to his elder brother. The old man was apoplectic with rage. Raising his stick, he ran after the two boys, who remained just beyond his reach.

'Are you an old shaman?' the taller of the boys shouted to him. 'Well, we're not afraid of your spells!'

Halfway across the field, the old man stopped and leaned on his stick, panting heavily. Far from calling their sons to heel, the woodcutters had gone on ahead. He could hardly believe his eyes. With parents as uncaring as that, how could these two youths grow into anything but hoodlums and vagabonds? But when he turned back the boys had gone, leaving the old man's hat at his feet. Racing across the field, they chased after their fathers.

The old man shook his stick at them, shouting: 'Show more respect for your elders! Your fathers should be ashamed of themselves.' But it was no use. The woodcutters were out of earshot, approaching the low ridge of wooded hills that sheltered Hamdok, the last village on their side of the border.

In the command bunker at Point 763, Yi Soong was putting the final touches to his plan for the destruction of the mercenaries.

'On the contrary, Colonel, I don't want your border guards near them. These are not your ordinary renegades, and besides, it has become a matter of personal pride to me and my men.'

The colonel nodded thoughtfully. He could imagine the sort of fuck-up that was being avenged. It was always the way: something would go wrong up-country – a coup attempt, a mutiny or a local rebellion; the survivors would try to flee to the South and those most responsible for causing the unrest in the first place would be the ones screaming loudest for revenge. But of course revenge would always be cloaked up in talk of national security; the colonel had heard the same claptrap a hundred times before. But whoever these runaways were, it was no longer any concern of his. Comrade Yi had taken personal control of the interception operation planned for that night and it was to be repeated every night until the enemy had been terminated.

When the colonel had gone and Yi was satisfied that only his own special forces officers and NCOs were present in the briefing room, he checked that everyone knew his part in the plan.

'We don't know where they will cross, but I believe it will be in this sector. Our intruder alarms and ground sensors should give us ample warning of their approach but in the last resort we can only rely on our own skills. I've had a network of sensors laid to cover the entire front. The border fence system, with its razor wire, dog runs, mines and machine-guns, will be the anvil and we, gentlemen, will be the hammer. At the first sign we will move in with the Quick Reaction Forces and crush them.'

Once they were back in the cover of some trees, Terry moved the party into a lying-up position and made the maximum use of the remaining daylight. The boys had crept into the outskirts of Hamdok and returned with an armful of corn-cobs and some apples, but not being prepared to risk the smoke of a fire this close to the border, Terry ordered the men to crush the corn, soak it in water and chew it raw. Since proving themselves over the incident of the old man, the boys had become trusted members of the team and delighted in sharing out their stolen rations.

When everyone had eaten, they stripped their kit to the bare minimum, burying the mess tins and the few other items that had helped them to survive until now. In the night crossing of the border, stealth would be essential and Terry wasn't prepared to risk being given away by a clanking tin or shining spoon.

Next the weapons were checked and the ammunition evenly distributed. Planning for the worst case, Terry decided to split the party into two roughly equal groups in case they had to withdraw using fire and manoeuvre, but when Danny tried to explain to the boys that one of them would have to go with each group, they refused to be parted, Little Chiao sobbing as he clung to Liang.

'OK, OK,' said Terry, relenting. 'Put them both in my team, but shut them up before they give the whole game away.'

Along with the two boys, Terry detailed Danny and Andy to join his group. Both he and Andy would carry Kalashnikovs and Danny his M16. Ken would take the other three men, with the two Kalashnikovs captured from the paratroopers in the earlier forest battle. The grenades were split fifty-fifty.

Lastly everyone cammed up, checking each other to make sure that their faces were well blacked and that nothing would rattle in the silence of the night.

This done, they lay down and waited, each man

locked in the privacy of his own thoughts and fears until, when it was completely dark, Terry stood up and hand-signalled everyone to their feet.

'As Danny's the only one who's seen the border before, my group will take the lead. Also, if we're challenged, the kids can reply that they're lost or something. Ken, you keep an eye on the rear. Once we close up to the actual fences, we'll leapfrog you through, OK?'

Terry looked around at the anxious faces staring back at him in the dark.

'Good luck, lads. All being well, we'll be in South Korea this time tomorrow.'

A couple of the men laughed nervously and with a final check of his safety-catch, Terry led the way out of the lying-up position, contouring slowly round the hillside before crossing a narrow track and starting the climb towards the ridge and the first of the border fences.

Before the small green light had flashed a second time, the soldier had tugged on the communication cord linking his wrist to his section commander. Without a word the NCO woke instantly, checked the reference number beside the tiny bulb, pressed the switch on his pocket radio and spoke into the throat mike in a barely audible growl.

In the command bunker, Yi strode to the map.

'Say again reference.'

'Contact point three-two-zero, over.'

Yi plotted it on the map. 'Roger, out.'

His luck was in. Tonight he could feel it as sure as ever. He had known that Dojo was far too professional to follow an existing track, but there were so many in the area that at some stage in his approach to the border he would be forced at least to cross one. Yi had allowed for this in his plan by covering all the tracks in the sector with a thin spread of ground sensors. Lightly buried in the earth, they could pick up the slightest tremor and measure the strengths to distinguish between an animal and a man. But the NCO who had just reported in had picked up not one man, but two groups, each of at least four.

Speaking into another handset, Yi had to suppress the excitement in his voice.

'Move to Kilo Golf four, out.'

He wanted these bastards who had thwarted him. He wanted them dead and in a short while they would be, their blood seeping into the earth of the fourth of the twelve separate killing grounds that Yi had prepared with painstaking effort.

At the top of the hill the ground levelled out into a broad plateau, sloping gently down towards a distant row of lights.

'The border,' Danny said flatly. 'Some areas are covered by bright spotlights, but others are blacked out. They vary it every night to avoid creating a standard pattern.'

'And the dark areas?'

'Covered by night-vision devices, image intensifiers, thermal imagers, infrared – you name it. Just because you can't see them, don't assume they can't see you.'

Terry scanned the ground ahead, mostly undulating folds of scrub and gorse. The bulk of the taller trees had been cleared to give open fields of vision, but there were a few patches here and there.

Following Terry's line of thought, Danny pointed to a shallow drainage ditch.

'That will probably run all the way up to the border fence but you can bet it'll be covered by ground sensors and filled with razor wire and anti-personnel mines.'

'Any more good news?'

'It's probably our best bet. In the open, however well we stalk, we'll be sitting ducks. At least if we're in dead ground we're invisible to all the other devices except the ground sensors. There's no answer to them. Let's just hope they haven't deployed any and have relied on booby-traps instead.'

Terry agreed. From his training with surveillance devices he knew that darkness no longer provided cover from view. Image intensifiers drew on the ambient light from stars and expanded it into a glowing green picture of the landscape; thermal imagers gave an accurate heat picture, showing men, animals, engines and any other heat source as easily identifiable white shapes against a dark background; and infrared torches could bathe an area in light invisible to the human eye, but not to the ambusher lying in wait with special goggles and a machine-gun.

The only way to counter this array of highly sensitive devices was to treat night as day and move across ground accordingly, using every fold, depression and piece of cover, trusting that the hidden observer was tired or careless, prone to the same human weaknesses as his prey. It was the latest twist in never-ending game of cat and mouse.

Crawling back to the others, Terry briefed them on his plan to use the drainage ditch. The going would be painfully slow and they would be lucky to make it completely across by first light, but it was their only hope. Andy pushed to the front of the group.

'Let me go first, Dojo. I'm a qualified assault pioneer. I did the combat engineer course at Chatham. I know all about booby-traps and mines. If anyone can clear a way through, I can.'

Terry checked with Danny.

'OK by me,' Danny said. 'I'll give him back-up.'

'That's settled then. My team will lead. Ken, you be prepared to pass your team through when we breach the first fence. I reckon we'll be knackered by then.'

'Or blown to fucking kingdom come.'

Leaving Ken to deploy his team into fire positions ready to give covering fire in case Andy and Danny had to pull back in a hurry, Terry waited until the little Scot and the big Indian had wriggled across the scrub and slipped down into the drainage ditch, before moving out of cover himself. Behind him, the two boys slithered as silently as snakes, so that Terry had to keep glancing round to check they were still there. But whenever he looked, he saw their two blacked-up faces close behind, stuck to him like shadows, their fear and excitement visible through the dirt.

Reaching the lip of the ditch, he dropped into it and slowly crawled forward. Ten yards ahead of him, Andy was probing the ground with the tip of a bayonet, his fingers feeling gently for trip-wires or pressure pads – anything that might indicate the trigger of a mine or booby-trap. Clearing a yard at a time, he worked his way along the ditch at an agonizingly slow speed. Terry couldn't help admiring his courage. He might be a vicious bastard in war, merciless with his enemy and almost as ruthless with his own side, but it took the coolest of nerves to deal with a hidden mine that could explode and blow your hands off at any moment. It was a different kind of courage from the red-hot ferocity of an attack, and as he watched the painstaking operation in front of him, Terry felt a new respect for the man.

Crawling level with Andy's feet, Danny was flat on his stomach, pulling aside stray branches and smoothing the path for those coming up behind him. So long as they kept their heads and backsides below ground level, he knew that they would be masked from every surveillance device except a ground sensor, and he hoped that because this was a drainage ditch, subject to flooding, it would either have been overlooked or any sensors would have been washed away or rendered inoperable by the water. It was a hell of a gamble, but it was the best they could hope for.

After two hours Andy reached the first fence. Although the drainage ditch continued underneath it, the gap had been closed with a coil of razor wire. Deciding not to risk cutting the fence in case it was alarmed, he took each lethal strand of the coil as delicately as he could, wrapped a cloth around it, and piece by piece, clipped a way through. Sliding up alongside him, Danny used the crook of his tomahawk blade to pull the loose ends apart, forcing a gap wide enough for the largest in the group to crawl through. If anyone got snared on the savage barbs it would take valuable minutes to free them, time they could ill afford. This was only the first of several fences and when daylight came clearance patrols would be sent out to check every scrap of dead ground such as the ditch.

Coming up beside Danny, Terry signalled them to stop.

'Well done, lads. We'll let Ken pass through now. I think he's got the hang of it.'

Ken and his team had closed up behind, ready to leapfrog into the lead. As Terry hugged the side of the ditch, Ken slithered past, winking as he drew level.

'Had enough, have you? We'll show you how it's done, mate. Last one to Seoul's a poofter.'

'Just take it easy.'

When the last of Ken's team had cleared the gap in the razor wire, Terry set the boys to keep watch and crawled alongside Danny. It was a good fifty yards to the next fence, beyond which they could see the dog runs that they would have to tackle before reaching the third and last fence and the minefields on the other side. After that they would have to cross a stretch of no man's land before climbing towards the first of the South Korean defences and home. Danny intended to use his tomahawk to silence the dogs. With luck they would only have to deal with one of them. Each dog had its own run of several hundred yards, separated from the next one by a fence. A thin wire was suspended the full length of the run, with a leash attached to the dog's collar long enough for him to cover the entire enclosure. Inadequately fed, they were the dogs who had proved untrainable, too savage even as compound dogs, and anything that ventured into their territory would be instantly attacked and killed.

Terry knew that the drainage ditch was unlikely to run through all three of the fences; they were lucky to have had use of its cover this far. But soon they would be forced out into the open. Luckily they were midway between two watch-towers and Terry hoped that the guards would be concentrating on the ground directly in front of them, not suspecting that anyone could have penetrated into the fence zone itself. Leave the fence zone to the dogs, Terry thought, as if, by willing it with all his might, he could make it happen.

When Jimmy Haynes missed the hidden trip-wire, snagging it with his elbow, the small charge of the booby-trap exploded upwards, taking his left arm with it. In an instant the whole area was flooded with light, and to the background baying of the dogs, straining at their leashes, mad with rage and hunger, bipod-mounted RPK machine-guns opened up from both watch-towers, hosing the area of the detonation with fire.

Screaming with the pain, Jimmy stood up and staggered into the open before Ken could stop him. But he hadn't gone more than six stumbling paces before the Korean gunners found his range and put a swift end to his agony. Firing as they went, Ken and the other two survivors wriggled backwards as fast as they could, not stopping to aim but spraying the bursts randomly over the lip of the ditch in the rough direction of the guard towers. From the base of the towers came the sound of shouting and running feet as soldiers poured out of the underground accommodation bunkers and closed in on the trapped mercenaries.

Springing to his knees, Terry rested his elbow on the side of the ditch and brought his Kalashnikov into the aim.

'OK, guys, let's give them some covering fire. Danny, snipe at the lights. Me and Andy'll take on the guards.'

But as he caught first sight of the approaching Korean soldiers, Terry's blood went cold. For by their black combat suits and the controlled precision of their fire and movement, he recognized them as special forces, and he knew that Ken would be lucky to escape from the killing ground alive.

Yi was furious, screaming into the handset.

'Why the hell did you open fire? I wanted to get them all in the killing ground first.'

On the other end of the line the special forces officer stammered in reply: 'We didn't, Comrade. They set off a booby-trap.'

'I ordered the colonel and his border guards to remove them before handing over the sector to us.'

'He must have overlooked one.'

Yi cursed. Why did he have to do everything himself? Nevertheless, at least half the mercenaries seemed to be trapped and from the reports it appeared that the others were pinned down beside the outer fence. If he moved quickly he could still trap them. Calming himself, he paused before speaking again to the company commander.

'OK. It's not your fault. Get your cut-offs into position immediately. If Dojo is the man I think he is, he'll stick around to help his friends rather than run away and save himself. I'm on my way and together we can have him yet.'

But at the border fence the decision was not being left to Terry. A second member of Ken's team had been killed and a moment later the third mercenary was hit in the chest. Checking the exit wound, Ken saw that the man had only minutes to live. The ground between him and the fence was alive with impacting bullets; from their vantage point high on the watch-towers, the guards were able to angle their fire downwards, directly into the ditch. It was only a matter of time before Ken himself was hit. Meanwhile, Terry and the others were making themselves into sitting ducks, doing their best to cover him, but Ken knew what he was up against and that if the Korean special forces were as good as they were supposed to be, they would be putting in a long-stop to block Terry's escape route even now.

He shouted at Terry and waved him away frantically, but although Terry could hear him he ignored the message. Realizing there was only one thing for it, Ken gritted his teeth and stood up, tossing aside his Kalashnikov and holding his hands high above his head.

'No!'

He turned at Terry's scream, stared across the open killing ground at him and grinned.

'Guess I'm the fucking poofter, mate,' he shouted. 'Clear off, there's a good fella.'

As Terry looked on in horror, the fire continued unabated, dancing in the raging earth at Ken's feet until it found the lone Australian and cut him down. Terry felt Danny's hand on his arm.

'Come on, Terry. Let's get out of here. Ken's given us a break. Let's make the most of it.'

Andy shot to his feet, blazing from the hip.

'The bastards! The fucking bastards!'

After pulling him back into cover, Terry and Danny dragged him back along the ditch.

With the last of Ken's team dead, the tower gunners redirected their fire at the furthest party of mercenaries while the special forces pursuers unlocked the gates and hurried through the safe lanes in the minefield towards the other side. When they entered the dog run, the raging beast leapt at them but was shot down with a burst from an AKM. Speaking into his throat mike, the commander checked on the progress of the cut-off teams.

'In position, over.'

'Roger, out.'

The commander sighed with relief; no one survived in Comrade Yi's bad books for long. Deciding to risk the casualties that his men would take if they ran into their own cut-off groups, he urged them on. Better that than lose the mercenaries again.

Terry reached the end of the ditch, burst into the open and led the way across the scrub towards the ridge line. Sprinting over the top, he careered down the hillside until he came to the first of the trees near the lying-up position that they had left only hours before. He crouched down and waited for the others to close up, frantically organizing his thoughts.

Steady, man, he thought, fighting to calm his breathing and clear his mind of the life-threatening panic that clawed for supremacy. He had seen that these were special forces troops, so Yi Soong was probably somewhere around. What would he be doing at this moment? Think, man, think. Of course! Nothing. If he had prepared one killing ground for the mercenaries to enter, there would be a network of others. He would already have back-stops out, using his forward troops to drive Terry back into the cut-offs. But the Welshman wasn't some pea-brained pheasant to be easily frightened straight into the muzzles of the waiting guns.

'Which was the way to Hamdok?' he asked as Danny skidded to a halt beside him, followed a moment later by Andy and the two boys. Trusting

Terry's judgement and knowing better than to question a commander in the white heat of battle, Danny pointed across the hillside.

'Two hundred yards. Path. Go left. Three hundred yards. Hamdok.'

'Roger. Move!'

Without giving anyone time to catch their breath or wonder where he was taking them, Terry led the way diagonally across the hillside, moving through cover whenever possible, hoping that the pursuing troops would carry on straight down the hill to the open fields. If he was Yi Soong, that's where he would have sited his cut-offs, writing off the village or at most covering it with a thin manpower screen.

When they were within fifty yards of the path, the bare earth glowed like a silver ribbon in the moonlight. Veering sharp left, they moved parallel to it, following it like a road sign down towards the village.

Hurrying through the night with his heavily armed escort, Yi paused to take the message from his radio operator.

'Ground sensor contact, Comrade. Kilo Golf eight.'

Yi smiled. So far so good. If Dojo was hoping to find something in Hamdok, be it a hiding-place, a hostage, transport or whatever, he would be sorely disappointed. Every villager had been evacuated and the streets converted into a viper's nest of interlocking machine-gun arcs, Claymore directional anti-personnel mines, booby-traps and razor wire, making Killing Ground Eight the one that Yi was most proud of.

A hundred yards out from the village outskirts, with

the first of the houses silhouetted against a peaceful backdrop of paddy-fields, Liang pointed excitedly at a thick grove of bamboo on the other side of a wide, fast-flowing stream. When Andy grabbed him by the scruff of the neck and tried to drag him away, he jerked loose and rushed over to Danny, whispering urgently.

'What's the hold-up?' Terry hissed, anxious to be getting on.

'I don't know,' Danny replied, frowning as he tried to calm the boy and translate using his sketchy Korean.

'We haven't got time. Thump him and let's get on.'

'No, hang on. This might be worth having a look at if it's what I think it is.'

Before Terry could stop him, Danny and the two boys had darted off towards the bamboo and plunged into the stream.

'Jesus Christ, this had better be good,' Terry groaned. Slipping into the stream, he and Andy gasped as the icy water soaked them to the skin. Their Kalashnikovs above their heads, they waded across, leaning into the current to avoid being swept off their feet. Danny and the boys were already across and heading into the shadows, from where a tall brick structure loomed out at them.

'What the fuck's that? It looks like some kind of shrine or something,' Andy asked when he and Terry caught up. But Danny had found a small alcove where a statue of a Buddha was poised on a stone plinth.

'If I'd known this was a shagging sightseeing tour I'd have brought my sodding camera,' said Andy.

Danny cursed the weight of the statue as he set his shoulder to it and shoved.

'Shut up and lend a hand.'

'What is it, Danny?' asked the Scot.

But before he could answer, the statue slid aside and Danny almost toppled headlong into the gaping darkness below.

11

Falling back on to the grass, Danny grinned up at Terry while Liang and Little Chiao danced with excitement.

'What's that? The door to the bloody underworld?'

'That, my fine Welsh friend, is our passage to freedom.'

'What do you mean?'

As Terry peered into the dark abyss, Danny explained how for years the North Koreans had been tunnelling under the border to allow infiltration teams to carry out sabotage and suicide missions.

'We've known for years that the border's honeycombed with these, but the problem's been finding them. When I was in the Rangers we had to track down a sabotage team that had taken out a whole desalination plant on the coast. We drove them back into their tunnel but before we could get at them they had blown it up and buried themselves alive. The Communists use labour gangs to dig them. Liang here recognized the village and remembered the shrine.'

'I thought you said he didn't know the area.'

'He doesn't. They were trucked in in covered vehicles and he didn't have a clue where he was. He only recognized it just now when he was virtually on top of it.'

Andy shoved them aside. 'Fuck me. Are you two going to stand there gabbing all night?'

'Hang on a minute, couldn't it be booby-trapped? Panji stakes or something?'

But before Terry could stop him, Liang had ducked between the three Westerners and dropped down into the hole. His voice came back to them out of the darkness.

'He says it's all clear.'

'Well, that's one way of finding out.'

One by one they lowered themselves gingerly into the hole. There was an eight-foot drop to the floor of beaten earth and when the last of them was in, Danny balanced on Terry's shoulders to ease the Buddha back into place as best he could. In the pitch-blackness he fumbled for his cigarette lighter, flicked it open and struck the flint. The small, yellow flame that sparked into life threw a thin glow on the five tired and dirty faces, the outer reaches of its weak light playing on the damp, earthen walls of the chamber. Liang pointed out the entrance to the tunnel itself, the roof of which was little more than four feet high. Out in the night, muffled and sounding far away, they heard the unmistakable sound of gunfire.

'Those assholes have run into their own cut-offs,' said Danny.

'Yeah, but it won't be long before they sort themselves out and pick up our tracks. We'd better get on,' Terry replied.

Liang tugged at his sleeve.

'He says he wants to show us the way,' said the Indian.

'Fine by me. Give him the light.'

With Liang and Little Chiao in the lead, the party

ducked into the tunnel and set off, the impenetrable blackness retreating grudgingly in front of the lighter, but swiftly closing in behind them so that the last two men had to feel their way forward along the slimy walls. Whereas the two boys hurried along with ease, Little Chiao barely having to bow his head, the three men had to double over, hobbling and cursing, going down on one knee every few yards to stretch aching limbs that rebelled with the effort.

After what seemed like an age, Liang suddenly stopped and called back to Danny.

'Go easy, gents,' Danny said, 'the buggers have rigged up a panji pit.'

Peering between the two boys in the flickering light of the flame, Terry saw that the floor of the tunnel dropped abruptly into a two-foot-deep pit. Sharpened bamboo stakes had been driven into the bottom, their fire-hardened tips black and deadly, waiting in the dark to spear the unwary.

'Nice work, Liang,' Terry said, patting the boy on the shoulder.

Danny laughed. 'He said it was him who had to fix them in the first place.'

With the butt of his Kalashnikov, Terry smashed a path through the forest of bamboo, moving stealthily across the six-foot gap until Liang was able to take the lead again at the far side. But after that progress became slower. As the tunnel went further under the border the booby-traps became more frequent. Liang found a trip-wire attached to the pin of a grenade that had been fixed into the tunnel wall at waist height. Then they came upon another panji pit, longer than the first, and this time the ground in between the stakes was sown with a scattering of anti-personnel mines. It took a full half hour to clear a way through and no sooner had they set off again than they almost blundered into another trip-wire, set to activate a necklace of four grenades embedded in the tunnel roof. The panji pit and the grenade necklace worked as a pair, each complementing the other, so that anyone clearing either obstacle could be expected to have their guard momentarily relaxed just in time to hit its waiting partner.

'Proper little theme park, isn't it?' Terry said as he stepped over the hair-thin wire.

By now they were all suffering badly from the strain, a combination of delayed battle shock, physical exhaustion and the agonizing tension of the dark, cramped tunnel packed with its lethal secrets. As he pulled himself painfully forward, Terry couldn't help admiring the stamina of the two boys, probing up ahead in the flickering light, chattering to each other, seemingly oblivious to the fact that they could all be blown to kingdom come at any moment. He found himself waiting for the sickening twang of a trip-wire or the metallic spring of a grenade pin and the five seconds of mad panic and confusion that would follow as the detonator fuse burned its way into the heart of the shrapnel-encased explosive.

Miraculously it never came. Further minutes went by and more ground was painstakingly covered. Terry had no idea where the boys had come from or how long they had been starving in the hills before the mercenaries had found them, but he was almost certain of one thing: they had saved his life. Even if he had been able to lead the party away from the immediate danger of the pursuit, they would have been forced to attempt another crossing of the border at some stage, and with the North Koreans alerted to their presence, their chances of success would have been minimal. The tunnel had come as a miracle – the one saving grace in a disastrous operation. Somehow he would have to find a way of repaying them.

Suddenly, a few yards in front of him, the boys stopped and Liang called back excitedly. They had reached the end of the tunnel.

On the outskirts of Hamdok, Yi Soong was consulting with his commanders. On the open farmland to the east of the village, one of the special forces platoons had taken four casualties when they had blundered into their own ambush party. In the darkness the fleeting figures had been mistaken for the runaway mercenaries and the machine-gunners had opened fire without a preliminary challenge. To add to the confusion, the platoon that was caught in the killing area assumed that they were being ambushed by the mercenaries and had immediately gone to ground and returned fire, while their depth sections executed a wide hook that caught the ambush in the flank and attempted to roll it up from the side. It had been precious minutes before the chaos had been unravelled, the parties disengaged and the bodies counted.

But what bothered Yi more was the apparent disappearance of Dojo and his team from the face of the planet. The losses suffered by his own men were due to their own incompetence, but if the surviving mercenaries managed to slip through his fingers again, he would not only lose face but his superiors would start asking some awkward questions that he would be sorely pushed to answer.

He had gambled that Dojo would go for Hamdok and had prepared a reception accordingly. The ground sensors had indicated that the mercenaries had indeed been going in that direction, but somewhere along the way they had apparently stopped and nothing more had been seen or heard of them since. Several hours had passed and at first Yi had assumed that they had gone to ground. But why? The eastern sky was already brightening and in full daylight it would be an easy task to comb the area. Cover was sparse and if the mercenaries were lying up in a patch of scrub or bamboo it would be no great problem to locate, isolate and destroy them. The logical thing to have done would have been to seek the deep cover of the forest again, regroup, move to another sector of border and try again. Failing that, Dojo might well try his luck along the seashore; find a fishing village, steal a boat and slip down the coast and into South Korean waters by night.

But the network of ground sensors had indicated nothing. Yi himself had checked on their deployment, ensuring that the entire area was adequately covered. In addition, he had placed covert teams of surveillance specialists with image intensifiers, night-vision goggles, thermal imagers and ground-surveillance radars in a broad arc covering every possible exfiltration route out of the killing grounds. Ever desperate to appease their commander, one of the surveillance teams had even reported the ambling passage of a fox. Lastly, a thin spread of snipers had been superimposed over the whole interlocking network, each man being allowed to select his own position. If anyone could catch a man with sniper training it was another sniper. Set a poacher to catch a poacher.

Nothing. If Dojo and the others had tried to leave the area Yi would have received word by now. Instead, they had simply disappeared.

It was only as the light strengthened and the tracker dogs were deployed that the scent was picked up and the mercenaries' trail was found. Starting from the last-known point of contact at the drainage ditch, the dogs easily followed the scent to the lying-up position and then down the track towards Hamdok. Losing the trail when confronted with the stream, they were urged across by their experienced handlers and after scanning up and down the far bank, quickly recovered the scent and followed it up to the shrine. Excited and confused, the dogs yelped and bayed at the mute stone which their puzzled handlers surrounded, waiting for Comrade Yi Soong to arrive.

Striding through the water, Yi shouted up at them.

'Tear it down, you morons. Do I have to do everything myself?'

'But, Comrade, the shrine belongs to the local village.'

Unfastening the flap of his holster and drawing his pistol, Yi was wild with rage, and in seconds the dog teams and their escorts were ripping at the stones with their bare hands while urgent messages were sent to bring picks and shovels.

Fighting to control his temper, Yi sat on the grass and threw stones into the water. Why hadn't he guessed? A tunnel. He had used them himself often enough in the past. But how the devil had the wretched mercenaries discovered it? It couldn't simply have been luck; it was too well concealed. They must have had intelligence that even he wasn't privy to. The details of the North Korean tunnel system were accessible to only a handful of the most senior intelligence officers, and the labourers who dug them were usually eradicated once the work was complete.

Be that as it may, the fact was that in all probability his quarry was now safely home and dry in South Korea. Of course they might well have fallen foul of one of the booby-traps with which the tunnels were always laced, but Yi discounted the possibility the very moment he thought of it: Dojo was far too clever for that.

One of the dog handlers approached him warily.

'We've found it, Comrade. It's a tunnel.'

Yi sighed heavily and smiled up at him. 'Well I never!' Getting wearily to his feet, he called across to the men working feverishly to dismantle the shrine.

'Forget it.'

'But Comrade, we can follow them.'

'I said forget it. Get your stupid dogs back to their kennels. They're pissing on the Buddha.' He turned to his radio operator. 'Call in the surveillance teams and the ambushes.'

The man blinked up at him uncertainly. 'Is it over?'

'For now.'

Brushing the grass from his combat trousers, Yi slung his assault rifle over his shoulder. There would be no more shooting today. The bodies of the dead mercenaries in the border fence zone had been identified and their details passed to Yi. As he walked back towards the Hamdok track, three names and three faces hung almost tangibly in the air before him. Andy Buchan. Danny Grey Wolf. Dojo Williams. Yi Soong knew that he himself would now be going undercover again.

* * *

Emerging into a chamber similar in size and proportion to the entrance under the Buddhist shrine, Terry breathed a sigh of relief as he stretched to his full height and felt his knees and joints crack into place. Seconds later, Danny popped out of the tunnel beside him, helping Andy, whose old leg wound was throbbing painfully from the exertion of the long, damp scramble underground. Little Chiao was already balancing on Liang's shoulders, scrabbling at the earth overhead with his small hands.

Danny took the lighter and held it up. Long tendrils of tree root dangled from the ceiling and as Little Chiao's efforts brought a shower of loose earth down on their heads, Danny and Terry reached up and joined in the excavation.

'It'll probably come up in a wood or somewhere,' Danny said. 'The one I saw before with the Rangers seemed pretty much like this. They put all this effort into digging them but only ever use them once. The surface shouldn't be more than about four feet up, and it'll be reinforced so that anyone walking over the spot by accident won't cave it in.'

Sure enough, after some more digging they came upon two sturdy wooden beams, which they manhandled to one side. They had only been digging for a few more minutes when there was a groan, a cascade of loose earth, and they were squinting up into the harsh daylight.

Little Chiao fell back into the hole and Liang picked him up, dancing and clapping with delight.

'OK, lads. Keep the noise down,' Terry cautioned them, unable to suppress a huge smile. Even Andy chuckled at the smell of the fresh, cool air that flooded into the chamber.

With a leg-up from Terry, Danny eased into the breach and cautiously poked his head through the opening.

'Yep. Middle of a wood,' he called down, and after pulling himself out of the hole, he reached down to help the others. Once the two boys had climbed out, Terry cupped his hands under Andy's boot and hoisted him up. Then, when Danny and Andy were both lying flat on the overhead grass, reaching down into the hole, Terry pulled the pins from two hand-grenades, rolled them as far as he could back down the tunnel, and grabbing the outstretched hands, was lifted bodily out of the hole just as the grenades detonated, collapsing the tunnel behind him. As the shock waves expanded, magnified in the confined space, they triggered the nearest of the booby-traps and anti-personnel mines, until a full hundred yards of roof had come crashing down, sealing the tunnel to all but a well-equipped party of engineers.

Rolling away from the opening as a cloud of dust and earth sprayed into the air and settled on the surrounding undergrowth, Terry felt the clean smells of the forest flood his nostrils and the dazzling light prick at his clenched eyelids. Looking at the broad smiles all around him, he sat up on the lush grass and spat the dirt from his mouth.

'I don't like to put a dampener on things, but how do we know we're in South Korea and not still on the wrong side of the border?'

'This,' Danny said simply, handing him a small piece of dark-brown plastic. 'US Army ration pack.' He brushed the inside with the tip of his finger and tasted it. 'Mm. Peanut butter.'

Terry laughed. 'I suppose you'll give me an eight-figure grid reference of our position next?'

'Well, let's see. We're probably well into the South Korean side of the DMZ. The gooks would have wanted their tunnel to penetrate far enough to avoid a messy clash with our own border troops. As the tunnel ends here you can bet there'll be an easy covered exit to a highway or something where they could have met up with their own agents or gone straight on to their target. It's a game they've been playing for years.'

Andy massaged his stiff leg. 'So what's the problem? We just walk to the nearest guard post and tell them who we are, right?'

Danny saw that Terry was deep in thought.

'I think Dojo's got other plans.'

'Oh shit,' said Andy.

'Well, what do you make of it?' Terry asked. 'We don't really know who set us up.'

'What do you mean? Yi did. He was some kind of double agent.'

'Yes, but who was controlling him?'

'Who the hell cares?' Andy growled. 'They can do what they damn well like. I'm going home.'

'I wouldn't bet on it. We don't know what story they've been putting around. For all we know the South Korean government might be after us too. We've caused them a fair bit of bother, after all.'

Danny kicked at a loose stone. 'Shit. He's right, man. We've been out of circulation for too long. It'd do no harm to check out the lie of the land before we go surrendering to anyone.'

'And what about Babs?' Terry added. 'How much did he know? I can't speak for you guys but I want some answers. We owe it to Ken and all the others who haven't made it back.'

'Fuck the answers. I want my money,' Andy said bitterly.

'Right. And there's only one bloke who can give it to you.'

Danny looked across at the two boys, who were listening intently to the conversation without understanding a word.

'What about them? Do we take them with us?' he said.

'You bet we do. If it wasn't for them we'd still be in North Korea, or worse. They stick with us until we've sorted this out and then we'll see if we can help them dig up some relatives in the South.' Terry smiled grimly. 'And you might find that Babsy wants to make a sizeable donation to their future welfare; a sort of orphan's fund.'

Making their way out of the clearing, they moved through a forest that was tamer than the sprawling wilderness they had become used to over the last days. Being close to the border it had been used for military exercises and the evidence was visible wherever they looked: bits of ration pack, blank cartridge cases, discarded scraps of military clothing, pieces of link from machine-gun ammunition belts.

'Don't think much of their field discipline,' Andy observed scornfully. 'These your boys?' he added with a wry grin at Danny.

'No way. You don't see the Rangers until they've got a knife to your throat, and the ROKs would be crucified if they left a heap of shit like this. These'll be the GIs – bums and college kids.' He spat in disgust. For years he had trained his men to move inconspicuously, taking out their rubbish or burying it too deep for wild pigs to dig it up again.

On reaching the edge of the forest, they located a farmstead and lay down to observe it until they were reasonably confident that they could account for all the occupants. The whole family was busy in the fields on the far side of the farm buildings. So, while the three men remained out of sight on the edge of the trees, Liang and Little Chiao crept forward and disappeared through a window into the farmhouse, returning ten minutes later with armfuls of clothing and food.

While everyone stripped off their prison fatigues, now caked with dirt and stinking, Terry made a note of everything taken from the house.

'Babs might also want to send the farmer an anonymous cheque repaying him for his kindness.'

In their new outfits they felt even more conspicuous than in their fatigues. It had been impossible to find anything big enough to fit Danny; in his borrowed jeans and sweatshirt he looked like the Incredible Hulk, his chest bulging through the Pepsi slogan and the trouser legs halfway up his shins. Andy, Terry and the boys had been easier to kit out and once they were happy that they looked as normal as they ever would, they put their weapons in a holdall that Liang had stolen and stepped out on to the metalled road.

'Right,' Terry said, trying hard not to laugh at Danny's ridiculous appearance. 'Erm . . . bus or taxi?'

'What about surfboard?' Andy said innocently, pointing at Danny's newly cut-off jeans, huge boots and skin-tight sweatshirt, and starting to whistle a Beach Boys number.

Later that same morning the cheque from Francis

Kwang was cleared and Babs discovered that he was richer than he had ever been in his life. He nipped out to the local supermarket and bought some Asti Spumante, the closest thing to champagne he could find, then rang Michelle and told her to come round immediately. She pressed him for the reason but Babs delighted in making her wait; he wanted to see the expression on her face when he told her of his plans for their future.

The sparkling wine was still warm when Michelle arrived, but unable to contain himself any longer, Babs popped the cork, filled two whisky tumblers to the brim, offered her one and then proposed a toast.

'To us.'

'What is it, Babsy? Tell me, tell me,' said Michelle, pulling at his jacket sleeve like a child wanting attention.

Babs pulled a slip of paper from his pocket and handed it to her. It was a printout of his bank balance.

Michelle went pale. 'This all yours?' she said with staring eyes.

'No, it's ours,' Babs said warmly. 'I've done it, my love. I've finally done it. You and me are going to take a little trip and we're not coming back. Bin that revolting job in It'aewan, bring your stuff round here and we'll fly out next week.'

Michelle stared blankly at him. 'Where we go?'

'Hell, I don't know. Anywhere away from here. We'll go to Tokyo first.'

'Oh, Babsy, I always want go Tokyo!'

He put his glass down and pulled her to him, her waist trim and slight in his plump hands. She had come straight from the club and was wearing a bright-red dress split up both sides to the thigh. He slid his hands underneath, drawing her closer, feeling her hips press against him.

'Then maybe we'll fly on to Hawaii. Cathay Pacific. First class, of course.'

The wine spilled from Michelle's tumbler as she kissed Babs full on the lips, feeling his mouth open and his tongue penetrate her. Arching her back, she ground into him until she felt him respond, then slipped a hand between them, fumbling with his trousers. When she had him in her hand, she slid to her knees, caressing him with her tongue until she heard him moan. Easing him down on to the carpet, Michelle pulled aside the flaps of her dress and manoeuvred herself delicately on top.

'You been good to me, Babsy. I repay you rest your life. You see.'

But Babs was beyond hearing. As he ran his fingers through Michelle's ebony hair, his body pulsated with every move she made, each motion slow and teasing, seeking out his weakness and pleasure with hips and hands until he longed for release. For the first time in her life, Michelle too found herself being carried away beyond her own control, lost in an unknown world where the pleasures of the body met the fondness of the heart, the two continuing together to explore the strange new region where neither she nor Babs had ever ventured before.

When the mid-afternoon sun pushed its lowering beams through the window blinds, slashing the room into thick strips of shadow and golden light, it found them in bed, Michelle's head resting on Babs's bare chest, her eyes open and wondering. Listening intently to his gentle snoring, she marvelled at all that had happened. He had been telling her the truth after all. Like many of her clients, Babs had always been full of stories. Some men needed to impress her, as if by filling her ears with their importance and exploits they could explain away their presence in a whore's room, assuaging some hidden guilt. As if she cared. Others compensated with a hostile silence, treating her as a sly enemy who had somehow lured them in and entrapped them; their lovemaking was savage and brief, and they seldom allowed their eyes to meet hers lest they be forced to confront the fellow-human beneath their brutal thrusts.

Babs had always been different. Sure, he had been full of stories, but somehow he had let Michelle know that he didn't really believe them himself either. It had been a game and she had grown to love it. But what surprised her now was the discovery that, in the process, she had grown to love him.

Slipping out of his arms, she dressed hurriedly, resolving to start their new life together as she meant it to go on. When Babs awoke he would find a cooked meal waiting for him. The apartment would be alive with the smells of the food and the noise of their laughter. She tiptoed into the kitchen, opened the fridge and surveyed the empty shelves. Finding the cupboards likewise bare, save for a packet of biscuits and two empty whisky bottles, she slipped on her shoes and took some money from Babs's wallet. The store on the corner would have everything she needed for now. In future she would dress like a proper housewife and shop at the market, haggling with the fishmonger and the vegetable man until they gave her their best produce at a reasonable price. Of course, she wouldn't haggle too much; that would be vulgar. No, she would do exactly what was expected of the wife of an ex-army officer and man of honour.

With a final check on her sleeping lover, Michelle eased out of the door, closing it behind her soundlessly. Once out in the corridor, she bounced down the flights of stairs, humming to herself with unbounded joy, stepping to one side when she reached the second floor to let a group of Westerners pass. A number of them lived in this block, though most of the inhabitants were middle-class Koreans, bank clerks and junior managers. She smiled generously at a strangely dressed giant, and winked at a couple of mischievous boys. Perhaps she would have sons of her own one day.

Last in line, an athletic man of medium build greeted her pleasantly. 'Morning, miss.'

'Morning.'

Babs had told her to drop the 'Good', making it sound more natural. As she looked after the strangers, Michelle wondered whether they would soon be neighbours. Perhaps she would pick up her things from the club that evening. Continuing on down the stairs, she resumed her humming, daydreaming of Tokyo, Mount Fuji and Honolulu.

12

'Darling!'

The bowl of ice-cold water struck Babs's face, waking him instantly.

'How simply wonderful to see you. You fucking bastard.'

Andy dragged the terrified man from the bed and threw him to the floor.

'Jesus, what a sight for sore eyes. There's more flab on that bum than on the dance floor of a gunner officers' mess.'

Terry pulled Andy away and hoisted Babs to his feet. 'Get a chair, Andy. We've got some questions to ask our friend here before we decide what to do with him.'

Behind Babs, Danny tested the blade of his tomahawk.

'Can I have first shot?' he asked.

'Sure. Why not. Add his foreskin to your scalp collection.'

When Babs had been tied to a chair, he stared forlornly at the three men looming over him.

'Listen, boys, I didn't know anything about the operation. Kwang simply hired me to recruit the best mercenaries money could buy.'

'Who's Kwang?'

'He's the bloke who put up the money. Yi was only his sidekick.'

'Keep talking.'

'He's something big in South Korean intelligence.'

'Then why would he cause his own government all this bother?'

'I don't know. You've got to believe me. He was probably fooled by Yi Soong, like the rest of us.'

Andy sprang forward. 'Us? Don't you dare count yourself as one of the team. You seem to have come out of it all right, don't you? And where's our money, and the money for all the boys who didn't make it back?'

'I haven't got it.'

Andy's fist slammed into Babs's mouth, splitting his bottom lip.

'Honest I haven't. Kwang's only paid me my share. The arrangement was that you would all be paid direct by him. I gave him your details and that was that.'

'And you can bet he hasn't parted with a fucking dollar since,' Danny added.

Terry walked over to the window and drew the blinds shut.

'Where's this Kwang guy now?'

'I'm not allowed to tell anyone.'

In an instant, Danny was beside the chair, his tomahawk resting lightly between Babs's legs.

'How do you want it, Babsy? Diced or sliced?'

Babs stared in horror at the big Indian and swallowed hard.

'Dojo, explain to him. You know how it is . . . if I break a confidence I'm finished.'

Terry shrugged helplessly. 'Danny-boy's got a mind of his own, I'm afraid. When he's set on something, there's no stopping him.'

Babs gritted his teeth as Danny moved the savage blade closer to his penis.

'All right, all right. He's got a country villa at Sorak-san, but there's no point contacting him – he's untouchable. When the news broke about the raid there was an investigation and Yi Soong took the wrap. If Kwang is a double agent – and I'm not saying he is, mind – but if he is, he's already covered his back. If you try to get to him he'll have the entire South Korean defence establishment down on you before you know what's happening. Believe me, Dojo. Don't mess with him.'

'What's his address?'

Babs sighed. 'You can't take no for an answer, can you?'

Terry put his face close to Babs's. 'Not when there's thirteen other blokes out there pushing up daisies. If Yi was a double, then Kwang fucked up with his screening procedure and I'll see that the widows and families get every penny that's owed to them. And if Kwang was in on it himself, then I'll find a way of getting even with the bastard.'

Babs nodded to a dressing-table. 'In there.'

Rummaging through the drawers, Terry came across an address book.

'This it?'

Babs nodded.

Sinking into the armchair, Terry began to leaf through the pages.

'Danny, why don't you see if you can find something that fits you in Major Butler's wardrobe. I'm sure he wouldn't mind. Andy, take the boys into the kitchen and get a brew on.'

'Right, boss.'

Stopping at one of the pages, Terry raised his eyebrows in surprise. 'Is Mike in town?'

'Mike Adams? Yes. He's with CNN now. Seoul desk.'

Terry whistled. 'He's come a long way since Angola.'

'Haven't we all?'

'No. Look, do you want some clothes? I don't like the way your prick's staring at me.'

'You don't like it? What about me?'

Cutting Babs loose, Terry kept an eye on him as he dressed, ordering him to sit again when he had finished.

'Ah, here we are. Kwang, Francis. Sorak-san. That's the National Park, isn't it?'

'Yes, but you're wasting your time.' Babs thought for a moment. 'What do you intend to do about yourselves? I mean, how are you going to get out of the country?'

'British Embassy. We discussed it on the bus on the way here. We reckon we'll give the Korean authorities a wide berth.'

Babs coughed lightly. 'And what about me? I really didn't know about any of this. Look at it from my side: why would I have set you up? First, I know that no bugger on earth could ever hold you for long, and second, the word would be out that Babs Butler was a turncoat. If I wasn't fixed in the night by some old chum of yours, I'd never be able to recruit anyone ever again. I'd be ruined. We were both stitched up, Dojo. You, me, the others, all of us.'

'Except you got paid.'

'I suppose Kwang reckoned it would throw me off his trail. Make it all seem legit.'

'Seems to have worked.'

Terry leaned back in the chair and looked at Babs calmly. He had worked with him before and in his heart he knew that it didn't add up. Babs could be selfish, stupid, idle and greedy, but he wasn't a double-crosser. And he wasn't imaginative enough to fall in with a devious plan like this. The odds were that he had been used as well. But perhaps that wasn't good enough. After all, Terry's life was still on the line.

When Andy and the boys had come back with mugs of sweet tea and Danny had found some clothes that looked almost normal on him, Terry had just tied Babs to his chair again to stop him escaping or raising the alarm, when the door opened and Michelle came in, screamed and dropped her shopping. Lunging past Andy, who tried to catch her, she flung herself protectively across Babs's lap, shouting insults at the three men and the two staring boys.

'Who the fuck's the tart?' Andy said, rubbing his cheek, which Michelle had clawed on her way past.

'Well, well, well,' Danny grinned, 'Babsy's got himself a squaw.'

'Leave her alone, lads,' Babs pleaded. 'Michelle knows nothing about all this.'

'You needn't worry about us,' Terry said. 'Our business is with Kwang.'

When they had calmed Michelle, Terry left her kneeling beside Babs's chair and went to call the British Embassy from the phone extension in the bedroom. After some minutes, the languid, disinterested voice that had first answered was replaced by the clipped, precise tones of another person who refused to give either his name or position.

'I think we can help you, Mr Williams, but you

mustn't come to the Embassy building. Nor can I say any more on this line. Do you know the Central Post Office?'

'No, but I can find it.'

'Good. Be outside it at nine-thirty tomorrow morning. We'll take it from there.'

'Want us to come too?' Danny asked afterwards as Terry pored over a street map of Seoul.

'Yes. But not with me. Babs, have you got a car?'

'No.'

Terry turned on him and glared. Babs sighed.

'A Blue Honda Civic, down in the basement. The keys are in my coat pocket. Dojo, please be careful. I only got it a few days ago.'

'Babsy, I used to drive armoured personnel carriers.'

'That's what I'm afraid of.'

'Danny, I want you and Andy to shadow me. Bring the hardware, just in case.'

'What about the boys?'

'They can stay here and keep watch. We'll make Babsy and Michelle nice and comfortable before we go and the kids can watch them for us. See they come to no harm.'

Andy was doubtful but Terry reassured him.

'Don't worry. The way I'll tie them up I doubt we'll even be able to undo the knots when we get back.' He turned to Babs. 'And when we do, I'll have to relieve you of your cheque card and account number. Simply as a precaution until things are cleared up and Mr Kwang's seen the error of his ways and paid all his bills.'

'Please, Dojo,' Babs pleaded, 'Don't take my money. It's all I've got. Me and Michelle were going away.'

Terry smiled, patting him on the back. 'Don't worry, mate. If you're clean and you've told us the truth, I'll buy you a wedding present and drive you both to the airport myself.'

'And if you've been lying to us,' Andy said severely, 'I'll put a match to the place with both of you in it.'

The next morning they were up at first light. As it was the first night they had spent under cover for some time, it had taken a while to get used to the soft mattresses spread on the floor. Michelle had been given the bed with Liang on one side of her and Little Chiao on the other; whereas Terry could trust the boys to keep an eye on her and no more, he wasn't so sure about the other two men. Babs was secured in his armchair and Terry, Andy and Danny slept on the floor, taking it in turns to keep watch in the event of any unwelcome visitors.

After an early breakfast that finished the last of Michelle's shopping, the three men prepared to leave, tying Michelle and Babs securely back to back using a combination of knots that even Houdini would have been unable to wriggle out of.

'Be good, now. As soon as we're back, we'll fix lunch.'

Turning to the boys he added: 'And you've done all right. We'll sort something out for you too, don't you worry. Tell them what I said, Danny.'

The Indian smiled. 'I think they got the drift.'

Once out in the street, Terry set off at a brisk pace for the centre of town. Feeling lost in one of Babs's jackets, he felt in the pocket for the 9mm Browning that he had taken from the major's desk, along with two spare clips of ammunition. As he touched the black plastic grip of the butt like a lucky charm, he was glad to have it in easy reach should things go wrong. He was too experienced to trust anyone at this stage in the game, and certainly not some posh-sounding diplomat or whoever he was, British or not.

As he sauntered along Chungmu-ro Street, he stopped to look at a display of Gucci shoes, checking in the shop window's reflection for the reassuring shape of the Honda Civic idling a block away. Moving on, he crossed over another street and found the Central Post Office opening for the day's business.

Stamping up and down in the fresh morning air, Terry scanned the crowds of shoppers and tourists. It didn't seem a day since he and the others had first arrived in Seoul at the start of the mission. Remembering the crowd of faces at Babs's reception party in the private dining-room of the restaurant, he felt anger mounting inside him. None of them had been saints, but they hadn't deserved to be butchered like that. No one did. He vowed to himself that he would get to the bottom of the whole affair if it was the last thing he did. If Kwang had merely been incompetent and Yi Soong had slipped through the South Korean screening process, then Terry would ensure that every last dollar reached the dependants of the dead mercenaries. If, on the other hand, Kwang himself was a double agent, Terry would sort him out personally. Francis Kwang might be able to pull the wool over the eyes of the South Korean intelligence community, but he would find Terry Williams and his mates a different kettle of fish.

Out of the heavy traffic, a sleek white Mazda pulled up alongside the kerb and the man in the passenger seat wound down the window and called across to Terry.

'Mr Williams?'

Terry nodded and made towards the car as the driver reached over and opened the back door. A second man was in the front passenger seat.

'Good morning.'

Terry recognized the passenger's voice as the cool one from his telephone call. The car pulled out into the traffic and turned north up Sogong-no Street.

'Presumably now that you've caused a major political embarrassment to our South Korean allies, you want us to clear up the mess and get you out of the country incognito?'

'I couldn't have put it better myself,' Terry replied, angered by the man's arrogant tone.

'Who are you, anyway? British intelligence, I suppose.'

The man smiled.

'As regards getting you out of the country, I'm afraid it won't be quite that simple.'

'I didn't think it would.'

'We'd like to know everything you can tell us about the whole operation. Who hired you, how you came into the country, who met you, your method of entry to the North and so on.'

Terry looked around at the bustling city streets. 'Here?'

'Here. We don't want you to be seen at the Embassy, I'm afraid, so this will have to act as the debrief.'

'And if I don't want to tell you.'

The man swivelled round.

'I hardly think you're in any position to refuse. You're going to need travel documents and identification papers. Were you the only one to escape?'

Terry was about to give him the names of the

other two but on the spur of the moment changed his mind.

'Yes. The rest were all killed.' It would be no big problem for the Embassy to arrange further papers for Andy and Danny later. For now, Terry wanted to see the lie of the land, as Danny had said.

The interrogator relaxed. 'I see. Congratulations,' he said grudgingly. It's no mean feat to get in and out of North Korea at the best of times, let alone with their security forces after you.'

Terry let the compliment pass and as the unmarked embassy Mazda toured slowly through the streets of the capital, he recounted the story of the Korean contract. The intelligence officer stopped him a couple of times, to slip a new cassette into his recorder or ask a question on a point of detail.

'So perhaps you should tell your friends in Korean intelligence to have a closer look at Francis Kwang,' Terry concluded.

'They already have and as far as they're concerned his name's been cleared.'

'And in your books?'

Without answering Terry's question, the man continued. 'Your operation was compromised by his assistant, Mr Yi Soong.'

Terry snorted. 'Tell me about it!'

'There was an investigation and Kwang was cleared of all blame. Once Yi had warned the North Korean government of the attempt to kidnap Professor Lim Choy, they decided to capitalize on the operation and turn it into a propaganda coup for themselves. It worked very nicely. Of course none of us seriously believed that American special forces would be involved in any massacre, but there were enough states in the UN that did believe it to cause severe embarrassment.'

'And the UN inspection of North Korean nuclear facilities?'

'Put on hold, I'm afraid. It seems that for the time being the Communists have won.'

Red-hot anger surged through Terry as he thought of the dead civilians at the resort, massacred by Yi and his men; of the dead mercenaries; of Dave, Ken, and in all likelihood Jules. Perhaps this man was right and Kwang was innocent, simply an incompetent who had allowed his organization to be penetrated by a double agent.

After driving in silence for a while, Terry remembered the money owed to him and the others, and broached the subject.

'Not my problem, old chap,' the intelligence officer replied. 'And if you know what's good for you you won't go near Kwang. Think yourself lucky to be alive, and get out of the country. We can have identification papers and travel documents ready in a couple of days.'

Terry's mind raced. He would be able to get money from Babs but it would never be enough for the dependants of the dead mercenaries. But was there any point in approaching Kwang? Perhaps he should take the man's advice and cut and run.

He was about to come clean and tell the officer about the existence of Danny and Andy, when he noticed the driver glancing in the rear-view mirror. They had come to a halt in a solid queue of traffic at a major intersection. The man in the passenger seat looked across irritably.

'What is it, Simon?'

The driver chuckled. 'The way these Orientals drive! Some impatient arsehole back there flashing his lights. Can't he see the red lights?'

Terry twisted round and saw the blue Honda Civic some way back in the queue. The headlights were flashing and the horn blaring. The doors were open and Danny and Andy were diving out of the car.

'Get out!' Terry screamed.

'What the . . .?'

The intelligence officer never finished his sentence. A burst of machine-gun fire raked the car, catching both front-seat occupants in the chest and face. Even as he screamed, Terry was flinging himself to the floor, fumbling for the handle and kicking open the door.

Slithering out on to the road, he pulled the Browning from his pocket and curled into a ball with his back to the car, clenching the pistol in a firm, two-handed combat grip. He glanced down the row of cars, but there was no sign of either Danny or Andy, though he could hear the sound of the Kalashnikov and M16 answering the much heavier bursts of fire coming at them from several directions.

Flat on his stomach, Terry scanned the ground underneath the cars, still jammed nose to tail in parallel queues. Most of the drivers and passengers had stayed in their vehicles, huddling for shelter and screaming with terror, but some were attempting to bolt for cover. To Terry's trained eye, it was obvious which of the people whose feet were visible under the packed cars were running in fear of their lives, and which of them were moving methodically towards him, pausing to fire, then moving still closer at a crouch.

Realizing that the attacking gunmen probably considered him dead or at least badly wounded, Terry watched silently as the nearest pair of feet approached round the side of the neighbouring car. Easing himself up into a kneeling position, he aimed the Browning, sighting with both eyes open ready for a close-quarters engagement. When the man appeared, his attention was on the occupants of the Mazda; he was doing a quick body count. Both rounds of Terry's double tap hit him in the middle of the chest, knocking him backwards too fast for alarm to register on his face.

Pivoting on his heel, Terry whipped his pistol round just in time to fire a second double tap at another Korean as he aimed his AKM. Again the man toppled backwards, but not before Terry had recognized him as one of the snipers from Yi Soong's team that had accompanied the mercenaries to the resort and that had later ambushed them.

'That one's for Ken,' Terry said bitterly.

Tumbling into a forward roll, Terry came up level with the Mazda's rear bumper and aimed round the corner seeking his next target.

'Dojo, catch!'

Looking up at the cry, Terry saw a grenade arcing towards him through the air, the pin pulled and the lever spinning free as if in slow motion.

'Shit!'

Keeping a hold on the Browning, he caught the grenade in his hands, hearing the fizz of the detonator in its lethal core.

'Behind you!'

Without looking, Terry flung the grenade over his head like a hot potato, hitting the tarmac as it exploded in an airburst of deadly splinters, showering down on the two gunmen who had been about to take him out.

He looked round at Danny's anxious face several cars away.

'Sorry, buddy. I couldn't be sure of reaching them from here.'

From a couple of blocks away the sound of sirens filtered through the noise of the machine-gun fire. The attacking AKMs faltered and fell silent as the ambushers pulled out, with shouted orders and the squealing of tyres on the cartridge-strewn tarmac.

'Better make ourselves scarce,' Terry shouted.

'Fine by me.'

Finding Andy blazing off a last volley after the retreating cars, Terry and Danny bundled him into Babs's car and Terry shunted back and forth until they had cleared a space big enough to slip through.

'Hope Babs is insured more than third party.'

Once they were out of the traffic jam, Terry gunned the engine and raced away with the tyres smoking. Swinging the car round a corner, he shot up a side-street, raced straight across two intersections, then slowed at the end of another side-street before turning lazily into a busy main road and losing himself as just one more frustrated motorist amid the Seoul traffic.

Several blocks away the sirens wailed as heavily armed police tumbled out into the killing ground to puzzle over the carnage and the slaughter of two British Embassy officials and several unidentified gunmen.

'Well, we can't go back to the flat,' Andy said, clipping a fresh magazine on to his Kalashnikov.

'Keep that fucking thing out of sight, will you? We don't have a choice. Babs, the kids and the bird are there. And another thing, I recognized one of those fuckers back there as a goon from Yi's sniper team.'

Danny stared grimly out of the window. 'So he's back in town. It didn't take him long, did it? You don't think he's taking it personally, do you?'

Terry turned into the road outside Babs's apartment. 'I hope to God he is. That way we can expect him to make a mistake.'

Instead of stopping at the main entrance, Terry drove straight past and went round to the back, pulling up by the fire escape that snaked up the side of the building. Getting out of the car, the three men moved away quickly, splitting in three different directions, checking every angle to ensure that their approach had been unobserved. Only when Terry was content that the coast was clear, did he hand-signal the others to cover him towards the fire escape.

Bounding up to the first level, he crouched by the rusty metal steps until Danny and Andy had joined him. Then, as they watched, Terry moved again, and so on, leapfrogging through the levels until they came to Babs's floor. He forced the lock on the window, eased it open and slipped into the corridor. As soon as Danny and Andy were crouching beside him, he moved stealthily past the other apartments and peered round the corner. At the end of the corridor Babs's door was ajar. Terry felt the hair on his neck bristle and without taking his eyes off the entrance, he gave the thumbs-down signal for enemy contact.

Leaving Andy to cover the rear, Terry and Danny sidled along the corridor, hugging the walls on opposite sides. Danny had flicked his M16 to automatic and Terry held the Browning in a combat grip, eyes wide open and every sense alert to the slightest hint of trouble.

Reaching the door, Terry signalled Danny into a

position a few yards back, where he knelt down and aimed his M16 at the centre of the doorway. Then, taking a deep breath, exhaling, and breathing again, Terry tensed like a spring and burst through the door into the middle of the sitting-room, coming up from his forward roll at the foot of Babs's chair.

'Who do you think you are? The man with the Milk Tray?'

Babs's fat white cheeks shuddered with laughter as Terry flopped back on to the carpet with relief.

'You stupid fat bastard,' Terry exploded. 'Why was the bloody door open?'

'Ask those two little devils you set to watch us. Michelle's been pleading with them to cut us loose but the swines told her to shut up. The eldest one even put his bloody hand up her skirt. Where did you find them? Biting the heads off kittens?'

Calling Danny and Andy into the apartment, Terry went through into the kitchen and found the boys stirring a huge pan of rice and meat.

'They went through my wallet and sent out for a bloody take-away! How's that for covert? Leave the recruiting to me next time.'

Terry took a knife from the worktop, went back into the sitting-room and cut Babs and Michelle free. In a blur the woman was on her feet and dashed into the kitchen. A second later there were howls and screams and it took two of them to pull her off Liang, who collapsed on the floor nursing his head, which she had clubbed repeatedly with the heavy wooden spoon from the rice pan.

When a modicum of order had been restored and Little Chiao had served out the food, everyone sat on the floor to eat, Michelle glaring at Liang over the top of her bowl, muttering curses in between cramming her mouth with rice. Terry reached across and switched on the television for the midday news bulletin. The screen was instantly filled with footage of the battle site in town.

'My, my,' Babs drawled, 'you boys have been busy. It says that two British Embassy officials were attacked and assassinated by three escaped criminals. I wonder who they mean?'

Danny slammed his bowl on the floor. 'Have we got to take on the whole of goddam South Korea as well?'

Terry stared at the pictures of the blood-soaked bodies of the British intelligence officer and his driver, referred to by the media as 'registry clerks'.

'So what do we do now?' Andy asked morosely. 'I don't reckon the Embassy will want to hear from us again.'

Terry wrestled with the blur of facts. How on earth had everything gone so terribly wrong? Obviously the Embassy's phone had been tapped and once he had got word, Yi Soong had decided to eradicate Terry and the others as soon as they had been forced out into the open. They would have been safer walking straight into the Embassy and asking for shelter, but the intelligence officer had insisted on playing his pathetic secret-agent game of intrigue. The poor sod had paid for it with his life.

Now, even though his men had bogged up the ambush, Yi had capitalized on the situation. The word had been sent out and Terry and the gang were down to take the rap. In addition to Yi's own hit team, the South Korean police and intelligence services would be after them, anxious to catch the murderers of two foreign diplomats and to regain the face they had lost by hosting a full-scale fire-fight in the heart of their capital city.

But the more he thought about it, the more Terry found himself coming back to Francis Kwang. Who else would have had the contacts both in the security services and the media? Yi had been discredited, at least publicly. Unless the whole edifice of the South Korean government was rotten, riddled with Communist sleepers, Yi would have been unable to pass the word himself. It would have had to have come from someone who was trusted, whose name had been cleared of any complicity. It must have come from someone at the top.

'I think it's time we paid a visit to Mr Kwang,' Terry said.

Danny looked at him thoughtfully, following his reasoning. 'I'd say it was overdue.'

Andy stabbed his thumb at Babs. 'What about this useless fucker?'

'I say!' Babs protested.

'That's just it,' Terry answered. 'He *is* a useless fucker. But he's not the bastard who set us up. The North Koreans are the most paranoid, security-conscious arseholes in the world. The last person they'd let in on their little plot is a foreigner. No. This is purely home-grown. Babs was used, like the rest of us. Kwang paid him off to cover his own back with his intelligence bosses here in Seoul. Made it seem above board as though he had intended to get the scientist out just like we were briefed. God, what fools we were! To think we fell for it.'

'And to think Kwang's got away with it as well,' Danny added.

'Sure. Why not? It was the easiest thing in the world

for him to finger Yi. So what if there was an investigation? The old-boy network probably runs as smoothly here as it does anywhere else. Kwang could have used his connections to get himself off the hook and before you know it, he's back in business. Probably planning his next little gem – trucking a nuclear bomb into the heart of Seoul and holding the government to ransom, for all we know.'

Terry snapped off the television,which was showing mugshots of Andy, Danny and himself, along with their names and details, and stalked to the window.

'We'd better get out of here fast. Babs, you're coming too.'

'Dojo, I . . .'

'Shut it. This is going to take every one of us. We'll need explosives. Can you get them?'

Babs sighed. 'Yes.'

He had seen Terry in this mood before and he knew there would be no escape until things had run their course, even though it was unlikely that by then anyone caught in the way would be left alive.

'Demolition charges. TNT. OK?'

'Got it.'

'Tetrytol boosters, det cord, electric detonators, masking tape – all the trimmings. And mines. Claymores and grenades.'

As he scribbled down the shopping list, Babs mumbled: 'Are you planning to start a war?'

'I hope I'm going to prevent one.'

'I get it,' Babs answered. He looked up and smiled. 'And I suppose this "useless fucker's" going to help you?'

'You've got it.'

'Just like old times.'

13

For the journey to Sorak-san, Babs gave Michelle some money and sent her out to hire a Toyota minibus. By now the police would be looking for the Honda and if Kwang was able to pull strings, there would undoubtedly be roadblocks on every approach to his country villa. Apart from that, if, as Terry insisted, they were all going to make the trip, it would take a minibus to hold the seven of them and all the hardware.

From the bottom of his bedroom cupboard, Babs unfolded an ancient pair of combat trousers.

'Hello, boys,' he said quietly as he held them up against himself in front of the mirror. 'It's been a long time.'

After putting them on, he went back into the sitting-room to hoots of laughter from the others.

'Blimey, it's Danny La Rue. How'd you squeeze into that little number? Dacron, isn't it?'

'Looks more like chiffon.'

Babs smiled good-naturedly. 'Actually they're jungle OGs. These were used in combat when you, Mr Buchan, were in kindergarten. Or was it the Glasgow branch of the Hitler Youth?'

They had spent an afternoon of feverish activity; Babs had been out with Terry's shopping list, to which he had added a few items of his own, and when he had returned he had staggered up the stairs with an enormous holdall in each hand and a bergen over his shoulder stuffed with still more hardware. For the next hour Terry and Danny sat cross-legged in the middle of the floor, preparing a variety of explosive charges. As the minutes passed the pile grew, and with it, their range of options. There were steel-cutting charges for severing metal beams or fences, charges for cutting timber, road-cratering charges, and breaching charges for attacking reinforced concrete.

'There,' Terry said at last, sitting back and admiring their handiwork. 'That ought to do the trick.'

Meanwhile Andy and Babs had been preparing the weapons. In addition to the two Kalashnikovs, the M16 and 9mm Browning pistol, all of which they stripped, thoroughly cleaned and then reloaded, Babs had brought back an M60 machine-gun, an M203 rifle with attached 40mm grenade-launcher, three more Brownings, grenades and plenty of spare ammunition.

When everything was ready, Terry went over each item of kit, checking and double-checking, before supervising the repacking of the holdalls.

It was late afternoon by the time they loaded the van and set off, Michelle driving, the two boys in front with her, and the four men tucked out of sight in the back.

'Just look like any mother out driving with her sons,' Babs called to her. She glared with distaste at Liang and his grubby companion, who both smiled back innocently.

Reasoning that the main roads were likely to be under surveillance, they turned away from the east–west Yongdong Expressway and selected a route that took them across country on a network of back roads. Once out of the city, Babs clambered up into the front passenger seat between Michelle and the boys and navigated from a map that he spread on the dashboard. Heading north-east towards Uijongbu and then east to Chunchon, they planned to approach the Sorak-san National Park by the lesser-used northern route.

Nevertheless, as they finally neared the park's outer boundaries later that night, Michelle pulled the van over to the side of the road when she saw a queue of cars ahead and the flashing blue and red lights of a police roadblock. In accordance with a pre-arranged plan, the four men piled out of the back and, shouldering the bags of weapons and explosives, disappeared into the night. Swinging back into lane, Michelle eased the minibus forward until she had closed up behind the queue of cars, to sit waiting her turn. She lit a cigarette, stuck her elbow out of the window and blew smoke in the face of the policeman who came up to ask her where she was going.

'Naksan beach.'

'At this time of year?'

'I need to get away with the kids.'

The policeman shone his torch on the two boys, by now curled up asleep in the back.

'They don't look anything like you.'

'No. Everyone says that. They take after their father.'

The policeman looked her up and down, taking in the dress and the make-up. He grinned at her. 'Which one?'

Michelle winked at him. 'A girl's got to earn a living.'

Further up the line a police sergeant shouted for

the minibus to get moving. The policeman stood back reluctantly and waved her on. As Michelle selected first gear and moved forward, she blew him a kiss. Weaving through the armoured cars, she noted the heavily armed police and a chill ran through her when she saw a handler restraining a sniffer dog close to her rear bumper. Her only experience of them had been when the police had raided the brothel for drugs, but she was sure that they could sniff out the scent of explosives just as easily, even if the TNT was no longer actually in the minibus.

In her rear-view mirror she saw the dog tense, its nose spinning round to the back of the vehicle. Seeing that the handler was looking the other way, chatting to a friend, Michelle gunned the accelerator and simultaneously trod hard on the clutch a couple of times, bouncing the van forward in a series of kangaroo jumps like a first-time driver. Now firm on the scent, the dog barked and strained at the leash, but Michelle jerked the van into a couple more violent lurches.

'Goddam useless fucking piece of shit!'

The policemen burst out laughing. 'Nice language for a lady.'

The dog tugged and yapped. Michelle turned on the officers.

'What the fuck are you staring at, idle sons of bitches! Can't you shut that fucking dog up?'

The boys woke up and Little Chiao burst into tears, terrified by the barking and the noise. But the handler just grinned and waved after the retreating minibus, pulling his dog to heel.

'Even my dog thinks your driving sucks, lady!'

'Screw you!'

Stepping on the accelerator, Michelle shot away from the roadblock, gripping the steering wheel with all her might to calm her shaking hands. Liang came up beside her, picked her cigarette off the floor and put it between her lips.

'Here you are, Mum.'

Two hundred yards up the road, with the police out of sight, Michelle pulled over again, turned off the lights and waited. After a while four figures emerged out of the darkness and Terry and the others climbed into the back of the minibus, Babs breathing heavily from their fast cross-country march, which had bypassed the roadblock in a wide hook.

'OGs pinching a bit, Grandad?' Andy smirked as he clambered past.

Babs wiped away the sweat cascading down his cheeks. 'Let's just see who's still standing when this lot is over,' he said quietly.

Lying in the darkness, Kwang listened to the light fall of rain outside. It had only started in the last half hour and he loved the sound of it on the wooden roof and the skylights. Feeling Lulu's naked body the length of his, snuggling safe and warm in their sheets, away from the night's discomforts, he found it reassuring to know that the villa was fully manned, his own guards reinforced by a complete police SWAT team.

He felt like a spider at the centre of a sprawling web, towards which the unwary fly was being inexorably drawn. The moment he had heard of the escape of Terry Williams across the border he knew that they would eventually be meeting. Dojo sounded an extraordinary man and Kwang regretted being unable to make use of his obvious talents. Such professionals were rare and it would be a pity to waste his expertise. But that was how it had to be. His own security came before everything. Williams had chosen the wrong man to make an enemy of.

Shifting gently on to his side, he looked at Lulu's face, her hair spread across the pillow like a Chinese silk fan. It would be morning in a few hours. Lulu would make breakfast for them both and if the rain had stopped they would later go for a walk in the compound. It would be unwise to go farther until the remaining mercenaries had been apprehended or killed, but Kwang didn't expect to have long to wait for that. Roadblocks were covering every approach to the secluded villa and his men had had every opportunity to recce their positions in daylight, carefully selecting their arcs and checking that every angle was covered.

Dangling the tip of his finger on the hollow of Lulu's throat, he lightly traced a line down between her breasts. She moaned in her sleep, turning slightly, then slipping back into her dreams. Her mouth opened and she moistened her lips. Pausing to feel the beat of her heart, the finger continued over the taut, smooth skin of her stomach, down past the well of her navel to the eternal secrets of her thighs under the white sheet.

As Lulu blinked awake, yawning, she smiled at Kwang with half-closed eyes and guided his hand. He thrilled at the touch of her, watching all the while with a detachment that she always found tantalizing. Outside, he knew that the web lay taut and waiting, its deadly arcs fanning out from the hub where he and Lulu were making love. It would take an army to storm the defences.

Moving beneath the sheet, Lulu's body writhed, her

fists clenching above her head, tightening on the pillow as she bit her lip to keep from crying out. Unable any longer to deny himself the same pleasure, Kwang eased himself on top of her, fighting to hold back the waves that shuddered through his body, kissing her breasts until she parted beneath him.

When the minibus got to within a mile of Kwang's villa, Babs indicated a side road leading off into the trees. Winding steeply up a hill, it soon became little more than a forestry track. Cutting the lights, Michelle edged the vehicle slowly forward, leaning over the steering wheel with her nose on the windscreen to make out the ribbon of track, almost invisible in the darkness. Terry thanked his lucky stars. The night was overcast and the light rain would not only interfere with any night sights that Kwang's guards would be using, greatly reducing their effectiveness, but in the thick undergrowth it would also muffle the sound of their footsteps on the forest floor.

'Perfect. We couldn't have planned it better ourselves.'

Babs grinned. 'You'll probably find that Kwang's pulled his men in close to the compound, shoulder to shoulder in a daisy-chain. He doesn't trust the wilderness. Never been in it.'

'Well, the wilderness is about to come to him. You know your position?'

Babs hoisted the M60 out of the carrying case. 'Don't worry. I'll be there.'

'Take Michelle and the boys to carry the ammunition.'

After backing the minibus into a thicket, Andy cut several boughs and camouflaged it as best he could. When they were ready, he, Terry and Danny shouldered the holdalls and set off on foot, Babs and the others disappearing into the trees in the opposite direction.

It took Terry a good hour to get his charges in place. Moving in a wide circle, he gradually worked his way around the villa, stopping whenever he came to a track. At each location, while Danny kept watch, he planted cratering and tree-cutting charges, so that he would be able to isolate his target from the outside world. While reinforcements tried to penetrate the network of demolitions and booby-traps, Terry would be dealing with the man in the centre.

Beyond and around the demolitions, Andy set trip-wires attached to Claymore mines, and in the trees on either side of the roads, he scattered anti-personnel mines so that anyone trying to outflank the obstacles would be forced to think twice. It would not be impenetrable, but it would cause sufficient delay and give them the time they needed to get to their man.

Shortly before dawn the three mercenaries dropped silently into a ditch fifty yards from the wire fence. Checking the defences, Terry decided on an entry point and crawled forward through the tall grass until he was close enough to attach a steel-cutting charge to the main fence post. Withdrawing as carefully as he had approached, he slipped back over the rim of the ditch and checked the demolition firing circuits on the panel of his control box. He looked up at the sky. Despite the dark blanket of clouds, the sky was lightening, but the drizzle was getting heavier and looked like persisting throughout the morning.

'We'll wait until it's fully light and then hit them.'

Terry knew that the change from night routine to

day routine was always a time of maximum vigilance for any defensive force. Kwang's guards would probably be going through some sort of stand-to drill, but once the day had fully broken they would be preparing to change shifts and thinking of breakfast.

As if to confirm his reasoning, a lone figure came into view, walking calmly around the inside of the compound. When he came to a hut, he paused beside it and Terry saw his lips moving, although the man kept his face to the forest. Terry glanced at Andy.

'Got him,' Andy replied, noting the concealed sentry position and slipping a 40mm grenade into his M203.

When the guard commander had disappeared around the corner to visit his next sentry post, Danny leaned across.

'Did you see the outfit? He's police. Kwang's got a SWAT team in there.'

'What's the strength?'

Danny shrugged. 'Could be eight, maybe twelve guys. They could be pretty good too.'

'Body armour?'

'You can bet on it.'

'Go for head shots then.'

Dressed in a trim pair of slacks and T-shirt, Kwang smiled at Lulu across the breakfast bar. He sipped his decaffeinated coffee and then deftly sliced the ripe papaya that Lulu had prepared with segments of fresh lime. It was a shame about the rain. They would have to spend the morning indoors, but casting his eyes over Lulu's tight cotton blouse he was sure they would find some way of passing the time.

The police commander had just been in to report that everything was secure, but Kwang didn't like the man. He was far too cocky and overconfident. Kwang had also noted that his men's uniforms had been immaculately ironed; normally he would have been the first to admire neatness, but somehow it didn't sit well with a SWAT team who were supposed to be hardened professionals. He hoped it wasn't an indication of a narrow, parade-ground mentality.

Feeling uneasy, he got up and walked across the room.

Lulu looked up, catching some lime juice on her chin. 'What is it?'

'I'm just going to check something, kitten.'

There would be no harm in checking that his own man was equally happy with the situation, even if he had been put under the command of the police.

Kwang pressed the intercom. 'Hello? Chun Jo, isn't it?' He laughed. 'Listen, Chun, will you have a look around? I don't trust that idiot police captain. Report back when you're satisfied.'

Feeling better already, Kwang stretched lazily. Walking briskly up to Lulu, he put an arm round her and kissed her tenderly.

'What was that for?'

He was just about to reply that he loved her, when the large glass doors that covered most of the wall leading out on to the terrace shattered in a hail of lethal shards.

As soon as Terry pressed the button to fire the cutting charge attached to the fence post, Babs Butler opened up from his position on the hill above. He had done his job well, finding a commanding position that gave him a broad view right across the compound and buildings, enabling him to direct the fire of his M60 into any part of the villa, dominating the battle with accurate machine-gun fire in close support of Terry's assault group.

Working through the buttons, Terry pressed one after another and from all around the valley came the answering reports of the detonations, echoing through the mountain passes as if the villa was being engaged by a battery of medium artillery. On every track and approach, explosions sent chunks of dry earth into the sky, as huge craters appeared, rendering the tracks and roads useless. As the tree-cutting charges shattered the trunks, giant pines toppled across the roadways like latticework, adding to the craters and the waiting booby-traps, cutting Kwang off from the outside world.

Before the roar of the last explosion had died away, Terry was on his feet and doubling towards the breach in the fence. The severed post had taken a good thirty yards of wire down with it, and the three men cleared the tangled mess in a single bound. Firing from the hip, Andy pumped his 40mm grenade into the hut where the police commander had given away the position of his own sentry. Splintering in an orange ball of flame, the hut and the man inside disintegrated.

Two men in police uniforms appeared round the corner. Had they been Kwang's men, Terry would have finished them with head shots. Instead, he engaged them with bursts of fire from his Kalashnikov aimed at the chest. Although their body armour saved their lives, the force of the bullets smacking into them at close range flung them backwards and smashed their ribs, knocking them unconscious.

The next one wasn't so lucky. Diving out of cover in a forward roll, he was scythed down by a long burst of fire from Babs's M60. Up on the hilltop, Babs couldn't afford the luxury of distinguishing between the enemy targets. For him, every one of them deserved and got the same concentrated hail of 7.62mm bullets.

Terry waited until Danny and Andy had both closed up beside him before pressing on to the centre of the compound, where the main villa was situated. With Babs raking the ground ahead of them, they made rapid progress until coming up against the first of Kwang's own men. Secure behind a wall of sandbags, he sprayed them with a burst from his AKM. Andy cried out and dropped the M203, blood soaking his right arm. Unable to retrieve the grenade-launcher, Terry and Danny hugged the ground, desperately trying to place their rounds through the narrow firing slit in the sandbags.

From his firing position on the hill, Babs spotted the target and swivelled on his belly, bringing his M60 to bear as Liang clipped on a fresh belt of ammunition.

'That'a boy,' Babs mumbled, his cheek squashed on to the butt. 'We'll make a soldier of you yet.'

Firing a long, continuous burst, he noted the line of tracer, adjusting his aim as if hosing a garden plant, until he found the bunker and, with finger firmly on the trigger, let the endless stream of copper-plated bullets chew their way through it.

Lying a few yards back from the sandbag emplacement, Terry and Danny cursed and hugged the ground as the bullets cracked past their ears. But in front of them the sandbags were dismantled, torn and finally ripped apart. Realizing that his shelter was disintegrating, Kwang's guard suddenly sprinted away from it, but once in the open he was cut down by Danny's M16, two well-aimed shots smacking into his back.

Retrieving the M203, Terry clamped a tourniquet

on Andy's arm. Although the wound wasn't severe, Andy had lost a lot of blood and Terry noted the first tell-tale signs of shock.

'Better sit this one out.'

'Fuck that,' Andy replied, struggling to his feet. 'I can still use this.'

Drawing his Browning, he limped after Terry and Danny. He had made it this far. There was no way he was going to let his mates down now. That was one of the reasons he was here, after all. To fight alongside men like Dojo Williams and Danny Grey Wolf, and to call them mates. If he deserted them now to sit beside the wall, he'd be nothing, a nobody. It was what drove him up the hill every time. It was what pushed him on.

By now Terry and Danny were out of sight, inside the villa itself. Lurching forward, Andy tightened the tourniquet on his arm, but fumbling with the knot, he dropped his pistol. From the hilltop, Babs Butler saw the figure emerge from a doorway behind Andy, and struggled to free the stoppage that had just silenced his M60. Liang and Little Chiao screamed for all they were worth, but their voices were lost in the vast, empty valley.

'Mr Buchan, isn't it?'

Andy froze at the sound of Chun Jo's voice. His hand was only inches away from his pistol but as he felt his heart go cold he knew that it might as well be a mile. The first kick caught him full in the ribs but it was the second that made him scream, landing on the gunshot wound in his arm. Rolling on to his back, Andy lashed out with his feet, but Chun Jo stepped aside easily.

'You Westerners really have no idea how to fight, do you?'

A barrage of kicks disabled the Scot, leaving him at the mercy of his attacker. When the final kick landed, it cut into the back of his neck. Tumbling on to his face, Andy started at the dirt as Chun Jo pulled back his fist and released the death blow. Up on the hill, Babs had cleared the stoppage and squeezed off a burst. But it was too late. The bullets found only empty space and the loose earth around Andy's body.

Having recovered a little from the shock of the explosion, Kwang had armed himself with the semi-automatic pistol that he kept in the drawer of his desk, and pulled Lulu into the relative safety of the corner farthest from the terrace. Rain slanted in through the shattered sliding doors, and crouching behind the bar where the remains of his uneaten breakfast lay covered with bits of glass, he cursed the police commander and wondered why his own guards hadn't come in to give him the close protection he wanted.

Entering the ground floor of the villa, Terry and Danny found themselves in a large vestibule. Tropical fish stared stupidly from a long ornamental tank and potted palms fringed the reception area. With his finger on the rifle trigger of the M203 combination weapon system, Terry edged round the side of the wall, eyes wide and senses alert. Standing hard up against a tall rubber plant, he covered Danny as he crept stealthily towards the corridor entrance, which led into the heart of the luxury building.

In the heated tank, a brilliant-turquoise fish swerved suddenly, alerted by a movement that Terry had missed. Swinging his weapon on to the source, Terry squeezed off a burst, the 5.56mm bullets ripping through the furniture and finding behind it the guard, who was aiming his AKM at Danny's back.

As if at a signal, the vestibule was suddenly alive with men, springing from cover to tackle the two intruders. Three of the SWAT team policemen burst from a side room, Heckler and Koch MP5 sub-machine-guns blazing. Dropping on to one knee, Terry knew that he had barely half a second before the tightly packed group fragmented into separate fleeting targets. Aiming at the centre man, he fired the M203's grenade-launcher. The snub-nosed 40mm round hit the policeman in the centre of the chest and exploded, cutting him clean in two and dismembering both his neighbours.

Pumping the barrel open, Terry ejected the spent casing and slammed in a fresh round, as Danny blazed at another of Kwang's men, who had darted between two chairs. But the man came up uninjured and hit Danny's M16 with a round from his AKM, smashing the stock, before rolling forward again, unwittingly giving Danny time to recover. Rather than go for his Browning, Danny pulled his tomahawk from his belt, and launched himself over the top of a sofa and on to the stunned Korean.

Seeking a clear shot, Terry didn't dare fire in case he hit his friend, but after a savage struggle Danny pinned the guard to the floor by the throat with one hand, while the other raised the tomahawk over his head and brought it down mercilessly on the man's grimacing face.

He wiped the blade on the man's shirt. 'It might not be high-tech, but it doesn't suffer from stoppages.'

At the top of a flight of stairs they came to a single wooden door, and kicking it open, entered a large comfortably furnished sitting-room. One wall had been of glass but it had been shattered either by one of the explosions or by Babs's M60.

Scanning the room, Danny tensed at the sound of whimpering coming from behind a bar in the far corner.

'Stand up. Now. Slowly, with your hands above your head,' he said, then, repeating it in Korean, moved in the opposite direction to Terry, his Browning trained on the beautiful Korean girl who came into view. He looked across at Terry, both of them realizing that they were at the heart of Francis Kwang's empire.

'Come on out, Mr Kwang,' Terry called, kneeling behind a chair and levelling his M203 at the bar. 'If you try anything, both you and the bird get it. I don't know what kind of peashooter you've got, but there's a 40mm grenade over here just begging to be fired.'

Slowly Kwang stood up, the pistol sliding from his fingers as his hands rose above his head.

'Don't shoot. I'm sure we can come to some arrangement.'

'I doubt it.'

'How much do you want?'

'Just what's owing to us and to the guys you had murdered in North Korea.'

'I knew nothing about that,' Kwang replied in an even voice.

Danny looked across at Terry. 'Cool bastard, isn't he? Staring down both barrels of an M203 and still lying his shit-filled heart out.'

'I told you, I knew nothing about it. I was cleared by a full investigation. You were hired to do a job. I'm sorry if it went wrong, but that's war.'

'And Yi Soong? He was your man.'

'Yes. But he double-crossed us all.'

Terry and Danny closed in on Kwang. Tossing his M203 aside, Terry knocked him to the floor. Lulu screamed and ran forward, but Danny caught her, holding her by the arms in a vice-like grip. Terry pulled Kwang to his feet and punched him again, holding his sagging body upright like a rag doll.

'You hired him, you fucker. Even if you're not working for the Communists, you let that murderer lead us into a trap.'

With the renowned Mr Kwang in his hands at last, Terry felt the rage surging through him, blinding him as he remembered Ken, Dave Bedford, Jules and the others. He drew back his balled fist.

'That'll do, Dojo.'

Fast in Terry's grip, Kwang twisted round to see the speaker. 'Chun Jo! Where the fuck have you been? Where are the police and the other guards.'

'Dead, I'm afraid. These devils have turned out to be really rather good.'

Rooted to the spot, his back to the speaker, Terry looked across at Danny, his alarm mounting.

'If either you or the Indian moves a muscle, you're dead. Release Mr Kwang. Now!'

Letting Kwang go, Terry turned round slowly until he was standing face to face with Chun Jo.

'Chun Jo, is it now?'

Yi Soong shrugged. 'Call me what the fuck you like, but keep it polite, please. There's a lady present.'

Cradled in his large hands, Yi Soong held a semi-automatic shotgun, short-barrelled especially for close combat. Terry knew that, however fast he moved, he could never hope either to recover the M203 or to draw his Browning. Likewise he knew that Danny too had fallen into the trap. With Lulu still locked in his arms, he could never get his pistol into the aim. Yi would cut them both down at the first twitch, probably not even caring to avoid the girl. He cursed himself for being so stupid. Just when they had made it to the centre of the lair, they had allowed their emotions to get the better of them. His only hope now lay in playing for time. Somehow he had to find a way of parting Yi from the shotgun.

'So. You win,' Terry said amiably.

Yi laughed, his eyes never moving or even blinking as he kept the shotgun barrel trained midway between the Welshman and the Indian, ready to switch and take out either target.

'You don't expect me to fall for any more of your little ploys, do you?' he said. He was clearly thinking hard, tilting his head on one side as he did so. He beckoned Kwang to move towards him.

'Shoot them!' Kwang screamed. 'That's an order!'

Yi glared at him. 'In my own time. Communist equality, remember? I'll do this my way.'

Ordering Danny to sit cross-legged on the carpet with his hands on his head, Yi had Lulu and Kwang bind him securely, keeping his gun trained all the while on Terry. Then, when Danny was secure, Yi directed Kwang to disarm Terry, throwing the Browning aside and checking that he had no further weapons.

'There now, that's better, isn't it?' he said. He moved across to Danny and slipped the tomahawk from his belt, grinning at it and shaking his head. 'You really haven't progressed very far from the caveman, have you? How does it work?' Testing the weight of the blade in his fist, he suddenly lashed out at Danny, hitting him in the face with the flat metal. With blood pouring from his nose, Danny tipped over backwards, gasping.

Terry lunged forward, but found himself staring down the shotgun barrel.

'Easy, Dojo, easy.'

Tossing the tomahawk through the window, Yi ordered Kwang to pull back the loose rugs that covered the floor.

'What are you playing at?' Kwang said, irritated by his subordinate's growing lack of respect in front of the two Westerners, but more particularly in front of Lulu.

With his eyes still on Terry, Yi handed the shotgun to Kwang. 'Here. Take this.'

But before releasing his grip on it, he added very slowly, the menace barely concealed: 'You will not use it. I will want it back when I've finished with him.'

Like a scolded child, Kwang took the shotgun and moved to one side, the peeled carpets and rugs laying bare the polished wooden boards underneath.

Yi smiled at Terry. 'Well, Dojo. What are you waiting for? Here I am.'

Slipping off his shoes and socks, Yi padded to the far side of the cleared area. Danny propped himself upright, spitting the blood from his mouth. 'Don't do it, Terry.'

But Terry knew there was no other way. Perhaps he had known since his first meeting with Yi Soong that one day the two of them would have to fight. Not in the detached blur and confusion of a fire-fight, but like this, across a cleared space of open ground, with only their natural weapons of hands and feet.

Keeping his eyes on Yi, he bent down and unlaced

his boots, stuffing his socks inside them. Testing the wooden surface with the balls of his feet, he noted the grip; although the boards were highly polished, there was a good enough purchase. Almost as good as the gym, he thought. But then in the gym he had never fought *sutemi*: to the death.

14

Facing Yi Soong across the cleared sitting-room, Terry couldn't help admiring the man's coolness. He moved with the grace and agility of a cat, a faint, ironic smile on his lips. In his eyes, however, Terry saw only the chill glint of death. Steeling his nerves, he drew on all his experience and training, forcing every other thing from his mind, bringing himself wholly and completely into the present. All the events of the past days since his arrival in Seoul, and the fire and mayhem of the contact battle only minutes before in the vestibule – everything was purged from his mind as he slipped into the total concentration of unarmed combat.

Yi appeared to be in no hurry to start things. He circled almost lazily, but Terry refused to be taken in by it, knowing full well that behind the semblance of carelessness a ruthless killer lay in wait, ready to pounce if given the slightest opening.

Sinking into a *kamae* fighting stance, Terry placed his hands to guard against both lower and upper attacks. Alternating between open-hand blocks and closed fists, he glided to the right, changing his stance and blocks as he went, his eyes following Yi's own counter-clockwise steps. Terry had fought Taekwondo experts at all-styles tournaments before and had learned a healthy respect for their superb kicking techniques. As Yi had twice been the world champion, it was painfully clear to Terry that he couldn't afford a single mistake.

However, although the Taekwondo kicking techniques were the best of any combat style in the world, he had also noticed how their hand techniques were less impressive. Concentrating on stunning leaping and jumping kicks, they often neglected basic hand blows. The result was that, while they were most proficient at the longer ranges, in the closest contact when punches were being traded, they tended to lack the variety of most Japanese karate styles. But more particularly, being used to enjoying the tremendous momentum of vast sweeping kicks, they had also neglected the development of *kime*, the focus that gave even the shortest karate hand blow its devastating power.

Focusing on the middle of Yi's chest, Terry concentrated on observing his every move. With his eyes on the centre, everything was visible, a change of stance, the lifting of a heel or a shift in balance that might signal the start of an attack. But as hard as he tried, Terry saw nothing, Yi was far too proficient to telegraph his intentions.

When the attack came, Terry only just managed to react in time, darting aside as Yi's heel spun past his face, the rush of air stinging his cheek. Jesus, this bastard's fast, he thought. He had known Yi would be good, but not how good.

No sooner had his kick failed to contact, than Yi was the far side of the arena again, his breath as steady as if he hadn't even moved. By comparison, Terry felt like a ton weight, fatally slow.

Wake up, you idle bastard, he thought. Wake up

or die. He knew that he couldn't play Yi at his own game and win. His own style concentrated on strength and power, solid stances and lightning hand blows. When Terry moved it was like a glacier, calm and unstoppable. Sure, he could deliver stunning kicks and rush at an opponent as fast as a cobra, but not with an enemy like Yi. Yi was the master of speed. Somehow Terry had to capitalize on his own strengths, combining them with Yi's weaknesses, to bring the bastard crashing down.

Yi's next attack started as a roundhouse kick, but halfway through it he switched and spun the other way into a jumping back-kick, seeming to defy gravity and hang in mid-air as his foot shot out, catching Terry in the chest and knocking him backwards across the floor. Aware that Yi would be on him the moment he landed, Terry forced himself to ignore the searing pain that shot through his ribcage, rolling to one side and up again to his feet.

Halfway to him to deliver a drop-punch, Yi skidded to a halt and backed off as he saw the speed of Terry's recovery.

'Not bad for an old man,' he mocked. 'Still, we're only just beginning.'

The next moment Yi was hurtling through the air towards Terry, his legs bunching for a flying side kick without having betrayed any sign of preparation, a feat that was only made possible by superb fitness and muscle control. Sliding aside in a *tae sabaki* body shift, Terry used the heels of both palms to deflect the lethal knife edge of Yi's foot, seeing an opening for the first time. As Yi landed and recovered his balance, Terry shot forward with the *kiai* shout welling from the depths of his midriff, firing a punch straight at Yi's waist. Catching the left floating rib, Terry felt it crack and saw the pain register on Yi's face. But even so Yi slipped smoothly out of reach, turning on his heel.

Not this time, Terry thought. If you're expecting me to follow up my attack and walk straight into your counter, you've got another think coming.

'No more smart-arsed remarks?' Terry said.

The last hint of a smile had gone from Yi's face. Instead the skin was drawn tight across the cheekbones and his lips were set in a thin line.

Terry wished with all his might. That's it, lose your temper, Mr bloody Soong. Terry smiled sweetly, changing to *neko ashi*, the cat stance, the rear foot taking his body weight, his front leg poised on the ball of the foot. At the same time his hands came up into a high guard position. Judging the time to be right, he edged forward, shifting his weight to his right foot and raising the left into the cat stance, his hands maintaining the guard at all times.

He was halfway across the floor when Yi struck. Even with a broken rib, the kick came at lightning speed, wheeling round. Despite Terry's block, Yi's foot scythed through and slammed into his cheek. Staggering to keep his balance, Terry reeled backwards, catching the look of triumph in Yi's eyes. Instantly another kick followed, and again Terry's guard was too slow to stop it powering into his stomach. With the breath knocked out of him, Terry shot backwards across the floor, executing the *ibuki* breathing technique to regain his wind, parrying Yi's increasingly ferocious kicks and punches as he did so.

This is it, Terry realized. The horns have been locked and only one of us is going to be standing at the end. Yi's seen I'm hurt and he knows that if he lets me recover he might not get another chance this good. He knows he has to close and finish it now.

It was the chance Terry had been waiting for. Lured on to his prey by the success of his attack, Yi pounded forward with a lashing series of punches. Backing away all the time, Terry blocked some but allowed others through until he was reeling, blood pouring from his nose and mouth.

I can't take much more of this kind of punishment, he thought, willing Yi to give him the only opportunity that could save him. Come on, you bastard, come on.

And then it happened. Blind with rage, the pain from his broken rib jarring through his body, Yi smelt the blood of his opponent and knew that he had him where he wanted. Now was the time to close in with his fists, now that he had the Welshman at his mercy. At last, after so many failures, and after so much loss of face.

Driving forward, intent upon his own attack, Yi ran straight on to Terry's *mae geri* front kick. As the *josokutei* ball of Terry's foot shot forward with the massive power of his hips and leg muscles, it found its path clear and open, straight through Yi's attacking move and drove deep into his solar plexus, Yi's own forward momentum doubling the power of the crippling blow.

Crumpling to the floor, Yi tried to freeze the pain in a superhuman effort to drag himself out of range before it was too late. But it was already too late. Dojo Williams was on top of him. Raining out of the sky like bolts of lightning, Terry's carefully aimed punches dismantled the fallen Korean, one by one destroying his ability to resist, until at last he lay broken and bleeding at Terry's mercy.

Glaring down into Yi's eyes, Terry gripped him by

the blood-soaked collar of his shirt, drawing back his right hand for the *nukite* finger-thrust that would bring instant death.

'This is for all the lads you killed, you bastard,' he said through gritted teeth, spitting out the words with the venom that was consuming him. But as he looked at the ruined creature on the floor, despite the pain and suffering Yi had inflicted, Terry's hand remained quivering at his side, ready and vibrant with death.

As he exhaled slowly, Terry's hatred left him, dissipating with his breath in the stale air of the room, rank with blood, sweat and the smell of cordite. Releasing his grip, he let Yi's head fall back on to the floor, unconscious. Straightening up, he turned towards the doorway, but instead of Kwang and the shotgun, he found himself looking into the soaked, filthy but triumphant face of Major Babs Butler. At his feet, Kwang cowed, holding his head in his hands, blood seeping between the fingers where Babs had clubbed him with the butt of the M60.

'I didn't like to disturb you, old boy. Didn't seem the sensible thing to do.'

Terry fell to his knees, his knuckles cut and bruised, the nauseous taste of blood in his mouth. Michelle had Lulu against the wall, the barrel of a Browning pistol stuck in her back, and beside the shattered windows, the two boys were busy untying Danny. With the situation once more under control, Terry knew that there was only one more thing to do.

'The CIA?'

'Who else is big enough to handle this? The South Koreans think Kwang's clean as a whistle and even once we show them that Yi was here, there's no saying how they'll react.'

Babs came back from the drinks cabinet with a bottle of whisky and some glasses. 'I agree with Terry. Don't forget, we've just taken out a Korean SWAT team. There are bits of policemen all over the place out there. I don't know about you, but I'd rather hand Kwang over to the CIA than to his own erstwhile colleagues, even if we can convince them he's a Commie plant.'

Danny took a long drink of the whisky that Babs was passing around. 'OK. The CIA it is, then. How do we get hold of them? Directory enquiries?'

Terry looked at Babs. 'You must know someone, don't you?'

'Yes, I think I can help. One of my drinking chums is CIA. Of course, he's never been so crude as to say so, but like all these sneaky-beaky fellows he can't resist dropping the occasional hint, especially when he's pissed. I'll give him a call and set up a meeting.'

While Babs went off to search for a phone amid the wreckage of the sitting-room, Danny secured Yi's hands and feet with a length of flex ripped from the back of the television. With another length he then bound Kwang's wrists.

As Michelle similarly tied Lulu, she winked at her. 'I bet the old man does this to you as well, eh?'

Lulu spat at her. 'Slut! Take your hands off me.'

Wiping the saliva from her face, Michelle gripped Lulu by the chin and sneered at her. 'The only difference between you and me is a couple of years of screwing. Where do you think you'd have ended up?'

Lulu jerked her head away. 'Francis, order them to let me go.'

But Kwang was staring morosely out of the window, his eyes glazed and baffled by the turn of events.

'I don't think they'd listen to me. So why don't you just shut the fuck up? There's a good kitten.'

Lulu burst into tears.

Escaping into the fresher air of the courtyard, Terry went to retrieve Andy's body. Babs had told him how he had watched helpless as Yi had slain the young Scot. Terry was glad that he hadn't heard about it until after he had won his fight with Yi; the anger might have destabilized his concentration, giving the vital edge to his opponent and altering the whole balance of skill between the two men.

When he found Andy, he was lying where Yi had left him, face down in the dirt. Rolling him over, Terry closed the eyes and brushed the earth from the face and hair.

'Poor sod,' he said quietly. 'Not much of an innings, was it?' He wondered what combination of circumstances had made Andy Buchan into the fierce, angry man he had been. Tucking his arms under the body, Terry lifted it and carried it back towards the villa. He was surprised to find it strangely light, as if the vanished life-force had somehow contained a weight of its own instead of the insubstantial mix of qualities, traits and quirks that together had composed the dead mercenary.

Laying the body on a sofa in the vestibule, Terry placed the M203 across Andy's chest and folded his arms across it as if on the stone tomb of a knight. Searching around, he discovered in an outhouse some jerrycans of petrol. He dragged them back into the house, opened the caps and emptied the contents on the walls and furnishings.

Babs and the others came down the stairs, bringing Kwang and Lulu with them. At the back, Danny half carried and half dragged the semi-conscious Yi Soong.

'It's on,' Babs said proudly. 'My chum says they would be delighted to get their hands on the bastards. They'll square everything with the South Koreans.'

Danny hoisted Yi Soong over his shoulder like a sack of coal. 'Let's just get rid of this shit soon. I'm going to need a shower to get myself clean after handling him.'

Taking their prisoners across the compound and out through the fence, Danny and Babs set off for the hidden minibus on the far side of the ring of demolitions that had isolated the villa before the main attack. In the vestibule, Terry took two grenades from his pocket and was about to pull the pins when he paused a moment, laid them on a table and disappeared back up the stairs to Kwang's sitting-room. It was a full ten minutes before he returned and took up the grenades again. With a last look at Andy, he strode out into the open air, pulled the pins and lobbed the grenades back into the villa.

Following hard on the twin explosions, a raging fire swept through the building. Halfway up the hillside, Babs and Danny turned to watch the mounting blaze, and the distant figure of Terry jogging away from the compound towards them. In the bowels of the villa, the searing heat detonated the ammunition of Kwang's dead guards like the crackling of Chinese firecrackers. Catching at the wooden terrace, the flames leapt into the sky, firing a shower of sparks above the waving tops of the pines. And lapping at the sofa where Andy lay, they found at last the M203 locked in his stiffening arms, a solitary grenade silent and waiting in the black metal chamber, waiting for the touch of fire to detonate and consume its dead master.

When Joe Lacorde heard what Babs Butler had to say, he had to pinch himself to make sure he wasn't dreaming. Privately he had had his doubts about Francis Kwang from the very first, but the South Koreans had insisted he was one of theirs, so who was he, a relatively minor CIA desk officer, to contradict them? Now here, if he was to be believed, was that drunken old bastard Babs Butler, a washed-out mercenary and professional bar bum, saying that he could hand Kwang to him on a plate. What was more, to clinch it Babs said that he had captured the North Korean agent Yi Soong and could link him with Kwang. It was as good as in the bag. All Joe had to do was arrange the pick-up.

The moment he put the phone down he informed his boss and then got on to Operations. He would need to put a team together immediately if they were going to collect the two Communist double agents before Babs and his friends ran into the South Korean police. If a complete SWAT team had been eradicated Babs could expect little in the way of understanding from the gooks.

With the preliminaries taken care of, Joe sprinted down the corridor of the Seoul office and stuck his head round the door of the Ops room to check that the boys were getting ready to roll. A dozen square-jawed operatives were strapping on shoulder holsters and passing round the Ingrams, the snug close-quarters weapon with the highest rate of fire in the business.

Jeez, Joe thought to himself, they must stamp these guys out of a mould. No matter where they came from, they all ended up looking the same, mean sons of bitches without two scruples to rub together.

Carrying on down the corridor, he slowed to a walk outside his boss's door. He knocked on the frosted glass panel and when he heard the deep, growling voice of Felix Carlson he went in, to find another man already there.

'Oh, sorry, boss,' Joe stammered. 'I just wanted to say that we're almost ready to go.'

'That's fine, Joe. Get the guys into the briefing room. We'll be along in a minute. This is Mr Masterson. He's going to be in charge of the Op.'

Two hours out from the RV, Babs swung the minibus on to the Sokch'o road and reached across to pat Michelle's knee. The daylight was fading and by the time they met the CIA they would be conducting the hand-over in darkness. That suited Babs fine. He felt himself to be a creature of the night, not in any flattering combat sense like Dojo Williams or Danny Grey Wolf, but because that was usually the time that Babs would set off on one of his drinking binges in It'aewan.

Michelle put her hand on his and squeezed it. She was a good girl, Babs thought; they would be very happy together. He was also happy because in addition to the money that he had received from Kwang, he had arranged with Joe Lacorde for a handsome pay-off from the CIA. After all, why shouldn't they reward him and the others for exposing the North Korean plot that had so embarrassed America and delayed the access of the UN inspection teams to the Communist nuclear facilities? OK, so the idea of going direct to the CIA had been Dojo's, but Babs couldn't help feeling a certain pride for having capitalized on the opportunity as a means of making a few more bucks.

In the back of the minibus, Kwang had given up his attempts to bribe Dojo. Keeping his eyes on the road, Babs called over his shoulder.

'Aren't you going to make us any more offers we can't refuse, Francis? I can call you Francis, can't I?' He chuckled merrily.

Kwang sat on the floor with his eyes closed, trying to doze, Lulu curled at his side, her head in his lap.

'Shut up, Butler. You'll always be a loser, however much money you make. You're in this way over your head and you've no idea what you're getting into.'

Danny prodded Kwang with the toe of his boot. 'Is that so? Seems to me you're not doing so great yourself.'

Chuckling to himself, Babs glanced in the rear-view mirror and in the light of a passing car, saw Terry at the back of the minibus. At first he thought he was sleeping, but as the headlights swept across his face, Babs saw that he was gazing out into the dark. The old mind's working away, Babs thought. What a man; after all that's happened, he's still plotting, evaluating, asking himself the essential 'what ifs' that have kept him alive all these years and through all these battles. What if an enemy machine-gun opens up from those bushes on the right? What if I reach the open ground and encounter a minefield? What if a meteorite's on a collision course with planet Earth and I've only got five minutes to save civilization as we know it? Babs smiled. Dojo Williams: he was truly one of a kind. Thank God.

The rest of the journey was made in silence, each person locked into their own thoughts. Yi Soong regained consciousness to find Danny grinning down at him, a firm grip on the end of the flex that bound the Korean's wrists and ankles. Lulu woke and sat up beside Kwang, who was staring out of the windows wide-eyed. Liang and Little Chiao sat behind Michelle, to whom they had stuck throughout the day; leaning together, their heads lolled in sleep as the minibus rolled round the corners. Michelle held the map up whenever Babs needed to check a turning, glancing over, one hand on her knee, the other on the wheel. In the back seat, Terry sat alone. Looking at his watch, he took the Browning from his pocket and checked the mechanism, stuffing the pistol in his waistband when he was happy that there was a round in the barrel and a dozen more in the magazine.

'Looks like party time.'

Babs eased the minibus down a gear, slowing as the headlights cut through the pitch-black of the quiet side road, picking out the isolated lay-by and the four black limousines strung out in line.

'That'll do, Babsy,' Terry called. 'Stop short.'

Pulling to a halt fifty yards from the front limousine, Babs switched off the engine. Terry and Danny kicked open the back door and jumped to the ground, pulling Kwang, Yi, and Lulu after them.

'Give us some light, Babs,' said Terry.

Pulling their prisoners by the scruff of the neck into the corridor of light that appeared, illuminating the lay-by, Terry and Danny went towards the limousines, stopping halfway there. Babs, Michelle and the boys got out of the minibus and came forward to join them, the nine figures casting long shadows towards the opening doors of the limousines.

Babs peered at the faces of the suited men who

sprang out of the sleek black cars and jogged towards them. 'Joe, is that you?'

Joe Lacorde came up and shook Babs firmly by the hand. 'Nice work, Babs baby. You sure as hell know how to play an ace.'

Babs and Michelle laughed with relief and Danny relaxed his grip on Yi as two CIA operatives jerked him away roughly. Another two took hold of Kwang and Lulu.

'Thank you, sir. We'll handle things now.'

Terry let go.

'We'd better relieve you of these,' one of the men said, taking Terry's Browning and Danny's M16. 'Just routine.'

'Fine by me,' Danny said, yawning. It had been one hell of a long day and he felt reassured by the familiar sound of his fellow-Americans, even if they were overly precise and polite. It was the same in the military, he thought. All these guys had a pole up their arse.

When the three prisoners had been removed to one side, another two men got out of the front limousine, stepped into the light and came towards Terry.

'You'll be Mr Williams?'

'Yes.'

'And Danny . . . Grey Wolf?'

Danny's eyes narrowed, catching the tone in the man's voice. 'You got it.' Whoever this man was, he didn't like Indians. But so what? There was nothing new about that. The military was full of bigoted fuckers.

'My name's Eliot Masterson. This is Felix Carlson. You've done a really terrific job here.'

He looked at Yi Soong. 'Well, well. Nice to meet you at last.' Balling his fist, he punched Yi hard in the stomach, dropping him to the ground. ''Cuff the son of a bitch.'

As two of the operatives pinned Yi to the ground and another slapped a pair of handcuffs on him, Masterson went across to Kwang and looked him up and down, shaking his head.

'What a mess. What a sorry fucking mess.'

He took a knife from his pocket and cut the flex binding Kwang's wrists, then turned to Lulu and freed her.

'I'm really sorry about this, Francis.'

Handing Kwang his own Walther pistol, Masterson waved his hand and the remaining CIA operatives surrounded Babs and the others, now unarmed and dumbstruck in the beam from the headlights. Standing in a semicircle, each of the CIA men cradled an Ingram sub-machine-gun in his hands, nursing it close to the hip ready at the touch of a finger to spray their helpless victims with a hail of bullets.

Joe Lacorde shrugged in apology as Babs gaped at him questioningly. 'Orders, Babs baby. You know how it is.'

With the comforting weight and feel of the pistol in his hand, Kwang rubbed his wrists, bruised from the flex. Walking over to the kneeling figure of Yi Soong, he looked down at the large man, humbled and broken at his feet. As Yi's expression turned from puzzlement to understanding and rage, he tried to struggle to his feet, but the hands of his CIA captors held him firmly in place. Without a word, Kwang put the barrel of his Walther to Yi's temple and blew his brains on to the tarmac.

Michelle and Little Chiao started to cry; Liang put a protective arm around them and stared defiantly at the closest of the CIA men. Out of the corner of his eye, Terry signalled Danny to freeze. He had caught the first tell-tale movement that told him Danny Grey Wolf was preparing to go into action and he knew that, against the CIA Ingrams, it would be the last move he ever made.

While one of the CIA men escorted Lulu to the waiting limousines, Kwang and Masterson conferred over the dead body of Yi Soong. After a few moments, they walked across to Terry and the others, but being careful to keep behind the semicircle of Ingrams.

'You've caused us a great deal of inconvenience. You don't know it, but you've screwed up our plans and I'm afraid there's only one thing to be done.'

Stepping back, Kwang signalled to the CIA men, who cocked their weapons and braced themselves to fire.

'Surely you're not going to leave us in suspense,' Terry called out.

'Not at all. I'm going to have you shot.'

'Without an explanation? Don't you think we deserve at least that?'

Kwang turned to Masterson and exchanged a weary smile with the American.

'We really don't have time,' Masterson called across to Terry. 'But seeing as it's the last thing you'll ever hear we'll indulge you. Francis is exactly what he always said he was, a senior officer in the South Korean intelligence service. Some time ago, however, he was recruited by the Communists to work for them. Yi Soong was sent across to act as his number two and, secretly, to keep a check on him. Yi was already a double agent working for Pyongyang; he had been planted in the South Korean special forces some years earlier but he was always a dyed-in-the-wool Commie.'

He glanced at the crumpled body on the floor, a dark pool of viscous liquid spreading from the head.

'But things are never what they seem, are they? I'm sure you can appreciate that now, Mr Williams. Because over and above all of that, Francis was working for us. He was our man inside the South Korean intelligence network, reporting to us on everything the Seoul government intended to do, and then the bonus fell out of the blue when he was suddenly able to give us inside information on the Communists as well.'

Terry shook his head. 'Clever, really clever. A triple agent. So what was the mission to the resort all about and who was Professor Lim Choy?'

Masterson laughed. 'There never was any such person. The North Koreans decided to stage the massacre of their so-called top nuclear physicists and their families to throw the UN off their trail. They reckoned that if they could finger America they could delay UN inspections of their nuclear facilities long enough to complete a bomb.'

'But surely you've helped them achieve that? You've seriously embarrassed your own government, even if they weren't behind the raid.'

Masterson smiled. 'You really don't get it, do you? I don't give a fuck about my own government. Because Francis set up the Korean contract, hired you and executed the mission, he convinced the North Koreans that he was truly their man. He was proving himself. Sort of like a stamp of guarantee. The embarrassment will blow over and we don't reckon the gooks have got the know-how to produce a bomb yet, anyway. But with the Commies fully confident that Francis was loyal to them, we would have had our man at the centre of the intelligence networks of both North and South Korea. Smart, eh? The CIA could have looked forward to a stream of the most tightly guarded secrets from both governments: their nuclear programmes, military strengths and deployments, their sleepers in Seoul and Pyongyang.'

Terry stared at him steadily. 'And what do you get out of it?'

'What do you think?' Masterson answered. 'Promotion to the top of the most powerful organization in the world.'

'And the innocent political prisoners who were butchered at the resort? The men that Babs hired in good faith but who were double-crossed, tortured and killed?'

'Small fry. Dross. Disposable waste. Sad by-products of our modern society.'

'I think I get the message. But why can't you leave Kwang in place and let us go?'

Masterson and Kwang swapped smiles. 'You must think us very stupid. After your conversion of Mr Kwang's country home into a latter-day Valhalla, I think even the North Koreans would feel the need to ask awkward questions. Even they might suspect that Francis had been compromised.'

'You blew my cover, Dojo,' Kwang added.

'And as for letting you go on your way,' Masterson cut in, 'I don't think that even merits a reply. I'd love to go on talking to you all night, and in other circumstances you're a man who could have worked for me, but not now. I'm afraid the lot of you are going to have to join your comrades in your own little twilight of the gods right here and now. You see,

Mr Williams, you've fucked up a seriously brilliant master plan.'

Terry glanced around at the dark trees beyond the reach of the harsh white beams from the minibus and the figures silhouetted in their glare. When he spoke, it was not with the voice of a man who was about to die.

'You've no idea just quite how much.'

In the CNN newsroom in Seoul, Mike Adams could hardly believe his luck. After years as an investigative reporter he had acquired a nose for a story. It was like a sixth sense. But to sniff out a lead took contacts, and Mike had always been one to recognize a good contact. It seemed to him that conflicts attracted two kinds of men, reporters and mercenaries, and of all the mercenaries he had ever met, none was as worthwhile a contact as Terry Williams. In Africa Terry had given Mike the tip-off when a guerrilla leader had wanted to air his views to the press, and later in the same war he had enabled him to be the first Western reporter to enter the liberated capital.

So when Terry had called him earlier in the day from some place in Sorak-san and given him the gist of what could be on the cards, he had known it would be worth following up. But in his wildest dreams he had never imagined it would be this good. It had been a hell of a scramble to get the low-light cameras and the directional mikes in place, but the technicians had done a great job as usual and he was receiving every word and every picture on his monitors as clear as crystal. It was dynamite.

Switching to the intercom, he spoke into his mike.

'Jerry, please say you're getting all this.'

Via satellite link from head office in Atlanta came the affirmative answer, preceded by a long whistle of admiration.

'Jesus, Mike. You bet. We're putting it out live now.'

As the world's leading twenty-four-hour news channel, CNN relied on the hottest news items from around the world as and when they happened. Broadcasting live across the globe, Ted Turner's empire had made Atlanta the communications centre of the world.

'Ted'll love you for this.'

Mike eased back in his chair, hands behind his head, a grin spreading from ear to ear.

'Go for it, Dojo. Go for it.'

In the lay-by, Masterson had gone very quiet. Even in the glow of the minibus headlights Terry could see him get visibly paler before his eyes. It had started when one of the CIA operatives had called Felix Carlson back to his limousine to take an urgent call. Felix was glad to get away from the unpleasant scene being enacted in the headlights. He had been pretty pissed off when Masterson had breezed into his office in the first place, arrogantly taking charge, but more particularly he had been uneasy with the whole concept of the operation.

When he came back from the limousine, Felix's jaw was set in concrete, his eyes as hard as ball-bearings. Drawing Eliot and Kwang to one side, he relayed the drift of the grilling he had just received from the director, who had been sitting at home in Washington in front of his television, just in time to see Francis Kwang commit murder, with Eliot Masterson, one of the CIA's high-fliers, an accessory. What was more, Eliot had outlined a completely unauthorized operation to the American public, including the President, whom he had told, obliquely, to go fuck himself: and all on prime-time TV!

After relieving Kwang of his Walther and Masterson of his ID card and passport, Felix detailed four CIA men to escort them back to the limousines, where Lulu, unaware of the turn of events, was getting impatient and wishing they would simply get on with the execution and head back to Seoul.

Leaning on the bonnet of the minibus, Babs and Danny listened to Terry with amazement.

'When I heard that Mike was in Seoul, I made a note of his number. Just before I set fire to Kwang's villa I gave him a ring, and you know Mike: anything for a good scoop.'

But Babs was working himself into a rage. 'You mean you let me believe I was about to die while knowing all the time I was on candid bloody camera?'

'It had to look convincing,' Terry explained. 'You're not the world's greatest actor, Babs.'

Babs swelled with anger. 'Why, you . . .'

Strolling up behind him, Joe Lacorde placed a big friendly paw on Babs's shoulder.

'Babs, baby. No hard feelings, eh?'

With a grace and speed never seen before, Babs spun on his heel with fist flying, laying his CIA drinking partner out cold.

A week later, sitting up in his hospital bed, Alex Leitner was feeling better than he had done for years. That morning the doctors had given him a clean bill of health and to complete his recovery he had told his employers to get lost.

He had been watching the TV on the day of the famous CNN broadcast, his heart monitor bleeping forlornly at the bedside, a cheerless hospital meal untouched on the tray. Moments later, the nurses had come rushing in to find Alex leaning back on his pillows, roaring with laughter. He even tried to send out for a bottle of champagne but the ward sister intercepted his message in time.

His miracle recovery had started that same day when his superiors had rung offering him the job vacated by Eliot Masterson. Deliberating for all of two seconds, Alex had said a polite no thank you and hung up before his mouth ran away with him. Whatever his faults, Masterson had been right about one thing: it was time Alex retired. He'd had enough of jogging in the park when he'd rather be tucking into a hamburger and fries, and he'd done enough arse-licking to wear out a whole yard of tongue. No. From now on he was going to devote himself to his family.

Picking up a copy of *Time*, he turned to the lead article and began to read once more about the intricacies of the North Korean plot and their submission at last to the UN nuclear inspection teams. *Newsweek*, on the other hand, devoted its own lead to the shake-up in the CIA initiated by the President in the wake of the renegade operation.

Pushing through the window blinds, the sun warmed Alex to the core. But the greater warmth was generated by his own expectations of the catch he would land at Chesapeake Bay when he and Stephen went fishing at the weekend.

* * *

Burning down the expressway, Babs sped the minibus towards Tonghae. He had been meaning to turn it in and get one of the new red Toyotas with the pop-up headlights, but he and Michelle had decided to hang on to the larger vehicle until after the skiing trip.

Glancing in the rear-view mirror, he smiled at her attempts to get Liang and Little Chiao to speak English. She could hardly speak it herself. But there would be time to take care of that now. In fact, there would be time and money for everything now. Kwang's cheque had been good, even if the man himself was rotting in jail awaiting trial for both murder and treason. In the event that he was released before the end of his life, he would probably find the North Koreans waiting for him, patiently biding their time to exact their own grim retribution.

It was funny how things turned out, Babs thought. Things rarely ended up the way you expected or initially hoped, but somehow one usually found a way of living. And that was what it was all about after all, living. Michelle, himself, the boys. It might not be the family he had dreamed of having, on all those endless lonely, drunken evenings in It'aewan, but it was a family nevertheless. His family.

Sitting up behind the wheel, Babs pulled in his stomach. He would have to be more responsible from now on. With other people depending on him, he owed it to them. He owed it to himself as well. After the sort of life he'd lived, it was a miracle he was still around to make any resolutions at all. But then, looking at his new family in the back of the minibus, Babs realized that life was all about miracles.

With the Sea of Japan and the island of Hokkaido

behind it, the United Airlines jumbo started on the long trans-Pacific haul to Seattle. Sinking still deeper into his first-class seat, Terry checked his watch to see if he would have time to nip upstairs to the bar before the start of the in-flight movie. Deciding he couldn't be bothered, he rang for the hostess and ordered another cognac. On the other side of the spacious cabin, Danny was sleeping, his long legs sprawled across the ample expanse of carpet. There had been a difficult moment at the airport when the security scanner had picked up his tomahawk, but Danny had reluctantly agreed that it could travel in the hold and they had made the flight only minutes before departure.

Terry wasn't sure how long he would spend in Montana, taking up Danny's offer of a hunting trip. A walk in the wilderness seemed about the daftest thing imaginable after what they had been through, but it would be a novel experience to go to sleep at night under the stars and not to have to worry about putting out Claymores, sentry posts or clearing patrols. Perhaps he'd return Danny's hospitality afterwards, but a wet weekend in Swansea probably wouldn't have quite the same appeal, although a Blackfoot Sioux Indian with a real tomahawk would go down a treat at The Bull.

At least Terry would have enough money now to fix the karate dojo. He could even ditch it altogether, although he wouldn't want to disappoint the kids. Either way, he had resolved to give Liz a call when he got back. They could go away somewhere nice and quiet. Maybe Llanberis Pass; there was some great rock climbing there. Terry sighed. Perhaps Paris would be a better idea.

With his cognac in his hand, he gazed lazily out

of the window, watching the billowing roof of white cloud passing beneath. At the front of the cabin the screen flickered into life with a news bulletin before the movie. A reporter was crouching behind a wall somewhere in South America, bullets flying overhead as guerrillas were driven out of the presidential palace that they had stormed earlier in the day. Summing up, the reporter concluded that the people's liberation struggle was likely to go on for many months yet.

Unable to keep his eyes open, Terry drained his glass and leant back, letting the fierce, seductive liquid pull him the last few steps towards sleep. The drone of the engines hummed in his ears, mingling with the closing words of the reporter.

'One thing is for certain, arms and equipment will never be enough. Without proper training the Liberation Front is doomed to a long and difficult struggle.'

Terry pulled off his headphones and settled back. Arms and equipment were never enough. How often would people have to learn the same old lesson? In the end it always came down to the man. The quality of the individual, his training and his will. It had been the case when Alexander the Great crossed into Asia and it would be the same if men ever dodged and dived between the stars. And filing away the name of the war-torn Latin-American republic, Terry allowed himself to sleep.

SOLDIER OF FORTUNE 3

THE VATICAN ASSIGNMENT

James Halliday

1

Jack Kelly swung his legs over the side of a deeply padded sun-lounger and stood up to stretch himself. Only his black swimming trunks broke the smoothly tanned surface of his firm body. He glanced at the other end of a thirty-metre pool where the source of his lavish, tax-free income for the past six months crouched beside a fountain, pulling the clothes off a skinny, bedraggled doll.

He made a face to himself and looked away, over a four-metre perimeter fence topped by razor-wire, down the rippling brown hills towards Cannes and the turquoise sea. He rolled his shoulder muscles and thrust his lower jaw into a smile that spread across his battered suntanned face. At least he had something worth spending his money on this evening. A few drinks with a beautiful woman, dinner somewhere small and intimate, and then, maybe, a moonlit boat trip to the islands.

The pleasurable thought was abruptly fractured by a shrill scream.

'*Jacques! Jacques! Ma poupée!*'

Kelly spun his head round and, almost simultaneously, started sprinting towards the four-year-old girl who leant over the rim of the fountain, wailing with frustration.

He reached the cascade, plunged his hand into the

few feet of bubbling warm water and fished out a Barbie doll clad only in elaborate underwear that had probably cost more than all his childhood clothing put together.

He shook it to get some of the water off and handed it to the girl. '*Voilà*,' he growled with a smile, not really wanting to blame the kid for the ignominy of the rescue he'd just performed.

'*Merci*,' the girl said, warmly enough.

'Béatrice?' An impatient young Englishwoman's voice reached them from a veranda above the pool. '*Qu'est-ce que tu as fait?* What happened?' The second question was addressed to Kelly.

Kelly looked up at the raw, red face of the girl's principal nanny. 'It's OK. Barbie was drowning,' he said in his leisurely Scouse drawl. 'I saved her and gave her the kiss of life.'

The nanny was scurrying down a flight of narrow stone steps now. Physical protection was Kelly's job; emotional protection was hers. She gave Kelly an exasperated look and ran beneath a pergola of purple bougainvillaea, across to the fountain. She knelt down beside the small child and put her arm around her.

Kelly shrugged and walked away, leaving the nanny to her ministrations. This will have to stop, he thought. He hadn't spent fifteen years perfecting techniques in survival, surveillance and close-quarters battle to rescue Barbie dolls.

A British Airways flight landed on the baking tarmac of Nice airport. A mixed bag of passengers stepped out of the plane, blinking in the midday August sun. Most of them were excited holiday-makers, naïve enough to think there was glamour to be found on the Côte d'Azur at this time of year. A few, who had read their papers for the whole flight like regulars on the London Underground, were businessmen in suits, bound for Nice or Monaco to occupy themselves with construction, scent, tourism or tax evasion.

A sleepy, now largely superfluous customs man looked perfunctorily at the stream of passengers claiming baggage and heading for taxis or greeters outside beneath the dusty palms. The only one to stir his interest – though he showed no visible reaction – was a tall Englishman in a quiet fawn suit. This passenger's short, dark hair was cut conventionally beneath a blemishless Lock's Panama. Around his neck, against a pale-blue shirt, was knotted a black and blue striped tie. His old-fashioned decorousness was in itself unusual in travellers on commercial flights into Nice these days, but it wasn't this that caught the attention of the French official. It was the pale-grey, almost motionless eyes – eyes with an opaque curtain just behind the pupil that permitted one-way vision only. He had seen eyes like this, in one or two men who had joined Customs after leaving the Deuxième REP. They were the eyes of a man trained to keep secrets very close; a man trained to kill, and to feel nothing while doing it.

The passenger glanced at the *douanier* and saw him looking. Unconsciously, the official straightened his back a little and acknowledged the Englishman with a polite nod. There was no cause to stop him. He had not waited for any luggage and carried only a slim, dark-brown briefcase. A man like that, the *douanier* knew, would not be wasting his time breaking petty or, for that matter, grievous customs regulations.

* * *

Sinking into the black leather upholstery of the white Mercedes which had been waiting for him outside the terminal building, ex-Major Piers Bowring relaxed. The French police didn't, on the whole, approve of his presence in their domain. There wasn't a lot they could do to prevent him being there, but given the chance, they were more than glad to waste his time asking questions and letting him know that they knew he was there.

The driver of the car, an ex-signaller who had served for eight years with the British Paras and four with the Royal Signals and Radar Establishment at Malvern, glanced over his shoulder as he swung the car on to the A8 towards Menton.

'Do you want to go to the villa first, boss?'

'Yes please, Terry.' Bowring's voice – concise, deceptively languid, Old Etonian – perfectly matched his clothing, though not his eyes. 'Have you got hold of Kelly yet?'

'In a manner of speaking.'

'Yes?'

'He took the bait. She's bringing him down tonight.'

'Michelle?'

Terry Haynes nodded with a grin which Bowring saw in the mirror.

'Are you still confident she's safe?' Bowring asked.

'Yeah. She's a career girl. So long as she never has anything big to sell, and you're paying her well, she'll be safe. So long as she thinks she's got prospects,' Terry added.

'And she still has no regular lover?'

'The day she has, sir, is the day to give her her cards.'

Bowring nodded. Michelle would need a good few

more wrinkles before she would require the emotional security of a committed lover. She was a spectacularly self-possessed woman; had she been less so, she would probably have been a movie star. She was certainly endowed with the acting skills which that might have called for.

'She's going to want more meaty jobs now, after Bosnia. How's her training going?'

'She can handle most small arms very effectively. She's getting good at CQB skills, and she could pass the RSRE operators' exams standing on her head; she speaks Italian, Russian, Serbo-Croat, German and Gulf Arabic, and she still looks like something off the cover of *Vogue.*'

Bowring nodded his head again but didn't speak. He looked out of the window at the parched, rocky foothills of the Alpes Maritimes, and awarded Kelly a minus for taking the bait so easily.

Kelly had agreed to meet the girl in a café on the main square in Vence. It had been her suggestion. She was the first French girl with whom he'd made any progress since he'd arrived at the Villa Diane to look after Béatrice Skiapoulos. Up until now, the local girls had ignored his advances and he'd written them off as snotty and arrogant. But this one hadn't made any pretence that she didn't fancy him.

He parked the Range Rover a couple of streets from the square and sauntered through the oblique early evening sunlight with a smile on his face; even the hint of a twinkle in his hard blue eyes.

What a turn up, he thought, finding a girl like that on the side of the road. Just standing there, two miles out of town, wearing a bikini top and a flimsy bit of chiffon wrapped around her waist. She hadn't told him why she was there. He'd asked her, but she'd just smiled. And she spoke brilliant English – better than his, really.

He strolled into the busy square, bought a newspaper and made his way unhurriedly across the square, crowded with busy shoppers and ambling tourists, to the café.

Although he was five minutes late, he hadn't expected her to be there before him. He found an empty table, sat down in a white plastic chair and ordered a pastis from a passing waiter. A glass of viscous yellow fluid and a jug of iced water were placed in front of him a few moments later. The waiter, almost as an afterthought before he turned to go, said: 'The young woman you are waiting for has telephoned. You're to meet her down in Nice, by the old port . . . Café Pelican.'

Kelly understood, despite the man's nasal Midi accent. He twitched with annoyance. In his experience, last-minute alterations to plans augured problems.

He watered his pastis, gulped back the glassful of now milky liquid and slapped a few coins on the table. Walking back to his car, he reminded himself that this wasn't a military operation; he was going to meet a girl – a very tasty-looking girl – at her suggestion. Who was he to complain if she'd had to change the venue.

Piers Bowring poured himself a deep measure of Stolichnaya with a splash of Perrier and carried it from the south-facing *salon* of the Villa Fleurie. He sat down at a table on a terrace beneath a pergola and a wandering vine from which dangled bunches of small, dry, tasteless grapes. For a moment, like tens of thousands along that coast at that hour, he gazed down at a sea which glittered in the setting sun, and the little green hump of Cap Martin which protruded into it. But his cold grey eyes registered neither appreciation nor disapproval.

'Terry,' he called towards the house.

Haynes appeared at the french windows a few seconds later. 'Yes, boss?'

Bowring half-turned to speak over his shoulder. 'Bring Kelly's file out here, please.'

Bowring returned his gaze to the tumbling coast beneath him until the small cockney placed a yellow folder on the table in front of him. 'Sit down, Terry. You might as well go through this with me.'

Haynes drew up another wooden chair, so that they could look at the contents of the file together. Bowring was already familiar with them; he wouldn't have selected Kelly otherwise. But he wanted to make sure there wasn't any small detail he'd missed, and he wanted Haynes to know with whom he would be working.

From the assortment of regimental reports – which Bowring should never have seen – and from the letters, applications, citations and security assessments which he had managed to accumulate, a clear, if two-dimensional, picture of Jack Kelly had emerged.

Kelly had been born in 1955, in Toxteth, Liverpool, the second of five children. His parents, Eamonn and Mary Kelly, had arrived from Ireland with their parents in the mid-thirties. Nothing remarkable or derogatory was noted about them, beyond the fact that Eamonn Kelly had never earned enough money in the declining Liverpool docks to bring up their children. One could almost sense the relief they must have felt when Jack, having acquired half a dozen City and Guilds certificates at St Francis Xavier's RC secondary school, had announced that he was joining the Irish Guards on his eighteenth birthday.

What they might have felt when, five years later, he told them he had been accepted into 22 SAS, was more ambiguous. Both their families came from Co. Cavan, an area closely connected with Ulster across the border. No doubt their feelings were mixed when he married the non-Catholic daughter of a wealthy farmer on the Welsh borders whom he had met in a Hereford disco.

The records showed that Jack Kelly was an exceptional soldier, of the highest physical and mental resourcefulness. He came back from the Falklands in 1982 with a Military Medal for his sheer gall in carrying out surveillance operations, and after five years in the SAS he had been promoted to sergeant. He had an aptitude for disguise and languages, having acquired fluent Arabic – both classical and local spoken dialects – at the Royal Army Education Corps school at Beaconsfield by the time the short war against Saddam Hussein was waged. Here he served with distinction inside the Iraqi lines, pinpointing Saddam's mobile Scud missile-launchers. He lost one of his closest friends to an Iraqi land-mine, and returned to Hereford to find he'd lost his wife as well, to an up-and-coming tractor dealer.

At the end of '91, Kelly left the British Army, divorced and childless. At the time he was confident that his considerable skills and experience had a substantial value on the open market. But he balked at the idea of getting involved in other people's conflicts. To his growing disgust, he found most of the jobs on offer were concerned with mundane security, and providing what was known as 'close personal protection' to persons of sufficient political or financial clout to be considered targets.

Dull and frustrating, these jobs were nevertheless very well paid. After a year with a Saudi prince, during which he was under the mistaken impression that other, more varied duties would eventually be on offer, he had applied for a job in the team which looked after the toddler heiress to a billion-dollar Greek shipping empire. And that was only because, after Saudi, the locations sounded more attractive.

Though these reasons weren't specified in his file, Bowring knew, fairly accurately, what Kelly's motivation and aspirations had been. News of ex-SAS men was traded widely among their informal network, and Bowring had made it his business to keep up to date. He hadn't any doubt that Kelly and his extensive, hard-earned skills were utterly wasted in his current job, and that Kelly resented this.

'Looks like an all-rounder,' Haynes said.

'He is. Weapons, explosives, combat, plenty of covert experience. Dowson's got a job coming in where it looks as though I'll only be able to field three or four men.'

'What about the girl?'

Bowring nodded. 'I'll need her. She's got talents none of us could ever acquire.'

'Where did you find her?'

'I've known her since she was born. Hugue de Lassy – her father – was the best combat officer in the Deuxième REP I ever knew. We were working together in Lebanon when he got sniped by a militiaman in West Beirut. Her mother drove her car off the road in the Gorges du Tarn five years ago.' Bowring shrugged. 'I'd been a sort of uncle to her, and she'd always said she wanted to work with me. Of course, I ignored that and encouraged her to go to work in one of the international secretariats. She was always good at languages, then she got a degree in economics from the Sorbonne; she could have done anything she wanted. Last year, she came and saw me in England – she was working for Exxon – and told me she was ready to take on something a little more challenging.'

Terry Haynes was impressed. Michelle had been based at the villa with him for six months now, and she had never once mentioned this connection with their boss. That Bowring had never mentioned it before was to be expected.

'She's a hell of a girl,' Haynes nodded. 'Hard?' He sucked through his lips. 'She could give Tyson the brush-off and leave him wondering what hit him.'

'I take it she hasn't had cause to give you the brush off?'

'Course not. Even if it hadn't been standing orders, I don't think I'd have tried. I wouldn't have got anywhere. I don't think she's that interested in leg-over.'

'Just selective, I dare say. Let's hope Mr Kelly is quickly disabused of any ideas he might have about her interest in him.'

'D'you know him well, boss?'

'Yes. He was in my squadron in the Falklands, and he was the best of them. His marriage went wrong after the Gulf, but that'll have done him more good than harm – she couldn't take the pressure.

He'll suit this contract of Dowson's very well – if we get it.'

'Who's the client this time?'

Bowring turned and looked at him for the first time since he'd sat down. He lowered one brow in mild censure. 'I'll let you know when it's in the bag.'

Monsignor Alfonso di Montefalco emerged from a motorway tunnel – it must have been the hundredth he'd passed through that day on his way up from Rome – and blinked at the sun dropping behind Mont Agel towards Monaco. He had enjoyed the drive round the Ligurian coast, but he was tired now and ready for a decent dinner, preferably with a good bottle of wine.

He had been told that the English mercenary was an exceptionally civilized example of his type; that was partly why Montefalco had chosen to try him first. In the one, discreet telephone conversation they had had, Major Bowring's spoken Italian had certainly impressed him. Archbishop O'Keane had stressed that discretion was as important as efficacy in whoever he instructed to do the job. Having listened to thousands of confessions as a priest, Monsignor di Montefalco had become an efficient judge of people's characters from their voices. And this man had sounded more than discreet.

The monsignor, if he had not been a cleric, would very likely have become a politician. He was a clever, good-looking man who possessed all the required characteristics – not least ambition and a taste for intrigue. It hadn't taken him long to work his way up from a curacy in a poor Umbrian parish into the bishop's office and thence to Rome, where his more worldly predilections and personal vanity were less noticeable.

At forty-five, a year or two younger than the man he was coming to see, he still had a full head of fine, black hair and a trim figure. He liked to think that his sharp, handsome eyes, the colour of espresso, missed very little. Now they caught the signs for the exit down to Roquebrune and he throttled the big Fiat back to a hundred kilometres per hour. He took the slip-road over the autoroute and snaked down the hillside towards the glittering waters of the Côte d'Azur.

Haynes inspected the car and its driver through the security camera as the Fiat waited outside the villa's wrought-iron gates.

'Are you expecting some kind of vicar, boss?'

'Yes. Let him in and show him into the office.'

Haynes opened the electronic gates and the large car crept in and up the steep drive between the rows of cypress trees.

'I'll see him on his own,' said Bowring. 'Then I imagine he'll expect me to buy him dinner. I'll be back at eleven when Michelle gets here.'

His second in command nodded. 'Right. I'll take a run down to the end of the *cap*. And, boss, I was planning to take the girl out to the mountains tomorrow evening, to give her some practice with the new sniper and check out the laser sights system.'

'OK, but be discreet. They don't like us here and they don't need much of an excuse to chuck us out.'

'I'm always discreet. We'll have a couple of twelve-bores with us, to look as though we're lamping bunnies like the rest of the peasants.'

Bowring nodded philosophically. Without the vast army ranges of the Welsh hills at his disposal, he had to let his team use their initiative when it came to weapons training. 'Fine, and I'll want you back here later tonight when Kelly arrives with Michelle.'

'Right, boss.' Haynes gave a nod that acknowledged Bowring's position of command while at the same time asserting his own independence.

Jack Kelly squeezed the Range Rover between two Citroëns on the edge of the port in Nice and climbed out. There was the usual hubbub of fishermen, sailors, tourists and fun-seekers. Still warm but now dropping behind the castle on its rocky lump, the sun lit the upper storeys of the buildings on the opposite, east quay, and the lights of the bars and restaurants began to flicker on the oily water of the harbour.

Kelly sucked in a sharp, fishy smell which reminded him of the docks in Liverpool where he used to go as a small boy and dream of adventure and travel.

He spotted the Café Pelican and walked round to it with a rather different sort of adventure in mind.

The girl was sitting at a table outside on a chair of woven plastic. She looked at least as stunning as she had leaning back in his passenger seat a couple of days before. There was a cigarette between her lips and a packet of Marlboro on the table beside a bottle of local *rosé* and two glasses.

Kelly walked up to the table and grinned down at her.

'*Ça va?*' he said.

'OK,' she smiled back. 'I'm sorry I couldn't get to Vence. I was tied up down here.'

Her very slightly accented English made the idiom sound as if it were meant literally.

'Was that nice?' Kelly asked, then wished he hadn't.

The girl didn't answer.

Kelly pulled out another chair and sat down opposite her. She filled the second glass with pink wine and passed it to him. 'With the compliments of the proprietor,' she said.

'Why's that?'

'He's a friend of mine.'

Kelly had developed a taste for the *rosé* of the region and took a good gulp of it happily enough, but he resented the fact that he wasn't controlling this encounter in the way he would have liked.

'Do you come from here, then?'

She shook her head. 'No, but I'm living along the coast at Roquebrune.'

He realized he knew nothing about her. When they had talked in the car, it had been about him. He didn't even know her name.

'What's your name?' he asked with what he hoped was disarming directness.

'Michelle.'

'*Michelle, ma belle*,' Jack crooned in his appropriately Liverpudlian accent, '*sont les mots qui vont très bien ensemble*.'

Michelle smiled in a way that suggested this wasn't the first time she'd had those particular *mots* sung at her. 'When I was in England, they called me Micky.'

'Micky? That's absurd. What were you doing in England?'

'I was in the oil industry.'

This sounded sufficiently unlikely for Kelly to think it was probably true.

'What did you do in the oil business, then?'

'Nothing very interesting. That's why I don't now.'

'Well, what do you do now?'

Michelle smiled. 'I'll tell you sometime.'

Kelly shrugged. At least this suggested that there would be other meetings, and he understood that some people had the need for mystery. He was used to being secretive himself, but that was as a result of training rather than character. Many times his civilian friends, or his family, had asked: 'Where are you off to, then?' as he announced a forthcoming absence, and he would reply: 'I could tell you, but if I did, I'd have to kill you, so I won't.'

'You were a soldier, weren't you?' she asked.

He had no reason to deny it. 'Sure. Is it that obvious?'

'From the job you have now, looking after the little Skiapoulos. And because you are very fit.' She added this with a definite sense of appreciation.

'You spotted that, then?' Kelly said, pleased. At least there was some point in keeping in shape besides the need to rescue Barbie dolls. 'But how did you know about the Skiapoulos girl?'

Michelle shrugged. 'It wasn't very hard.'

No, Kelly thought, it wouldn't have been.

'Anyway, what about eating? What's the food like here?' He emptied the bottle into their glasses.

'Not bad, but there's a better place on the Boulevard Carnot.'

They finished their wine and walked a few hundred yards to the restaurant Michelle had suggested.

It was a warm, intimate place, serving classic

Niçoise food, and had an air about it that relaxed and softened.

Kelly and the girl talked, playing a game, shadow-boxing with the truth about each other. They had both travelled, and obviously shared a reluctance to put down roots. But Kelly learnt more about the girl from her eyes, face and gestures than anything she said – and he was impressed.

This was no bimbo, nothing like the girls who used to arrive in Hereford by the busload, ready to discard their underwear for any hard man with a tan, short-cropped hair and steely eyes who looked as though he was in the Regiment.

When they had finished eating, he hadn't, as he would normally have done, worked out a game plan, a series of initiatives that would lead her back to his bed; Michelle wasn't the sort of girl you led. And anyway, she pre-empted him.

'Come back up to the house where I live,' she said as he dropped a 500-franc note on the table. 'We can drink champagne and look at the moon,' she added with a shadow of a sardonic grin.

Kelly looked back at her, seeing the grin. She seemed to have reached some kind of decision. He couldn't guess what that decision was, but he made up his mind to take a chance.

Monsignor di Montefalco was sitting in a straight-backed armchair, fastidiously running his thumb and forefinger along the indistinct creases of his black trousers. Bowring had a chance to inspect him unseen for a moment as he silently walked into the room that they called the office. It looked more like the library of an Edwardian country house.

'Good evening, Monsignor.'

The cleric rose quickly and neatly to his feet and held out a hand in greeting. 'Major Bowring?'

Bowring nodded and closed the door behind him. 'Did you have a good journey?'

'Yes, thank you, though a very unsatisfactory lunch with the bishop in Lucca.'

'I have a table booked at the Chèvre d'Or in an hour's time.'

The Monsignor's eyes gleamed. He had not misjudged this man.

'But,' Bowring went on, 'I must ask you to change from you clerical garments, and we will have to converse there in Italian.'

Montefalco understood. He was proud of his crimson trimmings, but for dinner at the Chèvre d'Or, and for the sake of discretion, it was a small price to pay.

There was a quiet knock on the door.

'Come,' Bowring called.

A small, dark maid entered the room with a tray bearing coffee cups and a tall pot, which she placed on a table. When she had disappeared, Bowring said: 'I hope you don't mind coffee?'

'After four hours at the wheel, it is exactly what I need.'

Bowring poured, and indicated that they should sit opposite one another, before saying: 'So, Monsignor, I can't deny that I'm looking forward to hearing what you think we can do for you.'

The cleric looked back at him for a moment before he spoke. 'What, as a matter of curiosity, do you think it might be?'

'I really couldn't say, I'm afraid.'

'A man of your experience and practical knowledge of the world must surely be able to make an intelligent guess?'

'Of course, but that's not the same as knowing. And I'm not privy to the detail, or even the general thrust, of Vatican foreign policy, if there is such a thing.'

The cleric smiled. 'There most certainly is. But tell me your intelligent guess.'

'The Vatican is sending a pro-nuncio to Tel Aviv, and certain Islamic bodies are not best pleased.'

The Papal officer smiled, with a nod of encouragement. 'And?'

'And you're expecting a spot of trouble,' Bowring said with a slight display of impatience.

Montefalco noted this. 'Quite, quite,' he said quickly. 'More than a spot of trouble. Our legation in Damascus has received some information about a group of zealous who go by the name of Sufuf Allah – The Ranks of God.' He pursed his lips in distaste. 'These people plan to make a name for themselves by . . . neutralizing – as I think you say in your trade – His Holiness.'

Bowring nodded without expression.

'You are not surprised, or appalled?' the monsignor asked him.

'No,' Bowring said quietly. 'It's a while since I was surprised or appalled.'

Montefalco appeared to accept this, quite gladly. 'I'm told that you saw service fighting with Arabs against Arabs in Dhofar, so I presume you have no ideological problems in that direction?'

'I'd say that I was fighting for the interests of the free world against the deadening spread of communism.'

'And is that the only reason you did it?'

'No. I did it because I was good at it, and I enjoyed it.'

The cleric nodded, sadly pragmatic, 'Someone has to do these things. There is no doubt that God grants His blessings to the defenders of the free.'

Bowring allowed himself a small smile. 'Let's hope so.'

'Now, the very apogee of God's church on earth is under threat. It is not the first time, and it will not be the last. But if followers of Islam were to succeed in destroying our Pope in the current state of world tension, it would go a long way to encouraging militant Muslims everywhere, as well as depriving us of a great and good spiritual father.'

Bowring expressed no opinion on this; he had none to offer.

'Not only must we make sure that this plan does not succeed,' Montefalco went on, 'but we must also be sure that no one even hears of it. There are only two people in the Vatican who are aware of this current threat, myself and Archbishop O'Keane, who is head of security. Bishop Rappacioli, the Nuncio in Damascus, knows, and now you do too.'

Bowring nodded.

'His Holiness, as you may know, is making two foreign tours in the near future,' Montefalco went on. 'Three days in India at the end of this month followed by six days in Britain during September. Our information is that the attempt will be made on one of these tours. It is difficult to approach him armed in the Holy City.'

'Is it? With all those crowds and audiences?'

'Our Guardia Svizerra are not entirely decorative.'

'Then why aren't you briefing them on this job?'

'Major Bowring, they are good, well-trained soldiers, but quite frankly they are not remotely in the same league as men trained in, for example, Russia's Spetsnaz, Israel's Sayeret Matkalz, or the French Deuxième REP, or of course, your own 22 SAS, who still reign supreme, do they not?'

2

Out of habit, Kelly pushed the Range Rover to the limit through the chicanes and hairpins of the Grande Corniche. If the girl was scared or impressed, she didn't show it. When they reached the hillside village of Roquebrune, she directed him concisely to the house where she said she lived.

There was a tall, purposeful gate across the bottom of a steep drive which led up to a large, well-lit villa.

'I'll do the gate,' Michelle said. She jumped down from the vehicle and walked to a video entryphone set into one of the tall stone gateposts. By the time she was back in her seat, the gates had silently swung open. They were already starting to close as Kelly drove between them. He wondered again, but Michelle offered no explanation for the security surrounding the house.

She didn't speak until she was ushering him into a high, cool, tiled hall lit by a small chandelier. When the oak front door was closed behind him, she said: 'This villa belongs to my boss. I'll introduce you to him.'

She opened one of a pair of carved fruit-wood doors into an old-fashioned French *salon*.

Kelly followed her into the room, expecting the unexpected.

'Evening, Kelly.' The voice entered the room as the speaker stepped in through french windows which opened on to the glittering panorama of the coast below.

Kelly's surprise at seeing Bowring lasted only a fleeting moment. Major Piers Bowring had in the past provided him with enough mind-jarring surprises to have made him largely immune to them.

With barely perceptible hesitation, he answered: 'Evening, boss,' as if he had seen Bowring the day before.

'Drink?'

'Your messenger promised champagne.'

'Champagne it shall be. Nothing but the best for an ex-hero of H Squadron.' He walked across to a walnut cabinet which contained a fridge in its lower part. He took out a bottle of Louis Roederer Cristal Brut and filled two glasses, which he handed to Kelly and Michelle before splashing a long measure of Stolichnaya into a tumbler for himself.

Kelly took a drink of the mellow, bubbling liquid and erased from his mind a lot of the questions that had been nagging at him for the last few hours. It was almost a relief to have them answered, and he wasn't going to let the girl see his disappointment. Thank God, he thought, he hadn't succumbed to the temptation to proposition or pounce on her.

'Sit down, Jack,' said Bowring.

Kelly lowered himself into a deep armchair. Bowring walked behind a handsome maple writing table and sat down behind it. Michelle walked over to the window and remained standing.

Kelly had accepted the obvious fact that the girl had sought him out and brought him here under instructions. That didn't necessarily mean that there was no mileage to be got out of her – unless, of course, she was Bowring's girl. He stiffened slightly at the thought, and thanked his stars again that he hadn't made a fool of himself with her.

'So, how are you enjoying life at the moment?' Bowring asked.

'What do you think?' Kelly asked and tossed back another gulp of champagne.

'I imagine you're bored rigid and ready for a change. Michélle wouldn't have brought you here otherwise.'

Kelly nodded with a grin. He hadn't set eyes on Bowring for nearly ten years, but the man hadn't changed at all; perhaps a touch greyer of hair, but the eyes and voice were as sharp as ever. They'd been through plenty of shit together, he and Bowring, on the slopes of Mount Kent and in West Belfast – been through it, saved each other's lives a couple of times and come out the other side. He'd heard rumours that his old boss had set up in business but nobody seemed to know where.

'But the money's good. Have you got a better offer?'

'Maybe. You'll have to decide that for yourself, once I've made you the offer. But first I need to be sure what sort of condition you're in.' He was scrutinizing Kelly as he spoke. 'You look in good shape. Do you still run?'

'Yeah. Eight, ten miles, most days.'

'Could you still do the Long Drag across Pen-y-Fan inside twenty hours?'

'I could do it quicker now than I did at Selection.'

'What about weapons training?'

'I've kept it up, at least with small arms. I joined the gun club in Nice when I first got down here, and in Saudi they let me use their army ranges.'

'Gimpies, Stingers?'

Kelly looked surprised. You would only need a General Purpose Machine Gun or a hand-held SAM launcher in outright open combat. 'I'd need a bit of practice,' he admitted.

'And you're not worried about live targets?'

Kelly shrugged. 'You know what it's like. A target's a target.'

'OK. I'll want to have a look at you in action. We've got some L96s with laser sights and a few other bits of high-tech which you may not have used before.'

'But what's the job, boss?'

'Jobs,' Bowring said. 'I'm glad to say there's no shortage of work at the moment.'

Bowring stood and walked round to the centre of the room. 'I'll tell you more about it when we've both decided that we want to work together. For starters, are you prepared to undergo my short selection process?'

'How long's "short"?'

'A day or two. When is your next week off?'

'Starting Monday.'

'Fine. Come here then. And tell no one. If I want you, I'll want you right away, so you'll have to think up some reason. Our doctor can fix you up with a certified broken ankle if necessary.'

He held out a hand. Kelly stood and took it, realizing the interview was at an end.

'See you Monday, then – 0800.' Bowring nodded farewell and strode out of the room, closing the door on Kelly and Michelle.

The girl hadn't spoken since showing him into the office. Now she picked up the bottle of champagne and refilled their glasses. She lifted hers. 'Good luck,' she said.

Kelly walked over and looked out of the french windows on to the bay below. Slowly he turned back, looked at the girl and shook his head. Shit, she's lovely, he thought – and hard as fucking granite.

'Did he put you through selection?' he asked.

'Oh yes.'

'Is he your boyfriend?'

The girl smiled. 'He's my godfather, actually.'

Kelly couldn't imagine anyone seriously entrusting their offspring's spiritual guidance to Piers Bowring. On the other hand, Bowring had a lot to teach in other areas, if he chose to. Kelly wondered who the girl's father was, but he knew he'd asked enough questions for now.

'Right. Thanks for the drinks. I'm off.'

'Thank you for dinner,' she said, smiling back politely.

She opened the front door for him and watched him down the steps to the Range Rover.

'Good night, Sergeant,' she called softly.

Kelly didn't answer and climbed into his vehicle.

He roared down the drive, guessing that the gates would be open before he reached them. They were, and he spun out of the entrance on to the narrow road, heading towards the Grande Corniche, trying to sort out what the hell he was feeling.

The four days until the following Monday dragged like a prison sentence.

Kelly's tiny charge and her team of nannies were really beginning to get on his nerves. But he was a professional; he didn't let it show. He'd stood six months of it and another few days weren't going to kill him.

But he could hardly believe how turned on he was by the thought of getting back to some real action. He felt as if he had just been treading water, killing time since he had left the SAS.

It was a common syndrome.

They trained you up to the eyeballs; after fifteen years, you were a top man in the most élite regiment in the world's finest army. You didn't have anything to prove to anyone. But you became addicted to the adrenalin so that the gaps between action became unbearable, and when you left you found yourself facing a gap that threatened to last the rest of your life.

All the organizations who preyed on the men leaving the Regiment promised the earth: lots of money, travel, action. But it was all bullshit.

Close personal protection; sitting around for hours outside casinos or government offices, getting rigid with boredom until you began to hate the poor bastard you were supposed to be protecting. It might have been all right, as it was for a lot of his former colleagues, if he'd had a wife and children to worry about and pay for.

But all that had fallen apart for him. He would have liked children, he supposed, but he was bloody glad he'd never had one by Susan. Of course, his family thought he was mad. They thought he was wrong to have left her, despite the tractor dealer. They thought he could have got a highly paid, safe job with the police, or Customs and Excise. They didn't trust him any more, didn't know what to say to him when he came home tanned, with a pocketful of money. So he'd stopped going.

The Regiment had become his family, although he'd only discovered that after he'd left.

Since then, he'd forced himself to get used to being alone. He liked women and his ice-blue eyes and obvious independence had kept him supplied, but he liked them for the excitement of the chase, the chat, the buzz of the early stages of encounter. He didn't want women to know him well enough to see his moods or his loneliness.

And now Bowring was proposing that he should join a new family, and he wanted it and the action it promised. Clever bastard, Bowring.

Kelly didn't concern himself with how the major had known that he was ripe for recruitment. Of course, Bowring hadn't known for sure, but he'd sent the girl to check him out, and she'd taken him in.

He turned over in his big bed, in the large, airy room just down the corridor from the little billionairess and wasn't sorry at all that this was to be his last night in that room.

Monday was one of those rare, stormy days that whip down the Côte d'Azur in August, with a sharp, wet wind that blew down off the Alps to fill a vacuum in the atmosphere somewhere out beyond Corsica.

The change in the weather suited Kelly as he hurled his suitcase and a couple of bergens into the back of his Range Rover and blasted his horn at the sleepy gatekeeper of the Skiapoulos villa to let him out. He didn't want to be a second late for whatever selection course Bowring might have devised and drove through Vence as the market traders put the finishing touches to their stalls at half-past six.

* * *

The door of the villa was opened at eight o'clock by a man Kelly didn't know – a Londoner, judging from his accent.

'Morning, Mr Kelly. Have you left your keys in your vehicle?'

Kelly nodded.

'Good,' the little cockney said. 'Come in. I'm Terry Haynes.'

The weasel-faced man held out a hand with a cheerful grin. Kelly shook it and made an instant assessment. Definitely ex-services, definitely not ex-Regiment, but sound nonetheless.

'Morning,' said Kelly, appreciatively sniffing a whiff of strong coffee wafting into the hall. You didn't get any of that before Selection in Hereford in the old days.

It turned out that you didn't get any in Bowring's outfit either.

Haynes opened a concealed door in the painted panelled wall of the hall and beckoned Kelly to follow. The door opened on to a flight of narrow stone stairs which led down into a cellar.

'Shut the door firm behind you,' the cockney told Kelly and switched on half a dozen fluorescent lights.

The vast stone cellar appeared to have been cut right into the hillside, and had a number of tunnels hewn from the solid rock. The man-made walls on the south side were lined with metal Dexion shelving like any quartermaster's stores. On the shelves were stacked tidy row upon row of military gear: all-weather kit, clothing, communications equipment.

Haynes swiftly pulled out olive-green fatigues, a green ribbed pullover, Gore-tex jacket, heavyweight bergen, net scarf, torch, prismatic compass, water bottles and webbing belts to strap them to – everything the fully equipped SAS trooper might be expected to carry – except his weapons.

He dumped it all on a folding table in front of Kelly and grinned at the look of surprise on his face.

'I suppose you thought all our gear would by Yves St Laurent.'

'I was just wondering where it all came from.'

'You can buy most of this stuff if you know where to look. Have you brought your own boots?'

Kelly nodded. 'Yeah. What about a knife?'

'No knife. No shooters. No weapons of any sort, I'm afraid. But there'll be an L96 7.62mm waiting for you when you get to your last RV – just to make sure you can still hit a target.'

Kelly shrugged. It looked as though he was in for a good old-fashioned yomp. Evidently Bowring hadn't accepted Kelly's own assessment of his fitness or weapons skills.

This was confirmed when Haynes gleefully stuffed the bergen with fifty-five pounds of engineering bricks.

'Right,' Haynes said, looking at his watch. 'You've got less than an hour to get to the start line and cross it fully loaded. And eight hours to get to the finish. Your maps and grid refs are already in your vehicle.'

'What? In my own Range Rover?'

'Sorry, mate. No company cars supplied till you're on the payroll. Don't worry. It's all clean roads up to the start, but you'll have to give it a bit of welly. I'll get your rations and fill your bottles while you're changing.'

Haynes disappeared into a room at the end of a row of shelves, and Kelly mechanically set about pulling on the familiar kit. He didn't know yet where he was headed, but it was a fair guess that it would be high ground. What was harder to judge was what the weather would be like by the time he got there. But then, he could decide if he needed the Gore-tex when he reached the start.

As Kelly buckled on his belt, Haynes came back with two water bottles and a handful of dry rations, – enough for a short day's yomp – and stuffed them into the bergen on top of the bricks.

Haynes looked at his watch again. 'Right. It's 0815. You've got to cross the start line at 0900 so you'd better piss off – out the back way.' He jerked a thumb towards one of the tunnels hewn in the rock-face. 'That takes you up and drops you on to the back road to the village. You'll find your vehicle parked directly outside. Don't worry about locking the door, we'll do that, but don't let anyone see you come out. Best of luck.'

'Thanks.' Kelly felt like an eighteen-year-old rookie as he entered the unlit tunnel. He unhooked his torch and followed the passage round a bend, up a steep flight of fifty steps until he reached a heavy, double-bolted iron door. He drew back the bolts and the door swung silently and smoothly towards him, letting in daylight filtered through a curtain of scrub oak and dangling vegetation.

He pulled the door to behind him and carefully edged his head forward through the leaves until he had a clear view of what lay beyond. He was on one side of a shallow cutting through which ran a narrow lane. Directly in front of him, six feet below, was the roof of his Range Rover parked in a passing place. There were no houses or people visible for fifty or sixty yards in either direction. A small Citroën van with corrugated sides laboured up the hill towards him, passed him and carried on east, towards the village, Kelly reckoned. He waited a few seconds after it was out of sight and hearing, to listen for any more approaching vehicles or pedestrians. Satisfied there were none, he parted the branches in front of him and scrambled down the bank.

The left-hand-drive Range Rover was facing down the hill, with the driver's door closest to him. He heaved off the bergen and removed his loaded belt and opened the door to chuck them in, then climbed in himself. The keys were in the ignition, and there were two maps folded on the passenger seat. Kelly switched on the engine; it was still warm. He wondered vaguely who had brought it round, and realized he hadn't a clue how many people Bowring employed at this place. But perhaps the girl knew; maybe she was watching him even now.

Then he put the Range Rover into gear and shot off down the hill. The lane took a couple of hairpins and came out on the Moyenne Corniche. He drove a hundred yards along the main road until he reached a safe pull-in, and began to study the maps. On the first were written two grid references marked 'start' and 'finish'.

Within seconds Kelly identified the start just above the village of Sospel, due north from where he was, on the edge of the Mercantour National Park, well up in the Alpes Maritimes. He checked the route – about six miles along the autoroute, then twenty miles of switchback road up the Carei valley. He quickly memorized the route and pulled off again with a scattering of wet gravel.

The rain had stopped for the moment, but the wind kept coming, and the sky hadn't cleared. Within five minutes Kelly was heading east on the fast lane of the A8 in a spray of surface water.

In another five minutes he was pulling off the highway on to the *route départementale* that led up into the foothills. He flicked the transmission to four-wheel drive and gave every ounce of his concentration to climbing that road as fast as was humanly and mechanically possible.

Kelly parked in a small, quiet square in Sospel at 0854 hours. The rain had been beating down for the last few miles of the journey, and the clouds up ahead didn't look forgiving. He decided to keep the Gore-tex.

He climbed out, pulled out the bergen and belt, slotted the map into a perspex holder, then, after locking the car, heaved the rucksack on to his back and set off for the start.

He saw no sign of anyone watching or monitoring him at the first reference point. But then he hadn't expected to. He shrugged his shoulders, hoisted the bergen a little higher on his shoulders and headed into the wind.

The first two miles were fairly easy going along a rutted track, but he knew he would have to strike off it, and over the shoulder of the hill to pick up the intermediate grid refs he'd been given.

The straps of his bergen had settled into his shoulders and he had found a rhythm in his walk – a good, steady three miles an hour, he judged. He pulled a Mars bar from his smock and munched it as he walked, and asked himself what the hell a man of his age and experience was doing playing at trainee soldiers.

There was a time when he might have written off this bogus 'selection' yomp as a load of bollocks. But somehow he couldn't associate that with Major Piers Bowring. The major was a serious man and always had been.

Bowring had been on his second tour with the Regiment when Kelly had first come across him. He already had the reputation from his first tour as a troop commander of not being quite like the other officers. Out in Dhofar, as a twenty-three-year-old 'baby Rupert', he had shown as much guts and tactical instinct as any hardened old sergeant-major, and his reputation was well established by the time he came back a few years later from his parent regiment, the 17th/21st Lancers, to command his own squadron.

The troopers and NCOs of 22 SAS enjoyed a tradition of easy relationships with their officers. It was one appropriate to the kind of operations in which they were engaged, where every man was equally exposed to danger and equally in need of the mutual support they could give one another.

But Bowring had always been a bit aloof. He made no pretence of being interested in drinking or fraternizing with his troop or his squadron and clearly disapproved of the idea of currying popularity with his men. He expected them to accept him for what he was, and what he had done.

Where they would be ogling *Penthouse* or *Playboy*, he would be reading *Newsweek* or Trollope or A.J.P. Taylor.

When he had rejoined the SAS, he had insisted, quite

unnecessarily, on undergoing a physical Selection all over again, along with a bunch of aspiring recruits. On a sixty-kilometre slog across the Brecons in mid-January, he had romped home with a sixty-pound load on his back, an hour before the next finisher.

In the Falklands, he'd shown supreme skill and tenacity in placing his squadron in critical observation posts, sometimes a mere hundred yards from enemy positions. He had personally led the raid on an airfield on East Falkland, destroying six Pucaras, three helicopters and twenty-eight Argentinians with the loss of only one of his own men.

Yet after the Falklands, something had gone wrong with Bowring's career. No one Kelly had ever asked seemed to know what had happened, but abruptly in the summer of 1985, Bowring had resigned his commission, and gone. Thenceforth, although his name lived on in the Regimental roll of honour, there was always a slight question mark over his reputation.

Whatever had been decided had been worked out between Bowring, the CO of 22 SAS and the Colonel of his own regiment. Surprisingly, not much had been heard of him since, though odd rumours floated around Hereford. After Kelly himself had left, he heard nothing more, despite regular contact with old colleagues and return visits to Stirling Lines.

But whatever Bowring was doing now, Kelly didn't have any doubt that it was serious, and that Bowring took it seriously. It was characteristic of him not to make any concessions in his recruitment of men for his own private operation, whatever it did. So Kelly was prepared to take this test seriously – now, he realized, as much for his own satisfaction as Bowring's.

From his reading of the map, Kelly wasn't too worried about completing the course in time, though he knew he couldn't be complacent. After half an hour of walking up a steady incline, he reached the point where he would have to leave the muddy track, and head up a scree-covered mountainside. He looked up the forty-five-degree slope at the surface of loose shale and the scattered, scrawny bushes. There was little grass to ease the going, and not much to hang on to. He jerked the bergen up his back, tightened the straps and checked his bearing once more before pushing on.

Kelly reached a triangulation point a little after midday. Despite the wet wind, sweat was pouring down his face; his feet and the back of his legs ached viciously. It was time for a halt; fifteen minutes' recuperation should get him back to the same condition he'd been in before he started the main ascent.

Just off the crest of the mountain to the north, there was a large outcrop of shaley rock. He slithered down to it until he was sheltered from the wind in its lea, and hauled off his bergen and unclipped his belt. Using the rucksack as a back rest, he sat down, gulped down a pint of water and ate some dry rations and chocolate.

He gazed out over the naked hilltops and listened to the wind. It was hard to believe he was little more than an hour from the fleshpots of Monaco; it reminded him of the silent hours he had spent in OPs below Mount Kent in East Falkland and on the flanks of the Mourne Mountains of Co. Down.

Suddenly he became alert. That extra sense which

in most of us is only vestigial told him – without being able see, hear or smell anyone – that he was not alone.

A second later, someone was on his back, dragging him sideways to the ground. Even as he keeled over, he had time to reflect ruefully that on an operation he should never have perched in a place like that without checking it out first.

A second man was grabbing his belt from the ground beside him and rifling his open bergen. He'd been jumped by a couple of gypsies.

Kelly rolled like a log out from under his first attacker, and leapt to his feet, poised for the gypsy to come at him. He wished to hell he'd at least been issued with a survival knife. He saw the determination in the hard, high-boned face as the wiry little man launched himself at him.

He looked for the glint of a steel blade, but saw none as he sidestepped the gypsy's attack at the very last moment, grabbed him by his clothing and hurled him headlong down the hillside.

Regaining his breath, he turned his attention to the other man, who scrambled to his feet and sprinted off with all the booty he could carry. Kelly was up with him in half a dozen strides, thrusting his fist into his windpipe. The man was already crumpling when Kelly heard the gunshot behind him. He twisted round, still clutching his captive to use him as a shield.

Piers Bowring, in boots, OGs and a battered Barbour, jumped lightly from the bottom ledge of the crag, holding a 9mm Browning handgun by his side.

'OK, Jack. Quite satisfactory. Now let him go.'

Kelly heaved a sigh of relief.

'For fuck's sake, boss! They never did that to us in the Brecons.'

'No,' Bowring agreed. 'It'd be too risky, but I write my own rules now.' He looked at his watch. 'You'd better get a move on. You've got a detour to make.' Bowring approached as Kelly's victim sank to his knees, gasping. In his hand was a slip of paper. 'Here's the grid ref. And you're still due for target practice at 1700 hours.'

Kelly stifled his questions, gathered up his scattered kit, took another swig of water and heaved the bergen on to his back. He gave Bowring a nod and started off down the hill without a word.

The first gypsy grinned at him as he scrambled back up the slope.

For the rest of the muscle-racking slog, Kelly kept his eyes about him for another attack. It was the first time he'd been on the alert like this since the Gulf. It got his nerves tingling and the adrenalin pumping in a way he had almost forgotten. He felt more alive than he had done at any time in the last three years.

But there were no more attacks. The wind dropped, the clouds broke up. When the sun beamed through by mid-afternoon, he had to take off the Gore-tex and stuff it in his pack. Although his course had been across the grain of the land, over three more peaks as high as the first, he had managed to work up a rhythm which deadened the pain in his calves and ankles. Besides, all his regular running and swimming had kept him at least as fit as he had been when he was fully operational.

And on the stretches of level ground, he was able to think. Whatever Bowring had to offer, if it required this kind of physical condition Kelly wanted it. There was no way he was going to fail this selection.

He guessed that someone must have checked him through the grid refs, but he saw no one besides a lone farmer with his shotgun and a dog, out looking for quail. The farmer had greeted him affably enough in French, without any surprise, probably thinking he was on an exercise up into the mountains from the big French military camp at Canjuer.

Kelly continued up a narrow valley, through a small forest of holm oak and parasol pine, with a mile to go and one last long drag up to the ruins outside Mille Fourches, the last RV. He stopped for a final swig of water and adjusted his straps once more. He had already covered sixteen miles – the detour had added four – one more wouldn't kill him, he thought, almost cheerfully.

The sun was shining obliquely through the tops of the pines, casting occasional beams on the thin scrub of the woodland floor. Birds which had finished foraging for the day were beginning to settle into an afternoon chorus as the remains of the wind lightly rattled the pine needles above and stirred the air, full of the fresh smell of resin and damp earth.

The ground steepened sharply and Kelly found himself alongside a brook, swollen with rain, leaping and glittering down the gully. He scrambled up beside a small waterfall, on to a level clearing twenty yards across. As he started for the further side, his eye was caught by a slight movement in the trees to his left. He stepped back into the bushes and glanced across as two figures emerged from the low scrub.

'It's OK, Jack. You can come out. You've passed your first test.'

It was Terry Haynes. The girl was with him. They both had sporting shotguns broken over their arms and, over his shoulder on a sling, Terry carried an L96 – the new Accuracy International PM sniper rifle, fairly recently added to the standard armoury of 22 SAS.

Kelly grinned back at the cheery weasel face and smiled briefly at the girl, who showed no reaction to his achievement thus far. 'Reminded me of the old days,' he said. 'Does Bowring put all his employees through it?'

'He certainly does. He's not after knackered ex-heroes. Right. Now we've got to see if you can still shoot straight.' Terry hoisted the L96 off his shoulder. 'You've handled one of these?'

'Sure, but I'm more used to the old SSG69.'

'All right. We've got a high seat rigged up on the other side of the clearing, and targets across the valley at eight hundred metres. We'll have a go at those, then we'll wait until the light fades. Michelle needs some practice with the image intensifying and laser sights on closer targets.'

Kelly raised an eyebrow at Michelle. 'You can handle one of those?'

'We'll compare targets later, shall we?' she said.

Kelly dumped the bergen at his feet and said: 'Don't I get an R and R break?'

'Nope. The boss wants to see how you do straight after your walk. The targets are set up.'

'Isn't it a bit risky?'

'Not really. There's a man in the target area making sure there's no one around, and if anyone comes up here, we're after a bit of game. We've got another man at the top of the track too.'

'OK, let's go,' Kelly said, looking forward to proving himself, and warming to the competition provided by the girl. Up in the makeshift highseat, he found he had a clear line of vision across the tops of the pines on the south side of the clearing to a sheer cliff on the other side of the valley, half a mile away.

Through his 12×50 binoculars, Kelly found the targets, two life-sized cut-outs of a French film star, as seen in cinema foyers.

'Which is mine?' he called down to Haynes.

'The one to the east. You've got eight shots and thirty seconds.'

Kelly spread-eagled himself on the timber-plank platform and clicked the bipod down from the front of the stock. He checked that the magazine held eight 7.62mm rounds, then drew back the bolt and slotted one into the breech. With his eye to the telescopic sight, he steadied his breathing and waited for Haynes to start him from his stopwatch.

'Ready. Fire!'

3

Bowring got up from his wicker chair on the terrace. He was wearing a crisp, multicoloured cotton shirt and a fawn linen jacket. He looked as though he had done nothing more strenuous than play bridge all day as he held out a hand to Kelly.

'Congratulations.'

Kelly shook his hand and nodded with a grin.

'No sweat.'

'I wouldn't say that. I can smell you from here. Would you mind changing before we have dinner?' It was not a request. 'We'll talk details then. Terry will take you up to the annexe; there's a room for you there. Dinner will be served here at nine o'clock.'

'Right, boss.'

Kelly walked back into the *salon*.

Haynes was waiting there for him. 'OK? We'll go up in your vehicle.'

Evidently the 'annexe' wasn't adjacent to the villa. Neither man spoke until they were outside the house, walking across to the Range Rover.

'How far is it?' Kelly asked.

'Just up in the village – small house but comfortable.'

'Who else lives there?'

'It depends.'

They climbed into the Range Rover and Kelly started off down the drive.

'I'm usually there, when I'm not on a job,' Haynes went on. 'And anyone else who's over for briefing or training – or sometimes just having a rest. It's not a bad place to be hanging around, here. One thing, though: no pussy on the premises. OK? The boss is very strict about that. As far as the locals are concerned, we're a bunch of guys running a water-skiing school down by the Cap.'

'Anyone else up there now?'

'Yeah. A Jock called Andy Gallagher. Celtic supporter, know what I mean?'

'Ex-military?'

'Yeah. Para. Failed selection for the Regiment; too "self-assertive", they said.'

'Sounds dangerous.'

'He is, but he's got himself under control now. He's done three ops with us, and he's very useful.'

'What sort of ops?'

'I'll leave it up to the boss to tell you all that kind of thing, in case you don't agree to his terms.'

'He wouldn't be letting you take me up to this house if he thought I wasn't going to,' Kelly remarked.

Kelly drove back down to the villa an hour later. He had showered his aching body and clad himself in clean, white cotton trousers and a pale-blue, open-neck shirt. There was no sign now of the morning's wind and rain and the sun had gone down with its customary August orange blaze.

The annexe had turned out to be a stone town house, thoroughly restored and well planned, with four bedrooms and bathrooms. The ground floor was taken up by a large open space which served as kitchen, dining-room and drawing-room. The kitchen showed little sign of regular use, and the whole house had the air of a more than usually sophisticated barrack-room. The small basement had been converted into a fully equipped gymnasium.

Haynes had shown Kelly to a room on the top floor, with a fine view over the roofs of the village to the hills dropping away to the sea. Through the open windows he could hear the sounds of music and laughter drifting up from a small bar two doors down the narrow lane.

The insistent bass thump of soul music seeped beneath the door of the room beside his. When he was on his way down after changing, the door opened.

'Hello.' The delivery was curt, the accent unmistakably Glaswegian.

Kelly nodded a greeting and saw a muscular man, a little younger than himself, in faded shorts, a singlet and flip-flops. Dark hair curled above a tanned, even-featured face from which implausibly innocent blue eyes gazed out at him.

'You the fella who did a selection today?'

'Yeah. Jack Kelly.'

'Andy Gallagher. What did you think of it?'

'I could do with forty-eight hours' serious kip.'

'But you did all right. I checked you through the start and the grid refs. You did a good time. How did you get on with Bowring's ambush?'

Kelly laughed. 'I was lucky. One of them chucked himself down the hillside and smacked his head on a rock. I was just killing the other when the boss showed himself.'

'You were lucky. They're a hard pair those two. And Bowring gives them a bonus if they win. That's why you had no weapons.'

'Sure. I'd worked that out.'

Gallagher had been eyeing Kelly up and down as they spoke. He gave him one last, thoughtful look and said: 'I'll see you, then. We'll have a couple of bevvies.'

The Scot stepped back into his room and closed the door.

Kelly shrugged and carried on down the stairs. As he had assumed, there had been no sign of Michelle at the house. He thought of her as he drove down the hill. And he thought he'd better get any ideas about pursuing her out of his head pretty damn quick. If she was going to be a colleague, there wasn't going to be any room for tricky relationships. And any relationship with a woman who could score as high as she had with the L96 would have to be tricky.

At least, he thought with some satisfaction, he'd scored better than her with the laser sights in the dusk.

He reached the gates and activated them using a remote control which Haynes had given him. As he drove up towards the villa, he took a detailed look at it for the first time.

Below the main floor where the front door and principal rooms were, and beneath the terrace where Bowring had received him earlier, there was another level of rooms, presumably backing on to the cellar where he had been issued with his kit that morning. The front was some sixty feet long, with small cellar windows.

Above were the windows of the *salon*, and possibly another one or two rooms beyond it. The upper two storeys both occupied the same two and a half thousand or so square feet, with half a dozen windows on each front. There was space to accommodate a lot of people and offices. It was, he realized, a much larger building than he'd first thought. And, being where it was, it must have cost a few million. Whatever Bowring was doing, it was clearly making him plenty of money.

Even the gardens, secure behind high walls and other less obvious defences, were beautifully tended and looked like full-time work for at least a couple of men. Kelly was pleased that he was going to be a part of whatever organization funded it all.

He parked the Range Rover on the large gravel forecourt, where a Mercedes 500SL and a brand-new long-wheelbase Land Rover, both French-registered, were already standing.

Strong floodlights, fixed high up the walls of the villa, had been activated as he came up the drive. He was in no doubt that he was already being monitored on a concealed CCTV camera.

The front door opened before he reached the top of the steps. A man, a North African servant of some kind, held the door for him as he passed through.

'Major Bowring waits for you in his office,' the man said in guttural English. He led Kelly up the wide shallow stairs to a room above the *salon* and ushered him in.

Bowring was sitting behind a desk. 'Hello, Jack,' he said. 'Thank you, Omar.'

The servant left, closing the door behind him.

Kelly nodded. 'Major.'

'When we're out and about, we never make reference to any kind of rank or anything that might suggest a military relationship.' It was not a rebuke, but an order. 'Not even "boss".'

'Am I on the team, then?'

'Unless you want to go on providing close personal protection for ungrateful plutocrats.'

Kelly gave a grunt of laughter. 'I think I've had enough of that to be going on with.'

'Good. In which case, sit down and I'll tell you the terms of employment in our organization.' He waved Kelly to a chair opposite him. 'Initially there is a one-year contract, renewable by mutual agreement, which carries a retainer of £50,000, payable in Liechtenstein. For every job in which they participate, team members share ten per cent of the profits. You will be provided with a vehicle, or reimbursed for the use of your own. There will always be accommodation available here, in the village, or at our HQ in England. There are a number of house rules which will be issued to you by our general administrator, Madame Dubrulle.' He looked down at a file open in front of him. 'You aren't married, nor are you conducting any kind of long-term relationship.' He glanced up at Kelly. 'As far as your prospects in this organization are concerned, that's a plus. There are a number of other standing orders, nothing particularly surprising, which you will be required to obey – without exception.' He paused for a few seconds to allow Kelly to absorb the information.

Kelly smiled and nodded.

'Do I take that as your assent to our terms?' Bowring asked.

'I've got a couple of questions,' said Kelly.

Bowring invited them with a raising of his brow.

'What sort of jobs do we do?'

'That's a very broad question. I should tell you right away that we do take on the odd fairly routine sort of work, but only as one-offs, never on long-term contracts – we're far too expensive. Our clients are governments who either do not possess special forces with our particular skills, or who do not wish to involve their own armed forces for one reason or another; and multinational corporations who have to engage from time to time in special projects for which they aren't equipped.' Bowring swivelled his chair round to face the floor-to-ceiling shelves of books behind him. He pressed a button and the whole bookcase slid back and to one side behind its neighbour to reveal a backlit wall map, currently showing Kelly's route march that day. He picked up a control pad and clicked to bring up a geopolitical map of the world.

'In the last year,' he went on, 'we have worked here.' He pointed at a spot in the Amazon basin of Brazil. 'In Uganda, Western Australia, South Korea and here in Bosnia – as well as a lot of one-off escort work.'

Kelly could make intelligent guesses at the nature of the contracts carried out in each location. He nodded appreciatively. 'And what's on the cards now?'

'I'll tell you that once you're signed up.'

'Show me where to sign.'

Bowring allowed himself a quick smile. 'Good man. Here's your contract.' He stood up and walked round the desk, carrying a densely typed three-page document which he handed to Kelly.

The Liverpudlian took it and glanced through it,

picking out the salient points. The contract was between himself and Special Operations Services S.A., registered in Willemstad, Curaçao. 'Got a pen?'

'Don't you want to read it more thoroughly first?'

Kelly shook his head. 'I trust you. Anyway, there wouldn't be a lot of point in your stitching me up, would there?'

Bowring handed him a large black and gold Mont Blanc pen. When Kelly had signed and dated the contract, Bowring picked another from the file on his desk. 'Here's a copy for you, signed by me, so you can have a look at what you've committed yourself to when you have the time.' He held out his hand. 'Welcome to SOS.'

Kelly stood and shook Bowring's hand. 'Thanks,' he grinned.

'Right. We'll go down and join my other dinner guests,' Bowring said, gesturing towards the door.

There were five people already assembled in the *salon*, only one of whom Kelly had seen before.

'I'd like you to meet our newest recruit,' Bowring announced as they walked in. 'Sergeant Jack Kelly, ex-22 SAS, veteran of the Falklands, the Falls Road and Iraq.'

There was a general murmur of approval. Bowring introduced them one by one. 'This is Madame Dubrulle, who looks after money and home comforts, flights and travel arrangements.'

Madame Dubrulle was a short, elegant woman in her mid-fifties. She looked like everyone's favourite aunt and her dark eyes sparkled with perceptive humour.

Bowring then introduced Kelly to a man of a

similar age to Mme Dubrulle, dressed in traditional English summer clothes, much like Bowring. 'Major Lyke, ex-RAOC, who is in charge of supplies and logistics.'

Kelly was introduced to two other men, Michael Dowson, who was described as the London agent, and a Frenchman, Paul Lestienne, Paris agent.

'And Michelle de Lassy, of course, you've already met.'

Michelle smiled. 'Congratulations, Jack.'

The gathering split into two or three groups, and Kelly was left with Michelle.

'Is this the whole firm, then?' he asked.

'No. Besides Terry and Andy up in the village, there are three other permanent soldiers. They're currently on a job in El Salvador. Nothing very exciting. When Major Bowring needs more men, he recruits on a job-by-job basis, but he likes to have about six permanent, selected operatives as a core, so he can always guarantee a certain standard at short notice.'

'Are you a "permanent soldier"?'

'Yes. The major likes to have a good mix of skills. He wanted you for your intelligence-gathering experience and your languages.'

'I've only really got Arabic, and a bit of rough French.'

'And that's always useful. Besides, we needed a replacement.'

Kelly wondered if this was as a result of a resignation, dismissal or death. Before he could ask, they were joined by Major Lyke.

'Welcome aboard, Jack.'

'Thanks, Major.'

'Call me Bob. You're not in the British Army now.'

'I can tell that by the lifestyle,' Kelly laughed, as a maid who had come in and circulated among the guests handed him a glass of champagne.

'There are downsides to that as well, though,' Lyke remarked, without wistfulness. 'Risking your life, not for Queen and Country, just for the money. Still, there it is. It's a dirty job, but someone's got to do it.'

'And what is the next job?' Kelly asked.

'That's what we're all here for. Piers Bowring doesn't give dinner parties out of any sense of social duty. So I suggest you don't drink too much. The briefing comes after.'

Dinner was served in a large, classically French dining-room which, like the *salon*, looked out towards the sea.

Kelly was placed between Mme Dubrulle and Michael Dowson. The conversation was generally not 'shop', as if it were tacitly accepted there would be more of that later.

Madame Dubrulle, who asked Kelly to call her Colette, wanted to know all about him: his childhood, his marriage, life in Herefordshire, his recent job looking after little Béatrice Skiapoulos, who was regularly featured as a poor little rich girl in the French gossip magazines.

Dowson was less talkative. Kelly discovered very little about him or his background. In his late thirties, on the face of it he was a typical ex-public school stockbroker type, except that he seemed exceptionally well informed on current world affairs. But he was friendly enough and treated Kelly as a colleague and equal. It appeared that he was well acquainted with his service record and was prepared to grant him the credit he deserved.

After dinner, towards midnight, the party moved upstairs to Bowring's office on the first floor. There were enough seats to accommodate them all, while Bowring stood behind his desk and clicked the map back into view. In his hand he held, from habit, his old cavalry whip as a pointer.

'Right, ladies and gentlemen, Operation Parson's Nose.'

Kelly smiled, but the others showed no sign of mirth. Evidently it was Bowring's wont to give his contracts silly names.

'Our client is the Vatican State. We are instructed by the second in command to Archbishop O'Keane, who is responsible for security. As you may know, the Vatican has one of the best intelligence services in the world – a result, no doubt, of skills learned in the confessional. With a few hundred million pairs of ears listening on their behalf, there isn't much they don't get to hear about sooner or later. Through their legation in Damascus, they have received the information that a group calling itself Sufuf Allah is preparing an attack on the Pope some time within the next four weeks.'

Bowring pointed at his map. 'His Holiness's itinerary takes him to India for three days at the end of this month, and then he starts his six-day tour of the UK, or, I should say, England, Scotland and Wales; kissing the ground of Ulster was considered too risky. Though they have as yet no information to confirm it, the Vatican officials feel that the attack will be made on one of these two tours.'

'Why not at the Vatican itself?' Bob Lyke asked.

'Security there is surprisingly sophisticated, particularly after the last assassination attempt. Don't forget, they have a force of four hundred Swiss Guards to draw on. In any event, phase one of our job is to try to make direct contact with their informant, establish if he is in it out of idealism, or for the money, and see if he can put us anywhere nearer Sufuf Allah.'

'What do we know about these Sufuf Allah?' Paul Lestienne asked.

'Not a lot. I'd never heard of them before. I suspect it's a very small organization, and probably too militant for most of the mainstream groups to have much truck with. If they are seriously planning the Pope's assassination, it will be an opening propaganda gambit, to establish their credentials and pull in more like-minded recruits.'

'Where are they based?'

'We assume in Lebanon, but it could just as well be Iraq or Jordan. Anyway, they could be drawing from Islamic extremist groups from several countries.'

'Do we assume,' Lestienne asked, 'that this imminent attack has some bearing on the Vatican exchanging ambassadors with Israel?'

'Of course.'

'Then is it not likely that there would be a strong Palestinian element to any group wishing to show their objection?'

'Not necessarily. The destruction of the State of Israel is a tenet vigorously held by a diverse number of Islamic groups. Naturally, there may be a Palestinian factor.'

He paused, aware of the scantiness of information. 'Once we've established where they're coming from, our brief is straightforward enough: to destroy the task force, as close to the projected attempt as possible, so they don't have time to regroup and send in others and so not waste whatever logistical arrangements they've made.'

Bowring put down his whip and leaned forward with both his hands flat on the table. He looked at each of them in turn.

Christ, Kelly thought, it's a terrible brief, and he knows it. Three weeks to track down and take out an unknown number of Muslim loonies planning to kill a man who would be publicly exposed to hundreds of thousands of people at a time.

No one spoke for several seconds, then Lyke asked: 'What's the money like?'

One side of Bowring's mouth twitched. 'That's the good bit. Top rate daily fee and all exes, and a million-dollar performance bonus.'

'I'm not surprised,' Lyke murmured.

Bowring turned to Dowson. 'You brought this job in, Michael. Is there anything you can add to what I've said?'

Dowson leant back in his chair. 'When I first met our contact in Rome, he did surmise that the original lead might have come from a source in Amman.' Dowson shrugged his neatly clad shoulders. 'But if he didn't tell you, I guess it was fairly conjectural.'

'He did. That will be our starting-point.' He glanced at Kelly. 'Jack and I will be leaving for Jordan, via Rome, tomorrow evening, Colette.'

Madame Dubrulle nodded and made a note on a pad on her knees.

Kelly felt a flush of elation that he was going into action so soon.

'Bob, you and Michael can go over all the details of the Pope's two tours and identify likely sites for a hit,' Bowring continued. 'In case it's planned for the UK, we'll have to top up the armoury at Summerfold – two full complements of weapons and ammunition for four men. Use the boat into a small east coast marina.'

Major Lyke nodded. 'Who will you want on the job?'

'Jack here, Andy, Terry for communications, and Michelle. If we have to, we can pull Mick Young back from San Salvador. It depends on the size of unit we're up against.'

'And will you be active?'

Bowring nodded. 'I will be on this one. It could get complicated.'

Kelly woke from a deep sleep to a standard Côte d'Azur summer morning.

Haynes was brewing coffee when he went downstairs. There was a bag of fresh croissants on the table. 'Morning, mate. Feeling better?' said the Londoner.

'Fucking stiff. I'm going for a run to loosen up.'

'You're expected up at the villa in just over an hour, so make it quick. I'll leave a few of these for you if you like.' Haynes nodded at the bag on the table.

'Thanks.'

Kelly set off at a comfortable lope through the lanes of the village and down the switchback road towards the coast. Half an hour and seven miles later, he was back in the kitchen with a bowl of coffee in front of him.

At the villa, he was shown down some back stairs, not behind the hall panelling this time, leading to the rooms below. There he found Madame Dubrulle and Bob Lyke, each in an office reflecting their own personal tastes; hers full of flowers, his lined with regimental photographs and paintings of recent engagements by units of the British Army.

Colette Dubrulle showed him round a further office housing two secretaries and an advanced communications room. 'This is Terry's domain, though Bob can operate most of it,' she said.

There was an air of quiet efficiency about the place. From the charts and maps on the walls, it was obvious that there was a lot more going on than Bowring had revealed.

'How come there are so many of you involved in administration here?' Kelly asked, wondering if he'd get an honest answer.

Colette gave him a smile. 'Major Bowring didn't have time last night to tell you much about the background to our organization. He asked me to explain. Come into my office. I'll get some coffee.'

They went back to the bright, Provençal furnishings of her room, where she sat Kelly in a wicker armchair.

'This villa and these offices belong to Achilles International Couriers S.A. We operate one of the largest courier services in this part of the Mediterranean. It is a successful and very profitable business in its own right. It is also a very effective cover for the operation of SOS. As far as the French authorities are concerned, Major Bowring has no connection with it. Bob Lyke and Ferdinand Gatti, who is a lawyer from Monaco, are the directors. We also own a small boat-hire and water-skiing company called Hydra-Jet, down at Beausoleil. As far as the locals are concerned, that's who you work for. You should put in an appearance there now and again, and if no one's using the boats, you can.'

'Quite a set-up, then,' Kelly said.

'There are a few other activities as well, but not important for you. Of course, the existence of SOS must be kept secret. If you've read your contract, you'll have seen that.'

Colette also gave Kelly a letter of agreement between himself and the boat-hire company, purporting to make use of his services as an instructor; a folder containing information about Achilles Couriers; and a set of house rules. 'Make sure you read them,' she said. 'Major Bowring won't take any deviation from them. It's all in your contract.'

Kelly felt inclined to resent this degree of regulation, but on the other hand, he was used to it from his army days, and it was a small price to pay for the chance of some real action again.

'Now,' the Frenchwoman went on. 'We need a set of photographs for IDs and passports and we must get a letter to your previous employers tendering your resignation. I have a certificate here that says your ankle is badly damaged and you will be unable to undertake any physical duties for at least six weeks. You shouldn't have a problem, but let me have your old contract and I will sort it out.'

Kelly didn't see Bowring again until that evening on the flight from Nice to Rome. They sat at opposite ends of the plane and didn't communicate or acknowledge each other. It was only when they had booked into separate hotels in Rome and Kelly was in his room that he got a call from Bowring.

'I'll be over in twenty minutes. Take a walk round the block to make sure you haven't been followed.'

Kelly was accustomed, from his years in the SAS, to the notion of maximum intelligence gathering – leaving as little as possible to even the slimmest chance. That anyone might have shadowed him from the town house in Roquebrune to the airport, and then arranged to have him trailed from Leonardo da Vinci to his hotel in Rome was very unlikely indeed. But it was possible, and it he could be absolutely certain one way or the other by going out to see if he picked up a tail.

Through the narrow streets behind the Corso Vittorio Emanuele II, he set off at a fast walk on a circuitous journey, but always heading in approximately the same direction to give plausibility to his route. He entered a quiet residential street with one or two shops and walked a hundred yards until he reached an antique shop. He glanced in the window, apparently spotted something that took his eye and went in.

Inside, waving away the attentions of the proprietor, he held up an unframed print of the Colosseum as if to study it. But he kept his eyes fixed on the window, through which he had a clear view of the street, checking every man and woman that passed on either side of the road. He took a mental photograph of each of them, identifying a particular characteristic in each that would help his memory.

After a minute, Kelly apologized with a polite shrug for the fact that the print wasn't quite what he wanted, thanked the proprietor and left. He repeated the process in a picture gallery three streets and four turns further on.

He recognized none of the passers-by from his first stop, but went through the same mental photography. He had reached a large, open *piazza* now. He gave himself an excuse to run by stepping in front of a tide of unforgiving traffic as the lights turned green.

Kelly sprinted, as if for his life, across the square and into a small street on the other side. Near the corner, he bumped into an old woman coming in the other direction, which gave him the chance to take a quick glance over his shoulder. No one else had followed his suicidal dash. He carried on, hoping that he would be able to double back on himself, and before long he found a small alley, opening to the left. Relieved to see that it was open-ended, he ducked into it. He walked very quickly to the far end, turned left again, and arrived back on the corner of the square he'd just crossed. He saw no one he recognized from his two stops at the galleries.

He went into a bar, ordered and downed a small espresso, then set off back towards the hotel, satisfied that no one was following him.

Bowring arrived soon afterwards with a woman.

'The Contessa di Francisci looks after our interests in Italy,' Bowring said without preamble. 'Anna-Teresa, this is Jack Kelly.'

Kelly shook hands with the woman.

'It's a pleasure to meet you,' she said with a slight American accent. She looked, Kelly thought, more like the editor of a fashion magazine than an agent for a bunch of mercenaries.

She turned to Bowring. 'Monsignor di Montefalco will see you tomorrow morning. I have also had lunch today with a friend of mine in the Vatican press office. He was surprisingly indiscreet.'

'I'm sure it came as no surprise to you,' Bowring said.

She smiled. 'I was able to learn a little about the monsignor's boss, Archbishop O'Keane, as you asked. The Archbishop comes from Chicago, where the Church is having a hard time from women's groups over female ordination. He feels that His Holiness takes too firm a line on the question. Besides they already have big problems there trying to sell the official line on contraception.'

Bowring was looking at her thoughtfully. 'You feel this has some relevance?'

The Contessa lifted a narrow shoulder. 'It could have.'

'What about our friend Montefalco?'

'He has a reputation for being very orthodox.'

'You don't surprise me. What's his background?'

'Rather a grand family, though impoverished. He was an outstanding student at the University of Florence; he read theology and history. There is no scandal about him, but he is not well liked.'

'Not really one of the boys, eh?' Bowring gave a short laugh. 'He found it hard to approve of me, yet, realistically, he knew he had to. I don't know much about the inner workings of the Catholic Church, but I suppose, like any successful organization, pragmatism gets the better of ideology. You're a Catholic, aren't you, Jack? What do you think?'

'I'm afraid pragmatism came out on top a long time ago,' Kelly said quickly. 'I've seen what lack of birth control can do to a family. But I'm not too up-to-date on it all now.'

'Really,' the Contessa said, 'for practical purposes, you're dealing with a political body here, rather than a religious organization.'

Bowring nodded. 'That's the impression I have already. What is important to us – I mean to our own personal safety – is just how discreet these people are.'

'Very. Knowledge of SOS or yourself will be restricted almost certainly to the few people who are closest to it now. I'm certain that Monsignor di Montefalco was telling you the truth when he said that His Holiness doesn't know about this plot, and they'll want to keep it that way. As few people as possible will be told, if any more than know already. It's possible, I suppose, that something might leak back from the legation in Damascus.' She shrugged. 'I don't know anything about Rappacioli, the nuncio there, but I doubt it. A man in that posting would be a diplomat above all else.'

Bowring was silent for a moment.

'OK, Anna-Teresa. Thanks. Keep your ears open and report back to Bob Lyke, We'll be leaving for Amman as soon as we've seen Montefalco tomorrow. Now, I propose dinner somewhere civilized but discreet.'

Kelly walked back from the small restaurant in the Via Sicilia. The Contessa was dropping Bowring back at his hotel in her car. Kelly wondered if it was more than a purely professional liaison, but decided it wasn't. Certainly, Bowring seemed very relaxed, almost intimate in his dealings with her, but then, such was his own self-assurance, he could adopt such an attitude at will if he thought it would serve his purpose.

Kelly had seen him do it, with senior police officers in Northern Ireland and his superiors in the Falklands. Bowring, he knew, was well versed in the petty political skirmishes that surrounded battlefield decision-making.

But Kelly was not prepared for his boss's appearance when he arrived at his hotel next morning. He didn't even recognize the bearded cleric until he spoke.

'I'm Father Babbington now,' Bowring announced, without a hint of humour, 'until further notice and as long as I'm in this outfit. I've seen Montefalco. He's organized all the documentation I need. Anna-Teresa will be round shortly with your ticket, ID and hotel details in Amman. You are there as a representative of a small British firm dealing in second-hand agricultural vehicles. Register with the Embassy as soon as you arrive and I'll have made various other arrangements for you. In principle, if possible you and I shouldn't make direct contact in Jordan. But I'll get instructions to you tonight. Best of luck, and keep your head down.'

4

The heat blasted off the runways of Amman's international airport, making them shimmer. Kelly stepped out of an ALIA aircraft and sniffed the dry wind blowing off the great Saudi desert and his nose twitched at the familiar smells. Bowring was already easing himself fastidiously on to an airport bus.

As well as documents identifying him as Father Henry Babbington, an English Catholic priest and a temporarily accredited member of the Vatican diplomatic service, Bowring was carrying in his shoulder bag two Browning 9mm handguns and fifty parabellum rounds which he had arranged to pass on to Kelly at the Intercontinental Hotel that evening.

He received a few stares but passed without trouble through the terminal building. The sight of a European in a clerical collar was not common in the streets or indeed the diplomatic receptions of Jordan, where barely five per cent of the population were Christian. But Bowring intended to be noticed, and expected questions to be asked.

He had arranged to stay at the residence of the British Defence Attaché, rather than the Papal legation. It hadn't been hard to organize; he had been in the same regiment as the man currently occupying the post. 'Why, may I ask, are you posing as a Catholic priest?' Bowring's host enquired. They were walking together in the privacy of the lush gardens of the Ambassador's residence before the small monthly reception for visiting British businessmen which was taking place that evening.

Bowring was unconvinced by Colonel Giles Wilkinson's display of bluff bone-headedness. At the same time, he was aware that he was seriously compromising his friend. He guessed Wilkinson had agreed to have him purely out of curiosity, and the possibility that there might be an intelligence quid pro quo.

'I'm following up some information for my clients.'

'I'm not sure that I should be harbouring a freelance spy, particularly one disguised like you.'

'Why not? I dare say you have plenty of so-called "friends" from MI6 in the embassy.'

'Look, Piers, unless you can tell me something about your current contract, I can't be much help. And if you want your cover left intact, you'll have to make sure you keep out of trouble.'

'Frankly, Giles, there's not a lot to tell. I'm gambling on the probability that the presence of a visiting Vatican diplomat in town will flush out an informant. It's a long shot, but of course, if I get anything of value to HMG, I'll pass it on.'

'Of course,' Colonel Wilkinson said drily. He, and his superiors, though in principle disapproving of all freelances, had too much respect for Bowring's reputation to dissuade or impede him – at least, until he had had a chance to discover something worthwhile. The Vatican wouldn't have called him in without a strong lead and, by the same token, a potentially dangerous one.

In a way that was almost uniquely British, the two men, by tacit agreement, dropped the topic and began to swap information about mutual friends.

As they talked, Bowring considered his own plans.

It made sense to him that the information which had reached the ears of Rappacioli, the nuncio in Damascus, should have filtered up from Amman. Despite the British-educated monarch's aversion to the more outspoken representatives of Islam, and his generally benign approach to the West, angry Muslims were relatively safe going about their business in the Jordanian capital, where Palestinian refugee camps had created an unmonitorable population of itinerants.

It was also logical that information of interest to the Christian community should have been passed up the line into Syria, with its substantially larger Christian population, there to reach one of the most important Papal legations in the Middle East.

Whether the informant's motive had been financial or ideological, there was a more than reasonable chance that the presence of a visiting Vatican diplomat would flush him, or her, out.

Kelly pushed one of the Brownings into his shoulder holster and pulled on a loose linen jacket. He had picked up the package containing the handguns and ammunition from the lavatories of the main lobby of the Intercontinental, from the cubicle just vacated by the sober-looking, bearded priest. Before that he had spent an hour reading what scanty information he had been supplied with on the state of the Jordanian market for tractors and combines, enough at least to get him out of trouble if he found himself in a corner.

In the two days he had worked for Bowring's organization, Kelly had been impressed by the efficiency and thoroughness with which such things as alternative identities and travel arrangements had been made. A complete set of documents and passport had simply been handed to him with his ticket an hour before he set off for Nice airport.

He had hired a car as instructed. His brief was to attend the reception that evening at the Ambassador's residence to establish his temporary credentials.

The following morning, he was to be ready at eight to tail Bowring from the Defence Attaché's house to wherever he might happen to go. He was only to make his presence felt in circumstances of extreme danger, either to Bowring or to any informant who might appear. Otherwise, his was a watching brief.

A hundred yards from the gates of the Defence Attaché's residence, Kelly waited in his hired Toyota, with the blinds down, the Browning in his holster, and a pair of binoculars and a Pentax with a compact 600mm telephoto lens on the seat beside him. He had to wait over an hour before he saw Bowring climb into a taxi and head for the centre of town.

Amman, built on rolling hills to the east of the Ajlun Mountains, had largely, and hurriedly, been constructed since the country had gained independence from the British Mandate in 1949. A thousand dusty alleys gave off wide, European-style two-lane thoroughfares. Bridges crossed the dry, litter-filled courses of the Wadi Amman and its tributaries. The city's population of a million or so was largely influenced by sporadic influxes of Palestinian Arabs, particularly after the Arab-Israeli War of 1967 and their expulsion from Lebanon. But the Palestinians, like their Israeli cousins, are an industrious tribe, and despite its natural shortcomings as a centre for industry and trade, and the lack of resources of the nation as a whole, Amman bustled with commercial activity, especially since the destruction of Beirut.

Kelly had to dodge buses, trucks, ramshackle cars, donkeys pulling carts and unwary, black-clad women to keep up with Bowring's taxi. But he stuck with it and after fifteen minutes it pulled up outside the Hotel Philadelphia, an uninspired sixties construction on the edge of the old quarter.

Bowring climbed out of the taxi and walked into the hotel. The driver stayed where he was, evidently instructed to wait. Kelly found a gap to park his car from where he could see the entrance to the hotel, pulled down all but one of the blinds and waited.

Systematically, he checked every man, woman and child he could see within the vicinity of the hotel. He made a note of the trickle of people entering and leaving it. Relying on his own judgement, he photographed all those he thought might have dealings with Bowring, or be interested in those dealings.

Bowring walked into the hotel's gloomy, lacklustre café, sat on a bentwood chair at a small table and ordered a coffee from a sleepy waiter.

Having cast his bait in the water so recently, he was almost suspicious that he had had a bite so soon. But the taxi had turned up without warning at the Defence Attaché's house, its driver announcing that he had come to take Father Babbington to his meeting. News of his presence could have been relayed by any of the Ambassador's Arab staff, who would have noted his presence at the reception the evening before. The success of this stage of the operation and, for that matter, his own personal safety, depended on which side had received the news.

Although he'd known that Kelly wouldn't be far behind him, he himself was unarmed. That he had been deposited at this seedy hotel gave Bowring considerable relief; it was unlikely that anyone had brought him here to kill him.

The waiter returned without his coffee.

'Come,' he said, beckoning Bowring to follow him.

With some misgivings, Bowring let himself be led from the room, across a small hallway and up a narrow flight of service stairs. They passed along a dingy first-floor corridor until they reached a door guarded by two young, slouching Palestinians who each placed a hand inside their denim jean jackets with a deliberateness that conveyed an obvious message. Bowring showed no reaction to them as the waiter opened a door to a small, plain bedroom at the back of the building. He walked in.

Sitting on the bed was a large, prosperous-looking Arab in a well-pressed linen suit. He was stout, respectable, with an air of benign cosmopolitanism. Bowring judged he was a businessman, rather than a politician, of about fifty.

The man climbed laboriously to his feet.

'Father Babbington?'

Bowring nodded.

'*Salaam a leykum.*'

'*A leykum, salaam.*' Bowring returned his small bow.

'I am Said Shalawi. I understand that you are on a mission from the Vatican State?' He spoke good

English but in the manner of someone who has learnt the language from out-of-date textbooks.

'That's correct.'

'I had been expecting someone to come. I was responsible for certain information reaching Damascus. Do you know what I am talking about?'

Bowring nodded. 'We are engaged in the same matter.'

'Good. As I thought. I can tell you nothing here, you understand. It was risky even for me to come here, but it is my cousin's place, so I can enter unseen. You may have been watched, but that was a necessary risk. I have certain documents which I can give to you elsewhere.'

'Where are they now?'

'In my office in Beirut. If you will meet me in Paris next week, I will take them there and show you them. It is also possible that I may have more information by then.'

'Are you selling this information?'

'I will tell you why I want you to hear it. It is in the best interests of the whole business community, here and in Lebanon, that there should be peace between Arabs and Israelis. If the problems with the West Bank settlers can be resolved, and the people of Palestine allowed to resume their lives in the place of their birth, it will bring untold benefits to the prosperity of the whole region. I myself have done a considerable amount of business with Tel Aviv,' he added with some smugness. 'However, an international incident of the type which is being planned will harden the resolve of the entrenched right-wing Israelis and convince the waiverers that the Arab world is still committed to their destruction. My greatest wish is to see the current peace process brought to a happy conclusion.'

Bowring searched the man's earnest eyes for signs of altruism. He came to the conclusion that he was dealing with a man whose commercial interests happened to coincide with the aims of the peacemakers. It was a sound, reliable enough motive.

'Good,' said Bowring. 'I am instructed by my superiors that we will naturally meet any expenses you may incur in relaying this information to us.'

Shalawi nodded. He wasn't averse to any bonuses that might be on offer. 'That is generous. One of my associates has a house near Paris. I will be there next week. I will be able to give you the information then. I cannot here – there are too many eyes watching, too many people ready to torture and to kill to guard their secrets. I will leave details of place and date for you at the Hôtel Griffon in St Germain. Do not go yourself. Send a messenger, who must ask for a letter to M. Lorin about the Nicosia Project. Now you must go. *Inshallah*, your visit to this place has not been noted.'

Bowring and Shalawi bowed to each other again and Bowring let himself out of the room and went downstairs to the waiting taxi.

Kelly flicked up the blinds, dropped his camera on the passenger seat and started the car. He had photographed a dozen or so possible watchers. But he had seen no one go into the hotel after Bowring who looked like a candidate for their informant.

He pulled out behind the taxi and followed it, several cars back, until it drew up outside the Inter-continental. He pulled in and waited while Bowring got out and walked briskly inside. He was about to follow when he spotted a man get out of a Subaru pick-up which had arrived behind Bowring's taxi.

His guts tightened with an adrenalin rush; it was one of the men he had photographed outside the Hotel Philadelphia. Slim, dark-skinned, denim-clad, the man was maybe in his twenties. He walked confidently into the hotel lobby.

Unhurriedly, Kelly slung his camera over his shoulder, got out of his car and sauntered into the hotel. The young Arab was talking earnestly to one of the uniformed hotel porters. Kelly allowed his leisurely passage towards the cigarette kiosk to take him close to them. Without obviously dawdling, he heard the porter insisting that he hadn't seen the English priest before. The other, in a harsher Palestinian accent, pressed him. Kelly was unable to hear any reply. But it seemed that the porter, not surprisingly, was entirely ignorant about Bowring's, or Father Babbington's, identity.

As he bought a packet of cigarettes, Kelly's eyes swept the lobby for a sign of Bowring. There was none. He bought the *Daily Telegraph* and walked across to lower himself into one of a group of club chairs scattered about the marble floor of the huge foyer. He opened his paper and lifted it no higher than would allow his eyes to continue scanning the hall.

He watched the slim, blue figure of Bowring's pursuer walk swiftly over to the hall porters' desk, where he was met with an angry shaking of heads. The man dithered for a moment then, making up his mind, headed for the main doors once again. Kelly waited until he was through them before he stirred himself.

A minute later he was quietly easing the Toyota out on to the road with four cars between him and his quarry's Subaru pick-up. He guessed the Palestinian had thought that a Vatican envoy in town might spell trouble, though any connection with their own plans was only a remote possibility. It was certainly possible, Kelly reckoned, that this group, these Sufuf Allah, had a source of general information within the British Embassy.

It seemed unlikely that a two-handed team had been on to Bowring, or that he himself had been identified as having any connection with Father Babbington. But he kept a close look in his mirror until he was convinced that he had no tail on him. The Subaru had by this time recrossed the seething centre of Amman and was on the main road south towards Jerusalem.

After a few miles they were approaching a sprawling refugee shanty town when, as Kelly had feared, the pick-up turned off and dived down among the makeshift streets. As a European, he couldn't follow there without arousing suspicion, for it was scarcely a recognized tourist destination.

He drove on for a mile or so, turned and drove back past the refugee camp. With a sense of anticlimax and disappointment, he allowed some of the tension to drain from his system. It came as a slight shock to him to discover just how turned on he had been by the thought that he might, after a long lay-off, have had a chance to deploy a weapon in anger.

In fact, what he had achieved was a lot more useful than disposing of Bowring's tail; he had a photo in the can of someone very likely connected with, if not actually a member of, Sufuf Allah.

He drove back to the Intercontinental with the

aim of getting in contact with Bowring through the Embassy. But Bowring had pre-empted him. There was a curt note waiting for him: 'Your return flight booked for tomorrow. Collect details from commercial section at embassy.'

Bowring, beardless and looking his usual elegant self in a creaseless lightweight suit, was waiting for Kelly at Charles de Gaulle. He had a hired Citroën in the car park. Ten minutes after clearing customs, Kelly was sitting beside his boss on the autoroute back into Paris.

'When did you stop being Father Babbington?' he asked.

'When I arrived here last night.'

'Why did you leave so fast?'

'I'd got all I was going to get in Amman, and I dare say you noticed I was followed back to your hotel.'

'I did. I'd already got a shot of him. When he lost you in the hotel, I followed him back to a refugee camp on the Jerusalem road. But there was no way I could go in there.'

'Quite right. That's very good news, that you got a photo.'

'What did you get in the Hotel Philadelphia?'

'My clerical persona worked like a mayfly on a hungry trout,' Bowring said with a trace of self-satisfaction. 'I was taken there on the instructions of a man, a Palestinian of pragmatic outlook by the name of Said Shalawi.'

'What's his brief, then?' Kelly asked.

'Frankly, I'm not sure of his motives. It's probably fair to say that he's a natural dove, but I suspect he's just beginning to get deals together between Beirut and Tel Aviv and he doesn't want to see them blown out of the water before they're launched.'

'What did he tell you?'

'Nothing,' Bowring said. 'But he'll be here next week, with some kind of documentary back-up to his information.'

'Does he want paying for it?'

'Yes, though, as I say, I think that is a secondary motive. Of course, it's possible he represents broader interests in Beirut. After all, now that the place is being rebuilt again and business is starting to flow back, no one wants to risk a return to the mayhem of the eighties. He was prepared to tell me very little, and I suspect he gave me a false name; he felt there was some possibility that if it were known I'd been in contact with him, someone might try to extract anything he'd given me.' Bowring cleared his throat. 'That's why I saw no point in hanging around.'

'Do you think you were checked out of the airport?'

'Impossible to say. I doubt it, though, and anyway, if they start looking, they'll find that Father Babbington has disappeared up his own cassock.'

Kelly laughed. 'And they'll never make the connection between him and you. I didn't know you had the talent.'

'It's one I've developed since my days in the Regiment. I once tested it at a family funeral. There were a couple of dozen people who knew me there, but not one recognized me. It's been rather useful from time to time, in an intelligence-gathering capacity.'

'Anyway,' Kelly said. 'What's the form now?'

'Instructions will be left for us at a place called the Hôtel Griffon. Shalawi is coming to Paris next week, but he didn't say when precisely. In the meantime, I want you to check it out, for any comings and goings. We mustn't overlook the fact that Shalawi could be a red herring.'

'You'd better turn back into Father Babbington, when you see him, just in case.'

'Naturally. In the meantime, we're both staying at Paul Lestienne's in suburban splendour in Maisons-Laffitte. As a matter of fact, as I recall you have a taste for that sort of thing, I can tell you there's a small race meeting there this evening. First race is at five-thirty. You could just make it if I start driving like a native.'

Since he had been working in France, Kelly had made a habit of following the form of French horses. He had been a regular visitor to the *hippodrome* in Cagnes-sur-Mer. It had given him the slightest touch of homesickness to see some of the British-trained horses and their entourages trying to score some prize money and early-season experience in February.

He went to the races that evening and made the most of it for an hour or two, though he had the feeling Bowring was giving him the chance to relax a bit before the real action started. He came away with a good profit and arrived back at Lestienne's small mansion in the woods feeling ready for anything.

Lestienne introduced his wife and suggested that they go out for dinner. Bowring would join them later. Anxious to find out more about Special Operations Services S.A., Kelly agreed. However, it was soon clear that either Lestienne didn't discuss his business in public places, or his wife had no idea what sort of business he was in. He asked Kelly a little about his experiences in the Falklands, discussed the political situation in Northern Ireland with a surprising amount of knowledge and insight, and led the discussion on to international politics in general.

When Bowring joined them, much later than expected and making no excuses for it, the conversation still remained firmly aloof from the job in hand. But later, over large glasses of cognac and calvados, as the three men sat comfortably in Lestienne's spacious drawing-room, the matter of Shalawi was finally raised.

'When we have an address,' Bowring said to Lestienne, 'we'll need to have the place thoroughly staked out, even though we won't have a lot of time to organize it. Get Andy and Terry up from Roquebrune tomorrow, and find me three or four locals. You should be able to get some from Paul's Bar, but no dross, please, and for God's sake don't tell them SOS are involved.'

Lestienne nodded. Paul's Bar was an earthy drinking dive off the Place de la République, where ex- and jobless mercenaries and legionnaires gathered, to keep their ears open for any work that was going. 'There's a trio of ex-South African Recon Commandos just arrived. They came to see me last week. They looked useful but they have a pretty grand idea of their own value.'

'I'll have a look at them,' Bowring said. 'Fix it up.'

On the Monday of the following week, Kelly took a morning commuter train into Gare St Lazare. At that time of year, the train, like the whole of Paris, was half empty. Kelly, in open-neck shirt, light tweed jacket and thin beige cords looked comfortable, like a graphic artist or journalist just back from his holidays.

Once in Paris, he took the Métro to Rue du Bac, emerged into the Boulevard Raspail, and walked into the nearest *café-tabac*. He bought *Le Figaro* and a packet of Gitanes, sat down and ordered an espresso. He pulled a small map of Paris from his pocket and checked the location of the Hôtel Griffon. It was less than two hundred yards from where he was sitting, but in the next street off the main thoroughfare, not visible from the café. He finished his coffee, folded his paper under his arm and sauntered out into the street. A few minutes later he was walking with a purposeful stride along a narrow, car-lined street of private apartment houses, small antique shops and a bakery.

Fifty yards from the junction with Boulevard Raspail, he passed the Hôtel Griffon. It was one of those small Parisian hotels which the proprietors have never found it necessary to update, since they are cheap enough to generate no great expectations of luxury from their clientele. Kelly judged it might contain twenty or thirty rooms. He looked around for a suitable OP. There was no bar in the street but almost opposite the hotel was an antiquarian bookshop. That would have to do for an initial recce. After Kelly had browsed and leafed through twenty books over an hour or so, the bookseller was becoming restive. But during that time, Kelly had been able to gain some idea from the comings and goings of the clientele of the Hôtel Griffon.

In addition to various Europeans – businessmen,

tourists and students – a large proportion of the people he had seen entering and leaving the hotel were Arabs, Middle Eastern rather than North African, for the most part reasonably prosperous and conservatively dressed in western business suits. There were many reasons for Syrians and Lebanese to be visiting Paris, commercially and culturally, so there was nothing odd about a particular hotel having built up a connection, with regular visitors from those countries. In any case, it was possible that the place was owned and managed by Arabs. On the face of it, it was a perfectly plausible place for this contact of Bowring's to leave his instructions.

Aware that he had used up his browsing time, Kelly gratified the bookseller by buying an 1840 edition of Balzac's *Le Père Goriot*, and walked out of the shop clutching it with the smugness of a contented collector. He had at least created a precedent for a few more long visits there.

Later, Kelly met his boss among the anonymous, bustling tourists in the Deux Magots. They sat at the back of the cavernous café and ordered beers.

'What have we got?' Bowring asked.

'Looks OK. Lot of Arabs. Not Gulf – not rich enough – but businessmen, mostly. Didn't see anyone that worried me, but I only watched for an hour or so; had to buy this book. Can I get it back on exes?' He dropped the leatherbound book on the table in front of Bowring, who picked it up and flicked through it with interest.

'Sure. It's a good edition,' Bowring said, closing the book carefully. 'How do you want to go about it now?'

'I'll need a car for an OP. Fifty yards or so from the entrance, out of sight of any of the bedroom windows. That's the only real chance of keeping a long watch without moving into a building opposite.'

'We haven't got time for that. OK, get a car . . . no, a van. You'll just have to sit there until Andy and Terry arrive tonight, then you'll have to roster with them.'

Bowring saw the look of resignation on Kelly's face. 'There won't be too much of this. I'm paying you too much to waste you on passive surveillance. And, who knows, you might get a target out of it.'

'You think so?'

'No. I think Shalawi's genuine. But you know how it is.'

Kelly knew how it was. The survival of a unit depended on reducing risks to the minimum, and eliminating intelligence deficiencies. It was bloody boring, but the more you knew about your enemy when you went in, the more confidently and efficiently you fought them.

By Wednesday, after sharing eight-hour turns with Gallagher and Haynes, they had seen no one who aroused their professional suspicions, or matched Kelly's shot of the young Palestinian who had tailed Bowring in Amman.

Bowring reverted to the persona of Father Henry Babbington and dispatched one of the South Africans to the hotel to ask, as instructed, for the letter to M. Lorin about the Nicosia Project. The burly ex-soldier returned to the rendezvous at the Solférino Métro station with an envelope. Bowring opened it and read the few words on the single piece of paper inside.

'He's not taking chances. I'll be met in front of the Hôtel des Invalides one hour from when you collected this letter. Tell Andy I want you all there, singly, staked out, and Terry in the van in case I get taken.'

Terry Haynes sat in the anonymous Renault van which Kelly had hired to watch the Hôtel Griffon. He was parked illegally, ready to drive round the block of the esplanade in front of the Hôtel des Invalides if he was moved on. The team of six men that Bowring was currently using on the job also had a big Toyota Land Cruiser parked handily in one of the side-streets.

Kelly, Gallagher and the three South Africans ambled and loitered in the open public space, watching the bearded priest stride in front of the pink mausoleum towards the great iron gates. They had already seen the tall, portly figure walking more slowly, a little ahead of Bowring.

It had occurred to the watchers that this exposed meeting place might have been chosen because the Arab did not have total confidence in Father Babbington. It seemed likely that there were others surveying this scene with interest.

Bowring caught up with the Arab just as they reached the corner of Boulevard de la Tour Maubourg and Avenue de la Motte Picquet. A group of three dark young men walked round the corner towards them. Abruptly, they turned behind Bowring. As they turned, a black Mercedes 500 limousine drew up to the kerb, its rear near-side door opened on to the pavement and Bowring was instantly and inevitably propelled through it.

Within seconds, Shalawi and his three young henchmen had climbed in after him. The doors were slammed and the car took off at a sprint, south-west down La Motte Picquet towards the École Militaire.

Haynes in the Renault van was already moving before Bowring was in the car. He stopped momentarily to let Kelly jump in beside him.

'Christ!' he hissed. 'They did that fucking neat.'

'They wouldn't have if the boss had wanted to put up a fight,' Kelly said. 'He reckoned that might happen – even if his guy Shalawi's for real.' He picked up the radio in front of him. 'I wonder how long Andy and those gorillas will take getting back to the Toyota.'

Haynes's eyes were fixed on the back of the Mercedes as it raced ahead of them. 'Try him in a moment. I hope to God they can catch us up. I'll need them to leap-frog behind these guys. Thank God there's plenty of traffic now.'

Despite the urgency in his voice, Haynes's manner and his driving were calm and competent. He knew exactly what he was doing, but he also knew that to do the job properly, he would need his back-up soon.

Kelly picked up the radio in front of him and tried to raise the Toyota. The Mercedes was heading up to the Porte de Sèvres before he got any response.

'Andy? Do you read me?'

'Yeah, sure. Where are you?'

'Getting on to the Périphérique, heading east. The traffic looks as though it's moving bloody slow. You might do better to cut down to the Porte d'Orléans. It'd be handy if you could get in front of them.'

'Right,' Gallagher's Glaswegian vowels rasped over the airwaves. 'I'll tell you when we're there. Shouldn't take long; this guy Heynrik drives like an orang-utan with a frontal lobotomy and a death wish.'

He cut out. Kelly grinned.

'Was that a good idea, sending him ahead?' Haynes asked. 'These people might come off before then.'

'They might, but we can still tell Andy to double back. My guess is they're heading for one of the autoroutes.'

Terry gazed at the five lanes of fuming traffic in front of him, moving in close order at no more than twenty miles an hour. 'We won't have any trouble as long as it's like this.'

The radio crackled into life a few minutes later as they crossed the Porte de Châtillon. 'We're at the Porte d'Orléans' – Gallagher said it like 'New Orleans' – 'Which way?'

'East,' Kelly said quickly. 'But try and let him catch up with you.'

Whatever had been causing the hold-up appeared to have cleared and, as if with a sigh of relief, the traffic surged forward once again.

'Shit!' Kelly said, gazing at the Mercedes ahead of them. 'They're pulling off towards the A6. Andy'll be on the Périphérique.'

Haynes shrugged his shoulders and followed the Mercedes.

'Hey,' Kelly shouted with a laugh. 'It's OK. There's the Toyota, look, about ten cars ahead of the Merc.' He looked at the map on his lap. 'That's bloody lucky. They couldn't have got on to the Périphérique if they'd wanted to.' He grabbed the radio and opened the channel. 'Andy?'

'Yeah. You arsehole. We've got filtered down to the motorway out to Orly.'

'I know. That's fine. Stay there. I can see you. You're only fifty yards ahead of the quarry. Keep your speed up. I'll tell you when to let them pass. Over and out.'

The black limousine containing Bowring and presumably at least five others settled in the inner lane of the motorway, remotely sandwiched by the Toyota and the Renault. It cruised past the spur to the airport and stayed in the stream of traffic heading south down the A6, the Lyons autoroute.

'I wonder where these geezers are taking him,' Haynes muttered.

'Shalawi told Bowring some associate had a house near Paris – he didn't say exactly where. The guy had to be careful, I suppose. If he's shopping this bunch of Muslim nutcases, he'll want to be bloody careful how he does it.'

'Yeah, and he'll need to check that Bowring's kosher first.'

Kelly laughed. 'I don't think kosher's the word.' He stared at the car ahead of them and their own back-up beyond it. 'I wonder if we'll have any trouble.'

'Maybe. Those Yarpies'll be handy.'

If there was trouble – Bowring had briefed them – Gallagher would be in command.

We'll see about that, Kelly had thought. But for the time being, he kept the thought to himself.

5

'Andy! They're getting off the autoroute,' Kelly snapped over the radio. The Mercedes had slowed and was pulling over to the right-hand lane. As Kelly spoke, the Toyota plunged across the following traffic to reach the exit road six cars ahead of their quarry.

'It's OK, Jack. We got them,' Gallagher replied calmly.

'Yeah. I can see. It looks as though they're going to Fontainebleau. Once they're committed, let them pass you, then stay behind them. We'll divert and come back to you.'

'Roger.'

The Mercedes was going fast down the old road, through the village of Ponthierry. It wasn't difficult for the South African driving the Toyota to let them pass convincingly. Once he had, both cars carried straight on, ignoring the right-hand fork to Fontainebleau, which Haynes took instead. Kelly got on the radio again.

'We've taken the N7. There are plenty of ways we can get back to you in a mile or two and leap-frog again. Let me know where you are.'

Haynes carried on towards the town. They were now in the thick of the ancient forest of dense conifer, oak and beech, broken by regular, ten-metre fire-breaks.

Gallagher reported the position of the Mercedes every minute or so, until he announced gleefully: 'I think we're getting there. They've turned into a village called Bois-le-Roi.' Then: 'They've turned up a track into the forest, about a quarter of a mile from the edge of the village, on the road towards Samois. Have you got that?'

'Sure,' Kelly said, as coolly as he could. 'We'll meet you at the crossroads between the two in ten minutes.'

He gave Haynes concise directions as they skirted Fontainebleau and headed back into the forest.

The Toyota was stationary in a parking place just short of the crossroads. It was a large clearing by the side of the road, with a few picnic tables around the edges. There were half a dozen other vehicles there and a couple of families sitting at the tables.

As Haynes drove the Renault in, Kelly spotted Gallagher sitting alone at one of the tables, reading a paper and smoking a cigarette. He had left the South Africans in the vehicle.

'You'd better talk to him,' Haynes said.

Kelly nodded, got out of the Renault and ambled over to the Scot, sat down opposite him and took out a pack of Gitanes.

'Hello, mate,' he said conversationally. 'We'd better sort out what we're going to do.'

'I've already decided,' Gallagher said. 'We'll have to go in.'

'Hang on,' Kelly said. 'Not so fast. It's much more likely these people are genuine. If they weren't, they'd have taken Bowring out in Amman.'

'Not necessarily,' Gallagher growled. 'If they're Sufuf Allah and they've sussed there's been a leak, they'll want plenty of time to see what information they can extract. And as far as everyone else was concerned, Bowring was a Vatican envoy in Jordan. If he'd gone AWOL there, there'd have been a hell of a stink and they're not going to waste time with hostages. No one got enough from the last lot to make it worth while. Anyway, if we go in and they are genuine, no problem – we don't shoot.'

'That's too dangerous, Andy. Whoever they are, they'll assume we're hostile and shoot back. If they think we're on Bowring's side, they'll top him.'

'Listen, Kelly, if Shalawi isn't what he says he is, they'll kill Bowring anyway; that's why we should go in.'

'Look,' Kelly said, aware that he had to make some display of compromise. 'Whatever they are, Bowring's going to be alive for a few hours yet. Let's get to this place they've taken him and give it a full recce. We can make a better judgement then. For Christ's sake, Andy, there's no bloody point risking Bowring's life and ours for nothing.'

The Scot, though reluctant to admit it, knew Kelly had far more experience of hostage rescue than he had. He knew he must have spent hundreds, if not thousands, of hours developing his close-quarters battle skills in the 'Killing House' in Hereford. Besides, behind the verbal compromise, there was an uncompromising steeliness in the Liverpudlian's eyes.

'OK,' Gallagher said quietly, pulling two cigarettes from his packet and giving one to Kelly. 'We've got about four hours of daylight before we can go in anyway. We should be able to get some idea of their strength and set-up by then.'

With command of the operation now balanced

uneasily between them, Kelly and Gallagher made plans. Haynes was sent back into Fontainebleau to buy the largest-scale map of the area that he could. The best he could find was the IGN 1:50,000, which at least confirmed that there was a largish house with outbuildings, a quarter of a mile up the track where Gallagher had seen the Mercedes turn in. Between the road and the house, the track crossed a bridge over the branch railway line that ran to Fontainebleau and on down the Loing valley. Kelly had passed under this same line less than a mile back from the picnic area where they were now parked.

Kelly and Haynes took the Renault van – less noticeable than the Land Cruiser – up the lane towards Bois-le-Roi to see what they could from the road. The pine woods on either side were particularly dense and, according to the map, there were no other houses among them. The opening to the track – an ill-kept rubble drive – had no signs to announce the presence of the house at the end of it and looked little used. Haynes drove by slowly, while Kelly scrutinized every aspect of this approach to the house. Two hundred yards beyond the opening, within sight of the village, a van was parked beside a telegraph pole. At the top of the pole, an engineer in the overalls of the local telephone company was perched with the tools of his trade dangling from his belt.

Kelly tightened up. 'The overalls are right,' he said through clenched teeth, as if the man might be able to read his lips, 'but he's in a plain van.'

'Yeah, and he's some kind of darky.'

'There's plenty of Algerians work for the phone

company, but the van's definitely wrong. He's either on guard duty from the house, or someone else is staking out this place.'

'Shit!' Haynes hissed. 'That's going to make it tricky. What do you reckon?'

'Let's drive into the village and take the next road west of here. It runs about a quarter of a mile behind the back of the house.'

'Right,' Haynes nodded, taking orders from Kelly quite naturally. 'What was Andy's idea?' he asked as they wound through the narrow streets of the village.

'He wanted to go straight in, as if the boss was a hostage. I can see why he never made Selection at Hereford.'

'Yeah, he's a bit of a hot head, but he's a great scrapper.'

'I persuaded him we needed more info first, and darkness, to do the job properly. What we'll have to do now is an old-fashioned four-man patrol, though it's a bit of a bugger having to do it in a forest with Joe Public wandering about. If I'd known we were going to be doing this kind of thing, I'd have got a bit of training in.'

'The Yarpies'll know what they're doing,' Haynes pointed out.

Haynes had turned on to a main road that ran south to Fontainebleau. The forest on their left consisted of big old oaks and not much undergrowth, and Kelly peered between the tree trunks as the Renault followed an old van trundling sedately along. Looking at the map, he said: 'We must be behind the house about now; I can't see anyone, but there could be a hundred men in there for all I know.'

'There's another van parked up ahead,' Haynes said urgently.

Kelly swivelled his eyes forward. Besides the van was a small plastic screen of the type usually put round a hole in the road. 'I wonder what the hell they're pretending to do?'

'Electric,' Haynes said. 'Checking an underground cable.'

There were two men this time, both correctly clad, but again with a plain van.

'There could be half a dozen more in each of those vans,' Haynes said.

'Maybe,' Kelly nodded, 'but the problem's going to be finding out whose side they're on. If they're Shalawi's men keeping watch – and Shalawi is genuine – and we do them any damage, that could jeopardize the boss's chances.'

'Why?'

'They'll assume he's not what he says he is. They're not going to let him out alive then. Trouble is, if these other people are Sufuf Allah, and they're on to the fact that Shalawi's selling information about their plans, they'll take out everyone in the building if they can. From what the boss said, Shalawi's no soldier, and those lads who helped get him into the car didn't look up to much.' Kelly stared into the forest, not expecting to see a lot now. 'I'll have to check them out myself.'

Fifteen minutes later Kelly was jogging up the road towards the bogus electricians. He was wearing a pair of bright orange shorts, a St-Tropez T-shirt, flashy trainers and what appeared to be a Walkman. The two workmen they had seen were standing smoking at the back of the van. Kelly slowed to a walk, puffing hard, and grinned at the two dark-skinned, dark-eyed men. 'Have you guys got any water?' he asked in French with a strong southern accent to hide any hint of Englishness.

They looked back at him suspiciously. The elder of the two spoke in Arabic to his colleague. Despite the guttural Algerian accent, Kelly heard him say: 'It's all right. Give him some.'

The younger man walked round to the passenger door and came back with a bottle of Evian, which he handed to Kelly.

Kelly gulped eagerly at the water and gave it back gratefully, taking the chance as he lowered his head to glance through the back windows of the van. He couldn't see anyone else inside and the two Algerians hadn't made any noticeable effort to block the view. He wiped his mouth with the back of his hand, thanked them effusively, grinned again, and carried on at a slow jog along the edge of the road.

A mile further on, out of sight of the van, he stopped at an empty forester's lodge and walked a few yards into the dense woods behind it, listening for any human activity. Satisfied there was no one around, he unclipped the Walkman from his shorts and spoke quietly into it.

'Terry? Do you read me?'

'Sure,' the reply fuzzed through the headphones.

'Are you in Bois-le-Roi now?'

'Yeah.'

'I'll start running towards the village. Come out and pick me up. Have you found anywhere we can have a talk?'

'Yeah. There's a café in the square with a few tables outside. Andy and the others are sitting around having a beer like a bunch of tourists.'

'Fine. See you in a minute, then.'

The three South Africans, silent, surly men, didn't look like typical tourists but they didn't look out of place. They were dressed in jeans and T-shirts covered by light, loose anoraks. No one was taking any particular notice of them, for there were a lot of similarly clad, genuine walkers wandering through the village who had obviously spent the day tramping through the woods.

Kelly walked over to their table with a jovial greeting and some backslapping. He sat down on a spare chair and ordered a beer, then pulled the map from his pocket and spread it in front of him. As the waiter brought his drink, he described a fictional cross-country route he had just run.

When he judged they weren't going to be overheard by anyone, he said: 'OK. There's definitely a team in there. They're Algerians. Contract men, I'd say. I think it's very unlikely they're Shalawi's. I can't tell you how many there are. I've only seen three, but there could well be some already in the woods. They'll be waiting until it's dark, but like us they'll have wanted to do a recce first.' Kelly paused and looked at Gallagher. 'Do you want to hear what I think we should do?'

Gallagher shrugged. 'Sure. But this is a bloody stupid place to talk about it.'

'Six guys like us look a lot less conspicuous sitting around having a beer here than we would huddled in one of the cars out in the forest. If anyone comes near us, I'll change the subject. Try and look as though I'm telling you a dirty story.'

Haynes and the South Africans assumed inane expressions of amusement, while Gallagher put on a sulky grin.

Kelly laughed. 'OK,' he said quietly, leaning forward. 'We'll have to go in pairs – we can't risk a four-man patrol. We'll report back our progress to Terry, who'll stay here. Only take your nine-millies, and for God's sake, keep them out of sight. Don't use them unless someone's coming at you and you have to. If you come across anyone and they see you, you're just a walker – unless they start hostilities. It's very unlikely they will, because any shooting too early will bugger up whatever raid they've got planned.

'Basically, just don't get seen. You'll have to go as you are, though. You can't wander around in the daylight in OGs and camouflage. We'll approach the house from three start points.' He indicated them on the map. 'Andy and Hennie go down the side of the railway from the north, where the road crosses it just outside the village here. Jan and Willy start from the bridge on the lower road, near the picnic park. I'll go in alone from the forester's lodge there. Terry, you wait in the Toyota with the rest of the weapons. Jan and I will leave the van in the picnic place and regroup there after an hour, then come back up here. Terry, find somewhere discreet in the village where you can park and use the radio. Tell us where you are, and we'll come back to you and decide the best plan of attack. We should have some idea of what we're dealing with by then. How does that sound to you, Andy?'

'Fair enough. But we can't hang about. If these

others are going in, we've got to be right behind them.'

'Sure. It's five now. We'll meet back at the Toyota at six-thirty. Good luck.'

Kelly sat back. The rest of them laughed as if he'd just delivered the punchline. 'OK, let's go and get our gear.'

Hennie, who had barely spoken since he had joined the team three days before, and Gallagher walked west out of the village towards the railway line. Beneath their anoraks they each carried, in a shoulder holster, a 9mm Browning High Power handgun. Gallagher also carried a small rucksack. After they had crossed the railway bridge and turned off left on to a track leading across a field towards the forest, he patted the rucksack and grinned at Hennie.

'What you got in there, man?' the South African asked.

'My little Uzi, just in case we have a spot of bother before Kelly thinks.'

'Does Kelly know what he's doing?'

'Depends what you mean. If this was a properly sanctioned military operation, he'd probably be as experienced as anyone in the Regiment. He was a bloody good soldier; he was in Princes Gate and a couple of sieges in Belfast. But the rules are different in this freelance game and I'm not taking any chances.'

They were nearing the edge of the forest.

'How do you want to do this, man?' Hennie asked without a trace of anxiety.

'You follow the fence by the side of the railway embankment, about five yards in. I'll move parallel, ten yards further in and ten yards behind. I'll keep you in vision. If you see anyone, just stop. They might be blameless citizens. I'll get up to you. Keep me in sight.'

Hennie nodded brusquely. He'd been on hundreds of bush patrols in Namibia and Mozambique, in far more challenging and hostile conditions. He squeezed through the wire fence that bounded the field and slipped into the darkness of the forest.

Gallagher followed at the distance he'd specified. The undergrowth in this part of the forest was patchy, consisting of knotted clumps of fern and bramble interspersed with empty clearings edged with tall rhododendrons. Andy had some difficulty keeping his partner in view. The South African, despite the unsympathetic clothing he wore, slipped low, silent and barely visible from cover to cover.

Moving forward at the same rate, Gallagher stopped every few yards to listen and sweep the forest with his binoculars. Occasionally he had a clear line of vision a few hundred yards through the trees, and once he saw a family – parents and three small children – retreating towards the main road, a quarter of a mile to the west. They appeared relaxed and unhurried; he even caught a faint peal of laughter. They evidently hadn't seen anyone to worry them in that part of the forest. He watched them for a moment, then glanced ahead to his left to see Hennie stock still, crouched behind a broad beech trunk.

Hennie turned, saw Gallagher and beckoned.

With barely audible movements, the Scot took fifteen seconds to reach his partner. Hennie stabbed a forefinger across a clearing in front of them. The canopy of the forest was broken sufficiently to let in enough light for a small patch of tussocky grass to grow. Buried in a grassy dip in the shadow of a large rhododendron, Gallagher could just see a prostrate body in blue jeans and a white T-shirt. The man's head, if it was a man, was facing away from them, propped on his elbows, apparently watching something through the leathery leaves of the rhododendron. But from where they crouched, neither Gallagher nor Hennie could see what. They glanced a question at each other. Gallagher indicated that they should watch and wait for a few moments, and they both locked their eyes on to the motionless body while they felt for their Brownings.

For a quarter of a minute, the man didn't stir; then they caught a movement. The denim-clad buttocks were raised above the long grass, and slowly lowered again. The head disappeared from sight. The buttocks were raised and lowered again, then again.

Hennie nudged Gallagher and mouthed a breathless whisper. 'Christ, man! He's screwing!' he said with hypocritical disdain.

Gallagher grinned. 'Lucky bastard. We'll go round them. No point disturbing them – they might make a noise.'

Hennie nodded, and set off first, skirting to the left of the lovers. Gallagher waited, then took a route to their right. As he passed, not more than ten yards away, he caught sight of a naked female foot protruding from beneath the man's leg, and the motion, more vigorous now, drew a shrill squeak of pleasure. Gallagher felt an involuntary hardening of his own genitals, but ruefully turned away to concentrate on the way ahead. He and Hennie covered another two hundred yards without incident, sight or sound of anyone else.

Hennie stopped again. Gallagher came up to him to find they were confronted with a heavy chain-link fence some fifteen feet high and topped with rolled barbed wire. On the other side of it there was cultivated woodland and a glimpse through the ornamental trees of open parkland.

'This has got to be the perimeter of the place we're after. Let's check it twenty yards either way.'

Hennie turned east towards the railway line which had emerged from the cutting he'd been following and was now on a level with the grounds of the house. The fence took a right angle and continued as far as he could see alongside the railway track. There was a small humpbacked bridge about three hundred yards down the line, where the track up to the house crossed.

Gallagher had followed the fence to the west until he reached a right-angled corner at what must have been the rear of the property. They made their recce and met up again at the point where they had split. Gallagher pulled his radio from his rucksack and raised Haynes.

'We've reached a fence at the northern end of the property. Not too serious – burglar deterrent, I'd say; chain-link; cuttable; no sign of electrification. No trip-wires.'

'OK. The others have reached it too. Jack's sent Willy and Jan back to the Renault to come here. He's somewhere on the western perimeter waiting for you.'

Kelly's voice crackled in. 'Yeah,' he said quietly. 'I guess I'm halfway down. I've seen no sign of the enemy yet. Work your way round to join me and we'll check the rest of it.'

Hennie hugged the fence. Gallagher lagged ten yards behind and twenty feet out from it. After six minutes of silent progress, they reached Kelly.

'They've gone in,' Kelly whispered, nodding down the length of fence beyond them.

There was a straight cut, a yard high, where the severed edges of wire had been pushed in.

Hennie walked up and crouched at one side of the slit, peering at the ground in front of the opening. The vegetation had been scuffed aside, revealing a small patch of bare earth. He carefully pulled away a few straggling brambles, and after a moment he stood up.

'I can't tell for sure, but I doubt if there were more than four or five men through there.'

'That's all they'd need,' Kelly said, nodding, 'if they know what they're doing.'

He unclipped his radio.

'Terry. Change of plan. They've already gone in. I don't reckon they'll strike for another hour, when it's dark. But we'll have to be right behind them. Tell Jan and Willy to take the seven-thirty-threes and a dozen flash-bangs and go in two hundred yards either side of the road entrance. Tell them not to cross the bridge. They'll have to cut their way in instead. When they've got a clear view of the front flanks of the building, they should contact me on this frequency.'

'Roger,' Haynes said. 'What do you want me to do?'

'Get to the outskirts of the village on the lane down to Samois and I'll tell you when we need you.'

Bowring wasn't surprised to be ushered, without the option of refusing, into the big Mercedes when he met

Shalawi outside the Hôtel des Invalides. Had he been in Shalawi's place, he would have wanted to know for certain what he was dealing with before delivering information which would invite a death sentence if its source were discovered.

Inside the limousine, as it powered off down La Motte Picquet, passed the Champ de Mars and the Eiffel Tower, Bowring was confident that his six-man team wasn't far behind him.

'I'm sorry to use such impolite methods,' Shalawi said solicitously to him as they settled side by side on the deep rear seat of the car. 'But I would only be happy to pass to you the information I have in circumstances most favourable to me. And I'm sure you understand, we must satisfy ourselves as to your bona fides.'

Sitting opposite them on large, rear-facing dicky seats, were the three men who had hustled Bowring into the car. Two of them had been guarding the door of the hotel room in Amman where Bowring and Shalawi had first met. Once again, their hands were tucked into their jackets, making it clear that they both carried handguns. Bowring observed this, but was glad, on balance, that he had decided not to arm himself for this meeting. Beyond the guards, on the far side of a glass partition, a driver sat with another man beside him. Six to one, Bowring reflected: impossible odds.

'Naturally I understand,' he said. 'Do you have the documents we spoke about in Amman?'

'They will arrive at the house where we are going now, once we are satisfied that you will not . . . abuse the information they contain.'

'And what are they?'

'I have many interests, Father Babbington. Mainly I deal in commercial computers and office equipment. I also have an office services company in Beirut, which is very successful – software, faxing, desktop publishing, photocopying and so on. Since I have no wish to be involved in the disruptive elements who do not desire peace with our neighbours, I arranged that our photocopiers retain extra copies of everything that is processed by our offices, both internally and for outside clients. A trusted member of my staff looks through them every night for anything suspicious or of possible interest to me. It has been a surprisingly useful source of information to me.'

'I can see that it might be,' Bowring observed drily.

'I'm sure you'll agree just how useful when you see what I have for you. But that is all I am prepared to tell you about it for now.'

'I see,' Bowring said. 'What business do you carry on here in Paris?'

'I buy a lot of goods here. We have good trading relations with various computer companies, who have been quick and co-operative in adapting to our needs. Also, though I am reluctant to talk of such things with a man of peace like yourself, I have some interest in the ordnance trade.'

Bowring raised an eyebrow. 'That's a strange admission from a self-confessed dove.'

'Not so strange, Father Babbington, when you consider that peaceful settlements are seldom reached when one party in a dispute is armed, and the other is not.'

Bowring smiled and half turned to Shalawi. 'I had already concluded that you were a pragmatist rather than an idealist. That's good; I'd always rather deal with a cynic than a romantic.'

Shalawi laughed. 'You are right. I think we will get on very well.'

As the Mercedes joined the crawling traffic on the Périphérique, Bowring decided there was no point in asking where they were going. But when they turned off two exits later on to the southbound autoroute, he had the satisfaction of seeing the Toyota a few cars ahead of them.

Conversation for the rest of the journey was sporadic. Shalawi evidently felt that he'd said enough, and restricted himself to the occasional comment in Arabic to one of the young men opposite them.

They left the autoroute and took a road leading into the forest of Fontainebleau. Bowring made no comment until finally they turned up a weed-covered drive and crossed a fine ornamental wrought-iron bridge to draw up in front of a faded but still handsome eighteenth-century mansion.

'What a splendid house,' he remarked.

'It is quiet. We are seldom bothered here.'

Inside, the furnishings were disappointingly new and lacked taste, although they couldn't obscure the fine proportions of the reception rooms. Bowring was ushered into a large *salon* at the back of the house. The deep windows allowed views across simple rose beds, an ornamental lake and large lawns to a forest of grand old trees to the west.

'First of all, Father Babbington, I hope you'll forgive the formality of a search for weapons. This was not possible in the car, which is why, reluctantly, my young associates may have seemed rather menacing.'

Bowring opened his hands in a gesture of compliance. One of the guards frisked him quickly but thoroughly and grunted a negative at Shalawi, who smiled with boyish charm and said: 'Now may I offer you some refreshment? Coffee, mint tea?'

'Coffee, thank you.'

Shalawi gave a curt order to a male domestic who had appeared in the doorway.

'Will you excuse me for a few minutes,' Shalawi said affably. 'I have a few things to deal with.'

'Of course,' Bowring said. He hadn't been anticipating a short session with Shalawi. Several tours as military adviser to Britain's allies in the Gulf had accustomed him to the Arab penchant for procrastination.

Shalawi and his bodyguards left the room and the door closed behind them. Bowring walked to one of the windows and stood stroking his full, bogus beard, gazing at the splendid grounds without really noticing them. He was by now fairly convinced that Shalawi was what he said he was, at least as far as his own dealings with him were concerned. It was just possible that there was an elaborate and potentially very profitable hoax in the offing. Certainly Bowring now thought it likely that, whatever else his motives, Shalawi expected to make money from his information; his opting for the Vatican as a customer displayed shrewd judgement.

But in the seven days since their last meeting, Bowring had been frustrated by his inability to pin an identity on Shalawi. In the old days, when he still had a working relationship with the Deuxième REP and other French security forces, he could probably have got a line on his host from them. Now these doors were firmly closed to him, and he had to rely on a handful of friends in Whitehall giving guarded and increasingly sparing snippets of information. On Said Shalawi, they said, they had nothing to offer.

It was some time before Bowring heard the door open. He spun round to see the servant wordlessly bear a tray with coffee – French, not Arabic – to a table in the centre of the room and leave it there.

When the man had gone, Bowring poured a cup for himself and carried it back to the window. He peered at the forest beyond the gardens and wondered how his small troop was deployed. Although nominally Gallagher was in command, he had made it clear that there should be a sensible division of responsibility between him and the more experienced Kelly. He was aware that the Scot was a loner, but he judged that he had developed sufficient self-discipline now to work with a team if he had to. At the same time he had not forgotten that it had been an erstwhile lack of such control that had put paid to his selection for the Regiment. But, set against that, he had confidence in Kelly's charm and strength of personality.

He had no worries about Haynes's competence as controller of communications and logistics, and he was relieved that he and Kelly seemed to be getting on all right.

The South Africans he had brought in to add a bit of muscle if anything went wrong. It was probably an unnecessary precaution, but he would only have them on the payroll for a week.

Unconsciously, Bowring started to tap his foot. He was beginning to get impatient. The coffee pot was cold; the golden globe of the sun was dropping fast into the tops of the oaks beyond the park. There had been no sign of Shalawi or his aides for more than an hour. Although Bowring had trained himself to be patient, he was not by nature a patient man. He looked at his watch and turned his lips down with a sharp breath through clenched teeth. He wondered what the hell Shalawi was up to.

Decisively, he strode across to the double doors of the *salon*, opened them both and walked out into an oblong hall. His metal-tipped heels clicked loudly on the marble floor. A second later, two of the guards appeared, running down a broad flight of shallow stairs on his left. Both held Makarov 9mm automatics.

'What you want?' the first of them asked.

Bowring took no notice of the Russian pistols trained on him. 'I want to see Mr Shalawi.'

'Later. He still checking you.'

'Forgive me, Father Babbington,' Shalawi's voice boomed down from a gallery at the top of the stairs. His head came into view a moment later. He saw the guns and barked an order; the guards tucked them back into their jacket with surly obedience. Shalawi glided down the stairs towards Bowring. 'I'm afraid I've been having a little difficulty establishing your credentials. No doubt all will be confirmed very soon, but you do not appear on any of the normal diplomatic registers.'

'Naturally,' Bowring said easily, inwardly cursing Montefalco's lack of thoroughness. 'Mine is purely a temporary posting which wouldn't normally appear on the registers.'

'As I say, Father Babbington' – Shalawi was now standing a few feet in front of him, gazing at him with large, disingenuous brown eyes – 'I'm sure it will all be sorted out very soon. In the meantime, I'm sure you appreciate our need for caution.'

Bowring nodded. 'Yes, of course. But I really would like to get on with the business in hand.'

'It will be worth waiting for, I can assure you. Perhaps, in the meantime, you would like to eat? There is a good chef here. I will send him to take your order,' Shalawi added with finality. With a gracious but unequivocal gesture of his hand, he indicated that Bowring should go back into the *salon*.

Controlling his frustration, Bowring complied and the doors closed behind him once more.

6

Kelly, Gallagher and Hennie squeezed their way through the slit which had been cut in the fence by the Algerians.

Once through, the big South African scrutinized a mess of fresh tracks, and after a few moments he whispered: 'They split into two groups here – three that way, and two there.' He nodded left and right.

'OK, Andy, have you got any cam paint in your rucksack?' said Kelly.

Gallagher nodded.

'Good. Slap some on, both of you, and cover your heads. I'll have a look on the other side of this lot.'

Directly in front of them was a large spread of ornamental rhododendrons blocking any view into the park-like grounds beyond. Presumably, this was why the Algerians had decided to go in at that point. Kelly unknotted a camouflage net from his waist and wrapped it round his head. He dropped on to his belly and started to crawl like a lizard beneath the lower leaves of the overgrown bush.

He advanced with short, irregular movements to disguise any rhythm in the small, inevitable sounds of his progress through the dry leaves beneath the thick canopy. When he reached the far side of the bush, he wrapped the net across the lower half of his face and edged forward until he had a clear view through the gap between the lowest branches and the long grass. In the fast-fading light, he took a slow, careful look from left to right, registering as much detail as he could.

To his left, the lawns stretched some sixty yards north, and were planted with a few, isolated ornamental willows and birches. Beyond these, at ten o'clock, was a copse of half a dozen immature beeches. Between these and the house was a fine, spreading blue cedar whose lower branches swept gracefully to the ground, providing cover impenetrable to Kelly's vision. He noted it, and continued his sweep.

Forty yards in front of him was a lake about a hundred yards wide and fifty across. Beyond the lake, with a wide terrace between them, stood the house. It was a simple but elegant, classical eighteenth-century building whose rear elevation was designed to make the most of the grounds and the sunny westerly aspect.

Across the width of this front, a series of tall, unshuttered windows, reaching almost to the ground, reflected a faint pink from the last remains of daylight. There were no signs of any external guards covering these vulnerable entry points. It looked as though Shalawi and his men were unaware of any threat of outside interruptions to their meeting with Bowring.

Kelly swung his eyes to the right, stopping regularly to take a firm fix. By the south-west corner of the house stood a massive oak, much older than the house itself, whose vast, spreading limbs ended on one side barely a few feet from the south front.

To the south, the lawns ran into a big bank of tangled, neglected shrubs. Kelly estimated that the perimeter fence was no more than a few yards beyond them.

He listened to the birds making their final pre-roost calls. A blackbird burst into a sharp *chit-chit-chit* of warning from the woodland beyond the beeches to his left. He felt for his non-reflective, image-intensifying 10×50 binoculars and put them to his eyes. Magnifying any ambient light, they presented him with a scene almost as clear as day. He began a systematic search, starting with the foreground, stopping every few yards, alert for any signs of action or changes on each sweep.

On his third sweep, Kelly spotted a fleeting movement between the young beeches and the denser woodland beyond. Holding himself stock still so as not to miss anything, he kept his binoculars trained on the small stand of trees. He was rewarded a few seconds later by the sight of a man sprinting, bent low, from the woods to the isolated trees nearer the house. Scarcely breathing, Kelly waited to see if any others followed. After two minutes he concluded that he wasn't going to see anyone else. Either there were only two, or he'd missed one earlier. He thought they would then work their way closer to the house by way of the great blue cedar.

What lay along the north side of the house and beyond, Kelly couldn't see from where he was, but he guessed the raiders had identified a way of getting in close to the house from that side. He lowered his glasses. It was still light enough to detect movement with the naked eye; it would be at least twenty minutes before they went in.

Quickly, he backed through the bushes and emerged to find Gallagher and Hennie dark-camouflaged, their anoraks discarded and their T-shirts smeared with earth. Gallagher was bolting together the two parts of his Uzi sub-machine-gun.

Kelly shook his head. 'I suppose I ought to be glad you brought that.'

Gallagher grinned. 'I thought I might need it.'

'Not yet you don't. I've identified the position of at least two of the enemy. You and Hennie'll have to get round and take them out as quietly as you can. What else are you carrying?'

'Kukri, wire,' Gallagher answered.

'Hennie?'

'I've got my Russian knives,' the South African said smugly.

Kelly gave them the position of the beech trees and watched them disappear into the woods along the inside of the fence. He unclipped his walkie-talkie.

'Willy, Jan, do you read me?'

'Ya, Jack.'

'Give me your positions. You first, Willy.'

'I'm between the fence and a kind of garage block to the north-east of the house.'

'How far from the house?'

'Thirty yards at most.'

'OK. Get yourself due north of the house, in the closest cover you can. There may be two or three hostiles looking for a way in there. If you see any, deal with them. Try not to use a gun, but if you have to, keep it silenced. If you can't get to them before they go, tell us, then follow them in. If they reach Shalawi or the boss, be ready to bung in a couple of flash-bangs when I tell you.'

'OK.'

'Right, Jan, where are you?'

'I'm behind a little wall, about a hundred feet from the south-east corner of the house.'

'Can you see a massive oak, due west of you?'

'Sure.'

'Right. Head for that and get up it. You should be able to get on to the top of the house from it with your abseiling rope. But be careful, there are two more hostiles somewhere on that side of the house. I'm coming round that way, so I may get to them first. Keep this channel open. Over.'

Kelly took some camouflage paint from his rucksack and smeared streaks across his chin and cheekbones. He then shoved two thirteen-round Browning magazines into the rear pockets of his jeans and strapped his old SAS fighting knife to his belt.

The adrenalin was flowing free now he was getting close to the real action, but he hadn't any illusions about their position: as a result of his earlier tactics, they were almost certainly underarmed. As a unit, though, they weren't so badly off; the South Africans had their Colt Commandos and handguns, and Gallagher had his Uzi with four magazines. What was more, Kelly was sure that they still had surprise on their side.

Leaving his rucksack, he headed along the perimeter in the opposite direction to Gallagher and Hennie, stopping to listen every few yards. He reached the corner of the fence and headed east until he reckoned he was due south of the house. He worked his way through the thick shrubs to the edge of the open ground and parted the leaves.

Between him and the house he could just make out a low brick wall, level with the lawn on the far side –

a kind of small ha-ha. He guessed it must be the same wall from which Jan had reported his earlier position. Beyond the wall, at eleven o'clock, was the huge oak. He wondered if Jan was in position there yet but he couldn't risk using the radio. He lifted his binoculars to get a better view.

Hennie and Gallagher reached the woods behind the beech copse in time to see a figure flit across from it and disappear among the spreading branches of the blue cedar. Just then a distinct human noise, suggesting pressure on the lower colon, drifted from the beeches.

Gallagher drew his short battle kukri from its sheath, nudged Hennie and said, almost inaudibly: 'Let's go.'

Holding the broad-bladed knife in his right hand behind his back, he sprinted across the forty feet which separated him from the copse. He reached it before the two men standing behind the narrow trunks had fully registered the sound of his trainers swishing through the grass.

The nearest to him had just started to turn as the kukri flashed up a foot behind his head, and the perfectly balanced, curved blade descended with a soft crunch on to the nape of his bare neck. With a short gasp and a sigh, the Arab pitched forward and crumpled in front of him.

From his left, Gallagher saw the other man lunge at him. He dived over the motionless body in front of him, hit the ground and rolled on to his back. He winced as his Uzi caught him between the shoulder blades but started trying to pull the Browning from his shoulder holster. At the same time, he stuck one leg out at forty-five degrees to catch his assailant in the guts or genitals.

The Arab came down with all his weight on Gallagher's leg, twisting it viciously in its socket, and fell heavily beside him.

With the strength that only real danger can give, Gallagher lifted himself and wriggled his way out from under the man, ready for him to turn on him – until he saw a short, thick, steel handle protruding from the Algerian's back. The six-inch blade of Hennie's favourite toy – a Spetsnaz-issue MR-1 throwing knife – was buried in the heart beneath.

Gallagher saw Hennie looming over him, outlined against the dark, starry sky. The South African knelt down beside him and helped him to his feet. Gallagher leant for a moment against one of the slender beech trees, flexing his twisted leg. Hennie listened and gazed at the black lump of the cedar tree, fifty paces away, to catch any reaction to the small sounds of death their victims had produced.

In the sky above the forest, the last hint of sunset had gone, taking with it Bowring's view of the parkland outside. There remained only a faint, flickering reflection of the house lights on the lake. He turned away from the window, his patience ready to crack, when the doors to the *salon* were opened and Shalawi walked in with two of his guards.

'All seems well, Father Babbington. My courier will be here in an hour with the documents I have for you. Now, we will eat. Please, let me show you to our dining-room, where dinner is ready.'

Bowring had no appetite, but he was so glad his

wait was at an end that he was prepared to be agreeable about the idea of eating. Shalawi ushered him out of the room where he had spent the previous three hours, and into an adjoining room of almost the same size.

A large walnut table was laid with a number of cold dishes – stuffed vine leaves, olives, cheeses, small spicy sausages – and two places for diners on either side.

One of the surly young militiamen pulled out a chair for Bowring, who sat down gratefully.

The guards left, and Shalawi, sitting with his back to the black night outside, smiled across the table. 'I don't know about you, Father Babbington, but I am very hungry.'

He leant across to pick a stuffed vine leaf from one of the plates. Before it reached his large mouth, the room was filled with a deafening explosion followed by a blast of smoke and broken glass from the window behind him.

With pain and terror in his eyes, Shalawi turned, shards of glass and stains of crimson blood in his hair. Bowring registered this in the instant it took him to decide to dive under the table. He crawled around the central pedestal towards Shalawi, beyond whose chubby legs he saw two more pairs of legs, clad in boots and DPM fatigues.

He heard the throaty chatter of a Heckler and Koch MP5. Splintered holes appeared in the table top above him; the lower half of Shalawi's body became suddenly limp. Bowring carried on crawling towards the Arab, and when he reached him, he felt up the man's fat, lifeless legs to the waistband of his trousers. Feeling deftly inside Shalawi's loosely cut jacket, he searched for the pistol that he knew was concealed there.

He found the Beretta and removed it quickly, still watching the legs, running round the table now, kicking the fragments of glass. They knew he was there; they must have seen him through the uncurtained windows. The door from the hall burst open. There was the sound of a double-tap from a handgun, followed by two simultaneous bursts from the MP5s. Bowring exploited the distraction to get to the end of the table. Clutching the Beretta and smiling with grim resignation, he aimed just below the edge of the table at the first pair of legs coming towards him.

Kelly gazed through his binoculars and tightened up. Directly in front of him, no more than fifty feet away, two men crouched below the line of the wall. They both carried assault rifles whose manufacture Kelly couldn't identify. As he watched, one of them slowly raised his head above the wall. It looked as though they were going to go in any minute. He hoped to hell Gallagher and Hennie had had some luck with the three on the other side. And he wished he knew where Jan was; he couldn't have made it to the oak tree – these two would have seen him.

He sank back into the foliage and silently pulled his Browning from beneath his left arm. He was beginning to ease himself through the leaves with minimal sound when he heard the two Algerians scramble up and over the wall. Less concerned about noise now, he quickly pushed himself out and caught an outline of the two men running across the light cast on to the terrace from the windows of the house.

Kelly took an arc to his left, to keep out of range

of the light. He found himself beside the lake with a good view of the west front.

The two men were moving quickly along the terrace, checking each window as they went. Suddenly a third appeared, running silently from the other direction. They converged outside one of the windows, twenty feet from it, then ducked down and disappeared from view. Kelly guessed they were on the steps that led from the terrace to the lake's edge, a drop of no more then two or three feet.

A second later, the ragged thump of a fragmentation grenade shattered the silence of the garden. Two men jumped up, silhouetted against the window, and ran towards it. A second later, the deep *rat-at-at* of an MP5 resounded across the lake.

Kelly was already running round to the terrace. At the corner of the house he almost collided with Jan, who was sprinting up the east side of the building.

'Give me your rifle,' Kelly snapped. 'When we get to the window, chuck in a flash-bang, then follow me.'

Jan, still running, passed Kelly his Colt Commando, and unclipped a stun grenade from his belt.

They were still forty feet from the blown entry point when Kelly pulled up in the darkness between two windows. Two men had gone in; the third must have stayed by the lake to cover their exit.

A quick double-tap echoed from the house, followed by a sustained burst of fire.

Kelly peered towards the lake, into the darkness, trying to gauge the third man's position. But his attention was diverted by the sound of running up the terrace from the north end of the house. Three figures flashed past the light of the *salon* windows. A burst of fire on Kelly's left showed him what he was looking for. He swung round the M16 and spurted half a magazine at the point of fire. When he stopped, in the sudden silence, he heard a human gurgle and the clatter of a dropped weapon.

Jan didn't need telling. He ran on until he reached the shattered window at the same time as Gallagher and Willy. He threw in his stun grenade and jumped back to flatten himself against the wall. Kelly ran across and joined them. Cautiously at first, with weapons in the fire position, they turned into the window and jumped through, Kelly and Gallagher first, followed by Jan and Willy.

At the far end of the room, through the mist of the flash-bang, an Arab in a combat smock swung his automatic rifle towards Kelly. Before he'd completed his turn, he was shaking and jerking like a demented puppet as Kelly emptied the other half of the magazine into him.

As the burst of fire ended, the sharp, ugly sound of Gallagher's Uzi filled the room. Two Arab guards who had just run in waving their Makarovs pirouetted and tripped over their dead comrades in the doorway as they fell.

Kelly unclipped his empty magazine and flipped it over to insert the replacement, taped end to end with it. He looked around the room again. 'Where the fuck's Bowring?' he growled.

A hand appeared among the shattered contents of the dining-table. A second later, a face puntuated by a pair of hate-filled eyes raised itself, followed by the muzzle of an MP5.

Kelly was raising his own weapon when there was a single shot, and the dark, Semitic features slowly slid back out of sight. In their place, those of Father Babbington appeared, obscured by a large, crimson silk handkerchief. In his hand, Bowring held an automatic Beretta. The major glanced down, aimed and placed one more shot in his target.

Bowring looked back up at Gallagher and Kelly, who were now advancing into the room with their guns at the ready. 'There's a driver, and some domestic staff,' he snapped. 'They won't give you any trouble, but round them up and lock them away.'

Gallagher and Kelly went through to the hall while Bowring made his way to the shattered window. He stepped out to find Jan and Willy.

'Are there any enemy left out here?' he asked.

'I don't know,' Jan said. 'I guess we'd have heard by now.'

'Do you know how many there were?'

'Jack said five. There's one gone, over there, by the lake – after he did for Hennie.'

'There are only two inside. Get out into the dark and watch this window in case they come back.'

The two remaining South Africans nodded silently and melted into the night.

Bowring stepped back into the house and walked across the devastated room to the hall. He listened for a moment for sounds of Kelly and Gallagher dealing with the servants. There was some shouting from the north end of the house. With his Beretta in the fire position, he walked quickly along the corridor towards the commotion.

When he reached the kitchens, there were five men and two women sitting on the floor in a line along the wall. Gallagher was covering them with his Uzi while Kelly trussed them up.

'Jack, there were five. We've got two in the house, and one by the lake. What about the other two?'

Gallagher answered before Kelly could. 'Hennie and I, we done them outside. Did they get Hennie?'

'Yes,' Bowring said.

'Shit!'

'Where's Terry,' Bowring asked brusquely.

'With the Toyota in the village.'

'Give me your radio, for God's sake,' Bowring snapped. He activated the walkie-talkie. 'Terry, do you read me?'

'I read you, boss. You're back with us, then?'

'Only just. Hang on.' Bowring looked at Kelly. 'What's the best way out of here without using the drive?'

'Down the railway line to the bridge on the road to the south, just down from the car park where we RV'd earlier.'

Bowring crisply conveyed instructions to Haynes and snapped off the radio.

'Kelly, why the hell didn't you get him here before?'

'Too busy, boss. I didn't have time. We had to come in right behind those guys.'

'Well, the whole thing's a total fuck-up. They shot Shalawi before he'd told me anything and the papers he was going to give me hadn't even got here. Right, that'll do,' he said, looking at the terrified servants. 'Let's get out of here.'

Outside, Jan and Willy quickly stripped their dead comrade of weapons and anything else that might identify him, strapped him to a boulder from the rockery by the lake and waded in to carry him out to deeper water. As he sank, they ran down the south side of the house to catch up with the rest of the team.

Bowring and his four remaining men were swinging over the wrought-iron sides of the bridge across the railway line when they heard the wailing sirens of a convoy of police vehicles roaring up the drive from the road. They were running, a hundred and fifty yards down the track, as the first blue light flashed over the bridge.

Ten minutes later, streaming with sweat in the Land Cruiser, Haynes, Bowring and Kelly were heading for the bridge that crossed the Seine at Vulaines. Gallagher and the two South Africans were behind them in the van. No one felt much like talking until the river was between them and the carnage they had left behind.

Bowring, in the front seat beside Haynes, started to strip off his beard and clerical collar. 'Head north until we hit the A4 and we'll go into Paris from the east,' he said as he did so. 'They may put a block on the autoroute between Fontainebleau and Orly. We'll have to stop and get rid of our weapons and clean up. Keep your eyes open for somewhere, Terry.'

'OK, boss.'

Bowring turned to address Kelly. 'Not such a great result for your first operation with SOS.'

'Couldn't be helped, boss. That hit team had the place staked out before we got there. Someone must have got on to Shalawi in Amman.'

'Any idea who these men were?'

'Algerians; definitely not Palestinians.'

'Local contractors?'

'I should think so.'

'You didn't see the man who tailed me in Amman?'

'No. I should think any Sufuf Allah kept well out of the way.'

'You're right. I'm not blaming you for what happened.'

'At least we got you out of the shit, boss.'

'That one satisfactory aspect of the operation hadn't escaped me,' Bowring said quietly.

Next morning, the headlines of newspapers across the world bellowed conjecture at their readers. One aspect of the death of Beirut businessman Rashid al-Hussaini and his aides on which most of the media were agreed was that it was a strictly inter-Arab dispute.

Paul Lestienne brought the daily papers back to the house in Maisons-Laffitte for Bowring.

'As long as they don't decide to dredge the lake and find the South African, they won't be looking for any Europeans involved,' the Frenchman said.

Bowring grunted. 'That depends on what the servants tell them. Jack and Andy were blacked up, but they saw me.'

'You were totally unrecognizable.'

'Yes, but the driver might have realized I was English. Fortunately, he didn't hear any of my conversation with Shalawi – al-Hussaini, rather – because there was a partition between us in the car. Of course, they may say nothing. They may have been told not to by al-Hussaini's associates.'

'It says here that the house belonged to some anonymous import-export group who used it to entertain clients. People in the village, Bois-le-Roi, say they never saw anyone there, besides a gardener and a housekeeper.'

'We may get away with it,' Bowring shrugged, 'but it cost us a man, and we gained nothing.'

'Didn't al-Hussaini tell you *anything*?'

'No. They'd spent hours checking me out. Montefalco hadn't been thorough enough; Father Babbington wasn't on any of the diplomatic registers. I think I'd got through that though, and everything was going to be produced after dinner.'

'Any idea what he had?'

'Some schedules or notes of meeting – something like that brought into one of his offices in Beirut for photocopying. He told me that he had all the copiers in his Beirut bureaux rigged up to take extra copies for his own database. It was a smart move. People can be very careless about what they put in those machines; I know, I've done it myself from time to time when I've been away from my own offices. Nothing vital, of course, but things which could have compromised me.'

'But you saw nothing?'

'Nothing, but there's no doubt that something's up or they wouldn't have gone to these lengths to silence al-Hussaini and Father Babbington.' Bowring smiled. 'Although they don't know it, they've definitely done away with Father Babbington. Now all we have is a surveillance shot Kelly got of the Palestinian who tailed me in Amman. I may be able to get somewhere with that in London.'

'What's your next move, then?'

'I've paid off the two South Africans, though they could come in useful again, and I've sent Gallagher and Kelly back to Roquebrune to sort out ordnance with Bob Lyke. We've never had an assignment inside the UK that needed much armoury. I think it's far more likely that Sufuf Allah will make their hit during the British tour, not in India, and on the strength of what happened yesterday I think we'll encounter some serious opposition.'

7

Kelly was getting bored. He'd been in Ghent for three days and he'd visited every gallery, abbey and historic public building in the ancient city. He had been obeying orders. 'Just behave like a tourist until Bob contacts you,' Bowring had told him, and for the first couple of days he had enjoyed himself. Every few hours, though, he had been back to his hotel to see if there were any messages.

He spent the afternoon of the third day in the Schone Kunsten, wandering through chambers hung with fine old Flemish masters. He enjoyed the brilliant clarity of them; sixteenth-century moments frozen in time; details of the women's clothing and the soldiers' weapons. But after two hours he'd had enough. He walked back into his hotel for the twentieth time and nodded at the receptionist on the way up to his room.

'Mr Watson,' the girl called. 'There's a gentleman waiting for you in the bar.'

Kelly, buoyed with relief, nodded his thanks and changed direction.

Bob Lyke was sitting at a table with a cup of coffee in front of him, reading the *European*.

'Hello, how are you?' he greeted Kelly like an old friend. 'It's great to see you. I've only just got here, but I'd love to get out and take a squint at the Schone Kunsten before it closes.

Kelly sighed. 'Great.'

Outside he said: 'I've just spent the last two hours in there.'

'OK, we'll go and take a look at the Van Eycks in the cathedral, then. I'll update your orders on the way.'

The two men strolled like seasoned tourists through the medieval streets, unnoticed, unobtrusive, with cameras round their necks and guidebooks in their hands.

Lyke looked at his watch. 'I'm picking up the cash for our purchases from the bank in an hour, and the goods should be ready to collect from Bruges tomorrow. We've ordered more than we need for this job, but Piers thought we might as well use this trip to stock up on arms at HQ.'

'How much is there, then?'

'Quite a bit. M60s, MP5s, M16s, nine-millies, and SSG69s, ten of each and ten thousand rounds. A few Stingers, some PPG 66mm rocket-launchers and 40mm grenade-launchers.'

'How are we going to get that lot back to England?'

'Shouldn't be a problem. Michelle and Terry are bringing the boat over now; in fact, she should be in Ostend already. Take the 7.40 train there tomorrow; Andy will meet you from it. Rent a van and take it to one of the big chandlers down at the port. Buy twenty second-hand big polystyrene and plastic fenders – the scruffier the better. You'll find you can get some about three feet long, eight inch diameter – white to match the hull of the *Santa Laura*. Get a couple of dozen sheets of two-inch foam rubber from the street market. Gallagher should have arranged for you to pick up a stock of five-kilo catering tins of food and a welding kit. I've already briefed him; he'll know what to do with it all.'

'So why have I been hanging around here?'

'Preferable to you hanging around Ostend, and I've got to give you the money. I'll do that back at the hotel. Our supplier's OK, but if you make it easy for him, he'll diddle us. I'll give you a list of what we've ordered and the prices agreed, which you must memorize then destroy before you leave in the morning.'

'What's all this bloody marmalade and beans for?' Kelly asked Gallagher. They were driving away from a large cash-and-carry on the edge of the channel port of Ostend. Stacked in the back of the Renault Traffic van that Kelly had hired were eighteen catering tins of assorted foods.

'To put the ammo in,' replied Gallagher.

'We won't need all that for ten thousand rounds,' Kelly observed.

'Bob Lyke may be a bit of an old woman, but he's a tight operator. He never lets you buy anything you don't need. We'll only empty half of them for the ammo; the rest we'll stack on top in the boat, in case anyone comes on board for a snoop.'

'And the fenders are for the guns?'

'Aye, that's right.'

Kelly turned the van on to the old Bruges road. Fifteen minutes later he pulled into a small yard full of tractors, seeders, ploughs and a couple of rusty combine harvesters. A large sign proclaimed that these were the premises of Jan Bekkevoort, dealer in agricultural machinery.

Kelly was still manoeuvring into a suitable parking

space when a small man in shirtsleeves and a grey-flannel cap walked over to them.

When Kelly turned off the motor, the little man poked his head into the window. 'Hello. Who are you?'

'Watson.'

'OK. Come in my office.'

Kelly and Gallagher climbed out and followed the Fleming into a small lock-up room tacked on to the side of a breeze-block-built warehouse.

'Are you Mr Bekkevoort?' Kelly asked.

'Of course I am,' the little man snapped. 'Have you got the money?'

Kelly nodded, but made no move to back up his claim.

'Well, let's see it.'

'When we've seen the merchandise,' Kelly said.

'Impossible. It's all crated up.'

'All the same, I'd like to check it all before I part with the money.'

Bekkevoort looked at the motionless blue eyes for a moment, then shrugged. 'It's not necessary. Do you think I cheat you?'

Kelly shook his head. 'Not now.'

'Come,' Bekkevoort said testily and led them out of the grimy office and in through a double door to the warehouse.

Four wooden packing crates, nailed up and strapped with steel banding, lay on the floor beside a fork-lift truck. In Flemish, the words 'Bekkevoort, Agricultural Machinery' were stencilled straight on to the wood.

Kelly tapped the closest to the door. 'Is this one of them?'

'No,' Bekkevoort shook his head hurriedly. 'The two behind.'

'Is that so?' Kelly gazed at him, nodding his head with a grin. 'Right. Open them up, then.'

With bad grace, Bekkevoort cut the steel band with a pair of shears and picked up a crowbar to prise off the lid of the first of the two boxes. He stood back to give Kelly and Gallagher a view of the contents.

The crates were packed with polystyrene bubbles in which nestled a number of packages swathed in black plastic. Gallagher picked up the top one and pulled out a Heckler and Koch MP5 wrapped again in soft, lightly oiled cloth. He quickly stripped down the sub-machine-gun and checked all the moving parts.

'It's fine,' he nodded at Kelly. 'In good nick.'

'Right. Let's do the rest.'

Bekkevoort lifted his eyebrows but didn't otherwise object. He showed no particular surprise, or contrition, when Gallagher and Kelly rejected ten of the sixty weapons.

'How long will it take to get replacements?' Kelly asked.

Bekkevoort heaved his shoulders. 'Tomorrow, next day.'

'Too late. You'll have to knock them off the bill.'

The arms merchant winced. Kelly suspected that Bekkevoort himself had been ripped off; but that was his problem.

Bekkevoort shouted a guttural summons into the back of the warehouse and a large, surly youth appeared.

Gallagher stood guard while the crates were repacked and resealed. Kelly went back to the office to settle up.

An hour later, they were parked among the noise and coming and going of a truckers' restaurant, where no one took any notice of the activity in the back of the van.

They dealt with the rocket-launchers first, reducing them to their smallest component parts, then the guns. They had made an incision in the top of the outer plastic skin of each of the fenders before peeling it off the polystyrene cylinder inside. Using a hot-wire cutter, they sliced the cylinders longitudinally and gouged out the inside, creating a tube with a one-inch skin.

Leaving the weapons wrapped in the soft cloth, they put each one into a black plastic bag, which they sealed before enveloping and taping it in a sheet of foam rubber. They packed all twenty fenders that Kelly had bought with the foam-rubber parcels, filling in the gaps with the polystyrene bubbles from Bekkevoort's crates.

With a plastic-welding kit, Gallagher neatly resealed the fender skins so that the earlier incisions were barely detectable among the scuffs and skid marks on the old fenders.

'Right,' he said when he had finished. 'The ammo. We need to take the bottom out of half these tins and get rid of the contents somewhere.'

'Where the hell do we chuck ten stone of baked beans,' Kelly laughed.

Each can, washed out and greased, accommodated about twelve hundred rounds – four deep – and weighed forty pounds. Gallagher re-welded the bases back on to the cans and he and Kelly stacked them the right way up, with the unopened tins on top.

'These things won't get past a real search,' Gallagher observed. 'But I reckon the chances of that are about a hundred to one.' He shrugged. 'I've taken bigger risks.'

Kelly nodded, unconcerned, and started stacking the fenders. Though heavier than they should have been, they seemed a better bet than the food tins.

They dumped the bags of jettisoned beans, marmalade and peas beside a pile of garbage outside the restaurant and headed back for Ostend.

Bowring's boat was berthed across the 'T' of a long pontoon, dominating the other craft in the yacht harbour beside the railway station in Ostend. Not for the first time during his two weeks of employment in Bowring's organization, Kelly was impressed.

The *Santa Laura* was an elegant, seventy-two-foot aluminium-hulled ketch, built twenty years before in one of Hamburg's leading boatyards. She had, Lyke had told Kelly, been twice round the world and broken a couple of Pacific race records earlier in her career. Now refitted internally to suit the kind of customers who could pay $10,000 a week, she spent half of each year paying for her keep with charters. Despite her vast sail area, she could be efficiently handled by a skipper and a crew of three.

Kelly drove the Renault van down to the harbour wall, sorry that he was going to miss out on the short trip across the Channel on board her this time; not least because, for this trip, the ostensible charterer of the *Santa Laura* was Michelle de Lassy. He didn't even see her in the ten minutes he and Gallagher spent alongside the marina. The skipper of the boat, an ex-marine, oversaw delivery of the stores and extra fenders and signed for them without a surplus word.

An hour later, leaning over the rails of the afternoon

car ferry, Kelly and Gallagher watched the yacht motor out of the harbour before heading off under sail into the calm, August waters of the Channel.

In Harwich, the two fit and tanned mercenaries strolled off the ship, each carrying a grip and genuine passport. A customs officer with a nose for incongruities identified them as the two most likely targets among a mundane bunch of passengers. He beckoned them over as they sauntered through the customs shed. Kelly was philosophical; at least he was clean. Gallagher scowled.

'No vehicle, then?' the official asked.

'That's pretty obvious,' Gallagher growled.

The customs man gave a nasty smile. 'Would you open your bags, please,' he said, nodding at the counter between them.

The Scot was fuming as they walked out of the shed half an hour later.

'Officious little bastard!'

He had just paid two hundred pounds' duty on his Rolex watch.

Kelly laughed. 'Listen, it was worth two hundred quid to see his disappointment. He was sure he was on to something with us.'

'Aye, well. He just pulled us at the wrong moment.'

They walked round the harbour to a van-rental company. A short while later, they were driving a small Luton-bodied lorry out of the port towards Colchester.

Next morning, after an unfamiliar, greasy English breakfast, Kelly and Gallagher sat in a café looking east up the River Crouch. They saw the *Santa Laura*'s sails across the flat, featureless landscape half an hour before they could see her hull.

They remained where they were as she berthed on the end of the pontoons, where, once again, she eclipsed the mass of smaller craft around her.

Kelly saw Michelle for the first time since he'd left Nice for Rome, standing at the bow of the boat as her crew neatly brought her in, under sail until the very last moment. When they were tied up, Michelle came ashore with the skipper and walked quickly up the pontoon to the harbourmaster's office. A few minutes later Haynes and the other crew members began to offload equipment – damaged sails, an Avon semi-rigid tender, a number of canvas grips, boxes of empty wine bottles and beer cans, a pile of large cans of peas, beans and marmalade, and twenty scuffed and battered fenders.

The crew came to the stone quay and collected small wire tolleys and took them back to fill them. After three trips each, the offloaded stores and equipment were piled on the quay ready for collection.

Michelle was walking back now with the skipper, who ran his eye over the unwanted stores and instructed one of his crew to stay with them until the van arrived. Meanwhile, the yacht was taking on fresh water and receiving a good swabbing-down.

Among all the activity in the busy marina on an August morning, it all looked very normal.

The two men watching in the café finished their third cup of coffee, got to their feet and walked to the car park where they had left the hired van. They drove down to the quay and crawled along until they were beside the stack of goods from the *Santa Laura*.

'Fenders first?' Kelly suggested.

'Aye.'

With the crewman, they had loaded all the fenders, the deflating Avon, and half the tins of food when they were approached by an official in white shirtsleeves and navy trousers. He stopped and looked inside the van, and then at the rest of the tins still to be loaded.

'Why are you taking off the food?'

Kelly, inside the van, picked up Gallagher's quick, uncomfortable twinge of anxiety.

The crewman answered. 'The skipper was trying to make a few extra bob on his food budget. He bought all this junk in Ostend, but the charterer won't touch it. It's all got to go back to our depot in Portsmouth. Christ knows what they'll do with it there,' he added with a laugh.

The customs man stepped forward, fishing a pen-knife from his pocket.

Kelly held his breath. The nine cans stuffed with 9mm and 7.62mm parabellum rounds were already on the van, along with five of those still containing what they purported to be. There were four undoctored cans still to be loaded.

The customs officer took a moment thinking about which can to go for. He reached into the van and put his hand on one which Kelly was just about to stack.

Kelly wasn't sure whether it contained baked beans or twelve hundred rounds of illegal ammunition.

'Let's have a look in this one.'

'Here, what are you going to do?' Gallagher asked indignantly. 'The stuff'll be worthless if you puncture the can.'

'It's not worth much anyway, is it? Seems a lot

of expense to be carting it all the way back to Portsmouth.'

The customs man slid the can across the ribbed metal floor of the van. Kelly noticed with a surge of relief that it didn't seem particularly heavy, but he still held his breath as the official stabbed a short, stout blade into the top and began to cut it away.

When he had cut a semicircle, he hooked back the top and revealed a pale-orange pool of baked-bean sauce. With a look of disappointment, he rolled up his right sleeve and plunged his hand into the unappealing quagmire. He felt around inside for a few moments and, evidently satisfied that no packages of heroin, cocaine or cannabis were floating inside, withdrew his hand with a shake of his head.

His hand and forearm dripped with the sauce. He tentatively licked a bit off, made a face, and asked if anyone had a cloth. Kelly promptly dived into his grip, already stowed in the van, and pulled out a dirty T-shirt. 'This any good?'

The man nodded and started to wipe himself clean. 'OK. You must have a very tight-fisted owner, wanting to save that muck, that's all I can say.'

Kelly didn't let his relief show until they were outside the perimeter of the marina.

'Shit! Bit fucking hairy, that.'

'Did you think so? I was enjoying myself,' Gallagher said, grinning broadly.

'Yeah, but you're a masochist. Right. Where's our RV with Michelle?'

'A wee village the other side of Chelmsford. There's a fella with a farm there, ex-Regiment. Mike Harding. Did you know him?'

'Sure. He was training when I first joined.'

He does a bit of close personal work for us, and a few other bits and pieces when Bowring needs him. He once came on a job in Australia. Getting on a bit, though. Too slow. He's got this farm; does a bit of horse dealing. It's pretty isolated, considering it's only thirty miles from London. We used it to lock up a fellow who was getting in the way on another job.'

'What's happening there?'

'We meet Michelle. She'll tell us.'

Kelly tried to detect any resentment in Gallagher's voice, but heard none. He glanced at the hard-nosed Scot.

'Have you ever worked an oppo with her?'

'Aye. We'd a wee job in Bosnia earlier this year.'

'The dam?'

Gallagher nodded. 'Something like that.'

'And what was she like?'

'Very fucking cool, man, I can tell you. I never saw a woman with less fear – not many men either.'

'How well do you know her?'

'If you mean, have I screwed her, the answer's no way. For a start, I don't fancy her that much. She's, you know, like, too good-looking. Good-looking women're always trouble. Besides, Bowring wouldn't stand for it.'

'Did he say so?'

'He wouldn't need to, man. You know what he's like; you know damn well he wouldn't approve of his soldiers screwing, even if they're the opposite sex.' Andy shrugged. 'So, if you want my advice, don't even think about it.'

'I'll try not to.' Kelly nodded reluctantly. 'She brought me in, you know.'

'Aye. She knows what Bowring's after, so she took

a good look and decided he'd want you. If she'd thought the other way, you'd never have known, would you?'

'No. He's managed to keep the whole SOS thing very quiet. It's amazing really. I never knew about it before.'

'It's in your contract: talk and you're out.'

'What about people who've been and gone?'

'There aren't many, and I don't know what he says to them before they go, but I can tell you, they're not interested in spreading the word.'

'But how does he get the jobs?'

'Through the agents, Dowson and Lestienne.'

'He seems to have made a lot of bread out of it.'

'He's made bloody millions, man, on all his businesses. He could pack up tomorrow and it wouldn't make any difference. That's what you've got to understand about Bowring; he does it because he likes doing it, and he likes doing it very well. He's got one of the best reputations in the business. Put it this way, if you're good enough for Bowring you're good enough for anybody.'

'But what does he spend his money on? He's not married or anything, is he?'

'No. I don't know what he does for women. But he spends all right. The only trouble is that everything he touches seems to make more money. Like that bloody boat. He bought it for nothing from an arms dealer's widow. Since he put it back in the water, he uses it when he wants, charters it the rest of the time, and he still comes out showing a profit. And you wait till you see HQ.'

Mike Harding had aged a lot since Kelly had last

seen him back in Hereford. He was still big and powerful – if anything his gut had expanded – and he'd allowed a grizzled grey beard to run riot across his big, square jaw.

He was standing in the centre of the three-sided Victorian brick-built farmyard into which Kelly had driven the van. He recognised Kelly at once, greeting him with coarse, cockney bonhomie. 'Well, bugger me old boots, it's Scouser Kelly. So we've got a boody Gulf War hero on the team now.'

Kelly took the hand Harding offered, and groaned as the man tried to crunch his knuckles into submission. With his free left hand, he gave a short hard jab to Harding's heavy stomach. Harding let out a loud 'oof', let go of Kelly's hand, and doubled up, grinning. 'Should've known better, shouldn't I?' he gasped.

'When you two have finished playing games,' Gallagher said, 'maybe you can tell us when Michelle's getting here.'

'She's on her way. My boy went to pick her up from Burnham. Then whatever you've got in that van has got to go into that horse trailer there.' Harding jerked a thumb at a standard double Rice box, hitched to a workaday Land Rover. 'Well, just the naughty bits. The rest you can leave here. I'll have a deal with the major on it.'

'I doubt it,' Gallagher said. 'Even you wouldn't take five-kilo cans of beans that had fallen off the back of a lorry.'

'Why not? The pigs'll eat 'em.'

'What about the marmalade?'

'I can give that to the quackers – ready-made duck and orange, eh?' Harding guffawed. 'Anyway, get a move on. I don't want your bloody illegal imports on the premises longer than need be. You can top the load up with hay.' He nodded at an open-fronted shed stacked high with bales. 'I'll get you a drink.'

He walked off, followed by three loping Dobermanns who had been sitting quietly behind him up until then.

Kelly unlocked the back of the van and rolled it up.

'He's got stuck into the good life, then,' he said to Gallagher.

The drive from the lane to the yard had taken them through a quarter of a mile of woodland and well-kept paddocks containing every conceivable equine type, from Shetland ponies to lumbering Shires. The house they had seen beyond the yard was a rambling timber-and-cob manor house set in front of a rush-fringed lake.

The Scot nodded. 'Aye, but like I say, he's gone a bit soft. Look how you creased him up.'

'I've creased up harder men than him,' Kelly said unemotionally.

Before they began transferring the weapons from the van to the horse trailer, they laid a row of hay bales on their sides along the outside edge of the floor of the box. Inside this lining they placed the fenders and the ammunition cans, bringing the load level with the bales. They filled up the rest of the trailer with hay until it would just protrude above the tailgate when they closed it.

As they finished, a new dark-blue Mercedes 500SL crunched down the drive and pulled into the yard. A young, beardless version of Mike Harding eased himself out of the driver's door, and Michelle got out of the other. Still wearing the denim shorts and deck shoes in which she had arrived on the yacht, she stretched her long, tanned legs ane walked over to them.

'Hello, boys,' she said with a smile, and not without an element of flirtatiousness. 'Is my hay all loaded up?'

'Aye,' Gallagher said. 'We were just about to put the ramp up.'

Michelle, carrying a small leather grip, walked over to see what they had done and nodded with approval at the barrier of bales around the bottom.

'OK,' she said. 'I've just got to change from sailing clothes to riding gear.' She walked towards an open stable door with her bag.

Mike Harding walked back into the yard carrying three cans of bitter. He saw the Mercedes and nodded at his son. 'All right, Jason?'

'No problem, Dad. No one came after us.'

'Good. If you want a drink, you'll have to get your own!'

Harding handed a can each to the other two, who pulled off the rings gratefully. When they had had a good mouthful, they heaved up the tailgate of the trailer and dropped the pins in to secure it. A few minutes later Michelle reappeared in a pair of well-worn jeans and a sweatshirt with 'I love Apaloosas' printed across the soft contours of her breasts. She had undone the loose bun in which her hair was usually gathered up and unexpectedly long tresses fell in golden profusion down her back and shoulders. She had generally contrived the appearance of a typical horsy Englishwoman, albeit an exceptionally attractive one.

Kelly looked at her appreciatively. 'Who the hell's Apaloosas?' he asked. 'I'm jealous.'

'A kind of spotty horse,' Michelle said, opening the driver's door of the Land Rover. 'You'll see. I keep one at HQ.' She climbed in and started the engine, then turned the trailer in the yard without any difficulty and drove off with a wave of her hand.

Harding gazed after her with admiration. 'She doesn't hang about, does she?' He turned his attention to the rest of the things that had been unloaded from the *Santa Laura*. 'Right, you better get the rest of this crap into the barn. Then drop the van off in London and hire an ordinary jam-jar, a Sierra or something like that, and get on down to Summerfold. Then I hope I don't see you for a while; I'm getting a bit too old for Bowring's capers.'

8

Gallagher drove the van into London. He and Kelly didn't speak much. Kelly bought a paper at a petrol station to see if there were any more reports on the incident in the Forest of Fontainebleau.

So far, at least as far as the reported accounts went, Kelly was relieved to find that no suggestion had yet been made of the involvement of European mercenaries. Which meant that the domestic staff must have kept quiet about them and no one had thought it necessary to dredge the lake holding Hennie's bulky corpse. The bogus telephone and electricity company vans had been found and traced to an Algerian gang in Marseilles. It was reported that those who hadn't been killed in the battle at the house had managed to escape down the railway track which ran alongside the grounds.

A week after the incident, Kelly still tingled at the memory of the action; he just hoped that Sufuf Allah didn't now decide to abandon their plans for the Pope's tour. In the meantime, he was looking forward to seeing the SOS set-up in England.

Summerfold House was a little over thirty miles from Hyde Park Corner; sited amid dense, mixed woodland on the southern slopes of Surrey's North Downs, it could have been a hundred miles from the capital.

Kelly and Gallagher didn't approach it by its long drive leading up from the small village that nestled at the foot of the hill. They went instead to The Hollies, a handsome early-Victorian villa, standing alone on the other side of the ridge behind Summerfold and about two miles from it by the deep, winding woodland lanes.

The Hollies was surrounded by neat paddocks. The original stable block and carriage house had been renovated and the presence of a horse trailer and a large fresh muck heap were evidence of the kind of equestrian activity which was popular among the wives and daughters of the commuters who lived in the area.

Gallagher parked the car and the two men walked round to the back door of the house. The door was open.

'Hello. Come in,' Michelle said from the light, airy kitchen. 'You're just in time for lunch.'

She was preparing a large French salad with *charcuterie*.

The two men helped her to carry the lunch and two bottles of Provençal *rosé* out to a flagstoned terrace behind the house.

As they ate, Michelle brought them up to date.

One of them – Gallagher – was to go with her to a small local horse show that afternoon. It was both her cover and her amusement to make an appearance at these events when she was in England; it decreased speculation about what else she might be doing, staying alone up at the isolated house.

Kelly was to go and see Bowring at Summerfold House.

'I'll show you the way before Andy and I go to the show,' said Michelle.

'No need. I've got the OS map,' Kelly said.

'But you're not going overland,' Michelle grinned.

After lunch, Michelle led Kelly down to the large, full-height cellars. 'Summerfold was built by a Victorian banker called Sir Joshua Bowring. Yes, some ancestor of the boss. Because the English were even more hypocritical in those days than they are now, if a man wanted to keep a mistress he had to be very discreet. Sir Joshua kept his mistress in this house for twenty years – but no one ever saw him come, or go.' Michelle pointed at a door set in the wall of the cellar. 'The tunnel is a mile long.' She walked to the door, turned a large iron key and swung it towards them.

Kelly shook his head in amazement. The cylindrical tunnel was brick-lined and over six feet high. Michelle fetched a torch from a hook at the bottom of the stairs and handed it to Kelly. 'It's a little damp in parts, but no real problems. I'll tell the major you'll be there in fifteen minutes.'

Kelly nodded, flicked on the torch and stepped into the tunnel. The door thudded shut behind him. He played a powerful beam along the dank brick cylinder as far as it would penetrate until it faded into black nothingness. With a shrug, he set off at a brisk walk, breathing in the damp but surprisingly fresh air.

The source of this air became apparent after he had walked for five minutes, when he suddenly came across a feeble shaft of light in the curved roof. He stopped under it and glanced up. Way above him, too far to judge the distance, was a small circle of light. The Victorian Bowring had evidently wanted to be sure he didn't reach his mistress short of breath.

Kelly thought of Bowring's set-up in France –

the passages and precautions that surrounded his operation there. At the house in Roquebrune, the other businesses provided cover for his mercenary soldiering; Kelly wondered how Bowring explained his presence to his neighbours in the depths of south-east England.

After the quarter of an hour that Michelle had predicted, Kelly found himself facing a large oak door with a big iron ring of a handle. He turned the handle and pushed. Contrary to his expectations, the door swung before him and he stepped into a brick-lined cavern some twenty feet square. In the middle of the room was the top of a well shaft a yard wide. Curious, he walked across and flashed his torch down the hole. An iron ladder disappered down it, out of sight and no glimmer of reflection reached him from the depths.

Shining his torch around the rest of the vaulted cavern, he saw a door on the far side, similar to the one he had just opened.

Once again he turned the handle. This time, he was out of luck.

He looked around for some way of announcing his arrival to what he assumed was Summerfold House above, but there was nothing. The room was completely empty, featureless, except for the two doors and the well-head.

He put his ear to the inward door to see if he could hear anything and was rewarded with the sound of metal-tipped heels clicking on stone.

A moment later, after the sound of a key turning in a well-oiled lock, the door swung back and the cavern was filled with light from the passage beyond.

'Hello, Jack.' In the spotlight of Kelly's torch stood

Piers Bowring, in linen jacket and silk tie, with the hint of a smile on his face.

Kelly gave a short laugh. 'Hello, boss. What a way in!'

'More extravagant than you might think. It cost my great-great-great-uncle Joshua the equivalent of half a million to have it constructed, and keep it secret. And while you're here, I'll tell you about the other exit route.' He nodded at the well. 'The water level's over two hundred feet down, but at about a hundred feet there's another horizontal tunnel, only a quarter of a mile long, which comes out in an ice house behind the south lodge. Both exits have had their uses since I decided to move in here.' He gestured towards the door through which he had just come. 'Now, come on up.'

Kelly followed Bowring along a short corridor and a flight of stone steps up to another door to a higher level of cellarage. Bowring closed this door, and with scarcely any effort, swung a solid slab of brick wall across it, leaving it undetectable to any but the most thorough of searches. 'Apart from regular oiling, nothing's been done to that mechanism since it was built,' Bowring remarked, as they continued through a range of wine cellars, binned and labelled with dates from the previous century. Bowring stopped beside a stack of cobweb-covered bottles and picked one out. He blew a thick layer of dust from it. 'Calvados, 1892. Should be ready by now,' he said. 'We'll have some after dinner.'

They ascended another flight of stone stairs and emerged through a panelled mahogany door into a daylit hall. Bowring clicked his heels across a floor of patterned ochre and terracotta tiles to a wide, green-baize door which swung on double hinges into a larger, grander hall. A broad, extravagant staircase swept up beside them, and half a dozen elaborately architraved doorways gave off the hall. Bowring continued to the one nearest the front door and swung it open in front of Kelly, beckoning him in.

The afternoon sun flooded into the room through tall windows which allowed a stunning view over the tops of the trees across the lower Sussex hills to the South Downs beyond.

'That's a hell of a view,' Kelly said, aware that it must have been said many times before.

'Yes. If it hadn't been for the view, and its, ah, unusual means of access. I wouldn't have bought the place back. It had been out of the family for twenty years. A rock star whose name I forget bought it from my parents. Fortunately, he seems to have spent most of his time here in a drug-induced haze. Anyway, he never discovered the well room. Sadly, though, it's not a very beautiful house.'

'Well,' Kelly said, 'you can't have everything.'

'No, I suppose not,' Bowring mused, as if the idea hadn't occurred to him before.

Kelly looked around at the room – a library, perhaps twenty by thirty feet, with a large, black-marble fireplace and heavy mahogany furniture. The lights looked at least a hundred years old, and the only concession to modernity was a telephone on a large writing-table in the centre of the room.

Bowring picked up the phone and pressed a single number. 'Terry, Jack's here. Come down and we'll carry on with the briefing.' He cut the connection but didn't put the receiver down. 'Coffee, tea?'

'Coffee,' Kelly answered. He hadn't drunk English tea for over a year.

Bowring punched another key and ordered coffee, then waved Kelly towards a leather buttoned Empire chair and sat down at the table. 'Did you ever get round to reading your contract?' he asked abruptly.

Kelly nodded.

'You know then that the existence of this place, in so far as it has any connection with SOS, is inviolably secret.'

Kelly nodded again. He had got the hang of Bowring's *modus operandi* by now.

'You will only ever come to this place through The Hollies or, in certain circumstances, by the ice house. And unless you've told someone here that you're coming, you won't get as far as the well room. For your information, I occasionally entertain here, more to keep the local gossip under control than for my own enjoyment. I only keep two permanent staff, who are totally discreet. James, my butler, as well as knowing more than the average Master about wine, could probably outshoot you with a handgun.'

'Soldier?'

Bowring nodded. 'An old soldier.'

Haynes walked into the room. Although he had been aboard the *Santa Laura*, Kelly hadn't seen him either in Ostend or Burnham-on-Crouch. He nodded affably at Kelly. 'Hello, Jack. You found your way, then?' he grinned.

'Right,' Bowring said. 'We've got work to do. The Pope goes to India next week. From his itinerary, it's clear that the Indian security services have persuaded their government to restrict large-scale public appearances to a minimum. If I were planning a hit, I would dismiss any possibility of doing it on this trip. However, our clients will expect us to be around, to show that we're taking the job seriously. So, Jack, I want you and Gallagher to go over there and keep as close as you can, but don't make yourselves too damned obvious. Montefalco will be there, but you shouldn't contact him unless it's absolutely essential; in other words, if you think something really is going to happen.'

Bowring was interrupted by a knock on the door, followed by the entrance of a neat, quietly dressed, grey-haired woman in her mid-sixties. She was carrying a tray with coffee pot and cups.

'Ah, thank you, Nanny,' Bowring said with unexpected mildness. 'You haven't met Jack Kelly, one of our new recruits.'

The woman put the tray down on a side-table and looked steadily at Kelly for a few seconds, assessing and committing his face to memory.

'Jack, this is Miss MacFarlane, who had the misfortune to be my childhood nanny.'

Jack stood up and shook a small, firm hand. 'How are you?' he said.

'Very well, thank you,' she replied primly, making Jack aware that he was guilty of some small social misdemeanour in his approach. He could see why Bowring had such rigid, old-fashioned manners. 'Will Mr Kelly be staying in the house?' Miss MacFarlane asked.

'No,' Bowring answered. 'He'll be at The Hollies tonight.' This was the first Jack had heard about this arrangement; he was careful not to let his pleasure show.

Miss MacFarlane nodded brusquely and left the room.

When the door had closed behind her, Bowring said: 'If the situation arises, you can always leave any message with Nanny – however confidential. She is as much a part of SOS as any of you. Now, while you're away we'll be recceing every single venue on His Holiness's British tour. With Shalawi – al-Hussaini – gone, we're not going to get any more information from that source, so we'll have to do the job by tactical pre-emption. In other words, we'll have to second-guess them, and hope they're good enough to choose the right places.'

Haynes made a face. 'I still think it's too wide open, boss. Frankly, with so little intelligence there's too many places to look.'

'We have some intelligence,' Bowring said impatiently. 'We have a photograph of one of their men on the ground in Amman. It's not much, but it's a start. I've given it to an old colleague in counter-terrorism. They'll spot him if he comes in – at least they bloody well should. And I think I can persuade them to leave him alone.'

'Without letting on what you know?' Kelly asked.

'Don't worry about that. By the time you get back from India, we'll have produced a short-list of likely hit spots. Michelle will be covering the Pope's visit for a news agency in Nice. She's got her press credentials; she'll be able to do a lot of the close reconnaissance while she's doing her local colour pieces.'

Kelly nodded. 'With a camera?'

'Yes. And Terry will be producing all the scale maps and layouts that we'll need.'

It was, as Haynes had said, a very wide brief, but

Kelly accepted Bowring's proposition that the right hit spots would be fairly predictable. 'Boss, what concerns me is that there won't be enough of us,' he said, however.

'There'll be five of us on the ground. If we get the right spot, we don't need to be more; if we get the wrong one, it wouldn't make any difference if we were a whole squadron. And if Sufuf Allah get on to us, we'll be severely hampered; the fewer of us there are, the less chance there is of that happening.'

'But they knew you met al-Hussaini in Amman,' Kelly said.

'True, but they know they've silenced him, and they're not going to see Father Babbington again. Of course, it's quite possible they may abandon the whole op.' Bowring shrugged. 'We'd still get our performance bonus, but I'd feel we'd earned it rather too easily.'

'But you nearly got your head blown off in Fontainebleau,' Kelly said with a grim laugh.

'It'd take more than a pair of trigger-happy Algerians waving MP5s to blow my head off,' Bowring replied unemphatically. 'Now tomorrow, Jack, I want you to familiarize yourself with the anti-intrusion devices around the grounds here. Obviously I've had to keep them fairly discreet.'

'What's the area?'

'About twenty-five acres. Apart from four acres of semi-formal garden, the rest is woodland. There's a perfectly normal chain-link perimeter fence – six feet high and unprotected on top. A yard in from that is a disturbance sensor wire. It gets triggered from time to time by deer, foxes and badgers, but the circuit's complete at the moment. A hundred feet inside the fence we've got a series of magnetic and seismic intrusion detectors. There are also concealed CCTV cameras with image-intensifying filters sited in six old oaks, and four fitted on the corners of the house.' Bowring shrugged and spread his hands. 'It's not ideal, but anything more elaborate would arouse suspicions; one of my boundaries is with a patch of National Trust woodland and there's always someone pottering around in there. Up till now I've had no cause to feel this place was a target, but then we seldom operate in the UK – nothing serious anyway. I want to take a few more precautions, in the unlikely event that Sufuf Allah latch on to us. I've got a couple of dozen American acoustic buoys on FM transmitters that need siting. You could do that while you're checking the others.'

'Have you got maps of the lay-out?' Kelly asked.

'Yes. You can have those so you can get on with it tomorrow and do a few checks with Terry.'

'OK, boss. When do we go to India?'

'At the end of the week. You'll need to arrive a couple of days before the Pope and run checks on his accommodation; you'll have Vatican IDs for that. But, whatever you do, keep a low profile.'

Bowring spent another hour with Kelly and Haynes looking at the Pope's British itinerary, highlighting the places to be recced first. Later, Bowring took them to his billiard-room and left them there with a well-stocked drinks tray and instructions to enjoy themselves for a couple of hours. A series of fiercely competitive games of snooker, accompanied by a post-mortem of the Fontainebleau fiasco occupied them until Bowring reappeared to tell them that dinner was ready.

James served the meal for them at a dining-table that would have seated twenty. Kelly watched him, impressed by what Bowring had told him of this suave, silent man's shooting prowess. He would never have credited it were it not that Bowring seemed to have a natural skill at attracting this unexpectedly multi-talented type of person to his entourage. Even Nanny looked as though she could handle herself in a fight, as well as issue instructions on the correct way to eat peas.

After dinner and some glasses of the ancient, silky calvados, Bowring rang The Hollies, and Kelly was seen off through the concealed door, down into the well room. Fifteen minutes later, Michelle was pulling back the door at the other end of the tunnel. She let him into the cellar, and bolted the door again.

Upstairs, she and Gallagher had just finished dinner.

It was only ten o'clock, and Gallagher suggested that they should go out for a drink.

Michelle shook her head. 'But you two go. Just don't tell anyone where you're staying or let them see you coming back here.'

Gallagher drove the car through a circuitous route of tiny lanes to a village pub called the Thomas à Becket. It was Saturday night and the pub was fairly busy, but they found a corner to drink their pints in relative privacy.

'Well,' Gallagher asked. 'What did you think of HQ?'

'It's a hell of a set-up, but I just wonder what Bowring does with himself up there all the time.'

'He works,' the Glaswegian said simply. 'He's got fingers in umpteen pies and he likes to keep up to date with all of them. He's got no interest in other people, and even though you might think he's sort of charming on the surface, you'll find he only ever talks about his own projects.'

'I suppose so,' Kelly agreed. 'He was always like that in the squadron, but he's even got his old nanny working for him up there.'

'She wouldn't be there if she wasn't bloody useful to him,' Gallagher said. 'He's a very hard man, is Bowring,' he added with obvious admiration. 'You could drag the Gorbals and not find a harder one. It's his English gent manners that fool most people, but I can tell you, they don't mean a thing. If you stopped being useful to him, he'd sling you out – or kill you. That's why I like him – I know where I am with him.'

'What do you think about this job we're on now?'

'To tell you the truth, I think it stinks. We don't know half enough.'

Kelly nodded. 'Just what Terry was saying, but the boss seems to think we can do it.'

'He always does; and usually he's right,' Gallagher said with a shrug. 'That's why I'm still here.'

'Do you ever feel you want to jack this lot in? You know, marry and settle down?'

'No way. I tried. Hated it. I couldn't stick knowing what was going to happen every day, nothing to get the adrenalin going. How about you?'

'I was married, for a year or so, but she couldn't take it. I was still in the Regiment, you know, going off for a few weeks here and a few months there. She just couldn't hack it – went off with a bloody tractor salesman. She's still got a car of mine. I'll have to go back to Hereford and sort it out sometime. I bought one of those Morgan cars; they make them near there, and I've never been back to collect it. I couldn't face having to be nice to the new husband.'

Gallagher nodded and took a long pull at his pint. When he spoke again, it was not of their personal problems. 'Did Bowring tell you he's sending us to India?'

'Yes. In four or five days.'

'That's what Michelle said, but he hasn't told me; I guess he will tomorrow, but I'm going to tell him he's crazy. If we have to work in close to the Pope, we'll get spotted. Even if these Sufuf Allah don't try anything in India, they're more than likely going to be there checking out personal security arrangements. If they see us in England after that, they'll be on to us.'

'But they'd just think we were part of the Pope's team.'

'Look, they'd know our faces, and we'd lose most of our advantage. I think it's crazy for us to go.'

'Will Bowring listen to you?'

'Sure, if you back me up.'

They were drinking coffee on the terrace early next morning when James arrived via the tunnel. He was dressed like the gamekeeper of a large estate. He introduced himself this time, with the voice of a north country vicar, as Jim Mason.

'I've come for the weapons. I'll be driving them straight up to the house in the horse trailer. Mr Kelly, when you get up there, you're to help me unload them and put them in the gunroom.'

Kelly suggested the butler sit and join them for a

cup of coffee, but he declined, got the keys to the Land Rover from Michelle and drove away.

'Unfriendly bugger,' Gallagher snorted as they listened to the vehicle rumbling away.

Kelly didn't see Bowring when he arrived at Summerfold House but James was waiting for him. The trailer was backed up to a door at the rear of the house that had been designed for the delivery of coal straight into the cellars down a well-worn wooden chute. James showed Kelly down the stairs from the back hall, then turned into a small passage at the entrance to the wine vaults.

The coal cellar, redundant since oil-fired boilers had been installed, contained only a supply of logs for the open fires. Beyond it, through a sturdy oak door similar to the one which gave into the well room, was the gunroom. This was no gunroom in the country-house sense: the only shotguns it contained were pump-action Remingtons and Franchi SPAS 15s. It was lined with concrete and steel, and the inside of the door was a solid iron sheet. The racks which lined two walls were designed to hold over a hundred weapons of various types and sizes and a two-ton walk-in safe contained ammunition, land-mines and 66mm rockets.

By the time James had passed down Kelly's recent purchases from Bekkevoort in Bruges, the racks were full. When they had finished, they made a complete inventory of what was now a comprehensive arsenal of light assault hardware. Upstairs, the butler gave Kelly the acoustic buoys and charts of the grounds as if they were a gift from the Queen.

Dressed in a Barbour and flat tweed cap courtesy of the house, Kelly set off for the woods to carry out Bowring's instructions of the evening before. He left by the back of the house and crossed a large expanse of lawn, surrounded by an extravagant display of huge azaleas. Dotted about the garden were ornamental trees of the varieties favoured in mid-Victorian times – monkey-puzzles, Douglas firs and soaring Wellingtonias. Beyond these, the woods were thick with well-established oak, ash, beech and conifer, with a dense undergrowth of laurel and bracken which liked the acid, sandy soil. Once in the woods, Kelly called up Haynes on his walkie-talkie handset.

'OK, Terry, you should be getting me on one of the mini seismic detectors now, if I'm where I think I am.'

'Getting you faintly,' Haynes came back.

The AN/GSQ-154 miniature seismic intrusion detector would pick him up from about eighty feet in this sort of terrain. Kelly took a bearing and headed deeper into the woods until Haynes crackled over the radio that he had him good and strong. They repeated the exercise with the other seismics, and then moved on to the MAGID Model T4 DT-516/GSQs, magnetic intrusion detectors that would pick up a human carrying weapons from about ten feet.

When they had located and checked all of the detectors, Kelly turned his attention to the tiny thread of wire that ran inside the perimeter fence. He cut and then repaired it in four places, having got a positive check that the breaks in the circuit were registering.

As he had made his rounds of the existing equipment, he made notes of sites for his bagful of US Army acoustic buoys. For the most part he suspended them, out of sight, from the branches of trees, ten to twelve feet above the ground with about two hundred yards between each. Their small, integral FM radio transmitters would relay any sounds within normal human hearing.

When he had placed and checked them all with Haynes, he was satisfied that, provided the receivers were adequately monitored, intruders by any route would be detected, even if the CCTV missed them.

As it happened, Haynes had reported Kelly within sight of the sweep of the cameras in the woods for about twenty per cent of the time. The cameras on the house would take in a close approach from almost all directions.

Back in the communications room in the attic, Kelly and Haynes ran through the receiving ends of the systems, most of which Kelly had previously used in some form. Gallagher, who had been summoned up the tunnel with him that morning, hadn't been seen since his arrival. Eventually he too came up to the communications room.

'The boss wants to see you,' he said to Kelly. 'He's in the library.'

Kelly nosed the Land Rover through the sunken lanes, down to the main road running westwards to Guildford. The steady rush of weekend traffic struck him as somehow unreal after the seclusion of Summerfold House and the quiet emptiness of the wooded hills only a mile or so behind him.

He turned, heading towards Guildford, the M4 and finally Hereford.

India was off.

Bowring had listened to Gallagher and agreed,

without any resentment, almost as if he'd been expecting the objections. Perhaps he had; perhaps he liked to see how much constructive input his team could provide. He had already arranged to bring two men back from El Salvador for a quick briefing in the UK before setting off to keep close to the Pope in the subcontinent.

Kelly, glad of the chance to follow up his vague plan of two evenings before, had been dispatched to stock up on clothing and equipment from a large army surplus store close to the Regiment's home base. Bowring had agreed to give him an extra day to sort out his own business while he was there.

Walking into a bar in Hereford a few hours later, tanned, fit, obviously in work, Kelly was greeted jovially by those of his old colleagues who were there. He'd fought beside several of them and the bond that that creates is never completely broken.

He'd booked into a small hotel in the town and spent the evening grumbling good-humouredly to his mates about the boredom of most of the work he'd been doing since leaving Hereford. But he said nothing about Major Piers Bowring and Special Operations Services S.A.

At the same time he kept his ears open for news of other old colleagues, in case Bowring needed more recruits in the future. He left late, with an invitation to come to the Sergeants' Mess the following day.

In the bright, cloudless morning, the ridge of the Black Mountains, twenty-five miles west of Hereford, and the steep bluff of Gospel Pass above Hay-on-Wye, stood out clear against a blue sky. It was Kelly's first sight of the Welsh mountains for three years. They reminded him sharply of his arrival in Hereford as a twenty-three-year-old, determined to show anyone and everyone that he had what it took.

Now here he was fifteen years on, with nothing to prove, reluctant even to talk about what he was doing; yet he preferred it that way.

He smiled at the warm, familiar landscape as he drove the khaki Land Rover west out of Hereford towards the village of Eardisley.

Twenty minutes later, he slowed down as he approached a garage forecourt where half a dozen new tractors stood with a gleam on their red paint which wouldn't last a week once they had found a buyer. His ex-wife Susan and her husband, Will, lived in a large, timber-framed house behind the garage. In the garden, Kelly could make out the signs of a small child's presence – splashes of red and yellow plastic on the lawn; tiny clothes on the washing-line. He hadn't heard about a baby. By choice, he'd heard nothing in the two years since his divorce had become absolute.

Now this evidence of fertility in the woman he had, he supposed, once loved, gave him a sharp rush of sadness. But, setting his jaw, he came to a halt, reversed the Land Rover into a track and drove slowly back to the garage.

Will saw him, recognized him at once, and came nervously out of his glass-fronted office.

Kelly turned the motor off, jumped down from the dusty vehicle and waited for the chubby, red-faced tractor dealer to walk up to him.

'Hello, Jack. I didn't know you were coming.'

'Nor did I until this morning.'

'What . . . er, what did you want?'

'Just to see how you were getting on.'

'Oh, we're pretty good. Business hasn't been so bad, considering. Better than it was, anyway.'

'Glad to hear it. I see you've been building on to the house. Susan must be happy about that.'

'She is.' Will shut his mouth, uncertain what to say next, unwilling to show how little he wanted this hard, almost legendary, samurai to stay, not relishing any comparisons his wife might later make between them.

'Is she in, then?'

'Yeah. With the boy.'

'It's a boy, is it? No one told me.'

'Well, I don't suppose Sue thought you'd be interested. Anyway, she wouldn't know where to find you.'

Kelly nodded and started to walk towards the back of the garage building. 'I'll go and find her. There was something I wanted to talk to her about.'

Will waddled along beside him. 'What's that, then?'

'It's OK. I'll talk to her about it.'

Will looked worried, dropped his shoulders and fell behind.

Kelly strode casually across a patchy new lawn towards a paddling-pool where he could see Susan leaning over, splashing the child and laughing with him.

'Hello, Susan.'

She straightened her back and spun round. Her big brown eyes showed gladness, sadness and remorse.

'Jack! What are you doing here?' There was a tremor to her soft, Herefordshire voice. Guilt? Excitement? Kelly couldn't tell.

'I was in Hereford. I thought I'd drop in and see

you.' He smiled. Susan relaxed; she looked better now than when she'd walked out on him. 'And I thought I'd pick up the Morgan. I quite fancy it where I'm working down in the South of France.'

Susan's eyes dropped; she appeared to be studying the hem of her short cotton skirt. 'You . . . you'll have to talk to Will about that.'

'Why? What's it got to do with Will?'

'You talk to him,' Susan said, meeting Kelly's eye for a second.

'OK. I will in a moment. Aren't you going to introduce me to your son?'

Susan turned back to the small boy, splashing eagerly in the pool. She bent down and picked him up, holding his wet little body to her tight cotton T-shirt. 'This is Bobby. Bobby, say hello to Jack.'

The boy glanced at Kelly without much interest before turning back to his mother's breast. Susan gave an embarrassed laugh. 'I haven't really started teaching him his manners yet.'

Kelly looked at Susan's nipple, standing proud beneath the damp T-shirt. He thought about the baby sucking it. 'How old is he, then?'

'Just eighteen months.'

'He looks well.'

'So do you, Jack. Too well, almost. What you been doing?'

'This and that. Nothing very exciting.'

'Doing all right, then?'

'Making a few bob.'

'Have you got yourself a house yet, then?'

Kelly shook his head.

Susan looked relieved.

'Well, would you like a coffee or something?'

'No thanks. I haven't got a lot of time. I'd better go and talk to your husband about my car, if you won't.'

'Right. Well, I'll see you another time, then, maybe.'

'Maybe. OK, love?'

Kelly looked at her for a moment, gave her a quick wink and turned abruptly to walk back to the garage.

Will was talking to a farmer who had drawn up in an old pick-up. He looked round quickly when he heard Kelly coming and began to jiggle from foot to foot. 'I'll have to talk to this gentleman who's been waiting to see me, Mr Pugh. You come tomorrow and we'll sort it out, all right?'

The farmer nodded warily, then started his engine and drove slowly away.

'Where's the Morgan, then, Will?'

'The Morgan?'

'Yes, Will, the fucking Morgan. I left it with Susan for her to look after until I could pick it up. Well, I've come to pick it up, but she says I should talk to you about it. So, where is it?'

Will's russet features glowed.

'It's . . . it's not here at the moment.'

'Where is it, then?'

Will gulped. 'It's gone.'

'What do you mean, it's gone? You mean it's been nicked, or what?'

'Well, to tell you the truth, when you never came and picked it up, Susan thought you weren't ever going to. So . . . she asked me to sell it.'

Kelly wanted to laugh at the man's discomfort. But he didn't. His eyes narrowed.

'So you sold it, did you? How did you deal with the logbook?'

'I signed it for you.'

'You forged my signature on the change-of-owner slip?'

Will bit his lower lip and nodded.

'Oh well. It's not the end of the world. How much did you get for it?'

'Fifteen grand,' Will said quickly.

Kelly looked at him without speaking for a moment. Then he shook his head once. 'I think we'd better talk about this inside.'

Will seemed suddenly paralysed.

'In your office, Will,' Kelly hissed.

The tractor dealer forced his legs to carry him through the showroom doors, past a pair of newish Land Rovers and into his office.

Kelly followed.

'Now,' he said. 'That Morgan was brand-new. It cost me eighteen grand, but you can get a premium of three or four on the list price. So, tell me again: how much did you get for it?'

'Fifteen, I promise you, Jack,' Will whined.

Kelly was facing him now, with barely a foot between them, looking him straight in the eyes. He smiled as he slowly drew his right fist back beside his waist.

Will saw it; his fleshy face twitched; frozen with fear, he couldn't move. Kelly's fist came forward like a steam hammer and buried itself in Will's flabby guts.

Will gasped and coughed, stumbling forward as Kelly's left fist caught him full on the nose.

Kelly stepped back and let him collapse on to the

floor in front of him. He got down on his haunches to continue their conversation.

'How much did you get for it?' he asked again.

Will coughed and groaned before lifting his head a few inches off the ground, leaving a splash of blood which had dribbled from his nostrils. 'Twenty,' he mumbled, holding his hand up to his nose. 'I'm really sorry, Jack.'

'Twenty grand's not so bad. Well done, Will. Where's the money.'

Will laid his head back on the floor. 'I haven't got it,' he whimpered.

'Haven't got it?' Kelly asked with mock astonishment. 'What are all those tractors out there, then? Every one of them's worth more than twenty grand apiece.'

'Yeah, but I haven't paid for them. Business was terrible and Susan needed a lot of things when the baby came.'

'I bet she did,' Kelly laughed. 'Even after all the money I gave her when we divorced.' He straightened his legs, leant down and lifted Will up by the collar of his jacket. He half dragged, half led Susan's cringing husband across his office and pushed him down on a desk covered with a mess of papers. The man was openly blubbering now.

'Right,' Kelly said, still holding the man's collar. 'I don't need it right now, as it happens. I can give you a bit of time.'

'Thanks, Jack,' Will whimpered.

'Meet me at the Merton Hotel with it, tomorrow, midday. Cash. All right?'

Will's face drained of blood, turning to a sweaty grey. 'I . . . I c . . . can't,' he yammered.

'You haven't got any choice.' Kelly's mouth twitched up. 'You can do it. You know you can. Ask your dad. Tell him what'll happen to you if you don't. That should do the trick.'

Kelly released his grip, thrusting Will backwards on to the desk as he did so. 'See you tomorrow, then.'

He turned and walked out through the showroom to his Land Rover.

Without looking back, he climbed in, gunned the V8 engine into life and skidded off the forecourt on to the Hereford road. There was a smile on his face. He didn't make a habit of bullying, but the fat, flash bastard had deserved it.

After half a mile, he turned into a narrow lane and headed across country to do the shopping Bowring had asked him to.

9

In a pair of ramshackle barns nestling beneath a wooded hill ten miles north of Hereford, Kelly found what he wanted. On rows of ancient metal racks in Bill Bache's Famous Army Surplus Stores was enough ex-military equipment to kit out a small army with everything except firearms. He could even have bought a couple of armoured personnel carriers and a tank, if he'd wanted. He wandered around happily for an hour until he had gathered up all the boots, belts, bergens, knives, survival kits, OG and DPM clothing Bowring had specified and loaded them into the Land Rover.

Satisfied with his purchases, though uncertain where Bowring expected them to be used, he drove back down the old Roman road towards the sleepy little city. After a few miles, he pulled up outside a black-and-white pub. The soldiers he'd been talking to in Hereford the day before had told him that it had recently been bought by Mick Jones, the son of an Ebbw Vale miner and another ex-member of H Squadron.

'Bloody hell! Jack Kelly!' His one-time comrade-in-arms almost leapt over the bar to greet him. 'How are you?'

Kelly grinned. 'Pretty good, Mick. You?'

'Bored fucking shitless,' the big Welshman said

out of the side of his mouth. 'Here, come into the dining-room – it's empty as usual. What do you want to drink? Want some lunch? Course you do.' He turned as he led Kelly through a low doorway. 'Angie! Bring us two bloody great sirloins.'

He ushered Kelly into a picturesque timber-framed room, full of rustic tables and chairs and chintz curtains. He waved him into a chair. 'Pint of the local?'

Kelly shook his head. 'I'd rather have red wine.'

'Turned into a poof, then, or what?'

Kelly laughed. 'No. Just working abroad, Mick. You lose the taste for bitter.'

'I'll get the best bloody bottle in the house!' The Welshman went out for a few minutes and returned with a venerable claret and two glasses. He pulled out a chair opposite Kelly and lowered his large frame into it.

'So, boyo,' Jones said as he heaved the cork out of the bottle. 'What have you been up to? I haven't heard a thing.'

Kelly shook his head and laughed. 'I'm glad to say I can't tell you.'

'You lucky bastard! Do you know, the biggest challenge I've got running this place is making sure the minibus turns up on the right night to collect the crib team, and the occasional ruck with the brewery about a dodgy barrel of beer. So you've seen a bit of action, then?' he asked enviously.

'Just a bit.'

'Where?'

'I told you, I can't say,' Kelly grinned. 'But the boys in Hereford told me you were still working – proper work, I mean – and your brother-in-law runs the pub.'

Jones gave him a sharp look. 'Did they? Well, they don't know fuck all. I do the odd bit of CPP. Usual, boring gigs,' he said dismissively. 'But you, you're obviously up to something. You look bloody fit. If whoever's paying you needs reinforcements, you let me know.'

'Could you get through another selection?'

Jones looked surprised. 'Not without a bit of training.'

'I doubt there's much chance of anything coming up, but you never know. Anyway, what news of the other lads?'

Kelly and his old friend settled down to a few hours of reminiscing. They had done ten years together, and there was a lot to talk about. From time to time, Jones tried to trick Kelly into giving away something about his current job, but Kelly neatly side-stepped with a laugh. As they talked, Jones took no notice of what was going on in the pub even though, to Kelly's surprise, it became quite busy as lunchtime wore on. But no one disturbed them in the little dining-room.

Kelly drove off a few hours later, leaving the Welshman shaking his head in envy at the sight of all the khaki tack in the back of the Land Rover.

Kelly was welcomed with more reserve in the Sergeants' Mess at Stirling Lines that evening. Despite the close comradeship that existed when you were in the SAS, once you'd left you were an outsider, no longer privy to the Regiment's more covert activities.

Nevertheless, Kelly was a multi-decorated ex-sergeant, part of SAS folklore, and as such deserved a respectful reception. Besides, those men who were reaching the compulsory end of their stretch were anxious to keep tabs on new job opportunities.

Kelly walked back to his hotel, too drunk to risk driving through the town. But he slept soundly enough and woke next day with plenty of time to set off up the steep hill east out of the city for a tough eight-mile run.

He treated himself to a large breakfast when he got back to the Merton Hotel, and sat with a paper, waiting for Will.

Kelly saw Susan walk into the bar and wondered if she had come to plead on her husband's behalf. But if she was feeling nervous or resentful, she wasn't showing it.

Kelly got up from where he had been sitting. 'Hello, Sue. What happened to Will?'

'What do you think happened to him? He was too scared to come. I left him at home crying like a baby,' she said disdainfully.

Kelly nodded his head. 'Do you want a drink?'

'Just coffee.'

Kelly walked over to the bar and ordered it. He came back and sat down opposite his ex-wife. 'Why was he scared? Hasn't he got the money?'

'No. He hasn't. He didn't dare go to his dad. I didn't know it, but he's borrowed a lot from him already over the last few years. In fact, as far as I can see, the whole bloody business is subsidized by the old man.'

'Couldn't he get it anywhere else?'

'No, of course not. He's too much of a prat.'

'What does he think's going to happen, then?'

'He thinks you'll kill him, or at least beat the living crap out of him. I told him you won't, but he doesn't believe me.'

'Do you think I won't?'

'I know you won't; you're not that much of a bastard.'

'Are you so sure?'

She nodded. 'You've never scared me, Jack. What you did used to – when you were away. I used to lie awake all night wondering where you were and if you'd been killed. Every time they reported a killing in Ireland or anywhere, I thought it was you, until they gave a name. I drove the Wives' Support Group mad.'

Kelly didn't say anything. He looked at her, with her deep-brown eyes and the good, strong features of a country girl.

'Anyway,' she went on, 'I've brought the money. My dad just picked it up from the bank. He wasn't too happy, but he said I was going to get it anyway when he died. Mind, he did say Will could do with a good thumping.'

Susan reached into a bag she had brought in with her and pulled out a large brown envelope. 'It's all in fifties. Do you want to count it somewhere? I've got a receipt here for you to sign.'

Kelly looked at the envelope. It seemed absurd that the contents of a small brown paper package should mean so much.

He shook his head. 'No. I don't want to count it.' He looked into Susan's worried eyes. 'I don't want it. I don't need it. You have it. Put it on deposit and keep it for some real problem. You never know, you may find you want to leave Will and it doesn't sound as if he could afford much maintenance.'

Susan looked at him, then down at the envelope, still clasped in her hands.

'But,' she said, against all her instincts, 'I can't . . . It's yours.'

Kelly shrugged. 'It's yours now. I've given it to you. Put it back in your bag and take it straight to the bank when you go.'

There was a look of intense gratitude, and excitement in her eyes. 'But Jack, I want to give you something back.'

Jack shifted in his chair, feeling an erection coming on. She was offering herself to him, there and then – and not just as repayment for a debt. He wanted her, had the opportunity, the time, a room upstairs.

He shook his head and cleared his throat. 'You don't have to give me anything.'

'But I want to, Jack.'

'No way. I didn't come back here to wreck your marriage. What's done's done between us.'

She looked at him bleakly, unwilling to have her offer rejected.

Wordlessly, she put the package back in her bag and stood up, leaving her coffee untouched.

She turned and took a couple of steps, then looked back. 'Thanks, Jack. I'll never forget.'

He watched her neat little bottom, firm in black leggings, leave the bar and he sighed. Hell, he thought, I could have done with it, too.

That evening, when Kelly arrived back at The Hollies with the supplies he had bought, Michelle was alone. He was struck by the great differences, and certain similarities, between her and his former wife. The main difference as far as he was concerned was that Michelle was totally unavailable.

In the previous nights he had stayed in the house

with her, she had treated him as if they were the same sex, or brother and sister. No put-down, no rejection – just complete indifference. Either there was something wrong with her, or she was just too dedicated to her work for Bowring. And though he was fairly sure that there was no sexual relationship between her and the boss, he couldn't restrain a feeling of envy at Bowring's influence over her.

This time, Gallagher wasn't there. Michelle cooked a dinner that would have passed muster at any Côte d'Azur restaurant he'd ever been to, though she did it, Kelly guessed, because she had been told to. As they ate together, she brought him up to date.

During his two days away, a lot of groundwork had been done on the Pope's UK tour. Details of every rally venue and all routes that had already been fixed had been given to them by Monsignor di Montefalco.

Lyke and Dowson had appeared, walking around Summerfold, as if they were weekend guests at a shooting party, Michelle said. With Bowring and Haynes, they had been poring over the maps Terry had made on his computer, approaching the task as if it were SOS who had been ordered to make the hit. Two SOS men who had been employed in El Salvador had arrived, spent three hours with Bowring and left immediately for India. Andy, Michelle said, had been sent to London.

When they had finished eating, Michelle looked at her watch. 'We have to go up to Summerfold now. Major Bowring has a guest from London he wants us to meet.'

Michelle phoned HQ to say they were on their way. Leaving the lights on in The Hollies, and the intruder alarms and a scanning CCTV camera to guard the place, she and Kelly set off up the tunnel. As they went, she pointed out some features of the underground passage that he had missed on his previous trips along it.

At either end of the tunnel, just inside the doors, was a narrow slot in the roof. Retracted in the slots were half-inch steel sheets which could be dropped to block off the way in or out to anyone who didn't happen to have an oxyacetylene lamp and a lot of time on their hands.

Also concealed in the roof, every twenty yards, were small explosive charges primed to release canisters of red phosphorus into the restricted air, a useful substance with the property of absorbing oxygen; in combat it was used in grenades to flush out armoured personnel carriers. Here, the charges were linked and could be activated by a continuous detonation cord.

There was also, Michelle said, a remotely operated choke on the air inlet which he had seen half-way along the tunnel. Similar systems were also installed in the lower tunnel that ran from the well to the ice house. All entrances were monitored by CCTVs.

Even without the overt presence of armed men or guard dogs, Kelly concluded, you could house a US President in Summerfold with reasonable peace of mind. It was, he thought, all a bit over the top, but then he'd already learnt that Bowring worked on the SAS principle of eliminating or diminishing every risk he could.

There was a group gathered in a large drawing-room at the front of the house, on the other side of the hall from the library.

Miss MacFarlane was sitting quietly on one side,

and James was serving drinks, but there was no doubt both were included in Bowring's conference.

Bowring, Haynes, Lyke, Dowson and a fifth man whom Kelly didn't know were sitting on large leather chesterfields in front of an unnecessary log fire.

Despite the brandy glasses and cigars, there was an air of sober alertness to the party. They all rose when Michelle and Kelly walked in.

'Evening, Jack. How did you get on?'

'Got all the gear, boss. Checked out the Sergeants' Mess. I've made notes on some potential recruits.'

'Good. Let Nanny have them in the morning. Did you see your ex-wife?'

'Yes,' Kelly said simply.

Bowring nodded without expression. 'Right. I want you both to meet an old friend of mine, Harry Cotterell, from MI6. He has very kindly agreed to tell us a bit about Sufuf Allah. Harry?'

Everyone sat down again except Cotterell. He was tall, blond and dressed in an impeccable three-piece tweed suit. When he spoke, his voice and every gesture suggested a background of Eton and a regiment Guards regiment, belying his first-class degree in modern history from Oxford.

'A bit, I'm afraid, is all I have to tell you about Sufuf Allah – the Ranks of God. We've only become aware of their existence fairly recently, but what we've heard has worried us. It seems to be composed of the more viciously militant previous members of several other organizations – Hezbollah, Al Fatah, Islamic Jihad, PLFP, Abu Nidal – all committed without reservation to the destruction of Israel, with representatives from half a dozen different Arab nations. In so far as they are administered at all, the administrative base is in

Beirut, though there is certainly a presence in Baghdad. Assad won't have anything to do with them in Syria. We don't know but we guess funding is largely Iraqi and Libyan. We have unconfirmed reports of training camps in the Bekhar valley. Anyway most members would have already received extensive training in their previous organizations. Unlike many of these Islamic groupings, there is no identifiable connection with any European terrorist group; we have, for instance, no evidence of liaison with the Provisional IRA or INLA. So far, we've positively identified five prominent members of Sufuf Allah.'

Cotterell reached behind him and picked up a folder from the table beside the sofa. He pulled out five eight by ten black and white photographs and passed them around to his audience, who studied them as he continued.

'The two known positively to have been actively involved in assassination and sabotage, and the ones to watch, are known as Abdul abu Said and Salah Mahmoud. Of course, it's perfectly possible the others have been too.' He turned to Bowring. 'Until Major Bowring is able to tell me where you expect these people to become active, I can't offer you our most recent monitoring of their movements, such as it is. I am here, as the major has explained to some of you, in an unofficial capacity, and it is only our respect for your organization and some of the operations it has successfully mounted that I'm prepared to tell you what I have. Of course, we fully understand why other governments find it necessary to employ people such as yourselves, and we are pragmatic about your own need for secrecy, but, in the end, we do expect a quid pro quo for any help we might give you.'

Bowring nodded with a smile. It was clear to Kelly that the two men knew and understood each other well.

Later, when Cotterell had completed his briefing with more details of the style and *modus operandi* of the terrorists he had identified, the party broke into smaller groups. Haynes and Kelly excused themselves and headed for the billiard-room.

Over a vicious game of snooker, they discussed Cotterell's presence at their HQ.

'Frankly,' Haynes said, 'it's a bloody miracle that a senior man from MI6 is prepared to come and brief a group of mercenaries.'

'I don't know,' Kelly answered. 'It seems to me that Bowring has spent a lot of effort keeping in with his Establishment mates. I mean, he's one of them after all; and I don't suppose he's ever done anything to embarrass them.'

'You mean he's never let them know if he's done anything that might. But to get right inside the intelligence services like that' – Haynes shook his head – 'it's amazing. Did you recognize any of them mug shots?'

Kelly shook his head. 'No. Abdul abu Said looks like the worst of them. If he's not the boss, he must be very close to him. Not a kisser you'd easily forget.'

'Yeah, well, if you want to stay alive on this job, you don't want to forget any of them.'

Bowring came to The Hollies in the morning.

'I want you to go to London and meet up with Gallagher. He's been watching a flat in South Ken for the last couple of days. He'll tell you what's going on.'

'OK, boss,' Kelly said, hardly excited about the idea of static surveillance.

'Take a set of these shots up,' Bowring said, giving him copies of the photographs Cotterell had produced the evening before. 'We may be able to get a cross-ref on them.'

Michelle took Kelly to Dorking station, since Gallagher had the hire car and there wasn't a spare at HQ. A little over an hour later, he was getting out of a taxi in Queen's Gate. He checked the address Bowring had given him: it was a slightly tatty hotel occupying one of the formerly grand terraced houses. He went in. There was no one at the reception desk so he let himself into a shoebox of a lift, took it to the fifth floor and walked down a poky landing to room fifty-three.

He knocked. There was no immediate reply. After ten seconds, the door flew open in front of him, to reveal a small, scruffy bedroom. 'It's OK, Andy. It's Jack,' he said, keeping dead still.

Gallagher stepped from behind the door, holding his nine-milly in both hands. He lowered the gun when he saw that Kelly was alone. 'Hello, Jack. I didn't expect you so soon. Welcome to my five-star accommodation.'

Kelly followed Gallagher into the room and closed the door. On a dressing-table in front of the window were a full ashtray, several empty Marlboro packets, a newspaper, a pair of binoculars and a Canon camera fitted with a massive 600mm lens.

'How's it going?' Kelly asked.

'It's a bummer,' Gallagher said sourly. 'A bunch of students. I've logged over twenty mugs. Of course, I haven't been at it round the clock.'

'What's the story, then?'

'Hasn't Bowring briefed you?'

'No. He said you would.'

'OK. I'll tell you. The boss sent me to a meet with one of his contacts – an old colleague of yours, as it happens.'

'What? H Squadron?'

'Aye. Though this guy's a bit older than you; a Taffy called Mick Jones.'

Kelly laughed out loud. 'The lying bastard!'

'What?'

'I saw him only yesterday in this pub he's got outside Hereford. He told me he was bored shitless running the place, and he tried like hell to pump me for information. I guess he must keep tabs on a lot of the boys when he's up there. Did you tell him about me?'

'No, course not.'

'Thank Christ for that.'

'Aye, but he'll soon know: we've got a date with him this evening.'

The meeting was in a big, anonymous, Victorian pub in Westminster, full of civil servants on their way home. The Welshman was standing at the bar reading the *Evening Standard* when Gallagher walked in with Kelly behind him. Jones nodded and took a couple of paces towards Gallagher to greet him. Then he saw Kelly and stopped, shaking his head with a rueful grin.

'Hello again, Mick,' Kelly said. 'Has your place got a crib game with this lot tonight?'

Jones laughed. 'I might have guessed you'd be with our old boss. Right, lads. We'll have a quick drink, and then we'll take a walk.'

While they were in the pub, they didn't mention the reason for their meeting, or make any reference to their own current employment. Outside, they got into Gallagher's car – Jones in the front passenger seat, Kelly in the back – and headed back to South Kensington.

Once they were in the car, Jones told Kelly the truth about his current employment.

'I'm sorry about that yesterday. Obviously, the blokes in the Kremlin know what I'm doing; they had to give the references, but apart from a few senior NCOs, none of the others do.' The 'Kremlin' was the SAS's name for the intelligence unit in Hereford. 'I've got a bit of a roving brief, actually, somewhere between the Anti-Terrorist Squad and Special Branch, with a particular interest in the mercenary activities of British nationals.'

'Does Bowring know that?' Gallagher asked.

'Of course he does. And he gives us a lot in return. He's told me that he's interested in a particular bunch of Arab loonies. We've said we'd keep our eyes open. Did you get anything much today?' he asked Gallagher.

'No. This Imam Hafiz Jadid you put me on to is more of a sort of religious guru than a terrorist.'

'What makes you think that?'

'The type of people coming to see him, the people he's been out with. None of them look like soldiers – more like serious students. You get to know what to look for.'

'You're right; he's a sort of holy man, but that doesn't mean he's not dangerous. We think he might be here on a recruitment drive.'

'Why don't you watch him yourself, then?'

Jones laughed. 'Have you any idea how much a stake-out costs us? We have to be bloody sure it's worth it to justify it. You know how tight-fisted all the departments are these days. But Bowring's prepared to do it, and we think there's a connection between this bloke and the Sufuf Allah he's so interested in. The fact of the matter is that there's more and more aggressive militancy developing among a lot of the Muslim students in this country, and a lot of them are very well educated and likely to achieve positions of influence, if not actual power, here.'

Gallagher, driving, shook his head. 'There's no one interesting going to turn up at that place.'

'I'd give it a while longer. Anyway, until your boss tells you to quit.'

'Aye,' Gallagher said, resigned. 'Anyway, Bowring's sent up some mug shots for you; five suspected members of Sufuf Allah. Show him, Jack.'

'We've got six, actually,' Kelly said. 'There's mine from Amman too.' He took the photographs out of an envelope and passed them forward to the Welshman.

'Are these for me?'

'Yes,' Gallagher said. 'But the deal is, you tell us first if any come in.'

'We can't guarantee that. Are you expecting them in?'

The Scot shook his head vaguely. 'Not particularly. But there are always reasons why they might be over here. Of course, we've got people in France and Switzerland looking out for them.'

'Right. You can drop me here,' said Jones. 'I've got a meet in Sloane Square. Let me know what comes up in Queen's Gate, and don't forget, I'll want a set of your shots from there, too.' He turned back towards Kelly. 'I don't suppose I have to tell you, but keep your bloody trap shut about me, or Bowring'll sling you.'

Kelly laughed. 'You didn't get much out of me at lunch yesterday, and that was after two bottles of your best plonk.'

'Plonk? Château-Lafite '75. Fifty quid a bottle, that's worth.' Gallagher stopped the car and Jones let himself out. 'Cheerio, lads. Keep in touch.' Seconds later he was swallowed up in the crowd heading for Sloane Square tube station.

Kelly spent another two days in Queen's Gate taking turns at surveillance with Gallagher. They'd booked a second room in the hotel so that they could get a decent bit of sleep.

At half-past three on the second afternoon, to alleviate his boredom, Kelly decided that he'd tail the first interesting-looking individual to leave the flat opposite.

As Gallagher had told Jones, most of the visitors to Imam Hafiz Jadid looked like earnest, book-loving students. But there was one, apparently a European, who displayed much more assertiveness as he descended the stairs and bumped into another man, who was minding his own business as he entered the five-storey building.

'Right,' Kelly said to his colleague, who'd just returned. 'I'll take my four hours off tailing that character.'

'What the hell for?'

'Something to do. And he looks a lot dodgier than any of our man's other visitors.'

'He hasn't had many whites, that's true. Are you sure he went to see the Imam?'

'I've got a snap of him, through the window of the bloody flat.'

'Good enough. You'd better go or you'll lose him before you've started. Have fun.'

Kelly didn't wait for the ancient lift. He ran down the stairs three at a time and came out of the door of the hotel just in time to see his quarry turning left into Old Brompton Road.

The man was in his mid-twenties, about five feet ten, with short brown hair. He was wearing jeans and a white drill jacket. There was a sort of thrusting arrogance about him as he strode along the busy pavement. Kelly could not have said precisely why he had decided to follow this particular man, beyond the fact that he looked like someone who enjoyed causing mayhem.

It was a slender reason for going to the trouble of tailing the man, and an hour later, Kelly was wondering why he had bothered. Via the Circle and Northern lines, the man led him to a building in Hampstead – a student hostel by the look of it and the people coming and going.

From a distance, Kelly watched the place for a few minutes and came to the conclusion that his quarry, having gone home, would probably stay there. He retraced his route to South Kensington, telling himself that he'd only undertaken the chase to kill a few hours. In any case, it was gratifying to know that his solo surveillance skills weren't too rusty. Street-wise as he undoubtedly was, the guy hadn't suspected a thing.

When Kelly reached the hotel, Gallagher was more cheerful than he had been earlier.

'The boss has been on. He wants us back at HQ, thank God.'

They were back at The Hollies by seven that

evening and were immediately summoned up to Summerfold.

The Pope was due to arrive in England in eight days' time. There was a palpable increase in controlled tension within the English headquarters of SOS; fewer jokes, less lavish hospitality.

Although Bowring was confident that the attempt on His Holiness's life would not be made in India, there was always the possibility, and he had only two men out there to handle it. It was, on his part, a calculated risk. He was ninety-five per cent sure the attempt would take place in Britain, and he wanted his best men on the ground there.

There had been a further complication. As soon as Kelly and Gallagher walked into the library, where James had directed them, Bowring got up from his desk holding a newspaper.

'The *Telegraph*'s man in Paris has picked up a rumour that there was a European mercenary unit involved in the fracas at Fontainebleau. That's going to get them very excited in Whitehall, especially as they know we're interested in Islamic groups at the moment. Frankly, I'd expected to hear from them by now.'

'Boss, why did you tell them what we were after?' Kelly asked.

'If I didn't tell them something, they'd go to a lot more trouble to find out for themselves. This way I at least control what they know; and of course, they give me something back.'

'But the photos we gave Mick Jones yesterday were given to us by MI6.'

'That's simple exploitation of interdepartmental

secrecy and rivalry. I've made it my business to keep contacts with most of them.' Bowring's top lip twitched. 'Sometimes I think they trust me more than each other. As far as France was concerned, it must have been the domestic staff at the house who told French security that they were tied up by Europeans, but there's no way any of us would be identifiable, and they haven't even specified that they're talking about Brits. Anyway, there's bugger all we can do about it now.' He sighed. 'We should have killed them.'

'That's what I thought at the time,' Gallagher said.

Kelly didn't say anything.

'Right,' Bowring went on, with a change of tone. 'Let's have a look at what you got in South Ken.'

Gallagher had brought with him a stack of shots that he and Kelly had taken over the last few days. Bowring took the prints and spread them out on the table in front of him. He inspected each one carefully. When he'd been through them twice, he asked: 'Did you follow up any of these?'

'Only that one,' Kelly said, pointing to the three shots he had taken of the one caucasion visitor to the Imam Hafiz Jadid. 'I tailed him this afternoon to Hampstead, to a hostel mostly used by LSE students. I left him there.'

'None of the others?'

'None of them looked any worse than the rest,' Gallagher said, shrugging. 'Frankly, boss, it was a bit of a waste of time.'

'We'll see. There's a growing amount of militant fundamentalism among Muslim students in this country. If I were planning a hit, I think I'd see if I could make use of them. After all, they know their way around, speak the language properly and I have no doubt there are a few who'd like to get close to the more extreme Islamic groups. In the meantime, we've identified a number of choice hit sites.' Bowring cleared the photographs from the table and laid several maps on it. The first was of the whole of England and Wales.

'If I were running Sufuf Allah, I'd choose either here,' he said, putting his finger on Cardiff, 'the rally in the Arms Park, or here, at Aintree Racecourse, where they're holding an open-air mass, or here' – he pointed at the heart of London – 'at the final rally in Hyde Park. Terry and Michelle are checking them out now, making a full photographic survey. Michelle is interviewing officials and should be able to establish the Pope's planned movements at each venue. I want you two to carry on checking on local Islamic groups. Jack, take Manchester and Cardiff. Andy, you follow up more of Jadid's visitors, or see where he goes to talk to any groups. What we're looking for is any connection with the six faces we already have.'

Kelly hired a Ford Sierra and drove straight to South Wales, where he spent a day trawling around the areas of Swansea and Cardiff where most of the Bangladeshi, Somali and Yemeni populations lived. He also looked at the mosques and other public Muslim buildings. Back in his hotel that evening, he rang Bowring.

'Hello, boss. I'd have to be here a month to get anything useful. I need some short cuts.'

'Leave it with me,' Bowring said, and rang off.

Kelly had swum forty lengths of the hotel's empty

pool by seven-fifteen next morning. As he climbed out and began to dry himself, a man appeared through the swing doors from the hotel and sauntered across the tiled floor.

'Mr Kelly?'

He was about thirty, prematurely balding, and dressed in a baggy linen suit, with a silk shirt open at the collar.

'Who are you?' Kelly asked.

'Mick Jones sent me,' the man answered with a broad Cardiff accent. 'Said you needed a hand.'

Kelly nodded. 'Great. I'll meet you outside in ten minutes.'

'Mine's the green Daihatsu.'

In the Japanese 4WD vehicle, the driver introduced himself. 'Barry Bevan. Freelance. Used to be in CID here. Didn't like the discipline – or the money. The residents think I deal drugs so they try not to take too much notice of me. Inspector Jones tells me you need to identify a few of the Muslim groups here. I can tell you the name of any of them who are anyone in South Wales. What exactly are you looking for?'

Kelly told him – without saying why – and pulled on a baseball cap and dark glasses while Bevan drove him around, pointing out houses and individuals from his all too conspicuous car.

As they drove, stopped, looked and waited, Kelly pressed Bevan for information on possible student groups, but the Welshman didn't have much to offer. At the end of the day, having told Bevan he'd contact him if he needed him again, and feeling frustrated, Kelly contacted Bowring.

'Look, boss, there don't seem to be any organizations of the type we're looking for. The man you got Mick to put on to me knew his stuff; he's been hanging around the ghettos for years and he had no real leads.'

'OK. Drop it. Get up to Manchester. Book into the Piccadilly. I'll have someone round to you first thing in the morning.'

'Right. How's Andy doing?'

'Getting somewhere. I may need you back in a hurry, so check in every hour.'

It was several years since Kelly had been to Manchester. As far as he could see, the most significant changes to have taken place, besides the general cleaning up of the city, were the new trams and the increase in the number of beggars and prostitutes on the streets. He didn't doubt, though, that the long-established Islamic presence in the city was as strong as ever.

It was an Indian with the accent of a native Mancunian who turned up to see him at his hotel next morning. Ahmed Qureshi's family were originally from the Punjab, but his grandfather had brought his family to England in the early thirties to found what was now a substantial textile trading company. Ahmed, in his mid-twenties, had been at Manchester Grammar School and was now a journalist on one of the big local dailies. Utterly irreligious himself, he had nevertheless found himself covering a lot of news concerning the city's diverse Muslim community.

Outside, in Kelly's car, Kelly told Qureshi what they were looking for.

'Fundamentalist Islamic student groups? Plenty of scope there. I don't know what the hell they think they're going to achieve; chance to sit around and shout at each other, I shouldn't wonder. There's a very active bunch of them in one of the University halls of residence. Let's take a look at that first.'

Qureshi directed him south towards the University, along Oxford Road. They turned right by a municipal park and pulled up just short of a large, ugly, sixties building.

'I doubt if there's much going on now, but I'll pop in and check.'

Qureshi leapt out of the car and strode purposefully into the students' accommodation.

Kelly waited twenty minutes, using the time to scrutinize the men and women going in and out of the building. Glancing in his mirror as he had done regularly while he'd been waiting, he received an abrupt shock. Walking towards the rear of his car, with three young Asian students, was the man he had followed from Imam Hafiz Jadid's flat in Queen's Gate to the hostel in Hampstead.

Instinctively, Kelly sank down in his seat and pulled the peak of his baseball cap lower over his face, even though he knew he hadn't been spotted by his quarry in London. His pulse quickened and his nerve ends tingled. The group were passing his car now. He heard the white student talking, with a sharp London accent – '. . . we'll have to finalize it tonight, though . . .' – and carry on out of Kelly's hearing.

With a jolt, he saw Qureshi emerge from the student building and walk towards the car. He prayed that the journalist wouldn't say anything until he'd got back in.

The others, walking towards Qureshi, took no

notice, and he let himself into the passenger side before he said anything.

Kelly didn't start the car at once. He held up his hand for a moment as he watched the Englishman and the three Asians disappear through the door by which Qureshi had just left. Once they were in, Kelly started the car and drove on past the entrance.

'I knew one of those,' he said with excitement. 'I've seen him in London – the English one – visiting some kind of militant iman.'

'There are quite a number of white Muslims up here,' Qureshi said. 'Funny lot, but they're very committed.'

'Did you find out anything?'

'Yes, I did. There's some kind of meeting tonight, of the Council of Muslim Students. I was trying to see if I could muscle my way into it, but I think it'd be tricky – them not knowing me. They didn't suspect anything, though; it's lucky my dad always made me keep up my Urdu. I just said I was interested in getting involved, but they said I'd have to come to the next open meeting.'

'Still, you could hang around, couldn't you?'

'Of course I can. And I'll be able to tell you if that white bloke's part of it.'

Kelly was surprised but relieved that what he had thought was going to be a wild-goose chase had yielded a hard connection. He couldn't keep the elation from his voice when he rang Bowring.

'I've met up with my chum from Hampstead,' he said. 'He's up here to discuss something with a group of Muslim students.'

'Good. Can you leave the fellow who's with you to keep an eye on him?'

'I'd rather stay up here.'

'I need you in London, Jack. Can this other chap cope?'

'Well, probably. He's quite on the ball.'

'Fix it, and make sure he keeps in contact. Then get back to South Ken and contact me as soon as you're there.'

'OK, boss.'

Kelly spent an hour briefing Qureshi, without giving him much of an idea of what might be going to happen. The journalist was aware that he was involved in something bigger than mere news gathering. It didn't take much to convince him of the need for discretion, particularly since, as Kelly told him, there'd be a much bigger story in the end.

10

Kelly turned wearily into Queen's Gate from busy Cromwell Road and parked on a double yellow line a short distance from the hotel where he and Gallagher had stayed. Bowring had told him to get there and await instructions. Kelly cursed the lack of a telephone in the hired car and hoped he wouldn't have to wait long.

He didn't. Within a minute of his turning off the engine, he saw Jim Mason walking up the tree-lined street towards him.

Kelly wound down the front passenger window. 'What's the story?'

The butler poked his head into the Sierra and said: 'Major Bowring's in his car, a grey Daimler round the corner. You're to go and see him. I'll stay here with this one.'

Kelly climbed out and left the driver's door open.

He found Bowring parked in the adjacent street and opened the back door.

'Get in, Jack.'

Kelly slid in beside Bowring. The interior of the Daimler smelt of cigar smoke and leather.

'We've had a bit of luck. Your Palestinian's shown up,' Bowring said curtly. 'Andy was on to Jadid. Followed him to a house in a mews at the end of this road. Then he came out after an hour or so, with the chap you photographed in Amman.' He grinned and went on. 'I'm glad we've had a result. Andy's whinging was getting tiresome and I was beginning to think Jones had given us a bum steer. And now you've picked up this English Muslim in Manchester. I think we're getting somewhere. Just in time, too. I imagine my friends in Whitehall have worked out what's going on, so we'll have to tread rather carefully. Our contract with the Vatican is unequivocal on the question of not alerting the authorities here.'

'But they'll be on to it PDQ.'

'Not quick enough. We're a lot further on than they are. But it means you'll have to tell Jones you've drawn a blank. He'll forgive us when it's all over – I hope.' Bowring shook his head. 'That's the trouble with working on one's own doorstep.'

A radio on the seat beside Bowring wheezed into life.

'Blackbird?' Kelly recognized Gallagher's voice. 'Coaltit here. Are you receiving me? Over.'

Bowring picked up the radio. 'This is Blackbird. Carry on, Coaltit.'

'I'm at 57K142.'

Bowring opened a London A-Z and flipped through it until he found a page covering an area half a mile west of them.

'Go on, Coaltit.'

'I have Polecat in view. He's talking to a Joshua Reynolds in the street outside the tube station. Which shall I take?'

'Stick with Polecat. Keep in contact. I'm sending Wagtail to join you. Over and out.'

Bowring turned to Kelly. 'You're Wagtail.'

'You don't say. Who's Joshua Reynolds?'

'One of the five mug shots Cotterell gave us.'

'Shit. They're coming in fast.'

'But complacent, if they're chattering in the street. We can only take one, so we'll stay with Polecat for now. He's likely to be a general-purpose gofer and getting around more than the high-ups.'

Bowring picked up a dark-blue tourist's rucksack from the floor of the car. 'Here's a radio, an A-Z and a nine-milly in the wash-bag. To give your position, reverse the page number and add a digit to the grid. They're in Earls Court Road now. If Polecat takes the tube, you won't get anything from Andy until they come up for air. Once you've caught up with him, try and keep them in vision. I'll be cruising nearby. If you need back-up, I'll come in.'

'OK. You just want him tailed – no contact?'

'Yes. We don't want to touch them until we know which of them is doing the shooting, and preferably from where. I thought that balls-up in France might put them off the whole plan, but they're obviously anxious to make their mark as soon as possible. Besides they won't get a crack at His Holiness like this for some time. Now, just brief me on what you saw in Manchester.'

Kelly gave him a more detailed description of the Englishman he had seen go into the hall of residence with the three Asians, and told him what Qureshi had said about the meeting that was due to take place there that evening.

'This Qureshi should be OK,' Bowring said when Kelly had finished. 'He doesn't know it, but he's worked for me a couple of times before. His editor's an old friend of mine; he was the son of the gardener at Summerfold. Bright man. Got a scholarship to Manchester University from Guildford Grammar School.'

Kelly couldn't help a smile at the diversity of Bowring's contacts.

'Jack, most people like to be used, provided you tell them that's what you're doing, and reward them, of course. Tell James to get back here, will you.'

Kelly nodded, took the rucksack and let himself out of the car.

Back in the Sierra, Kelly took the radio from the bag and opened the channel. He also unpacked the Browning – fitted with a silencer – pushed thirteen rounds into the magazine and stuffed it into a pocket of his leather jacket.

In the absence of any communication from Gallagher, he started the car, pulled on his baseball cap and sunglasses and drove unhurriedly towards the mews where Bowring had said that Gallagher had followed Polecat.

On the way, he stopped to buy an *Evening Standard* from a newsvendor. He pulled into a gap opposite the eastern exit of the double-ended mews which gave him a clear view down it. He turned the motor off, lit a cigarette and opened his paper like any bored minicab driver.

The radio buzzed. 'Blackbird. This is Coaltit, are you receiving me? Over.'

Kelly picked it up.

'This is Wagtail. Where are you?'

'Polecat's turning back into the mews.'

Kelly glanced down the mews. Seconds later, he saw a sallow man of medium height walk into the cobbled street from the other end – too far for Kelly to positively recognize him as the man who had tailed Bowring in Amman.

He started his car and drove leisurely into the mews. He glanced at the front doors of the small houses, as if searching for a number. The man walking towards him looked briefly at him without breaking his step. Kelly drew level with him, and with a rush of adrenalin, saw that Gallagher hadn't been mistaken. The Palestinian was even wearing the same clothes as in the shots Kelly had taken outside the Hotel Philadelphia.

Kelly drove slowly by; Polecat ignored him. He carried on until he passed under a white-stucco archway at the end of the mews. Gallagher was waiting on the far side of it, out of Polecat's sight. Kelly made no sign of recognition. He pulled up fifty yards away, put on a tiny throat mike and a headset and put the radio in his pocket.

He opened his *Evening Standard* again.

'Coaltit?'

'I've got you.'

'What's the score?'

'Polecat's back in his den. We sit.'

'I'll go back and take the other end.'

Kelly started the Sierra again and took the next road on the right which backed on to the mews. He ended up where he had been parked before Polecat came back. This time he got out of the car and walked a few yards out of sight of the narrow lane.

He had smoked three more cigarettes when a black taxi turned in and rattled over the cobbles. As Kelly strolled back towards his car he saw the cab stop halfway down the mews. He got back into his car and his radio fizzed into life.

'Wagtail?'

'Receiving.'

'He's taken a cab, my way.'

'OK. I'm on to him. You take one too. I'll tell you where.'

Kelly turned into the mews as the taxi drove through the archway, indicating right. He reached the other end in time to see it heading up towards Cromwell Road. There was only one other car between them.

He had no trouble sticking with them, trusting that the anonymous beige Sierra wouldn't arouse Polecat's guard if he looked back. He followed the taxi through the thickening early-evening traffic as it crossed the main radial routes of Cromwell Road and Kensington High Street, heading north.

Gallagher came on the air.

'I've got a cab stopping. Where to?'

'Head towards Notting Hill Gate. I'll give you a number in a moment.'

Polecat's cab turned east on to Bayswater Road. Kelly grabbed the A-Z and opened it on his steering wheel, ready to give Gallagher a reference as soon as he could. Meanwhile his quarry carried on along the broad thoroughfare for half a mile, before diving abruptly to the left into a maze of white-stucco streets, where every other building was an hotel or guest-house catering mainly for Middle Eastern visitors.

The taxi stopped in a narrow, leafy square and Polecat got straight out and walked across the pavement, up the steps of one of the hotels.

Kelly drove past and round to the far side of the square, where he still had a view of the hotel entrance. He switched off his engine and flipped through the pages of the A-Z as he got through to Gallagher.

'Coaltit?'

'Hello, Wagtail,' the Scot said huskily from the back of his taxi.

'95K476. Polecat's gone to ground. Arrive here on foot and raise me. Over.'

'OK. Over and out.'

For the third time, Kelly picked up his newspaper, of which he had so far read no more than the front-page headlines, and kept his eyes on the hotel. There was nothing in particular about it to help him; it was like thousands of others in the area – just the sort of place to house an Arab associate of Polecat's. Kelly wondered which particular associate; perhaps another of Cotterell's mug shots.

'Wagtail?'

'Receiving you, Coaltit.'

'I'm on foot, walking into the south side of the square.'

'Clock my car. Our man's dead opposite.'

Gallagher sauntered into Kelly's view and strolled down the far side of the square, slowing his pace almost imperceptibly as he passed the hotel. He carried on, crossed over into the square's gardens and sat on a bench beneath the canopy of a large plane tree. He pulled his A-Z from his pocket and began to study it.

An hour dragged by. Groups of Arabs in djellabas and their womenfolk in yashmaks arrived back at the hotels, on foot and in taxis, with great bags of shopping. A younger generation in leather blousons and jeans came out, on their way to hang around the shopping malls in Queensway.

Gallagher and Kelly kept silent; they had no need to communicate until, at last, Polecat reappeared. He came out of his hotel and turned north, seemingly unaware of Gallagher sitting under his tree. Kelly started the Sierra and drove round the square in time to see Gallagher turn left into a road at the far end.

Kelly glanced down the road as he drove past. Apart from Gallagher, he saw no one. There were cars and vans parked tightly along both sides of the narrow road, and a 'No Entry' sign. Kelly could see that the other end gave on to a busy shopping street. He drove on and took the next left, running parallel to Gallagher's turning. He accelerated up to the busy street, then nosed left into the traffic and left again, towards Gallagher.

He had gone fifty yards when he saw Polecat, twenty yards ahead, leaning motionless against the back of a van, with a hand in the bulging pocket of his bomber jacket.

Kelly's guts tightened. Gallagher was strolling along the pavement towards the van, quite unaware of what was waiting for him behind it. Kelly glanced in his mirror. No other vehicle had followed him into the road. He dropped his speed to a crawl, winding his window down, as if he were looking for somewhere to park. Ten yards from the Palestinian, he pulled the Browning from his pocket.

At the same time, Polecat had discreetly pulled something from his jacket. He glanced down the otherwise empty road at Kelly, angrily impatient for him to drive past. When Kelly stopped fifteen feet from him, Polecat's eyes flashed wild with suspicion and indecision.

Calmly, without haste, Kelly lifted the Browning.

A double-tap, two muffled shots, straight to the head. There was just time to see a look of amazed disbelief on the man's face before he crumpled to the ground.

Before the Palestinian's body had completely come to rest on the oily grit of the road surface, the Sierra was in gear and roaring up the road, and Gallagher had reached the van.

'Coaltit. Walk on. Polecat's retired.'

'What the fuck happened?' Gallagher's voice was thick with shock.

'Just walk on past. Leave it,' Kelly said, trying to convey urgency without giving away to any airwave eavesdroppers the momentousness of the balls-up he and his colleague had just caused.

Gallagher's step faltered as he glanced down at the motionless body between the back of the van and a battered old Jaguar. 'OK, Wagtail,' he said, swivelling his eyes to look fifty yards straight ahead where a trio of young Arabs had turned into the road, walking towards him.

He carried on at a casual walk, burning up inside at the incompetence he had displayed in getting sussed so easily. He passed the Arab boys, reached the busy main road at the end and crossed straight over into a vast shopping mall that had been created from one of London's grand old department stores to cater for the unending stream of visitors to that part of London.

He walked briskly through the browsing crowds and out the other side, then turned up a quiet street leading to Bayswater Road.

'Wagtail? Are you receiving?'

'This is Blackbird,' Bowring's voice came back to him. 'Go ahead, Coaltit.'

'I'm clear.'

'Double check. I'll pick you up at 95K571, westward in twenty minutes. Wagtail, take that car back to the hire company immediately.'

'Roger, Blackbird,' Kelly's Liverpudlian drawl sounded unruffled.

Gallagher checked his A-Z, zigzagging through a maze of small roads towards Notting Hill Gate, where he dived down into the tube station, bought a ticket and switchbacked through the system of escalators and tunnels before emerging on the south side of the road to walk east back up Bayswater Road. Even if Polecat's people had put a team of watchers on him, which he very much doubted, he would have stretched them too far by now.

He spotted Bowring's Daimler cruising towards him as he reached his RV point. The car slowed and the rear door was opening before it came to a stop. Gallagher was in and the car moving off in less than three seconds.

'What happened?' Bowring asked tersely.

'Dunno, boss. He must have sussed me.'

'That was bloody careless of you,' Bowring hissed through tight lips. 'I've given the police an anonymous tip-off. With luck they'll have Polecat out of the way before his friends find out what's happened to him. With luck. Then we'll just have to keep our fingers crossed that no one took the number of Jack's car. If it gets traced back to us, it's not going to be easy to explain things to our Whitehall friends.'

'Aye, well, I'm sorry, boss. I was certain he wasn't on to us.'

'It may not be the end of the world. In fact, if his friends simply lose him, that could help; it's only if they know it was us who hit him that we'll have problems.'

Bowring arranged to pick up Kelly outside Gloucester Road tube station.

'Did you have to kill him?' Bowring asked as soon as he was in the car.

'Yes, I did. He was on to Andy. He'd have taken him out and gone back with the information that they'd been sussed and we'd have lost the lot of them.'

'And they'd have cancelled their operation, which is what we're being paid for.'

'And I couldn't let him kill Andy, could I?'

Bowring nodded. 'It's OK. It'll be much more satisfying to take them in the act.'

Satisfaction, that's what you're in it for, Kelly thought.

'Right,' Bowring went on. 'We'll go for a walk in Hyde Park. James, drop us by the Queen Mother's Gate.'

There was the usual summer crowd milling around the south-eastern corner of the Park. Bowring and his two soldiers strolled unobtrusively among them.

'The Pope's final rally is being held here. His motorcade will leave Westminster Cathedral, go round in front of Buck House and up Constitution Hill to give the punters a good look. They're opening the gates under the Quadrica Arch at Hyde Park Corner. He'll come through that, in front of Apsley House then turn up Park Lane. They'll go the full length of Park Lane and turn into the park at Cumberland Gate. The platform is being erected up there at the top end.' He waved up towards Speakers' Corner and looked at his two mercenaries. 'If they haven't had a crack at him in Cardiff or Aintree, where would you think they'd try and hit him here?' he asked, as if he were setting them a casual brain-teaser.

They stopped. Kelly swept his eyes along the route, that part of it which they could see, from the back of Apsley House to Marble Arch.

'Shit, there's about a dozen useful spots. But anyway, they could just do it from the crowd.'

'Unlikely, no exit,' Bowring said shortly.

'That wouldn't matter to a *hara-kiri* fanatic. They'd think they were going straight to heaven.'

'They wouldn't get near enough,' Gallagher said. 'Even if the DP Squad haven't sussed by then that somebody's going to try and pull something, they'll have hundreds of men on the ground. They'd be mad if they thought they could hit him out there. No, I reckon it'd have to be from one of the buildings along the other side of Park Lane, and they'd try and take him as he goes past.'

'In an armour-plated vehicle?' Bowring said.

'You could pierce the Pope-mobile with a 7.62 round.'

'No guarantee.' Bowring shook his head. 'They'd need something a lot heavier.'

'OK,' Kelly ventured. 'They could set up in any of those hotels – Inn on the Park, Lanesborough, Intercontinental, Londonderry House, The Hilton, Dorchester, Grosvenor House. Bloody hell, that gives them a choice of a few hundred rooms.'

Bowring nodded. 'Correct. We've got rooms booked in most of them for two nights before. Not the Hilton, Londonderry House or the Inn on the Park. I wouldn't choose any of them – too restricted an arc of fire. If no hit's been made by then, I'll have a fifteen-post surveillance team in operation, starting the Tuesday before. Right now, our job is to latch back on to those faces we've got. That gives us the flat in Queen's Gate, the mews house in Earls Court and the hotel in Bayswater. I'll get Michelle and Terry back to support you. Andy, you take Terry; Jack, you can have Michelle . . . and don't look so bloody pleased about it – you know the standing orders.'

The next morning, Michelle joined Kelly in the scruffy hotel opposite Imam Jadid's flat in Queen's Gate. They were watching from a room one floor higher than the previous OP. There wasn't a sign of life in the flat.

'I'll go and make some enquiries,' Michelle said.

In spite of Kelly's arguments, she left and he watched her cross the road and disappear into the building.

Two minutes later, she came out and back to their room.

'He's gone,' she announced. 'I told the caretaker I'd just started teaching at the Lycée in Old Brompton Road and needed a flat in a hurry. He said one had just come vacant – a Lebanese man had taken it for two weeks, but left last night in a hurry with a week paid for. It looks as though you have scared them away.'

A similar story came back from Gallagher at the mews house. The hotel in Bayswater didn't seem worth watching but Kelly and Michelle were able to book themselves into a guest-house opposite after dark that evening and watched it continuously for two days. By now they knew every wrinkle and characteristic of the five 'Joshua Reynolds'. None of them, nor anyone else who particularly excited suspicion, came or went.

Despite their physical proximity and their shared sense of purpose now that they were really on the scent of Sufuf Allah, Michelle maintained the polite, invisible barrier she had erected between them.

Kelly was philosophical; even if she had shown that she was interested in reciprocating his urges, they had a job to do which needed one of them permanently at the window with binoculars and a camera. He adopted a new tactic, and restricted his conversation purely to their immediate task.

'Why are you so quiet?' she asked at the end of the first day. 'Did it upset you to kill that man?'

Kelly shook his head without looking up from the newspaper he was reading.

'So it means nothing that you took his life?' she persisted.

This time Kelly looked up. 'You've never killed anyone, have you?'

'No,' she answered neutrally. 'Not with a direct shot.'

'When you're dealing with a target, you get used to the idea that it's not a person, just a problem to be dealt with. If you worried about upsetting their mums, you'd never be able to do it. I was brought up to think that it was a sin to kill; and so it is, if you know the person or they're not an enemy in a particular conflict. Anyway, this guy was planning to kill the Pope, so they couldn't hold it against me that much – in fact I suppose it's worth a few heavenly brownie points.'

'Did . . . did he die fast?'

Kelly snapped his thumb and forefinger. 'Like that.

Two shots, one hole. The only thing that worried me was I was using high-powered rounds. That's why I had to go for a head shot, otherwise the bullets might have passed right through his thorax and the van behind him where Andy was walking.' He shrugged. 'You have to think of these things as well as everything else, all in a second or two.'

Michelle turned back to the window. 'They say you were quite a hero in the SAS.'

'Do they?' Kelly said unenthusiastically.

'Well, you must have been, to win your Military Medal.'

Kelly laughed. 'That didn't seem very heroic at the time. I got it mainly for getting bloody wet and not leaving my post.'

'But you must have done something more than that.'

Kelly sighed. 'I was the leader of a four-man patrol, dug into a soggy pit above Port Stanley. They dropped us in Sea Kings from *Hermes* with a week's rations, early in May. You should have seen the way the mist rolled off the sea in the mornings. Anyway, we were there nearly four weeks. We sent in Harriers on half a dozen raids to wipe out Argy Chinooks and Pucaras and we sent back a lot of useful stuff on the state of the enemy troops we could see. Even then I could tell the Argies weren't keen to fight. They looked more miserable than we did, and we couldn't even cook ourselves a decent meal for over a fortnight in case they spotted us. It wasn't much of a laugh, and I was bloody pleased to get back, but the brass were chuffed.'

'Was that all?'

'It was enough, but we also took out an enemy

patrol – ten of them, four of us. We had to; at that stage the Argies didn't even know we were on the islands and it would have blown the whole oppo, and we couldn't take them prisoner – we didn't have any food.'

'And you worked in Ireland?'

'Yeah, but I'll tell you about that another time, all right? I'm just trying to crack this crossword.' He nodded at *The Times* on his knee.

Bowring gave Michelle and Kelly two days in Bayswater before he agreed with them that any Sufuf Allah there must have moved out at the same time as the others.

'I wish to God Andy had been more careful, Jack,' he said to Kelly in private back at Summerfold. 'When this job's over, you'll have to give him some refresher training.'

'I don't know if he'd take it from me,' Kelly said.

'He will if I tell him to. In the meantime, all our hot leads in London have gone cold and I'm having trouble getting anything else out of Harry Cotterell and Mick Jones. And I can't tell them any more now – not without revealing our involvement in Polecat's death, which would be tricky. Incidentally, I don't think anyone's reported your car to the police or we'd have heard by now.'

'I don't reckon anyone saw it, unless they happened to be looking out of a window at the time. The gun was silenced, and he went down without any fuss between a van and a car.'

'I'm glad you haven't lost your touch, anyway. In the circumstances it was the only option. The trouble is, all we've got to go on now is your white Muslim in Manchester. He's the only connection with the imam, and that doesn't necessarily mean he's with Sufuf Allah. Qureshi's been in touch, but I'm afraid he doesn't seem to have got much yet, so you and Michelle are going to Manchester in the morning. I'll see what I can do to revive the leads in London.'

Next morning, at the wheel of yet another mundane saloon, this time a Vauxhall Astra, Kelly wished he'd brought his own Range Rover across from France. Not that he'd had an opportunity, and anyway it would only have been more conspicuous. But he did have Michelle for company. It occurred to him how much he would have liked to have stopped and had a long, leisurely lunch with her in some country restaurant, but they didn't have time, and it probably wouldn't have got him anywhere with her. On the whole, they restricted their conversation to the job in hand, and some guarded revelations on her part about Bowring and SOS.

'What made you want to join?' he asked.

'It was a good opportunity for me,' she said. 'There are no other ways I could have done what I'm doing now, not in any official force.'

'They've got a few women attached to the Regiment now,' Kelly said. 'Mind you, I don't think they get to do much killing, mostly surveillance. I suppose that's where Bowring got the idea. Is that what you wanted to do?'

She didn't answer, but Kelly had no doubt at all that she had the strength to go through with anything that Bowring was ever likely to ask of her. And there were certainly advantages in having a resourceful woman on the team; she could make approaches which would be much more difficult for a man without raising suspicions. The only trouble was, she was too pretty for most people not to notice her, and that was a disadvantage. But he didn't press her on her reasons for coming to work for Bowring.

In Manchester, they booked into separate rooms in the Piccadilly. Ahmed Qureshi, bursting with excitement, arrived soon afterwards.

Bowring and Dowson were in the library at Summerfold House, reviewing Operation Parson's Nose.

'It's not going well, Piers. Sooner or later someone's going to draw a connection between us and that balls-up in Fontainebleau.'

'Relax. The French are much more pragmatic than our people about that sort of thing. The only French nationals involved were a handful of Algerian hoodlums from Marseilles; nobody's going to lose much sleep over them. It would suit the security services in Paris much better to treat the whole thing as an inter-Arab dispute of some sort. Certainly if they had conveyed any suspicions of a British involvement to Whitehall, I'd have heard by now.'

'You may be right, but gunning down that Palestinian in a London street in broad daylight, for God's sake!'

'It was the only option. Thank God Kelly still knows how to think on his feet – and how to shoot straight.' He walked over to the window, where the view of the South Downs was obscured by low cloud. In the immediate foreground, though, a large black saloon was winding its way up the long drive from the lodge. 'Here's Cardinal O'Keane's man. I wonder why Montefalco isn't coming.'

'He's probably on his way back from India. And

that's another thing. Frankly, we're bloody lucky nothing happened over there. I think it was a hell of a risk to make the assumptions you did.'

'Well, I was right, and besides, if there had been a plan to make the hit there, our chances of getting on to it were so slim as to be negligible. I was going to send Gallagher and Kelly; I'm rather glad they didn't want to go, because even though the trail's gone tepid for the moment here, we've made a lot of progress.'

'But your man in the AT Squad isn't going to give you any more, is he, and what else have we got to go on?'

'The Manchester connection looks promising, though I think we might be dealing with another branch of the organization. The only common link we've established is the Imam Hafiz Jadid, the religious leader who was staying in Queen's Gate. Unfortunately, I know very little about him or where he's coming from. MI5 have him logged as an ex-member of Islamic Jihad, but that's all.'

The official car from the Papal nunciate had disappeared from view round the side of the house and a few moments later, Bowring and Dowson were interrupted by a knock on the door, followed by Miss MacFarlane announcing, 'Father Sullivan,' and showing in a short man wearing a dog-collar and a well-cut black suit.

Father Sullivan was in his forties, sharp-eyed and with a pugnacity discernible in his manner and his handshake.

When the three men had introduced themselves, Bowring offered drinks.

'Bourbon,' the priest specified in a strong Midwest accent and a way that suggested that, though he might be a man of the cloth, he was also a man of the world.

Bowring waved the American into one of the leather Empire chairs, while he and Dowson sat at each end of the writing-table.

James brought the drinks and poured them. When he'd left, Father Sullivan came straight to the point.

'Look,' he said in a voice that was surprisingly gravelly for his small frame. 'The cardinal wants you guys to pull out of this deal.'

Bowring let neither his surprise nor his exasperation show. 'Pull out? But Father Sullivan, we have established that there are a number of people already in the country almost certainly planning to kill the leader of your church. Surely you can't ignore the seriousness of that threat?'

'We don't think there is a threat any more. We've had information that the plans for the assassination have fallen apart.'

'Where did you get this information?'

'I can't tell you that,' the priest said curtly. 'You know damn well we receive a lot of intelligence through our Middle Eastern legations. For God's sake, it was us who picked up on Sufuf Allah's plan in the first place.'

Dowson leant forward in his chair. 'But Father Sullivan, we have a contract with your government. Unlike the Catholic Church, we are not a charity, and we entered into the contract on the basis that we stood a good chance of earning our performance bonus.'

'Don't worry about that. If His Holiness doesn't get shot, you get your bonus, and all your expenses to date.'

Bowring took a deep breath and leaned back in his

chair. 'You're the client. It's up to you. But I'll want this alteration to your terms in writing.'

Dowson looked at his principal, who deflected him with a glance and went on: 'But until I'm able to assess the quality of your intelligence, I think you'd be very unwise to dispense with our services.'

'Cardinal O'Keane is adamant. He feels we could do ourselves a lot of damage by being involved in this unofficial killing that's been going on.'

'Why? There's absolutely nothing to connect you to it.'

'Except you, Bowring.'

'I'm hardly likely to offer that information to our authorities, or the French.'

'You may not have the choice.'

'Believe me, Father Sullivan,' Bowring said coldly, 'you can have absolutely no doubt that the choice will always be mine. But before I accept your alteration to our agreement, I should like it confirmed directly to me or my representative by your superior.'

'You don't think the cardinal has time to come round to clandestine meetings with mercenaries, do you?'

'Possibly not, but our agent, Mr Dowson here, is quite ready to leave for Rome immediately. So, you arrange it. Then, of course, we'll cease all active involvement at once.'

The priest took a moody swig of his whisky. 'OK,' he said decisively. 'I'll fix it. Just one thing, though. Cardinal O'Keane hasn't had a chance yet to talk about this to Monsignor di Montefalco, who's not back from India yet. If Montefalco gets in touch, just stall him, OK?'

Bowring nodded. 'No problem. But in the meantime, I think you should consider what you're saying. Although the Diplomatic Protection Squad will be in operation as a matter of course, they are not aware as we are of Sufuf Allah's original intentions. Are you going to tell them about this?'

'No point. Like I say, we consider, from the intelligence we have received, that there isn't a risk any more. And we don't want to put any kind of diplomatic strain on His Holiness's visit here.'

Bowring turned to Dowson. 'You'd better get off to Rome then, Michael.'

11

The same dense blanket of cloud which had hidden the South Downs from Bowring's view extended across the rest of England, swallowing up the treeless ridges of Howden Moor.

Kelly peered through his Zeiss 10×50s down into the valley where the brook that was the young River Derwent flowed off the north-eastern flanks of Bleaklow Hill in the High Peak between Sheffield and Manchester.

'Bloody hell,' he said in a husky undertone. 'He'll have to do better than that if he thinks he's going to have a fair crack at the job.'

Michelle was beside him, likewise prostrate in a shallow hide of heather and bracken. They had walked three miles up to the ridge from the next valley. Once they had hit the skyline, Kelly had insisted that they crawl. In a battered bergen, one which he had bought on his trip to Hereford, he had carried a rudimentary camouflage kit.

'You could do better then that,' Kelly added with a laugh.

'I suppose all soldiers are chauvinists by definition,' Michelle observed lightly. 'Even when you know I could probably do better than you.' She also had her glasses trained on the two men who stood amid waist-high bracken, two hundred and fifty yards below them.

One was a dark-skinned Palestinian who'd spent the previous five years being educated at the University in Amman, and in the Bekhar valley. He had learnt to parse an English sentence and strip down an AK47 with equal facility. Now he was teaching, not English, but the handling of small arms to his English pupil.

Kelly and Michelle had heard enough about this Englishman to feel they were beginning to know him.

Michael Duckett, born and brought up in Wandsworth, South London, abandoned at the age of six and taken in by Barnardos, had eventually won a place at Westminster Polytechnic to read Economics and History. But he had never reconciled himself to his early abandonment. His burning resentment had deflected the few people who had ever made any attempt to like this unlikeable boy. When it had been expounded to him by an Islamic fundamentalist group in the Poly, he had hungrily grasped to his bosom the notion of universal Muslim brotherhood. He was deeply grateful to belong, grateful to the point of being ready to risk his life to demonstrate his commitment.

But even if he was prepared to die hitting out at the world's most prominent Infidel, he must do it effectively. He must learn how to place the shots, in quick succession from a distance that was likely to be the closest he would come to his target. And, as his Arab brothers had told him, because he was white he would be able to get much closer than they would.

Duckett felt honoured, and at the same time anxious not to let down his Muslim mentors. He gritted his teeth and clutched the wooden butt of the .375 Colt he had acquired two days before in a tacky bar in Moss Side. Ahmed Qureshi had been there in the bar to watch the negotiations.

Qureshi had not seen the gun, or the money, but he knew Duckett was there to do a deal, and that he wasn't buying crack.

Kelly and Michelle, outside the bar, had watched him walk back to his digs up the Oxford Road. After that, one of the three of them had stayed near him for the next forty-eight hours, until, that morning, he'd been picked up by a young Arab in a new BMW and driven out of Manchester on the M67, through Glossop and up into the High Peak by the Snake Pass.

Qureshi had followed and reported back when the BMW had turned up the small road to the Howden Reservoir, deep in the upper Derwent valley.

They had tried to guess the purpose of Duckett's journey there. And Kelly had worked out from the map where the two men might have gone.

Duckett and his trainer had chosen as isolated a spot as they could have found on a grey Tuesday morning. They had brought with them a bagful of empty Coca-Cola cans, now lined up on a rock ledge twenty yards from where they stood in the bracken.

The pistol was silenced, though Kelly could make out another weapon in the Palestinian's hand – an airgun, probably, to explain their activity to any possible, though unlikely, passer-by.

Duckett reloaded and fired another six rounds in quick succession. This time he hit two of the cans, an improvement on his previous best score of one.

'He's very nervous,' Kelly whispered.

'How can you tell?'

'From the way he's standing; he's much too uptight.'

They watched him load and empty the six chambers a dozen more times. He was beginning to show more consistency.

'If he gets near enough, and he's not too worried about getting caught, he could do damage,' Kelly pointed out.

'Then we should get rid of him now, surely,' Michelle whispered back.

'No. They'll have a back-up. The only way to be sure they fail is to be there when he's about to make the hit. They'll have no time to replace him then. Right, we've seen enough of this. We'll try and get back to the car before they leave.'

Kelly led the way, flat on his belly up to the ridge, staying in the bracken so that the hump of his bergen wouldn't show.

On the other side, they stopped a moment for Kelly to raise Qureshi on the walkie-talkie.

'We're coming back down to our car now. We may get there before them, in which case we'll wait. But you stay in yours on the main road. They'll probably head back to Manchester. Stick with them until you know we're on to them, then we'll have to leap-frog. And get Bowring on the phone and tell him we need at least three more men up here.'

Kelly had parked the Astra twenty feet into the woods off a hairpin in the road and thrown a camouflage net over it.

The two men in the BMW following the lane down the side of the reservoir to the main road wouldn't have seen it, even if they'd been looking. Michelle and Kelly watched them go past.

'We'll leave Qureshi to pick them up first,' said Kelly. He squelched his radio to raise the journalist and told him to be ready for them. Qureshi was waiting a hundred and fifty yards east of the junction with the road that snaked across the bare hills from Sheffield.

'Men, I asked for,' Kelly said to Haynes. 'And he sends his old nanny.'

Haynes laughed. 'You don't want to worry about her. She knows what she's doing; he's trained her himself. And no one ever susses they're being watched by an old lady like that.'

Michelle, Kelly and Haynes were in Kelly's bedroom in the Piccadilly Hotel. Miss MacFarlane and Gallagher were taking a four-hour watch outside the large, gloomy house where Duckett had taken digs.

'I hope you're bloody right. The Pope arrives tomorrow, goes to Buck House; next day, Westminster Cathedral; Saturday, private audiences; Sunday, mass in Cardiff; Tuesday, Aintree.'

'Where do you think our man will try his hit?' Haynes asked.

'Could be any of them, though as he's up here, and his back-up, I'd say Aintree was favourite.'

'Yeah, that's what the boss thought, too,' Gallagher said, nodding. 'Especially as you didn't find any real heavy Muslim militant groups in Cardiff. Buck House trip's no good; he goes by too fast and disappears into the palace. And matey wouldn't risk trying to go into the Cathedral with a weapon, would he?'

'No. His best chance is definitely one of the open-air gigs – Liverpool or Hyde Park. But it makes no odds.

Provided we don't lose him, we'll know where he's going for it.'

Bowring met his London agent in Dowson's house in Lord North Street, near the Houses of Parliament.

'Well?'

'O'Keane's adamant there's no threat – at least, not enough to justify the risk of us getting tangled up with our own security services. I think he's having a dose of cold feet about employing us in the first place.'

'Why should he get cold feet now, for God's sake?'

'I don't know; he didn't tell me and I'm not a mind-reader. I suspect his diplomatic colleagues got wind of it and are kicking up a fuss.'

'What's he like, then?'

'Big, tough bastard; more like a fight promoter than a cardinal, though I gather he's on the liberal wing of the Catholic Church.'

'He's wrong about the absence of a threat. Kelly and this chap Qureshi are on to an Englishman, a crank called Michael Duckett who's become a fanatical Muslim. He's already got a record for ABH at an anti-Salman Rushdie rally. He was in contact with Jadid before he disappeared, and he's been buying weapons and taking shooting lessons from an ex-PLO soldier.'

'Where is he now?'

'Manchester.'

'Aintree, do you think?'

'No guarantee. I've got five watchers on him at the moment, plus Qureshi, who's pretty useful. They'll know soon enough when Duckett makes his move.'

'Aren't you going to call them off, now I've got

confirmation of the revised terms from the cardinal?'

Bowring shook his head. 'No, I'm not. It's possible that Duckett and whoever's put him up to it aren't part of Sufuf Allah, but I think it very likely there's at least a connection through the Imam Jadid. Besides, I'm not sure about O'Keane's motives, and I want to be sure we get our performance bonus.'

'What are you implying about O'Keane, exactly?'

'I'm not sure. But apart from any financial considerations, as you well know, once I've taken on a job. I'm very disinclined to drop it; it's not good for our reputation.'

'You won't get any more exes paid from now on,' said Dowson, whose fees in part depended on the profitability of a job.

'But if His Holiness goes home walking in his own white leather slippers, we get a million dollars; seems worth a small investment to make certain of it.'

'As a matter of curiosity, Piers, do you have any personal feelings about saving the Pope's life?'

Bowring lifted his shoulders. 'He seems a perfectly nice chap, with sound views on homosexuals, but I'm C of E myself.'

Dowson burst out laughing. 'Who are you kidding? You're not C of anything.'

His Holiness John Paul II was greeted with rapturous cheers by a seething crowd outside Buckingham Palace. Interspersed among the crowd were several hundred alert, hard-faced men, too busy to cheer. Special Branch and the Diplomatic Protection Squad had been deployed in strength.

Certain people in M15 and the Anti-Terrorist

Squad had deduced, without firm intelligence, that a new militant fundamentalist Muslim faction was planning an introductory propaganda coup.

The problem was that every known activist of that persuasion who had recently entered the country had ducked clean out of sight. Mick Jones reckoned he was owed a quid pro quo by his old boss; Bowring was stonewalling, claiming he'd lost them too. But Mick knew they had to be still here; no one had seen them leave.

In the isolation of his quite separate department, Harry Cotterell felt cheated by his old friend, but he had nothing to bargain with. He didn't want to fall out with Bowring – God knew, he could have had Piers's hide if he'd wanted – but he was damned if Bowring's gang of hirelings were going to upstage his own department.

In Manchester, Kelly and his team had scattered themselves around several small hotels, and restricted their meetings to cells of two. They only had one tail to watch, and if they lost that, they had no other tracks to follow. Even though they hadn't been sussed, they couldn't afford the smallest risk to their cover.

Miss MacFarlane in her silver Metro proved invaluable, while Michelle's striking looks had to be disguised with spectacles, straggly hair and the dowdiest clothes she could find in the local Oxfam shop.

'Christ, you look terrible,' Kelly said when he saw her.

'Maybe that'll stop you thinking you want to get me into bed all the time.'

'What the hell are you talking about? I've never even suggested it.'

Michelle laughed in a way that instantly neutralized Kelly's annoyance at his own transparency.

'Oh well, if it isn't true, then of course, I apologize.'

'Well,' Kelly said. 'I don't now.'

'I won't look like this for ever, you know.'

Over the next four days neither Duckett nor any of his half-dozen Arab colleagues behaved as if they thought they were being watched. They appeared supremely confident of their cover, all attached as they were in one way or another to the University. Kelly guessed that if they were connected with the heavyweights of Sufuf Allah, the link was fairly remote; certainly none of the 'Joshua Reynolds' appeared in Manchester. Not, that is, until the day before the Pope was due to say Mass at a rally of two hundred thousand Liverpudlian Catholics in the middle of the world's most famous racecourse.

It was Michelle who made the connection, almost by chance as she was just finishing a surveillance stint outside the hall of residence where Duckett and his Muslim brothers most often gathered. Kelly had agreed with Bowring that, through lack of manpower, they wouldn't be able to watch any of Duckett's collaborators, but Michelle, in a newly hired Ford Fiesta, had spotted the Arab whom she and Kelly had watched coaching Duckett out on the moors.

The man got into his BMW and drove, with Michelle close but discreetly behind, a few miles south to Stockport. In the old centre of the town, he parked in a dingy side street and walked into a scruffy restaurant called the Scheherazade Lebanese Kebab House.

Michelle drove on past, parked the car in the next street and, pulling up the collar of her well-worn, ankle-length man's raincoat, sauntered dreamily down the far side of the street. She lost the rhythm of her walk for only a fraction of a second when she saw the Palestinian come out again, look up and down the street, paying her no attention and speaking to someone over his shoulder. A second later Abdul abu Said appeared behind him, and they walked together to the BMW and got in.

Michelle didn't dare turn at once, let alone run back to her car. She could only look in frustration as the car screeched off and turned out of sight. As soon as they were gone, she tried to raise Kelly on her walkie-talkie. But she was out of range; there was no response.

Incensed at her bad luck in getting caught out, she turned back. She forced herself to stay at the same dozy pace, in case anyone was watching from the restaurant, ambled back to the corner, then ran to her car.

There was just a chance she might catch up with them if they were heading back into Manchester.

But she didn't.

Fifteen minutes later, she burst into Kelly's room in a small hotel in Lever Street.

'What the hell are you doing here?' he asked.

'I've just seen Abdul abu Said, with one of Duckett's friends.'

Kelly jumped to his feet.

'Shit! Where?'

'I followed the PLO man, the one who was training Duckett, down to a kebab place in Stockport. I left my car, and saw him come back out with this other guy

– definitely Abdul abu Said, I'm sure of it. But they drove off fast and I couldn't catch them.'

'Bloody hell, I wish we had more men! They must be going for the hit at Aintree tomorrow and this guy's come up to take charge.'

'I think so.'

'Right! We can't let Duckett out of our sight. The five of us, and Qureshi, we'll have to put a six-man watch on him, to cover the back entrance of anywhere he goes. He's going to be a lot more nervous and careful now it's so close. Especially if abu Said's here now; he's not going to take any chances, and he knows how to keep out of sight. You get on to Miss MacFarlane and Terry and tell them what's going on. They're to join up with Andy and Qureshi. I'll talk to the boss and catch up with you. Make sure Andy and Terry have a few spare magazines, too.'

'And me,' Michelle said coolly.

'Yeah, sure, you too.'

Bowring put the phone down, pleased with himself. He'd got his men in the right place at the right time – a fundamental prerequisite for success in battle. They knew what to do at Aintree, and how to do it.

However, he hadn't expected any known representatives of Sufuf Allah to turn up there. But if they were involved, they were unlikely to be deterred by one failure and the loss of one English Muslim. Quite probably, they were prepared to treat the thing as a dummy run if it didn't come off.

He looked out of his library window for a few moments at the beeches in his woods, turned to gold now by the sinking sun. He reached forward and picked up the phone again. He dialled a number and listened thoughtfully to its ringing. When it was answered, he spoke quietly.

'We start watching tomorrow. Confirm the rooms and have everyone in place by midday.'

'OK, sir.'

'I'll let you know how to contact me in the morning. Be available to take my call at eight-thirty.'

'Understood, sir.'

Kelly was right. Having been a basic, simple task, the surveillance had now become more complicated. Suddenly Duckett and his supporters seemed to have been made aware of the possibility that they were being watched, for they had taken to moving around separately and using alternative exits to the buildings they entered. Kelly, in no doubt now that Duckett was to be the hit man despite his inexperience, concentrated his restricted manpower on the Englishman.

The next morning Gallagher watched Duckett walk a short way down the Oxford Road, turn off, and get into a small Ford van which he hadn't used before. As Kelly and his team had expected, the van headed west out of Manchester on the M62. Between them, the SOS task force had five inconspicuous vehicles: two driven by single women and one by a scruffily dressed Asian. Haynes went with Kelly to co-ordinate communications.

Duckett surprised them by not turning north on to the M57, but then he'd almost certainly been told to be careful.

Kelly got on the radio. 'Brenda and Qureshi, stay with him. We'll get on up and wait on the A59 on the way out. Give me any significant direction changes.'

From the bulletins issued every so often by Miss

MacFarlane and Qureshi, Duckett drove on into central Liverpool to make a few inept attempts to shake any tail before he inevitably headed north for Aintree.

More significant was Miss MacFarlane's next report.

'He's picked up some support.'

'Switch channels to specify,' Kelly snapped.

She came back on a new wavelength. 'I've seen two. A blind mouse and got no knickers.'

'Thanks, Brenda,' he laughed.

He cut off and turned to Haynes in the driver's seat. 'Did you get that? Registration letters ABM and GNK. Neither of those is local, so with luck we won't get on to a red herring. Anyway, I should get the numbers from her later.'

Kelly wasn't surprised that Duckett had back-up, but he doubted that they would keep too close to him when they reached the racecourse, if they went in at all. At least SOS would be ready for them.

There was a steady stream of traffic with them on the motorway now, a lot of it, Kelly guessed, heading for the Papal rally. Once they had turned off to follow the signs to Aintree, cars and coaches were converging from every direction, eventually bottle-necking in the approaches to the car parks.

Kelly called Gallagher on the radio.

'Carry on and pick them up on their way up the A59. Keep in vision, then take close order. Report your position before you leave your car.'

'Roger.'

'You too, *chérie*.'

Kelly watched Gallagher and Michelle overtake them and carry on past the entrance to the racecourse. Despite the density of the traffic, he didn't think they would have too much trouble picking out the white van and Qureshi and Miss MacFarlane's cars. With luck they would also identify Duckett's back-up from the registrations.

Haynes drove the Astra where they were directed into the main car park, to the west of the stands. He parked, and stayed in the car. Kelly got out, wearing his headset, as if he were listening to the live radio commentary of the event, and a hidden throat mike. Round his neck, like many another experienced rally-goer, hung a pair of binoculars. He wandered back towards the entrance and leant against a fence post to watch the crowds flock in to pay their respects to the leader of the world's most numerous religion.

Haynes's voice fizzed in his headphones. 'Brenda's given me the numbers, I've relayed them to Andy.'

Five minutes later he came on again more urgently. 'Andy's followed matey round to the car park on the other side, by the Canal Turn. So did his back-up.'

Kelly pushed himself off his fence post and started to walk with the rest of the crowd through the main gates behind the old grandstand.

Out in the centre of the course, a vast platform had been erected, facing the stands. It was eight feet high, some sixty feet long and thirty deep, to accommodate the Pope, his entourage and Britain's leading Catholics. At the back of the platform, on its own dais, was set a large, neo-gothic throne beside an altar with all the paraphernalia of crucifixes, lecterns, candles, thuribles, and bells, as well as microphones to relay the words of the Mass through banks of loudspeakers dotted among the already vast crowd.

Kelly climbed a short way, as far as he could, up the steps of the stands, which were jammed full by then. He gazed with frustration across a sea of heads to a point on the far side of the course where thousands more were pouring into the area ringed by the racetrack.

The excited murmur of the crowd was joined by the music of a brass band accompanying the opening hymns. Kelly came back down from the stand, muttering as he went, 'Terry, I'm going to try and make it across, but tell Andy he's on his own.'

Gallagher parked his car twenty feet from Duckett's van. He put on his Walkman headphones and turned up his collar. To comply with Bowring's explicit orders, he wasn't carrying his Browning, but tucked inside his denim jacket in a tough, slim leather sheath was a freshly honed, nine-inch stiletto of dark steel.

He got out of the car, and his flesh tingled at the sight of his target within easy calling distance. He looked around, smiling affably at anyone and everyone, to show that he was sharing in the excitement and goodwill of the occasion.

Duckett's bony features were pale, framed by his lank brown hair. Gallagher could almost feel the tension in him now his Muslim brothers had left him on his own to make his grand gesture for Islam. Certainly there were no Middle Eastern faces in the crowd immediately around him.

Duckett carefully locked his van and began to walk stiffly with everyone else in the direction of the huge platform, four hundred yards away.

Gallagher slipped in behind him, never more than twenty feet away, but always with at least half a dozen people between them.

Duckett did glance back now and then, nervously

and not expecting to see any face he recognized, not really seeing at all. Gallagher carefully avoided his eyes, mingling with the people closest to him, exchanging pleasantries with them.

As they got closer to the platform where Catholic dignitaries in white vestments were beginning to gather, the crowd became denser, but not impassable, as people had seated themselves on the ground on rugs or on small collapsible chairs, unscrewing vacuum flasks of tea and waving banners of welcome for the Pope.

Duckett wormed his way deeper into the throng, drawing closer to the platform where shortly His Holiness Pope John Paul II would arrive to give his first blessing to the great gathering. He stopped beneath a cluster of loudspeakers, and leant against the scaffold tower that held them.

Gallagher hung back for a moment before taking a wide arc to approach the tower a little in front of Duckett, but keeping out of his direct line of sight.

The people were all singing now, in the ragged disharmony of an outdoor congregation. Gallagher mimed along to it as he slowly worked his way to the scaffold tower, until he was on the other side of it to Duckett, with barely eight feet separating them.

They were fifty feet from the platform, well within the range of Duckett's competence with a gun. This was undoubtedly going to be his point of fire. What the Scot had to judge was how soon after the Pope's appearance, Duckett would take his shot.

His Holiness had been driven through a well-stewarded gap to the back of the dais. As he appeared, with the sun gleaming off his white garments and skullcap, the crowd gave a thunderous cheer and surged forward a few feet, Duckett with them.

Gallagher took his chance and slipped round the scaffold poles until he was two feet from the hit man, jostling shoulders on either side. All eyes except his were fixed on the shining figure of the frail septuagenarian on the platform above them.

Duckett stood stock-still, transfixed, it seemed, by this first sight of his target, unconscious of the people closely packed around him. Gallagher's eyes didn't leave him for a second as he watched for a movement. Surreptitiously he slipped on a pair of gloves and felt inside his jacket for the narrow hilt of his weapon. He drew it slowly from its sheath.

As soon as Duckett's right shoulder moved, as his hand went to grasp the gun in his pocket, Gallagher closed the gap between them to a few inches, but still not touching Duckett or doing anything that might alert him or disturb his concentration. He undid the three copper buttons of his jacket and waited until the gun was about to be pulled into view.

As soon as Duckett's hand had emerged from his pocket, Gallagher leant back slightly. In a single, continuous movement, he pulled out the thin blade, held it parallel to the ground at chest height and pushed himself forward.

He felt the man tremble and gasp, though any sounds he made were drowned by the roar of welcoming cheers all round. No one except Gallagher saw the gun fall from the white, bony fingers. He bent down and quickly stuffed it in his pocket.

As the man crumpled, Gallagher, leaving the handle of the stiletto protruding from his back, took hold of him beneath his shoulders and lowered him solicitously to the ground, where he propped him against the scaffold tower.

A few people on either side glanced down with fleeting concern at a man who had obviously found the excitement of the event too much. Gallagher didn't look up; he crouched in front of the stricken man and talked to him. 'Wait here, Jimmy. I'll go and find a doctor.'

The sound of the Pope's characteristically accented English boomed from the loudspeakers above, while everyone hung on to each word of his greeting.

Gallagher stood up. 'I'll be right back,' he said to the corpse in front of him.

He squeezed his way through the crowd, who were now intently muttering the Lord's Prayer. 'Forgive us our trespasses . . .'

As Gallagher smiled apologetically and shoved his way towards the car park, he wondered if he would be forgiven this trespass. Or could it be deemed a trespass at all to have killed a man about to kill the Pope.

Kelly stood at the back of the gathering on some railings, muttering the prayers of his childhood out of ineradicable habit, angrily scrutinizing the sea of heads through his binoculars for any sign of Duckett, Gallagher or anyone else involved in his operation.

The Pope had been visible for fifteen minutes now and Mass was about to begin, when he would move from the front of the dais, further back to the altar.

Presumably Duckett knew this. He must have watched what happened at the other open-air events. Maybe he had chickened out at the last minute – it often happened with amateurs. Or maybe he hadn't been able to get within range.

A short burst on a St John's Ambulance siren made itself heard above the sound of hymn-singing and the brass band. Kelly turned sharply to watch the ambulance head into a mass of slowly moving people to his right. He held his breath. Maybe, he thought fervently, Gallagher had got there and Duckett was already dead. He swung his binoculars to the left, towards the Canal Turn, where the two of them had parked. But it was useless; he couldn't pick out any individual at that distance.

Haynes's voice in his earphones took him by surprise.

'Andy's leaving.'

'Has he done the repair job he was supposed to?'

'Yeah, no more trouble there.'

'Good. Tell everyone to go south. I'll see you in a few minutes.'

Kelly picked up Haynes's copy of the *Sun* from the passenger seat and chucked it in the back. He got in, closed the door and gave his signaller a big grin.

'We cracked it, then.'

'Andy was bloody sure of it. Sounded very pleased with himself.'

'Where is he now?'

'He'll be on the motorway.'

'What about the others?'

'Michelle and Brenda were watching his back-up. They stayed outside, didn't move.'

'Did they recognize any of them?'

'I think so, but we were being careful, of course.

I think Michelle was trying to say it was the geezer who took matey out for his target practice.'

'What about Abdul abu Said?'

'Nah. They didn't say so, anyway.'

'I wonder where the hell he was, then.'

'Well, wherever he was, he didn't get in Andy's way. Are you going to tell the boss?'

'Not over the mobile, not here. Too risky. I'll do it from a call-box later. Now, let's try and catch the others up. We'll have to think of somewhere for a pull-in.'

The SOS team, minus the temporarily seconded Qureshi, met up in a large, noisy pub on the outskirts of Oxford. Kelly felt safer south of Birmingham. He bought the drinks, then went to phone Bowring.

He came back from delivering the good news looking subdued. 'Sorry, we've got to move. The boss wants a briefing in two hours at HQ.'

12

'For some reason, somebody's decided to sit on it,' Bowring said. 'There's been nothing on the news or Ceefax about a fatality at Aintree, though they must have had him in hospital nearly four hours ago.' He turned to Gallagher. 'You're absolutely certain you neutralized him?'

'Aye, course I am. No question about it. I put the blade straight through his heart. He'd stopped breathing by the time I left him.'

'Hmm. Even if his back-up don't know he's dead yet, they certainly know he didn't shoot the Pope.'

Bowring was sitting on the writing-table in his library at Summerfold House. His eclectic band of mercenaries sat scattered around the room in a state of exhaustion. None of them had slept for thirty-six hours. He had congratulated them handsomely enough on their success, but made it clear that they had won only half the battle.

'With Abdul abu Said involved and over here, it's unlikely that he'll leave without trying another hit, and he's still got a prime opportunity the day after tomorrow in London. I've already put a very expensive surveillance exercise into operation along the vulnerable parts of the Pope's route, so all of you are going back to London tonight, except Miss MacFarlane, who's had enough excitement for one day. You're all booked into Londonderry House; it's the closest we could get.'

'But boss, you don't think they'll try another hit from the crowd, do you?'

'No, I didn't before, and I certainly don't now – not after they failed at Aintree. Frankly, if I'd been them, I'd have gone along with the Duckett plan, hoping but not really expecting it to work. I'd certainly have had a more substantial scheme worked out as a fall-back. So, we know they're here, and we know they mean business.'

Bowring looked at each of his employees, assessing their state of mind and fitness. Apparently satisfied, he said: 'Now, there's some food being prepared for you before you leave. I'll continue the briefing over dinner. I think in the meantime, you might be permitted a bath – in Michelle's case, that's an order; pity we haven't got a decent wig for you – and a glass or two of champagne.' He picked up his phone, pressed a button and said: 'James, a few bottles of Cristal, please.'

When James appeared, sooner than expected, he wasn't carrying champagne. There was a look of consternation on his stony face.

'Excuse me, sir. There's been a break in the perimeter circuit.'

Bowring glanced at him sharply. 'Where?'

'Somewhere up by the top of the hill behind the house.'

'Terry, get up to the monitors at once and check all the systems.'

Haynes was already on his feet, his fatigue overcome by the adrenalin rush as he left the room at a run.

Bowring then turned to Kelly. 'Is there any chance there was a tail on you back here?'

'No way. We left Duckett's back-up facing the wrong way and looking in the wrong direction.' He looked at Michelle. 'Isn't that right?'

'Sure, if those two cars were his only back-up.'

'But,' said Miss MacFarlane, speaking for the first time since coming into the house, 'we didn't see abu Said there, and I feel sure he must have been in the vicinity.'

'Yes,' Bowring nodded. 'That's right. Michelle, you saw him only once, leaving the restaurant in Stockport?'

She nodded her greasy, spiky head. 'Then I'm afraid I lost him. I never saw where the Palestinian took him.'

The telephone on Bowring's table trilled. It was Haynes in the communications room. 'Boss, we're picking up human movement from two of the MAGIDs.' That meant armed humans.

Bowring banged the phone down and jumped to his feet. 'We've got visitors. You must have been watched coming back from Liverpool; that means they know about The Hollies. All of you come up to the signals room; I'll brief you there.'

Up in the attic, surrounded by the radios, receivers, and CCTV monitors, Bowring checked the position. Haynes, with headphones on, was picking up something on the acoustic buoys hanging in the trees. 'I just got a whisper, couldn't understand it, sounded like Arabic.'

'There's two moving up on The Hollies, boss,' Kelly said, staring at the monitor from the television camera mounted on the villa's roof.'

'There are at least six more in the woods,' Haynes added urgently.

'Right,' Bowring said calmly. 'We're definitely about to come under attack. Kelly, Andy, Michelle and Terry, arm up lightly, use your headsets. Miss MacFarlane, take over the radio. James, get on the roof with an L96 with a night-scope. They won't come on until the light's completely gone. That gives us half an hour for you four to get down to the ice house and deploy in two groups up around the inside of the fence. Jack, you and Michelle take the western perimeter; Andy and Terry, come up the east side of the house to the top of the hill and circle back down towards it. Move in and neutralize any enemy as you find them. And be quiet about it. I don't want the locals calling the police. You'll have the advantage, since Brenda can give you their positions and they won't be expecting you from behind. Now, go.'

Haynes had already relinquished his place to Miss MacFarlane. Kelly led him, Gallagher and Michelle down the stairs to the armoury. They blacked up and slipped on battle smocks and belts. They each took a Browning and fitted a silencer; Kelly and Gallagher also took Colt Commandos, as weapons of last resort, with braces of magazines taped end to end. When they had pulled on their headsets they ran through the cellars and the brick door, down to the well room.

Kelly flashed his torch down the well and swung himself over the side to grab the iron rungs. The others followed and they swarmed down the shaft until the opening into a horizontal tunnel showed up in Kelly's torch beam.

It was similar in size and construction to the one

from The Hollies and they barely had to crouch to run its three-hundred-yard length. At the far end, Michelle knew the mechanism for getting through into the ice house. Before they stepped through the door, Kelly reiterated Bowring's orders. He and Michelle would take the west flank of the woods. The other two would take the east, which was the quickest way up the hill, to come back down towards the rear of the house.

In the signals room, Bowring stood behind Miss MacFarlane. On the VDU in front of her was a map of the grounds, showing the position of each surveillance device that had been triggered.

Only one breach in the perimeter wire was showing, but the pattern of disturbances from the seismic and acoustic monitors showed that the intruders had split into three or possibly four groups.

Bowring was staring now at the CCTV monitors banked above the VDU. The cameras were fitted with light-intensifying lenses which amplified whatever ambient light remained in the woodland dusk. One of them had picked up two shadowy figures who had stopped within its field of vision.

They appeared to have settled down to wait, confirming Bowring's view that the attack would not start for a while yet. But every few seconds his eyes flashed back to the monitor from the camera covering The Hollies' entrance to the tunnel. He hoped the two men who had come into the house would search it thoroughly enough to find the tunnel.

Excluding these two men, he assessed that his four soldiers out in the grounds were outnumbered two to one. With the element of surprise and regular position information from Miss MacFarlane, he could live with those odds. In addition, he and James were in a position to pick off any who came within sight of the house.

'OK, Nanny, I'm going next door to the window overlooking the stable block.' He picked up a walkie-talkie and an L96 which James had brought up for him. He checked the magazine, nodded at Miss MacFarlane and walked through the attic to the back of the house, where a small mansard window in what was once a maid's room gave him a view of the wooded hill behind and the cluster of outbuildings that had housed his ancestor's horses and carriage.

Kelly and Michelle worked their way through the gathering gloom of night, through the patchy woodland at the edge of Summerfold House's boundary. Kelly was glad now of the day he had spent in these woods checking and installing systems, although, at the time, it had seemed a very remote possibility that he would have to fight in them.

Miss MacFarlane quietly relayed over his headphones each new piece of intelligence provided by the network of surveillance devices and the TV cameras.

Kelly had a clear picture of the map of the grounds in his head and even in the darkening conditions was fairly sure of their own position.

'There are two men in vision, five yards west of camera two,' Miss MacFarlane's soft Scottish voice came through his headphones. 'There are two or three more twenty yards due south of them, currently static.'

Kelly knew where he was in relation to camera two. They were well placed to hit the other group of three. He signalled Michelle to stop behind him and indicated that they were going to take a right angle eastwards into the woods. He spaced them fifteen feet apart and started forward. At first the ground cover was sparse. They flitted from tree to tree to cover thirty yards before they came up against a mountainous bank of rhododendrons. When they stopped and slipped their headphones off to listen, they caught a few faint sounds of movement, the crunch of a human foot on woodland detritus that no native animal could have made. They were no more than twenty feet away, on the far side of the gigantic shrub.

Kelly replaced his headphones, to hear the message: 'The two men by camera two have moved off towards the east . . . They're now giving readings north-east on seismic seven.'

Kelly racked his brains for the location of seismic seven. He calculated from the sequence of numbers that it was about three hundred yards from his present position. That left them a clear field to deal with whoever was in front of them. But he wished he knew how many there were. He slipped his phones off and indicated to Michelle that she should go round the far side of the bush, so they would hit them on two flanks.

Pausing between each step, they slowly arced round until they were on the point of coming into sight of their targets. Inch by inch, Kelly brought his head round until he could make out three dim figures standing in a small clearing with their backs to him, peering intently through the trees towards the open lawn in front of the house. The nearest man to him stood alone, a few yards from his colleagues – like a lamb on the edge of the flock, Kelly thought.

He withdrew and devised an instant plan. Silently,

without even a creak of his bones, he lowered himself to a crouch and picked up a stout, two-foot length of dead beech. He straightened himself and with his left hand pulled his knife from the sheath on his belt. He stretched his other arm behind him, clutching the short branch, and swung it up and over like a cricketer throwing the ball in from the outfield.

He aimed his projectile between the trees in front of him and it flew in a silent parabola beyond the enemy to land with a noisy crash and a thud on the ground thirty feet ahead of them. They started, and one of them muttered something as they tried to see what had caused the disturbance.

Kelly transferred his hunting knife to his right hand and stole across the few feet that separated him from the nearest man, hoping that Michelle would take the cue. Three strides took him to just behind his target. The broad blade of his knife was slicing through the gristle of the man's windpipe before he knew he'd been attacked. As he fell to the ground with a last cough, his comrades swung round, momentarily disorientated, staring sightlessly into the gloom.

Kelly dropped his knife and reached for the Browning at his belt. Before he had drawn it, the next man was swinging an AK47 towards him. The Arab hadn't completed his turn when two muffled coughs of a silenced handgun carried across the clearing and he froze in mid-turn, jerked again and pitched headlong into the undergrowth, crunching his ribs on the butt of his rifle.

As he fell, another double-tap from the bushes to Kelly's right took out the third man while he was still trying to work out what was happening.

Kelly had got his own gun out now. He stepped

across to the fallen men and quickly put two more shots into each of the three bodies. Bowring's orders had been to neutralize the enemy, which meant making sure they wouldn't pick up a weapon again, ever.

Michelle walked into the gloom of the clearing, slipping her Browning back into a webbing pouch on her belt.

Kelly put his headphones on again.

'There is movement by acoustic buoy one, one hundred feet due north of the coach-house,' Miss MacFarlane was intoning. That was Gallagher's territory.

Kelly turned towards Michelle and put his mouth to her ear. 'Thanks, pal,' he breathed and turned to head up towards the two men last monitored at seismic seven.

Bowring had ordered one-way radio traffic to avoid the slightest temptation to any of his men on the ground to give themselves away. But the lack of incoming information was frustrating. He heard Miss MacFarlane give the position of the enemy a hundred feet above the house. One of his patrols ought to have been behind them. Holding his L96 lightly at the ready, he strained his ears and eyes into the last remnants of daylight.

Miss MacFarlane's voice came through the receiver clipped to the lapel of his jacket: 'Tunnel entry camera showing enemy intrusion . . .'

Bowring put down his gun and walked briskly back to the signal room. He arrived there in time to see activity on the last monitor. Two soldiers, clearly lit by the lights in the cellar at The Hollies, were trying to open the door to the tunnel. He couldn't see their faces, but he could see they were well loaded – dressed in DPM combat gear with a belt full of knives, grenades and ammo pouches. He smiled to himself; not unexpectedly, they weren't carrying respirators. He held his breath until they found the switch which unlocked the door and let it swing freely into the tunnel.

They stepped through the doorway and out of sight.

Bowring made himself wait a few more seconds to be sure they were in and going on. When he was satisfied that they were, he leant in front of Miss MacFarlane and pressed three switches in quick succession.

'They're in the trap now,' he said bluntly.

The steel shutters at either end of the tunnel slid into place; and the choke closed on the air-shaft.

Bowring gave Miss MacFarlane a quick glance of justification and flicked a red switch at the side of the console.

They didn't hear the small explosion, deep in the ground beneath them, which transmitted its shock wave down the detonation cord which ran the length of the tunnel. At almost imperceptible intervals, six charges were activated, producing small blasts which impacted through the confined brick tube, releasing clouds of oxygen-devouring red phosphorus.

Gallagher and Haynes had the two intruders behind the house in sight, silhouetted against a solitary light that glowed from the old stable-yard and filtered through the trees. Gallagher guessed that the terrorists were waiting for an order, or a sign, to launch their attack. According to the bulletins from Miss MacFarlane, they were the only enemy on this side of the house. Whatever strategy these Islamic warriors had, it had to be very sketchy, with no maps or plans of the house to go by.

Gallagher nudged his colleague and pulled his Browning from its holster. He had a Colt Commando slung across his chest, but that was only to be used in an extreme emergency. He beckoned Haynes to come with him and started moving soundlessly across a soft floor of pine needles towards their target.

It was a soft thud, deep in the earth beneath them, that distracted Gallagher, momentarily but long enough to let him miss a thick, protruding root of the large ornamental deodar round which he had been creeping. The Arabs heard the explosion too, instantly on their guard, alert to the thump and rattle of the Scot hitting the ground with his weapons. They spun round, both wearing night-vision goggles, AK47s cocked and ready.

Haynes, behind his fallen comrade, had barely acknowledged the crisis before a burst of 5.45mm high-power rounds ripped into him, jerking him like a scarecrow in a gale as he screamed in pain and fear of death.

Before Haynes hit the ground, Gallagher had rolled behind the broad trunk of the deodar, scrambling to his knees as he grabbed up his sub-machine-gun and brought it around the side of the tree. The weapon spat angrily as he emptied half a magazine into the silhouetted figures, saw them shudder and collapse to the ground, one bellowing with the agony of a blasted abdomen.

A flood of light from a row of five-hundred-watt

halogen lamps set beneath the eaves of the house suddenly bathed the whole place in a stark glow.

Gallagher glanced a few yards to the huddled, lifeless khaki lump which had been his friend. He bit his lip and turned his gun again on the whimpering bodies in front of him, pumping the trigger until the metal bit into the flesh of his finger and the magazine was empty.

Kelly and Michelle were keeping ten to fifteen feet apart as they worked their way across two hundred yards of tangled woodland towards the surveillance device designated seismic seven.

There was no new information from Miss MacFarlane through Kelly's headphones as he moved with a stealth which was second nature to him. He stopped and listened every few yards and picked up small sounds of Michelle's progress, sounds which blended convincingly enough with the woodland's natural creaks and rustles. He couldn't condemn her for them; she hadn't spent the months that he had in the jungles of Borneo, or even the tamer forests of Powys and Ulster, where he had learnt his skills; besides, she'd just saved his life.

Another sound, a low, guttural murmur, reached him on the easterly breeze. He prayed that Michelle had heard it too and would have the sense to stay where she was until he'd gone forward. In the few moments he took to plan his next move, the gentle noises of the wood were abruptly shattered by a burst of powerful automatic fire, somewhere behind the house; and a terrible, agonized scream, answered by a short, sharper discharge.

The bushes a few yards in front of him erupted and

two figures broke cover to run across the wide, open space of Summerfold's lawns. Kelly and Michelle emerged together through a border of large azaleas as the floodlights on the house lit up the ground all round it.

One of the soldiers in front of them drew back his right arm and swung it towards the house. A few seconds later, a shattering blast blew a small crater in the border where the grenade had fallen short of the library window.

A sharp crack echoed between the stately Victorian conifers and monkey-puzzle trees standing on the well-mown lawn, then another. The running figures stopped abruptly – reversed as if tugged back by a bungee cord at their collars.

'Get back in!' Kelly yelled at Michelle.

They dived back together through the tall border of shrubs that fronted the woods and crouched side by side. Kelly heard Michelle's breath coming hard, could almost hear her heart beating.

'That must have been James from the roof,' Kelly whispered. 'He wouldn't have identified us from there.'

Michelle nodded. 'Sure. Thanks.'

They waited. Everything was quiet around the floodlit house. The seconds stretched themselves into minutes; still no movement.

Bowring stood behind Miss MacFarlane at the console in the communications room.

'What do you think?' he asked.

'I don't know, not for sure. The pattern of movements through the systems indicated that they split into three separate groups after they breached the fence. One unit went down to the south-west, another up to the north side of the house, and a third in between them.'

'Judging by the gunfire behind the house, that unit's been neutralized. There was only one burst from their weapons, and two from ours. The middle unit would have been the two men that James took out on the lawn,' Bowring concluded.

'But someone moved up towards them. That might have been one of our patrols, or it might have been theirs.'

'Get them to report in. We'll have to risk it.'

Miss MacFarlane flicked her mike switch and said: 'Come in, Coaltit, and report your position.'

They could hear the gloom in Gallagher's voice. 'Fifty feet north of the stable block. Two enemy accounted for; we've taken one fatality.'

Bowring gritted his teeth and winced.

'Get Kelly,' he said tightly.

'Come in, Wagtail, and give your position.'

'South-western corner of the lawn, due west of the two hit from the house.'

'Have you met any other hostile units?'

'Yes; three men, all accounted for.'

Miss MacFarlane looked at Bowring, who said: 'Tell them to come in via the stable block. It looks as though we've neutralized the attack, but James and I will keep them covered, in case there are any more still on the loose. You keep your eyes fixed on those monitors for any signs of extraneous movement.'

'Control to both units. Come in under cover, via the stable block. The door will be released as you reach it,' said Miss MacFarlane into the mike.

Gallagher listened to the order, aware from it that

the attack on their HQ must have been successfully averted, but unable to feel much elation about it. He heaved Haynes's body over his left shoulder, clutching his automatic rifle in the other, and ran the short distance to the stable-yard, which led through to a door into the back of the house. When he reached the door, the lock was released remotely and he pushed through it with the dead weight of his load.

Kelly and Michelle came in a few minutes later.

The whole team, minus their dead colleague, gathered in a small office at the centre of the house on the ground floor which was Bowring's operations room.

'No movements besides yours have registered on the surveillance monitors for over twenty minutes; I'm sure we've dealt with the immediate problem. Unfortunately some public-spirited citizen heard the firing and alerted the police. Fortunately, I'd pre-empted them with my own call of complaint, but the police will be here any time now, so get out and retrieve the bodies; get them to the ice-house tunnel if you can and we'll deal with them later. Andy, take yours down to the well room; and you'd better put Terry there too for the time being. I'll stall a search for as long as I can but I want no bodies, weapons, or soldiers found here; you'll all just have to lie up in the well room until I come and give you the all-clear. You can't go into The Hollies' tunnel; it's full of red phosphorus and two more of our visitors and it'll take the pumps at least two hours to clear.'

The house was in darkness once again. Only a chink of light showed through the library curtains. Kelly was carrying the second body off the lawn when the sound of a siren reached him, winding up the hilly lanes from the A25. He and Michelle had already heaved their first three victims down to the ice house and dumped them inside the tunnel. Once they had got the next two in, they sat on the floor of the tunnel beside them, sweating and panting heavily.

'Christ, I'd forgotten how much a dead man weighs,' Kelly said. 'Still, we've got time for a rest now. The boss isn't going to get rid of the police in a hurry.'

James helped Gallagher to bring in the two men he had riddled after they had shot Haynes. Neither spoke as they wrapped the bodies in tarpaulins to avoid bloodstains and manhandled them through the cellars to the concealed brick doorway into the well room. Then they laid Haynes's ravaged carcass beside the two dead terrorists, and James left Gallagher alone with the corpses.

The local police sergeant, a natural cynic, and the constable with him were at first impressed by the suave ex-Guards officer who greeted them at the front door of Summerfold House. They'd heard of Summerfold, of course, and the rich family which had occupied it for over a century – apart from the short time it had been the home of the drug-abusing rock star, when it had been a regular target of police raids.

About the current incumbent, the sergeant, like most people in the district, knew very little.

'Come in, Sergeant,' said Bowring. 'Sorry to drag you out, possibly quite unnecessarily, but I did hear some odd noises in the woods near the top of the hill. From my rather out-of-date experience of firearms, it sounded like some kind of automatic rifle.'

'How long ago was this, sir?'

'I told the officer at the station maybe half an hour ago.'

'That concurs with another report we had,' said the sergeant. 'Only they said it sounded like some kind of explosion. Has there been any more since?'

'No. Not a sound. I went out and had a walk around. I didn't see or hear anything else. But I really think you ought to put a search party up through the woods. I'd say fifty men could sweep it in a couple of hours.'

'Fifty men, out at this time of night, for an unconfirmed report of something that sounded like gunfire? There's no way anyone here could sanction that.'

'What?' Bowring said with sharp indignation. 'Who's the senior station officer? I'd like to speak to him, right away.'

This was just the kind of high-handed behaviour the sergeant loathed in members of the so-called upper classes, who always treated the police as if they were their own personal servants.

'That won't be necessary, sir,' he said. 'There's no point in searching this place in the dark. I've posted a man down at your front gate. He'll stay for the rest of the night with a back-up squad car, in case there's any further outbreak,' he added with a hint of disbelieving sarcasm, which pleased Bowring. His face no longer expressed the slight awe with which he had entered the house. 'It's possible, sir, isn't it, that it might be someone after the game?'

'Well,' Bowring said as if the idea hadn't occurred to him before, 'we do put down quite a few pheasant and there are a lot of last year's birds still around. And of course, there are the deer up in the top woods.

Good Lord, you might be right.' He became sterner. 'But poaching's still a crime, Sergeant. Putting one officer on the gate isn't going to catch anyone.'

'Yes, sir. Poaching is still a crime, but it wouldn't justify bringing in a search party of fifty men, in the dark, when the poacher's probably been gone half an hour.'

Bowring looked at him, trying, it seemed, to overcome his exasperation. 'Yes, well, I suppose you're right, but I shall institute a search first thing in the morning, and if I find any evidence and report it, I'll expect immediate action.'

'Yes, of course, sir. Now we'll just have a look around outside. We'll let you know if my superiors decide to put fifty men through the woods tomorrow.' His tone made it clear that there wasn't a hope in hell of that.

Bowring stiffly showed him out and watched as he and the constable walked across the lawns with their torches flashing.

'Let's hope they don't find any spent cartridges, sir,' James's voice came from behind him.

'That's a risk I had to take, but frankly I shouldn't think they'll look hard or long. They're only going into the woods to stop me from complaining to the station superintendent. Get out through the stable block now and collect up what you can from where you picked up the two Arabs. Take a radio and a set of headphones. Miss MacFarlane can tell you if the policemen decide to go that way.'

James came back ten minutes later with a bag of fifty spent 7.62mm and 5.54mm cartridges.

'That's all I could find, sir,' he reported to Bowring.

'That looks about right. Now, we'd better find

out who the hell we've neutralized. Get down into the well room with a Polaroid and photograph the bodies. Then we'll have to dispose of them ourselves. There's no point in bringing Harry Cotterell into this yet. I'll break it to him afterwards, and Mick Jones, if the need arises.'

'I could probably deal with them, sir. Hydrochloric acid should do the trick. But Terry Haynes's relatives might like to bury him properly.'

'I'm sorry to say that I can't let that happen. If we manage to get away with this shoot-out tonight, I don't want there to be any more questions asked by Terry's family about it. He'll have to go missing on a job abroad, in a month or so.'

'I understand, sir.'

Gallagher, Michelle and Kelly, who had all three grown to like the little cockney signaller very much, also understood. But any sense of victory they might have felt after their activities that day was nullified by the loss of a member of their small team.

When seven of the dead terrorists were lined up along one wall of the well room, James photographed them. The police had left after a perfunctory search which, as Bowring had gambled, produced nothing to excite their interest, and he decided it was safe to let his soldiers back up into the house. They didn't change out of their military gear and kept their weapons beside them, in the remote event that Sufuf Allah still had a presence in the grounds. They sat around in the library, eating food prepared by the versatile butler.

'Something went seriously wrong today,' Bowring said as they ate. 'I'm very concerned that you were tailed back here, and we may have done irreparable damage to our cover by allowing a shoot-out in the grounds; we won't know for a few days yet whether or not we've got away with it. I'm blaming no one in particular, but we should never have been traced here.'

'Boss, none of us know how the hell we led them here,' Kelly said. 'We all took the usual evasive actions. Only Miss MacFarlane actually drove up to the house, and frankly I checked her for tails two or three times on the way from Liverpool – there was certainly no one on to her. And we all arrived separately at The Hollies.'

'On the positive side,' Bowring went on, 'you eliminated Duckett, and nine members of Sufuf Allah, assuming the two who found their way into the tunnel at The Hollies are dead. I think we've probably accounted for a large proportion of the enemy. Of the original five faces Cotterell gave us, three were killed outside. Maybe the other two are in the tunnel; we'll be able to have a look in an hour or so.'

'What do we do now, boss?' Gallagher asked.

'As soon as the tunnel's clear, you go straight to London. This time, do everything you have to to be sure you're not followed – if it takes all night. Tomorrow you start on-the-ground coverage of the buildings we've identified as the most likely hit sites. There are only three of you, which will make it tight, but we've got fifteen fixed OPs in operation. They'll need regular checking. They've got the "Joshua Reynolds", and they'll be told which are no longer relevant. If they're in doubt, they'll need one of you. It'll be a long, hard day and there may be no movement until Thursday. If there's anyone left from Sufuf Allah to make the hit, they may well lie low until that morning.'

'Who else is going to be on the lookout for these people?' Kelly asked.

'The DP Squad will be out in force, and Special Branch will have guns on the rooftops; I dare say a few dozen of Harry Cotterell's men, as well as MI5. But unless they've worked it out from Duckett's corpse at Aintree, I doubt if they've made a connection with Sufuf Allah yet – Duckett was English, and Andy removed his gun.' Bowring shrugged and went on. 'The one thing that could give them a lead is the fact that they know we're interested. I just hope to God the local police don't think of checking with Jones's unit in London.'

Kelly shook his head. 'They must have realized by now that something's going on. They know we've got a few soldiers in the country; we wouldn't be here unless there was work to be done.'

'That's my problem, so don't worry about that, Jack.'

'OK, but how the hell are three of us supposed to deal with a hit, even if we manage to find out where it's going to happen?'

'I'll be on the ground too, and James. And if we know where the hit's going to happen, it won't take a lot to stop it, you know that.'

'Aye,' Gallagher said. 'But how do we know what's going on?'

'Brenda will run central control. With all the radio traffic that'll be going on, you'll have to keep in contact by phone. James will issue you with mobiles, but use land lines where possible. Brenda . . . Miss MacFarlane will make her base at Londonderry

House, where she'll have three direct lines. Here are the numbers.' He handed each of them a slip of typed paper. 'Memorize and destroy.'

He looked at his small team – Kelly, Gallagher and Michelle. 'Personally I don't care too much about the money, but you might bear in mind that if His Holiness goes back to Rome unscathed, there's the thick end of thirty thousand dollars in it for each of you.'

13

Jim Mason went in Gallagher's car to London; Kelly went with Michelle, who drove while the Liverpudlian lounged in the passenger seat like a man who'd overdone the cognac. 'If Bowring doesn't care about the money, why the hell's he going through with this?' he asked, mostly for the sake of talking.

'He hates to be beaten,' Michelle said.

'I suppose I knew that. But he doesn't seem fanatical or anything. I mean, tonight, when we almost blew the cover off HQ, he took it calmly enough.'

'He has the same control over his anger as he has over all his other emotions.'

'I suppose that's quite an attraction in a man,' Kelly observed casually.

'It can be.'

They were driving east past Heathrow along the A4. They had zigzagged across country from The Hollies, and doubled back on themselves twice. They had checked the car for bugs and were certain that no other vehicle had stayed with them.

It was two hours since Bowring's briefing. The tunnel had been cleared of the asphyxiating red phosphorus and two more bodies. The face of one of the bodies matched one of the two remaining photographs in their gallery of mug shots.

Only Abdul abu Said remained unaccounted for. He seemed very much the sort of man who would take serious exception to having his plans interfered with by outside agencies. But looking for him in all the hundreds of places where he might choose to make his attack, among the hundreds of thousands of people who would be milling around the area of the Pope's route and rally seemed like a hell of a challenge.

'Basically, Bowring's plan's a bloody great punt,' Kelly said.

'You could say that every decision you take is a gamble. Bowring's way is to reduce the odds as much as he possibly can.'

'Well, he hasn't reduced them enough on this gig.'

It was around midnight when the SOS team checked into their rooms at Londonderry House. It had been a long day. When he was lying in his bed on the tenth storey of the hotel, it seemed to Kelly like a week since they had started tailing Duckett to Aintree that morning. But with well-trained will-power, he closed his eyes, emptied his mind of the day's events and the next day's doubts, and slept.

The wind had picked up during the night and dispersed the gloomy cover of cloud. The sun slanted mistily across Hyde Park at seven the following morning. Kelly ran the complete circumference of the park with his phone in one pocket and his Browning High Power in the other. As he neared the end of his run, the phone trilled. Miss MacFarlane sounded crisp.

'Good morning, Mr Kelly. All the observation posts are in operation. I'll be reporting to you regularly with all relevant sightings. You're to take the top end of Park Lane, from the Grosvenor House north.'

'OK, Miss M. Talk to you later,' he answered with a light-heartedness he didn't feel.

In his hotel, he changed into a well-cut, lightweight Italian suit and went back out into the hazy sunshine. He spent the next three hours prowling unopposed through the corridors of all the hotels, office blocks and apartment buildings that faced west across the park and into which he had cheerfully bluffed his way.

He checked every Middle Eastern face he saw – and there were many – but he hadn't forgotten Duckett, the fanatical white Muslim. At the same time, he was checking everywhere for any unusual signs – furtiveness, men carrying bulky, unlikely packages, anything that might have suggested preparation for attacking a hugely public figure with a security screen of several hundred men around him as he progressed in an armour-plated vehicle along the far side of the wide avenue.

It was a ridiculous brief, he thought to himself more than once, but those were Bowring's orders.

By two o'clock, he had seen nothing that seriously aroused his suspicions, and he was hungry. He ordered a sandwich in the lobby of one of the hotels, and used the time he took to eat it to watch everyone who came in and out. He was wiping the last crumbs from his mouth when someone he had not expected to see strolled in confidently but, in his white, open-neck shirt and tight Terylene trousers, quite out of place in this grand hotel.

The newcomer was also clearly taking note of everyone who crossed his line of vision. He spotted

Kelly before he had time to avoid it. He gave a slight smile and headed straight across the lofty hall and sat down in the chair beside him.

'Hello, boyo. What a surprise seeing you here.'

'Hello, Mick. Ditto. Are you chasing an African revolutionary on a recruitment drive or what?'

'Why, are you waiting to see him?' Mick Jones laughed. 'Course I'm not, Jack. I'm doing the same as you.'

'Are you? What's that, then?'

'Seeing what unsavoury characters are coming in and out. Have you finished your lunch, then?'

Kelly nodded and dropped a ten-pound note on the low table in front of him. 'That was a bloody expensive beef sandwich.'

'I'm sure Major Bowring will pay for it. Come on, let's take a walk. We may be able to help each other.'

On the wide, as yet uncrowded, pavement outside, they started to stroll northwards.

'I won't ask you directly what's going on,' Jones said. 'It wouldn't be fair and I don't suppose you'd tell me; anyway, I can guess. But you know, you may need help.'

Kelly grinned at him. 'We may. But I'm not going to ask for it.'

'All right, but you can tell Bowring. Look, I'm not interested in compromising whatever you're doing, but if you've got material information, you shouldn't be keeping it to yourselves. We know damn well the Sufuf Allah unit that came into the country hasn't left. Trouble is, they've dropped right out of sight, and it worries us.'

'Why, what do you think they might be up to?'

'For Christ's sake, Jack! Don't piss about,' the Welshman said with sudden sharpness. More conciliatory, he went on: 'You don't happen to know anything about somebody called Michael Duckett, do you?'

'Duckett?' Kelly shook his head. 'Doesn't sound very Islamic.'

'Well, he is. He goes by some Arab name now, or should I say, went. He was at the Papal rally in Liverpool yesterday and someone stuck a nine-inch blade into him.'

'Why would they do that?'

'To stop him taking a crack at the Pope, wouldn't you say?'

'You didn't say he had a gun on him.'

'Yeah, well, he didn't, but he has a record of disturbance at Islamic rallies and suchlike, and we'd had our eye on him as a possible fatwa merchant. One thing's for sure: he wasn't at that rally because he loves the Pope.'

'Well, he won't be causing any trouble tomorrow, will he, so you must be grateful to whoever neutralized him.'

'If only we knew who to be grateful to.'

'I'll let you know if I hear anything.'

'Look. If Bowring steps out of line tomorrow, and anything regrettable happens, there'll be trouble. As you can imagine we're not too keen on the privatization of the security services; not before our political masters decide it for us, anyway. I see you've got a mobile on you. Here's a number which will get me any time you want, all right? If you do, we may be able to overlook what's already been done.'

Kelly took a small piece of card on which Jones had scribbled a telephone number.

'OK, Mick. Now I'd better get on. I want to check the decorations up on Marble Arch.'

Jones shook his head. 'You've got my word, Jack. Contact me at the right time, and you're in the clear.'

'I'll remember that, Mick. Thanks.'

He gave the Welsh policeman a jovial nod, and extended his pace purposefully up Park Lane.

Mick was right, he thought, if anything went wrong, and SOS could be shown to have held back their intelligence from the security forces, of whichever branch, the faeces would hit the fan very hard.

He was crossing Upper Brook Street when his phone bleeped at him. It was Bowring.

'What's your position?'

Kelly told him.

'Are you on to anything?'

'Nothing hot.'

'Get yourself down to the Lanesborough, now.'

Bowring gave him a room number and cut off. Kelly, not too abruptly, turned around and began to stroll back down the other way, looking over his shoulder for a taxi. He got one before he'd walked twenty yards and was climbing out at the vast stucco building on Hyde Park Corner three minutes later.

Upstairs, in a fifth-floor room, he joined Bowring and two of his surveillance team. He introduced them briefly as John and Charlie. They looked like ex-policemen. Kelly wondered where Bowring had found them.

A telescope and camera with a 1000mm lens on tripods were pointing through the window that overlooked the constant whirlpool of traffic that spun round the triple arch of the Wellington Memorial. John sat on a chair with his eye glued to the telescope.

Newly developed black-and-white shots of a variety of individuals were clipped to a makeshift line to dry. Dozens more lay scattered on the double bed and dressing-table.

Bowring picked two up. 'Take a look at these,' he said, handing them to Kelly.

Kelly studied them for a few seconds, then nodded. 'You could be right. Can we blow them up more?'

'We're doing that right now. Is it ready yet, Charlie?'

'Give us another minute,' Charlie's voice came from the bathroom.

'Where was he, exactly?' Kelly asked.

'Over there, going into the front entrance of Apsley House with a crowd of other punters.'

'Was he with any of them?'

'Impossible to say, but he was the only Arab.'

'Here's the blow-up,' Charlie said carrying a dripping photograph from the bathroom which had become a temporary darkroom.

Bowring took it and laid it, still damp, on the bed.

From another stack of shots, he took one of the five which Harry Cotterell had given him ten days before and laid it beside the fresh one.

In the new shot – grainy from enlargement – a man was turning, looking around him, giving a three-quarter view of his heavy, dark features.

'Christ!' Kelly exclaimed, almost unwilling to believe that Bowring's strategy may have paid off. 'That's him.'

'Abdul abu Said,' Bowring said quietly. 'Yes. I think it is. And I doubt that he has more than a passing interest in the Duke of Wellington, if any.'

'That's the site, then,' Kelly said with a flurry of elation.

Bowring nodded his head, displaying no particular surprise that they had identified it. 'Not definitely, but probably. He may still be checking out the possibilities.' As he spoke, he picked up the phone beside the bed and punched out a number.

'Andy? Wherever you are, get down to Apsley House. Our last Joshua Reynolds went in about twenty minutes ago . . . main public entrance. Get to it.'

He put the phone down. 'He's outside the Inn on the Park. You should see him in a minute, John.'

'Hang on!' John said, 'Our man's just come out!'

'Shit.' It was the first time Kelly had ever heard Bowring utter any kind of obscenity. 'Jack, get down there now. As soon as you're out of the building, I'll get you on the mobile and tell you which way he's gone.'

Kelly was out of the door before Bowring had finished the sentence. He almost sprinted down the deep-carpeted, silent corridor to the lifts, and clenched his fists with impatience as he waited the fifteen seconds it took for one of them to arrive and open its doors. It already contained a large, powerfully scented woman. Kelly grinned at her and hoped nobody else got in on the way down. To his frustration, the lift stopped again two floors down, and he calculated the advantage of getting out and finishing the descent by the stairs. He took a chance on the lift. It didn't stop again.

When the door opened on the ground floor he pushed past the later entrants and strode like an Olympic walker across the lobby to the main entrance on Hyde Park Corner.

He pulled his phone out and headed for the pedestrian tunnel leading to Hyde Park Corner tube station. As he reached the entrance, the phone trilled. He stopped and put it to his ear.

'Kelly?'

'Yeah.'

'He went down into the subway nearest Apsley House. Head for the ticket office.'

'Right.'

He stuffed the phone back in his pocket. It wouldn't be any use underground. He plunged down the stairs, trying not to push too many ambling tourists out of his way and followed the signs through the complex of tunnels to the booking hall. As he walked into it, he slowed to a sensible walk and headed for the ticket machines.

Abdul abu Said was there before him. Kelly hung back to put half a dozen people between them. He watched the self-service machine where the terrorist selected his ticket. He couldn't read the names from where he was, but when he reached it he punched the same destination – Tottenham Court Road – and hurried down to the eastbound platform.

When he got there, the platform was fairly full, but not so crowded that he couldn't see every person on it. Abdul abu Said wasn't among them.

Kelly did his best to disguise his panic as he looked

around him and tried to guess where the Palestinian had gone. He rushed through to the westbound platform, walked briskly along it, checking all the faces, fighting the urge to become frantic with frustration. The rush of wind that preceded the arrival of a train hit him with its musty smell. He moved to the back of the platform, to see if his quarry emerged from somewhere at the last minute; but Abdul abu Said didn't appear.

Kelly raced back to the other platform, where he could hear an eastbound train pulling in. He tried to take in all the people who surged towards the opening doors. No abu Said. Almost beside himself with despair, Kelly realized he'd lost the scent. He climbed back up the stairs, checking the interlinking passages as he went, but he knew the Palestinian had been following routine behaviour to throw off any possible surveillance, and he'd done it well.

Kelly emerged into the sunlight on the north side of Hyde Park Corner, and pulled out his phone again. He called one of Miss MacFarlane's numbers.

'I need to speak to the boss,' he said as soon as he heard her clear-cut voice in his ear. Without any preamble, she gave him a number which he stabbed angrily on the instrument.

Bowring answered.

'He lost me,' Kelly said bleakly.

There was a momentary pause before Bowring spoke. 'That's a great pity,' he said.

'It's a fucking disaster. I'm sorry, boss. He knew what he was doing.'

'Get back up here, then.'

'I'm sorry, boss,' Kelly said again when he was back

in the hotel bedroom that was now their *ad hoc* HQ. Gallagher, James and Michelle had arrived while he'd been running around the tunnels of the tube station.

'It's OK, Jack. These things happen. I should have got Andy down there sooner; two of you would have kept on to him.'

'Do you reckon he'll still go for it, then?'

'That's what he came here for. He'll have realized by now that he's lost the rest of his men and he's on his own.'

'Do you think those nine we took out yesterday were the whole of his unit, then?' Kelly asked.

'I wouldn't be surprised. In fact, the way things look, it's quite possible Abdul abu Said is the last active member of Sufuf Allah. If he wants to retain any credibility with his rivals back home, he's got to pull this thing off now. I would think too many people there know about it by now. And if there's no one left to do it for him, he'll have to do it himself.'

He was interrupted by Miss MacFarlane on the phone.

'Monsignor di Montefalco has been trying to reach you,' she said. 'Shall I put him through?'

'Yes, please.'

The cleric was on the phone himself a few seconds later.

'Major Bowring?'

'Yes, Monsignor?'

'What has happened?' Montefalco sounded agitated. 'We have been informed, somewhat reluctantly, by your MI5 that an English Muslim was killed at the Papal Mass at Aintree. They thought he may have been there to make an attempt on His Holiness's life.'

'Yes, Monsignor. We know all about that.'

'You do?'

'We knew about it four hours before they did.'

'Thank God.' The priest sounded relieved. 'Did a man called Father Sullivan come and see you?'

'Yes.'

'Did you do as he asked?'

'No. We're still attending to the matter.'

'That is what I hoped. I am most grateful to you. There has been some . . . confusion. I can't explain now.'

'I understand.'

'And I may be sure you are continuing with the job?'

'You may, Monsignor.'

'Do we still have cause to be concerned?'

'You had, but we have the situation well under control.'

'That is good news. If you need me, you will be able to contact me at the nunciate until tomorrow morning. After that I shall be accompanying His Holiness to Hyde Park. I pray that you will be successful.'

'So do I, Monsignor, though I dare say to less effect.'

'Thank you, Major. And God bless you.'

Bowring put the phone down with a grin. 'We have a blessing straight from the Vatican; that should do the trick,' he said. 'But I suppose we'd better make plans as well.'

With a swing in her stride and a camera fitted with a

zoom lens over her shoulder, Michelle walked through the doors of 'Number One, London', Apsley House – the London home of the Dukes of Wellington since it was built by the first of that line in the 1820s.

The staterooms and the fine collections of pictures, tapestries and Wellington militaria were all open to the public that day. Michelle found herself going in with a party of French tourists who seemed happy to absorb her into their group. She bought every guide to the place that might contain plans or information, and photographed the staircases and the wide, open corridors.

On the first floor, as the other sightseers were engaged in more innocent research, she spotted a door marked 'Private', tried the handle, found it open and slipped through. She was ready with an explanation in rudimentary English, that she was looking for a lavatory.

But in the surprising hush of the private quarters, there was no one to challenge her. She flitted along the passage on the other side of the door until she found what she was looking for: a flight of stairs up to the next floor.

While Michelle was inside the house, Charlie, the more competent photographer of the surveillance team, was photographing the south, east and north elevations from the outside. More specifically, he was trying to identify and capture on film the most suitable windows, or other apertures for aiming and firing some kind of ballistic device at the centrepiece of the Papal motorcade.

Kelly and Gallagher made as thorough a survey as they could to assess the ranges and the weapon most likely to be used, approaching the task, as they had done all along, as if they had been granted the contract to shoot the Pope themselves.

Back in the Lanesborough, Michelle gave them her findings – an approximate, incomplete plan of the first and second storeys of the building. She'd been interrupted early in her search, and bluffed her way out, but hadn't found another opportunity to carry on. She'd had to guess at the dimensions and exact positions of the private rooms, but with the help of Charlie's external research they were able to put together a working diagram of the house.

'Not quite as much information as we had for the Iran Embassy siege, but then it's a much smaller job,' Bowring observed.

Kelly and Gallagher presented Bowring with the consensus of their opinions.

'If the guy knows what he's doing,' the Scot said, 'he'll use some kind of rocket – a Carl Gustav, maybe, or if they're using old Soviet weapons, an RPG7.'

Bowring shook his head. 'Too bulky to get in and too much blow-back. Unless he was in a sixty-foot gallery, the risk of setting fire to the place would be too high.'

'But he's not going to give a bugger about burning the place down, is he?' Gallagher argued.

'Yes, he is. I'd say that Abdul abu Said is far too interested in staying alive so he can wield his bit of power to risk either getting caught or fried alive. Why don't you think he'd use a simple high-power rifle? A 7.62 round would pierce the Pope-mobile without too much trouble.'

'No, boss,' Kelly said. 'He'd only have the one shot, and a bloody tricky shot. It might penetrate the glass, but the chances are it would get deflected.

What about an American 66mm rocket – an M66? Less blow-back and breaks down into two pieces, maybe three foot each.'

Bowring thought for a moment. 'I agree,' he said. 'Of the options available, I think that's what I'd choose. However, we're not certain that Apsley House is the hit site. Our friend may have just been making a recce, choosing his spot, and there are other possible sites. I'm keeping all observation posts in operation while we concentrate on this one. But you're going to have to be ready for a complete change of venue. At least our surveillance know exactly what they're looking for.'

'So we get back on the streets, then?' Kelly asked.

'That's right. You take the tube station. James, take the subway exit by Apsley House. Andy, you cover the bottom of Park Lane. Michelle, you stay up here and help John and Charlie. Abu Said's not going to be able to do anything after the place closes, so you can come off then, but I want you all out again tomorrow from seven onwards, and remember, there'll be a lot of other people out there watching, so make sure they don't pick you up.'

Kelly flopped on to his bed at ten that night. He was deciding whether or not he really wanted to watch the next film that was being broadcast on the movie channel when he heard a knock on his door.

Instantly, he was on his guard. He got up silently, picked up his Browning and shoved the holster under the bed with his foot. He walked across the room without a sound and stood with his back to the wall, a few feet from the opening side of the door. He reached across and released the lock.

The person outside knocked again.

'Come in,' he said sleepily, directing his voice into the corner.

The door handle turned and the door swung open. No one came in. Kelly's nerves tingled: he prepared himself and lifted his gun a little higher. He held his breath, one, two, three, four, five seconds.

Michelle walked in.

'It's only me,' she said, turning to him with a smile as he stared at her along the barrel of his gun.

'Why didn't you ring me and tell me you were coming?' Kelly said, breathing freely once again.

'I just decided, as I was walking past your room. You don't mind, do you?'

'Not much.'

She closed the door behind her. 'I didn't feel like watching the television and I don't think I'll get to sleep too easily.'

'Too much excitement for you?'

'Probably.'

'Do you want a drink, then?'

'Not really.'

'I do,' Kelly said and walked to the fridge in the corner of the room, opened it and poured himself a large whisky.

'Sit down,' he said, waving at one of the two armchairs, then sat himself in the other. 'What do you want, then?'

She raised her shoulders. 'I don't know really; maybe just to know what to expect tomorrow.'

Kelly grunted. 'That's anybody's guess. Trouble is, we haven't got a clue how many we're up against.'

'It can't be many, if abu Said is making the preparations himself. He didn't let himself be in the firing line at Summerfold.'

'We don't know that, not for sure. But it's all right, I don't think he's got anyone with him either.' He put his feet on the glass coffee table between them and took a long slug of his drink. 'I just wish I knew for certain, because if we do find out where and when he's going to make his hit, when we go in we won't have time to look over our shoulders. Is that what's worrying you?'

She shook her head. 'No. I just don't want to mess it up, that's all.'

'Well, if you do, you won't be around to regret it, so what's the worry?' Kelly said, throwing his hand in the air. 'But look,' he said, more gently, remembering well the times before his first operations with the SAS, 'I know what it's like, and to tell you the truth, there's no advice I can give you. You just get used to it. Come on, have one big drink, then go to bed.'

She gave him a long, slightly quizzical look and abruptly stood up. 'No thanks. I don't need a drink. I'll watch a movie.'

'Do you want to watch it with me?'

She smiled down at him. 'Not yet. Maybe another time. Thanks for talking to me.' She walked to the door. 'See you in the morning.'

'Yeah, sure,' Kelly said without moving in his chair. He watched her leave, and give him a last quick smile before she closed the door and was gone.

Maybe another time. Kelly shook his head and switched on the television.

Thursday morning, the morning of the last day of

Pope John Paul II's visit to Britain, dawned lightly swathed in a veil of mist. There was a definite chill to the air as Kelly and Michelle met up to jog along Rotten Row.

'OK?' he asked her.

'Sure.'

She looked it. There was not a hint of nervousness as she ran beside him with her hair flowing behind her.

The park was already busy at a quarter to seven with other runners and riders and a string of black Household Cavalry horses returning from exercise. In the top corner of the park, a few dozen men were making final adjustments to the stage and equipment that would be used for the open-air mass scheduled to begin at eleven o'clock which a hundred thousand people were expected to attend.

To reach it, the Pope's motorcade from Westminster would be passing around Hyde Park Corner at ten-thirty.

'There's not a lot we can do until Apsley House opens at nine,' Kelly said. 'But we may as well stay in our track-suits and watch for an hour until Andy and James replace us.'

They sat, like a pair of lovers who had spent the night together, on a bench a hundred yards from Apsley House. As they watched, they talked not about the day in front of them, but about Kelly's past, his experiences in the desert campaign, in Ireland and the Falklands, which helped to put into perspective the risks they might face in a few hours' time.

Bowring telephoned soon after seven to check that they were in place. He could see them from where he was, he said, so could the OP in the Intercontinental.

Reassured by this, Kelly and Michelle settled down for a few more hours of waiting.

14

Three hours later, Kelly was beginning to sweat. The mist had cleared to uncover a strong sun, but it was lack of information, not heat, that was causing his discomfort.

They had seen nothing. The OPs had reported nothing. Even Bowring in his regular progress calls was starting to sound irritable.

Kelly, changed now from his track-suit into jeans and denim jacket, was sitting on the bench while Michelle was jogging round the block where Apsley House stood. He glanced up from his *Daily Telegraph* to look west along Knightsbridge for the hundredth time to see if anyone of interest was approaching from that direction. Since before nine o'clock there had been a steady stream of pedestrian tourists and people coming to the Papal Mass. Most turned through the gate into the park before they reached him.

He spotted the bulky figure from fifty yards – a very stout Arab in a spotless, creamy-white djellaba, walking slowly, with the air of a man who suffered from his own self-inflicted burden. Of medium height, heavily bearded, wearing dark glasses and with a black-and-white checked *shemagh* swathing his head, he didn't turn into the park but waddled on up towards the corner.

Kelly was reading his paper as the Arab passed by

without looking at him. He waited a few moments before he stood up and walked through the gate among a steady stream of the Pope's followers, out of sight of the bulky figure. He pulled out his phone and called Bowring at the Lanesborough.

'Have you clocked a very fat Arab, passing opposite you about now?'

'Yes. We've got him. He's gone on past Apsley.'

Kelly felt a stab of disappointment. 'There's something not right about the way he's moving.'

'We've already photographed him. We'll check him out. The motorcade is passing Buckingham Palace now,' he added tightly. 'Should be with you in about ten minutes. Hang on! He's turning back! Michelle's just come round from the other side. I think she's on to him.'

'Right,' Kelly said, turning back towards Knightsbridge. I'm on my way.'

'Good luck, Jack.'

Kelly moved as fast as he could without breaking into a run. He was just in time to see the Arab join a short queue of tourists going into Apsley House. Michelle was a few yards behind.

He could hear the cheering now as the Papal motorcade progressed slowly up Constitution Hill. The Arab had disappeared though the doorway of the house, followed by Michelle. He couldn't see Gallagher or James. He broke into a run, dodging and weaving through the dawdling pedestrians to the great wrought-iron gates. He sprinted now up the steps to the main door, but before he got there, his way was blocked by a commissionaire and a uniformed police constable.

'What's the hurry?' said the policeman.

Kelly couldn't risk an argument or a scene.

'Special forces,' he said crisply. 'I've got to get in there, quick.'

'ID?'

'Of course I'm not carrying ID.'

The policeman and commissionaire, joined by another, moved to more effectively stop Kelly entering as a small tail-back of sightseers built up. He was ready to burst with frustration. 'Listen, you arseholes, this is bloody vital.' He had a sudden inspiration, and pulled his phone from his pocket and punched the number Mick Jones had given him.

His fists clenched and unclenched as he waited ten rings for the call to be answered.

'Jones,' Kelly heard with a surge of relief.

'Mick. Jack. I've got to get into Apsley House. I've got a copper barring the way.'

'Tell him to radio central control right now.'

Kelly looked at the immutable constable. 'Call your control – now,' he snapped.

The policeman doubtfully clicked on the radio on his lapel. 'Control. B157 at Apsley House. There's a character come rushing up, wants to go in.' He waited and listened for fifteen nerve-shredding seconds, watching Kelly all the while.

'What's your name?' he asked him at last.

'Kelly.'

'Last rank and regiment?'

'Sergeant, 22 SAS.'

The policeman stepped aside.

Kelly ran in, up the first flight of stairs, looking around him for the Arab or Michelle.

On the first floor, he sprinted to the door at the end of the gallery which Michelle had told them about in her briefing the evening before. He went through into the relative calm on the other side. Again there was no one about. He listened but heard nothing to tell him if Michelle and the Arab had come that way. He looked for the stairs up to the next storey, found them without meeting anyone else and ran up.

On the second floor he had to take a gamble. He weighed up the options and headed east; that was where the closest shot could be taken. Then he saw Michelle. She had her Browning drawn and was standing with her back against the wall beside a door at the end of a wide corridor.

He stopped five yards short of the door and beckoned her to him. She reached him in a few silent strides. He put his mouth to her ear.

'What's the story?'

'He's gone in and managed to lock the door.'

'Does he know you saw him?'

'No. I hadn't reached the top of the stairs when he went in.'

'I hope you're bloody right. Let's go.'

Kelly walked along the soft, sound-deadening carpet until he was three feet from the door. He lifted his right leg, bending his knee, brought it back and powered his heel into the lock set in heavy mahogany.

It cracked, but the door was still in place. He gritted his teeth, aware that he'd already blown fifty per cent of their chances, lifted his leg again and with the desperate strength which that knowledge gave him, smashed his heel at the splintered lock once more.

The door shuddered open with the impact.

Kelly and Michelle sprang to each side of it. Kelly raised a hand for her to wait until he gave a sign. Gripping their Brownings in both hands, they spun round together and crouched in the doorway.

The Arab had his back to an open window, where a curtain flapped in the breeze and the noise of the Pope's approach was rising in a crescendo.

He had shed his bulk and his djellaba, and was facing them now with pure hatred on his face and a loaded M66 rocket-launcher on his shoulder.

Twelve silenced shots spat from both Brownings. The rocket-launcher crashed to the ground. The Arab's dark bearded face seemed to disintegrate and the ravaged T-shirt he wore turned crimson as he stumbled back and collapsed to lie with sightless eyes gazing at the fine plasterwork of the ceiling.

Kelly ran into the room and placed two more, needless 9mm rounds in the mangled, bloody mess of the Arab's torso. He reached down beside the dead man and deactivated the rocket-launcher.

Michelle had followed Kelly into the room. She was by the window watching the Pope-mobile and its squadron of motorcycle outriders pass at ten miles an hour between Apsley House and the hotel opposite. She turned and looked down at the man whose brains she had just blown out. Unconsciously, she made a sign of the cross.

The sound of running up the stairs and several heavy sets of feet pounding towards them echoed down the corridor.

Mick Jones burst into the room, followed by Bowring and two plain-clothes policemen, all with weapons drawn.

They stopped inside the splintered door.

'Shit!' Jones hissed. Kelly didn't miss the sweat that was pouring off the Welshman's forehead.

'Close the door,' Bowring snapped at one of the policemen, who obeyed without question.

Jones turned to Bowring. 'Christ, you cut that fine. You're bloody lucky you got to him.'

'So are you, Mick,' Bowring said more calmly. 'Because if we hadn't, your people certainly wouldn't have. How did you know he was here?'

'I told him,' Kelly owned up.

Bowring looked at Jones. 'There you are. Nobody could call us uncooperative. And what's more, we're going to quietly slip away from here while you and your men take all the credit for saving the Pope's life and deflecting some nasty repercussions in the Middle East peace talks. I wouldn't be surprised if you got a nice gong for it.'

A policeman now, but always at heart a member of the Regiment, Jones looked at his old squadron commander. 'You always were a jammy bugger, boss.'

Bowring looked back at him and nodded slowly with a faint smile. 'And don't you forget it.' He turned to Kelly and Michelle. 'Right, let's get out of here.'

For once, Piers Bowring looked as though he was enjoying one of his own dinner parties at Summerfold House that evening. The only outsider to join the SOS team at table was Harry Cotterell from MI6 – a gesture of appeasement on Bowring's part.

'I suppose we ought to be grateful to you,' Cotterell said. 'You seem to have wiped out the whole of Sufuf Allah in the last three days.'

'I hope so. They were a particularly nasty bunch.'

'But Piers, we can't let this kind of thing happen.

You should have brought our people in and let them deal with it.'

'Stop fussing,' Bowring said lightly. 'His Holiness is going home intact. As far as those who are aware of what happened are concerned, the AT Squad were responsible. Where's the problem?'

'We've still got the small matter of a Palestinian shot in the streets of West London, and an English Muslim stabbed to death at Aintree.'

'Sorry, Harry. Can't help you there.'

Cotterell shook his head, resigned. 'What have you done with the rest of them?'

Bowring looked at James, who was bringing in bottles of calvados, port and brandy. 'James?'

'All gone, sir,' the butler said curtly.

'We do have some photographs for you, though,' said Bowring. 'But we won't look at them now. They're not a pretty sight.'

'Did you lose anyone?'

'I can't tell you that, Harry.'

'Look, Piers. Of course, you know that it would be too messy for me to start making a fuss about this, but for God's sake, please don't take on any more jobs inside the UK.'

'That I'm happy to agree to. I found it very disagreeable to have my privacy here threatened. No more operations in Britain, I promise.'

'I'll drink to that,' Cotterell replied. 'But I'm amazed anyone from Sufuf Allah found their way here, with the precautions you take.'

A look of annoyance passed across Bowring's face. 'There was what you might call a minor cock-up with a major result. Somewhere, perhaps when they stopped outside Oxford, a bug was put on Miss

MacFarlane's car. No one checked when they left to come here – James found it later that evening before he and Andy went to London.' He lifted an eyebrow. 'It would have been a doddle for them after that, and Miss MacFarlane's was the only car that actually came back to the house.'

Cotterell nodded, glancing round the room. 'And am I right in thinking there's one less of you than there was?'

There was a moment's silence in the room. No one wanted to admit to an outsider what had happened to Terry Haynes. At the same time, to deny his existence and the part he had played in the eradication of the small but deadly Sufuf Allah seemed disloyal to the memory of the gutsy little cockney.

Bowring picked up his team's mood and nodded.

'Yes. We did lose a man, a very useful soldier, and a good man. He's quite a loss to us.' He sighed. 'But there it is. He knew the risks of working in an operation like this; we all do and we've all learnt to live with it; otherwise we wouldn't be here.'

Bowring met Monsignor di Montefalco at Dowson's house in Lord North Street next morning.

'Major, I should like to thank you. The security services here informed us last night that they had found and neutralized a serious threat to His Holiness's safety.' The cleric paused. 'I got the impression that they were slightly embarrassed about it.'

'They'll get over it, Monsignor. We didn't tell them until the job was done, as per our terms of engagement with you.'

'I understand. The contract will be honoured. I'm

also grateful that you chose not to act on the instructions of Father Sullivan and, er, Cardinal O'Keane.'

Bowring looked at Montefalco with a smile in his still, grey eyes. 'If you tell me what's going to happen to O'Keane now, I'll take you to lunch at Greens.'

Montefalco struggled for a moment. 'Well, it will be a matter of public record soon. He is retiring from active ministry, going back to Chicago.' He shrugged his narrow shoulders. 'Better than a South American posting, anyway,' he said fastidiously.

While Bowring and the monsignor talked in London, Kelly woke up in his room at The Hollies. The sun was streaming in through the windows and a light breeze wafted in the scents and sounds of the woodland beyond the neat Victorian garden.

He heard a soft step on the stairs and glanced across the bed to the door. Michelle, in a flimsy dressing-gown and with her hair tumbling in disarray over her shoulders, came in with two large French cups of coffee. She put them on a table beside the bed, and climbed under the duvet beside Kelly.

He put out a hand and ran it through her hair, then allowed it to wander down to her breasts.

'What made you change your mind?' he said quietly.

'Does it matter?' she answered.

'Not much, but I'd still like to know.'

She bent down and kissed his battered face and stroked his chest with a hand which, slowly, tantalizingly, slipped down to touch his tight-muscled stomach, his thighs and burgeoning erection. 'I'll tell you later,' she murmured between kisses.

* * *

A long, blissful while later, he asked her again.

'I slept with you,' she said slowly, 'because the Boss said you deserved it.'

Kelly tightened up, ready to protest.

She calmed him with a caress of her long, gentle fingers. 'And because he said it would do me a lot of good.' She smiled serenely. 'And do you know something? He was absolutely right.'